A Labour Theory of Value

Luigi L. Pasinetti was one of the most significant figures in the history of post-Keynesian economics. In his final book, he reflects on the history and future of post-Keynesian economics, as well as a broad range of issues relating to his previous work. He argues that the economics profession has reached a critical impasse, unable to grasp the true nature of the unprecedented world we now inhabit. He examines how modern economic thought has diverged from addressing real-world challenges, challenging outdated frameworks to offer, instead, a path for reflection and reorientation. With a rigorous critique of prevailing paradigms, Pasinetti proposes an alternative framework of analysis extending an invitation for economists to rethink foundational assumptions. Providing his final statement on these issues, this book delivers a compelling critique of the current state of economics and political economy and offers a vital contribution for reimagining these disciplines in extraordinary times.

LUIGI L. PASINETTI was a distinguished economist and a leading figure of the Cambridge School of Economics. Renowned for his pioneering work in structural economic dynamics, income distribution and growth theory, Pasinetti profoundly influenced modern heterodox economics. As a professor at Università Cattolica del Sacro Cuore in Milan, he authored landmark works such as *Growth and Income Distribution and Structural Change and Economic Growth*. Honoured with numerous international awards, his legacy endures as a cornerstone for those rethinking economic paradigms.

A Labour Theory of Value

LUIGI L. PASINETTI
Università Cattolica del Sacro Cuore, Milan

CAMBRIDGE
UNIVERSITY PRESS

CAMBRIDGE
UNIVERSITY PRESS

Shaftesbury Road, Cambridge CB2 8EA, United Kingdom

One Liberty Plaza, 20th Floor, New York, NY 10006, USA

477 Williamstown Road, Port Melbourne, VIC 3207, Australia

314–321, 3rd Floor, Plot 3, Splendor Forum, Jasola District Centre, New Delhi – 110025, India

Cambridge University Press is part of Cambridge University Press & Assessment, a department of the University of Cambridge.

We share the University's mission to contribute to society through the pursuit of education, learning and research at the highest international levels of excellence.

www.cambridge.org
Information on this title: www.cambridge.org/9781009694841
DOI: 10.1017/9781009694865

When citing this work, please include a reference to the DOI 10.1017/9781009694865

First published 2026

A catalogue record for this publication is available from the British Library

A Cataloging-in-Publication data record for this book is available from the Library of Congress

ISBN 978-1-009-69484-1 Hardback

This book is published posthumously.

Despite multiple illnesses haunting his last few years, he devoted each single day to reviewing his papers and finalising this book. He left having put together an almost full-fledged work with only the last chapter, in full draft, to be reviewed.

I do apologise for the time it took me to come to an end. Not being an economist, I had a hard time, though I should admit I've become more and more fascinated by the subject as I went through.

I would like to express my most sincere gratefulness to all dad's colleagues and pupils who supported and encouraged me throughout this task, in particular Alberto Quadrio Curzio, Enrico Bellino and Nadia Garbellini.

Contents

Figures

Tables

Preface

The present book is mainly addressed to my professional colleagues, the economists. The basic purpose is a strong invitation to reflect, observe, consider and ponder over the present state of the economics profession that seems to me to have wound up in a blind alley which does not reveal the true nature of the new world in which we have come to live.

What I am stating in the whole book is basically a critique of the present state of political economy, as I have expressed it over the course of my entire professional career.

My pupils (who are behind the insistence on me to gather my writings from various sources and put them together, at last) are convinced that only in this way will I be able to convince my colleagues of the real extraordinary and unprecedented times in which we have arrived. Only in this way, by insisting on what I have tried to say, would the readers at large be able to see what I have tried to repeat and yet has remained unheard, or misunderstood for years, owing apparently to the difficulty of connecting and understanding the pieces, which I presented separately in too many different places.

Here, therefore, are my pieces, all together, according to their wishes, while I am of course extremely grateful for all their support, insistence and encouragement.

LLP

Prologue

Humans have changed the way the world works. Now they have to change the way they think about it.

"Welcome to Antropocene", The Economist's Editorial (2011). 28 May–3 June

The third millennium has been opened by an unprecedented succession of economic crises and major financial collapses in the whole industrialised world and, by inevitable repercussion, also in many of its least-advanced regions. In short: a world-wide disaster.

The situation could not be worse: unemployment has reached a massive scale, never experienced before, even among qualified workers and people (particularly youth) who generally have, with respect to their older counterparts, a reasonably higher level of education. Most of all, a widespread sense of dissatisfaction and unhappiness is felt among large strata of the population, which itself has become unprecedentedly large.

When, in early 2008, the current economic crisis broke out, Paul Samuelson, then the most authoritative still living economist, having written the most widely sold economics textbook ever in the whole world, did promptly react in a somewhat instinctive flush of writing. He entirely pinpointed what he singled out as 'the seven sins' of prevalent (mainstream) economics, sadly suggesting that the economics profession 'may get rough handling when facing St. Peter at the portals to heaven'.[1] But, since then, there seems to have been a retreat. In spite of plenty of articles and books and comments, that have invaded both the

[1] See Samuelson (2008).

scientific and the popular press, one can hardly find among the majority of economists any hints on admitting any sort of responsibility.[2]

What is most astonishing is that the opinions advanced on the current state of affairs are extremely varied. There does not seem to be any clear, commonly shared, view at the basis of any conviction. Any view that is proposed is regularly faced with other views, which often go in the opposite direction, and not merely on trifle matters, but with respect to major aspects of the crisis. The result is that since the beginning of this unparalleled economic and financial disaster, widespread confusion reigns supreme: among the leaders of the *elite* economies, among their politicians and among their supposed experts and advisers.

What has happened? Sheer common sense would seem to suggest that there must be something wrong, perhaps something very wrong somewhere, maybe even entrenched in the views that the whole profession of economists are currently taking for granted.

Shouldn't perhaps the economists – I mean the whole profession of economists, as Paul Samuelson seems to have innocently, but wisely, suggested – undertake a serious self-examination of their convictions?

To begin with, there is something which is rather surprising, though never generally perceived. While most fields of modern-day established learning have a long history behind them, this is not the case of economics, or more appropriately, of *Political Economy* as the field began to be called. *Political Economy* is a relatively recent subject. It only started to emerge not much more than two centuries ago (in the second half of the eighteenth century). It was of course promptly welcomed and admired as a supposedly much needed 'social science'. Since then, it has continued to gather growing success and, most of all, astonishingly high prestige. So much so that a few decades ago – in parallel

2 Cassidy (2012, pp. 5–6) mentions in his introduction, as an exception, Alan Greenspan, Governor of the Federal Reserve (from 1987 to 2006), who in testifying before the Vigilance Committee of the US Senate, had the courage to say: 'I made a mistake in presuming that the self-interests of organisations, specifically banks and others, were such that they were best capable of protecting their own shareholders and their equity in the firms [. . .]. The problem here is that something, which looked to be a very solid edifice, and, indeed, a critical pillar to market competition and free markets, did break down. And I think that, as I said, it shocked me. I still do not fully understand why that happened and, obviously, to the extent that I figure out what happened and why, I will change my views'.

to the generally admired prestigious prizes set up by the initiative of the philanthropist Alfred Nobel with the noble intention of honouring the best scientists – the Bank of Sweden decided to finance an entirely new, parallel, and in all forms analogous, 'Prize in Economic Sciences in Memory of Alfred Nobel', which in fact immediately became known as the Nobel Prize in Economics.

This makes it even more surprising that *Political Economy* proper, as a discipline, should have started its existence so recently.

It is of course true that historians of economic thought have promptly discovered many hints and thoughts in many treatises, which today are classified as pertaining to *economics*. They are on problems that undoubtedly are now dealt with as part of economics. They were written, however, with other purposes and within other subjects – mainly law, social behaviour or elaborations in various fields, mostly as parts of moral philosophy. The relevant point surely is that they were not originally conceived as part of a common, autonomous, prestigious discipline as nowadays it is felt necessary. Only now, apparently for the sake of convenience, are they made to fit together and presented as antecedents to that magnificent subject known as *Political Economy*.

It is therefore tempting to begin by asking: how is it that, all of a sudden, two centuries ago, at the end of the eighteenth century, the need was felt for bringing this new field of knowledge – *Political Economy* – strikingly into existence? More practically perhaps, we may turn the question around and more appropriately ask: what happened two centuries ago to be so special as to generate the need to set up a new specific field of knowledge, which has now become so influential in research and so relevant in social action?

It is enough to put the question within this more precise time-frame to immediately generate a more helpful answer.[3] Yes indeed, we can see very clearly, in the major nations of the Western World, even more now than before, from a reasonable (two and a half century) distance, that the emerging, the unravelling, the opening-up, the evolving of

[3] The most curious and astonishing event has perhaps been the unprecedented decision of Queen Elisabeth II in November 2008 put her questions to the whole profession of economists. How did it happen that such a crisis should have arrived in such an unexpected and most of all, so inexplicable manner? 'Why did no-one see it coming?'. These are the sort of questions she submitted to the economists on her well-advertised visit to the London School of Economics.

Political Economy – undoubtedly a new field of research – was clearly and directly induced by a historical event of striking, indeed huge and irreversible proportions: what the economic historians have by now called the *Industrial Revolution.*

In fact, in these terms, it should even come as no surprise. The *Industrial Revolution* was a really sharp and terrific break with the past. And yet – we may well add – it took some time before the profession of economists began to perceive what was inexorably and irretrievably happening.

It becomes extremely important, at this point, to sharpen our questions and search further back, deep into the past. Historians are openly telling us, without any hesitation, that in order to find a comparably similar event, we must go very far back, no less than ten millennia! It is generally agreed by now that, most probably in a well-defined region between the Tigris and the Euphrates, in the eighth to sixth millennium BC, an event took place which – with reason – economic historians, did indeed call, by analogy, the *Agricultural Revolution.* What was it? It started at the dawn of the Neolithic era and certainly marked nothing less than, as is by now widely perceived, the passage from pre-history (about which we know very little, even if it lasted thousands of years) to documented *history* – that is, to a stage, in the existence of humanity, in which the anthropological species (*homo sapiens*) grew beyond its primitive, savage, most certainly nomadic, life and got organised in more structured communities. But in what sense? The crucial point seems to have come when mankind learnt to cultivate land and domesticate animals, which in fact came to imply much, very much, more than that! What then? It seems reasonable to think, that at a certain stage in the history of mankind, there presumably were a series of crucial innovations, which irreversibly generated a terrific jump forward in the quality of life, away from a primitive, presumably more nomadic, life, and marked by a definite sharp break with the past and a keen projection into the future. This may well have generated ambivalent tendencies: just when the acquired stability of people on the territory was imposing the necessity to develop and multiply means of communication. This meant not only physical communication but also, and even more importantly, the communication and transmission of knowledge. The most typically crucial event in this respect undoubtedly was the invention of *writing*, which made it possible to communicate knowledge to other people across space and time.

It would of course be ridiculous to pretend to provide here even an extremely compact vision of what happened after that remarkable beginning, by pretending to compress millennia of human activity in a few lines. But, it should also be quite clear, almost obvious, from these very simple reflections that the very basic and fundamental characteristic of mankind that strikingly began to emerge was its *sapientia*, that is, that unique anthropological species that has been called the *homo sapiens*, or more recently, and even more specifically, the *homo sapiens sapiens*.

Curiously enough, economists seem to have neglected, or forgotten this, or at least to have been rather reluctant to bring into evidence this basic human characteristic.

Adam Smith, to whom the whole economics profession without much dispute attributes the appellative of father of Political Economy, had no hesitation in devoting the very initial pages of his masterpiece (*The Wealth of Nations*, Smith (1776)) to recognise that in that 'early and rude stage of society', consisting of 'hunters and fishers', the only 'factor of production', as he began to call it (and originator of economic value), was human Labour, (or, as later more accurately minded economists called it, unassisted labour). He did not devote more than a few lines to such a state of the human community, going straight through the *Agricultural Revolution*, to add another 'factor of production', namely: Land, or as we might like to say more generally today, *Natural Resources*.

Thus stated, we have little space and time to consider anything else. Labour, exerted on externally given natural Land, had become the economically relevant stage of society that came to dominate the scene since the outburst of the *Agricultural Revolution*. Quite surprisingly it has remained so ever since – for around 10 thousand years!

For our purposes, there is no willingness or pretence, in fact no need to go into detail. Historically, there are however two really crucial features worth pondering as they are singularly and basically relevant from an economic view point. The first refers to the effect on the sheer size of the human population that has come to invade the entire planet. The second refers to the way in which people have tried to develop devices – which we may well call *social institutions* – to organise social relations among themselves.

On the first feature, the amazing, recent anthropological discovery is the singularity of the *homo sapiens* species. Anthropologists by now seem to be in agreement that the *homo sapiens* originally came from a single ethnic group (almost certainly from a single couple, probably originating in central Africa). If this is the case, one can imagine how it must have taken millennia (in fact thousands of millennia), for this unique, extraordinary, single-couple species, to spread over the surrounding free land. It is also amazing to realise how, by starting from that single couple, the human species did in fact eventually occupy the entire planet, except for a few impossible corners (like Antarctica or the Himalayan peaks). Even more amazing is the realisation of the unique identity[4] kept by the species, by the extraordinary process of growing and developing. Critical points must have come when the available space seemed saturated. And it is not difficult to imagine how inevitable clashes must have been the origin of wars, while these historical events must have happened at different times in different parts of the planet. How total population did move through its fluctuations is obviously difficult to figure out. A few historians[5] have had the courage of trying to present some reliable estimates. They have tried to estimate the global population roughly at the end of the Neolithic age – that is, not far away from the *Agricultural* Revolution – to not much more than 1 million, then slowly growing, by the time of the Roman Empire, almost ten millennia later (!), towards roughly 250 million. In between the ten millennia that elapsed between these two delimiting points, from what historians can tell us, we may well imagine that slowly, a delicate equilibrium must have come into being between people and lands (and seas), giving specific identities to those marvellous civilisations (so different from one another and so complementary) which represent the cultural wealth of the ancient world.

It is important to notice, however, from what historians have been able to tell us, that for roughly ten millennia – that is, roughly since the beginning of the *Agricultural Revolution* – the rate of increase of the world population could not have been but rather slow: in fact, *to each single generation*, almost imperceptible. In various parts of the ancient world, prosperity, as we may imagine, alternated with famines,

[4] The recent amazing discovery of DNA has been decisive in achieving this conviction, even if dispute remain open on whether the two single members of the original couple were contemporary or not.

[5] See, e.g., Cipolla (1978), but more appropriately the works of Cavalli-Sforza, Menozzi, and Piazza (1996).

abundance with dearth, accompanied by epidemics, sometimes by terrible wars and even natural catastrophes. In the mentioned regime of 'Labour and Land', it was slave labour that undoubtedly made up the majority of the workers, and it was a limited elite of leaders who were in command of society. For centuries, the average returns obtained from that primitive life must have been rather meagre in terms of socio-economic development, at least in the sense we intend it today. And, over the long run, as we may imagine, the achievement of a roughly established relative stability, when looked at from the viewpoint of any single generation, must have appeared as almost near to zero. Under such conditions, each single generation must have felt the impression of an 'economic' world, as we might say today, that by and large was repeating itself in a kind of circularity. And nevertheless, as our researchers have come to know, this came to be characterised by the appearance now and then of exceptional geniuses as expressed by singular, extraordinary personalities, we might well say by absolutely exceptional representatives of the *homo sapiens sapiens* species. When we look at this from the angle of what it means to us, it is impossible not to realise that, what it essentially means is the cumulated *sapientia*, which in the various subsequent generations, we have been able to inherit from our predecessors. Ancient history is rich of singularly relevant, extraordinary personalities fulfilling this role.

In particular, there was one, a single one, who so uniquely and exceptionally came to mark the whole history of mankind as to compel historians to single out the specific time of his coming on this earth, and call that point in time 'time zero', thus sharply splitting the whole history of mankind into two phases: before and after time zero (to be respectively denoted as BC and AD – that is Before Christ and *Anno Domini*, which has come to mean after Christ[6]).

It might sound paradoxical to say that as formidable and penetrating as this event was in so many extraordinary respects, it passed unnoticed to the overall majority of contemporary people of the time, especially to those in command of the day-to-day historical destiny of humanity. It did not appear to interrupt the overall continuity of that splendid stationarity that had lasted (for millennia) since the

6 Year zero does not exist. The succession of historical years goes from year (−) 1 BC to year (+) 1 AD; time zero is reduced to just one infinitesimal point in time in between year 1 BC and year 1 AD.

Agricultural Revolution. It took time, a few centuries, before even the historians began to realise the relevance of what had happened and to actually suggest a reckoning of the elapsing of time from time zero.[7] In addition, the period around time zero happened to turn out to be exceptionally (relatively of course) peaceful. Historians later called it *Pax Romana*.

But there was a clash – a tremendous clash. The obvious signs were the brutal persecution of Christians by the Roman emperors, which we find historically revealed in myriad ways (documents, monuments, catacombs, churches etc.). If we take the two features mentioned previously, referring respectively to Labour and natural Land, we immediately realise quite well where the clashes did lie, and they were drastic, even if not usually stated in these terms. The Christian affirmation of every single person's dignity as an individual human being was in striking, drastic contrast with any form of slavery. But that conviction could not be achieved at the time. It is not entirely achieved *even today*! In Roman times, the attitude of most Christians was to affirm it, without contrast, at the cost of martyrdom. Even more interesting were the Christians' claims with reference to the rights towards individual property, Land and natural resources. The Early Church Fathers attempted to construct a proper set of guidelines for human relations that, following Christ's teachings in the Gospels, envisaged a radical regime of change of the *institutions* concerning individual property of wealth, entailing a voluntary renunciation of the ownership of wealth, within a surrounding social context of extended poverty. It induced a distribution of purchasing power in relation to the actual needs of the poor, rather than basing the right of ownership of wealth exclusively on the entitlement to the provenance of inherited wealth. Some scholars have referred to the life of these early Christian communities as the best, perhaps the only, actually achieved historical examples of truly communist institutions.

Here one must recall however that – although observed by small minorities of devout Christians, or in communities such as monasteries – these rules of life, excellent though they might have been on ethical grounds, could never be *socially* achieved. They clearly and simply

[7] It began of course (not even generally) only with the Gregorian calendar, a change proposed by Dionysius Exiguus in the sixth century.

could not be enforced. They remained voluntary exceptions outside the prevailing rules of Roman Law.

In fact, on these matters of private property, the institutions of Roman Law had been very sophisticated. We must perhaps acknowledge that it is Roman Law that achieved the apex on this matter. To go back to what happened over the whole stretch of the long ten millennia, when the production process of the various economically relevant goods was slowly progressing within the regime of *Labour* and *Land*, the produce of the cultivated land and of the domesticated animals had obviously to provide the sustenance for all the Labourers, even if sometimes kept at the brink of subsistence (partly free labour, but mostly, as it was then taken for granted, slave labour) while the surplus – as we might call it today – was absorbed by the owners of Land. Over a period of ten millennia, of course, conditions may have varied enormously in many different ways, according to space and time. What is relevant for us is that looking back, the various communities must have been able to set up social institutions that regulated these relations. Roman Law was, undoubtedly, the best symbol of this institutional setup. Its norms took for granted that any piece of land had at its origin an owner (a person or an institution). The land was gained most of the time from inheritance and at other times as a consequence of conquest. The ownership of property could be clearly defined and protected. It was framed within an institutional organisation that was obviously based on the power of a successful, overall, public and/or private, governance, as to grant a series of rights and protections.

There is a whole literature, developed from Roman times, on the subject of public and private property of land and dwellings. Some of those norms have been thought out in such clear and logical terms as to be taken as a reference by jurists even today. The aspect to underline here is that Roman Law succeeded to construct a legal system of peaceful institutions, built upon centuries of successful governance of private and/or public property.[8]

What is interesting for us however, is simply that in the early period of Christianity, when newly converted Christians happened to live within the social context of Roman Law, especially after (but,

[8] See for all Max Weber's (1864–1920) published dissertation: Weber (1967), chapter IV.

even before) the Constantine Edict of 313 AD, which after so many persecutions, allowed religious freedom, the rules of Roman Law prevailed and persisted.

We shall simply underline here the *institutional* origin of the success of these Roman regulations. The whole of the social relations were constrained within the network of the Roman Institutions – political, legal, cultural. They were even able to absorb the spreading force of Christianity, most probably simply because this force was aimed at rewards to be obtained in a different world.

But, if we resume our story since the beginning of the AD era, a really new outlook had started to act on mankind from time zero. The first millennium of the new era was characterised by many historical vicissitudes. Yet, the two basic economic features considered previously (the size of the global population and the social framework of the relations of the various categories of people to land and natural resources) seemed to maintain a surprising continuity. To the external world, things did not appear to change significantly in the first millennium AD. The High Middle Ages acted as a kind of external closure to the internal activities that seemed to be inspired by entirely different principles. In the internal peace and silence of the spreading number of monasteries, things really seemed to be intent on a different world. The whole world of the BC historical stages seemed to have fallen into oblivion. And perhaps it would indeed have been buried and forgotten altogether if it were not for an extraordinary and minute process that took hold and kept going under-way, inside the monasteries, to *copy* all the works of the ancient civilisations for the future. This took place without publicity, but it turned out to be a gigantic undertaking. It meant transmitting to future generations the accumulated knowledge behind Roman Law and architecture, Greek literature and philosophy, Jewish and Christian spirituality, and in fact, all the works of the ancient civilisations that could be copied. And this was done – we may well say (when nobody even dreamt of the means of future communication yet to be invented) out of sheer love for humanity, within an aura of duty to subsequent generations that few could understand. It was a capillary process that was carried out during the whole first millennium. We may well say an extraordinarily bright inner source of light, in a millennium of obscurity and destruction, during which the world of the future would appear to remain waiting.

Material conceptions regained momentum in the early part of the second millennium. First, within the flourishing commerce and trade of the maritime Mediterranean republics, and then with the Western development of the Atlantic nations, entering the scene – slowly at first, and then amazingly fast – on the spur of the initial powerful motor represented by the outburst of the *Italian Renaissance*. It quickly spread to the whole Western world. What happened was quite amazing, or perhaps simply fantastic: impossible even to be hinted at, let alone described in a few sentences. To take just two historical events as symbols of the fabulous upturn that came to take place, we may simply consider two events: the invention of the printing press, which carried with it the possibility to immediately replicate written material in as many copies as needed, and the geographical discovery of new continents, especially the Americas, sparsely populated and extraordinarily rich in natural resources. Both occurred almost exactly at the same time: at the very middle of the second millennium.

But at this point, the time has come for us to explore, with dutiful and more intense attention what happened in the *second* tiny part of the second millennium (if compared with the many preceding millennia!). At the macroscopic level, the startling realisation that was first perceived was imposed by the size of the population. And the novelty was striking.

After an almost-stationarity that covered the previous ten millennia of which we have reasonable knowledge, including the striking almost-immobility of the first millennium AD, the world population, from the sixteenth century onwards, began to grow as never before, and to grow in a way that immediately appeared frightening. From the beginning of the sixteenth century (1500 AD) to the beginning of the eighteenth century (1700 AD) – in the course of two centuries – the world population grew from roughly 400 to about 700 million,[9] this means that it almost doubled! But the most stupefying growth took place in the eighteenth century. In slightly over *one* single century, the world population doubled for a second time. Ever since, the world population has literally 'exploded'! At the beginning of the twentieth century – thinking of myself, this means when my parents were born – it was just surpassing 1.5 billion. At the beginning of the following

[9] See footnote 5.

century, that is, at the opening of the third millennium – that is, now, when all my grandchildren have been born – it has surpassed the 7 billion mark!

Let us pause for a moment and reflect. After roughly ten millennia of almost-stationarity, that came after the *Agricultural Revolution*, in three centuries (*centuries* not millennia!) the total world population multiplied almost tenfold!

It was an English economist (and Anglican priest), Robert Malthus, who drew attention to this extraordinary fact with a famous little book (*The Principles of Population*, 1798). Framing the obvious question of where the means of subsistence could come from, a whole profession of Classical economists (in particular Malthus, Ricardo, Torrens, West) at the beginning of the eighteenth century, became famous for developing what has been hailed in all the economics textbooks as the 'economic theory of rent'.[10]

They argued that Land is given and limited. As population increases, Land becomes scarcer and scarcer. Less fertile pieces of land, when available, may be put into cultivation (or be cultivated more intensely). But if the population keeps on increasing, a growing number of hungry mouths, working on less and less productive land, will only achieve *decreasing returns* from the newly cultivated lots of land. The immediate future looked catastrophic.

Yet, it was enough to wait a few decades to see another even more stupefying realisation emerge. With the benefit of time, it could be seen that in terms of world total Gross National Product (GNP), even leaving aside some uncertainties of measurement, another most astonishing outcome emerged: since Malthus's time, world per-capita GNP not only never lagged behind population growth, but most surprisingly, it increased more! This means that it increased *more* (not less) than tenfold! However, and this is the worrisome aspect, the increase was not uniform. Growth was strikingly different from country to country. The simple fact is that while the growth of the population was indeed 'global' (in the sense that it did take place everywhere), the growth of per-capita income was not uniform at all: the distribution of its increases was revealed to be frighteningly unequal.

[10] See also Pasinetti (2015) 'On the Origin of the Theory of Rent in Economics'.

This should not have been surprising! What the above-mentioned facts reveal is simply that with the beginning of the *Industrial Revolution*, productivities in a few nations took off and began persistently to grow at steady rates of change; in other nations the take-off was delayed by a few decades; in others by a century or so; in others they are beginning to take off only now; and still in others the take-off has not happened at all, and the respective countries are now struggling on the brink of starvation and despair, with their citizens induced to leave their country and try to migrate to others!

Let us not mince matters. This is the problem we must face today, at the beginning of the third millennium. The economics profession should wake up and start reflecting.

A warning first of all. We seem to be continually taken aback by extremely relevant events which the current economic theory has blatantly or inexplicably disregarded, and we seem surprised when the neglected aspects or events emerge as being responsible for reversing our expectations! Let us, therefore, look at least at some quite obvious and relevant facts.

There seems indeed to be something in the background to indicate the need for a profound re-shaping of our entire mode of thinking. Radical changes have taken place in our *immediate* past: that is, *only over the past three centuries*! Yet, there have been previous millennia of almost-stationarity which cannot be forgotten. They pose a real problem that concerns the whole of mankind and, even more for us, the whole profession of economists! We must probe more in depth, and very simply and most humbly, investigate what the causes are of this strikingly relevant monster, or good fortune, as it may be, that has fallen upon us: the *Industrial Revolution*.

The economics profession is persistently showing to be scandalously slow to wake up. It has taken two centuries, from Malthus to Keynes (actually to Roy Harrod, a pupil of Keynes's) to wake up and realise that it was time to abandon the exclusive concentration and fear of scarcity (or, rather and more reasonably, face scarcity within a different and more imaginative context) and open-up to the fact that such a fantastic process of growth as that of the new industrial world cannot exclusively have behind it the pressure of population growth (which by the way must more reasonably be regarded as an effect, not a cause) of the present situation, but perhaps more imaginatively begin to be considered also as an ensemble of thinking brains rather than of mouths to feed. If sheer data are showing that growing GNPs are the effect of increasing productivities, we may look at what is behind these growths of productivities. And, if we find, as very simply Roy Harrod pointed out, that they are due not only to population growth, but also to further basic elements relevant to production activities namely: technical change and capital accumulation, we must open up our enquiries to them. This should be done even if we shall note that not only they are both typically new, but also that (i) they are both characteristic of the last three centuries, and (ii) paradoxically, they are both revealed as precisely the crucial economic features on which *mainstream economics* has inexplicably and almost totally failed to be helpful!

For millennia, since the *Agricultural Revolution*, humankind had produced the goods which it needed by using *Labour* and *Land* (or more generally, Labour and Natural (given) Resources, as was pointed out previously).

At the end of the eighteenth century, something radically new appeared on the world scene. One may indeed understand that the official view was to open up a novel branch of investigation that had not existed before: it was called *Political Economy*! And this suggested to what had appeared as a new factor: a 'third factor of production', to be added to the previous two more traditional ones (*Labour and Land*). It was called *Capital*. But this was too easy a way out. The new phenomena were much more complex than simply the discovery of another 'factor of production'.

Of course the appearance of physical capital was a typically new feature of the new world, a collective name which stands for the material goods which are employed as means of production – together with Natural Resources and of course Labour – to obtain both final goods for consumption and indeed other capital goods. But the strongly dynamic new process under way was a terrifically much more complex reality!

The mere emergence of the new organisational system (first with workers exerting their work in factories) entailed a much more radical change, which escaped immediate attention, and yet came to change not only the production processes themselves but also the social relations, as it penetrated down even to the family structure.

There was a profound difference with respect to the slightly earlier 'phase of commerce' that had characterised the first part of the second millennium. For those workers, transformed in the eighteenth century into 'proletarians', who did not possess anything except the possibility of offering their labour, it meant a separation of their place of work from the place where their families lived, which forced them to leave the family in order to go to the *factory* – the symbol of the new era – with rigidly determined working hours, in a subordinate position, and again, at least in the initial phases, with long and heavy work shifts, while the ample supply of labour was keeping wages at the limit of subsistence.

Owing to this process, the commerce that developed in the first part of the second millennium, was actually transformed into *capitalistic* economies (in the sense of production with Labour as means of production).[11]

The whole phenomenon is the result of an entirely novel technological and social process – we may well call it a *capitalistic transformation of production* which began to take place in the eighteenth century and which was much more than, or perhaps something different from, the simple addition of a 'new factor of production'.[12] Originally, it was generated by the invention and diffusion of machines, no-longer moved by human or animal energy, but, by a series of new sources of energy which have been, and continue to be, discovered and developed by a cumulative process in a variety of sources and qualities. This is the novel feature that led to an extraordinarily unprecedented increase of total production. Immediately evident was the fact that this novel process had not been accompanied by an equitable or reasonable distribution of the benefits which ensued. We no-longer doubt nowadays, on reconsidering the appearance of industrialisation, that the increase of wealth was socially concentrated in the hands of those restricted groups of people and of nations, who organised the production process in factories, themselves to become a symbol of the new era.

[11] I am using the term *capitalist* economies for that institutional form in which all the decisions are concentrated in the hands of the owners of the means of production: the capitalists. The capitalist economies are a particular institutional type of modern organisation. But *capitalistic* economies are a *more general* phenomenon: namely the production *with already produced physical goods*. This is what *all* our economies are today.

[12] If at all, it should induce us even to question whether the concept of 'factor of production' is appropriate to deal with it.

It should be clear that it is this feature, which Harrod called Technical Progress (or rate of growth of productivity) that came into being in parallel to the earlier features (population and capital accumulation) that was the basic characteristic of the new dynamically moving world of the *Industrial Revolution*. Paradoxically, this should not appear as entirely new. The products of human thought were inherent in the *sapiens sapiens* species since its origin. It was mentioned, previously, as something that characterised those very early innovations that spurred the *Agricultural Revolution*, but then it was always behind human action ever since. In the eighteenth and nineteenth centuries, there clearly was something *extraordinarily new*. We might well say that it began in the Renaissance and continued afterwards. Few economists perceived all its positively radical effects. In fact, the economists were extraordinarily blind as even to induce a literary polemicist, like Thomas Carlyle, who had become quite acquainted with the extraordinary opportunities available in his time, to mock the pessimistic unrepentant economists with his famous term 'the dismal science' of Political Economy! So we might apparently conclude that the common-sense-non-economists seemed to be more alert than the economists themselves on the effects of the *Industrial Revolution*.

We may of course say now very simply that the *Industrial Revolution* coincided with the beginning of the age of science and technology. But how is it that so few economists perceived all its amazing effects? A mere attentive evaluation should have led to pay more attention to population, rather than to scarcity, which was quite obvious, and go on to the fabulous developments, precisely in the communications field, as a consequence of the change from the use of the typical energy sources of the agricultural era (animal and human) to the multifaceted forms of energy that became available towards the end of the eighteenth century/beginning of the nineteenth century. This meant a shift to the more modern world in which we live.

Let us look concisely but significantly at a few details. How is it that so meagre attention should have been paid to what all people with common sense could see? We all know quite well that, beginning from the end of the seventeenth century, over the following two centuries, with unprecedented rapidity, people in Western Europe witnessed such a terrific series of innovations that seemed almost unbelievable. Let me simply list a few: the steam engine, which revolutionised land and maritime communications; the internal combustion engine, which caused the switch from the stagecoach to motor cars and air planes; electricity and electric motors, which ever since have begun to move a series of multiform and growing sorts of mechanisms; the reaction engine, which perfected and broadened intercontinental transport and made travel into space possible. Within the information communication field, one could later see the appearance with breath-taking speed of the telegraph, the radio, the television, the fax, the world-wide-web (internet). At the same time, the development of chemistry was leading to the creation of completely new and previously entirely unknown materials. Lastly, let me simply mention the appearance of nuclear energy, which for the first time in the history of mankind, has made a truly 'global' responsibility emerge for the people of the whole world!

There are also paradoxes. At the time we began to be able to land on the moon, and then even to prepare to be able to reach Mars, and to dream of conquering new territories in outer space, we became capable of annihilating not only ourselves, but also the whole of life on Earth!

Let us embrace, however, the more attractive idea and prospect of social responsibility – of usefully and beautifully transforming the surface of the Earth to make it a more pleasantly inhabitable planet.

But let us concentrate a little on questioning ourselves.

If I were to ask the reader to have a look at the photos that show how the Earth appears now from any space-craft going round it, could we – for a moment – imagine how much the surface of the planet has changed since time zero?

No surprise there: we may well learn, from what anthropologists have already realised, that the anthropological species has by now so transformed the face of the Earth as to require some new definitions.

Anthropologists have already characterised the phase which our planet has now reached by a new term: ANTHROPOCENE. After the succession of all the previous geological eras of the past, it is undeniable that a radically new geological phase has started in which the new (anthropological) species (*homo sapiens sapiens*) has come to so strongly dominate and shape the global face of the Earth, as to justify the clear conviction that we are going to live in a shockingly new era, that carries extraordinarily exciting marvels but also – *helas* – frightfully diffused dangers.

For us economists, we have the duty to seriously reflect on this.

The prevailing *political economy*, following from its traditional archetype, Adam Smith, has proposed a view according to which the whole economic world has been generated by a productive activity depicted as the upshot of three 'factors of production': labour, land and capital.

But is this not a disguised way of differentiating diverse sorts of the same human activity?

Essentially, why not at least recognise that in general it is human activity that encompasses everything. Simply put in economic terms: it is Human Labour, and nothing else, that is behind everything. In these terms, Labour emerges as the only and single 'factor of production': always present in any human activity, throughout the world. All the rest is given to us from outside.

A counter-factual thought should bring into evidence this objective and basic truth. As will emerge, at a certain point in our discourse later on, try to make a counter-factual thought. Imagine an event that were to destroy all existing accumulated capitalistic goods that human activity has produced – a terrific disaster. Yet, in time, those human beings that survive would build it up again, and in less time than in the past. As an opposed counter-fact, imagine the opposite event: the destruction of the human species while all produced goods, buildings, palaces, etc., remain intact. What would happen next? Ask even a child: *Nothing!* All beautiful cities that had been built before would stand frightfully still and empty. Nothingness would follow and no-one would care!

Only one conclusion stands: the only real 'factor of production' is Human Labour!

It may be surprising to affirm this at the beginning of the book. But, I shall provide further evidence in the pages that follow.

Perhaps the really surprising thing is that one should need to write a whole book in order to give evidence to something which is so unmistakably obvious.

PART I

The Basic Conceptual Approach

1 *Theory of Value: Source of Alternative Paradigms in Economic Theory*

There is a dichotomy that happens to have been created, in economic analysis, between production-oriented theories and exchange-oriented theories. In this chapter, I will argue that the source of such a dichotomy can be traced back to a much deeper dichotomy, which lies at the very basis of the whole economic theory itself and more specifically on the theory of value.

1 *Justum pretium*: The Pre-theoretical Stage

Value and, more specifically, prices represent an old subject for discussion and disquisitions among scholars. However, the formulation of economic *theories* of value is an extremely modern concern, which began to emerge only towards the end of the eighteenth century. In earlier times, we find, for many centuries, a series of disquisitions about the *ethics* of prices and, more specifically, about the concept of 'just price' (*justum pretium*). These disquisitions originated as a result of the preoccupation of moral philosophers specifying what is justified and what is not justified in the fixation of prices.

The historians of economic thought have by now distilled the sentences of the ancient and medieval moral philosophers from many angles. Without going into detail or trying to give exhaustive lists, let me recall schematically a few representative points.[1]

[1] I may mention, for the interested reader, at least a few references. The development of the concept of 'just price' from the Romans to the Scholastics may be seen in Baldwin (1959). In Haganauer's (1931) article, the just price is seen as an anticipation of the labour theory of value; see also Sapori (1955). An interesting article in which both 'objective' and 'subjective' hints are singled out is that by Roover de (1958). See also Schumpeter (1951, Part II, chs. 1–2), Hollander (1965) and Spicciani (1977).

(i) *Justum pretium* (or *verum pretium*) has its origins in Roman law. It is, however, from the ancient Greek philosophers that we have received the most notable arguments on the subject. Aristotle (384–322 BC) is credited with condemning the price of the single seller (or monopolist, in the etymological sense of the word, μόνοσπωλεῖν) as contrary to justice, as it arises from artificial scarcity. He is also credited – from sentences such as 'There will be reciprocity, . . . as farmer is to shoemaker, so the amount of the shoemaker's work is to that of the farmer's work, for which it exchanges' (*Nichomachean Ethics*, 1133 17; Ross (1925)) – with trying to find a sort of cost principle and, more specifically, a sort of labour principle underlying the notion of a *just price*. What is certain is that Aristotle explicitly faced the problem of what he called 'commutative justice' in the pricing process. In trying to single out a common standard on which to gauge the 'equivalence' of what is given and what is received, he used various arguments, among which freedom from artificial scarcities and labour costs appear to be the most prominent.

(ii) Among the scholastic philosophers, St Thomas Aquinas (1225–1274) and many others – notably Albertus Magnus (1206–1280) and John Duns Scotus (1266–1308) – have all resumed the Aristotelian arguments and have developed them further. St Thomas's main references are his *Commentaries* on Aristotle's *Nichomachean Ethics* and his famous 'Quaestio LXXVII' (*Summa Theologiae*, pt II, 2), where the ethics behind *justum pretium* is spelt out. The Aristotelian flavour of the disquisition is unmistakable. Historians have seen in the references to *aestimatio* an implicit admission of subjective elements and in the reference to expenditures, particularly to *expensae et labores* (in the search for a standard of 'equivalence' in 'commutative justice'), an explicit reference to the cost and, more particularly, to the labour principle in price determination.

(iii) The moral philosophers who, in the following centuries, dealt with the pricing problem did perfect the disquisitions of the Scholastic philosophers in many directions and added further details; notable to this effect are the works of St Antonius of Florence (1389–1458) and of Luis de Molina (1535–1600). But the basic approach, in spite of increasing sophistication, remained the same.

My conclusion is that it would be wrong to try – as so many modern scholars are continually trying – to look meticulously at the works of the moral philosophers for hints that anticipate one of the modern theories of value. When one takes this approach, one inevitably ends up either straining the meaning of words and seeing in the works of the moral philosophers whatever one would like to see in them or concluding with words of surprise at the 'contradictions' between the various principles that those moral philosophers were 'unable' to distinguish. This is not only unfair, but also – it seems to me – incorrect.

We can trace, in the arguments of ancient and medieval philosophers, hints at subjective elements (coming from the concept of estimation), hints at objective elements (referring to costs and labour), hints at the working of a possibly efficient mechanism (competitive markets) and other hints too. But clearly, they were *not* aiming at proposing theories. They were trying to state standards of ethical behaviour and – given this purpose – it was not contradictory for them to try to set out, not one, but many separate arguments, provided that they all helped, in various cases and occasions, to achieve the final effect. Far from considering these various arguments as being in contradiction with one another, they regarded them as enriching their discussion.

2 Ferdinando Galiani: A Remarkable Symbol of Pre-Theoretical Writing

Perhaps the most symbolic of all pre-theoretical writers on 'value' is Ferdinando Galiani, who has bequeathed to us that delightful chapter II from book I of *Della Moneta*, first published in 1751. Galiani wrote it only 25 years before Adam Smith's *Wealth of Nations* was published. Galiani wrote as an economist, in the modern sense of the word, rather than as a moral philosopher, yet he wrote as an economist still at a pre-theoretical stage. Anyone looking, from today's standpoint, at his rather sophisticated arguments can choose the hints to the theory of value that he likes. Consider, as examples, the following excerpts:[2]

[2] Galiani's remarkable book (which the author published at the age of 23!) has never been published in English. I discovered, however, after the publication of the present Essay in 1986, that a translation in English by Peter Toscano exists and can be obtained 'on demand' from University Microfilm International, Ann Arbor, Michigan ©1977. I have however preferred to stick

The value of things . . . is by many people defined as the estimation men have of them. (Galiani 1751, p. 27)

Value therefore is a relationship ('ragione') and this is composed of two relationships, which I call: *utility* and *rarity*. (Galiani 1751, p. 28, author's italics)

I call *utility* the attitude of things to generate happiness. (Galiani 1751, p. 28, author's italics)

But most people, like Bernardo Davanzati, argue as follows: 'An actual calf is nobler than a golden calf yet how less is it valued?' I answer. If an actual calf were as rare as a golden one, it would have a higher price than a golden calf, as the utility and need of the former is higher than the latter. These people think that value derives from one single principle, and not from many which combine to form a composite relationship. I hear others saying: 'a pound of bread is more useful than a pound of gold'. I answer. This is a shameful paralogism, deriving from not knowing that *more* or *less* useful are relative terms which are measured according to the subjective conditions of people . . . but for he who is satiated, is there a thing more useless than bread? He is therefore doing well if he satisfies other inclinations . . . Hence, when Davanzati says that 'an egg, which is worth less than half a grain of gold, was enough to keep conte Ugolino alive in the tower, even on his tenth day [a famous scene from Dante's *Inferno*], which all the gold in the world could not have done', he fails to make a distinction between the price someone might pay for an egg, when that person does not fear starvation without it, and the needs of conte Ugolino. Who has said that conte Ugolino would not have paid even a thousand grains of gold for an egg? . . . here he has actually admitted that *dear* and *cheap* are relative terms. (Galiani 1751, pp. 34–35, author's italics)

I call *rarity* the proportion between the existing quantity of a thing and the use made of it. (Galiani 1751, p. 38, author's italics)

Going on now to tell of the quantity of things, I say there are two classes of bodies. For some of them, it depends on the different abundance with which nature produces them; in others only on the different toil and trouble, and work, that is bestowed upon them. (Galiani 1751, pp. 38–39)

to my own translation – which seems to me more reasonably accurate. The references given here are to the original Italian texts, all of which can be found in Pasinetti (1986).

I now begin to speak of toil and trouble ('*fatica*'), which, not only in all creative works or art, such as pictures and sculptures, etc., but in many objects such as minerals, stones and wild fruits... etc., is the only thing that gives value to things. The quantity of matter for nothing else contributes to the value of these things, but because the toil and trouble increase or diminish. (Galiani 1751, pp. 39–40)

What a splendid collection of arguments and hints! The modern economist can see very clearly in these excerpts the concept of utility, the concept of decreasing marginal utilities and the relativity of all these concepts. One can also see the concept of cost of production and, more particularly, the principle of labour cost ('fatica', an expression corresponding to Adam Smith's 'toil and trouble'), which is defined as nothing less than 'the only one that gives value to things' ('l'unica che dà valore alla cosa'). One may go much further, however. Consider these other excerpts:

If, for example, in a village, fifty thousand casks of wine are harvested and consumed; if suddenly an army were to come, the price of wine will increase because more of it will be drunk. (Galiani 1751, pp. 48–49)

Since men own unequal wealth, so to each degree of wealth there always corresponds the purchase of certain goods and services. If the prices of the latter fall, those people who are at the lower level of wealth will also buy them; if their prices increase, those who used to buy them will begin to give them up. (Galiani 1751, p. 49)

fashion is the illness of the soul... If a reason for it is to be found, we must say that this variety of tastes springs from the imitation of usage of the predominant nations. (Galiani 1751, p. 49)

Who cannot see in all this the interplay of demand and supply, the concept of *elasticity* of demand with respect to both prices and income and, in fact, also a clear enunciation of the hierarchy among goods (which was later to be known as Engel's law)? Who cannot see even a clear indication of the 'demonstration' and 'imitation' effects, and thus of the interdependence among individuals' preferences?

I have quoted at length precisely to show the many principles referred to. Ironically, it has become difficult for us today to give Galiani all the credit he deserves, precisely because – carried away by our modern theories – we tend to see contradictions among the various principles (only later clearly perceived) he has so remarkably anticipated.[3]

3 The Emerging of Theories

There was a dramatic change in the approach to discussions on value in the second half of the eighteenth century. From the ethical pronouncements on value, writers began at last to move on to *theories* of value.

Theory entails abstraction. It means making a choice from among the maze of interconnections that a superficial glance can capture, and then trying to get down the fundamentals. In social sciences, this also means simplifying, sometimes very crudely, by minimising what appears as secondary, and singling out and magnifying what the theorist (with his intuition) identifies as the major or basic element that is capable of providing the explanation that is sought.

Since the end of the eighteenth century, economic theorists have concentrated on fewer and fewer basic elements. On the concept of value, they have narrowed themselves down to a choice between two quite different and alternative routes: the 'objective' route of a cost-of-production and, more specifically, of a labour theory of value; and the 'subjective' route of a 'marginal utility' theory of value.

I think the source of each of these two alternative theories may well be symbolised by the following two quotations, taken from Adam Smith and William Stanley Jevons, respectively:

> In that early and rude state of society which precedes both the accumulation of stock and the appropriation of land, the proportion between the quantities of labour necessary for acquiring different objects seems *the only circumstance* which can afford any rule for exchanging them for one other. If among a nation of hunters, for example, it usually costs twice the labour to kill a beaver which it does to kill a deer, one beaver should naturally exchange for or be worth two deers. It is natural that what is usually the produce of two days or two hours labour, should be worth double of what

[3] Schumpeter himself (Schumpeter 1951, pp. 300–302), though a great admirer of Galiani, cannot refrain from pointing out how abruptly Galiani jumps from one theoretical principle to another.

is usually the produce of one day's or one hour's labour. (Smith 1904, p. 49, my italics)

The Science of Political Economy rests upon a few notions of an apparently simple character… it is in treating the simple elements that we require the most care and precision, since the least error of conception must vitiate all our deductions… Repeated reflection and inquiry have led me to the somewhat novel opinion, that *value depends entirely upon utility*. (Jevons 1871, p. 1, author's italics)

Both Smith and Jevons have taken precisely the same step, but in opposite directions. In striking contrast with Galiani, for example, who chided those who 'thought value derives from one single principle' ('Costoro immaginansi che il valore derivi da un principio solo'), both Smith and Jevons concentrate precisely on *one single principle* to be put at the foundation of their elaborations. This does not, of course, mean closing their eyes to everything else. But it does mean putting everything else in a secondary, or subordinate, position. It means that everything else must be excluded from the first skeleton of the theory, and only be introduced later on, at a second, third or even subsequent stage. This is not merely a sort of successive approximation process; it is something much more basic to the theorising process, because whatever does not fit properly into the core of the theory must impiously be omitted or left to play a subordinate role.

It should be added that individual writers may not always be themselves clear about which features are secondary and subordinate to the basic propositions. But the unmistakable sign of a basic principle is that it can never be left out. Conversely, the unmistakable sign of subordination is that when, or if, in successive developments and re-elaborations, any logical difficulty arises, the subordinate elements are the ones to be sacrificed, in the sense that, by one assumption or another, they are further minimised or modified, or even eliminated, through a process of logical abstraction, in order not to invalidate the major, or basic, elements characterising the theory.

It will be useful to consider succinctly, but with the aid of some formalisation, the essentials of the two major theories of value so far proposed. For each of them corresponds to one of the two alternative paradigms that have characterised the whole economic theory ever since.

4 The *Subjective* Theory of Value (A Pure Exchange, or Pure Preference, Model)

It may be useful to start with the subjective theory of value, which – although proposed, chronologically, after the objective theory of value – is the one about which most efforts of formalisation have been carried out.

To single out the essentials of the theory, one must look for those bare elements, and only for those bare elements, that the theory cannot do without. The elements that a subjective theory of value cannot do without are all contained in that simple formalisation known as the model of *a pure exchange economy*, but which I would rather call a model of *a pure utility*, or *pure preference* economy, since it is the utility, or preferences, of the individuals that plays the crucial role. Such a model can be found on the first pages of almost all standard treatments of economic theory. I shall follow here, very synthetically, a formalisation given by Mosak (1944), which has the advantage of being complete for all general purposes and, at the same time, more accessible to the general reader than the more sophisticated and recent formalisations by Arrow and Debreu (1954) and Debreu (1959).

Suppose there is a society of individuals, each of whom earns, or – as is also said – has been 'endowed' (we do not enquire by whom) with a certain set of 'resources'

$$\bar{x}_1, \bar{x}_2, \ldots, \bar{x}_n, \tag{1.4.1}$$

which in general are different from one individual to another. Each individual can freely exchange his/her resources with those of the other individuals, at the prices

$$p_1, p_2, \ldots, p_n, \tag{1.4.2}$$

which are accepted from a competitive market. The only constraint each individual faces is budget:

$$p_1\bar{x}_1 + p_2\bar{x}_2 + \cdots + p_n\bar{x}_n = p_1x_1 + p_2x_2 + \cdots + p_nx_n, \tag{1.4.3}$$

where $\bar{x}_1$, $\bar{x}_2$, ..., $\bar{x}_n$ are the physical quantities he/she starts with and $x_1, x_2, \ldots, x_n$ are the physical quantities he/she ends up with.

Each individual is supposed to have a complete and well-defined set of preferences, in the sense of being able to rank any combination of goods in order of preference. More specifically, he/she can specify all possible combinations of goods among which he/she is indifferent,

$$u(x_1, x_2, \ldots, x_n) = \bar{u} \qquad \text{(a constant)}, \tag{1.4.4}$$

and can also specify all combinations of goods that are preferred to (1.4.4) (i.e. give rise to a higher constant – a higher utility), and those that are not preferred to (1.4.4) (i.e. give rise to a lower constant – a lower utility). Hence, a utility function exists for each single individual:

$$u = u(x_1, x_2, \ldots, x_n). \tag{1.4.5}$$

This is supposed to be only ordinally (not necessarily cardinally) measurable. In other words, if u is an index of utility for the combination $x_1, x_2, \ldots, x_n$, then any arbitrary function $F(u)$ of u is also a suitable index of utility, provided that $F' > 0$. It is also assumed that relation (1.4.5) is continuous and has partial derivatives of the first and second order:

$$u_s = \frac{\partial u}{\partial x_s}, \quad u_{st} = \frac{\partial^2 u}{\partial x_t \partial x_s}, \qquad s, t = 1, 2, \ldots, n. \tag{1.4.6}$$

Moreover,

$$u_{st} = u_{ts}, \tag{1.4.7}$$

which means that utility does not depend on the *order* in which the goods are arranged.

Suppose now that each individual behaves rationally and maximises his/her utility function, subject to his/her budget constraint, then

$$u + \lambda[\Sigma p_s \bar{x}_s - \Sigma p_s x_s] = \text{a maximum}, \tag{1.4.8}$$

where λ is the usual Lagrange multiplier. The solution to this problem is well known. To find a maximum, we must take all the first partial derivatives with respect to x_s and equate them to zero:

$$u_s - \lambda p_s = 0, \qquad s = 1, 2, \ldots, n. \tag{1.4.9}$$

And to ensure that equation (1.4.9) defines a maximum (and not a minimum), we must impose the second-order condition:

$$\mathrm{d}^2 u = \Sigma\Sigma u_{st} \mathrm{d}x_s \, \mathrm{d}x_t < 0, \tag{1.4.10}$$

the meaning of which is that the multidimensional hyper-difference curves (1.4.4) taken for all $\bar{u}$ must be convex towards the origin. When the necessary condition (1.4.10) is satisfied, then (1.4.9) and (1.4.3) form $n+1$ equations, which determine λ and the n physical quantities $x_1, x_2, \ldots, x_n$. This is the solution that defines the *equilibrium of the single individual*.

It may be noticed that the solutions to equation (1.4.9) are characterised by

$$\frac{u_s}{p_s} = \frac{u_t}{p_t}, \qquad s, t = 1, 2, \ldots, n. \tag{1.4.11}$$

In other words, each single individual's equilibrium is characterised by the equality of *all* the partial derivatives (i.e. the *marginal utilities*) divided by the corresponding prices. Of course, the equilibrium of each single individual is *relative* to his/her set of preferences, initial endowments *and* market prices, which the individual takes as given but which the individual takes as given though determined by the market. Now, if any price were to change, each individual's equilibrium would also change. This means that, for each physical resource x_s $(s = 1, 2, \ldots, n)$ and for each single individual i $(i = 1, 2, \ldots, m)$, we can formulate a *demand function*:

$$x_{si} = f_{si}(p_1, p_2, \ldots, p_n; \bar{x}_{1i}, \bar{x}_{2i}, \ldots, \bar{x}_{ni}). \tag{1.4.12}$$

It can be shown that, under the assumptions taken, this demand function is homogeneous of the zero degree in all prices (i.e. for any given amount of physical resources, the multiplication of all prices by the same multiplicative factor leaves each single individual's demand unchanged).

At this point, we may sum up the demands of all individuals for the same 'resource' to obtain the *aggregate* demand function for that 'resource'. Then, by equating this aggregate demand function to the corresponding aggregate amount that is available, we obtain the n equations,

$$\sum_{i=1}^{m} \bar{x}_{si} = \sum_{i}^{m} f_{si}(p_1, p_2, \ldots, p_n; \bar{x}_{1i}, \bar{x}_{2i}, \ldots, x_{ni}), \qquad s = 1, 2, \ldots, n, \tag{1.4.13}$$

which, with the budget constraint extended to the whole market,

$$\sum_{s}^{n} \sum_{i}^{m} p_s x_{si} = \sum_{s}^{n} \sum_{i}^{n} p_s \bar{x}_{si}, \tag{1.4.14}$$

define the general equilibrium of the market.

Equation (1.4.13) make up n equations, which are, however, constrained by (1.4.14), so that they form in fact only $(n - 1)$ independent equations. These yield $(n - 1)$ solutions for $(n - 1)$ prices. Hence, the general equilibrium of the market determines *relative* prices, whereas the general level of prices remains indeterminate. Also, to determine the absolute level of prices, one should at this point go on to introduce money, but we don't need to go into this field for the time being. We may well remain at the stage of determination of the $(n - 1)$ *relative* prices, which define the *general equilibrium* of the market as a whole.

5 The Meaning of Prices in a Pure Preference Economy

As may be noticed, the pure preference model is a beautiful theoretical construction. It proposes a clear and well-defined problem: the problem of allocation, through exchange, of given resources, and it provides a well-defined and elegant solution. If individuals behave rationally, a set of relative prices will emerge, which lead to the equilibrium of each single individual and the market as a whole. The resource allocation thereby reached can be shown to have optimal properties. At the equilibrium point, no individual can be made better off without making some other individual worse off (a situation which has been called Pareto optimality – optimality relative to given endowments and given individual preferences). The set of prices associated with the equilibrium (optimum) solution has a very evident economic meaning – it provides an index of relative scarcities.

It is sometimes said that this is a static model, but it would be more appropriate to say that time is not a relevant element in the model. The problem which is posited is a once-for-all problem (how to allocate given resources), and the solution which is provided is a once-for-all solution (optimal allocation). Once the solution has been given, there is nothing more to be done, except to investigate the mathematical conditions that make it meaningful (existence, uniqueness and stability) or to illustrate the elegant properties it possesses (optimality). It might also be observed that the theoretical choice that is implied in the formulation of the pure preference model, and with it the subjective theory of value, springs from a particular way of looking at society. It springs, so to speak, from a particular 'social philosophy'. This social philosophy relies on the individual's social behaviour; on the idea of the consumer's sovereignty over the whole economy; on a great faith in the market as an institutional mechanism that brings about the utilisation of all resources; and on the private property of all goods, as an institution that must in fact be taken as a basic postulate of the theory.

It is interesting to note how all these features are inherent in the pure preference model. They are all there, without the need to consider anything else or to introduce any other phenomenon. In fact, from this point onwards, the introduction of any complication becomes possible *only if* it does not affect any of these basic features.

6 Extensions of the Pure Preference Model

The model of a pure preference economy, if taken at face value, would refer to a very limited problem. But the theoretical construction has proved flexible enough to afford extensions and generalisations in many directions.

I have had the opportunity elsewhere of pointing out how the first phenomenon to be introduced into the model was of course the phenomenon of production.[4] This was done by replicating all the functions and concepts of a pure preference economy – a convex, continuous, differentiable 'production function', in all analogous to a utility function; 'marginal productivities', in all analogous to marginal utilities; a postulate of profit maximisation, in all analogous to the postulate of utility maximisation; and so on and so forth. Labour, which does not explicitly appear at the basic stage, has been introduced by considering it as one of the many 'endowments' that an individual possesses and can market, etc.

But, most of all, the 'generalisations' have taken place by way of 'shaping', by a series of assumptions, the phenomena to be investigated in such a way as to make them suitable for the applications of the ready-made analytical tool. In other words, the 'generalisations' basically consist in *looking at* all the economic problems *as if* they were problems of optimum allocation of given resources. When the analytical tool and the phenomenon to be investigated do not match, it is not the tool but the phenomenon that has to be changed (by assumption) so that it can be made to be 'well behaved' (i.e. suitable for the application of the analytical tool). In this way, the very basic analytical tool of the model – maximisations under constraints – has become the 'foundation of economic analysis'.[5]

[4] This can be seen very clearly on the historical scene. The theory of marginal productivity was developed twenty years *after* the theory of marginal utility, as an immediate and direct extension of it. Further details will emerge in Chapter 2 Section 1. See also Pasinetti (1981, Ch. 1).

[5] This is precisely the basic claim of Samuelson (1947).

Without going into further details here, I may simply mention a very significant and symbolic case in this respect; namely, the way in which the theory has recently responded to the discovery that an aggregate production function does not exist in general and that an inverse monotonic relation between the rate of profit and the 'quantity of capital' was a false 'intuition' (deriving from a too naive extension of the pure preference model) that has turned out to be without foundation. Capital goods have always created trouble in this model. But the new criticism has elicited the most logical response. The solution has been found by adopting an interpretation that had not been taken very seriously, when originally proposed, but that had to be resumed later simply because it revealed itself as the only logically consistent one. It consists of an inter-temporal reinterpretation of the transactions that have been represented by the model. The capital goods, as all goods, that exist at the beginning are taken as given resources, and all the goods (capital goods or consumption goods) that become available or may become available in the future are taken as themselves transacted on present markets for future deliveries, or on contingency markets, which are supposed to be held at the very same point in time. This maintains the basic once-for-all character of the problem. At a unique point in time, a gigantic higgle-haggle is supposed to take place, which allocates all resources from now to eternity. Thereby, nothing is changed in the model; only its symbols are *reinterpreted* at a higher level of abstraction. All the properties of the solution, as well as the meaning of prices, are preserved.

This is perhaps the extreme stage reached by the generalisation of the pure preference model, but it is a most logical one. A theory can admit no exception to logical consistency. If 'anomalous' cases arise, they must be excluded or modified by assumption so as to be reabsorbed at a higher level of abstraction.

7 The *Objective* Theory of Value (a Pure Production, or More Specifically, a Pure Labour, Model)

The objective theory of value, on which the earlier classical economists took their first steps, has undergone considerably less analytical work, especially by way of formalisation, than the subjective theory of value. It is, however, also possible for the objective theory of value to present a bare skeleton of a theory that includes those essential elements, and only those essential elements, that the theory cannot do without.

I think that the essentials of the objective theory of value can be found in what may be called a model of a *pure production*, or more specifically, of a *pure labour model*.[6] One must go back for this to the very initial intuition of Adam Smith. However, it is not necessary to refer such a model to a primitive society, as Adam Smith did. In our theorising, we may well refer it to a technologically advanced society, which has the characteristic of using only labour. On this subject I shall follow a formalisation I have given myself in earlier works (see Pasinetti (1962, 1981, 1993), Chapter 2).

Suppose there is an economic system in which a society of individuals carries out an activity of production and an activity of consumption. All consumption goods are made by labour alone; labour is therefore the only 'factor of production'. The activity of production is carried out with extensive division of labour and thus with a marked specialisation. Each individual produces only one type of good, or even a *fraction* of one type of good, thereby being able to achieve a very high productivity. This means that each individual will then need to obtain all the consumption goods he/she needs through exchange. This is the way in which a series of rates of exchange, or prices, come into being.

Suppose technology is represented by a series of labour coefficients $\ell_1, \ell_2, \ldots, \ell_m$, for the production of m consumption goods, and suppose that per-capita demand is represented by a series of consumption coefficients $c_1, c_2, \ldots, c_m$. Let us denote the physical quantities produced by $Q_1, Q_2, \ldots, Q_m$, the prices of the m consumption goods by $p_1, p_2, \ldots, p_m$, the total quantity of labour by L and the wage rate by w. Then we can represent the economic system, in a closed Leontief model fashion (see Chapter 3, Section 6), by two linear and homogeneous systems of equations:

[6] This term (after calling the model presented in Section 4 a 'pure preference' model) seems to me more appropriate to characterise the initial stage of the present model than the term 'pure production' model used earlier (in symmetry to the term 'pure exchange' model) in Pasinetti (1981).

$$\begin{bmatrix} 1 & & & & -c_1 \\ & 1 & & & -c_2 \\ & & \ddots & & \vdots \\ & & & 1 & -c_m \\ -\ell_1 & -\ell_2 & \dots & -\ell_m & 1 \end{bmatrix} \begin{bmatrix} Q_1 \\ Q_2 \\ \vdots \\ Q_m \\ L \end{bmatrix} = \begin{bmatrix} 0 \\ 0 \\ \vdots \\ 0 \end{bmatrix}, \qquad (1.7.1)$$

$$[p_1, p_2, \dots, p_m, w] \begin{bmatrix} 1 & & & & -c_1 \\ & 1 & & & -c_2 \\ & & & & \vdots \\ & & & 1 & -c_m \\ -\ell_1 & -\ell_2 & \dots & -\ell_m & 1 \end{bmatrix} = [0, 0, \dots, 0]. \qquad (1.7.2)$$

The necessary condition for non-trivial solution is

$$\sum_{i=1}^{m} c_i \ell_i = 1, \qquad (1.7.3)$$

and the solutions for relative quantities and for relative prices, respectively, are

$$Q_i = c_i L, \qquad (1.7.4)$$

$$p_i = \ell_i w \qquad i = 1, 2, \dots, m. \qquad (1.7.5)$$

Necessary condition (1.7.3) turns out to be the Keynesian effective demand condition for full employment and comes to link together the economic system as a whole. Solutions (1.7.4) evince a demand-determined theory of production, and solutions (1.7.5) a *pure labour theory of value*.

In perfect analogy with the previous case (see end of Section 4), the solutions determine *relative* prices, whereas the absolute level of prices remains indeterminate. Here, again, one should go on to introduce money (and other things) in order to deal with the determination of the absolute level of prices. But, for our purposes, we do not need to go any further and may remain at the stage of relative prices (at least for the time being). Relative prices turn out to be proportional to physical quantities of labour. If the wage rate were to be used as *numéraire*, prices would actually turn out to be *equal* to physical quantities of labour. The beauty of this basic model is that it can give rise to no ambiguity or complication. Value is labour. It makes no difference whether it is referred to as 'labour embodied' or as 'labour commanded'. Any good or service can 'command' an amount of labour that is always equal to the amount of labour it embodies. This is the really basic and original feature of a pure labour theory of value.

8 The Meaning of Prices in a Pure Labour Economy

As may be seen quite clearly, the explanation of value that emerges from the theoretical scheme of a pure labour economy, and indeed the whole conception of an economic system, are strikingly different from those emerging from the pure preference model presented in the previous sections.

The economic phenomenon at the very basis of the model is the technological process of production, with division and specialisation of labour. And the explanation of prices that emerges follows as a consequence. Prices, that is the rates of exchange among commodities, arise from the fact that each individual specialises in producing only one (or even a fraction of one) consumption good but at the same time needs, in principle, *all* consumption goods. These must therefore be obtained through exchange. Production and exchange are inherently linked by labour specialisation. In this context, prices express Smith's 'toil and trouble' of production. Hence the physical quantity of labour emerges as the clearest objective standard with which to compare all goods and services. The most elementary notion of cost of production ('labour embodied') coincides with the most elementary notion of purchasing power ('labour commanded') to give a concrete expression of that old Aristotelian intuitive idea of a homogeneous common constituent of all goods.

In synthesis, prices simply emerge from the necessity of an extensive division of labour – this is their *raison d'être*. And their meaning is consequential: they represent indexes of costs in terms of the ultimate constituent of all commodities – physical labour.

As far as time is concerned, it may be noted that, already at its essential and simple stage, the theoretical scheme is inherently sequential. Production and labour services are flows, that is, they have a time dimension. The solution to the problem which is proposed refers to a particular period of time. But this period of time will be followed by another period of time and therefore by another solution, which in its turn will be followed by yet another period of time, and yet another solution, and so on. One may well start by assuming a production process that repeats itself unchanged in time (a stationary economy), but this is clearly an extreme case. Different periods of time will be characterised by different technical coefficients and therefore by *different* solutions. The model naturally leads to the investigation of *changes* and movements through time (i.e. to *dynamic* analysis).

It may here be added too that the theoretical choice implied in the formulation of a pure labour model – and with it the objective theory of value – springs from a particular way of looking at society, from a particular 'social philosophy' so to speak, which is indeed different from the one pointed out with reference to a pure preference model. It is a social philosophy that, through division of labour, stresses the necessarily *cooperative aspects* of an organised society and that looks for the responsibility of society as a whole in bringing about situations that are considered socially desirable. Of this, the fulfilment of the necessary condition (1.7.3), which expresses Keynes's requirement of an effective demand sufficient to ensure full employment, is the clearest indication. And it is important to realise that it is there, right at the initial and essential stage. Postulates concerning private ownership, or for that matter public ownership, are not made, and the problem of how the net product is distributed, both at a given point in time and through time, is thrown wide open for investigation.

These are clear and sharp features, which are to be maintained, from this point on, in any elaboration of this theoretical scheme beyond the simplest and essential stage of a hypothetical economy of pure labour.

9 Extensions (Generalisation and Achievements) of the Pure Labour Model

The theoretical process of *extending* (and even more of generalising) the model of a pure labour economy has been more laborious and roundabout than the analogous process for the pure preference model. There can be little doubt that, at the stage considered so far, a process of generalisation has remained far from having been completed. There are many reasons for this state of affairs. To begin with, the *type of economy* the model envisages is more complex than the one envisaged by the pure preference model. The model of a pure exchange economy could, in essence, have been developed centuries ago, for the concept of individual preferences and the process of exchange that are at its basis are centuries old. By contrast, the process of production with division of labour, which is at the basis of the pure labour model, though of course originally just as old, has become crucially relevant only with the development of industrial societies. The conceptual magnitudes that have come into being are more numerous (commodity physical quantities, in addition to labour, and rates of wage and profit, in addition to commodity prices).

Adam Smith was himself unable to extend the pure labour theory of value beyond its simple stage of a pure direct-labour economy (which he associated with a primitive society; see Section 7). When he came to deal with an advanced society, in which there is accumulation of capital and appropriation of land, he could do no better than adopt an 'eclectic' approach, consisting in considering the cost of production, and thus value, as made up of three components: wages, profits and rents, without being clear on how they could be determined, and, most of all, without being able to maintain the logically beautiful simplicity of the original version.

It looked as if the central problem to be faced was that of income distribution. And it was Ricardo (1821) who took the really remarkable theoretical step forward. In one stroke, Ricardo was able to 'eliminate' rent from the determination of value (by his differential theory of rent) and extend the pure labour theory to production with capital (circulating or fixed) by relying on the assumption of uniform capital intensity in all production processes, or rather by relying on the 'hope' that, when uniformity of capital intensity is not realised, deviations from pure labour proportionality might be empirically negligible. It was precisely the difficulty of answering the objections to this assumption that got Ricardo into an *impasse*, from which his followers have been unable to extract him.

After Ricardo, Marx (1894) made the boldest attempt at a complete solution to the problem of value, but on alternative lines. He overturned the whole approach of the Classical economists by *defining* value as labour embodied, which implied throwing on the intrinsic characteristics of the capitalist economies the fault of making production prices deviate from values (owing to their institutional necessity of uniformity of the rates of profit and labour exploitation). This was a powerful way of cutting a really Gordian knot, by a direct indictment of the whole capitalist institutional set-up. But in this way, the emotions and passionate discussions that were generated by Marx's controversial works, and his calls for a social revolution, came to complicate enormously the analytical work of theoretical economists. On pure analytical grounds, this may well have contributed to discouraging a dispassionate pursuit of the generalisation of the pure labour theory of value along genuine Classical lines.

It is only with Sraffa (1960) – and parallelly, though independently, with Leontief (1941, 1951) – that rigorously based discussions have recently been resumed, by going right back to the point where they had been left by Ricardo. Sraffa's analysis has clarified the meaning of Ricardo's 'elimination' of rent from the determination of value. Land and natural resources are claimed by Sraffa to play a role which, in reverse, is analogous to that of the non-basic commodities: they do not affect the determination of prices of basic commodities nor the relations between profits and wages. Secondly, the enrichment of the production model into a full-fledged inter-industry scheme and the analysis of its mathematical properties have clarified enormously the complex input–output framework (see Leontief (1951, 1966)) and the relations between prices and quantities of labour, besides those between prices and distribution of income, both in the simple case of single production and in the more intricate case of joint production. Thirdly, through the analytical construction of Sraffa's 'Standard commodity', expressing what, from Ricardo's work, could only appear as the *chimera* of an 'invariable standard' of value, it is shown that income distribution is indeed a phenomenon that can be dealt with independently of value.

The field has thereby been cleared of the many conceptual difficulties into which Ricardo's analysis had stumbled. Indeed the whole field of Classical analysis has been shown to be quite open to the application of the modern tools of formal rigorous logic and mathematics. But the major analytical work on the way to a complete generalisation has not been carried out. Sraffa (too modestly) claimed to only have provided a 'prelude' to further the work to be left to the younger generation.

10 Analytical Breakthroughs

The present work started from the conviction that, from the analytical work done so far, the logical process of generalisation can and must proceed till its end.

An examination of the development of the theories of value would seem to evince, within the theorising process, an internal logic that imposes on the modern theorist a strict discipline on the use and development of concepts and on the relation of assumptions to deductions, that were unknown in older discussions. This is not merely due to requirements of conciseness and elegance but to more profound requirements of rigour and logical consistency, with few and simple principles at the basis of any theory that deserves this name.

The 'eclectic' treatment of value used by the old moral philosophers may appear to have taken advantage of wider degrees of freedom. But there is obviously no question of going back to that stage. Those degrees of freedom, if they are to be recovered, will have to be recovered at a higher level of investigation.

A theoretical approach in itself, once taken, becomes quite demanding. It can allow no compromise, and yet it has to cover the whole hypothetical world it is supposed to represent. So a theory *must* be general or must be generalisable so as to cover, in principle, the whole reality it is supposed to refer to.

Not surprisingly, Debreu did not call his theory *a* theory of value; he called it *Theory of Value* (1959), without any qualification. The alternative, and competing, labour theory of value, to the extent that it has not yet done so, will have to aim at doing the same. It will have to aim at being general, or at being generalisable, so as to cover the whole of economic reality.

The advantage of this generalising impetus is enormous, for it allows us to extricate ourselves, on the guidance of a few simple principles, in the middle of a very complex economic reality, by never losing the sense of direction.

It will be seen later on that this can be done precisely through a very logical and indeed complete generalisation of the *pure* labour theory of value. It will be shown that, through a further development of a labour theory of the rate of profit and of a (separate) labour theory of the rate of interest, which together imply a theory of income distribution based on physical quantities of labour, both at a given point in time and through time, a complete generalisation is possible in terms of the pure labour theory of value for which the original equality of 'labour embodied' and 'labour commanded' is realised in general (i.e. in a complete, full-fledged production model, even with joint production) and not only in the hypothetical case of Adam Smith's original pure direct-labour economy.[7]

11 Further (Methodological) Breakthrough

If this theoretical construction stands, the consequences for economic theory become far reaching. For they inevitably imply a revolutionary change in economic methodology in terms of a separation of those economic relations that are to be investigated at a *normative* level (giving a complete content to the Classical notions of natural features of an economic system), and those relations that are to be investigated at an *institutional* level (on rules and criteria that include a wider scheme of individual's behaviours), in a way that is no longer constrained but includes characteristics of particular, widely accepted, institutional relations as part of a more general framework, stretching to the extreme stage of a complete coverage of *all* economic phenomena (though to be faced in a different way and at a higher level of investigation).

[7] See Parts III and IV of the present work.

2 *The 'Production Paradigm' in Historical Perspective*

1 Conceptual Foundations

A historical, brief and selective, review of the path recently followed in economics by an emerging 'production paradigm' will now be attempted in the present chapter.

The conceptual foundations of this paradigm can of course be traced back very early in the history of human societies. But it is only very recently that it has become of overwhelming importance.

1.1 Production as a Basic Characteristic of Modern Human Societies

It is worth stressing immediately that it is one of the most outstanding characteristics of human societies that they *produce* the goods and services which they need. This phenomenon was less conspicuous in primitive societies. Early mankind lived on what was immediately offered by the natural environment through hunting, fishing, gathering berries and wild fruit. In the course of human progress, however, man learned to *transform* what he/she found in his/her surroundings, to use and control those processes of nature which are useful and to eliminate or tame those which are harmful. The history of mankind is also a history of the continual improvement of the process of production of goods and services, of the increasing emancipation of humankind from the caprice and whims of the natural environment, of a persistent effort at making the goods and services which they consume and of shaping the whole environment in which they live.

1.2 Two Epochal 'Revolutions' in the Process of Production

The evolution in the process of production has of course taken place continuously. But it has also undergone qualitative leaps and remarkable discontinuities. In particular, the *Agricultural Revolution*, as it has been called by the economic historians, which led to the cultivation of land and the domestication of animals (i.e. to the production of the means of subsistence), was the first major leap (about 8000 to 5000 BC) towards the independence of human societies from the variability and unreliability of the natural surroundings.

Many changes took place, of course, after that major event and slowly continued to take place ever since, but in order to find a second comparably crucial qualitative leap in the organisation of human societies, we must go through a long stretch of centuries and come very much near us. More precisely, we must come to what the economic historians have called the *Industrial Revolution*, which, in the eighteenth-century AD, led to the production of the very place (the factory) in which the process of production was going to take place and to mould (and hopefully – or at least ideally – protect) the whole environment within which we live.

It is the Industrial Revolution that is absolutely important for the purposes of the present work. The contemporary economists perceived the rapid and enormous increase in productive capacity which was being generated as an increase in the wealth of nations. The phenomenon was, however, far more variegated, complex and deep-rooted. One basic aspect marked it very deeply, namely a change in the very *conception* of wealth, which had itself evolved, because of the evolution in the process of production.

1.3 Two Different Notions of 'Wealth'

The concept of 'wealth' appears perfectly clear and familiar at first sight. It is traditionally defined as 'the abundance of goods and services at the disposal of an individual or of a community'. But a closer look immediately reveals sources of ambiguity in this as in other definitions.

The principal distinction to be made is that 'abundance of goods' might mean an endowment, or fund, of existing goods, that is, wealth as a given *stock* of resources, commodities or claims, or it might mean an increasing periodic flow of goods and services, that is, wealth as a *flow* of commodities and services – an increasing national income. These two meanings are often confused, even today. Yet they embody very different concepts. Although the two kinds of wealth are not, of course, unconnected, the relation between the two is not at all simple or clear; nor is it unchanging with the evolution of the economic systems themselves.

It is a fact that, when speaking of the wealth of single individuals, one usually finds it most convenient to refer to the concept of wealth as a stock (i.e. to the size of their total ownership). But, when speaking of rich and poor nations, one usually refers to the average income per head of their inhabitants, that is to their average annual ability to produce, and then enjoy, goods and services that are produced. It is the concept of wealth *as a flow* that has recently become increasingly relevant with reference to the wealth of nations.

1.4 Natural Resources versus Produced Wealth

For centuries, the wealth of a nation was identified with the wealth of its King. It is not surprising, therefore, that the concept of wealth as a stock, to which one usually refers in relation to single individuals, was almost inadvertently but rather generally extended to nations and to the whole world. This is particularly evident in the work of moral scientists (and economists) who wrote *before* the Industrial Revolution.

More specifically, in the three centuries during which human societies were moving towards the Industrial Revolution (i.e. in the fifteenth, sixteenth, and seventeenth centuries) wealth continued to be taken as the endowment of available economic resources, especially with particular reference to the precious metals. This was the approach that came to be known as *Mercantilism*. The dominant idea was that the total stock of wealth is given, for the world as a whole, and that the wealth of one nation can therefore increase only at the expense of some other nations.[1] (Hence, the close connection between Mercantilism and the aggressive policies of the national states.)

The really outstanding merit of having broken away from this ancient tradition goes to the French Physiocratic School, of the middle

[1] Consider, for example, statements like the following, reported by Heckscher (1955, vol. II, p. 26): 'It is said that no one ever loses without another gaining. This is true and this is borne out in the realm of commerce more than anywhere else... (Montchrétien)... It is likewise to be remembered that... an increase in any Estate must be upon the Foreigner, for whatsoever is somewhere gotten is somewhere lost (Francis Bacon)'.

of the eighteenth century. It was at that time that François Quesnay drew a *Tableau Économique*, in which he focused attention precisely on the net annual product of a nation. In the various analyses of the *Tableau*, the *production et distribution des richesse* are continually referred to. And the synthesis of Physiocratic thought which Turgot wrote towards the end of the eighteenth century was, indeed, entitled: *Réflexions sur la formation et la distribution des richesses*. The terms *production* and *distribution* essentially refer to the concept of wealth as a flow. Yet the implications had already reached much further. When the 'stock' consists of *produced* goods, it is itself continually consumed and replaced by the very process of production; it is no longer something which is accepted as given, but something which is itself produced, renewed and enlarged.

Jean-Baptiste Say himself divided his *Traité d'économie politique* (1803) into three books: (i) *De la production des richesses*; (ii) *De la distribution des richesses*; and (iii) *De la consommation des richesses*.

An essential change of view had gradually asserted itself. It was not only the distinction between wealth as a stock and wealth as a flow that was seen important but also the contrast between *produced* wealth (whether as an annual flow or as an accumulation of means of production) and exogenously given natural resources.

Later on, the English Classical economists were no longer in any doubt over this matter. Whatever the endowments of natural resources and the climatic characteristics of a country might be, it was in their conviction *produced* wealth (as a flow of goods and services and as accumulated capital goods), which was going to increasingly characterise and condition the emerging industrial societies.[2]

This crucial passage from Mercantilism to Physiocracy, almost immediately perceived by Classical Political Economy, is so important for the purposes of the present investigation as to deserve some further, more articulated (even if concise), series of remarks and reflections, before coming to consider a more logically consistent framework of the production paradigm, which will absorb the whole of our analysis, from Chapter 3 onwards.

[2] See the very first pages of Adam Smith's *Wealth of Nations* (1776), to which we shall come back in a moment (references in the text are to the 1904 ed.).

2 Eighteenth-Century Physiocracy and a Discovery of the New Concept of Wealth

I should like to draw the reader's attention, though within the limit of a few pages, to the profound and complex process – the awareness of which even today is not sufficiently perceived – that immediately preceded, and in the end generated, the Industrial Revolution.

2.1 From Mercantilism to Physiocracy

To begin with, one should not be surprised to find that the immediate responses stimulated among the early economists by the inception of the modern world (by which is here meant the world from the Renaissance onwards) should have been of a 'mercantilistic' type. As is well known, Mercantilism – with its central tenet that a nation, in order to increase her wealth, should aim at an excess of exports over imports – is a doctrine that dominated economic thought in the sixteenth, seventeenth, and the first half of the eighteenth centuries. The Mercantilists' arguments and their over-enthusiasm about the merits of trade have subsequently been proved faulty, but this only underlines how strong must have been the impact of the benefits of trade on the minds of the scholars who, during those centuries, tried to analyse and understand the relevant economic aspects of the commercial environment of the time.

But, as the approach to the Industrial Revolution was proceeding, it was unmistakeably the other aspect of the modern world – the aspect connected with production – that forcefully began to be brought to evidence.

It is important to realise how, in the second half of the eighteenth century, Physiocracy – by submerging Mercantilism – became the new doctrine which came to dominate economic thinking. It was indeed centred precisely on *production* and – understandably enough in the eighteenth century – on agricultural production as the basic source of wealth of the nations.

As already hinted in the previous paragaraphs, it is to the Physiocrats that we owe the first table representing the circulation of commodities in an economic system (François Quesnay's celebrated *Tableau Économique*). This document marked a turning point. The radical change of perspectives introduced by the elaboration and implications of this table started with a change of the very conception of 'wealth'. No longer the accumulated stock of precious metals, advocated by the Mercantilists, but the *produit net*, the annual net production, was singled out as the true source of wealth of a nation.[3] The economists of this school of thought were then able to go on and also consider the trade in the commodities which are produced and to develop those arguments in favour of free trade, which came to break the mercantilistic recipe, after two and a half century of undisputed domination.

It may be interesting to make a remark straight-away, the relevance of which had already emerged in the definitions of the two paradigms sketched out in Chapter 1, but which will emerge ever clearer in the following pages. A theorist is able to analyse trade without any reference to production. In fact, in order to isolate this problem, he/she will very likely ignore production altogether. But when a theorist concentrates his analyses on the process of production, the horizon widens up, and he/she is also bound to consider the trade in the commodities which are being produced, although he/she may tend, for simplicity of arguments, to leave aside the goods which are not produced – the natural resources.

2.2 *François Quesnay and the* Tableau Économique

A few words may be useful on the importance of Physiocracy as the basic economic achievement of the eighteenth century. François Quesnay was its central figure.[4] Curiously enough, he was not an economist.

[3] Consider the following propositions reproduced from Mirabeau (1762, pp. 14–15), and generally attributed to *Docteur* François Quesnay, as after all is done in the recently published version by INED (1958) of the works of Quesnay: '*C'est cet excédent que nous appellons revenu. C'est la seule richesse, parce que c'est la seule proportion disponible, tout le reste étant nécessairement engagé à l'entretien indispensable du rouage de la machine économique.*'

[4] It may seem unfair – to any historian of economic thought – to begin our selective review straight with Quesnay, jumping over all precursors, especially those that made their contributions in the field of the quantitative aspects of economics, but we need conciseness and selective significance. To make some, though obviously insufficient, amendments, I shall mention at least three earlier major personalities: Fra Luca Pacioli (1447–1517), who with his *Summa de arithmetica, geometria, proportioni et proportionalità* (1494) gave

He was a surgeon physician by profession. But, at the court of Louis XV, the King of France, he suddenly surged to universal fame as the author of the *Tableau Économique*,[5] which aims to represent the circulation of commodities in the whole economy. François Quesnay remained for a couple of decades at the centre of practically all the major economic discussions in the whole of Europe.

To understand the relevance of François Quesnay's masterpiece, we need to make an effort of imagination and go back in time to the amazingly rough rural economic society characterising mid eighteenth-century France, under its politically authoritarian (and by then obsolete) regime, of absolute monarchy. Yet it is here that we find the birth of that exciting and extraordinary intellectual movement – the *French Enlightenment* – that produced the *Encyclopedie* of Diderot and D'Alembert.

Within that society, Quesnay had the merit of propounding, together with Mercier de La Rivière (1767), the idea of an *ordre naturel et essentiel des sociètès politiques*, that is a fundamental 'natural order' in social interchange, of which enlightened scholars should take upon themselves the task of discovering and illustrating, so that appropriate Government institutions could be put together in order to bring it into existence. From here comes the term 'Physiocracy' (etymologically 'government of Nature') that Quesnay and his followers coined for the school of economic thought they founded.

The scheme which Quesnay developed is very simple. There is in it an identification of social classes and their economic functions (identification that will be kept later by the Classical economists and by Marx).

the first description of double-entry book-keeping; William Petty (1623–1687), whose *Political Arithmetick* [1690] started the conception of economic 'science' as measurement (see the excellent treatment not only of Petty but also of other – though only British – empiricists in Stone (1997)); finally, Richard Cantillon (1680–1734) who – with his *Essai sur la nature du commerce en general* – stands out quite sharply at the point of the passage from the treatment of Trade to the Physiocratic concepts of 'production'. See its re-publication, both in English and in French, made by the Royal Economic Society (Cantillon 1931).

[5] The *Tableau Économique* was first published in Versailles in 1758 and was immediately acclaimed as one of the greatest discoveries of all times (see further details later). Abridged versions were elaborated by Quesnay himself and by Mirabeau. It has since been reproduced many times. Its most recent and accurate reproduction may be found in Kuczynski and Meek (1972). An excellent, detailed account of it may be found in Giancarlo de Vivo (2009).

The members of society are grouped into three classes: the productive class, the so-called sterile class and the aristocratic class. Each class has particular rights and performs particular functions. The 'productive' class consists of those employed in agriculture and mining. This class is termed 'productive' because the physical quantity of goods it obtains by working on the land can directly be seen to be greater than the physical quantity of the same goods which had to be used up. The land thus comes to be thought of as the only factor that generates a 'net product'. The 'sterile' class consists of the craftsmen and those engaged in manufacturing. It is called 'sterile' because, in Quesnay's naive conception, it adds nothing to the net product; it merely transforms what has been produced by the productive class. Finally, the landlords class consists of the King, and of the noble and ecclesiastical Aristocracy. This class does not work, owns the land and receives the rents from its property.

Given this social structure, it is clear that exchanges must occur, that is, flows of physical commodities from one class to another must take place at the end of each production period, in order that the wealth produced may be distributed among the various classes, and in order that the production process may then continue in the following period. The purpose of the *Tableau Économique* is precisely to represent these flows.

The *formule arithmetique* originally used by Quesnay to represent these exchanges (known as the zigzag, because of the crossed, slanting lines joining the various figures) is rather cumbersome and is now only of historical interest.[6] Various devices have been used ever since to clarify these relations. We may ourselves take advantage of two of them, one graphical and one in terms of a double-entry table. They may well look primitive to modern economists, so extensively trained in sophisticated mathematical arguments, yet a more attentive examination will show them to be more significant than they may at first appear.

2.3 A Simple Graphical Representation

Let us suppose that the production process takes place within a finite period of time (which we may call a 'year') and that the exchanges take place at the end of such period. Quesnay's *Tableau* could be

[6] See its recent reproduction in Kuczynski and Meek (1972).

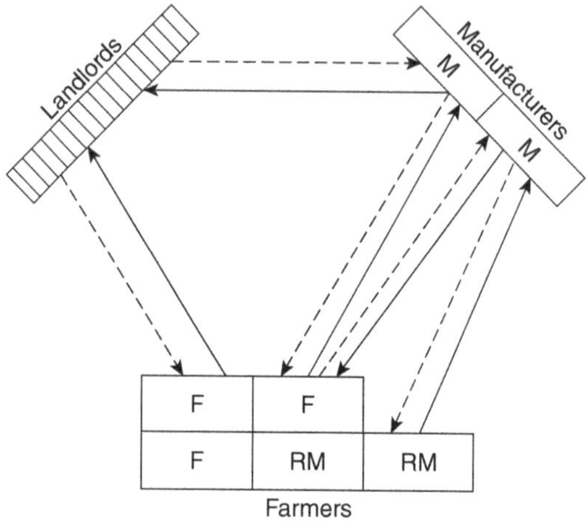

Figure 2.1 Graphical representation of the *Tableau Économique* (before exchange).

represented[7] as shown in Figure 2.1. Each rectangle represents a physical quantity of commodities having a value, say, of 1 million *livres*. Total gross production is therefore worth 5 million *livres*. *F* denotes production of foodstuffs; *RM*, production of raw materials; and *M*, production of manufactured goods. The two finer and dashed rectangles represent 2 million *livres* in money (i.e. means of payment, introduced here merely for accounting purposes). Finally, the broken arrows show the *monetary* flows, and the solid arrows the *real* flows (opposite but symmetrical to the monetary flows).

When the process of exchange is completed, the situation is as shown in Figure 2.2. The 2 million *livres* in money which are shown in the possession of the farmers will, at the beginning of the following period, return to the landlords as rents for the use of land. The initial situation will thus be re-established, the production process will go on, and at the end of that period the same circular flows of commodities will take place all over again.

At the end of every period, the landlord class is thus able to obtain goods for the value of 2 million *livres*. These 2 million *livres* worth of goods, which constitute the physical excess emerging over and

[7] These figures are those used in the original Tableau. The graphical representation follows the one given by Shigeto Tsuru (1942).

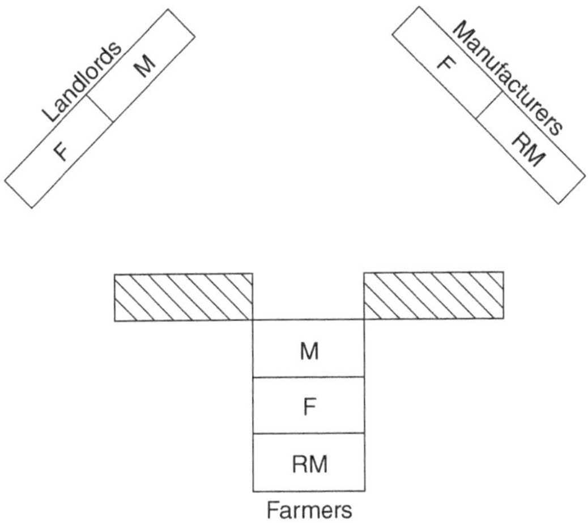

Figure 2.2 Graphical representation of the *Tableau Économique* (after exchange).

above what is needed to maintain the production process, represent for Quesnay the 'net product' of society.

As can be seen, Quesnay's schema is very simple and may well appear rather primitive to us. Yet, in order to find any markedly superior schema of inter-industry relationships, we had to wait until the contemporary economic literature, and more precisely until Leontief presented his input–output analysis, which will be considered in Chapter 3.

2.4 A Double-Entry Table Representation

It is not difficult to express Quesnay's *Tableau Économique* in the more modern form of a double-entry table. The flows of material goods and of money considered by Quesnay may be rewritten as in Table 2.1

This table is a genuine input–output table,[8] as may be seen quite clearly by looking at Leontief's scheme, to which we shall turn in the Chapter 3. The farmers and the manufacturers (first two rows and columns) represents what is today called the inter-industry part of the table, while the landlord class (third row and third column) represent the 'final sector'. The 'net product' of the system – all of which,

[8] Phillip (1955) was the first to represent it in this way.

Table 2.1 ***The* Tableau Économique *as a double-entry table. The figures are supposed to be in million livres***

		Outputs			
Inputs		Farmers	Manufacturers	Landlords	Totals
Farmers	Foodstuffs	1	1	1	5
	Raw materials	1	1	–	
Manufacturers	Manufacturing	1	–	–	2
	Luxuries	–	–	1	
Landlords		2	–	–	(2)
Totals		5	2	(2)	7

according to Quesnay, goes to the landlords – is shown both in the third column and in the third row. It appears in the third column as the bundle of material goods available to the final sector, and it appears in the third row as the 'value added' to the means of production.

We are clearly put in a position, at this stage, to realise how one may grasp from the *Tableau Économique* of Quesnay surprising anticipations of many concepts which later on were developed by the economic theory now so familiar to us.

2.5 Important Anticipations of Modern Theoretical Concepts

Without exerting any forcing of the evidence and avoiding to talk of a specific theoretical model, at least in the sense we would talk of it today, we can nevertheless immediately perceive a set of ideas, very clearly emerging from Quesnay's *Tableau Économique* that will constantly characterise the subsequent economic literature. Here is a list:

(i) The idea of a surplus, or net product (*produit net*), that is of a physical excess of produced commodities over and above the commodities which must be set aside, and then must re-enter the production process. In Quesnay's scheme the whole net product originates from the primary sector, where it can objectively be seen that, at the beginning of the production period, 3 billion worth of commodities enter as inputs, and then, at the end of the same 'year', 5 billion worth of the same commodities are produced as output.

(ii) The idea of economic activity as a circular process that, besides producing a surplus, reproduces all the physical commodities used up during the production process, so that the production process itself can re-start and then take place again, exactly in the same way, in the following period. Notice that this circular process is something absolutely fundamental to the very conception of Quesnay's analytical framework. In fact, primary goods (food and raw materials) are necessary to feed the process of production of manufactured commodities, and at the same time manufactured commodities are necessary to feed the process of production of primary goods. In Piero Sraffa's terminology today, we would say that both the primary goods and the manufactured goods are *basic* commodities, while the commodities consumed by the aristocrats (luxury, cultural, and military commodities) are *non-basic* commodities. Quesnay considers the latter as finally incorporating the net product of the whole economic system. In fact, this physical surplus has been originated in the primary sector and then has been transformed – by the inter-action of the primary and of the manufacturing sectors – in such a way as finally to emerge in the form of those two billion worth of commodities that the Aristocracy can afford to consume.

(iii) The idea, indeed essentially analytical, of the subdivision of time into finite periods, so that the production process and all the operations technically required by it take place in each period. At the end of each period, precisely at the point that separates it from the subsequent one, the analytical attention, so to speak, pauses to consider the exchanges taking place. Such exchanges are necessary for the whole economic system in order to provide the Aristocracy with the net product and, at the same time, to re-create the initial conditions that allow the production process to start again in the following period.

(iv) The concept of 'capital' as an advance, that is, as a set of necessary means of production, that must regularly be provided and replaced by the economic system. (On this respect the role of a social class was originally associated with the provision of savings *before* the production process may re-start.)

(v) The symmetrical roles of the flows of physical commodities produced in the economic system and of the counterpart flows of money. Money had basically been considered for its intrinsic value. With the *Tableau*, it comes to evidence also as means of payment and (very importantly) as a unit of account.
(vi) Finally, the realisation that these newly discovered conceptions were relevant for decisions of economic policy.

And here we may pause for a moment, simply taking cognisance of the incredible list of anticipations, concerning both economic theory and policies, that emerged out of the turmoiled elaborations of that remarkable group of intellectuals, in eighteenth-century pre-Revolution France, who, for the first time, called themselves *les economistes*.

2.6 *The Beginning of Political Economy*

It is of course all too easy to see the vital relevance of these ideas for us today, after the development that economic theory has gone through ever since, but can we imagine what was the impact at that time? Of course, the concepts – and even more their analytical expressions – were rather cumbersome and even confused, given the historical background within which they were presented. But the interesting aspect is that the convictions of the people who entertained them were remarkably strong and deep-rooted. They created the belief of something absolutely new and of enormous importance for the whole mankind. Schumpeter, one of the most perceptive economic historians, was so impressed as to define the whole movement as representing the very first true school of economic thought, in the full sense of the word. It had a master (François Quesnay), it was founded on a few basic concepts (see the list given above), and it was given an analytical expression (the *Tableau Économique*); it was common to a group of strongly convinced propounders (Mercier de La Riviére, Mirabeau, Turgot, Dupont de Nemours, Baudeau, Le Trosne, to mention only the most well known of them), who could take advantage of a channel of expression and diffusion (the *Encyclopedie*) that exerted an extraordinarily effective and widely felt intellectual impact.

This movement, which – for fear of personal consequences – was talked about from outside as a 'sect' (while the scholars concerned normally wrote anonymously), reached perhaps its apex during the forty years that go from 1738 (the year of first publication of the *Tableau*) to the disappearance of its inventor, François Quesnay (who died in 1774).

During those years, its intellectual impact was terrific, not only in France, but also in Great Britain and in the whole continent. It attracted in fact attention from the whole of Europe.

To mention two major figures that have already appeared in our arguments in Section 2 of Chapter 1, I shall recall that both Ferdinando Galiani and Adam Smith spent a non-insignificant period of their time in Paris, precisely in that period, though at different junctures in the development of their ideas.

Galiani was in Paris for ten years, from 1760, as an assistant to the Neapolitan ambassador to Paris. At that time, he had already written his masterpiece (his famous *Trattato della Moneta*), mentioned in Section 2 of Chapter 1 as containing economic arguments which I called of a pre-theoretical nature. His stay in Paris led him to write a further book, in French: *Dialogues sur le commerce de blés*, also notable, though not as outstanding as his *Trattato*.

For Adam Smith, the intellectual adventure was probably even more important. His stay in Paris was definitely influenced both on the analytical and on the conceptual level. Smith's *Theory of Moral Sentiments* had already been published (1759). He had resigned his chair at the University of Glasgow (1764) and had seised the opportunity of a remunerative job as tutor of the son of an Aristocrat – the duke of Buccleuch. He could in this way accompany him on a tour of Europe. In France, he met Voltaire, D'Alembert, and, most importantly, in Paris, he got in touch with Quesnay and the other Physiocrats, right in the fervour of the Paris cultural atmosphere of discussions on subjects of reason and progress. Only in 1767 did he return to his home town, Kirkaldy, where he could devote himself full time to draft what turned out to be his masterpiece, the *Wealth of Nations*. In 1773, he moved to London, to follow the last stages of the publication (in 1776), which were to give him universal fame. François Quesnay had meanwhile died (in 1774), but the impact of his ideas is evident in Adam

Smith's process of writing the *Wealth of Nations*. So much so that his colleague and biographer (Dugald Stewart) revealed that Smith had, at a certain point, entertained the intention of dedicating the *Wealth of Nations* to Quesnay.[9] This intention was not finally maintained (but Quesnay had meanwhile died).

It is nevertheless impressive that in the *Wealth of Nations*, he should give a very extensive quotation of Mirabeau's famous evaluation of the *Tableau Économique* as one of the three great inventions since the beginning of human civilisation![10,11,12]

[9] See Dugald Stewart's (1811) *Biographical Memoirs of Adam Smith* (read by Stewart himself at the Royal Society of Edinburgh on 21 January 1793).

[10] The following quotation, as it appears in the *Wealth of Nations*, is worth reproducing, in spite of the ambiguous detachment with which Adam Smith gives it:

> There have been, since the world began – says a very diligent and respectable author, the Marquis de Mirabeau – three great inventions which have principally given stability to political societies, independent of many other inventions which have enriched and adorned them. The first, is the invention of writing [. . .]. The second is the invention of money [. . .]. The third, is the Œconomical Table, [. . .]; the great discovery of our age, but of which our posterity will reap the benefit. (See Smith 1904, Vol. II, p. 177)

[11] On the other side, it is interesting to reflect on how high in France was the enthusiasm that characterised *les economistes*. On this respect, one may quote the conclusive evaluation, attributed to Dupont de Nemours, of a comparison he gave of Jacques Turgot and Adam Smith. With regard to the *Wealth of Nations*, he stated:

> Tout ce qu'il y a de vrai dans ce livre estimable, mais pénible à lire, en deux gros volumes [. . .] se trouve dans les *Réflections* de Turgot; tout ce qu'Adam Smith y a ajouté manque d'exactitude et même de fondement. (Quoted in his *Eloge de Turgot* by Schelle 1888, p. 159)

[12] A whiff of national pride would lead me to mention a group of economists mainly in Lombardy who have become known as constituting the Italian (mainly Lombardy) Enlightenment at the end of the eighteenth century. The most remarkable among them was clearly Cesare Beccaria (1738–1794), who became instantly well known in the whole western intellectual world thanks to the publication of a small book in which he advocated the suppression of the death penalty Beccaria (1764). In our contest, the really crucial piece of thought that is relevant is Beccaria's doubts about the appropriateness of the institutional principle of private property of the means of production to which he referred with the epithet ('*Quel terribile diritto*') 'that terrible right'. It is really surprising to find it mentioned as early as in the eighteenth century at the time of the breaking out of Industrial Revolution.

3 *Classical* Political Economy

3.1 Beginning and Time Coverage

The stream of economic thought, conventionally referred to as 'Classical', which started with the *Wealth of Nations* of Adam Smith (1776), is generally thought to end with John Stuart Mill's *Principles of Political Economy* (1873). It started directly on Physiocratic lines, but under a much more powerful impact, namely, the actual impact of the English Industrial Revolution. It was, not surprisingly, the industrial aspect of the modern world that impressed the Classical economists as being undoubtedly the most important feature of a new society. Trade was also a substantial topic, but it was the trade of manufactured goods. This had obvious consequences on the attitude that the Classical economists adopted towards the economic reality they wanted to investigate. This attitude can be caught immediately in the very opening pages of their works, when they are outlining the subject of their inquiries.

Without, of course, any pretence of going into any definite and, even less, exhaustive evaluation of the development of economic thought in the eighteenth century, it suffices for our purposes to consider very briefly the basic concepts as they were developed by the two most prominent, and by far most influential, figures of the British Classical school of thought: Adam Smith and David Ricardo.

3.2 From Adam Smith to David Ricardo

Adam Smith begins his *Wealth of Nations* with an analysis of 'the causes of the improvements in the productive power of labour', which are immediately singled out as the main source of the wealth of nations. At the very beginning of the work, when sketching out the plan of the whole inquiry, Smith explains that 'the proportion [of the produce] to the number of those who are to consume it' – namely per-capita income, as we may say in modern terms – 'must in every nation be regulated by two different circumstances; first, by the skill, dexterity, and judgement with which its labour is generally applied; and, secondly, by the proportion between the number of those who are employed in useful labour and that of those who are not so employed. Whatever be the soil, climate, or extent of territory of any particular nation, the abundance or scantiness of its annual supply must [...] depend upon these two circumstances'.[13] But Smith insists further. He wants to underline the pre-eminence of the 'skill, dexterity, and judgement with which its labour is generally applied' over the quality of 'the soil, climate, or extent of territory' and he points out how 'the savage nations of hunters and fishers [where] every individual who is able to work is more or less employed in a useful labour [...] however, are so miserably poor [... while] among civilised and thriving nations, though a great number of people do not labour at all [...] yet the produce of the whole labour of the society is so great that all are often abundantly supplied'.[14]

These sentences are worth meditating on even today. Under the compelling pressure of the striking disparities between developed and under-developed countries, it is with a sense of achievement that we have recently been re-discovering the same factors accounting for differences in per-capita incomes that Adam Smith had clearly singled out two centuries ago!

At this point, I may simply start by recalling what has been said (see pages 34–38) on how Smith was able to sketch out a pure labour theory of value, with reference, however, only to a supposed primitive economy. But, not surprisingly, he immediately got into difficulties when he tried to go beyond the most primitive stage. Only half a century later could Ricardo come to some help.

David Ricardo, by becoming more analytical, had already missed Smith's emphasis on the effects of improvements in technology. But his basic approach to economic reality remained the same; indeed, he centred his analysis on production in a way much more suitable for analytical elaboration, as he had a clear conviction (his enemies could even say a 'stubborn' conviction) that, when simplifications are necessary, these ought to be made in the direction of eliminating from the analysis what in practice is least important. Like Smith, he considered the phenomena connected with the commodities which are given by nature as 'by far' less important than those connected with the process of production. Therefore, when faced with a choice, he never hesitated in devising his analytical apparatus with reference to the latter, even if

13 Smith (1904, vol. 1, p. 1).
14 Ibid., p. 2.

that sometimes implied some crude simplifications with regard to the former.

It is in the first two pages of his *Principles* that Ricardo draws a distinction which seems to me of crucial importance. It sets out, precisely in terms of types of commodities, the evolution of the analysis from trade to manufacture. Ricardo says that 'there are some commodities the value of which is determined by scarcity alone'.[15] We may call these the commodities of the *natural endowment* type. They are given (by nature, by particular circumstances or by peculiar skills) in a fixed quantity, and they have to be accepted as they are. They become economically relevant when they are scarce, that is, when their fixed quantity is insufficient to meet all needs (*scarce goods*). For Ricardo, they have very little economic importance. 'These commodities', he adds, 'form a very small part of the mass of commodities daily exchanged in the market'.[16] Therefore, he chooses not to consider them at all. He is interested in a different, more relevant, type of commodities. 'By far the greatest part of those goods, which are the object of desire, are procured by labour, and they may be multiplied, not in one country alone, but in many, almost without any assignable limit, if we are disposed to bestow the labour necessary to obtain them'.[17] We may call these the commodities of the production type. It is on these commodities exclusively (the produced – or reproducible – commodities) that Ricardo concentrates his analysis.

With this approach the next difficulties arose. Natural resources are goods which are provided by nature; they belong to the category of *scarce goods*; nevertheless, they do enter the process of production. Ricardo solved this problem by following the logic of his basic approach. It was essential for him not to blur the picture of the most important phenomena – those connected with production – with secondary complications from the existence of non-homogeneous natural resources. Therefore, he referred his analysis to that piece of land which, by being at the limit of cultivated lands, yields no rent, namely to that land which is no longer scarce. All the other lands (or natural resources, in general), which have better intrinsic qualities than those at the limit of cultivation, yield a net gain or *rent* to the person who

15 Ricardo (1951, vol. 1, p. 12).
16 Ibid.
17 Ibid.

happens to own them. After deduction of this rent, all lands are put on the same footing of non-scarce land. The problems of scarcity had been 'eliminated'[18] from his analysis of production, and Ricardo could carry on his inquiry into the commodities which he really wanted to investigate – the produced commodities, which are 'by far the greatest part of goods' and 'which are the object of desire'.

Another difficulty was bound to arise in connection with short-run situations. As Ricardo says, the 'wants and wishes of mankind' may suddenly change, and the various processes of production may require some time for adaptation to the new requirements. Meanwhile, even produced goods may become *temporarily* scarce, and their market prices may diverge from what they would be on the basis of their fundamental determinants. Again, Ricardo solves the difficulty within the logic of his basic approach. He simply refuses to follow 'accidental and temporary deviations', because in the long run they become irrelevant. These deviations only come to blur, without influencing, the fundamental picture which is behind them. And Ricardo is mainly interested in the fundamental picture, namely in those values of economic variables which are – as he calls them – 'primary and natural'.[19]

3.3 The Logical Strength of Ricardo's Theoretical Scheme

There can be little doubt about the substantial jump ahead in economic analysis that was achieved by David Ricardo at the beginning of the nineteenth century. Historians will rightly point out that it is to Adam Smith that we owe the discovery and absorption of the Physiocratic contributions and then of stressing the centrality of Labour in the processes of production of industrial societies. But there can also be no doubt that it is to David Ricardo that we owe the merit of completing a logically tenable analytical framework within which one can see clearly the basic features of the whole Classical theory of 'natural prices', in the context of an *industrial* economic system.

Those recent economists who have tried to apply modern mathematical tools of analysis to express Ricardo's ideas[20] have always been

[18] See the reference, in the next section, to a letter to McCulloch.
[19] Ricardo (1951, vol. 1, p. 88, and also chapter XIX).
[20] And I am one of them: see Pasinetti (1960).

impressed by the clearness of Ricardo's logic and by his ability in setting together a remarkable logically consistent economic model.[21] It is also quite impressive to find how determined he was in defending (against his many critics) his (sometimes daring) assumptions – all of which were (even if inadvertently) made for the purpose of keeping his elaborations on a logically consistent ground.

To realise the superb level of his achievements, within a discipline that was struggling to become a 'science', let me briefly review how, even with his rough analytical tools, all essentially based on verbal logic, he was able to expound a remarkably complete economic 'model', which included the following:

(i) A theory of Rent (which became known, and is still called nowadays, the 'Ricardian' theory of differential rent) – a theory that came to fill the theoretical gap due to the absence of any theory of rent in Adam Smith's analysis. The analytical relevance of this theory was, as Ricardo himself put it to McCulloch, that it immediately allowed him (on purely analytical ground) of 'getting rid of rent'.[22]

(ii) A consequent theory of Income Distribution, which allowed him to narrow down his investigation to the roles played by the capitalists and the workers, forgetting about the landowners.

(iii) A 'dynamic' conception of such a theory, as an immediate effect of capital accumulation, since the profits would continually decline and the system would eventually settle down to a (Ricardian, as it was later called) stationary state.

(iv) Finally (and most importantly) a labour theory of value, valid no longer with exclusive reference to a primitive economy, as it was in Adam Smith, but extended to a full-fledged capitalist economy, with only one (rather baffling) assumption, namely that the proportions of labour to capital are the same in all branches of production. This was (analytically) the ingenious device which allowed him to keep logical consistency throughout. But it exposed him to a whole barrage of criticisms, which he bravely

21 See, for example, Piero Sraffa's remark in his *Unpublished Papers*: 'The problem is that of ascertaining the conditions of equilibrium of a system of prices and the rate of profits, independently of the study of the forces which may bring about such a state of equilibrium' (D3/12/15:2).

22 See Ricardo (1951, vol. 8, p. 194).

> defended by claiming that it was 'the nearest approximation to the truth' (Ricardo 1951).

And yet, this was not all!

Ricardo's analysis was rich of many other contributions. To mention only two of them, I may recall that he also propounded the principle (at that time borrowed from an anonymous pamphlet) of 'comparative cost advantages' that came to be a major addition to his theory of international trade.[23] On purely analytical grounds, another of his efforts was the search for a sort of 'average commodity' that could represent an 'invariable standard of value'; an idea whose usefulness to him was that it gave substance to his daring claim, mentioned above, of equi-proportionality of labour and capital in the production processes. There was here of course a real problem, which he was unable to solve – a problem which persisted not only during the whole of his lifetime but also after, as we shall see later.

All this being said, we may well conclude that, after Smith, it was with Ricardo that the 'production paradigm' reached the apex of the Classical economics' contributions.[24]

3.4 Post-Ricardian Anti-climax

It is commonplace, as already hinted Section 3.1, to consider the dominance of Classical economic theory as extending from Adam Smith's *Wealth of Nations* (1776) to John Stuart Mill's *Principles of Political Economy* (1st ed. 1848, 7th ed. 1873). This span of time includes almost all the British Classical economists, and almost all the economists of the time in Europe. The list is long, yet it would be of little help for us to consider it in detail. The general characterisation

[23] This principle was crucial to his prescription-claim of appropriateness to England of specialising in manufacturing and importing agricultural goods, thus halting the decreasing returns to scale which were thought to be prevailing in agriculture.

[24] This may also explain why, in the latter part of the nineteenth century, when Classical economics fell under strong critical attacks, it was on Ricardo, much more than on any other Classical economist, that criticisms were concentrated. Recall the persistence of the expression, proposed by Schumpeter (1954, p. 473), of calling his most daring simplifying assumptions a 'Ricardian vice'! All critics missed the point that it was precisely due to those crude assumptions that he could keep logical consistency all through his arguments.

of the whole period as 'Classical', and even more the tendency[25] to consider what immediately followed Ricardo as a period of 'decline of Ricardian economics' is – I think – misleading. In terms of a so much needed development of a 'production paradigm', clearly not of a decline one should talk, but rather of a failure of economic theorists to proceed and go ahead, beyond Ricardo.

What by now clearly appears is that economists (after Ricardo) reached a sort of anti-climax. There was a failure to grasp the basic fundamental elements of the revolutionary event – the *Industrial Revolution* – that was under way, and, more deeply, there was a failure, in economic analysis, to keep separate, from such an exceptional and unprecedented event, the consequent institutional changes that could, or would, or might, be made. The prevalent economic profession somehow felt it was then its duty to defend the existing institutions as they had been inherited. We must admit it was not easy to do otherwise. These institutions were basically founded on private property as the basis of social relations, on *laissez-faire* in government's economic policies, and on a reasonably free-market framework of the whole institutional set-up. This attitude accorded well with the political Restoration brought about, in the whole of Europe, by the Treaty of Vienna (1815), which substantially came to govern the European political scene for the whole new century after the Napoleonic era.

But the truth is that, within the economic profession, opinions had already been shocked by the implications of Quesnay's Physiocracy and of Ricardo's crude elaborations. Economic theorists were in great difficulties to proceed further. At the institutional level, theories and policies were shuffled in various ways and directions but did not go further. They essentially remained at the stage of knowledge and of analysis reached by David Ricardo, who had died in 1823.

More basically, therefore, one should say that Ricardian economics, far from falling into a 'decline', failed to go ahead! It came to a standstill.

Paradoxically, Ricardo himself provided many asides which were used, by his less inspired followers, to look backward, rather than to push forward.[26] As far as Ricardo is concerned, one must say that

[25] See, e.g., Meek (1950) and Pashkoff (2012).

[26] Consider the acute, perspicacious, concluding remarks of Ronald Meek's (1950) in his article on the 'decline' of Ricardian economics: 'Ricardo's

he was always saved in his arguments by his iron-strong logic. He had undoubtedly underestimated the great achievements of the technological age of his time, but he was always careful not to deny that 'improvements might take place in agriculture' (Ricardo 1815, p. 11). But, quite remarkably, he decided, for clarity of arguments, to ignore them (a powerful analytical device!). He cut short of all hesitations: 'We will, however, suppose that no improvements take place in agriculture, and that capital and population advance in the proper proportion' (Ricardo 1815, p. 12). Notice the qualification: 'in agriculture'. In this way, the absence of technical progress in agriculture was turned into an explicit *assumption*! And the surprising result is that, once granted, this assumption was by itself sufficient[27] to salvage the logic of all Ricardo's conclusions. His model remained terrifically clear and, on logical ground, unassailable. It grinded out, in strictly logical succession: lower fertility of the lands that had to be brought into cultivation, higher rents, lower rates of profits, a higher price of corn; hence, a movement towards the gloomy conditions of a *stationary state*, with wages compressed to subsistence, profits at their minimum and rents at their highest. The results of these analytical conclusions led Ricardo to extol the new class of capitalists that appeared to him as the really dynamic class of the new emerging society.[28]

The strong *analytical* point to note is that technical progress in manufactures, *however pronounced it could be*, did not make the slightest difference to Ricardo's (logically derived) conclusions. It was the process of production of the agricultural goods that acted as a bottleneck for the whole economic system.[29] The argument was indisputable, but

disciples, like the later followers of Quesnay, through overboard their master's most essential principles, while still claiming to speak in his name' (Meek 1950, p. 62).

27 This can be seen clearly even from a simple two-commodity version of his 'model'. See, on this, Pasinetti (1960, pp. 81–84).

28 Lets reflect on his conclusion: 'It follows then, that the interest of the landlord is always opposed to the interest of every other class of the community... High rent and low profits, for they invariably accompany each other, ought never to be the subject of complaint, if they are the effect of the natural course of things' (Ricardo 1815, p. 20).

29 We know what Ricardo's way out was free external trade. If corn were imported, the country would specialise in manufactures, and the process of diminishing returns (which, as it was imagined, only affected agriculture) would be brought to a halt!

it stood on the crucial assumption of a 'law of diminishing returns' in agriculture.

The majority of the profession did the rest, nay much worse! After starting by accepting the 'law of diminishing returns' in agriculture, the profession proceeded to extend such law to production in general, as if it were a *universal law*! It is interesting to note that various economists objected, but this was of no avail. James Anderson (1777), for example – an agriculturalist and a critic of Adam Smith – claimed that, in his experience, the 'diminishing returns' were not even the case in English agriculture. Others, such as H. C. Carey (1837), pointed out, more forcibly, that the way in which the 'law' was illustrated, namely by the process of cultivation starting on the most fertile land, was contradicted by historical facts, especially in newly settled countries, as it clearly was the experience in the United States!

Very few economists realised that this was a crucial turning point. Inexplicably, the 'Law of diminishing returns' became one of the cornerstones of nineteenth-century mainstream Political Economy. Already James Mill in his *Elements of Political Economy* (1821) expounded the law of diminishing returns as a general rule. Unlike Ricardo, he neglected even to mention the possibility of new discoveries or improvements. When John Stuart Mill, his son, finally wrote his *Principles of Political Economy* (1848) – which became the conventionally accepted synthesis of Classical economic theory – he reserved to the *Law of diminishing returns* a special chapter dealing with 'the Law of the Increase of production from Land' (as *different* from that of labour), warning that '[t]his general law of agricultural industry is the most important proposition in Political Economy. Were the law different, nearly all the phenomena of the production and distribution of wealth would be other than they are' (Mill 1848, 1st ed., vol. I, p. 212). Half a century later, Edwin Cannan – perhaps the most attentive critical editor of Adam Smith's *Wealth of Nations* (Smith 1904) – remarked that John Stuart Mill must have felt uneasy, and not at all on solid ground, as he kept on continually modifying his presentation of the *Law* in the subsequent editions (seven in the end!) of his *Principles*.[30]

[30] In examining the succession of John Stuart Mill's many qualifications and exceptions, Edwin Cannan pointed out that J. S. Mill ended up by admitting a surprisingly high number of exceptions. Cannan commented:

In spite of all this, the crucial fact was that the 'Law of diminishing return' was accepted generally.

This means that, for dominant economic theory, the effects of the combination of the differential theory of rent with what Cannan sadly defined the 'pseudo-scientific law' of diminishing returns turned out to be fateful. It generated, in the economic profession, an extraordinarily unjustified pessimism concerning the future of industrial economies.

Looking at these events two centuries later, they really appear astonishing.

Let me recall that the beginning of the nineteenth century, in the advanced countries of Europe, was historically a period of extraordinary development in all fields of knowledge.[31]

In the *actual* world of economic *activity*, meanwhile, the 'Industrial Revolution' was in full swing. Yet the dominant academic profession of John Stuart Mill's generation seemed scarcely to notice.

The contrast between what was happening in the actual economies of the real world and the surprisingly *non-chalant* atmosphere within which the academic profession of economists had settled down to argue is really striking.[32]

> ...we should be at a loss to conceive why Mill should be at the trouble of developing a law which: 1) does not operate in the very early date of the history of society; 2) is liable to temporary supersessions; and 3) has been made head against by an antagonizing principle, namely, the progress of civilization, throughout the whole known history of England. (Cannan 1903, p. 177)

But what kind of 'law' can this be? Cannan (1903) ended up by calling it 'the pseudo-scientific law of diminishing returns' (p. 181), pointing out that it was based on 'pseudo-historical characteristics' (p. 175).

31 Think of what was happening in all other fields of knowledge, outside economics! Think of what was happening in literature, philosophy and all moral sciences, not to speak of the arts (music, painting, sculpture etc.). But think, most of all, of what was happening in all the sciences (physics, medicine, biology, evolutionary zoology and anthropology), and, more significantly, in mathematics! (The famous Bernhard Riemann's lecture which started the development of non-Euclidean geometry was presented in 1854, although it was published only in 1866). Its impact had been revolutionary ever since. I am grateful to Edoardo Vesentini, a former president of the Lincei Academy, for bringing my attention to this.

32 For a more detailed presentation of the failures of economists to pick up the technical and scientific novelties of the early part of the nineteenth century, see Pasinetti (2015).

Curiously enough, the lack of justification of the economists' pessimism was perceived more quickly by external observers than by the internal practitioners of the new 'science'.

Thomas Carlyle, the Scottish poet and writer, unwarrantedly happened to pick up the striking contrast. His epithet, defining Political Economy as the 'dismal science', has become famous ever since.

4 Karl Marx Scheme

4.1 *Premise*

With all these events in the background, and at the same time with the social discontent very widely spreading in the industrial countries, it cannot be surprising that something had to happen on the socio-economic scene.

And it did happen, in the second half of the nineteenth century, when a personality of the stature of Karl Marx swept the scene of the discussions and debates on the impending changing social relations.[33]

[33] There were of course many precursors, who did perceive the dramatic social impact of the impending industrial age. Their mild, peaceful attitude quickly pushed them out of the centre of the discussions and quickly condemned them to oblivion. I may cite the example of Robert Owen (1771–1858), the utopian philanthropic 'socialist'. But there were many others, among whom it is worth mentioning that group of early 'socialists' (William Thompson, John Gray, Thomas Hodgskin, John Francis Bray), who at the beginning of the nineteenth century clearly and innocently wrote that, for them, according to all logical and practical evidence, it was clear that the whole product of society belonged to the working people who had produced it. They were quickly set aside and forgotten, until, at the end of the nineteenth century, Herbert Somerton Foxwell – the great Cambridge bibliophilist – in collecting their works was so impressed as to feel it necessary to draw attention to them. He rightly called them the 'Ricardian Socialists', and went on to write a long Introduction to the translation into English of the work of another economist of the same category – the Austrian Anton Menger, ironically brother of Carl Menger, one of the marginalist 'counter-revolutionaries' (see footnote 40), whose book appeared, with Foxwell's introduction, under the title *The Right to the Whole Produce of Labour* (1899). Esther Lowenthal devoted to them a book, precisely called *The Ricardian Socialists*. She synthesised their whole position as follows: 'Their criticism of the existing order was destructive; their plans of reforms subversive of it; but they expected to create the new society by peaceful means within the framework of the old' (Lowenthal 1911, p. 101). Not surprisingly, their philanthropic, peaceful, mild, quiet approach ended up by having absolutely no effect on the masses and in fact also on public

Marx occupies, as we all know, a unique place in the history of economic thought, and not only in the history of economic thought. The sheer volume of his writings is huge. But here we must concentrate our remarks selectively on those concepts and tools of analysis which refer to the theory of value, in connection with what was the evolving 'production paradigm'.

The shortest way to do this – I think – can be achieved quite well by considering the simplest of Marx's production scheme: what has become known as the model of simple reproduction.

4.2 Karl Marx's Scheme of Simple Reproduction

Marx's writings rely on a production schema which displays all the characteristics of Quesnay's *Tableau Économique*, and, at the same time, immediately contains, though in a different form, all the difficulties that Ricardo came to face in his efforts towards the formulation of a pure labour theory of value. But Marx cut them short.

For Marx the 'value' of a commodity is, by definition, the quantity of labour 'socially necessary' for its production. Human labour has the characteristic of being able to produce more commodities than are strictly necessary for mere survival, and this would be a source of joy and happiness if the capitalist society in which we live were not such as to cause certain lamentable distortions. Starting from the Classical belief that free market competition reduces the prices of commodities to their cost of production, Marx argues that the 'capitalist' society has the peculiarity of reducing human labour itself to a commodity like any other. Thus the ruthless logic of market competition also reduces the price of labour to its cost of production, that is, for him, to the subsistence wage which is strictly necessary for the maintenance of the worker and his family. The excess of what a worker produces over what is strictly necessary for this maintenance, which Marx called 'surplus value', is appropriated in full by those in the privileged position of being the owners of the means of production – the 'capitalists'. The 'surplus value' thus becomes the tangible measure of exploitation.

The 'value' of any commodity is represented by Marx as the sum of three components:

opinion. In terms of impact on the accepted mainstream economic theory, Ricardian socialism turned out to be a complete failure.

$$c + v + s,$$

where c denotes the quantity of labour needed to replace the 'constant capital', defined as all the commodities and machines consumed in the production process; v denotes the quantity of labour needed to replace the 'variable capital', defined as the stock of wage goods advanced for the maintenance of the workers; s denotes the 'surplus value', or the quantity of labour in excess of replacement needs, which ends up in the commodities appropriated by capitalists.

Consider a simple economic system in which there are three sectors, producing respectively means of production, wage goods, and luxury goods, the corresponding variables being denoted by the subscripts 1, 2, 3 respectively. If the system has to be capable of reproducing itself from year to year, the following equations will have to hold:

$$\begin{cases} c_1 + v_1 + s_1 = c_1 + c_2 + c_3, \\ c_2 + v_2 + s_2 = v_1 + v_2 + v_3, \\ c_3 + v_3 + s_3 = s_1 + s_2 + s_3. \end{cases} \tag{2.4.1}$$

The value of the commodities produced in sector 1 must be equal to the value of the means of production required by all three sectors. The value of the commodities produced in sector 2 must be equal to the value of the wage goods needed by the workers in all three sectors. Finally, the value of the commodities produced in sector 3 will make up the value of the luxury goods purchased by the capitalists, or the surplus value of the economic system as a whole.

This is, in brief, the Marxian schema of simple reproduction. As may be seen, it reveals a close kinship with Quesnay's *Tableau*. Social classes are here completely identified with specific economic roles. As with Quesnay, production is represented as a circular process which reproduces, from year to year, all the means of production used up in the production process and yields, in addition, a surplus of goods, here called the 'surplus value', which is appropriated by the owners of the means of production.

4.3 Marx's Claim of a Process of 'Transformation' of Values into Prices of Production

The ratio between surplus value and variable capital, which will be denoted by σ, is by Marx called the 'rate of surplus value':

$$\sigma = \frac{s}{v}. \tag{2.4.2}$$

If the subsistence wage is the same in all sectors (as a result of competition) and if the value of each commodity is (by Marx's definition) equal to the quantity of labour socially necessary for its production, then it follows that the rate of surplus value must be the same in all sectors, so that in our example,

$$\sigma = \frac{s_1}{v_1} = \frac{s_2}{v_2} = \frac{s_3}{v_3}. \qquad (2.4.3)$$

In a capitalist system, however, this equality of the rates of surplus value will never be realised because market competition will drive capital into the various sectors in such a way as to tend to equalise, not the rates of surplus value, but rather the rates of profit, which we shall denote by π_i, and which Marx represents by

$$\pi_i = \frac{s_i}{c_i + v_i}, \qquad i = 1, 2, 3, \qquad (2.4.4)$$

that is, as the ratio of surplus value to total capital (constant capital plus variable capital) in each sector.

We can now denote by γ what Marx calls the 'organic composition of capital' and define it by the ratio

$$\gamma_i = \frac{c_i}{v_i}, \qquad i = 1, 2, 3, \qquad (2.4.5)$$

which obviously is an index of the capital intensity in the various sectors. Substituting (2.4.3) and (2.4.5) into (2.4.4), one obtains

$$\pi_i = \frac{\sigma}{1 + \gamma_i}, \qquad i = 1, 2, 3, \qquad (2.4.6)$$

from which the following proposition can be immediately obtained:

(i) the rate of profit is positive if, and only if, the rate of surplus value is positive;
(ii) the rate of profit is always less than the rate of surplus value, except in the extreme case in which $\gamma_i = 0$ and hence $\pi_i = \sigma$;
(iii) the rate of profit is a monotonically increasing function of the rate of surplus value.

It can also be seen immediately from (2.4.6) that equality of the rates of profit in the various sectors and equality of the rates of surplus value in the same sectors can hold simultaneously only in the very special case in which the 'organic composition of capital' is exactly the same in all sectors.

In the general case, in which the 'organic composition of capital' differs from one process of production to another, it will be the equality of the rates of profit which is realised in any capitalist system and not the equality of the rates of surplus value. The result is that prices will come to diverge from quantities of embodied labour (i.e. from what Marx calls 'values', by definition). This once again contradicts, in a framework different from Ricardo's, the pure labour theory of value.

But Marx, like Ricardo, did not give up in the face of these difficulties. On the contrary, and here in contrast with Ricardo, Marx went on to counterattack. After carrying out the whole of his analysis in Volumes I and II of *Capital* by adhering to the rule of proportionality between values and quantities of embodied labour, in Volume III, Chapter IX (see Marx 1894), he turned to 'prices of production' and developed an argument which can, in essence, be expressed as follows.

In a capitalist system, 'prices of production' certainly diverge from quantities of embodied labour, or 'values'. Such a divergence is, nevertheless, for Marx, nothing more than merely one of the distortions of capitalist economies. The primary magnitudes, Marx argues, are the 'values', and thus all the fundamental relationships must be expressed in terms of 'values'. Prices are *derived* magnitudes. They are derived from the 'values' and simply effect a redistribution of surplus value according to the logic of a capitalist system, which needs to place capital at the heart of the production process. What happens in a capitalist system is that the market acts like a kind of pool which receives surplus value and redistributes it in the form of profit. It is as if, ideally, the capitalists would pay surplus value into a common fund and would then redistribute it, through the price system, no longer in proportion to wages (i.e. in the way in which it was created), but instead in proportion to total capital. In the system (2.4.1), the common fund would consist of $(s_1 + s_2 + s_3)$ and the average rate of profit would be

$$\frac{s_1 + s_2 + s_3}{c_1 + c_2 + c_3 + v_1 + v_2 + v_3} = \pi. \qquad (2.4.7)$$

The market would force the prices of the outputs of the three sectors so as to become:

$$\begin{cases} c_1 + v_1 + \pi(c_1 + v_1), \\ c_2 + v_2 + \pi(c_2 + v_2), \\ c_3 + v_3 + \pi(c_3 + v_3). \end{cases} \qquad (2.4.8)$$

The prices of commodities produced by processes with an above-average capital intensity will prove to be higher than the quantities of embodied labour, while the prices of commodities produced by processes with a below-average capital intensity will prove to be lower than the quantities of embodied labour. Appearances would thus become more complicated, but the substance would nevertheless remain unchanged. Finally, on the basis of two further assertions, namely: (i) total profits are equal to total surplus value and (ii) 'the sum of the prices of production of the commodities produced is equal to the sum of their values', Marx concludes that the 'transformation of values into prices of production' effected by the market serves merely to create the mystification that capital is 'productive' and that profit is its reward, while in reality the former is embodied labour and the latter is disguised surplus value.

4.4 The Beginning of a Long Dispute on the 'Transformation Problem'

The ingenuity of these arguments can hardly be disputed. What had been an insurmountable analytical difficulty for Ricardo was turned by Marx into a further indictment of the capitalist system.

However, critics of Marx soon pointed out a logical inconsistency in the original Marxian argument. If the conditions of simple reproduction are to be satisfied, the totals of the three rows in (2.4.8) must be equal to the totals of the three corresponding columns, as in (2.4.1). If this were not so, the economic system would not be able to reproduce itself from year to year. Now it is not difficult to show that, when this condition of logical consistency is met by (2.4.1), it cannot be satisfied by (2.4.8), unless the three sectors have the same organic composition of capital, in which case the very problem of transformation would simply not arise. The drastic conclusion was therefore drawn that Marx's whole argument was mistaken.

But the whole problem of the 'transformation of values into prices of production' was given new life by Ladislaus Bortkiewicz, a Russian economist of Polish descent (and one of the teachers of Leontief, as will be mentioned below), in an article published in 1907 (translated into English and published in Sweezy 1949). Bortkiewicz showed that, while Marx had certainly fallen into a mistake, this was due not to the intrinsic difficulty of the problem but rather to his inability to give a correct mathematical formulation of his simple model.

The dispute on the 'transformation problem' regained momentum and developed ever since into an enormous literature.

Let me synthesise it in a few brief sentences.

Marx was too hasty in thinking that he had solved the problem of the relation between prices and quantities of labour. His two assertions, (i) and (ii), mentioned in the end of the previous section, are incorrect; furthermore, the expressions which he suggested for the rate of profit, (2.4.4) and (2.4.7), are also incorrect. At the same time, however, the accusation, made by his critics, that there is an inherent logical inconsistency in the problem of the 'transformation of values into prices' has also been shown to be incorrect. A relation between quantities of labour and prices *does* exist, even if it is rather complex, and not so easy to interpret. In the economic literature on Marx, these problems have given rise to a long series of debates which, even today, show no sign of coming to an end. As Bortkiewicz taught us, new tools of analysis (especially novel mathematical tools) were required. But these have become available to economists only later. We shall return on these problems subsequently, in Chapters 5 and 6, where we shall be able to take advantage at last of the analytical framework following from the elaborations of Leontief and most of all of Sraffa, before concluding our analysis in Chapter 15. But we shall again return to Marx.

4.5 Marx versus *(or Complementary to?) Ricardo*

Meanwhile, a few remarks may be helpful to clarify what might look a tricky discontinuity, inside the same (production) paradigm, within which both Marx and Ricardo were moving.

Marx had grasped remarkably well the extraordinary leap ahead that the industrial society had brought about with respect to the previous (agricultural/mercantile) framework. He had learnt from Quesnay and Ricardo that all attention had to be concentrated on the profound implications of the production process, and more specifically: (i) on the centrality of what most people perceived had emerged as the new crucial 'factor of production' – capital (besides land and labour) – and (ii) on the emerging in society of a new class of economic agents – the capitalists (or *bourgeois*, in Marx's terminology). However, his attitude on this second aspect could not but be going in a diametrically opposite direction with respect to that of Ricardo.

The judgements (and the exhortations) on the new emerging class (the capitalists) were extolled by Ricardo, who considered them as representing the really dynamic class of society – hence a class to be favoured. On the contrary, Marx condemned them as the class that was exploiting the others and hence had to be overturned through a radical social revolution. Marx did not entirely realise that, at the very basis of Ricardo's analysis, there were the same conceptual elements of the production process, which he himself was considering, and moreover, he did not realise that both he and Ricardo were repeatedly stumbling against the same analytical difficulties, which needed to be solved. It was clearly of no use for either of them to push these difficulties aside by assuming that they did not exist!

Marx, in his usual disparaging mood, went on to dissect the 'disintegration' of the Ricardian school, but the sense and purpose of these terms were quite different (in fact the *opposite*) to those of the anti-Ricardian post-Classical economists. So much so that Marx, in his history of economic ideas – his *Theories of Surplus Value* (1869–1872) – had to devote to Ricardo more space than to any other economist, and the explanation should not be difficult to grasp. Ricardo's concepts (besides Quesnay's) were unmistakeably essential to Marx's elaborations. Had he followed them more analytically, he would have found Ricardo's basic analysis, not opposite, but complementary, to his own.

If only the distinction could have been clearly perceived between the stage of the fundamental relations and the stage of the institutional organisation of society, what a great contribution could have been made to economic theory on the one side and to the (institutional) construction of modern societies on the other side. Alas such a distinction, far from being perceived at those times, still escapes most of the economists' theories even nowadays![34]

4.6 Beyond Economic Analysis

Quite understandably, Karl Marx was overwhelmingly too sure to have struck at the very centre of the features of the new industrial society. Neither the clever insights of an English gentleman of great repute such as Ricardo (of Jewish stock besides) nor the rigour and precision of competent mathematicians, such as Ladislaus Bortkiewicz, supposing,

[34] This is what I have argued at length in Pasinetti (2007) and I shall be arguing (here and) most definitely in the final chapter of the present investigation (Chapter 15).

by a paradoxical, counterfactual, rhetorical figure, that they might have been available to him (which of course they were not), could have tamed him. He conducted analysis and discussion to their extremes. The process of production of material goods appeared to him so overwhelmingly important as to induce him to undertake his great efforts to conceive a whole theory of the history of social relations – which, after him, became known as *historical materialism*. In brief, according to his conception of history,

> Men... begin to distinguish themselves from animals as soon as they begin to *produce* their means of subsistence, a step which is conditioned by their physical organization. By producing their means of subsistence men are indirectly producing their actual material life.
>
> The way in which men produce their means of subsistence depends first of all on the actual means of subsistence they find in existence and have to reproduce. This mode of production must not be considered simply as being the production of the physical existence of the individuals. Rather it is a definite form of activity of these individuals, a definite form of expressing their life, a definite *mode of life* on their part. As individuals express their life, so they are. What they are, therefore, coincides with their production, both with *what* they produce and with *how* they produce. The nature of individuals thus depends on the material conditions determining their production. (Marx and Engels 1865, p. 42; authors' italics)

But, in this way, Marx had gone much beyond pure economic theory to enter territory fraught with philosophico-sociological political controversy. The whole of the Classical economic theories of Smith, Malthus, Ricardo, together with their Physiocratic precursors, were themselves unjustly turned upside down by the Marxian cyclone.

There was bound to be a reaction, and of course there was one – a major one! The repercussions thereof could not but affect and shake the very foundations of the whole of economic theory itself.

5 The Counter-revolution of Marginal Economic Theory at the End of the Nineteenth century and the Need to Rescue the Paradigm Lost

5.1 The Missed Opportunities of Classical Economics

I hope the reader will not consider it too ambitious a statement if I say that, significantly enough, this is the point where a *true* and solid post-Ricardian economic theory (had it been developed by true Ricardian pupils!) could have come to help.[35]

Dominant economic theory was in a desperate need of responding not only to the challenge of Marx's writings but also, more effectively, to the widespread and crucial weight of enlarging actual social unrest. But the academic profession of economists had lost any vitality, especially since Marx had learned the principles of Classical economics much better than the *bourgeois* economists – as he disparagingly called them – all essentially bent on trying to defend the existing institutional set-up.

The historical juncture was dramatic. As far as academic discussions are concerned, Classical economics was bound to come under the fire of criticism at the very moment at which – as it was happening in the second half of the nineteenth century – economists turned their attention to problems connected with the side of demand of the economy. The Classical economists had neglected demand almost completely. On this aspect, criticism was legitimate.[36] But what happened is very curious and sad. The economists who, at the end of the nineteenth century, criticised the Classics (and Marx) did not correct them on this point (we shall come back to this aspect in Chapter 10).

They did something else. They went back to deal with an entirely different order of problems: namely the problems related to those commodities – the scarce goods – which the Classical economists had left aside as unimportant (recall on this Ricardo's attitude stressed in Sections 3.2 and 3.3). This might sound extraordinary at this point, as in this way, they were moving into an entirely different field of investigation, concerning no longer the objective phenomenon of production, that is, no longer the major social feature of the Industrial Revolution, which was there, apparent to anybody who could open their eyes and attention to look at it, but concerning the *subjective* individualistically based phenomenon of utility and, more particularly, as it happened, of 'marginal' utility. Even more surprising to an attentive critic is that, in so doing, they gained approval and astonishing success.

[35] Alas, what happened instead was what Ronald Meek concluded, which I mentioned already in footnote 25 and footnote 26.

[36] See how strongly Ken Arrow (1991), in his vest of a 'modern economist', is criticising Ricardo for his neglect of the demand aspects of economies, calling this no less than the major fault of Classical economists.

5.2 That Baffling 1870s

The sudden theoretical rising to success of marginal utility theory in the 1870s is something to be pondered upon. What strikes one about it is that it took off apparently out of nothing. Utility had been no novel subject of discussion among economists,[37] and the marginal principle was not new either.[38] But before the 1870s, these concepts had been taken as rather secondary, and in any case always as complementary to the (more basic) ones coming from the sphere of production.[39] By contrast, in the 1870s, all of a sudden, they were laid astonishingly down as the very foundation of economic analysis. What is even more fascinating is that this happened not in one place alone but almost simultaneously all over Europe,[40] and, moreover, precisely the same concepts, in precisely the same places, had already been tried before, but without success.[41]

A satisfactory and comprehensive explanation of such a striking turn-about may yet require a long time to emerge clearly. But it seems to me that in the end it cannot be abstracted from the combined effects of two major features of the European environment of the time: the appearance of Marx's critique of economic theory (Marx's *Das Kapital* first appeared in 1867) and the widespread and serious social unrest which, in the real industrial world, characterised those troubled years.

At a basic level, Karl Marx was a Classical economist in the full sense of the word. He picked up and pursued the Classical (both Smith's

37 The numerous writings of Jeremy Bentham had very prominently introduced utility (and the measurement of utility) into economic discussions since the end of the eighteenth century. Even with reference to the specific problem of value, discussions had been widespread. See, e.g., Galiani (1751) and Say (1803).

38 Ricardo, as we have seen above, had used it for his own theory of rent.

39 Jean-Baptiste Say, to take an authoritative example, always took the line that 'le prix des produits s'établissait en chaque endroit au taux où les portent leurs frais de production, pourvu que l'utilité qu'on leur donne fasse naître le désir de les acquérir' (Say 1841, p. 321, 6th and last edn).

40 The 'marginal revolution' is by now jointly attributed to Jevons (1871), Menger (1871), brother of Anton Menger (see footnote 33), and Walras (1874), even though they all wrote their works independently of one another.

41 The list of 'precursors' is long and is continually being lengthened (Galiani, Lloyd, Longfield, Senior, Dupuit, Jennings etc.). Some of them actually are more than precursors, as is the case of Cournot and Gossen, who were marginalists in the full sense of the word, with only the bad luck of having published their works before the 1870s (Cournot (1838); Gossen (1854)).

and, especially, Ricardo's) approach to economic reality. This gave a sweeping drive to his analysis, since production – and production with capital – undoubtedly is the central feature of any modern industrial system. At an institutional level, however, he used Classical theory for purposes which were diametrically opposite to those of the Classical economists. The Classical economists (in a line descending directly from Physiocratic thinking) had accepted the society in which they lived as part of the order of Nature; Marx regarded it as a passing phase in the transition from the feudalism of the past to the socialism of the future. The Classical economists had generally been arguing in terms of harmony of interest among the various sections of society; Marx conceived economic life in terms of conflicts of interest and class struggle. The Classics (and the Physiocrats) had aimed at finding out how the established system works in order to help it work better; Marx aimed at uncovering its contradictions in order to hasten its end through turmoil and revolution. Even the purest of all analytical problems was turned upside down. Consider Ricardo's labour theory of value, bogged down by the difficulty of relative prices changing when income distribution changes, even if relative quantities of embodied labour remain the same. Marx could waste no time to untwine such Gordian knots: he just cut them. He *defined* values as being embodied quantities of labour and then turned the argument against the capitalist system. Marx argued that if, in practice, prices turn out to be different from 'values', that is the fault of the capitalist system, which, by disguising 'surplus value' under the form of profits, distorts the 'price of production' from 'values'. Precisely those features that appeared to the Classical economists as different, perhaps even insoluble analytical difficulties, were turned by Marx into further indictments of capitalist economies.

This was upsetting. To many people it sounded preposterous. Yet Marx's overall arguments were not easy to challenge. The obvious procedure to follow would have been to question the premises. But this is precisely what was so difficult to do. Marx's premises were exactly the same as those of Quesnay, Smith and Ricardo, that is, of all established Classical economics.

If only one could find an economic theory that made no reference to labour, no reference to means of production, possibly even to production itself... that would surely be the sort of thing that a frightened

Establishment could not but most warmly welcome. Marginal utility theory provided precisely that.[42]

It is worth recalling that the whole of Europe had just been under the impact of shivering revolutionary waves. A concentration of events had taken place precisely in those years. The First Socialist International – founded in London in 1864 – had held its four congresses in the four successive years of the late 1860s (1866 in Geneva, 1867 in Lausanne, 1868 in Brussels and 1869 in Basle). And, at the end of the Franco-Prussian War of 1870, Europe had witnessed the first communist revolutionary attempt ever to be made (the Paris Commune, March–May 1871). The Papacy itself was openly acknowledging the challenge. Shortly afterwards, Pope Leo XIII was going to overcome all hesitations and take the unprecedented step of pronouncing on social matters (Encyclical Letter *Rerum Novarum*, 1891) – not without reasons, after all.[43]

It cannot be surprising that when, in the 1870s, peace-loving academic economists began strongly to press with a theory which sharply drifted attention away from all the features which had so ruthlessly been put at the basis of the revolutionary trends of the time, the public

[42] There is absolutely no need to think that the marginal utility theorists developed their theories with such a purpose in mind. Marginal utility theory may well have been, as Schumpeter (1951, p. 888) puts it, 'a purely analytic affair without reference to practical questions' (actually too much so). The point which is made here is that historical circumstances made the 1870s, in sharp contrast to earlier decades, exceptionally receptive to such a theory.

[43] Consider how Leo XIII, on the first page of his *Rerum Novarum* (1891), opened the subject:

> That the spirit of revolutionary change, which has long been disturbing the nations of the world, should have passed beyond the sphere of politics and made its influence felt in the cognate sphere of practical economics is not surprising. The elements of the conflict now raging are unmistakable, in the vast expansion of industrial pursuits and the marvellous discoveries of science; in the changed relations between masters and workmen; in the enormous fortunes of some few individuals, and the utter poverty of the masses. [...] The momentous gravity of the state of things now obtaining fills every mind with painful apprehension[.]
>
> [...]
>
> In any case we clearly see, and on this there is general agreement, that some opportune remedy must be found quickly for the misery and wretchedness pressing so unjustly on the majority of the working class: [...] surrendered, isolated and helpless, to the hard-heartedness of employers and the greed of unchecked competition.

to whom theoretical economic works are addressed should have had a second look at what was proposed, no matter how unimportant or queer it had been considered before.[44] And what happened is indeed striking. Wherever, in the 1870s, marginal utility theory was proposed, it struck an astounding success.

5.3 Highly Sophisticated Analysis Framed within a Pre-Physiocratic Paradigm

An attentive examination of this new course of events, in academic economic theory of the end of the nineteenth century, allows us to uncover some more plausible reasons behind what at first appears an inexplicable explosion of the subjective paradigm.

It is after all natural to expect – if the thesis of a confrontation of paradigms is correct – that, from a radically different approach, a polarisation of the whole analysis should take place on the other aspect – the trade aspect – of the modern economic world. This theoretical movement began in the 1870s with the elaboration of the concept of *marginal utility*. It took up an approach to economic reality which appears as exactly opposite to the Classical one. The Marginalists began to study the real world not in what is most important but in what is easier to begin with. An analogy taken from the field of mechanics suggested to them to investigate the static aspects of reality

[44] Cournot and Gossen provide the impressive examples. Their books (in 1838 and 1854 respectively) were complete failures. Cournot thought at first that economists might not have paid attention to his work because of lack of acquaintance with mathematics. He patiently rewrote the whole work in plain words, making it three times as long (*Principes de la théorie des richesses*, Paris 1863). But the second version was as bad a failure as the first one (and remained so). Gossen, in his turn, was deeply disappointed. His book did not arouse any interest: it remained practically unsold. He died (in 1858) without glory. But three decades later a shrewd publisher (R. L. Prager of Berlin), after realising that marginal utility had become fashionable, got hold of the old printed material, which was still lying unsold. He added a short foreword, put up a new titlepage with the new date (1889) and with the simple addition 'neue ausgabe' and reissued the book. This time it was a great success. These aspects were pointed out to me, in conversation, by Piero Sraffa, who could show me, as proving pieces in his private library, the original first and subsequent editions of the relevant books. I was able to resume these arguments in my *Foreword* to the publication of the Catalogue of the Books of Piero Sraffa, see (Pasinetti 2014).

first: not because these aspects are supposed to be more important than the dynamic ones, but because they seem to offer the first logical step to take. From a formal point of view, the analysis which has come out is impeccable. It starts from clear premises and, by the use of the most elegant analytical tools, arrives at logically consistent conclusions.

The relevant fact is that, over the 100 years after that, hundreds of economists has carried out an enormous amount of analytical work along these lines, and by now marginal analysis have been cleared of the sundry small traps that the original arguments contained. The analytical tools themselves have been perfected through time and have become more and more elegant. A first generation of Marginalists using diagrams was followed by a second generation using calculus and eventually by a third using set theory. As was to be expected, through this long analytical process, the model has been schematised and stripped down to essentials so that the basic approach has by now emerged most clearly.

We may indeed say that the typical marginalist scheme of general equilibrium, as it has been called, is a model of what has become known as a *pure exchange* economy.[45] The model presupposes the existence of given natural resources in fixed quantities and of a given number of individuals, who are endowed with them. These individuals own the resources in a way in which is accepted as given and they have well-defined utility preferences. The economic problem that is investigated is that of finding those prices (equilibrium prices) which bring about, through exchange, an optimum allocation of the given resources; this optimum allocation being defined as that situation at which the individuals maximise their utilities, relative to the original distribution of resources among them. This model is worked out, in its basic features, with no reference whatever to a process of production. The only type of commodities that exist are given by nature and, in equilibrium, their prices will be either zero (and they will be called *free goods*) or positive, and they will be called *scarce goods*, the only ones to be economically relevant. In such a context, the economic problem is only one of *rational choice*. The individuals of the community, if they behave rationally and act atomistically, will exchange among themselves the given commodities up to that point where the ratios of

[45] As shown in Section 4, Chapter 1.

marginal utilities are equal to the corresponding ratios of prices. At this point their utilities are maximised. No individual could become better off without some other individuals being made worse off (a situation which has become known as one of *Pareto-optimality*). Most typically, the whole problem may be represented by a mathematical function to be maximised, subject to certain constraints to be accepted as fixed.

This is a perfectly valid theoretical scheme. Perhaps the Classical economists themselves would not have objected to it. They certainly would not have denied that there exists a rational problem of optimum allocation of the existing scarce goods. But they would never have dreamt of making of it anything more than a minor problem and an easy one to solve, so easy in fact that they felt justified in taking it for granted. The Marginalists, on the other hand, went to the other extreme. After analysing the problem of optimum allocation of given resources, they began to advance a disproportionate claim. They began to think that they had discovered a principle of *universal* validity, which *alone* would allow them to analyse the whole of economic reality.

From this point on, a vast theoretical movement started, the task of which has turned out to be that of *extending* the same elegant tools of marginal utility analysis to all branches of economic analysis. This tendency became clearer and clearer in the twentieth century and is in fact being continued nowadays by the great majority of economists, especially in the United States. Paul Samuelson, at the very beginning of one of the clearest versions of marginal economic theory, claimed precisely this. He claimed to have been able to isolate a simple principle, which, by being applied again and again, is behind every economic investigation: a mathematical function to be maximised under constraints. This is the *foundation of economic analysis*.[46] For Paul Samuelson (and for all Marginalists), the whole of economics can be reduced just to that principle (and mathematical tool).[47] Under this generalising form, marginal economic analysis has eventually even been

46 See Samuelson (1947), especially chapter I: *Introduction*. The same concepts are resumed and expanded by Koopmans (1957, pp. 4–5). Still more recently, they have been reformulated by Arrow and Hahn (1971).

47 Samuelson has restated his conviction that maximisation is 'the very foundation of our subject' in his Nobel Memorial Lecture: 'Maximum Principles in Analytical Economics', *Les Prix Nobel en 1970*.

called 'neoclassical' (a term that sounds ironical if one considers the opposition between the Classical approach and the marginalist one).

It was with reference to this vast movement and with a deep conviction on the generality of its approach that Lionel Robbins, at the apex of the marginalist era, epitomised the new conception of economic analysis with a celebrated definition. 'Economics', Robbins said, 'is the science which studies human behaviour as a relationship between ends and scarce means which have alternative uses'.[48]

But this is precisely the question. Is economics really all here – in a problem of optimum allocation of scarce goods[49] – or is this not rather a narrowing down of the subject of economics itself to one aspect, perhaps not even the most important aspect, of economic reality? Unfortunately, the Ricardian distinction between produced commodities and scarce commodities had by this time been pushed aside and forgotten,[50] and it was no longer so easy to see that the Classical economists had been talking about different things.

5.4 What Happened to the Theory of Production? (The Artificial Construction of Marginal Productivity Theory)

It is worth considering in detail and, more attentively, what happened to the theory of production within the marginal economics framework. Clearly, the marginal utility theory had to be extended beyond its original field (the optimum allocation of scarce goods) – it would have

48 Robbins (1935, p. 16).

49 Paradoxically enough Arrow (1991), in his retrospective review of Ricardian economics, reproaches Ricardo for not having understood that the centre of economic theory is the analysis of the optimal allocation of resources.

50 The process through which this has happened is itself very interesting. Economic goods have positive prices. Now, within a pure exchange model, the only goods that have positive prices are the 'scarce' goods. The Marginalists have therefore turned things upside down and *defined* the scarce goods as those goods that have positive prices. But this procedure, though justified in a pure exchange model, is illegitimate in general. All the produced commodities do have positive prices, and yet they are not 'scarce', in the Classical sense of the word. But the Marginalists did not go back to check their definitions. The consequence has been that they went on to (illegitimately) apply to produced goods the conclusions of their theories about scarce goods. For the Marginalists, all economic goods have become *scarce*, not because they are really *scarce* in our world, but simply because by definition they have been *called* so,

had a rather limited impact otherwise. And an extension (or, using a word which sounds deceptively more attractive, a 'generalisation') was soon made to the more important problems of production. Thus, in the 1890s, the theory of marginal *productivity* emerged.

The point is worth stressing. Historically, Marginal productivity theory did not spring from a factual examination of the problems to which it was meant to apply: the problems of production. It came from an *extension* to these problems of a set of ready-made analytical tools developed for completely different purposes.

The starting point was again provided, not by what is most important in an actual industrial society, but by what could most easily be fitted in, namely land (a scarce natural resource). Labour was immediately assimilated to land as one of the many scarce resources. A check is significant: all the original illustrative examples of this extension are in terms of land and labour. But there was a big stumbling block, represented by the treatment of capital goods. Capital goods are not 'given': they are themselves produced. Early attempts to deal with the problem had spontaneously considered capital goods as accumulated labour and time.[51] But this labour-time approach has put the natural resource model into such a series of inextricable difficulties as to be abandoned and resumed and abandoned many times. There is in fact only one logical solution compatible with that scheme: namely to assume that capital goods are in no way different from land.[52] This is the approach that has prevailed in the end. All means of production have either been merged into a homogeneous factor, called 'capital', which is put on exactly the same footing as labour and land, or have all been considered as many land-like factors, to be put on the same footing as many different types of labour and land. In the latter case, there is not even the necessity of insisting any more on any distinction between capital, labour and land of various types, as they are all

[51] See, e.g., Jevons (1871, chapter VII). It is interesting to notice that Jevons, who in general was harsh on the Classical economists, is in no opposition to them on this point. See also Böhm-Bawerk (1889).

[52] Consider, e.g., the involution that took place in Pareto's own analysis. In the *Cours* (1986), he tried to apply Walrasian analysis to capital goods, but he was not satisfied and in the *Manuel* (1909) he abandoned all the processes of production of capital goods altogether. What he continued to call *capitaux* are quantities which are given and not produced: they are in no way different from land-like scarce resources.

treated in the same way. They are all assumed to be land-like 'factors of production'.

Thus, with a series of natural-resource-like factors of production, one could go on and faithfully duplicate the marginal utility scheme. The same convex smooth differentiable 'well-behaved' function was assumed – called 'production function' instead of utility function: the same partial derivatives were considered – called 'marginal productivities' instead of marginal utilities. But there was a further difficulty. Production (unlike utility) must be measurable, which implies that marginal productivities must actually be equal (and not only be proportional) to the 'factor prices'. And since the total net product, by being always appropriated by somebody, can always be written as the sum of the various factor quantities multiplied by the corresponding factor prices, marginal productivities had to be such that they could be freely substituted for the factor prices without affecting the total (i.e. without leaving any positive or negative residual). Analytically, there is only one type of mathematical function that gives this result: namely, a linear and homogeneous function. So production functions, far from being observed, have been *assumed* to be linear and homogeneous.

A striking feature is that any difficulty that came in the way was eliminated by introducing further assumptions. No concern was ever shown about the essence of such assumptions, only with the logical consistency which they obviously required. For the Marginalists, it was rigour, not relevance, that counted. No hesitation had ever been shown, for example, on promptly extending, by assumption, the properties of giveness and definiteness, which are characteristic of scarce natural resources, to the state of technical knowledge, namely to something which is exactly the opposite. What is interesting is that, by adding, onto that fixed framework, a rational behaviour postulate (profit maximisation, parallel to utility maximisation) the theory provided a well defined and fixed relation between final (produced) goods on the one hand and the natural resources which go into them on the other. To take the former or to take the latter is the same thing in this model: there is a one-one correspondence between the two. Demand for the final commodities is thereby transformed into demand for the scarce resources. The two poles – utility on the one hand and natural resources on the other – had thereby been re-established, with everything in between reduced to irrelevance. For all essential purposes, the model had, so to speak, *eliminated* the process of production from the analysis, in the sense that all conclusions drawn at the stage of the scarce resources could be carried over, directly and without the slightest modification, to the final commodities.[53]

We may note that this is exactly the opposite of what the Classical economists did. The Classical economists eliminated from their analysis the complications raised by scarce goods in order to concentrate their investigations on produced commodities. The Marginalists have eliminated from their analysis all the relevant features of the production process in order to maintain intact the model they had built for the problem of optimum allocation of scarce goods.[54] Out of this symmetry – as we may see – there emerges a deep contrast, which reduces to a basically opposite criterion for the choice of the hypotheses: practical relevance (i.e. the singling out of those problems that are thought to be the most important ones) in the case of the Classical economists; logical consistency with a pre-conceived pure exchange theoretical scheme in the case of the Marginalists. This so well diffuse attitude of continuing to forget strictly logical criticisms, as if they did not exist, is beginning by now to appear absurd.[55] It has led economists such as

53 The analytical procedure of, one may say, trivialisation of the aspects concerning production is not just something that has happened once. It is happening all the time now! In what is known nowadays as general equilibrium analysis, all problems, all theorems are, generally, first of all, framed and proved within a pure exchange model – i.e., for a hypothetical world in which the process of production does not exist. Then – when all the things look fine for a pure exchange model – a production process is introduced. But at this stage, obviously, a production process can be introduced only if it does not upset the already built scheme. And what inevitably happens is that all aspects that might upset such a scheme are taken away by assumption. All important problems concerning production are either ignored altogether or stripped of their relevant features, devitalised and reduced by one assumption over another, to an innocuous form that does not upset the pre-conceived scheme of the optimum allocation of scarce goods.

54 It is interesting to compare this procedure with the one opposite to it adopted by Ricardo, who, faced with the problem of consistency, in his Theory of Distribution decided, as he pointed out, 'to get rid of rent' and concentrate his analysis on the distribution between profits and labour. His criterion, as we may realise, was to eliminate from the analysis what was *less* important (for him: land) and concentrate on what was most important (see Chapter 1, Section 9).

55 I have had other occasions to come back to this critique of Neoclassical economics; see, e.g., Pasinetti (2000).

Charles Ferguson to refer to it as 'a statement of faith' (Ferguson 1969, p. 269). Harcourt and Kriesler have found a way to facetiously refer to it by quoting the old proverb 'He who is convinced against his will is of the same opinion still' – very witty, but far from being scientific![56]

6 A Sharp Bifurcation of Economic Theory at the End of the Nineteenth Century

Some summarising reflections are in order at this point. As we may now realise, the end of the nineteenth century and beginning of the twentieth century marked a crucial turning point in economic analysis and theory. In the immediate, it took the form of a sharp bifurcation, of which very few scholars seemed to have become aware, or if they did, they preferred to react by shying away from it.

On the one side, Marx had picked up the Classical stream of thought, had acknowledged its analytical achievements and had accepted them as the very basis of what he thought to be the economic theory that should be developed for the industrial societies that had come into being. Unfortunately, he did not distinguish in his analysis the fundamental (what I have called *natural*) features of the industrial systems from the whole set of civil *institutions* of the society that had meanwhile come into existence, which he considered as a superstructure.[57] He took the former for granted and violently opposed and rejected the latter. This had the effect of placing him in flat opposition to the Classical economists, rather than in continuation and complementarity to them, which he actually was, or should have been considered. This turn-about gave Marx's works the character of a devastating critique of the existing institutions, of which he actually did advocate, as if to them there were no alternative, their destruction. This meant, openly and flatly, the advocacy of a social revolution; the very end of all the 'civil institutions' of the 'capitalist' economies, no one excluded, even those that might with some reasons be considered the proud achievement of the new society that had just emerged. Could this be done? Or, more reasonably and alternatively, could there be a set of institutions that should be set up in the place of those that

[56] Introduction to the *Oxford Handbook of Keynesian Economics*, (Harcourt and Kriesler 2013, p. 25).

[57] From *Critique to Political Economy* (Marx 1867–1970).

Marx singled out for un-pious destruction? Something was missing in this approach; its other side, that is, its positive side, which however needed to be entirely constructed! Nobody had the courage or the force or the guts to effectively put the problem in these terms. Yet, the relevant questions were precisely in these terms, and they remained in the air. Nobody dealt with them, which means they are still there: lingering in the air up to this day!

At the opposite extreme, the great majority of the economic profession turned out to be of no help in facing this real problem. The academic economists of the time who represented and created the other horn of the bifurcation were apparently unable to see any other alternative except retreating into the pursuit of a stubborn and straight defence of what turned out to be indefensible: namely the defence of the existing institutions, even if they had put the industrial world in the tongs of unbearable, inhumane living conditions of the working population, as those that characterised the end of the nineteenth century.[58] In front of a failure to propose any effective constructive opening, the economists of the time closed their ranks and proceeded straight into what actually became a 'counter-revolution'.

The real substance of what has paradoxically been called the 'Marginal Economic Revolution', that cropped up everywhere in the 1870s, was precisely that. Yet, it had an extraordinary and almost unbelievably attractive feature, of which it is now worth and important becoming aware by bringing it out into the open.

7 Elegance and Beauty versus Substance and Truth

Hence, the Marginal School of economics did represent the other horn of the economic theory bifurcation. It needs to be carefully considered because the phenomenon is indeed very interesting. As was shown in Section 5.4, in order to be logically consistent, the Marginal School of economics was compelled to abandon the production theory of the Physiocratic and Classical Schools and return to pre-Physiocratic and pre-Classical traditions. This meant a revival of the attempt to build

[58] Well known were the conditions of excessive length of the working week, under-paid hours of work, loss of the leisures of rural societies and over-crowded living conditions in the cities.

theoretical economic theory on that, other and older, traditional conceptions of wealth which had prevailed before. It meant a return to the concept of wealth conceived as an endowment of given resources to be optimally allocated. Substantially, it meant a return to the past while giving up any effort to trying to understand the future. Clearly it could not have succeeded, if done in the simple old unrealistic way, no matter how modified and updated. There had to be something new, possibly something dramatically new. And that is what happened!

Unexpectedly, an elegant and ingenious way was found to pursue the more primitive version of the economic system, namely that of an exchange economy. It was wrapped up in terms of the development of an apparently more modern, more 'rigorous', economic analysis.

No doubt, this was an ingenious turnabout. And it struck a remarkable success.

The device consisted in re-expressing the old basic economic concepts of the search for an optimal allocation of given resources, but by carrying them out with the use of new analytical tools. These were the *mathematical* analytical tools. Academic economists discovered that they could heavily make use of a language – mathematics – which had meanwhile become the language that was providing prestige to science! Many economists sincerely believed (or had the illusion to believe) that the use of mathematics was actually the way of transforming economics into a science. This was not an innocent or idle device. Mathematics had itself meanwhile, in the nineteenth century, undergone a remarkable evolution. It could indeed provide new tools of analysis. Let us be careful! We should notice that this aspect had nothing to do with the economic theory and substance of the subject under investigation. The new tools for the search of the analytical truth could well be applied to any discipline.[59] Advocating the help of mathematical tools of analysis, when these are helpful, or useful, to clarify procedures and results, and even to find out new relations, was – it must be admitted – a great and exciting innovation. But it concerned the efficiency, or elegance, or even the beauty of carrying out analytical arguments, not the *substance* of the subject or the relevance of the economic problems to be investigated, or the truth of achieved propositions. Any progress in the analytical tools of investigation as such

[59] See footnote 31 concerning Riemann's non-Euclidean geometry.

must clearly and perfectly be welcome if compatible with any logical framework, no matter within which paradigm, in economics, or in any subject.

However, nobody seemed to point this out. The majority of the production-paradigm-inclined economists – with the exception of very few, and we shall come to them in a moment – quite justly thought that *they*, not the marginalists, were dealing with the really relevant economic problems of production in the new industrial society. They underestimated the complexity of the type of society that had come into existence, which required not only a renovated conceptual paradigm but also new analytical tools! They underestimated, in particular, the attraction of the innovation: the elegant and beautiful tools for carrying out analytical investigations that the profession could have come to take advantage of in the new era of the emergence of science.

They left these ideas and tools of analysis to the Marginalists. This was a tragic mistake.

8 Efforts to Rescue the Paradigm Lost

Due to the vicissitudes just described in Sections 6 and 7, the twentieth century in academic circles opened with an almost complete absence of substantial works within the 'production paradigm'.

In fact, there did exist a few scholars who perceived the importance of pursuing the production paradigm by taking advantage of the mathematical tools of analysis. These extremely few scholars were ignored and remained almost unknown, only to be discovered later on (in fact, decades later). Hence, we should not be surprised to find that most of those economists who (with delay) were recognised as relevant in the development of the production paradigm, at the end of the nineteenth and beginning of the twentieth centuries, are precisely those who presented their fruitful theories by using mathematical methods. The most renowned among them are perhaps Vladimir K. Dmitriev [1904] and Ladislaus Bortkiewicz (1907) – the latter having already been mentioned in Section 4.4 as the scholar who successfully corrected the most obvious mathematical errors contained in Marx's formulation of the 'transformation problem'.

These economists did present mathematical formulations of simple economic models of production. Perhaps, due to the mathematical complexity for the majority of economists, these models remained largely ignored or misunderstood at the times they were presented. They remained largely ignored until much later than their conception. In fact, practically until they were translated, at last, into English, which happened in (1974) and (1952), respectively. Very recently, there has even been a further discovery: Maurice Potron, a cleric, who was brought to our attention first by Abraham-Frois (see Abraham-Frois and Lendjel 2004) and then by Christian Bidard (see Bidard, Erreygers, and Parys 2009b). Almost incredibly, both these works were only published in the twenty-first century![60]

But of course, even apart from the general practical ignorance of these predecessors in economic literature, we must also reckon the fact that, since the Classical economists and Marx, we had to wait for almost a century (till the middle of the twentieth century) before a decisive resumption of the production paradigm could take place in economics, and –even this– only owing to that minority of scholars in the economic profession who were alert at following the publications of the works of Wassily Leontief and Piero Sraffa, the two economists who have the merit of having rescued –in the middle of the twentieth century– what by their time had become a 'Paradigm Lost'.

9 Inter-industry Analysis in the Twentieth Century

Thanks to Wassily Leontief and Piero Sraffa, it has become clear that the new development which they brought back to centre stage has direct links with the Physiocratic *Tableau Économique* and with the theoretical investigations of the Classical economists.

Wassily Leontief (1906–1999) – an economist of Russian origins – was first a pupil of Ladislaus Bortkiewicz in Berlin, then an economic

[60] Potron was a French Jesuit who, even though knowing very little of economics, remarkably made use, in anticipation of the modern linear algebra in economics, of Perron-Frobenius theorems, in his search for the understanding of the problems of production in industrial economies. Interesting enough, his stimuli came from applying the old moral concepts of just prices and just wages in a society which had deviated from these principles. By knowing practically nothing about economics, Potron gathered his stimuli from the stands of Pope Leo XIII's Encyclical Letter *Rerum Novarum*, already cited above in footnote 43.

researcher and later a professor, at Harvard University in the U.S., till the end of his career.[61]

Piero Sraffa (1898–1983) was an Italian who emigrated to England in the 1920s (due to troubles with the Fascist regime in Italy) and then remained there (a very reserved man always escaping publicity) for the whole of his life.

Inter-industry analysis has by now proved to be a fruitful field of enquiry in which economic theory, analytico-mathematical tools, and direct empirical applications have reached an effective combination, as we shall see in the following chapters.

Curiously enough, it fell upon Paul Samuelson – the unrivalled author of that major work on *The* neoclassical *Foundations of Economic Analysis* that contributed substantially to the return of economics to the pre-Physiocratic conception of wealth! – the task of describing this remarkable occurrence. In 1991 (in the *Journal of Structural Change and Economic Dynamics*) Samuelson wrote a retrospective review of those crucial events, in the form of a Preface to the publication in English (at last!) of the basic lines of Leontief's doctorate thesis which had been presented in Berlin as early as in 1928 (the English publication can now, belatedly, be seen in Leontief 1991). It is from this work that we have come to know Leontief's original conception of what he called in his title 'The economy as a circular flow', a notion resumed by him straight from the works of Eighteenth Century Physiocracy and of Marx.

It is interesting to note how Paul Samuelson coupled the appearance in the economic literature of Wassily Leontief with that of Piero Sraffa, two people who had never met each other. Piero Sraffa arrived at Cambridge, England, precisely around the same time as Leontief arrived in the U.S. Finally, at the end of long elaborations, Sraffa came

[61] He was awarded a Nobel Prize in economics in 1973! The event was perhaps due more to a fortuitous circumstance (the preoccupation by the leadership of the USA, then engaged in a 'cold war', of being over-taken by the Soviet Union on matters of over-all economic programming, and thus keen to endorse Leontief with a generous research project) than to any conversion of the economic profession to the production paradigm, still very strongly opposed even today.

to publish his extraordinarily compact and important theoretical work (*Production of Commodities by Means of Commodities* (1960)).[62]

At this point we have arrived, in this brief but selective review (of the analytical surge of the production paradigm), at the end of the twentieth century. We shall now immediately go on to consider the basic contributions of Leontief and Sraffa, the two major scholars who have done so much to revive the *production paradigm* of economics in the twentieth century, and in this way – through their inter-industry analysis – to rescue what until then had remained a *paradigm lost* in economic theory, though being undoubtedly the most relevant and appropriate paradigm to be adopted in order to understand the features of the industrial society and the objective theory of value which is appropriate to it.

[62] It is even more interesting to realise the alertness with which Paul Samuelson was able to seize the opportunity to write a few lines that were inserted as a *Foreword* to Bidard's book on Potron (2009a).

PART II

The (Objective) Theory of Value in Inter-industry Analysis

3 *Wassily Leontief Input–Output Model*

1 Leontief's Starting Point

In 1941 Wassily Leontief startled the community of economists with the publication of what turned out to be his masterpiece (Leontief 1941). The initial page of such a work (the very first page of its Part I) opened with the following sentences:

> The statistical study presented in the following pages may be best defined as an attempt to construct, on the basis of the available statistical materials, a *Tableau Économique* of the United States for 1919 and 1929.
>
> One hundred and fifty years ago, when Quesnay first published his famous schema, his contemporaries and disciples acclaimed it as the greatest discovery since Newton's laws. The idea of general interdependence among the various parts of the economic system has become by now the very foundation of economic analysis.[1] (Leontief 1941, p. 9)

Isn't this astonishing? In 1941 Leontief was jumping back, over a century and a half – precisely over that century and a half in which Political Economy had come into existence and had developed up to its present-day highly sophisticated analytical elaborations – and dared to go back and resume basic ideas and aims that were conceived by a community of economists living in the intellectual infancy of economics, within the early formation of that *Enlightenment* movement that was indeed to shape the dawn of modern society, yet at a stage, which politically at that time, was still under the obsolete ancient regime of pre-Revolution France.

Astonishing as this may be, the previous chapter, Chapter 2, should by now suggest many helping hints to an understanding of Leontief's claim.

[1] This acknowledgement was not stated in isolation. It preceded, right on the verso of one of the title pages, a long quotation taken from the writings of François Quesnay expounding what he called *Premier problème économique*.

2 Remarks on Method

The economists of the eighteenth century had naively set themselves the impossibly ambitious task of studying economic reality, in all its complexity, while still using crude and primitive analytical tools.

Today economists are much more conscious of the complexity of real economic relationships and adopt the procedure of assuming simplified economic systems to begin with, in order to analyse them in as a rigorous way as possible, that is, with analytical methods which should leave no room to ambiguity. It is only after having studied simplified economic systems that the attempt is then made to introduce more complex hypotheses, one at a time. This is, of course, the procedure which will be followed in the present work as well, from now on.

3 The Transaction (Input–Output) Table

We may well adopt what might appear at first as the reverse of a normal procedure and take advantage of what has been shown already in Chapter 2, where we have used a double-entry table to present, in more modern terms, François Quesnay's *Tableau Économique*.

Suppose we actually *observe* an economic system which we suppose as simplified to such an extent as to be in a perfectly stationary state, with respect to the labour force, technical knowledge and consumption decisions. We assume that exactly the same physical flows of goods and services are effected year after year. A set of commodities are inherited from the previous period of production (let us say from the previous 'year') and are used up in the present period and reproduced: simple reproduction with no expansion.

A more general treatment of such a simple economic system can be carried out in algebraic terms.

Suppose, quite generally, that the transactions table contains n rows and n columns, representing the inputs and the outputs, respectively, of n industries (where the term 'industry' is broadly interpreted). Denote by $q_{i1}, q_{i2}, \ldots, q_{ij}, \ldots, q_{in}$ the physical quantities of the ith commodity which are delivered to industries $1, 2, \ldots, j, \ldots, n$; and by p_i the price of the ith commodity. Since $i, j = 1, 2, \ldots, j, \ldots, n$ (i.e. there are n rows and n columns), the transaction (to be called input–output) table will appear as Table 3.1.

As may be seen in this table, there appear n prices, p_i, $i = 1, 2, \ldots, n$, and n^2 physical quantities, q_{ij}, $i, j = 1, 2, j, \ldots, n$. These physical

Table 3.1 *Transactions table*

Inputs	Outputs					
	Industry 1	Industry 2		Industry j		Final sector (n)
Commodity 1	$q_{11}p_1$	$q_{12}p_1$	$\cdots$	$q_{1j}p_1$	$\cdots$	$q_{1n}p_1$
Commodity 2	$q_{21}p_2$	$q_{22}p_2$	$\cdots$	$q_{2j}p_2$	$\cdots$	$q_{2n}p_2$
$\vdots$	$\vdots$	$\vdots$	$\ddots$	$\vdots$	$\ddots$	$\vdots$
Commodity i	$q_{i1}p_i$	$q_{i2}p_i$	$\cdots$	$q_{ij}p_i$	$\cdots$	$q_{in}p_i$
$\vdots$	$\vdots$	$\vdots$	$\ddots$	$\vdots$	$\ddots$	$\vdots$
Final sector (n)	$q_{n1}p_n$	$q_{n2}p_n$	$\cdots$	$q_{nj}p_n$	$\cdots$	$q_{nn}p_n$

quantities are classified both by the kind of commodity (classification by the rows) and by the type of industry (classification by the columns). The symbol q_{ij} thus denotes the physical quantity of the ith commodity which is used in the jth industry. In other words, the two subscripts indicate the position of the corresponding physical quantity in the table – the first shows the number of the row and the second shows the number of the column.

The physical quantities which appear on the same row are clearly homogeneous (the first row might refer, let us say, to the commodity wheat), while the physical quantities which appear in any column are heterogeneous (e.g. wheat, coal, iron etc., used in the wheat-producing industry). Nevertheless, since every physical quantity has been multiplied by the corresponding price, the magnitude appearing in every cell is expressed in current values. It is thus possible to carry out the sums both across the rows and down the columns. From the purely accounting nature of the table, it follows that the sum of each row will be identically equal to the sum of the corresponding column. Thus, if we denote by $Q_1, Q_2, \ldots, Q_n$, the total quantities of the commodities $1, 2, j, \ldots, n$ we have

$$\sum_{j=1}^{n} q_{ij} = Q_i, \qquad i = 1, 2, \ldots, n.$$

Table 3.1 can also be expressed, alternatively, by two systems of accounting identities corresponding to the sum of the rows and to the sum of the columns, respectively. We obtain:

$$\begin{cases} q_{11}p_1 + q_{12}p_1 + \cdots + q_{1n}p_1 \equiv Q_1p_1, \\ q_{21}p_2 + q_{22}p_2 + \cdots + q_{2n}p_2 \equiv Q_2p_2, \\ \cdots \\ q_{n1}p_n + q_{n2}p_n + \cdots + q_{nn}p_n \equiv Q_np_n. \end{cases} \tag{3.3.1}$$

$$\begin{cases} q_{11}p_1 + q_{21}p_2 + \cdots + q_{n1}p_n \equiv Q_1p_1, \\ q_{12}p_1 + q_{22}p_2 + \cdots + q_{n2}p_n \equiv Q_2p_2, \\ \cdots \\ q_{1n}p_1 + q_{2n}p_2 + \cdots + q_{nn}p_n \equiv Q_np_n. \end{cases} \tag{3.3.2}$$

4 An Algebraic Reformulation

The two systems of accounting identities (3.3.1) and (3.3.2) are somewhat unmanageable for mathematical purposes because they present a marked asymmetry. Each equality in (3.3.1), for example, can be immediately simplified by dividing through by the price (which is the same for each term). This cannot be done in (3.3.2). Yet it is possible to introduce some definitions which, by rendering the algebraic formulation symmetrical, make it analytically more interesting. Let

$$\frac{q_{ij}}{Q_j} = a_{ij},$$

and hence

$$q_{ij} = a_{ij}Q_j, \qquad i, j = 1, 2, \ldots, n.$$

Using these definitions to eliminate the q_{ij} from (3.3.1) and (3.3.2) and then simplifying, we obtain

$$\begin{cases} a_{11}Q_1 + a_{12}Q_2 + \cdots + a_{1n}Q_n \equiv Q_1, \\ a_{21}Q_1 + a_{22}Q_2 + \cdots + a_{2n}Q_n \equiv Q_2, \\ \vdots \\ a_{n1}Q_1 + a_{n2}Q_2 + \cdots + a_{nn}Q_n \equiv Q_n. \end{cases} \tag{3.4.1}$$

$$\begin{cases} a_{11}p_1 + a_{21}p_2 + \cdots + a_{n1}p_n \equiv p_1, \\ a_{12}p_1 + a_{22}p_2 + \cdots + a_{n2}p_n \equiv p_2, \\ \vdots \\ a_{1n}p_1 + a_{2n}p_2 + \cdots + a_{nn}p_n \equiv p_n. \end{cases} \tag{3.4.2}$$

It will be seen that the two systems (3.4.1) and (3.4.2) are now perfectly symmetrical. The first sets out relationships between the physical quantities $Q_1, Q_2, \ldots, Q_n$, and the second, relationships between the prices, $p_1, p_2, \ldots, p_n$. Both contain the same magnitudes a_{ij} $(i, j = 1, 2, \ldots, n)$, but the rows and columns are interchanged – the same a_{ij} which in (3.4.1) appear on the rows, in (3.4.2) appear on the columns, and *vice versa*.[2]

5 Leontief's Two Systems of Linear Equations

Consider once again the two systems of accounting identities (3.4.1) and (3.4.2) which, in matrix notation, may be written out in full as

$$\begin{bmatrix} (a_{11}-1) & a_{12} & a_{13} & \cdots & a_{1n} \\ a_{21} & (a_{22}-1) & a_{23} & \cdots & a_{2n} \\ \vdots & \vdots & \vdots & \ddots & \vdots \\ a_{n1} & a_{n2} & a_{n3} & \cdots & (a_{nn}-1) \end{bmatrix} \begin{bmatrix} Q_1 \\ Q_2 \\ \vdots \\ Q_n \end{bmatrix} \equiv \begin{bmatrix} 0 \\ 0 \\ \vdots \\ 0 \end{bmatrix} \tag{3.5.1}$$

$$\begin{bmatrix} (a_{11}-1) & a_{21} & a_{31} & \cdots & a_{n1} \\ a_{12} & (a_{22}-1) & a_{32} & \cdots & a_{n2} \\ \vdots & \vdots & \vdots & \ddots & \vdots \\ a_{1n} & a_{2n} & a_{3n} & \cdots & (a_{nn}-1) \end{bmatrix} \begin{bmatrix} p_1 \\ p_2 \\ \vdots \\ p_n \end{bmatrix} \equiv \begin{bmatrix} 0 \\ 0 \\ \vdots \\ 0 \end{bmatrix} \tag{3.5.2}$$

where the a_{ij} denote the coefficients of production (broadly interpreted), the Q_i, denote the physical quantities and the p_i, denote the prices $(i, j = 1, 2, \ldots, n)$.

From the economic meaning of the coefficients, it follows of course that

$$a_{ij} \geq 0, \qquad i, j = 1, 2, \ldots, n. \tag{3.5.3}$$

[2] At this point, it becomes important to investigate the mathematical properties of (3.4.1) and (3.4.2) considered as two systems of linear equations.

The solutions and the properties of systems of two or three linear equations are well known from elementary algebra. In the present context, however, the number of equations could become very large indeed. To facilitate and speed up our analysis, an extensive use will now be made of matrix algebra.

For the reader's convenience, the basic concepts of matrix algebra used in the following pages can all be found synthesised in a *Mathematical Appendix* of Pasinetti's (1977a) *Lectures on the Theory of Production*.

That is, the coefficients of production and of consumption are all positive or, at the very least, equal to zero. Negative coefficients would have no economic meaning.

As will be seen, the matrices of coefficients for these two systems of accounting identities contain exactly the same elements, but each matrix is the transpose of the other. All this comes from what we suppose has been an actual observation of our (very simple) economic system.

The systems (3.5.1) and (3.5.2) are supposed to come from observation; hence, they are – by construction – two systems of identities: they are identically true.

But now we take an important analytical step by introducing a crucial assumption. This assumption is that we rely on our coefficients – after obtaining them simply by observation at a certain point of time – even if the scale of operation were to change. This assumption comes down to suppose that all the technical coefficients a_{ij} are taken as remaining constant when the Q_i and the p_i vary $(i, j = 1, 2, \ldots, n)$. On logical ground, this is an important step since it transforms the two systems of identity (3.5.1) and (3.5.2) into two systems of equations. From here on, they are no longer identically true. They are true only if the hypothesis made (constant returns to scale) holds. They thus come to express a 'theory', which could, for example, be rejected by empirical tests. It is in this shape that they come to represent what has been called the Leontief system (or schema or model), *closed* with respect to final demand, or more simply the closed Leontief system.[3]

6 The Closed Leontief Model

6.1 The Term 'Closed' Explained

The reason for calling (3.5.1) and (3.5.2) a 'closed' system is that the final sector is treated as if it were an ordinary 'industry'. The nth

[3] This system was presented by Leontief in the first edition of his work (Leontief 1941).

By the way, we may perceive quite clearly, at this point, the importance that the use of matrix algebra has come to take in the development of this analysis. For shortness, I shall continue to refer the reader to Pasinetti (1977a) for mathematical details and proofs.

column, which contains final demand, is treated in the same way as every other column, as showing the inputs required by the industry to which it refers. And the nth row, which contains the value added in the various industries, is treated, in the same way as every other row, as representing the outputs distributed to the various industries.

This interpretation acquires an immediate meaning in the context of a stationary system in which the labour force is constant from year to year and new investment is zero (since only that investment needed to replace the used-up means of production is carried out). This is, in effect, the case to which Leontief referred the theoretical formulations of his closed model. The nth column and the nth row appear as an industry that requires a set of consumptions as inputs and produces a set of services as outputs. These services are composite services – of labour and productive resources – which are, however, simply paid an all inclusive income – value added – comprising wages, salaries, profits and rents. In other words, at this stage of his analysis, Leontief preferred in fact not to distinguish between the various kinds of income and to accept value added as an entity in itself, irrespective of its composition.

6.2 A Necessary Condition for Economically Meaningful Solutions

Consider now the formal aspects of our two systems of equations. These equation systems are linear and homogeneous. From their mathematical properties, we know that systems of this kind always have at least one solution, namely,

$$Q_i = 0 \qquad i = 1, 2, \ldots, n, \tag{3.6.1}$$

$$p_j = 0 \qquad j = 1, 2, \ldots, n. \tag{3.6.2}$$

These, however, are the so-called trivial solutions. When all outputs and all prices are equal to zero, the economic system does not exist. This is, indeed, a solution to these systems of equations, but it is a solution completely devoid of any economic interest. We are obviously interested in situations in which there are other solutions, namely, solutions with economic meaning - positive solutions.

Now, if linear and homogeneous systems are to have solutions other than zero, the determinant of the matrix of coefficients must be *equal* to zero. Since, in our formulation, the matrix of coefficients is the same for both systems, although transposed, this condition is the same for both systems:

$$\begin{vmatrix} (1-a_{11}) & -a_{12} & \cdots & -a_{1n} \\ -a_{21} & (1-a_{22}) & \cdots & -a_{2n} \\ \vdots & \vdots & \ddots & \vdots \\ -a_{n1} & -a_{n2} & \cdots & (1-a_{nn}) \end{vmatrix} = 0 \tag{3.6.3}$$

In other words, a necessary condition for the existence of non-zero solutions is that at least one column of the coefficient matrix is linearly dependent on the others.

We must therefore reconsider the economic meaning of the various columns to see whether they permit the satisfaction of (3.6.3). Now we know that the first $(n-1)$ columns represent the technical coefficients of the production processes. These coefficients are given by technology. In general, then, we cannot expect to find among the first $(n-1)$ columns one that just happens to be linearly dependent on the others (i.e. that is a linear combination of the others). If that were to occur, it would be a truly exceptional coincidence indeed. And even then that coincidence could be observed only at a precise moment in time. The very smallest change, in even only one coefficient among the production processes concerned, would suffice to destroy that coincidence.

For all practical purposes, therefore, one must exclude the possibility that the first $(n-1)$ columns are linearly dependent.

Only the nth column remains to be considered. This column clearly can be linearly dependent on the others, since it contains a set of magnitudes concerning consumption which are not technically given and which can be adjusted. Condition (3.6.3) therefore simply amounts to stating that this column *must* be linearly dependent on the others for the two systems of equations to have non-zero solutions. And that is fairly obvious. There can be no economic system in which per capita consumption levels are independent of the matrix of technical coefficients. In common sense terms, the consumption possibilities (represented here by the nth column) are limited by the technical production possibilities (represented by the other $n-1$ columns). Or, alternatively, we may say that in a stationary system, it is physically impossible to devote to consumption more than can physically be produced.

Yet the previous discussion does not exhaust the full meaning of condition (3.6.3). This condition does not merely say that the determinant in question cannot be lower than zero, it says also that the determinant must be *equal* to zero. This implies that final demand not only cannot exceed the technical production possibilities (which would be physically impossible) but must not fall short of them either. Actually, a final demand smaller than the technical production possibilities is quite possible, physically at least. It is just this eventuality which is ruled out by (3.6.3), which implies that, if final demand were less than the technical production possibilities, at least one of the equations would not be satisfied. More precisely, the sum of the outputs of each industry would be less than the sum of the inputs to that industry (accumulation of stocks, i.e. under-utilised productive capacity) and/or the sum of the labour requirements would be less than the total supply of labour power (unemployment).

Condition (3.6.3) can thus also be interpreted in economic terms as expressing the well-known Keynes condition that the total volume of final demand must be equal to the productive capacity of the system, if full employment is to be ensured. In other words, the satisfaction of the macro-economic condition (3.6.3) turns out to be a way, in the present context, of expressing Keynes's principle of Effective Demand.[4]

7 The Solutions of the Closed System

7.1 Relative Prices and Relative Quantities

Suppose, then, that the condition (3.6.3) is satisfied so that, in economic terms, final demand is such as to require full employment of the existing productive capacity and labour force. In this case, there are also non-zero solutions, that is, economically meaningful solutions.

From the arguments in Section 6.2 (leading to the conclusion that for all practical purposes the matrix of the two systems contains $(n-1)$ linearly independent columns), it follows that the matrix itself is of rank $(n-1)$. This implies that each of the two systems (3.5.1) and (3.5.2) contains $(n-1)$ independent equations. Since there are n unknowns,

[4] For these two alternative ways (Leontief's and Keynes's) of expressing, in different contexts, what Keynes called the principle of Effective Demand, see also Pasinetti (1974, pp. 41–42).

any one of them may be fixed arbitrarily. Then the solutions for the other $(n - 1)$ unknowns will be uniquely determined.

For the price system (3.5.2), the meaning of these conclusions is immediately apparent. The system determines only relative prices and not the absolute level of prices. The price of any commodity can thus be fixed arbitrarily; the system will then determine all the other prices relative to the arbitrarily chosen price. In other words, any commodity can be adopted as the *numéraire* (which is equivalent to setting its price equal to unity), and all the other prices can then be expressed in terms of that *numéraire* commodity. As is well-known, for centuries the commodity adopted as *numéraire* was gold. In modern economic systems, the determination of the price level has become more complex. However, without going into questions of a monetary nature, it will suffice to point out that the real system offers the possibility of a choice here. As is apparent from the set of relations considered, each price only expresses a ratio -the exchange ratio between physical units of two goods. The absolute level is open to choice.

The interpretation of these same formal conclusions is rather less obvious with respect to the system of physical quantities (3.5.1). Here, too, one could say that the system of equations determines the relative quantities or the proportions in which the various commodities are produced, but not the absolute levels of the outputs; that is, it determines the structure of the economic system but not the scale of operation (provided, of course, that the assumption of constant returns to scale holds good). However, the concept of a relative quantity is not so intuitively evident as that of a relative price. There is, moreover, a more compelling question, resulting from the fact that in practice not all of the Q_i, $i = 1, 2, \ldots, n$, are open to being determined within the economic system. One of these quantities – Q_n, in our formulation, the available labour force – is, as it is normally put, an exogenous quantity; in the sense that, for the purposes of economic argument, it is generally taken as given. In other words, while $Q_1, Q_2, \ldots, Q_{n-1}$, – the physical quantities of commodities to be produced – are subject to economic decisions, the total labour supply is not. Therefore, in system (3.5.1), if Q_n is thought of as an exogenous quantity, the unknowns are reduced to $(n - 1)$, and they will all be determined by the $(n - 1)$ independent equations of the system.

7.2 A Sufficient Condition to Ensure Non-negative Solutions

The reader will perhaps have noticed that condition (3.6.3), when it is satisfied, ensures that there are non-zero solutions but does not necessarily ensure that they are positive. Since negative solutions for $Q_1, Q_2, \ldots, Q_n, p_1, p_2, \ldots, p_n$ would have no economic meaning, some further condition in addition to (3.6.3) must be satisfied to ensure that the two systems of equations (3.5.1) and (3.5.2) have positive solutions.

This condition can be stated quite simply by taking advantage of the fact that the coefficient matrix of the two systems (3.5.1) and (3.5.2) is, from (3.6.3), a non-negative matrix. It may be noted, in fact, that the coefficient matrix of the two systems (3.5.1) and (3.5.2) is the special case of the matrix $(\lambda\mathbf{I} - \mathbf{A})$ in which $\lambda = 1$. Thus, when condition (3.6.3) is satisfied (i.e. when the determinant of the coefficient matrix is zero), unity is an eigenvalue of the coefficient matrix of the two systems. It is easy to show that this eigenvalue is also the maximum eigenvalue.[5] Then, the Perron-Frobenius theorems[6] guarantee immediately that the solutions of the two systems (3.5.1) and (3.5.2), that is, the components of the two eigenvectors associated with the maximum eigenvalue, are all non-negative.

To conclude, given the way in which the coefficients have been obtained, condition (3.5.3) suffices, in conjunction with condition

[5] Call $\mathbf{Z}$ the matrix of the quantities q_{ij}, of Chapter 2 $(i, j = 1, 2, \ldots, n)$. In order to go from the q_{ij} to the a_{ij} $(i, j = 1, 2, \ldots, n)$, we divided each column of matrix $\mathbf{Z}$ by the corresponding total quantity Q_j $(j = 1, 2, \ldots, n)$, i.e., we performed the operation $\mathbf{Z}\widehat{\mathbf{Q}}^{-1}$, where $\widehat{\mathbf{Q}}$ is a diagonal matrix with the $Q_1, Q_2, \ldots, Q_n$ on its main diagonal. If, instead of performing the operation $\mathbf{Z}\widehat{\mathbf{Q}}^{-1}$, we had performed the operation $\widehat{\mathbf{Q}}^{-1}\mathbf{Z}$ (which means dividing the rows of $\mathbf{Z}$, instead of its columns by the corresponding quantities $Q_1, Q_2, \ldots, Q_n$), we would have obtained a matrix in which, by construction, the sum of each row is equal to unity. Such a matrix, i.e., $\widehat{\mathbf{Q}}^{-1}\mathbf{Z}$, has a maximum eigenvalue equal to unity (owing to Perron-Frobenius Theorem 6; see Pasinetti (1977a), Mathematical Appendix, p. 274). But matrices $\widehat{\mathbf{Q}}^{-1}\mathbf{Z}$ and $\mathbf{Z}\widehat{\mathbf{Q}}^{-1}$ are similar, and this implies that they have the same eigenvalues (see Pasinetti (1977a), Mathematical Appendix, p. 261). It therefore follows that (*all* q_i's and Q_i's being non-negative) matrix $\mathbf{Z}\widehat{\mathbf{Q}}^{-1}$, i.e., the coefficient matrix $[a_{ij}]$, has a maximum eigenvalue equal to unity.

[6] See Pasinetti (1977a), *Mathematical Appendix*, Theorems 1 and 1b, pp. 269 and 275.

(3.6.3), to ensure that the solutions are not only non-zero but are actually non-negative, that is, economically meaningful.

8 Hint at the 'Open' Leontief System

When Leontief published the second edition of his book (in 1951, ten years after the first edition), he reproduced without any change to the first edition but added a new Part that doubled the length of the book. In this new Part, he developed another version of his model, which he called 'open'. This version was aimed at more concrete 'applications' of the model. For this purpose, he 'opened' the model to the final demand of the economic system. Essentially, what he did was to take the column of final demand, for consumption and investments, out of the inter-industry relations, thus considering final demand as exogenously determined, and in this way stimulating the whole economic system from outside.

We shall not deal explicitly with this Part of Leontief's analysis, which is essentially concerned with the physical quantities of the economic system rather than with its prices.[7] I shall stress the important point, however which, relates to the type of approach which is used, relying essentially not on hypothetical magnitudes or behavioural assumptions but on *actual observation*.

It is moreover worth considering, though briefly, the first attempts that were made in the economic literature to go, from a stationary conception of a production economic system, on to its dynamics. These attempts were made with reference to a hypothetical system in which growth is exclusively due to population expansion with absolutely constant technical coefficients. Although not realistic, and open to a critique, which we shall express explicitly at the end of this chapter, this configuration of the system (open to investments and growth) was

[7] The reader may see it in detail in Pasinetti (1977a, pp. 59–70). To deal with the price structure of the economic system, we shall make use of the Sraffa system (see the following chapter). Let me mention that perhaps the most relevant concept that emerged from the Leontief open system is the concept that was called the *Leontief inverse matrix*. For its economic interpretation, see Pasinetti (1977a, pp. 63–65); see moreover Section 9, where a version of the Leontief inverse matrix will emerge in its application to proportional dynamics. See also Chapter 4, (p. 121), where its economic meaning will be shown to be useful with reference to the concept of viability.

the first new product of the 'open' Leontief model. We shall justify it in the following Sections 9.1 to 9.8 in terms of an intermediate analytical step taken with the purpose to go on to a full dynamic system.

9 Analytical Attempts in the Direction of Economic Dynamics

9.1 *Population Growth and Constant Technical Coefficients*

As an immediate follow up of the purpose just stated, the following few pages are concerned with the problems which arise in a hypothetical economic system undergoing a growth of population (and of the labour force), but no technical change. The assumption is made that technical knowledge and consumers' preferences remain unchanged. Strictly speaking, an economic system of this kind cannot be considered a truly 'dynamic' one, and it has also been called 'quasi-dynamic' or, from another point of view, 'quasi-stationary'. For, although it embodies those dynamic aspects which are inherent in the growth of the labour force and of the system of physical quantities, it continues to exhibit features which are typical of stationary systems, mainly constancy of the structures of prices, of production, and of consumption. Such a system gives rise to a type of dynamics in which all sections of the economy expand at the same percentage rate as the rate of population growth, while keeping all proportions constant. This is obviously a simplified type of dynamics, which we shall call *proportional dynamics*: it means that growth concerns the total quantities, while per capita quantities remain absolutely constant.[8]

One must acknowledge that in this direction, that is, in the direction of population growth with constant technical coefficients, there have been two outstanding attempts, which, for our purposes, it may be useful to say a few words about, also because the economic literature has paid so much attention to them. They are due to Wassily Leontief himself and to John Von Neumann.[9]

8 Almost all the mathematical models of growth presented in the post-World War II economic literature refer to economic systems with *proportional dynamics* (or with a slight variation of it). The present work (which started in Pasinetti 1965) is an exception.

9 See 'Dynamic Analysis', chapter 3 of Leontief (1953b) and Von Neumann (1945).

Let me begin, owing to the large fame that it has achieved, by considering Von Neumann's celebrated mathematical model, which is built on a set of assumptions that may be listed as follows: (i) there is a wide, well specified, and invariant set of technical methods for producing separately or jointly the various commodities; (ii) there are constant returns to scale in the employment of all inputs of production (labour included, in the sense that labour is supposed to require a subsistence wage rate and is treated, like any other commodity, as an output which requires a series of inputs of subsistence consumption); and (iii) the excess of the output of each commodity over the input of the same commodity in the production process is accumulated. Given these assumptions, Von Neumann shows that there exists a particular set of techniques and corresponding set of relative prices, and certain proportions among the various commodities, at which a uniform rate of growth of all products is at maximum. At this rate of growth (which in Von Neumann model turns out to coincide with the economically meaningful rate of profit), the economic system grows uniformly, that is, all its sections are multiplied in the same proportion, while the composition of production and the structure of prices remain constant over time.

Wassily Leontief arrives at results which are similar to these, although he does not go into the problem of choice of techniques and starts instead by immediately taking given production coefficients for each process, as they might actually be observed. He begins with his input–output flow matrix and adds to it a matrix of capital coefficients. Then, he shows that there is a well-defined composition of the initial stocks of capital goods (determined exclusively by the structural coefficients), which yields a maximum uniform rate of growth for all industries. Even if the economic system does not start from this particular composition of the initial stocks, it will all the same tend to produce it eventually, although in the meantime it may run into various difficulties.

With this approach, deriving from a much more empirically minded attitude than Von Neumann's, Leontief succeeds to investigate the relations concerning a hypothetical growing economy at fixed coefficients in a much simpler way, basically due to Leontief, which we shall try to follow from the end of this chapter.

9.2 A Prototype Model of Proportional Dynamics

Consider now an economic system which, as far as our data are concerned, is the same in all respects as the Leontief system considered in the earlier sections of this chapter, except that population is supposed to grow through time.

More precisely, assume, as in Sections 3 to 7, that the technique for the system as a whole is represented by $(n-1)$ single-product industries:

$$\begin{bmatrix} \mathbf{A} \\ \mathbf{a}_n \end{bmatrix}. \tag{3.9.1}$$

We may well suppose – to pay some tribute to Von Neumann – that this technique has been uniquely chosen from a wider range of alternative techniques, that is, from a technology:

$$\begin{bmatrix} \mathbf{A}^{(\alpha)} \\ \mathbf{a}_n^{(\alpha)} \end{bmatrix}, \begin{bmatrix} \mathbf{A}^{(\beta)} \\ \mathbf{a}_n^{(\beta)} \end{bmatrix}, \ldots, \begin{bmatrix} \mathbf{A}^{(\omega)} \\ \mathbf{a}_n^{(\omega)} \end{bmatrix}. \tag{3.9.2}$$

But in any case, we take it that, once the choice has been made, the chosen technique remains unchanged for all time.

Population N, by contrast, increases at a given percentage rate *per annum* $\bar{g} \geq 0$ (so that our previous analysis constitutes the particular case in which $g = 0$).[10] Denoting time by t, we can write

$$N(t) = N(0)[1 + \bar{g}]^t. \tag{3.9.3}$$

Assuming that the total labour force, Q, is proportional to total population, we have

$$Q_n(t) = \mu N(t), \tag{3.9.4}$$

where μ denotes the (constant) proportion of the total population which is active in the process of production. Hence

$$Q_n(t) = \mu N(t) = Q_n(0)[1 + \bar{g}]^t. \tag{3.9.5}$$

Now our task is to look for those relations which must hold in order that the economic system, which we assume to be in equilibrium at time zero (by which we mean with full employment of the labour force and full utilisation of productive capacity), may remain

[10] The letter g therefore denotes a *percentage* annual rate of growth. For brevity, whenever no misunderstanding is possible, we shall simply call it 'rate of growth'.

in dynamic equilibrium (i.e. may maintain full employment and full capacity utilisation) through time.

9.3 Growth of the Physical Quantities

All the physical quantities will obviously have to grow. We denote them by the symbols used previously with the addition of the suffix t to indicate that they refer to the time period ('year') t. Hence

$$\mathbf{Q}(t) = \begin{bmatrix} Q_1(t) \\ Q_2(t) \\ \vdots \\ Q_{n-1}(t) \end{bmatrix}, \quad \mathbf{Y}(t) = \begin{bmatrix} Y_1(t) \\ Y_2(t) \\ \vdots \\ Y_{n-1}(t) \end{bmatrix}, \tag{3.9.6}$$

where $\mathbf{Q}(t)$ is the (column) vector of the total physical quantities of commodities $1, 2, \ldots, n-1$, in year t; and $\mathbf{Y}(t)$ is the (column) vector of the physical quantities of the same commodities which, in the same year, make up the net product, or surplus, or net national income, of the economic system as a whole.

The complete system of physical quantities can be represented, in a manner analogous to that used previously, by the system of equations

$$\mathbf{Q}(t) - \mathbf{A}\mathbf{Q}(t) = \mathbf{Y}(t), \tag{3.9.7}$$

to which we must add the equation

$$\mathbf{a}_n\mathbf{Q}(t) = Q_n(t) = \mu N(t), \tag{3.9.8}$$

expressing the condition of full employment of the labour force.

Since $N(t)$ grows through time, according to (3.9.3), we must now investigate how the other physical quantities should grow too.

9.4 Net Product Divided between Consumption and New Investment

We can say at once that, if the labour force is growing, it will be necessary to provide the new workers with new capital goods, that is, with new productive capacity. This implies that at the end of each year, it will no longer suffice, in a growing economic system, to set aside the quantities $\mathbf{A}\mathbf{Q}(t)$ as replacements of the means of production. It will also be necessary to set aside other quantities to permit the expansion of the means of production. In other words, the net product of the economic system, $\mathbf{Y}(t)$, can no longer be devoted entirely to consumption.

A part of it must be devoted to new investment. We therefore define two new vectors

$$\mathbf{C}(t) \begin{bmatrix} C_1(t) \\ C_2(t) \\ \vdots \\ C_{n-1}(t) \end{bmatrix}, \quad \mathbf{J}(t) = \begin{bmatrix} J_1(t) \\ J_2(t) \\ \vdots \\ J_{n-1}(t) \end{bmatrix}, \tag{3.9.9}$$

where $C(t)$ denotes the (column) vector of the physical quantities of the commodities $1, 2, \ldots, (n-1)$, which are devoted to consumption, and $J(t)$ denotes the (column) vector of the physical quantities of the same commodities $1, 2, \ldots, (n-1)$, which are set aside for new investment. By definition, of course,

$$\mathbf{Y}(t) = \mathbf{C}(t) + J(t). \tag{3.9.10}$$

Equation (3.9.7) may now be written as

$$\mathbf{Q}(t) - \mathbf{A}\mathbf{Q}(t) - \mathbf{J}(t) = \mathbf{C}(t). \tag{3.9.11}$$

This makes it necessary to seek the relation between $J(t)$ and the pre-existing means of production. But before doing this, we must specify how consumption $C(t)$ evolves through time.

9.5 *Growth of Total Consumption with Invariance of Its Composition*

The evolution of the components of $C(t)$ through time is, in fact, very simple within the present model. Although there is a problem of choice over the composition of consumption, to which we shall return in Section 9.8, we can say immediately that, since consumers' preferences, technology and the structure of prices are all assumed to be constant through time, the choice of the composition of consumption is made once for all. This means that if we define a new column vector

$$\mathbf{c} = \begin{bmatrix} c_1 \\ c_2 \\ \vdots \\ c_{n-1} \end{bmatrix} = \frac{1}{N(t)}\mathbf{C}(t), \tag{3.9.12}$$

representing the per capita consumption of the commodities $1, 2, \ldots, n-1$, this vector will remain constant in dynamic equilibrium. (We have therefore written it without the t suffix.)

Hence, we may write

$$\mathbf{C}(t) = \mathbf{c}N(t) = \mathbf{c}N(0)[1 + \bar{g}]^t, \tag{3.9.13}$$

in order to represent the evolution of the demand for consumer goods in dynamic equilibrium (i.e. the evolution of demand given that full employment is maintained). Equation (3.9.13) states that the average individual always demands the same goods, so that the composition of demand remains constant through time. However, since the number of individuals increases, total demand for each consumption good increases at the same percentage growth rate of population (g).

9.6 *New Investments*

Let us now consider the new investments. If the demand for each consumer good increases at the annual percentage rate $\bar{g}$, then a necessary condition for the corresponding production to take place without there being any unutilised productive capacity is that all the means of production increase at the same annual percentage rate $\bar{g}$. This condition gives us the expression for investments we have been looking for:

$$\mathbf{J}(t) = \bar{g}\mathbf{AQ}(t). \tag{3.9.14}$$

This means that, at the end of every year, all physical quantities making up the means of production $\mathbf{AQ}(t)$ will have to increase at exactly the same percentage rate.

9.7 *The (Quasi-Dynamic) Equilibrium Solution for Physical Quantities*

Substituting (3.9.14) and (3.9.13) into (3.9.11), we obtain the system of $(n-1)$ equations:

$$\mathbf{Q}(t) - \mathbf{AQ}(t) - \bar{g}\mathbf{AQ}(t) = \mathbf{c}N(t). \tag{3.9.15}$$

We can solve immediately and obtain

$$\mathbf{Q}(t) = [\mathbf{I} - (1+\bar{g})\mathbf{A}]^{-1}\mathbf{c}N(t), \tag{3.9.16}$$

or, in greater detail, using (3.9.3)

$$\mathbf{Q}(t) = [\mathbf{I} - (1+\bar{g})\mathbf{A}]^{-1}\mathbf{c}N(0)[1+\bar{g}]^{t}. \tag{3.9.17}$$

Since all the coefficients on the right side of (3.9.17) are constant through time, and since the only factor which varies is the exponential scalar function $(1+\bar{g})^t$, it follows that (3.9.17) implies that each of the total physical quantities in $\mathbf{Q}(t)$ grows through time at exactly the same percentage rate of growth $\bar{g}$ as do the physical quantities in $\mathbf{C}(t)$.

The solution (3.9.17) defines, so to speak, a 'dynamic path' along which productive capacity for each commodity is increased from year to year by exactly the amount required by the increase in the corresponding demand. Along such a dynamic path, the growth of the system is perfectly balanced and proportional. Consumption $\mathbf{C}(t)$, net investment $\bar{g}\mathbf{AQ}(t)$, the means of production $\mathbf{AQ}(t)$ and hence the total physical quantities $\mathbf{Q}(t)$ all increase at the same percentage growth rate $\bar{g}$. All proportions remain constant through time.

We can see here in detail what is the meaning of the proportional dynamics of the economic system under consideration.

9.8 The Full-Employment Condition

For every given exponential evolution of consumption, $\mathbf{C}(t)$, through time, the solution (3.9.16) gives the evolution of the total physical quantities $\mathbf{Q}(t)$ which are required – as direct, indirect and, we might add, hyper-indirect requirements (meaning by this last the requirements for new investment) – to keep the economic system in dynamic equilibrium. The inverse matrix

$$[\mathbf{I} - (1 + \bar{g})\mathbf{A}]^{-1} \tag{3.9.18}$$

has in fact been called the 'Leontief dynamic inverse matrix'.[11]

It must also be pointed out, however, that the solution (3.9.16) involves a well-determined evolution of labour requirements $L(t)$, namely

$$L(t) = \mathbf{a}_n\mathbf{Q}(t) = \mathbf{a}_n[\mathbf{I} - (1 + \bar{g})\mathbf{A}]^{-1}\mathbf{c}N(0)[1 + \bar{g}]^t. \tag{3.9.19}$$

Hence, if our dynamic equilibrium solution is to ensure not only full utilisation of productive capacity but also full employment of the labour force, then we must impose the further condition:

$$L(t) = \mathcal{Q}_n(t), \tag{3.9.20}$$

or, after substitution into (3.9.19)

$$\mathbf{a}_n[\mathbf{I} - (1 + \bar{g})\mathbf{A}]^{-1}\mathbf{c}N(t) = \mathcal{Q}_n(t). \tag{3.9.21}$$

[11] After Leontief (1970). Leontief attempted at the outset to go over to a dynamic version of his model by assuming the initial conditions to be given independently of technology. But he encountered numerous difficulties which were never solved completely. See Leontief (1953b).

The left and right sides of this equality condition are indeed compatible with one another, since *ex-hypothesis* $N(t)$ and $Q_n(t)$ are growing at the same annual percentage rate $\bar{g}$. But this does not mean that the two sides will always automatically be equal to one another. This will be so only if the initial situation is an appropriate one. No doubt: a strong condition indeed.

10 A Concluding Note

The 'dynamics' attempts of Leontief and Von Neumann are clearly not yet satisfactory. However, we must acknowledge that their elaborations – in spite of their limitations – have undoubtedly been most important contributions to the development of dynamic economic analysis. To begin with, they represent a most radical departure from marginal economic theory, as they entail the abandonment of the concepts of given scarce resources and a return to Classical economic theory: all goods considered are *produced* goods. This character is so basic that John Von Neumann, as a true mathematician always looking for symmetry, even applied the scheme to an imaginary society where the workers themselves are treated as if they were like any other produced goods.

There is in fact nothing in the schemes considered in the present chapter which is incompatible with the dynamic analysis which is going to be developed later on in Part III of this book. Especially, if we take Von Neumann model as a reference, we might say that all Von Neumann-type models represent a concentration of powerful analytical tools on one particular set of technical hypotheses, namely the case of constant returns to scale with absolutely constant technical coefficients (i.e. with no technical progress). From an analytical point of view, this is an elegant and exciting case, an analytical framework that has fascinated hundreds of clever minds. However, taken as such, on strictly empirical grounds, it can have very little practical relevance. We can make a sense of it only if we consider it *as an intermediate analytical step* to a more relevant type of dynamic analysis, which is substantially what we are going to aim at in Chapters 4 to 10.

But, before proceeding further, we must first complete the concepts developed within the framework of inter-industry analysis by considering Sraffa's remarkable work, which has enabled us to reach a whole series of new results.

4 *Piero Sraffa's Price System*

1 Production of Commodities by Means of Commodities

The basic relationships already considered in the previous Chapter 3 will now be reformulated in terms of a theoretical schema, considered by Piero Sraffa (1960), for pre-eminently theoretical purposes, which he called *Production of commodities by means of commodities.*

The version of the Sraffa system presented in the present chapter is the least complex one – concerning single product industries. Unlike Sraffa, whose analysis is in terms of elementary algebra, we shall take advantage of the notions of matrix algebra, which are by now so widely diffused.[1]

2 The Assumptions

The assumptions underlying the analysis of this chapter can be briefly stated as follows:

(i) We assume that we are observing a certain economic system which is in a perfectly stationary state. Each 'year' the system produces exactly the same physical quantities of commodities.

(ii) The methods of production are such that each industry produces a single commodity by using a certain physical quantity of labour and a set of certain physical quantities of commodities. These commodities (required as means of production) are completely used up in each period, so that they have to be replaced entirely.[2]

[1] In any case, the reader will find them in an Appendix to Pasinetti (1977a).

[2] This is the assumption of 'single-product industries'. Sraffa also carries out his analysis with reference to the more general case of 'joint production', which he uses for his treatment of fixed capital and land. The principal theoretical results thereby obtained do not, however, basically differ from those obtained for the case of single product industries.

At the end of each 'year' the total output of the system must therefore be divided into two parts: one part must be devoted to the replacement of those commodities which have been used up in the production process; the remainder represents the final net output, or net national income, or net product, and can be devoted to consumption (the system being in a stationary state).

The technical methods of production will be represented by a matrix of interindustry coefficients, denoted by **A**, and by a row vector of direct labour coefficients, denoted by $\mathbf{a}_n$:

$$\mathbf{A} = \begin{bmatrix} a_{11} & a_{12} & \dots & a_{1,n-1} \\ a_{21} & a_{22} & \dots & a_{2,n-1} \\ \vdots & \vdots & \dots & \vdots \\ a_{n-1,1} & a_{n-1,2} & \dots & a_{n-1,n-1} \end{bmatrix}, \tag{4.2.1}$$

$$\mathbf{a}_n = \begin{bmatrix} a_{n1} \, a_{n2} \, \dots \, a_{n,n-1} \end{bmatrix}, \tag{4.2.2}$$

where

$$a_{ij} \geq 0, \qquad j = 1, 2, \dots, n-1; \qquad i = 1, 2, \dots, n.$$

We shall call $\begin{bmatrix} \mathbf{A} \\ \mathbf{a}_n \end{bmatrix}$ the *technique* of the system. It is important to add that Sraffa does *not* introduce the assumption of constant returns to scale, although he warns that 'If such a supposition is found helpful, there is no harm in the reader's adopting of it as a temporary working hypothesis. In fact, however, no such assumption is made'.[3]

(iii) The value added in the economic system, which is equal to the value of the commodities which make up its net national income (or net product), is distributed to the members of the community at the end of each 'year' in two forms: *wages* and *profits*. Wages are distributed in proportion to the physical quantity of labour which has been contributed; profits are distributed in proportion to the value of the means of production. It is assumed that labour is of a uniform quality and that both the wage rate and the rate of profit are uniform all over the economic system.

[3] Sraffa (1960). The reason why Sraffa's analysis is kept free from any assumption on returns to scale is that he is interested in investigating an economic system in which nothing changes except the distribution of income between wages and profits.

3 The Price System

We begin by considering the system of prices. The value added in the economic system is here divided into two categories: wages and profits. Let us denote the wage rate by w (a scalar) and the rate of profit by π (also a scalar).

Given the technique $\begin{bmatrix} \mathbf{A} \\ \mathbf{a}_n \end{bmatrix}$ and assumption (ii) concerning the distribution of value added, the prices will be defined by the system of equations

$$\begin{cases} (a_{11}p_1 + a_{21}p_2 + \cdots + a_{n-1,1}p_{n-1})(1+\pi) + a_{n1}w = p_1, \\ (a_{12}p_1 + a_{22}p_2 + \cdots + a_{n-1,2}p_{n-1})(1+\pi) + a_{n2}w = p_2, \\ \vdots \\ (a_{1,n-1}p_1 + a_{2,n-1}p_2 + \cdots + a_{n-1,n-1}p_{n-1})(1+\pi) + a_{n,n-1}w = p_{n-1}, \end{cases} \tag{4.3.1}$$

where $p_1, p_2, \ldots, p_{n-1}$ are the prices of the commodities $1, 2, \ldots, n-1$. In a more compact notation, system (4.3.1) can be rewritten

$$\mathbf{pA}(1+\pi) + \mathbf{a}_n = \mathbf{p}, \tag{4.3.2}$$

where $\mathbf{p}$ denotes the (row) vector of prices.

As may be easily verified, this system contains $(n-1)$ equations in $(n+1)$ unknowns, namely w, π, and the $(n-1)$ prices $p_1, p_2, \ldots, p_{n-1}$. We therefore have two more unknowns than we have equations; this means that two of the unknowns can be fixed exogenously.

We may begin by setting the price of any arbitrarily chosen commodity equal to unity. The number of prices (which thereby become relative prices) is reduced to $(n-2)$, and the total number of unknowns is reduced to n. We still have one degree of freedom. To render the system determinate we have to fix another unknown. And, since it would have no economic meaning to fix arbitrarily a relative price, we are left with a choice between the wage rate and the rate of profit. Within the context of (4.3.1) we can therefore fix arbitrarily either the wage rate or the rate of profit.

It must not, of course, be inferred from this conclusion that in a real economic system the wage rate or the rate of profit can be fixed at will. Our conclusion simply means that the system of equations (4.3.1) is not sufficient to determine all the unknowns. The determinants of one of these unknowns will have to be sought outside the equations (4.3.1).

4 Search for a Relation that May Render the Price System Determinate

The problem just referred to has behind it a long history in the evolution of the economic thought. The Classical economists were aware of the indeterminateness of the system of prices (4.3.1) and solved the problem by taking the wage rate as determined by a relation outside the economic system. They thought of the biological needs of subsistence, appropriately assessed with reference to social conditions. If we accept this approach (by setting $w = \bar{w}_{\text{subsistence}}$), the system equations (4.3.1) do indeed become determinate.

It need hardly be added that this approach is not normally followed today. At most one might think of the wage rate as consisting of two parts: a part which is necessary for subsistence and which is comparable to the commodities constituting the means of production (its composition being rigidly determined by biological necessity), and a part which represents a 'surplus' relative to subsistence requirements. But, if this distinction is accepted, the subsistence part of the wage rate takes up a character which is similar to that of the technical data and could therefore be thought of as being already included in the matrix of technical coefficients. We could then have to reinterpret our system, taking w to mean the surplus wage. Thus, the problem of the division of the total surplus between π and w would remain unchanged.

The inclination of most modern economists with reference to system (4.3.1) is to reverse the Classical approach and seek a relation from outside the system (4.3.1) which may determine the rate of profit. Sraffa himself gives a clear indication that he thinks in these terms, although he does not explicitly state which relation might determine the rate of profit. He rather confines himself to considering alternative solutions to system (4.3.1) for any possibly given values of the rate of profit. In this chapter, we follow Sraffa's approach.

5 Relative Prices with Reference to Various Levels of the Rate of Profit

5.1 Extreme Cases and Intermediate Cases

To examine the properties of the possible solutions of the system of equations (4.3.1), corresponding to various assumptions about the level of the rate of profit, it is instructive to consider the two extreme cases in which the rate of profit is at its minimum level and at its maximum level, respectively, separately from the general case in which the rate of profit is fixed at any intermediate level in between the two extremes.

5.2 A Pure Labour Theory of Value

We may begin by considering the extreme case in which $\pi = 0$. In this case, profits being zero, the entire net product, or surplus of the economic system, goes to wages. Equations (4.3.1) become a system of $(n - 1)$ linear equations in n unknowns: the wage rate and the $(n - 1)$ prices. There is only one degree of freedom. If any one of the commodities is chosen as the *numéraire*, its price being set equal to unity, the equation system determines uniquely the wage rate and the other $(n - 2)$ prices in terms of the chosen commodity. Alternatively, if we take the wage rate as the *numéraire* (by setting $w = 1$), the system determines uniquely the $(n - 1)$ prices in terms of the wage rate.

Whichever convention is adopted, when $\pi = 0$, the system (4.3.2) becomes:

$$\mathbf{p}(\mathbf{I} - \mathbf{A}) = \mathbf{a}_n w. \tag{4.5.1}$$

Since the matrix $(\mathbf{I} - \mathbf{A})$ is nonsingular, we can multiply both sides of (4.5.1) by $(\mathbf{I} - \mathbf{A})^{-1}$ to obtain

$$\mathbf{p} = \mathbf{a}_n(\mathbf{I} - \mathbf{A})^{-1} w, \tag{4.5.2}$$

which, for the special case $w = 1$, becomes

$$\mathbf{p} = \mathbf{a}_n(\mathbf{I} - \mathbf{A})^{-1}. \tag{4.5.3}$$

Since $\mathbf{a}_n$ is a non-negative vector (see Section 2) and $(\mathbf{I} - \mathbf{A})^{-1}$ is a non-negative matrix, it follows that the prices $\mathbf{p}$ are all non-negative in both systems (4.5.2) and (4.5.3).[4]

[4] The so-called Leontief inverse matrix $(\mathbf{I} - \mathbf{A})^{-1}$ is a particular case of $(\mathbf{I} - t\mathbf{A})^{-1}$ when $t = 1$; hence, thanks to theorem Perron-Frobenius theorem (in its strong version), we have $(\mathbf{I} - \mathbf{A})^{-1} \geq \mathbf{0}$ as long as

$$\lambda_m < 1, \tag{4.5.4}$$

where λ_m is the maximum eigenvalue of $\mathbf{A}$. Condition 4.5.4 may be interpreted as a *viability* condition of the technique; in the 'open Leontief system' it assures that the system is able to produce a positive surplus of at

These expressions have an economic meaning which deserves to be emphasised. Each component of the vector $\mathbf{a}_n(\mathbf{I}-\mathbf{A})^{-1}$ is the scalar product of $\mathbf{a}_n$ (the vector of direct labour coefficients) and the corresponding column of the inverse matrix $(\mathbf{I}-\mathbf{A})^{-1}$. It is known that the ith column of $(\mathbf{I}-\mathbf{A})^{-1}$ represents the physical quantities of commodities which have been used, directly and indirectly in the economic system as a whole, to obtain one physical unit of the ith commodity as a final commodity (see, e.g., Pasinetti (1977a, chapter IV, section 7.1)). Multiplying each of these physical quantities by the corresponding labour coefficient and summing the products thus obtained, we clearly obtain the quantity of labour used, directly and indirectly in the economic system as a whole, to obtain one physical unit of the ith commodity as a final commodity, $i = 1, 2, \ldots, n-1$. Therefore the vector $\mathbf{v}$ defined as

$$\mathbf{v} = \mathbf{a}_n(\mathbf{I}-\mathbf{A})^{-1}, \tag{4.5.5}$$

contains what may be called the *vertically integrated labour coefficients*. In Classical terminology, we can also say that $\mathbf{v}$ represents the quantities of labour directly and indirectly 'embodied' in each physical unit of the commodities which make up the net product of the economic system (what Marx called 'values', by definition).[5]

Thus, equations (4.5.2) state that, when $\pi = 0$,price are proportional to the physical quantities of 'embodied labour'. Indeed, in the particular case $w = 1$ prices are prec isely equal to these physical quantities of labour. This conclusion should cause no surprise. Profits being equal to zero and the entire net product being absorbed by wages, prices cannot but be proportional to quantities of labour. We have thus arrived at a rigorous definition of the case for which the pure Classical labour theory of value holds.

5.3 The Maximum Rate of Profit

We now turn to the other extreme case: that in which the rate of profit is at a level so high as to render the wage rate equal to zero. Profits

least one commodity (for further references see Pasinetti 1977a, pp. 61–63); in the present context the same condition assures the semi-positivity of the price system in the particular case of $\pi = 0$.

[5] See Chapter 5, Section 3.

are so high as to absorb the whole net product.[6] In this case the rate of profit is at its maximum possible level, which we may denote by Π, defined as

$$\Pi = \pi_{w=0}, \tag{4.5.6}$$

that is, as the rate of profit corresponding to a zero wage rate.

We can find the system of prices for this case setting $w = 0$ in equations system (4.3.2), which thus becomes:

$$\mathbf{pA}(1 + \Pi) = \mathbf{p}, \tag{4.5.7}$$

or

$$\mathbf{p}[\mathbf{I} - (1 + \Pi)\mathbf{A}] = 0. \tag{4.5.8}$$

Further, writing for convenience

$$\frac{1}{1 + \Pi} = \lambda, \tag{4.5.9}$$

we obtain

$$\mathbf{p}(\lambda\mathbf{I} - \mathbf{A}) = 0. \tag{4.5.10}$$

This is a homogeneous system. A necessary condition for its having solutions other than zero is that the determinant of the matrix of coefficients, that is, $\det(\lambda\mathbf{I} - \mathbf{A})$, be zero. We can find the values of λ which satisfy this condition by solving the characteristic equation

$$\det(\lambda\mathbf{I} - \mathbf{A}) = 0. \tag{4.5.11}$$

As the reader will note, the roots of equation (4.5.11) are the eigenvalues of matrix **A**. It is known that there are $(n - 1)$ such eigenvalues (although some of them might be repeated). There are therefore $(n - 1)$ values of λ that assure non-trivial solutions. These eigenvalues, and the connected eigenvectors, might not have an economic meaning, however. Indeed, since **A** is a non-negative matrix, we can say immediately that only one of the $(n - 1)$ eigenvalues, that is, the maximum eigenvalue, λ_m, is certainly such as to yield an eigenvector with no negative components. Since in the present context the components of such an

6 The reader may find it hard to imagine a hypothetical economic system in which wages are reduced to zero. But one may use the device of interpreting w as the 'surplus' wage rate, in the sense suggested by Section 4. In other words, that part of the wage rate which represents subsistence (duly specified in physical terms) may be considered as already included in the technical interindustry coefficients. With this reinterpretation of matrix **A** the whole analysis of the present section remains formally unchanged.

eigenvector are prices (and negative prices would have no economic meaning), it follows that only the solutions corresponding to the maximum eigenvalue will certainly have an economic meaning. Thus, even though from a mathematical point of view there are $(n-1)$ values of λ satisfying (4.5.11), only one of them, the maximum eigenvalue λ_m, is certainly such to have an economic meaning. Hence, we shall always take Π to be the rate of profit which is associated with λ_m.[7]

If we substitute this rate of profit Π into (4.5.8) and λ_m into (4.5.10), we obtain a linear and homogeneous system of equations with a zero determinant.

Thus, the $(n-1) \times (n-1)$ matrix $[\mathbf{I} - (1+\Pi)\mathbf{A}]$ will, in general, be of rank $(n-2)$, that is, the system (4.5.8) will contain $(n-2)$ independent equations. This ensures the existence of determinate solutions for the prices, which we shall call $\mathbf{p}^*$, if anyone of them is fixed arbitrarily. To conclude, substituting the rate of profit Π into (4.5.8) and λ_m into (4.5.10), we are enabled to obtain determinate, non-negative solutions for all the $(n-2)$ relative prices.

5.4 The Viability Condition

There is a further condition which must be satisfied in the case $w = 0$. The unique rate of profit

$$\Pi = \frac{1}{\lambda_m} - 1, \tag{4.5.12}$$

to which there certainly correspond non-negative prices (i.e. prices with an economic meaning) must itself be economically meaningful. It must not be negative or

$$\Pi \geq 0, \tag{4.5.13}$$

which implies, from (4.5.12),

$$\lambda_m \leq 1. \tag{4.5.14}$$

If (4.5.14) were not satisfied, we should be dealing with an economic system so technically backward that it could not generate a profit even with a zero wage rate. Such an economic system could clearly not survive; it would not be *viable*.

7 Actually the non-negative solution for relative prices, which is associated with the maximum eigenvalue λ_m, is also a unique solution. The only proviso needed is a condition to be discussed later (Section 10.7).

It will be noted that (4.5.14) is precisely the condition for the viability of an economic system discussed in footnote 4. Thus, relation (4.5.12) between Π and λ_m provides a new interpretation of the economic meaning of that condition.

5.5 A Pure Capital Theory of Value

It might be asked what kind of theory of value is implicit in the prices $\mathbf{p}^*$, corresponding to a zero wage rate. To give an answer to this question, it is useful to adopt the device suggested in Section 4 of supposing that the goods constituting the subsistence wage are already included in the matrix of technical coefficients, so that $w = 0$ may be taken to mean a zero *surplus* wage.

In such a system the quantities of labour required in the process of production come to be treated in the same way as any commodity. 'Men are like horses', so to speak. The inputs to the production process, including the workers, are all represented by commodities evaluated at their mere cost of reproduction. This is obviously a slave economy. Prices become proportional to the cost of the means of production, that is, to the cost of the capital goods. The prices $\mathbf{p}^*$ – the solution to (4.5.7) – thus express a theory of value which, bearing in mind the proportionality to the cost of the capital goods, we could call a 'pure capital theory of value'.[8]

It is interesting to note that theories of both Ricardo and Marx can be interpreted as referring to such an economic system. We can now better understand the nature of their theoretical difficulties. They both thought, intuitively, in terms of a pure labour theory of value, that is, of exchange ratios such as those given by (4.5.2). But they found themselves grappling with an analytical scheme the logic of which led them to the opposite extreme, that is to prices such as those given by (4.5.7), which imply a pure capital theory of value. Ricardo responded by building his theories largely on the special case in which the ratio of capital to labour is the same in every sector, that is, as we may now realise, precisely to the special case in which the prices (4.5.2) come to coincide with the prices (4.5.7).[9] (He then thought of the

[8] Torrens (1965, pp. 25, ff.) and, later, the Russian economist (Dmitriev 1974, pp. 50–80) both came very close to this conclusion.

[9] In an economic system in which the proportions of capital to labour are the same in all production processes, prices proportional to capital are clearly also

more general case as giving rise to only insignificant deviations from this case). For his part, Marx faced the difficulty by resorting to the analytically equivalent device of assuming the 'organic composition of capital' to be the same in all industries,[10] and then, for the general case,

proportional to labour. The conditions under which this happens are, however, very restrictive indeed. In analytical terms it must be possible to substitute prices (4.5.3) for prices (4.5.8), which we have called $\mathbf{p}^*$, so that

$$\mathbf{a}_n(\mathbf{I}-\mathbf{A})^{-1}[\mathbf{I}-(1+\Pi)\mathbf{A}]=0,$$

or rather, owing to definition (4.5.5),

$$\mathbf{v}[\mathbf{I}-(1+\Pi)\mathbf{A}]=0. \tag{4.5.15}$$

It should be clear that these expressions hold only for very particular vectors $\mathbf{a}_n$ and $\mathbf{v}$. More precisely, we can see immediately that (4.5.15) holds if, and only if, $\mathbf{v}$ is a left-hand eigenvector of matrix $\mathbf{A}$ (corresponding to its maximum eigenvalue λ_m, since $\mathbf{v} \geq 0$). Now call $\mathbf{v}^*$ that particular vector of vertically integrated labour coefficients which is an eigenvector of $\mathbf{A}$, and $\mathbf{a}_n^*$ the vector of direct labour coefficients from which it derives. Since by definition

$$\mathbf{v}^*=\mathbf{a}_n^*(\mathbf{I}-\mathbf{A})^{-1},$$

wc havc

$$\mathbf{a}_n^*=\mathbf{v}^*(\mathbf{I}-\mathbf{A})=\mathbf{v}^*-\mathbf{v}^*\mathbf{A},$$

or

$$\mathbf{a}_n^*=\mathbf{v}^*-\lambda_m\mathbf{v}^*=(1-\lambda_m)\mathbf{v}^*=\frac{\Pi}{1+\Pi}\mathbf{v}^*. \tag{4.5.16}$$

That is, $\mathbf{a}_n^*$ too, by being proportional to $\mathbf{v}^*$, is an eigenvector of $\mathbf{A}$. We may conclude that the necessary and sufficient condition for prices such as those given by (4.5.2) to coincide with prices (4.5.7) – in other words, for a pure labour theory of value to coincide with a pure capital theory of value – is that the vector of vertically integrated labour coefficients (which also implies the vector of direct labour coefficients) be a left-hand eigenvector of the matrix $\mathbf{A}$.

10 In analytical terms this assumption also may be expressed by saying that the vector of direct labour coefficients must be a left-hand eigenvector of matrix $\mathbf{A}$, i.e., must be a particular eigenvector $\mathbf{a}_n^*$ such that

$$\mathbf{a}_n^*(\lambda_m\mathbf{I}-\mathbf{A})=0.$$

For, if this expression holds, then

$$\mathbf{v}^*=\mathbf{a}_n^*(\mathbf{I}-\mathbf{A})^{-1}=\mathbf{a}_n^*(\mathbf{I}+\mathbf{A}+\mathbf{A}^2+\mathbf{A}^3+\cdots),$$

$$\mathbf{v}^*=\mathbf{a}_n^*+\lambda_m\mathbf{a}_n^*+\lambda_m^2\mathbf{a}_n^*+\lambda_m^3\mathbf{a}_n^*+\cdots,$$

$$\mathbf{v}^*=\mathbf{a}_n^*\left[1+\frac{1}{1+\Pi}+\left(\frac{1}{1+\Pi}\right)^2+\left(\frac{1}{1+\Pi}\right)^3+\cdots\right]. \tag{4.5.17}$$

And since

$$\lambda_m=\frac{1}{1+\Pi}<1,$$

by resorting to the problem of the 'transformation of values into prices of production'.[11]

5.6 The General Case

We can at last turn to the more general case in which the rate of profit lies between the two extremes. Setting $\pi = \bar{\pi}$, such that $0 < \bar{\pi} < \Pi$, we can write (4.3.2), after a few obvious algebraic manipulations, as

$$\mathbf{p} = \frac{1}{1+\bar{\Pi}}\mathbf{a}_n\left[\frac{1}{1+\bar{\Pi}}\mathbf{I} - \mathbf{A}\right]^{-1} w, \tag{4.5.19}$$

or

$$\mathbf{p} = \mathbf{a}_n[\mathbf{I} - (1+\bar{\Pi})\mathbf{A}]^{-1} w. \tag{4.5.20}$$

Here, again, any one price can be set equal to unity, so that a determinate system will be obtained for the other $(n-2)$ prices and for the wage rate w. Or we can adopt the wage rate as the *numéraire*, setting $w = 1$, so that (4.5.19) and (4.5.20) become, respectively

$$\mathbf{p} = \frac{1}{1+\bar{\Pi}}\mathbf{a}_n\left[\frac{1}{1+\bar{\Pi}}\mathbf{I} - \mathbf{A}\right]^{-1}, \tag{4.5.21}$$

and

$$\mathbf{p} = \mathbf{a}_n[\mathbf{I} - (1+\bar{\Pi})\mathbf{A}]^{-1}. \tag{4.5.22}$$

Expression (4.5.21), or (4.5.22), is a determinate system of equations in the $(n-1)$ prices, expressed in terms of the wage rate.

$$\mathbf{v}^* = \mathbf{a}_n^* \frac{1}{1-\lambda_m} = \mathbf{a}_n^* \frac{1+\Pi}{\Pi}, \tag{4.5.18}$$

which is the same expression as obtained in footnote 9. Thus, if $\mathbf{a}_n^*$ is an eigenvector of $\mathbf{A}$, then $\mathbf{v}^*$ is also an eigenvector of $\mathbf{A}$ (while it was found in footnote 9 that, if $\mathbf{v}^*$ is an eigenvector of $\mathbf{A}$, then $\mathbf{a}_n^*$ is also an eigenvector of $\mathbf{A}$).

It is now easy to grasp the economic meaning of (4.5.18). The proportion between each component of vector $\mathbf{v}^*$ and the corresponding component of vector $\mathbf{a}_n^*$ is exactly the same for all components. This means that the quantity of direct plus indirect labour required by each commodity (in Marxian terminology, the quantity of labour embodied in constant plus variable capital) is *for all commodities* the same proportion of the corresponding quantity of direct labour. This is precisely the meaning of a uniform 'organic composition of capital'.

[11] See Chapter 5, Section 6.

Since $\bar{\pi} > 0$, $\mathbf{a}_n \geq \mathbf{o}$, and, moreover, $[1/(1+\bar{\pi})] > \lambda_m$, which implies that[12]

$$\left[\frac{1}{1+\pi}\mathbf{I} - \mathbf{A}\right]^{-1} \geq \mathbf{O},$$

it follows that all the prices (4.5.21), and thus all the prices (4.5.19), are non-negative.[13]

It can now be verified that, when $\bar{\pi} = 0$, (4.5.19) and (4.5.21), or (4.5.20) and (4.5.22), reduce to (4.5.2) and (4.5.3), respectively, and prices become proportional to the quantities of embodied labour. But, as soon as $\bar{\pi} > 0$, this is no longer so. The quantities of indirect labour come to acquire a greater 'weight' relative to the quantities of direct labour because of the profit which has to be reckoned on them. In general, therefore, the proportionality between prices and quantities of labour (i.e. the pure labour theory of value), which was so dear to the Classical economists, breaks down. As is clear from (4.5.19), the structure of prices depends, in general, on both the technical coefficients (i.e. on the quantities of embodied labour) and the particular level of the rate of profit.[14] Given the technique of the economic system, a particular structure of prices, corresponding to each level of the rate of profit, will obtain.

It is to this general case that most of the following analysis will be referred. Note that, in this general case, the rate of profit is taken as exogenously given and the *numéraire* is chosen arbitrarily. Of course, any time that the choice of the *numéraire* does make a difference to our arguments, the *numéraire* itself will be explicitly specified. But in most cases our arguments will be such as to hold whichever *numéraire* is chosen. We shall, however, make a point of always specifying the *numéraire* explicitly whenever the wage rate is set equal to unity. In other cases this will be unnecessary. Therefore, whenever in the following pages we refer to vector $\mathbf{p}$ without any specification, we shall mean a vector of $(n-1)$ prices in which it does not matter which one of them (or which linear combination of them) is set equal to unity.

12 See Pasinetti (1977a, *Mathematical Appendix*, pp. 273, 276).

13 In the system of equations (4.3.1) the prices are therefore non-negative at each of the two extreme levels $\pi = 0$ and $\pi = \Pi$, as well as at all intermediate levels $0 < \pi < \Pi$.

14 These assertions will be further illustrated in Section 7.2.

5.7 Price Changes as an Effect of Changes in the Rate of Profit

A question that may be asked at this point is how prices change, relative to one another, as a consequence of the changes in the rate of profit. Unfortunately, this is not a question to which any simple answer can be given.

One can infer from (4.5.22), in which $w = 1$, that, as π increases, *all* prices in terms of the wage rate will increase or, in extreme cases, remain constant[15] (the extreme cases in question being those of commodities, if there are any, which require for their production only direct labour unassisted by any intermediate commodity).

However, although all prices in terms of the wage rate increase (or do not decrease) as π increases, some of them will increase faster than others, so that, relative to any given *numéraire*-commodity, some prices will increase and others will decrease.

Returning to equation system (4.3.1) and setting $w = 1$, we can consider the ratio

$$\frac{p_j}{p_1} = \frac{a_{nj} + (1+\pi)\sum_{i=1}^{n-1} a_{ij}p_i}{a_{n1} + (1+\pi)\sum_{i=1}^{n-1} a_{i1}p_i}, \qquad j = 1, 2, \ldots, n-1,$$

which is equivalent to changing the *numéraire* or, more precisely, to expressing the price of the jth commodity, $j = 1, 2, \ldots, n-1$, in terms of commodity 1. By finding the derivative of this ratio with respect to π, one can verify immediately that, at least in the neighbourhood of π,

$$\frac{\mathrm{d}}{\mathrm{d}\pi}\frac{p_j}{p_1} \gtreqless 0,$$

according as

$$\left[p_1 \sum_{i=1}^{n-1} a_{ij}p_i - p_j \sum_{i=1}^{n-1} a_{i1}p_i\right] + (1+\pi)\left[p_1 \sum_{i=1}^{n-1} a_{ij}\frac{\mathrm{d}p_i}{\mathrm{d}\pi} - p_j a_{i1}\frac{\mathrm{d}p_i}{\mathrm{d}\pi}\right] \gtreqless 0,$$
$$j = 1, 2, \ldots, n-1. \qquad (4.5.23)$$

In other words the price of the jth commodity in terms of commodity 1 will increase or decrease (as π increases) according as the expression (4.5.23) is positive or negative.

[15] This follows from Pasinetti (1977a, *Mathematical Appendix*, Theorems 5 and 5a of Perron-Frobenius, pp. 273, 276). According to these theorems each single element of matrix $[\mathbf{I} - (1+\pi)\mathbf{A}]^{-1}$ is an increasing (or at least non-decreasing) function of π.

Expression (4.5.23) is rather complex. However, it has been possible to split it up into two parts which have been enclosed in square brackets. The first square bracket expresses a comparison between the proportion of the price of the jth commodity ($j = 1, 2, \ldots, n-1$), which is due to the cost of its means of production. The effect exerted on (4.5.23) by the expression in this bracket can therefore be called the *capital intensity effect*. This effect will always be positive for all commodities produced by technical processes having a capital intensity greater than that of commodity 1 (used as the Standard of comparison or *numéraire*); and it will always be negative for all commodities produced by technical processes having a capital intensity lower than that of commodity 1. By contrast, the expression in the second square bracket cannot be related to any property which may be defined in a simple manner. It depends on how *all* the prices change in the whole system. Its effect on (4.5.23) can thus be called the *price effect*. This effect could be either positive or negative, depending on the entire network of interindustry relationships.

Thus, whereas the capital intensity effect always acts on each single price in a well-defined direction (which can be determined unambiguously at the level of the corresponding production process of the *numéraire*-commodity), the price effect depends on the entire economic system and is therefore not predictable at the level of any single industry. In some cases it will strengthen the first effect (when it works in the same direction) and in other case it weaken it, when it works in the opposite direction, or indeed even reverse it, when it is particularly strong.

To conclude, in predicting price changes in the neighbourhood of any particular rate of profit,[16] a probable, but not so absolutely certain, indicator is provided by the degree of capital intensity of the various processes of production. Thus, we can say that an increase in the rate of profit will be associated in most cases with an increase in the prices of commodities which for their production require a

[16] This qualification is necessary. The degree of capital intensity (defined as the ratio of the means of production component to the wage component in each price) is a notion which is itself dependent on the rate of profit. Some production processes might turn out to be more capital intensive at some rates of profit, and less capital intensive at other rates of profit, than the production process of the *numéraire*-commodity.

ratio of means of production to direct labour which is greater than that required by the *numéraire*-commodity (processes with high capital intensity). And, at the same time, that it will be associated in most cases with a decrease in prices of commodities which require a ratio of means of production to direct labour which is lower than that required by the *numéraire*-commodity (productive processes with low capital intensity). However, as has already been said, these propositions hold *in most but not all cases*. There might always be commodities for which the price effect is not only in the direction opposite to the capital intensity effect but also is so strong as to more than offset it and cause a reversal of the overall effect.

This would seem to be about all that can be said concerning the changes of the prices (4.5.19) corresponding to changes in the rate of profit. The relationships are highly complex precisely because the structure of prices depends on the technical coefficients and on the particular level of the rate of profit.

6 The Relationship between the Wage Rate and the Rate of Profit

6.1 *Income Distribution and Changes in Relative Prices*

There is an important relation, that between the wage rate and the rate of profit, which is influenced in a very complicated way by the unpredictable behaviour of prices, examined in Section 5.7. When the structure of prices changes as the rate of profit varies, the relation between the wage rate and the rate of profit is influenced by two different phenomena: the change in the distribution of income between wages and profits and the variation of the structure of prices as this distribution changes.

The role played by the distribution of income stands out clearly if we start with a particular net product in physical terms, $(\mathbf{I} - \mathbf{A})\bar{\mathbf{Q}}$, and then consider the distribution of shares of this net product (in physical terms) to wages and to profits. If we denote by ω the proportion or share of $(\mathbf{I} - \mathbf{A})\bar{\mathbf{Q}}$ distributed to wages and by $(1 - \omega)$ the share distributed to profits, all the possible distributions of income are obviously represented by a straight line with a slope of 45° (see Figure 4.1).

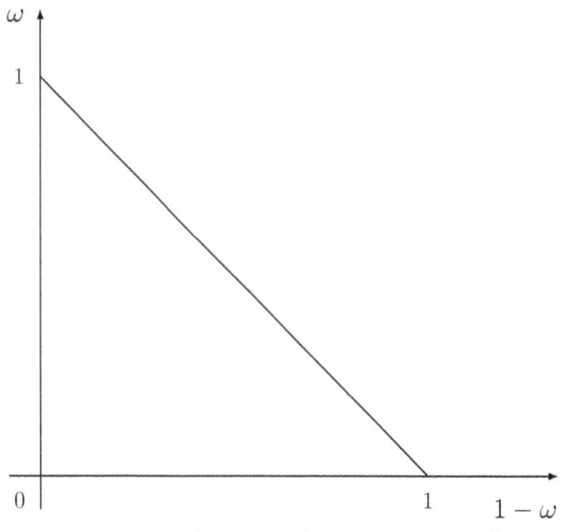

Figure 4.1 Distribution of net income by shares to wages and profits.

However, as long as we consider not just the *shares* of the net product which go to wages and profits (which can be thought of in physical terms) but rather the wage rate and the rate of profit, the introduction of the price vector $\mathbf{p}$ becomes unavoidable, and the relation immediately becomes more complicated.

It is still always possible to preserve the equality of the wage rate and the share of the net product which goes to wages (i.e. of ω and w) by adopting the convention of setting the net product per worker of the system equal to unity, that is, of setting $\mathbf{p}(\mathbf{I} - \mathbf{A})\bar{\mathbf{Q}} = Q_n$, where Q_n is the available labour force, assumed to be exogenously given. But, with respect to profits, the transition to considering their *rate* rather than their share involves the introduction of the total value of capital. Indeed, the rate of profit is precisely a ratio between the value of that part of the net product which goes to profits and the value of total capital. In general, it can be represented here as

$$\pi = (1 - \omega)\frac{\mathbf{p}(\mathbf{I} - \mathbf{A})\bar{\mathbf{Q}}}{\mathbf{p}\mathbf{A}\bar{\mathbf{Q}}}. \tag{4.6.1}$$

Now, when $\omega = 0$ and the prices become those given by the solution of (4.5.7), that is, $\mathbf{p}^*$, we have

$$\frac{\mathbf{p}^*(\mathbf{I} - \mathbf{A})\bar{\mathbf{Q}}}{\mathbf{p}^*\mathbf{A}\bar{\mathbf{Q}}} = \Pi. \tag{4.6.2}$$

But, as soon as $\omega > 0$, we have $\mathbf{p} \neq \mathbf{p}^*$. And, since the composition of capital, $\mathbf{A}\bar{\mathbf{Q}}$, differs in general from the composition of the net product, $(\mathbf{I} - \mathbf{A})\bar{\mathbf{Q}}$, the ratio $\mathbf{p}(\mathbf{I} - \mathbf{A})\bar{\mathbf{Q}}/\mathbf{p}\mathbf{A}\bar{\mathbf{Q}}$ will vary continually, as the distribution of income changes, because of variations of $\mathbf{p}$. This means that (4.6.1) will be influenced both by the variation of ω and by the variation of $\mathbf{p}$.

6.2 *The Special Case of Uniform Capital Intensity*

It may be of interest to note that there is a special case in which these complications disappear. It is the very special case (considered by Ricardo and Marx) in which the price vector, which we shall call $\bar{\mathbf{p}}$, remains invariant to changes in the distribution of income (the case of uniform capital intensity or uniform 'organic composition of capital' in all sectors). In this case, since $\mathbf{p} = \bar{\mathbf{p}}$, we have

$$\frac{\bar{\mathbf{p}}(\mathbf{I} - \mathbf{A})\bar{\mathbf{Q}}}{\bar{\mathbf{p}}\mathbf{A}\bar{\mathbf{Q}}} = \Pi, \qquad (4.6.3)$$

for all values of ω $(0 \leq \omega \leq 1)$, not only when $\omega = 0$, so that, by substituting into (4.6.1), the latter reduces to the simple linear relation

$$\pi = \Pi(1 - \omega). \qquad (4.6.4)$$

If we then adopt the convention of taking the net product per worker of the system as the *numéraire*, that is, of setting $\mathbf{p}(\mathbf{I} - \mathbf{A})\bar{\mathbf{Q}} = Q_n$, ω coincides with w and the relation even becomes

$$\pi = \Pi(1 - w), \qquad (4.6.5)$$

a linear relation between the rate of profit and the wage rate (see Figure 4.2). This relation reflects the income distribution phenomenon alone, simply because the price structure remains invariant to changes in the distribution of income.[17]

[17] The same linear relation may be obtained (but in a more labourious way) from the expressions of footnote 10. It was proved there that, if the vector of direct labour coefficients is the particular vector $\mathbf{a}_n^*$, defined as the eigenvector of $\mathbf{A}$ corresponding to λ_m, then relative prices turn out to be the same at the two extreme points $\pi = 0$ and $\pi = \Pi$. It is not difficult to prove now that relative prices remain the same also at *all* intermediate levels of the rate of profit $0 < \pi < \Pi$. If we put $\mathbf{a}_n = \mathbf{a}_n^*$ in (4.3.1), that is, if we consider the special case

$$\mathbf{p}\mathbf{A}(1 + \pi) + \mathbf{a}_n^* w = \mathbf{p}, \qquad (4.6.6)$$

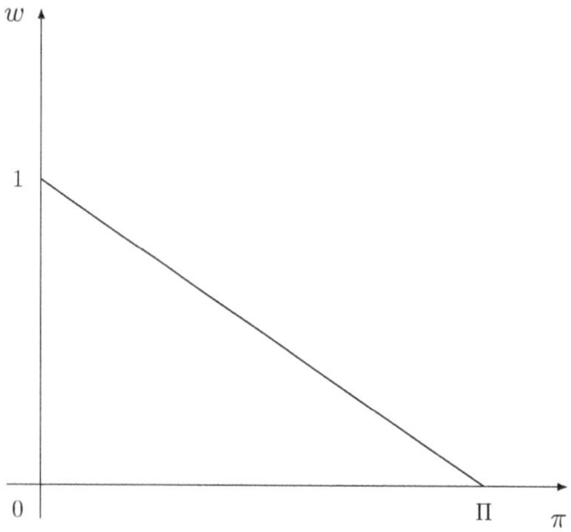

Figure 4.2 Relation between the wage rate and the rate of profit in the special case of uniform capital intensity.

it is sufficient for us to verify that (4.6.6) holds if we substitute in the price vector $\mathbf{p}^*$ (which is by definition an eigenvector of $\mathbf{A}$). Since $\mathbf{p}^*\mathbf{A} = \lambda_m \mathbf{p}^*$, by substitution we obtain

$$\mathbf{p}^* = \mathbf{a}_n^* \frac{w}{1-(1+\pi)\lambda_m}. \tag{4.6.7}$$

We may therefore say that this expression holds if $\mathbf{p}^*$ and $\mathbf{a}_n^*$ are proportional to each other. But $\mathbf{p}^*$ is an eigenvector of $\mathbf{A}$ by definition, and $\mathbf{a}_n^*$ is an eigenvector of $\mathbf{A}$ by hypothesis (i.e. the two are indeed proportional to each other). Therefore, whatever the scalar

$$\frac{w}{1-(1+\pi)\lambda_m}, \tag{4.6.8}$$

may be, that is, whatever the rate of profit, π, and the wage rate, w, may be, expression (4.6.7) does indeed hold. (Note that for no other $\mathbf{a}_n$, which is not an eigenvector of $\mathbf{A}$, (4.6.7) does hold).

We know also from footnote 10 that $\mathbf{v}^*$ is proportional to $\mathbf{a}_n^*$. And, since the price vector contains one degree of freedom (i.e. prices are determined up to an arbitrary constant), we may well set $\mathbf{p}^* = \mathbf{v}^*$, which is equivalent to choosing the unit of embodied labour as the *numéraire* of the price system (and therefore to fixing at $0 \leq w \leq 1$ the range of variation of the wage rate). In this case the coefficient of proportionality between $\mathbf{p}^*$ and $\mathbf{a}_n^*$ from (4.6.7), must coincide with the coefficient of proportionality between $\mathbf{v}^*$ and $\mathbf{a}_n^*$ from (4.5.18), that is,

$$\frac{w}{1-(1+\pi)\lambda_m} = \frac{1}{1-\lambda_m}, \tag{4.6.9}$$

from which we obtain

$$\pi = \Pi(1-w), \tag{4.6.10}$$

which is precisely the linear relation obtained in the text.

6.3 The General Case

In the general case the relation between the rate of profit and the wage rate is very complicated. For the purpose of analysing its properties it is helpful to return to our earlier convention of expressing prices in terms of an arbitrary commodity, chosen as *numéraire*. We might start by choosing, for example, commodity 1, that is, by setting $p_1 = 1$. By post-multiplying expression (4.5.20) by the first unit (column) vector $\mathbf{e}_i$, we obtain

$$1 = \mathbf{a}_n[\mathbf{I} - (1+\pi)\mathbf{A}]^{-1}\mathbf{e}_1 w^{(1)}, \tag{4.6.11}$$

where $w^{(1)}$ denotes the wage rate expressed in terms of commodity 1.

It will now be noted that (4.6.11) is an implicit function, of polynomial form, relating π and $w^{(1)}$. More specifically, (4.6.11) is in general an $(n-1)$th degree polynomial in π (where $n-1$ is the order of the matrix $\mathbf{A}$, which we shall here assume, for simplicity, to be irreducible). If the graph of this polynomial is drawn, using the usual Cartesian axes, its shape will therefore be far more complex than that of a straight line. One could, for example, obtain a curve such as that shown in Figure 4.3.

Unfortunately, one can really say very little about the shape of this curve. One can only say that: (i) its intercept on the horizontal axis is necessarily Π (by definition); and (ii) the curve itself is everywhere strictly decreasing throughout the positive quadrant. Actually, every element of the matrix $[\mathbf{I} - (1+\pi)\mathbf{A}]^{-1}$ is a strictly increasing function of π. And this necessarily implies that each of π and $w^{(1)}$ is a monotonically decreasing function of the other.

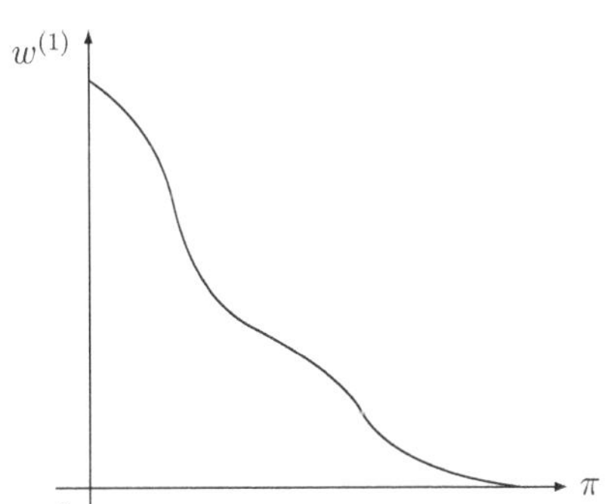

Figure 4.3 The wage rate–rate of profit relationship in the general case.

One could, of course, repeat this argument with respect no longer to commodity 1 but to commodity j, j being any one of the other commodities $2,\ldots,n-1$. In general, for each commodity $j, j = 1,2,\ldots,n-1$, one obtains a particular relation of the type (4.6.11) and a particular curve of the type shown in Figure 4.3. Each of these relations (and each corresponding curve) is different from each of the others, being dependent on the particular production conditions for the commodity in question. These relations are all polynomial functions of degree $(n-1)$, they all intersect the π axis at Π, and they are all strictly decreasing in the positive quadrant. However, nothing whatever can be said in general about their shape.

We may now conclude. In an economic system with single product industries, the wage rate, expressed in terms of any commodity, is a monotonically decreasing function of the rate of profit.[18] However, this function is expressed by a complicated polynomial curve which assumes a specific shape for each particular commodity chosen as *numéraire*. This prevents a clear perception of the phenomenon of the distribution of income between wages and profits, since this phenomenon becomes intertwined with the other complex phenomenon of the variation of the entire structure of prices.

At first sight this conclusion might appear to destroy not only the Classical pure labour theory of value, but also the Ricardian attempt to separate the problem of income distribution from the problem of value. But we shall return to this question in Section 12.

7 Reduction of Prices to 'Dated' Quantities of Labour

7.1 A Convergent Series of Quantities of Labour

Despite the difficulties met thus far, which might seem to stand in the way of any attempt to consider the system of prices in terms of quantities of labour, equation (4.5.22) lends itself to an interesting analysis which actually places the quantities of embodied labour at the centre of the stage once again. The matrix $[\mathbf{I} - (1+\pi)\mathbf{A}]^{-1}$ can be expanded as a power series in $\mathbf{A}$ provided only[19] that $(1+\pi) < 1/|\lambda_M|$, where λ_M

[18] Not even this proposition holds when there is joint production.
[19] See Pasinetti (1977a, *Mathematical Appendix*, p. 265).

is the eigenvalue of **A** with the greatest modulus. In the present context, the eigenvalue of greatest modulus coincides with the maximum eigenvalue,[20] and this condition is therefore satisfied for every

$$\pi < \Pi \equiv \frac{1}{\lambda_m} - 1.$$

Equation (4.5.22) can therefore be written as

$$\mathbf{p} = \mathbf{a}_n[\mathbf{I} + (1+\pi)\mathbf{A} + (1+\pi)^2\mathbf{A}^2 + (1+\pi)^3\mathbf{A}^3 + \cdots], \qquad (4.7.1)$$

or

$$\mathbf{p} = \mathbf{a}_n + (1+\pi)\mathbf{a}_n\mathbf{A} + (1+\pi)^2\mathbf{a}_n\mathbf{A}^2 + (1+\pi)\mathbf{a}_n^3\mathbf{A}^3 + \cdots. \qquad (4.7.2)$$

Consider first the special case in which $\pi = 0$. Since $w = 1$, $\mathbf{p} = \mathbf{v}$ from (4.5.3); and (4.7.2) reduces to

$$\mathbf{p} = \mathbf{v} = \mathbf{a}_n + \mathbf{a}_n\mathbf{A} + \mathbf{a}_n\mathbf{A}^2 + \mathbf{a}_n\mathbf{A}^3 + \cdots. \qquad (4.7.3)$$

It is not difficult to realise that this sequence of powers of **A**, pre-multiplied by $\mathbf{a}_n$, has a precise economic meaning. It can be seen[21] in fact that in the series of powers $\mathbf{I}, \mathbf{A}, \mathbf{A}^2, \mathbf{A}^3, \ldots$ the columns of each matrix represent the quantities of commodities which are (conceptually) required in each 'round' of production in order to obtain each unit of the corresponding commodities as final commodities. The pre-multiplication of these matrices by the vector of direct labour coefficients therefore yields an infinite series of vectors which represent the quantities of labour required in the various successive rounds of production. Since the elements of the matrix $\mathbf{A}^s, s = 1, 2, 3, \ldots$, become ever smaller as s increases, these labour requirements become ever smaller as one moves backwards in time through the various rounds. They actually tend to zero as s tends to infinity. Thus, the first term on the right side of the (4.7.3) is the vector of direct labour requirements, while the sum of all the following terms is the vector of indirect labour requirements. The total sum thus represents the vector of the total (direct and indirect) labour requirements, that is, the vector of the vertically integrated labour coefficients or quantities of embodied labour, which was obtained earlier in a compact, timeless way from (4.5.5).

But each of these quantities of labour also appears in (4.7.2). The latter expression, indeed, contains exactly the same quantities of labour

[20] See Perron-Frobenius Theorems.
[21] Pasinetti (1977a, pp. 67–69).

as (4.7.3), with the difference that they are multiplied by the factor $(1+\pi)^s$, where s is the round of production in which the quantity of labour is required. Thus, the same quantities of labour, which in (4.7.3) are summed as they stand, in (4.7.2) are *dated*; a different weight is attributed to each quantity of labour according to the particular date, in time, at which it is required. It is to be noted that each term in the series, and thus also the sum of them, is an increasing function of π. Hence, all the prices increase as the rate of profit increases. In the limit, (4.7.2) ceases to be convergent, and the prices, in terms of the wage rate, tend to infinity. This occurs, however, only at the extreme limiting point at which the rate of profit reaches its maximum level, Π. For all rates of profit in the interval $0 \leq \pi < \Pi$, the series (4.7.2) is convergent and effects the reduction of all the prices to quantities of labour of different 'dates', appropriately weighted by the corresponding compound interest factor $(1+\pi)^s$.

7.2 A Series of 'Layers' of Wages and Profits

We can now make use of the series (4.7.2) to illustrate the assertion made at the end of Section 5.6 that each price depends on both the quantity of labour directly and indirectly embodied in the respective commodity and the particular level of the rate of profit. Writing (4.7.2) in terms of an arbitrary *numéraire* as

$$\mathbf{p} = \mathbf{a}_n w + (1+\pi)\mathbf{a}_n \mathbf{A} w + (1+\pi)^2 \mathbf{a}_n \mathbf{A}^2 w + \cdots, \qquad (4.7.4)$$

it can be seen at once that, with each variation in the distribution of income, each term in the series is pulled in opposite directions by the variations in the wage rate and the rate of profit.

The net result of these opposing pulls will, however, differ from term to term and from commodity to commodity, being dependent on the particular characteristics of the various powers of the matrix $\mathbf{A}$. As w and π vary in opposite directions, some terms will increase while others will decrease,[22] and each price will increase or decrease in accordance with the net effect of the sum of all these complicated variations.

[22] A detailed analysis (with numerical example and graphical illustration) of the variations of all these addenda as an effect of changes in the rate of profit can be found in Sraffa (1960, pp. 35–38).

Expression (4.7.4) can also be thought of as representing the superposing, backwards through time, of the infinitely many 'layers' of profits and wages of which the price of each commodity consists. For each commodity each 'layer' of wages and profits depends on the particular proportions of labour to means of production required, at the corresponding 'date', by the technical characteristics of the production methods for that commodity. The reason for the variations in prices as the distribution of income between profits and wages varies can thus be traced back to the particular proportions of labour to means of production required by each commodity in each of the infinitely many 'layers' of wages and profits which make up its price.[23]

8 The System of Physical Quantities

We turn now to the system of equations relating to the physical quantities to be produced, and we begin by formulating this system as 'dual' to the price system. Leaving aside the last column, we can write

[23] Consider, by contrast, the very special case in which the proportions between labour and means of production are the same everywhere in the economic system (uniform capital intensity). In this case, $\mathbf{a}_n^*$ is an eigenvector of $\mathbf{A}$ (see footnotes 9 and 10). Therefore

$$\mathbf{a}_n^*\mathbf{A} = \mathbf{a}_n^*\lambda = \mathbf{a}_n^*\frac{1}{1+\Pi},$$

so that (4.7.4) becomes

$$\begin{aligned} \mathbf{p} &= \mathbf{a}_n^* w + \frac{1+\pi}{1+\Pi}\mathbf{a}_n^* w + \left(\frac{1+\pi}{1+\Pi}\right)^2 \mathbf{a}_n^* w + \left(\frac{1+\pi}{1+\Pi}\right)^3 \mathbf{a}_n^* w + \cdots = \\ &= \mathbf{a}_n^*\left[1 + \frac{1+\pi}{1+\Pi} + \left(\frac{1+\pi}{1+\Pi}\right)^2 + \left(\frac{1+\pi}{1+\Pi}\right)^3 + \cdots\right]. \end{aligned} \qquad (4.7.5)$$

The succession is perfectly regular. As may be seen, there appears within square brackets a geometric progression which is exactly the same for all prices. Therefore, whatever variations may take place in w and π, these variations affect each price by exactly the same multiplicative factor, thereby leaving their ratios (relative prices) unchanged.

It also follows from (4.7.5) that for all commodities the proportions of labour to means of production are exactly the same *at each single* conceptual stage of the production process, and not only at the vertically integrated stage. (As we saw, $\mathbf{v}^*$ is proportional to $\mathbf{a}_n^*$). The remarkable consequence is that it makes no difference whether one talks of uniform capital intensity at the level of single industries, at the level of the integrated sectors or at any one of the intermediate stages. Uniformity at one level necessarily entails uniformity at *all* levels.

$$\begin{cases} a_{11}Q_1 + a_{12}Q_2 + \cdots + a_{1,n-1}Q_{n-1} + Y_1 = Q_1, \\ a_{21}Q_1 + a_{22}Q_2 + \cdots + a_{2,n-1}Q_{n-1} + Y_2 = Q_2, \\ \quad \vdots \\ a_{n-1,1}Q_1 + a_{n-1,2}Q_2 + \cdots + a_{n-1,n-1}Q_{n-1} + Y_{n-1} = Q_{n-1}, \end{cases} \tag{4.8.1}$$

where $Q_1, Q_2, \ldots, Q_{n-1}$ are the total quantities to be produced of the various commodities, and $Y_1, Y_2, \ldots, Y_{n-1}$ are the quantities of the various commodities that can be devoted to final demand (the surplus of the system seen in physical terms).

If we were now to make explicitly the assumption of constant return to scale, this system of equations would appear to be nothing but the 'open' Leontief system, the quantities $Y_1, Y_2, \ldots, Y_{n-1}$ being displayed on the left-hand sides in order to draw attention to these quantities as constituting those portions of the total physical quantities which are in surplus relative to those portions which must go back into the production process.[24] To emphasise this point further it will be useful to express the various quantities of commodities which are devoted to final use in relative terms, that is, in terms of physical rates of surplus, which we shall call R_i, $i = 1, 2, \ldots, n-1$, and which we define as

$$R_1 = \frac{Y_1}{Q_1 - Y_1}, \qquad R_2 = \frac{Y_2}{Q_2 - Y_2}, \qquad , R_{n-1} = \frac{Y_{n-1}}{Q_{n-1} - Y_{n-1}}. \tag{4.8.2}$$

The system of physical quantities may now be written in the alternative form

$$\begin{cases} (a_{11}Q_1 + a_{12}Q_2 + \cdots + a_{1,n-1}Q_{n-1})(1 + R_1) = Q_1, \\ (a_{21}Q_1 + a_{22}Q_2 + \cdots + a_{2,n-1}Q_{n-1})(1 + R_2) = Q_2, \\ \vdots \\ (a_{n-1,1}Q_1 + a_{n-1,2}Q_2 + \cdots + a_{n-1,n-1}Q_{n-1})(1 + R_{n-1}) = Q_{n-1}. \end{cases} \tag{4.8.3}$$

Just as the quantities $Y_1, Y_2, \ldots, Y_{n-1}$ in (4.8.1) have been considered as given from outside, so in the alternative version (4.8.3)

[24] It may also be pointed out that in this chapter we are considering a stationary system, so that all physical quantities $Y_1, Y_2, \ldots, Y_{n-1}$, making up the net product, are entirely devoted to consumption.

the $R_1, R_2, \ldots, R_{n-1}$ can now be considered as given from outside. In version (4.8.1), the problem is to find the total quantities $Q_1, Q_2, \ldots, Q_{n-1}$ which must be produced in order to obtain the given set of final commodities $Y_1, Y_2, \ldots, Y_{n-1}$. In version (4.8.3), the corresponding problem is that of finding the total quantities $Q_1, Q_2, \ldots, Q_{n-1}$ which must be produced in order to obtain a given set of physical rates of surplus $R_1, R_2, \ldots, R_{n-1}$. These physical rates of surplus will, of course, normally differ from one commodity to another (just as the proportions among the quantities $Y_1, Y_2, \ldots, Y_{n-1}$ are usually different from one another in (4.8.1)). Moreover, they must be non-negative, that is,

$$R_i \geq 0, \qquad i = 1, 2, \ldots, n-1, \tag{4.8.4}$$

(just as $Y_i \geq 0,\ i = 1, 2, \ldots, n-1$).[25]

The two formulations carry different implications, however. This becomes apparent as soon as one rewrites system (4.8.3) in the form

$$\begin{bmatrix} \left(a_{11} - \frac{1}{1+R_1}\right) & a_{12} & \cdots & a_{1,n-1} \\ a_{21} & \left(a_{22} - \frac{1}{1+R_2}\right) & \cdots & a_{2,n-1} \\ \vdots & \vdots & \ddots & \vdots \\ a_{n-1,1} & a_{n-1,2} & \cdots & \left(a_{n-1,n-1} - \frac{1}{1+R_{n-1}}\right) \end{bmatrix} \begin{bmatrix} Q_1 \\ Q_2 \\ \vdots \\ Q_{n-1} \end{bmatrix} = \begin{bmatrix} 0 \\ 0 \\ \vdots \\ 0 \end{bmatrix}. \tag{4.8.5}$$

It will be noted that this system, by contrast with (4.8.1), is homogeneous. A necessary and sufficient condition for the existence of non-zero solutions is therefore that the determinant of the coefficient matrix be zero, that is,

[25] To get an idea of the meaning of these physical rates of surplus, it may be useful to refer them to an example presented by Sraffa (1960, chapter I, § 3) and modified by Pasinetti (1977a, chapter II, § 1.3), where the quantities devoted to the final sector are set equal to $Y_1 = 180$, $Y_2 = 0$ and $Y_3 = 30$.

	Q_i	$Q_i - Y_i$	Y_i	$R_i = \frac{Y_i}{Q_i - Y_I}$
Tonnes of wheat	450	270	180	66.66%
Tonnes of iron	21	21	0	0%
Gross of turkeys	60	30	30	100%

$$\begin{vmatrix} \left(a_{11} - \frac{1}{1+R_1}\right) & a_{12} & \cdots & a_{1,n-1} \\ a_{21} & \left(a_{22} - \frac{1}{1+R_2}\right) & \cdots & a_{2,n-1} \\ \vdots & \vdots & \ddots & \vdots \\ a_{n-1,1} & a_{n-1,2} & \cdots & \left(a_{n-1,n-1} - \frac{1}{1+R_{n-1}}\right) \end{vmatrix} = 0. \quad (4.8.6)$$

If this equation is to be satisfied, it is necessarily implied that the physical rates of surplus $R_1, R_2, \ldots, R_{n-1}$ cannot all be taken as given. At most $(n-2)$ of them can be taken as given; the remaining one must be such as to satisfy the algebraic equation (4.8.6).

Let us assume therefore that at least one of the R_i, $i = 1, 2, \ldots, n-1$, is determined so as to satisfy (4.8.6). Then, (4.8.5) becomes a linear and homogeneous system of equations with a zero determinant. Such a system will yield solutions for the physical quantities $Q_1, Q_2, \ldots, Q_{n-1}$, which are determined only up to a scalar multiple, that is, it will determine the *structure* of production in the economic system, leaving the scale of operation indeterminate.

The contrast between this formulation and that given in (4.8.1) (the Leontief 'open' system) now becomes clear. In system (4.8.1) all the Y_i, $i = 1, 2, \ldots, n-1$, can be taken to be exogenously given; in system (4.8.3) at least one of the R_i, $i = 1, 2, \ldots, n-1$, since it has to satisfy equation (4.8.6), cannot be taken as given but itself becomes unknown. On the other hand, the solutions to (4.8.1) refer to a well-defined scale of production, while the solutions to (4.8.3) relate to 'relative quantities' and thus are independent of the scale of operation.

Version (4.8.3) has the advantage of retaining a degree of freedom, which might be used, for example, to take account of the labour requirements in relation to the existing labour force. In other words, we could now add equation

$$\mathbf{a}_n\mathbf{Q} = \bar{Q}_n. \quad (4.8.7)$$

By means of this equation, the size of the available labour force would determine the scale of operation of the economic system under consideration.[26]

[26] The elaborations of this section have been presented in such a way as to make them directly comparable with those of the Leontief system. It may therefore be easier for the reader to consider them under the assumption of constant return to scale. It must be specified, however, that Sraffa himself always keeps his analysis free from such an assumption. His arguments on the proportions

9 The 'Standard System'

9.1 A Logical Exercise

We now set ourselves a particular problem which we shall, for the moment, face as a purely logico-mathematical exercise. Since all but one of the R_i, $i = 1, 2, \ldots, n-1$, can be taken to be determined from outside the system of equations (4.8.5), we may set all the R_i equal to one another, that is,

$$R_1 = R_2 = R_3 = \ldots = R_{n-1} = R, \qquad (4.9.1)$$

where R denotes a uniform rate of surplus throughout the economic system.

Substituting a single R for the various R_i in system (4.8.5), $i = 1, 2, \ldots, n-1$, and defining, for convenience,

$$\frac{1}{1+R} = \eta, \qquad (4.9.2)$$

we obtain a system of equations which can be written in compact form as

$$\mathbf{AQ} = \eta\mathbf{Q}, \qquad (4.9.3)$$

or

$$(\eta\mathbf{I} - \mathbf{A})\mathbf{Q} = 0. \qquad (4.9.4)$$

This system of equations is formally the same as system (4.5.10), although here the (column) vector $\mathbf{Q}$ multiplies the rows of $\mathbf{A}$, while in (4.5.10) the (row) vector $\mathbf{p}$ multiplies the columns of $\mathbf{A}$, Here too a necessary condition for the existence of non-zero solutions is that the determinant $|\eta\mathbf{I} - \mathbf{A}|$ be zero. Thus, we can obtain the solution (or solutions) for η from the characteristic equation

$$\det(\eta\mathbf{I} - \mathbf{A}) = 0, \qquad (4.9.5)$$

which has, in general, $(n-1)$ roots, although some of them could be repeated roots. These roots are simply the eigenvalues of the matrix $\mathbf{A}$, while $\mathbf{Q}$ is a right-hand eigenvector of $\mathbf{A}$. But $\mathbf{A}$ is non-negative and is the same matrix as appears in system (4.5.10), where $\mathbf{p}$ is its left-hand

among various industries are carried out on a purely hypothetical basis, as a preparation for the construction of the Standard commodity, which we consider in following sections.

eigenvector. It follows that the values of η satisfying (4.9.5) coincide with the values of λ satisfying (4.5.11), so that

$$\eta_i = \lambda_i, \qquad i = 1, 2, \ldots, n-1.$$

As before, however, not all of these eigenvalues have an economic meaning. In fact, only one of them, the maximum eigenvalue η_m, is certainly associated with a strictly non-negative eigenvector,[27] the elements of which represent physical quantities in the present context. It is therefore to this eigenvalue that there corresponds, via (4.9.2), the unique R having an economic meaning, that is, the unique R which, on being substituted into (4.9.3), always yields non-negative solutions.

Moreover, since $\eta_m = \lambda_m$, it also follows that

$$R \equiv \frac{1}{\eta_m} - 1 \equiv \frac{1}{\lambda_m} - 1 \equiv \Pi, \tag{4.9.6}$$

that is, the uniform rate of surplus of the system is identically equal to the maximum rate of profit. This is a remarkable result, deriving from the mathematical properties of the equations which represent a production system.

Thus, R and Π provide two different economic interpretations of the maximum eigenvalue of $\mathbf{A}$, the matrix of the interindustry technical coefficients. Every $\mathbf{A}$ matrix is characterised by a particular maximum eigenvalue, which is related, by the same relation (4.9.6), both to the uniform rate of surplus and to the maximum rate of profit, which consequently coincide.

9.2 *The Viability Condition Once Again*

A further condition must, of course, be satisfied by system (4.9.3):

$$R \geq 0,$$

which implies that

$$\eta_m \leq 1.$$

But, since $\eta_m \equiv \lambda_m$, this is nothing other than condition (4.5.14), which we have already discussed. Thus, the identity $\eta_m \equiv \lambda_m$ now provides an alternative interpretation of that condition. If the condition

[27] The result of Theorems 1 and 1a, Pasinetti (1977a, *Mathematical Appendix* pp. 269, 275).

were not satisfied, it would mean that the economic system considered is so technically backward as to yield a negative rate of surplus, that is, to use as means of production greater quantities of commodities than it would then be able to produce. Such an economic system could obviously not survive; it would not be viable. This is in effect the interpretation of the viability condition for the system which was anticipated in footnote 4 at page 121.

9.3 'Standard Commodity' and 'Standard Net Product'

Once the uniform rate of surplus, R, has been found, it can be substituted into system (4.9.3), thus enabling us to obtain the solutions for the Q_i, $i = 1, 2, \ldots, n-1$, which satisfy the problem which we posed at the outset. Since the system (4.9.3) becomes linear and homogeneous with a zero determinant, it yields solutions for the physical quantities Q_i, $i = 1, 2, \ldots, n-1$, which are determined up to a scalar multiple. It thus determines the structure of the production system but not its scale of operation. To determine the latter a further relation is required.

We may now suppose such a relation to be introduced by adding, for example, (4.8.7). We may thus write

$$(1 + R)\mathbf{A}\mathbf{Q} = \mathbf{Q}, \tag{4.9.7}$$

$$\mathbf{a}_n\mathbf{Q} = \bar{Q}_n. \tag{4.8.7}$$

Equations (4.9.7) and (4.8.7) now form a system of n equations and in n unknowns: R and the $(n-1)$ physical quantities Q_i, $i = 1, 2, \ldots, n-1$. We shall denote the solutions for the Q_i by $Q_1^*, Q_2^*, \ldots, Q_{n-1}^*$.

An interesting problem now arises. If the **A** matrix is an irreducible matrix, the Perron-Frobenius theorems guarantee that the solutions are all strictly positive. If, on the other hand, the **A** matrix is reducible, the same Perron-Frobenius theorems (in their weak form) guarantee only that the solutions are non-negative.[28] This means that some of them will be positive while others might be zero. The positive solutions clearly satisfy the equalities (4.9.1). For the zero solutions, by contrast, a physical rate of surplus cannot be defined. However, precisely

[28] See Pasinetti (1977a, *Mathematical Appendix*, pp. 269, 275), Theorems 1 and 1a.

because these solutions are zero, we may remove the corresponding rows and columns from the coefficient matrix. This means that we can eliminate the corresponding industries and commodities from the system of equations.

Let the number of positive solutions be k ($k = n - 1$ if the matrix $\mathbf{A}$ is irreducible, and $k < n - 1$ if the matrix $\mathbf{A}$ is reducible). It may now be noted that these solutions possess a very interesting property concerning their proportions. If we denote by $Y_1^*, Y_2^*, \ldots, Y_k^*$ the quantities for final use corresponding to the solutions $Q_1^*, Q_2^*, \ldots, Q_k^*$, we shall have by definition

$$R = \frac{Y_1^*}{Q_1^* - Y_1^*} = \frac{Y_2^*}{Q_2^* - Y_2^*} = \cdots = \frac{Y_k^*}{Q_k^* - Y_k^*},$$

from which it follows that

$$\begin{aligned}[Y_1^*, Y_2^*, \ldots, Y_k^*]' &= R[(Q_1^* - Y_1^*), (Q_2^* - Y_2^*), \ldots, (Q_k^* - Y_k^*)]' = \\ &= \frac{R}{1+R}[Q_1^*, Q_2^*, \ldots, Q_k^*]'. \qquad (4.9.8)\end{aligned}$$

Thus, the positive physical quantities which represent the solution of system (4.9.3) are such that the *proportions* in which the various commodities are produced are equal to the proportions in which the same commodities are used as means of production in the economic system as a whole and are also equal to the proportions in which the same commodities are devoted to final uses (in the present context, consumption).

Sraffa has called an economic system which exhibits these proportionality relations a 'Standard system'. And he has called the net product of that particular Standard system in which the scale of operation is such as to require a quantity of labour equal to that employed in the actual economic system, as in (4.9.7) and (4.8.7), the 'Standard net product'. It will be noted that vector $[Y_1^*, Y_2^*, \ldots, Y_k^*]'$ represents a particular composite commodity into which the various commodities enter in precisely determined proportions. Sraffa has called this composite commodity, or any multiple of fraction thereof, the 'Standard commodity'. And he has called the ratio R, expressing the uniform rate of surplus, the 'Standard ratio'.

The Standard system, as derived (4.9.3)–(4.9.8), is, of course, simply a logical construction. For any given economic system, characterised by a particular coefficient matrix **A**, there logically exists a corresponding Standard system in which each commodity from the actual system is produced in the Standard proportions or is not produced at all.

9.4 Labour Embodied in the Standard Net Product

By calling $\mathbf{Q}^*$ the vector solution of (4.9.7)–(4.8.7), we have

$$\mathbf{AQ}^* = \frac{1}{1+R}\mathbf{Q}^*. \tag{4.9.9}$$

and thus, in general

$$\mathbf{A}^s\mathbf{Q}^* = (1+R)^{-s}\mathbf{Q}^*, \tag{4.9.10}$$

It follows that

$$\mathbf{Y}^* = (\mathbf{I}-\mathbf{A})\mathbf{Q}^* = R\mathbf{AQ}^* = \frac{R}{1+R}\mathbf{Q}^*, \tag{4.9.11}$$

and hence, after substitution into (4.9.9), that

$$\mathbf{AY}^* = \frac{1}{1+R}\mathbf{Y}^* \qquad \mathbf{A}^s\mathbf{Y}^* = (1+R)^{-s}\mathbf{Y}^*. \tag{4.9.12}$$

Thus, $\mathbf{Y}^*$ is also found to be an eigenvector of **A**. ($\mathbf{Q}^*$ and $\mathbf{Y}^*$ are indeed proportional to one another, as they contain the same commodities in exactly the same proportions).

Let us now consider the problem of finding the quantity of direct and indirect labour which is required for the production of the Standard commodity, that is, the total quantity of labour 'embodied' in it. By making use of (4.7.3) and post-multiplying by $\mathbf{Y}^*$, we obtain $\mathbf{vY}^*$, the labour embodied in the Standard net product expressed as the sum of the (infinite) series:

$$\mathbf{vY}^* = \mathbf{a}_n\mathbf{Y}^* + \mathbf{a}_n\mathbf{AY}^* + \mathbf{a}_n\mathbf{A}^2\mathbf{Y}^* + \mathbf{a}_n\mathbf{A}^3\mathbf{Y}^* + \cdots, \tag{4.9.13}$$

where the first term on the right-hand side is the quantity of direct labour and the sum of the remaining terms is the total quantity of indirect labour, the latter being divided up according to the dates at which the various quantities of indirect labour were required. On substituting from (4.9.12), we obtain

$$\mathbf{vY}^* = \mathbf{a}_n\mathbf{Y}^*\left[1 + \frac{1}{1+R} + \frac{1}{(1+R)^2} + \frac{1}{(1+R)^3} + \cdots\right], \tag{4.9.14}$$

and thus,

$$\mathbf{vY}^* = \mathbf{a}_n\mathbf{Y}^*\frac{1+R}{R}. \tag{4.9.15}$$

This is a remarkable expression. The total quantity of labour embodied in the Standard net product, $\mathbf{v}\mathbf{Y}^*$, is obtained by simple multiplication of the quantity of direct labour, $\mathbf{a}_n\mathbf{Y}^*$ by the scalar $(1+R)/R$. As is shown by (4.9.11), $(1+R)/R$ is the ratio between the total quantities of the Standard system and the corresponding quantities of the Standard net product.[29] The remarkable conclusion obtained is thus that for the Standard commodity, the quantity of direct labour bears the same ratio to the quantity of embodied labour (direct labour plus indirect labour) as the Standard net product $\mathbf{Y}^*$ bears to the total outputs $\mathbf{Q}^*$. And, as a consequence, the quantity of direct labour $\mathbf{a}_n\mathbf{Y}^*$ bears the same ratio to the quantity of indirect labour (the latter being $R^{-1}\mathbf{a}_n\mathbf{Y}^*$) as the Standard net product $\mathbf{Y}^*$ bears to its means of production $\mathbf{A}\mathbf{Q}^*$. Hence, the Standard ratio R also expresses the proportion between the quantity of labour embodied in its means of production.

9.5 *Numerical Example*

It may prove helpful to illustrate an algebraic operation of finding the Standard system by making use of the numerical example presented by Pasinetti (1977a, chapt. II, § 1.3), here reproduced in footnote 25. The matrix of interindustry coefficients that can be derived from that example is

$$\mathbf{A} = \begin{bmatrix} \frac{186}{450} & \frac{54}{21} & \frac{30}{60} \\ \frac{12}{450} & \frac{6}{21} & \frac{3}{60} \\ \frac{9}{450} & \frac{6}{21} & \frac{15}{60} \end{bmatrix} \simeq \begin{bmatrix} 0.4133 & 2.5714 & 0.5 \\ 0.0266 & 0.2857 & 0.05 \\ 0.02 & 0.2857 & 0.25 \end{bmatrix}. \tag{4.9.16}$$

This is an irreducible matrix. We can infer immediately that all three commodities will enter the Standard net product. The maximum eigenvalue is[30]

$$\lambda_m \simeq 0.674, \tag{4.9.17}$$

[29] It should be noted that the Standard commodity has the remarkable property of reproducing precisely that proportion between direct labour and total embodied labour which characterises each commodity in the hypothetical case of uniform capital intensity (or uniform 'organic composition of capital'). Moreover, it reproduces precisely the same temporal succession of labour requirements. Compare expressions (4.5.18) and (4.5.17) in footnote 10, p. 126.

[30] As may easily be verified, the other eigenvalues are 0.2 and 0.074, both positive but smaller than $\lambda_m = 0.674$.

from which the maximum rate of profit and the uniform rate of surplus can be derived as

$$\Pi \equiv R \equiv \frac{1}{\lambda_m} - 1 \simeq 48\%. \tag{4.9.18}$$

(The sign $\simeq$ is used because some decimal places have been rounded off.) On substituting the matrix (4.9.16) and the corresponding maximum eigenvalue (4.9.17) into (4.9.3), we can now compute the *relative quantities* for the Standard system corresponding to the economic system considered in our numerical example.

Furthermore, if we add equation (4.9.17), after having substituted therein the total quantity of labour in the system and the vector of direct labour coefficients, which are supposed to be, respectively, $\bar{Q}_n = 60$, and

$$\mathbf{a}_n = \begin{bmatrix} \frac{18}{450} & \frac{12}{21} & \frac{30}{60} \end{bmatrix} \simeq [0.04 \quad 0.5714 \quad 0.5]. \tag{4.9.19}$$

We can now compute the absolute quantities of the Standard net product. These quantities are

$$Y_1^* \simeq 141.77, \qquad Y_2^* \simeq 11.58, \qquad Y_3^* \simeq 14.47. \tag{4.9.20}$$

The same results may be obtained by an alternative method which proceeds directly from the numerical example just considered, which is in fact the alternative procedure employed by Sraffa. The procedure consists in finding appropriate multipliers which, when applied to the corresponding industries in the original system, effect an expansion (if greater than 1) or a contraction (if lower than 1) of each industry so as to make the total quantities produced stand in the same proportion to the total quantity of the corresponding commodity used as means of production. In our example, with three industries, the respecting multipliers being denoted by q_1, q_2, and q_3, the problem becomes that of solving a system of three equations:

$$\begin{cases} (186q_1 + 54q_2 + 30q_3)(1+R) = 450q_1, \\ (12q_1 \;\; + 6q_2 + \;\; 3q_3)(1+R) = \;\; 21q_2, \\ (9q_1 \;\;\; + 6q_2 + 15q_3)(1+R) = \;\; 60q_3, \end{cases} \tag{4.9.21}$$

in which there are four unknowns: q_1, q_2, q_3 and R. We must therefore add another, normalising equation which, from (4.8.7), is

$$18q_1 + 12q_2 + 30q_3 = 60. \tag{4.9.22}$$

As may readily be checked, the unique positive solution (i.e. the economically meaningful solution) of system (4.9.21) and (4.9.22), is

$$\begin{aligned} q_1^* &\simeq 0.968, \\ q_2^* &\simeq 1.695, \\ q_3^* &\simeq 0.741, \\ R &\simeq \ 0.48. \end{aligned} \tag{4.9.23}$$

The meaning of these results will be clear enough. Industry 2 (producing iron) will have to be expanded by a factor of 1.695, while industries 1 and 3 (producing wheat and turkeys, respectively) will have to be contracted, by being multiplied by the factors 0.968 and 0.741, respectively. In this way the sizes of the industries will all be such as to yield a physical rate of surplus of 48% for each of the commodities, while requiring neither more nor less labour than is employed in the actual system.

Using either the solution (4.9.18) and (4.9.20), or the solution (4.9.23), we can construct the hypothetical Standard system with a Standard net product – which we may call the 'normalised Standard system' – corresponding to the original economic system. The results are brought together in Tables 4.1 and 4.2.

It will be seen that both the original economic system and the normalised Standard system employ sixty workers. In the former, the workers produce a net product consisting of 180 tonnes of wheat, 0 tonnes of iron and 30 gross of turkeys, with corresponding rates of surplus of 66.6%, 0% and 100%, respectively. In the normalised Standard system the same number of workers produce a Standard net product consisting of 141.77 tonnes of wheat, 11.58 tonnes of iron and 14.5 gross of turkeys, with a physical rate of surplus of 48% for

Table 4.1 *Actual economic system*

		Industries						
Commodities		(1)	(2)	(3)	Q_i-Y_i	Y_i	Q_i	R_i
(1)	Wheat (tonnes)	186	54	30	270	180	450	66.66%
(2)	Iron (tonnes)	12	6	3	21	–	21	0%
(3)	Turkeys (gross)	9	6	15	30	30	60	100%
	Man/years	18	12	30			60	

Table 4.2 *Normalised Standard system*

Commodities	Industries (1)	(2)	(3)	$Q_i - Y_i$	Y_i	Q_i	R_i
(1) Wheat	180.04	91.52	22.24	293.80	141.77	435.57	48%
(2) Iron	11.62	10.17	2.22	24.01	11.58	35.59	48%
(3) Turkeys	8.72	10.17	11.12	30.01	14.47	44.48	48%
Man/years	17.42	20.34	22.24	–	–	60	–

each commodity. It will be observed that the proportions between the quantities of wheat, iron and turkeys are always the same, whether one considers the means of production, the net product or the total outputs. It is also to be noted that the uniform rate of surplus (48%) lies between the lowest (0%) and the highest (100%) of the rates of surplus in the original system.

10 Basic Commodities and Non-basic Commodities

10.1 Definitions

It was pointed out in Section 9.3 that, in going from the actual economic system to the corresponding Standard system, the latter may prove to contain fewer commodities (and industries) than the former. In such a case there are commodities (and industries) in the actual system which do not appear in the Standard system (or, if one prefers, which appear with zero quantities). The methods of production of these commodities, which do not appear in the Standard system, therefore play no role whatever in the determination of the prices of those commodities which do enter the Standard system and moreover play no role whatever in the determination of the maximum rate of surplus for the economic system as a whole.

These commodities, which do not appear in the Standard system and therefore have a limited role to play, are called *non-basic commodities*. By contrast, the other commodities, those which do appear in the Standard system, and which therefore contribute to the determination of all prices and of Π and R, are called *basic commodities*.

10.2 A Definition in Terms of Reducible and Irreducible Matrices

The distinction between basic and non-basic commodities clearly derives from certain properties of the technical processes of production. In the case considered in this chapter this distinction can be characterised very precisely in simple mathematical terms. If the matrix of technical interindustry coefficients is an irreducible matrix, then all the commodities in the economic system are basic commodities; on the other hand, if the matrix is reducible, some of the commodities are basic commodities, while others are non-basic commodities.

More precisely, suppose that the interindustry coefficient matrix so far considered, **A**, is reducible by appropriate interchanges of rows and corresponding columns to the block-triangular form see Pasinetti (1977a, Mathematical Appendix, p. 242) definition 5.4:

$$\mathbf{A} = \begin{bmatrix} \mathbf{A}_{11} & \mathbf{A}_{12} \\ \mathbf{O} & \mathbf{A}_{22} \end{bmatrix}, \tag{4.10.1}$$

where $\mathbf{A}_{11}$ is an irreducible square submatrix of the kth order ($k \leq n-1$), and $\mathbf{A}_{22}$ is a square submatrix of the $(n-1-k)$th order (reducible or irreducible). Then, the first k commodities on the rows of **A** are basic commodities and the remaining $(n-1-k)$ are non-basic commodities.

If $\mathbf{A}_{22}$ is an irreducible submatrix, we assume that at least on element of $\mathbf{A}_{12}$ is strictly positive. If $\mathbf{A}_{22}$ is a reducible submatrix, then (4.10.1) may be reduced further to the general form

$$\mathbf{A} = \begin{bmatrix} \mathbf{A}_{11} & \mathbf{A}_{12} & \dots & \mathbf{A}_{1s} \\ \mathbf{O} & \mathbf{A}_{22} & \dots & \mathbf{A}_{2s} \\ \vdots & \vdots & \ddots & \vdots \\ \mathbf{O} & \mathbf{O} & \dots & \mathbf{A}_{ss} \end{bmatrix}, \tag{4.10.2}$$

where all submatrices $\mathbf{A}_{11}, \mathbf{A}_{22}, \dots, \mathbf{A}_{ss}$ on the principal diagonal are irreducible.

In this case we assume that each of the submatrices $\mathbf{A}_{12}, \dots, \mathbf{A}_{1s}$ on the first row contains at least one strictly positive element. The reason for this assumption is that we want to consider a single economic system. If the submatrices to the right of $\mathbf{A}_{11}$, on the first row of (4.10.2) or of (4.10.1) were zero matrices, then matrix (4.10.1), or matrix (4.10.2), would not refer to a single economic system, but to a multiplicity of quite separate economic systems, disjoint from, and simply put side by side with one another. (See also Section 10.7.)

By simple inspection of matrix (4.10.1) or matrix (4.10.2), we can now see clearly the economic meaning of the distinction between basic and non-basic commodities. Since the columns of the interindustry coefficient matrix represent production processes, the basic commodities are revealed to be commodities that are required (directly or indirectly) for the production of all commodities (basic and non-basic). By contrast, the non-basic commodities are commodities that are not required for the production of the basic commodities (though they may be required for their own production).

10.3 A Reformulation

We may partition the vectors **Q**, **p**, and $\mathbf{a}_n$ as follows:

$$\mathbf{Q} = \begin{bmatrix} \mathbf{Q}_1 \\ \mathbf{Q}_2 \end{bmatrix}, \tag{4.10.3}$$

$$\mathbf{p} = \begin{bmatrix} \mathbf{p}_1 & \mathbf{p}_2 \end{bmatrix}, \tag{4.10.4}$$

$$\mathbf{a}_n = \begin{bmatrix} \mathbf{a}_{n1} & \mathbf{a}_{n2} \end{bmatrix}, \tag{4.10.5}$$

where subscript 1 refers to the first k components (i.e. to the basic commodities) and subscript 2 refers to the remaining $(n-1-k)$ components (i.e. to the non-basic commodities).

It may be noted immediately that, when the matrix **A** is of the form (4.10.1), a vector **Q** of the form

$$\mathbf{Q} = \begin{bmatrix} \mathbf{Q}_1 \\ \mathbf{O} \end{bmatrix}, \tag{4.10.6}$$

that is, a vector **Q** in which $\mathbf{Q}_1 = \mathbf{O}$ is a solution of equation system (4.9.7). It follows that the Standard system will simply be defined by the solution of the system of equations

$$[\mathbf{I} - (1+R)\mathbf{A}_{11}]\mathbf{Q}_1 = \mathbf{O}. \tag{4.10.7}$$

The non-basic commodities are thus eliminated completely. Vector $\mathbf{Q}_1^*$, the solution of (4.10.7), defines the Standard commodity. Hence, both $\mathbf{Q}_1^*$, the Standard commodity, and R, the Standard ratio, depend exclusively on $\mathbf{A}_{11}$, the production processes of the basic commodities, while being entirely independent of $\begin{bmatrix} \mathbf{A}_{12} \\ \mathbf{A}_{22} \end{bmatrix}$, the production processes of non-basic commodities.

It may be noted, moreover, that, when the matrix **A** is of the form (4.10.1), the inverse matrix $[\mathbf{I} - (1+\pi)\mathbf{A}]^{-1}$ may be obtained by parts (see procedure in Pasinetti (1977a, *Mathematical Appendix*, pp. 242–243)), so that

$$[\mathbf{I}(1+\pi)\mathbf{A}]^{-1} =$$
$$= \begin{bmatrix} [\mathbf{I} - (1+\pi)\mathbf{A}_{11}]^{-1} & [\mathbf{I} - (1+\pi)\mathbf{A}_{11}]^{-1}\mathbf{A}_{12}[\mathbf{I} - (1+\pi)\mathbf{A}_{22}]^{-1} \\ \mathbf{O} & [\mathbf{I} - (1+\pi)\mathbf{A}_{22}]^{-1} \end{bmatrix}. \tag{4.10.8}$$

This means that the general solution for the price system (4.5.20) takes the form

$$\mathbf{p}_1 = \mathbf{a}_{n1}[\mathbf{I} - (1+\pi)\mathbf{A}_{11}]^{-1}w, \tag{4.10.9}$$
$$\mathbf{p}_2 = \mathbf{a}_{n1}[\mathbf{I} - (1+\pi)\mathbf{A}_{11}]^{-1}(1+\pi)\mathbf{A}_{12}[\mathbf{I} - (1+\pi)\mathbf{A}_{22}]^{-1}w, \\ + \mathbf{a}_{n2}[\mathbf{I} - (1+\pi)\mathbf{A}_{22}]^{-1}w. \tag{4.10.10}$$

As may now be seen explicitly, vector $\mathbf{p}_1$ (the prices of basic commodities) depends exclusively on the submatrix $\mathbf{A}_{11}$, that is, on the production processes of the basic commodities, while being entirely independent of the submatrix $\begin{bmatrix} \mathbf{A}_{12} \\ \mathbf{A}_{22} \end{bmatrix}$, that is, the production processes of the non-basic commodities. By contrast, vector $\mathbf{p}_2$ (the prices of the non-basic commodities) depends both on $\mathbf{A}_{11}$ and on $\begin{bmatrix} \mathbf{A}_{12} \\ \mathbf{A}_{22} \end{bmatrix}$, that is, both on the production processes of the basic commodities and on the production processes of the non-basic commodities.

Finally, expression (4.6.11), which gives the relation between π and $w^{(1)}$ (the rate of profit and the wage rate expressed in terms of commodity 1), takes the form

$$1 = \mathbf{a}_{n1}[\mathbf{I} - (1+\pi)\mathbf{A}_{11}]^{-1}\mathbf{e}_1 w^{(1)}. \tag{4.10.11}$$

This means (provided only that the wage rate is expressed in terms of a basic commodity) that the w–π relation depends exclusively on the production processes of the basic commodities and is entirely independent of the production processes of the non-basic commodities.

10.4 Numerical Example

In order to appreciate the economic meaning of the preceding presentation, it will be helpful to consider again the numerical example of

Section 9.5. Let us suppose an economic system which, in addition to producing wheat, iron, and turkeys as previously assumed, also produces a fourth commodity, which we shall call ostriches. And suppose that the production of one unit of this commodity requires, on average, 0.2 ostrich, 0.005 tonne of wheat and 0.005 tonne of iron. The matrix of technical coefficients for this new economic system (containing four industries and four commodities) will thus be

$$\begin{bmatrix} 0.4133 & 2.5714 & 0.50 & 0.005 \\ 0.0266 & 0.2857 & 0.05 & 0.005 \\ 0.02 & 0.2857 & 0.25 & 0 \\ 0 & 0 & 0 & 0.200 \end{bmatrix}. \tag{4.10.12}$$

As can be seen immediately, this is a reducible matrix. One can easily verify that, on moving from the system described by this matrix to the corresponding Standard system, the fourth commodity disappears (i.e. the corresponding solution turns out to be zero) and the Standard system comes to be characterised simply by the submatrix

$$\begin{bmatrix} 0.4133 & 2.5714 & 0.50 \\ 0.0266 & 0.2857 & 0.05 \\ 0.02 & 0.2857 & 0.25 \end{bmatrix}, \tag{4.10.13}$$

which is the same matrix (4.9.16) as for our earlier example. Commodities 1, 2, 3, (wheat, iron, turkeys) are thus basic commodities, while the fourth commodity (ostriches) is a non-basic commodity. It is also easy to see that the maximum eigenvalues of (4.10.12) and (4.10.13) are the same, namely 0.674, corresponding to a maximum rate of profit of 48%. (The eigenvalue, which in (4.10.12) is added to the three previous eigenvalues, is 0.2, as can be seen by inspection, and is thus smaller than 0.674.)

If the matrix (4.10.12) is now examined more closely, it will be seen that it is the three zeros appearing in the last row which render it reducible. These zeros have a precise economic meaning; they imply that commodity 4 is *not* used in the production of the other three commodities, while these other commodities are required for its production (wheat and iron directly, and turkeys indirectly – through the production of wheat and iron). It follows that a zero output of commodity 4 is compatible with the production of positive quantities of commodities 1, 2, 3. By contrast, it would not be possible to produce a positive quantity of commodity 4 without also producing positive quantities of commodities 1, 2, 3. There is thus a sense in which we can say that the basic commodities are 'more necessary' to the system than the non-basic commodities. This is the reason why the Standard system, which represents the system's essential nucleus, so to speak, necessarily includes the basic commodities but excludes the non-basic commodities.

10.5 The Economic Meaning of the Distinction Between Basic and Non-Basic Commodities

The findings in Section 10.3 make it necessary for us to emphasise further the economic significance of the contrast between basic and non-basic commodities. We have seen that a basic commodity is a commodity which is technically necessary for the production of all the other commodities. It follows that a zero production of even just one basic commodity necessarily implies zero production of all commodities (basic and non-basic). It also follows that, when any one of the production coefficients for a basic commodity changes, this causes the prices of all commodities (basic and non-basic) to change. It also causes a change of the maximum rate of profit and uniform rate of surplus for the whole system and a change of the whole w-π relation.

A non-basic commodity, by contrast, is not technically necessary for the production of basic commodities, whereas the latter are required for its production. Even if all the coefficients of the production process for a non-basic commodity changed, while the price of that commodity and those of the non-basic commodities which use it as a means of production would certainly change, the prices of all basic commodities in terms of any basic commodity would remain unchanged. The maximum rate of profit and the uniform rate of surplus of the system and the whole relation (4.6.11) between w and π would also remain unchanged.

10.6 Relations with the Distinction between Necessary and Luxury Goods

It may be of interest to point out that the distinction between basic and non-basic commodities corresponds to the distinction which the Classical economists made between 'necessary' or 'subsistence' commodities and 'luxury' goods. In the theories of the Classical economists, subsistence commodities are always needed in the production of all commodities. By contrast, luxury commodities require subsistence commodities for their production but are not used in the production of the latter.

Yet the Classical economists thought of this distinction as being based on the *use* to which the two categories of commodities were devoted. The novel feature of Sraffa's analysis is that the distinction is shown to arise from the technical properties of the production processes

10.7 An Assumption on the Physical Own-Rates of Reproduction of the Basic and Non-Basic Commodities

The preceding discussion enables us to consider two assumptions which it has not been possible to discuss explicitly until now, even though they have been present throughout the analysis.

The first assumption is that there always exists at least one basic commodity[31] and that it requires labour for its production. This assumption implies that all commodities require, directly or indirectly, both commodities and labour for their production.

The second (rather more complex) assumption concerns the maximum eigenvalue of the matrix of technical coefficients. It is known that the eigenvalues of a reducible matrix (when it is reduced to a block-triangular form) coincide with the eigenvalues of the square submatrices which lie on its principal diagonal.[32] The assumption which is now to be made explicit is that the maximum eigenvalue of the matrix **A** is the maximum eigenvalue of the submatrix on the principal diagonal which refers to the basic commodities. (This assumption is obviously satisfied in our earlier numerical example, where the maximum eigenvalue of the matrix (4.10.12) is $\lambda_m = 0.674$ and coincides with the maximum eigenvalue of its submatrix (4.10.13), which refers to the basic commodities).

From a purely mathematical point of view this assumption might seem somewhat arbitrary. It is less so, however, if we consider its economic meaning. To assume that the maximum eigenvalue is that of the submatrix relating to the basic commodities is to assume that

[31] If this were not so, we should not be considering an economic 'system', but a multiplicity of different systems, set alongside each other.

[32] See Pasinetti (1977a, *Mathematical Appendix*, p. 258)

the physical own-rate of reproduction of the basic commodities is smaller than the physical own-rate of reproduction of the non-basic commodities.[33]

Given the economic meaning of basic and non-basic commodities, discussed in Section 10.5, this seems to be a rather plausible assumption.[34] This is a case in which our knowledge of the economic system permits us to accept certain assumptions in preference to others, even when they might appear, from a formal point of view, to be symmetrical to one another.

In any case the effect of this assumption is that, at the analytical level, it enables us to make some further important assertions. First of all, if the maximum eigenvalue of the (irreducible) submatrix referring to basic commodities is larger than the maximum eigenvalues of all the other submatrices on the principal diagonal, we know that the maximum eigenvalue of the corresponding characteristic equation is a simple root.[35] This implies that the Standard ratio R (a real number) is associated with a vector $\mathbf{Q}^*$ which not only has all non-negative components (as we said in Section 9.1) but is also *unique*. Similarly, we can say (in addition to what was said in Section 5.3) that the system of prices, $\mathbf{p}^*$, associated with the same real number $\Pi \equiv R$, is *unique*. Indeed, with respect to the latter vector, we can even assert that its elements are all strictly positive. (In other words, prices are always positive, both for basic commodities and for non-basic commodities.[36])

10.8 An Unusual Case

It is nevertheless natural to ask what would happen in the case (which Sraffa considers a 'freak case') of a non-basic commodity whose

33 In our previous numerical example, the physical own-rate of reproduction of basic commodities is 48% (uniform rate of surplus). This means that basic commodities cannot be reproduced at a rate larger than 48%. The non-basic commodity, by contrast, has a physical own-rate of reproduction of

$$\frac{1}{0.2} = 400\%.$$

34 An interesting discussion of this problem has taken place between Piero Sraffa and Peter Newman (Sraffa and Newman 1970), following Newman (1962).

35 Theorem 1 of Perron-Frobenius, (Pasinetti 1977a, *Mathematical Appendix*, p. 269).

36 This follows from the theorem stated in footnote 9, p. 275, of Pasinetti (1977a, *Mathematical Appendix*).

physical own-rate of reproduction were so unusually low as to be lower than that of the basic commodities; for example, the case in which, in the particular economic system considered in Section 10.4, the own-coefficient of reproduction of ostriches was, say, 0.8 (rather than 0.2), corresponding to an own-rate of reproduction of 25% (rather than 400%). The answer is that in such a case the non-basic commodity could not be produced at a rate of profit greater than 25%. The basic commodities, by contrast, could perfectly well continue to be produced at a rate of profit greater than 25%. In other words, the maximum rate of profit for the economic system would continue to be determined by the maximum eigenvalue of the submatrix which relates to basic products (i.e. in our example it would continue to be 48%), and the whole of our earlier analysis would continue to hold with respect to the basic commodities. However, the price of the non-basic commodity would now behave in a rather peculiar way. The formal solution for the system of prices shows that in this case the price of the non-basic commodity (in terms of a basic commodity) is positive for rates of profit less than 25% and becomes negative for rates of profit greater than 25%. In practice, since infinite or negative prices have no meaning, this simply means that, for rates of profit equal to, or greater than, 25%, it would not be possible to maintain the assumptions of a uniform rate of profit in all sectors and of a uniform price for all units of the same commodity.[37]

11 Autonomy of the Two Systems Considered (the Price System and the Physical Quantity System)

Considering the preceding analysis as a whole, it must now be emphasised that, all the similarities and the formal analogies notwithstanding, the system of prices and the system of physical quantities are two separate systems, neither of which carries any implications for the other. The Standard system, for example, is a logical construction which relates to physical quantities and which implies nothing about the price system. Although, from a formal point of view, the particular system of prices in which $w = 0$ appears as 'dual' to the Standard system, the former in no way implies the latter and, similarly, the latter in no way implies the former. If, for example, a certain economic system were

[37] A special appendix is devoted to this case in Sraffa (1960, pp. 90–91).

actually to be in the Standard proportions, that would not imply that the system of prices would necessarily have to be that for which $w = 0$. Any other system of prices would be perfectly possible. Similarly, if the (surplus) wage were actually zero in an economic system, that would in no way imply that the proportions of the physical system would necessarily have to be those of the Standard system. Any other set of proportions would be possible.

In practice, of course, the ruling price system is usually a system with a rate of profit lying somewhere between the two extremes, while the system of physical quantities actually being observed will usually be a system in which the proportions are not those of the Standard system. Thus, actual economic systems are usually highly complex and, from a formal point of view, distinctly inelegant. It is precisely this complexity which justifies the analysis of the corresponding (hypothetical) Standard systems, which, in addition to being formally more elegant, are conceptually easier to grasp. These hypothetical systems possess the important property of having the same coefficients matrix as the actual system. It follows that all those properties *of the actual system* which depend on the structure of the coefficient matrix can be better analysed, studied, and understood by considering the Standard system and the extreme cases of the price system. The significance of these remarks should already be clear from the preceding analysis; however, a further important illustration is given in the following section.

12 Price System and Income Distribution

12.1 The Standard Net Product as the Numéraire of the Price System

We are now going to consider one of the most interesting applications of the notion of a Standard system (and of a Standard net product and of a Standard commodity). This is an application which has been carried out by Sraffa in order to solve a theoretical problem that had remained unsolved since Ricardo.

Suppose we are observing a certain economic system and suppose that the corresponding physical quantities and prices are represented by the two systems of equations which were obtained earlier, namely,

$$\mathbf{AQ} + \hat{\mathbf{R}}\mathbf{AQ} = \mathbf{Q}, \tag{4.12.1}$$

$$\mathbf{pA}(1+\pi) + \mathbf{a}_n w = \mathbf{p}, \tag{4.12.2}$$

where $\hat{\mathbf{R}}$ is a diagonal matrix with $R_1, R_2, \ldots, R_{n-1}$ on the principal diagonal.

We have seen that, although the rate of profit is taken as exogenously fixed, a normalisation problem arises with reference both to (4.12.1) and to (4.12.2). For the former determines only relative quantities and the latter only relative prices. In each case there is room for a further equation.

For the quantity system it will prove convenient to add the equation

$$\mathbf{a}_n\mathbf{Q} = 1, \tag{4.12.3}$$

which sets the total quantity of labour equal to unity. This means, in comparison with our previous convention under which the labour coefficients were expressed in terms of workers/year, that here those coefficients have been divided by Q_n and are thus now expressed in terms of the total quantity of labour.

For the price system we know that any commodity, or any linear combination of commodities, can be chosen at will as the *numéraire* by setting its price equal to unity. Now we consider the choice of a very particular *numéraire*, namely, the Standard commodity. More specifically, we choose as *numéraire*-commodity that particular bundle of commodities, a composite commodity, which forms the Standard net product.

To effect this normalisation we must first find the Standard system corresponding to the actual system (4.12.1). By using the normalisation which also yields the Standard net product, we obtain

$$[\mathbf{I} - (1+R)\mathbf{A}]\mathbf{Q}^* = 0, \tag{4.12.4}$$

$$\mathbf{a}_n\mathbf{Q}^* = 1, \tag{4.12.5}$$

where, of course,

$$\det[\mathbf{I} - (1+R)\mathbf{A}] = 0.$$

The Standard net product is represented by the column vector $\mathbf{Y}^* = (\mathbf{I} - \mathbf{A})\mathbf{Q}^*$ and the convention adopted here is thus to set equal to unity the value of the composite commodity represented by this vector, that is,

$$\mathbf{p}(\mathbf{I} - \mathbf{A})\mathbf{Q}^* = 1. \tag{4.12.6}$$

This is the extra equation we need. By adding it to (4.12.2), the system of prices is closed (for any given rate of profit) and the $(n-1)$ prices and the wage rate all come to be expressed in terms of the particular composite commodity $\mathbf{Y}^*$, the Standard net product.

The value of the Standard net product having been set equal to unity it should be noted that the value of the actual net product will, in general, differ from unity so that, in general: $\mathbf{p}(\mathbf{I}-\mathbf{A})\mathbf{Q} \neq \mathbf{p}(\mathbf{I}-\mathbf{A})\mathbf{Q}^* = 1$, except in the special case in which $\pi = 0$. In this case, prices are given by $\mathbf{p} = \mathbf{v}w$, that is, they are proportional to the quantities of embodied labour, and the value of the net national income, whatever its physical composition, will simply be equal to the total quantity of labour multiplied by the wage rate. In the present case, thanks to normalisations (4.12.3) and (4.12.6), it even follows that, for the special case $\pi = 0$,[38]

$$\mathbf{v}(\mathbf{I}-\mathbf{A})\mathbf{Q} = \mathbf{v}(\mathbf{I}-\mathbf{A})\mathbf{Q}^* = 1 = w.$$

In other words, the normalisations adopted here fix the two extreme limits (between which the wage rate can vary) at zero and unity respectively. (As one can easily see, $w = 0$ for $\pi = \Pi$ and $w = 1$ for $\pi = 0$.) Hence, the wage rate w now also expresses the proportion, or relative share, of the Standard net product which can be purchased by total wages.

12.2 The $\pi - w$ Relation in the Standard System

Before going on, a brief digression will prove useful. If the very special case of an actual economic system being exactly in the Standard proportions were to occur, and if the net product or net income of that system were to be distributed between profits and wages in such a way that both profits and wages consisted of Standard commodity, then the rate of profit could be seen in physical terms, that is, it would be

[38] From (4.12.3) and (4.5.5) we have

$$\mathbf{a}_n(\mathbf{I}-\mathbf{A})^{-1}(\mathbf{I}-\mathbf{A})\mathbf{Q} = 1,$$

$$\mathbf{v}(\mathbf{I}-\mathbf{A})\mathbf{Q} = 1,$$

and similarly, from (4.12.5),

$$\mathbf{a}_n(\mathbf{I}-\mathbf{A})^{-1}(\mathbf{I}-\mathbf{A})\mathbf{Q}^* = 1,$$

$$\mathbf{v}(\mathbf{I}-\mathbf{A})\mathbf{Q}^* = 1.$$

independent of prices. Indeed, with total profits and means of production consisting of the same commodities, in the same proportions, the ratio between the physical quantity of any commodity in total profits and the physical quantity of the same commodity in the means of production would express the rate of profit as a physical ratio. Even if all the physical quantities were multiplied by their prices, any given price, by appearing both in the numerator and in the denominator, would cancel out leaving the ratio unchanged.

It follows that the Standard system (in which $\mathbf{Q} = \mathbf{Q}^*$) is another special case in which the ratio $\mathbf{p}(\mathbf{I}-\mathbf{A})\mathbf{Q}/\mathbf{pAQ}$, which we met in (4.6.1), remains the same at all levels of the rate of profit. (It will be remembered that the other special case in which this occurs is that in which the prices remain the same at all levels of the rate of profit, that is, the case of uniform capital intensity in all sectors.) In the Standard system, therefore (as in the case of uniform capital intensity in all sectors), we always have $[\mathbf{p}(\mathbf{I} - \mathbf{A})\mathbf{Q}^*/\mathbf{pAQ}^*] = \Pi$, for all levels of π within the interval $0 \leq \pi \leq \Pi$.

In the present context, since $\omega = w$, owing to (4.12.5) and (4.12.6), the relation (4.6.1) between π and w becomes

$$\pi = \Pi(1 - w), \tag{4.12.7}$$

that is, it becomes a linear relation between π and w (see Figure 4.4.) The simplicity of the linear relations contrasts sharply with the complexity of the polynomial relation between w and π in the general case

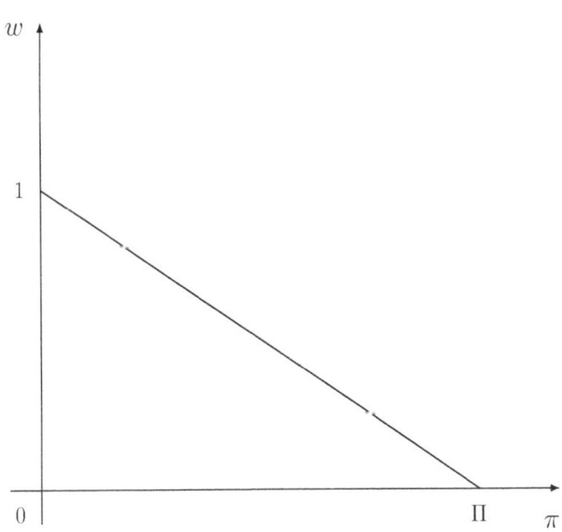

Figure 4.4 Relation between w and π in the Standard system.

discussed in Section 6.3. It is clear, however, that so a simple relation, derived for a special case, will be of interest to us only if it is in some way relevant to the general case.

12.3 The Same Linear Relation Valid for the Actual System, with the One Provision that w Be Expressed in Terms of the Standard Commodity

Let us return to the actual economic system for which the prices have been expressed in terms of the Standard commodity (in the particular size of the Standard net product):

$$\mathbf{pA} + \mathbf{pA}\pi + \mathbf{a}_n w = \mathbf{p}, \quad (4.12.2)$$

$$\mathbf{p}(\mathbf{I} - \mathbf{A})\mathbf{Q}^* = 1. \quad (4.12.6)$$

Post-multiplying both sides of (4.12.2) by the column vector $\mathbf{Q}^*$ and rearranging, we obtain

$$\mathbf{pAQ}^*\pi = \mathbf{pQ}^* - \mathbf{pAQ}^* - \mathbf{a}_n\mathbf{Q}^*w,$$

$$\mathbf{pAQ}^*\pi = \mathbf{p}(\mathbf{I} - \mathbf{A})\mathbf{Q}^* - \mathbf{a}_n\mathbf{Q}^*w.$$

But $\mathbf{p}(\mathbf{I} - \mathbf{A})\mathbf{Q}^* = 1$, from (4.12.6), and $\mathbf{a}_n\mathbf{Q}^* = 1$, from (4.12.5). Hence,

$$\mathbf{pAQ}^*\pi = 1 - w,$$

or

$$\mathbf{pAQ}^*\pi R = R(1 - w). \quad (4.12.8)$$

Consider now the term $(\mathbf{pAQ}^*R)$. Returning to (4.12.4), pre-multiplying by the row vector of prices $\mathbf{p}$ and rearranging, we obtain

$$\mathbf{pAQ}^*R = \mathbf{pQ}^* - \mathbf{pAQ}^*,$$

$$\mathbf{pAQ}^*R = \mathbf{p}(\mathbf{I} - \mathbf{A})\mathbf{Q}^*.$$

But $\mathbf{p}(\mathbf{I} - \mathbf{A})\mathbf{Q}^* = 1$ from (4.12.6). Thus, $\mathbf{pAQ}^*R = 1$; so that, by substituting into (4.12.8),

$$\pi = R(1 - w). \quad (4.12.9)$$

Since $R = \Pi$, this is precisely the same linear relation obtained in Section 12.2. But here it has been obtained for the actual system (4.12.2) and (4.12.6)!

This is a truly remarkable result. The relation (4.12.9) between the wage rate and the rate of profit is found to be valid in general, and not only for the Standard system, provided only that the wage rate is expressed in terms of the Standard commodity.[39] In the actual system, of course, the rate of profit will no longer appear as a ratio between physical quantities, but as a ratio between values. Nevertheless (the price system being independent of the system of physical quantities), the relation between w and π will always be the same, both for the Standard system and for the actual system. To put it the other way round, we can say that, although the w-π relation is the same for both systems, the particular proportions of the Standard system have the property of 'rendering visible', in terms of ratios between physical quantities, that which in the actual system can only be seen in terms of ratios between values.

Returning to our numerical example, if, in the actual system, we distribute to wages a sum that can purchase $\frac{3}{4}$ of the Standard net product, the remaining part of the actual net product, which goes to profits, will be such that, at the corresponding prices, its ratio to the means of production will yield (just as in the corresponding Standard system) a rate of profit equal to $\frac{1}{4}$ of 48%, or 12%.[40]

12.4 No Assumptions on Return to Scale

It is important that explicit emphasis be given to the absence of any assumption concerning returns to scale in the preceding sections. The two systems (4.12.1) and (4.12.2) represent observed quantities. Thus, no change in those quantities has been considered. For its part, the

39 The fact that the wage rate is expressed in terms of the Standard commodity does not mean that it will necessarily be spent on buying Standard commodities (in the same way as, in our previous cases, the fact that the wage rate is expressed in terms of any commodity, for instance gold, does not mean that it is necessarily spent on buying gold). What it means is that the physical goods which the workers can buy (whatever their physical composition) have a value, at current prices, which is equal to the value of that quantity of Standard commodity which makes up the wage rate.

40 It should be noted that, the actual net product being different from the Standard net product, the part of the actual net product which is left over for profits (after deducing $\frac{3}{4}$ of the Standard net product for wages) will be equal neither to $\frac{1}{4}$ of the actual net product (since the already deducted $\frac{3}{4}$ refers to the Standard net product) nor to $\frac{1}{4}$ of the Standard net product, since the already deducted $\frac{3}{4}$ of the Standard net product has been deducted from the actual net product. Yet its ratio to the means of production will be exactly 12%.

logical construction (4.12.4) and (4.12.5) is an imaginary system, the sole purpose of which is to define those proportions between the basic commodities which constitute the Standard commodity, to be used as *numéraire*. Thus, no assumption about returns to scale is needed to obtain the linear relation (4.12.9) between the rate of profit and the wage rate.

Strictly speaking, it is not even necessary to adopt any explicit convention concerning the measurement of prices, since no price appears explicitly. It was shown in Section 12.3 that the *numéraire*-commodity $\mathbf{Y}^* = (\mathbf{I} - \mathbf{A})\mathbf{Q}^*$ implies the linear relation (4.12.9) between the wage rate and the rate of profit. But the converse is equally true: (4.12.9) implies (4.12.6), since no other *numéraire* would satisfy such a linearity condition. Hence, if we impose the requirement that the system of prices be such as to produce the linear relation (4.12.9) between w and π, then the wage rate and prices will *ipso facto* be expressed in terms of the Standard net product. The system of prices (4.12.2) and (4.12.6) can therefore also be written more simply as

$$\mathbf{p} = \mathbf{pA}(1 + \pi) + \mathbf{a}_n w, \tag{4.12.2}$$

$$\pi = R(1 - w), \tag{4.12.9}$$

where without explicit reference to any construction, the very simple relation (4.12.9) has replaced (4.12.6). In this way, wages and prices come to be expressed in terms of the Standard net product, without it even being necessary to compute the Standard system, that is, without it even being necessary to know what the Standard commodity consists of. The only quantity which needs to be calculated is the Standard ratio R, that is, through relation (4.9.6), the maximum eigenvalue of the matrix $\mathbf{A}$.

12.5 'Labour commanded' and the Standard net product

We may note that, from (4.12.9), it immediately follows that

$$\frac{1}{w} = \frac{\Pi}{\Pi - \pi}. \tag{4.12.10}$$

The total quantity of labour and the value of the Standard net product being equal to unity by definition, and the wage rate being expressed in terms of the Standard net product', the ratio $1/w$ clearly represents 'the quantity of labour that can be purchased by the

Standard net product', that is, Adam Smith's notion of 'labour commanded'. This quantity of labour varies from 1 to ∞, as π varies from 0 to Π, according to the simple relation (4.12.10). We thus obtain the remarkable result that the quantity of labour which can be purchased by the Standard net product, while being a function of (i.e. while varying with) the rate of profit, is entirely *independent of prices*. This means that expressing the prices in terms of Standard net product is equivalent to expressing them in terms of that quantity of labour which, at the given rate of profit, can be purchased by the Standard net product.[41]

12.6 Perfect Regularity of the 'Layers' of Wages and Profit in the Standard Net Product

It was seen in Section 9.4 that 'the quantity of labour embodied in the Standard net product' can be obtained by multiplying the corresponding quantity of direct labour by the ratio $(1+R)/R$. We can now draw attention to a more deeply rooted property. If we reduce the Standard net product to quantities of 'dated' labour by using the expression (4.7.4) we obtain

$$\mathbf{pY}^* = w\mathbf{a}_n[\mathbf{I} + (1+\pi)\mathbf{A} + (1+\pi)^2\mathbf{A}^2 + (1+\pi)^3\mathbf{A}^3 + \cdots]\mathbf{Y}^*, \tag{4.12.11}$$

and since

$$\mathbf{AY}^* = \frac{1}{1+R}\mathbf{Y}^*,$$

we have

$$\mathbf{pY}^* = w\mathbf{a}_n\mathbf{Y}^*\left[1 + \frac{1+\pi}{1+R} + \left(\frac{1+\pi}{1+R}\right)^2 + \left(\frac{1+\pi}{1+R}\right)^3 + \cdots\right]. \tag{4.12.12}$$

As already noted at the end of Section 7.2, this series can be thought of as the sequence, backwards through time, of the 'layers' of wages and profits of which the Standard net product $\mathbf{Y}^*$, at prices $\mathbf{p}$, consists. But (4.12.12) exhibits another remarkable property. The quantities of labour which follow one another in the various 'layers', namely

[41] Sraffa points out that '... it is surprising that the Standard commodity which has been evolved ... here should be found to be equivalent to something very close to the Standard suggested by Adam Smith, namely 'labour commanded', to which Ricardo himself was so decidedly opposed' (Sraffa 1960, p. 94).

$\mathbf{a}_n\mathbf{Y}^*, \mathbf{a}_n\mathbf{Y}^*(1+R)^{-1}, \mathbf{a}_n\mathbf{Y}^*(1+R)^{-2}, \ldots$, form a perfectly regular geometrical series. The quantity of labour (and hence the wage bill) needed in any 'layer' is always equal to $1/(1+R)$ times the quantity of labour (and the wage bill) which is needed in the 'layer' immediately following in time. Consequently, the reckoning of a rate of profit on the regular sequence of wage bills generates a geometric progression of profits which is also perfectly regular through time. It follows that the sum of profits and wages in any 'layer' is always equal to $(1+\pi)/(1+R)$ times the sum of profits and wages in the 'layer' immediately following in time. Thus, each 'layer' is structurally the same as every other 'layer': it differs from the other 'layers' only by a scale factor while having the same proportions. In other words, the proportions between labour and the means of production are always the same, in all the infinitely many 'layers' backwards through time.[42]

This is, in fact, the essential property of the Standard commodity: that of reproducing exactly the same proportions between labour and the means of production in each of the infinitely many 'layers' backwards through time of which it consists.

12.7 The Standard Commodity and the Theory of Income Distribution

We may now draw some conclusions concerning the theoretical significance of the linear relation (4.12.9), associated with the use of the Standard commodity as *numéraire* of the price system.

It was seen in Section 6.3 that, in general, the relation between w and π is highly complex. This results from the fact that one can never exclude all the prices for that relation; at least one price, that of the commodity in terms of which the wage rate is measured, is always implicitly present. It is precisely the peculiarities of the methods of production of the commodity used as *numéraire* which cause a whole series of complications. We have seen the source of these complications

[42] Compare expression (4.12.12) with expression (4.7.5) in footnote 23 on page 139. It will be seen that the succession through time is identical. The Standard commodity therefore reproduces, *ex-constructo*, in all its infinite number of 'layers', that constancy of proportions between capital and labour which, in the very special case of uniform capital intensity, is assumed *ex-hypothesis*. (The nature of this contrast seems to have escaped many of Sraffa's critics. For example, cf. Burmeister 1968).

in Section 7.2. The peculiarities of the methods of production of any commodity translate themselves into the different proportions between labour and means of production in each of the infinitely many 'layers' of wages and profits of which the commodity consists. As wages and profits vary, they give rise to irregular movements in each of these 'layers', and, *a fortiori*, in their sum. Thus, in expression (4.6.11) and in the corresponding Figure 4.3, changes in the distribution of income between profits and wages cannot be seen clearly because they are, so to speak, 'disturbed' by the many complex effects of the variations in the components of the price of the *numéraire*-commodity. And since these effects or 'disturbances' differ from one commodity to another, the relation between w and π will differ, even within the same economic system, according to which particular commodity is used as the unit of measurement of wages.

However, a very special commodity, the Standard commodity, has now been discovered, which enables us to formulate the distribution relations independently of prices. A commodity has been found which has a price whose infinitely many 'layers' of wages and profits (which for an arbitrary commodity are superimposed in the most disparate way, depending on the technical characteristics of its methods of production) here always follow one another in a perfectly regular way, at any level of the rate of profit, according to a geometrical progression which always reproduces, to infinity, the same proportions between labour and means of production. The use of such a commodity as the unit of measurement for prices thus has the remarkable analytical property of eliminating any 'disturbance' due to the peculiarities of the methods of production of the *numéraire*-commodity from the relation between the wage rate and the rate of profit. With the linear relation (4.12.9) we are at last able 'to see', as it were, the alternative possible distributions of the net national income between wages and profits in ideal conditions, free from any interference due to price changes specific to the commodity used as the unit of measurement.

After a century and a half, Sraffa's Standard commodity has thus fulfilled Ricardo's dream of an 'invariable measure' of value.[43] It would, of course, be merely fanciful to think that such a commodity might

[43] This, at least, with reference to the property of being 'invariable' with respect to changes in income distribution.

be found in the real world (and it is scarcely surprising that Ricardo never found it); yet it can always be constructed from the commodities actually produced by taking them in the proportions defined by the Standard system.

The most remarkable theoretical implication of this construction is to be found in the demonstration that it is possible to treat the distribution of income independently of prices and in the demonstration, moreover, that this possibility is not tied to the pure labour theory of value.[44] It is at last possible to state rigorously that the shortcomings and inadequacies of the Classical pure labour theory of value or indeed even the abandonment of such a theory, leave quite unscathed the possibility of treating the distribution of income independently of prices.

[44] Ricardo's insistence on an 'approximate' validity of the pure labour theory of value had ended up by hampering awareness of this result. In the economic literature the rejection of Ricardo's pure labour theory of value has generally been associated also with the rejection of his (quite legitimate) claim that his theory of income distribution is independent of his theory of value.

5 *The Marxian 'Problem of Transformation of Values into Prices of Production' after Sraffa*

1 Introductory Remark

The analysis of Sraffa price system also gives us a deeper understanding and a more appropriate presentation, which is entirely new and, even today, puzzling, of the discussed problem of the transformation of values into prices of production, which Marx set out in Volume III of *Das Kapital*[1].

2 An 'Ideal' Price System

Imagine an economic system of the kind considered in Chapter 4 with single-product industries. The technique of the system is represented by a matrix of interindustry coefficients **A**, assumed to be viable (i.e. to have a maximum eigenvalue $\lambda_m < 1$), and by a row vector of (direct) labour coefficients $\mathbf{a}_n$.

An 'ideal' system of prices, as understood, for example, by the 'Ricardian socialists'[2] (who had claimed at the beginning of the nineteenth century that the whole net product of an economic system ought to go to the workers), might be:

$$\mathbf{p}\mathbf{A} + w\mathbf{a}_n = \mathbf{p}. \tag{5.2.1}$$

This is a linear system of $(n-1)$ equations. It determines $(n-2)$ relative prices and a wage rate which absorbs the entire net product per worker of the economic system. This has been regarded as the 'maximum' wage rate in Chapter 4, since it corresponds to a zero rate of profit and

[1] See Marx (1959, chapter IX). Mathematical formulations of Marx's system have been frequent in recent economic literature. See especially Brody (1970) and Morishima (1973). But other formulations have also been given. A few will be mentioned in the following pages. The simplest of all formulations (intuitively immediate, though analytically incorrect) has been anticipated already in Chapter 2, Section 4.

[2] See, e.g., Lowenthal (1911).

thus absorbs the whole net product. We may call it the 'ideal' wage rate here, or from a different point of view, the 'complete' wage rate, and denote it by w^*. It also represents the per-worker net product of the economic system.

As we know, the system of prices (5.2.1) can be expressed in absolute, rather than in relative, terms by adding an equation defining the *numéraire*. To this end we may adopt our usual procedure of setting the price of an arbitrarily chosen commodity, for example the ith commodity, equal to unity, or of setting the wage rate equal to unity. In the first case we have

$$\mathbf{p} = \mathbf{a}_n(\mathbf{I} - \mathbf{A})^{-1}w^*, \tag{5.2.2}$$

$$p_i = 1, \tag{5.2.3}$$

where the exchange ratios prove to be proportional to the quantities $\mathbf{a}_n(\mathbf{I} - \mathbf{A})^{-1}$, which represent the vertically integrated labour coefficients, or quantities of labour 'embodied' in the corresponding commodities.[3] In the second case, explicitly denoting the solution vector by $\mathbf{v}$, we have

$$w^* = 1, \tag{5.2.4}$$

$$\mathbf{v} = \mathbf{a}_n(\mathbf{I} - \mathbf{A})^{-1}. \tag{5.2.5}$$

The exchange ratios become exactly *equal* to the physical quantities of embodied labour. It is precisely these quantities of embodied labour that Marx called 'values'.

It should be noted that system (5.2.4) and (5.2.5) has the property of making 'labour embodied' coincide with 'labour commanded'. Each commodity i, evaluated at the corresponding v_i, $i = 1, 2, \ldots, n-1$, can purchase in the economic system a quantity of labour ('labour commanded') exactly equal to the labour 'embodied' in it.

3 The Marxian 'Value System'

Marx carries out his analysis in terms of 'values', defined here by (5.2.5), but focuses his attention on what is for him a fundamental distortion that occurs in a capitalist society. The owners of the means of production (the 'capitalists') find themselves in a privileged position, which allows them not to pay the 'complete' wage rate w^*.

[3] See page 122.

Suppose that we are able to define in physical terms, that is, as a bundle of heterogeneous commodities, a set of h quantities $d_1, d_2, \ldots, d_h$, which together constitute the subsistence real wage, which we shall denote by the column vector

$$\mathbf{d} = \begin{bmatrix} d_1 \\ d_2 \\ \vdots \\ d_h \\ 0 \\ \vdots \\ 0 \end{bmatrix}. \tag{5.3.1}$$

(It will be assumed that the matrix $\mathbf{A}$ is so ordered that its first h rows and h columns refer to the h subsistence commodities and industries.) Of course, $h < n - 1$.[4] Marx argues that

$$\mathbf{vd} = \delta w^*, \qquad \text{where} \qquad \delta < 1. \tag{5.3.2}$$

That is, the capitalists pay the workers only the subsistence wage $\mathbf{vd}$, which represents a fraction $\delta < 1$ of the 'complete' wage w^*. What remains, that is, the fraction $(1-\delta)$ of w^*, represents the 'unpaid wage' or 'surplus value', in Marx's terminology, which is appropriated by the capitalists.

Using the solutions (5.2.4) and (5.2.5), in which $w^* = 1$, and substituting (5.3.2) therein, we can rewrite (5.2.1) as

$$\mathbf{vA} + \frac{1}{\delta}\mathbf{vda}_n = \mathbf{v}, \tag{5.3.3}$$

or

$$\mathbf{vA} + \mathbf{vda}_n + \frac{1-\delta}{\delta}\mathbf{vda}_n = \mathbf{v}. \tag{5.3.4}$$

It may now be noted that the ratio $(1-\delta)/\delta$, which we shall call σ, so that

$$\sigma = \frac{1-\delta}{\delta} = \frac{1}{\delta} - 1, \tag{5.3.5}$$

represents what Marx calls the 'rate of surplus value', that is, the unpaid part of w^*, expressed as a percentage fraction of the part which

4 Notice that, as a consequence of the hypothesis that all commodities require labour, directly or indirectly, to be produced, wage goods are necessarily *basic* commodities.

is paid. Or, as it is also said (all the quantities involved being expressed in terms of physical quantities of embodied labour), σ represents the ratio of 'surplus labour' to 'necessary labour'. Or again, $(1 - \delta)$ also represents the fraction of the working day (or of the 'working year' if a 'year' is the unit of time) in which the worker works for the capitalist, and δ represents the fraction in which he works for himself. This was Marx's reason for calling their ratio σ not only the 'rate of surplus value' but also the 'rate of exploitation'.

It may also be noted that, since the subsistence wage (5.3.2) is assumed to be the same for all workers, the rate of surplus value (or of exploitation) σ proves to be the same in all industries. In fact, (5.3.4) may be rewritten

$$\mathbf{vA} + \mathbf{vda}_n + \sigma\mathbf{vda}_n = \mathbf{v}, \tag{5.3.6}$$

or

$$\mathbf{vA} + \mathbf{vda}_n(1 + \sigma) = \mathbf{v}, \tag{5.3.7}$$

or

$$\mathbf{v}[\mathbf{I} - \mathbf{A} - (1 + \sigma)\mathbf{da}_n] = 0, \tag{5.3.7 bis}$$

where σ is indeed the same in all industries. The solutions for $\mathbf{v}$ and σ (and δ) are, of course, still those obtained from (5.2.4) and (5.2.5), together with (5.3.1), (5.3.2) and (5.3.5).

The same solutions for $\mathbf{v}$ and σ can, however, be obtained in an alternative way directly from (5.3.7) – or from (5.3.7 bis) – if one adds the equation

$$\mathbf{vd}(1 + \sigma) = w^* = 1, \tag{5.3.8}$$

which – as in (5.2.4) – defines the value of a unit of embodied labour to be the *numéraire* for the system of 'values'. The method of solution is by now familiar to us. Expression (5.3.7 bis) is a system of linear and homogeneous equations in the 'values'. A necessary condition for the existence of non-zero solutions is that

$$\det[\mathbf{I} - \mathbf{A} - (1 + \sigma)\mathbf{da}_n] = 0. \tag{5.3.9}$$

Solving this equation, we obtain the value of σ, which, when substituted into (5.3.7) and (5.3.8), enables us to determine the $n - 1$ elements of $\mathbf{v}$ (from $n - 1$ independent equations).[5]

[5] It may be interesting to note that, from a pure analytical point of view, (5.3.9) is much simpler than the corresponding equation in the price system, i.e.,

As emerges clearly from (5.3.6), the 'value' of each commodity may be regarded as the sum of three components: (i) replacement of the means of production, or 'constant capital' (each element of the vector $\mathbf{vA}$); (ii) replacement of the capital advanced by the capitalists as wages, or 'variable capital' (each element of the vector $\mathbf{vda}_n$); and (iii) 'surplus value' (each element of the vector $\sigma\mathbf{vda}_n$). In the same way, if $\bar{\mathbf{Q}}$ is the (column) vector of the physical quantities of all commodities produced in a given economic system, the total gross product $\mathbf{v}\bar{\mathbf{Q}}$ may be expressed as the sum of three components:

$$\mathbf{vA}\bar{\mathbf{Q}} + \mathbf{vda}_n\bar{\mathbf{Q}} + \sigma\mathbf{vda}_n\bar{\mathbf{Q}} = \mathbf{v}\bar{\mathbf{Q}}, \qquad (5.3.11)$$

which represent the 'constant capital', the 'variable capital' and the total 'surplus value', respectively, for the whole economy. All the physical quantities, being multiplied by $\mathbf{v}$, come to be expressed in terms of 'values' or quantities of embodied labour.

Notice that the rate of surplus value can also be derived as the ratio between the two aggregates which are shown as the third and second terms, respectively, in the sum on the left side of (5.3.11). On the other hand, contrary to what was thought by Marx,[6] the rate of profit for the system as a whole, as we shall see in a moment, cannot be obtained, in general, as the ratio between the third term (total 'surplus value') and the sum of the first two terms (total capital) of (5.3.11). To obtain the rate of profit, one must turn to a different system of

(5.4.7), which will be obtained in Section 4. For matrix $\mathbf{da}_n$ is the product of two vectors and therefore has rank 1, i.e., cannot contain more than one linearly independent vector (see Pasinetti 1977a, p. 251, theorem (i)). This means that σ will have at most one non-zero solution, by contrast, with π in (5.4.7), which may have up to $n-1$ non-zero solutions.

Alternatively, (5.3.9) can be rewritten

$$\det[\mathbf{I} - (1+\sigma)\mathbf{da}_n(\mathbf{I}-\mathbf{A})^{-1}] = 0, \qquad (5.3.10)$$

which is an expression formally of the same type as (5.4.7) of Section 4, but precisely with the simplification that σ emerges as having at most one non-zero solution, owing to $\mathbf{da}_n$, and therefore also $\mathbf{da}_n(\mathbf{I}-\mathbf{A})^{-1}$, both being matrices of rank 1 (see Pasinetti 1977a, p. 258). It may also be interesting to point out that the elements of matrix $\mathbf{da}_n(\mathbf{I}-\mathbf{A})^{-1}$ have a precise economic meaning, i.e., that of vertically integrated subsistence consumption coefficients, as may be realised from an analysis of the type developed in Pasinetti (1973).

6 See, e.g., Marx (1959, p. 42).

equations, referring – not to the 'Marxian values', but to the 'prices of production'.

4 The 'Price-of-Production System'

The system of equations in Section 3, which may be called 'the Marxian-value system', cannot be observed in the practice of a capitalist economy, because that part of the net product which is not paid in wages is distributed in the form of profits. And profits are distributed in proportion to total capital, not in proportion to total wages (as, by definition, surplus value would be).

This implies that the exchange ratios, or 'prices of production', which can be observed in a capitalist system, will differ from the 'Marxian values'. Now, if we assume that wages are advanced by the capitalists at the beginning of the production period, and hence that the wages fund is itself part of capital, the 'prices of production' will be given by the system of equations

$$(\mathbf{pA} + w\mathbf{a}_n)(1 + \pi) = \mathbf{p}. \tag{5.4.1}$$

Moreover, if we assume, as in Section 3, that the wage rate can be specified in physical terms as $\mathbf{d}$, defined by (5.3.1), and thus that

$$w = \mathbf{pd}, \tag{5.4.2}$$

we obtain, after substitution in (5.4.1),

$$(\mathbf{pA} + \mathbf{pda}_n)(1 + \pi) = \mathbf{p}. \tag{5.4.3}$$

That is,

$$\mathbf{p}[\mathbf{I} - (1 + \pi)(\mathbf{A} + \mathbf{da}_n)] = 0. \tag{5.4.4}$$

The matrix $(\mathbf{A} + \mathbf{da}_n)$, which may be called $\mathbf{A}^{(+)}$, that is,

$$\mathbf{A}^{(+)} = \mathbf{A} + \mathbf{da}_n, \tag{5.4.5}$$

is a matrix of inter-industry coefficients which is, so to speak, 'augmented' by the consumption coefficients needed for the maintenance of the workers. We have already referred to this matrix several times,[7] but without ever having had to distinguish it explicitly from the matrix $\mathbf{A}$ (our analysis being exactly the same, in *formal* terms, whether the inter-industry coefficients matrix was interpreted as including the

[7] See page 120 and page 123.

subsistence consumption coefficients or as excluding them). But the distinction has now become necessary.

Using (5.4.5), we can rewrite (5.4.4) as

$$\mathbf{p}[\mathbf{I} - (1+\pi)\mathbf{A}^{(+)}] = 0. \tag{5.4.6}$$

We thus obtain a system of linear and homogeneous equations of a kind which we have already considered several times. We know that a necessary condition for the system to have economically meaningful solutions is that

$$\det[\mathbf{I} - (1+\pi)\mathbf{A}^{(+)}] = 0, \tag{5.4.7}$$

or

$$\det[\mathbf{I} - (1+\pi)(\mathbf{A} + \mathbf{da}_n)] = 0. \tag{5.4.7 bis}$$

Furthermore, we know that the rate of profit satisfying the characteristic equation (5.4.7), to be denoted by $\Pi^{(A+)}$, is non-negative if the maximum eigenvalue of $\mathbf{A}^{(+)}$ is less than or equal to unity, which we shall of course assume. In symbols, we assume that

$$\lambda_m^{(A+)} \leq 1, \qquad \text{which implies} \qquad \Pi^{(A+)} \geq 0, \tag{5.4.8}$$

where $\Pi^{(A+)}$ is derived from (4.5.12), in correspondence to $\lambda_m^{(A+)}$. After substituting this rate of profit into (5.4.6) and adding whatever further equation we choose in order to define a *numéraire* for the price system, we can determine all the 'prices of production' in terms of the chosen *numéraire*.

5 A Comparison

It is not difficult now to understand why the 'Marxian-value system' (5.3.7 bis) differs from the 'prices of production' (5.4.4). The fundamental diversity lies in the different ways in which the part of the net product which is not paid as wages is distributed among the various industries. In the 'Marxian-value system' it is distributed (as 'surplus value') in proportion to the wages advanced to the workers (or 'variable capital'); in the 'prices of production system' it is distributed (as profits) in proportion to the sum of 'variable capital' and 'constant capital'. The rate of profit will therefore be *less than* (or, in the limiting case in which there is no constant capital, equal to) the rate of surplus value, simply because the same physical quantities, of which both surplus value and profits are made up, must in the case of profits be spread over a larger amount of capital (total capital, and not merely variable capital).

Rigorous confirmation of this intuitive[8] argument can be found in the fact that the rate of surplus value and the rate of profit are the solutions of the characteristic equations (5.3.9) and (5.4.7 bis), respectively. A straightforward comparison of these two equations provides immediate confirmation of Marx's three well-known[9] propositions, namely, that: (i) $\pi > 0$ if and only if $\sigma > 0$[10]; (ii) $\pi < \sigma$, except in the limiting case of $\mathbf{A} = \mathbf{O}$, when π and σ become equal; and (iii) π is a monotonically increasing function of σ and *vice versa*.[11]

It may be of interest to note that, from the standpoint of the formulations of Chapter 4, Section 5.1, the 'Marxian-value system' and the 'prices-of-production system' formally correspond to two extreme (opposite) cases considered there for exogenous determination of the

[8] The argument is 'intuitive' because of the analytical complication that, although the physical quantities which constitute both total surplus value and total profits are the same, their evaluation is different according as it is made at the 'Marxian values' or at the 'prices of production'.

[9] For details see Pasinetti (1977a, § 4. 2, pp. 20–22).

[10] Morishima (1973) calls this proposition 'the fundamental Marxian theorem'.

[11] Equations (5.3.9) and (5.4.7) may also be written

$$\det\left[\frac{1}{1+\sigma}\mathbf{I} - \left(\frac{1}{1+\sigma}\mathbf{A} + \mathbf{d}\mathbf{a}_n\right)\right] = 0, \tag{5.5.1}$$

and

$$\det\left[\frac{1}{1+\pi}\mathbf{I} - (\mathbf{A} + \mathbf{d}\mathbf{a}_n)\right] = 0. \tag{5.5.2}$$

As is easily seen, these two equations coincide only in the two particular cases in which $\mathbf{A} = \mathbf{O}$ (no constant capital) and in which $\mathbf{A}$ and $\mathbf{d}$ are such as to yield the solution $\sigma = 0$, which also implies $\pi = 0$. In all other cases (where both $\sigma > 0$ and $\pi > 0$), it must be the case that $\pi < \sigma$. For

$$\frac{1}{1+\sigma}\mathbf{A} < \mathbf{A},$$

and therefore

$$\frac{1}{1+\sigma} < \frac{1}{1+\pi},$$

or $\sigma < \pi$, owing to the Perron–Frobenius theorems. Since both σ and π are decreasing monotonic functions of each single element of the corresponding inverse matrix, and since $\sigma > \pi$ at any of their positive values, the rate of profit proves to be an increasing monotonic function of the rate of surplus value, and conversely.

distributive variable, but with respect to two different coefficient matrices. 'Marxian values' are derived by setting the rate of profit equal to zero in a system involving the matrix **A**, while 'prices-of-production system' are derived by setting the (surplus) wage rate equal to zero in a system involving the matrix $\mathbf{A}^{(+)}$. These being two different systems of equations,[12] it is hardly surprising that they should have different solutions. Hence, in general, $\mathbf{v} \neq \mathbf{p}$.

It follows, for example, that for any total output, given in physical terms by the (column) vector $\bar{\mathbf{Q}}$, the evaluation of this output will differ

[12] One can thus understand why Samuelson may have got impatient to the point of making the sarcastic remark: '... the "transformation algorithm" is precisely of the following form: "contemplate two alternative and discordant systems. Write down one. Now transform by taking an eraser and rubbing it out. Then fill in the other one. *Voila*! You have completed your transformation algorithm"' (Samuelson 1971, p. 400).

But one must beware of superficial impressions. Although matrices **A** and $\mathbf{A}^{(+)}$ are different from each other, they do not differ in an arbitrary way. All their differences reduce to the specific matrix $\mathbf{da}_n$ which has the important property of distributing subsistence goods over the columns of $\mathbf{A}^{(+)}$ in proportion to the labour coefficients. Hence, it would be a mistake to think – from a superficial look at (5.4.6) – that proportionality of profits to capital is the sole criterion adopted there for the distribution of the net output. This is not so, because that part of the net output which refers to subsistence goods has already been distributed, within matrix $\mathbf{A}^{(+)}$, in proportion to the labour coefficients. Actually one can see that, as **d** is increasing, the 'prices-of-production system' (5.4.6) tends to the 'Marxian values', until eventually they coincide with them at the extreme point at which **d** has absorbed all the net product and nothing is left over for profits. Let us consider this extreme case. If, *ex-hypothesis*, the maximum eigenvalue of $\mathbf{A}^{(+)}$ is 1, which means $\Pi^{(A+)} = 0$, then (5.4.4) becomes

$$\mathbf{p}(\mathbf{I} - \mathbf{A} - \mathbf{da}_n) = 0.$$

And, if the wage rate is set equal to 1, i.e.,

$$\mathbf{pd} = 1,$$

we obtain, after substitution,

$$\mathbf{p} = \mathbf{pA} + \mathbf{a}_n,$$

and thus

$$\mathbf{p} = \mathbf{a}_n(\mathbf{I} - \mathbf{A})^{-1} = \mathbf{v}.$$

This is precisely the expression (5.2.5) defining the 'Marxian values'. In other words, when $\Pi^{(A+)} = 0$, the 'prices-of-production system' (5.4.4) coincides with the 'Marxian values' (5.2.5), simply because profits are zero and all the net product (relative to matrix **A**) has already been distributed within the columns of matrix $\mathbf{A}^{(+)}$ in proportion to the quantities of labour.

according as it is done in terms of 'Marxian values' or in terms of 'prices of production'; that is, in general,

$$\mathbf{v}\bar{\mathbf{Q}} \neq \mathbf{p}\bar{\mathbf{Q}}. \tag{5.5.3}$$

Moreover, the ratio of total surplus value to total capital, expressed in 'Marxian values', will differ from the rate of profit (more specifically from the ratio of total profits to total capital) for the system as a whole; that is, in general,

$$\frac{\sigma \mathbf{v} d\mathbf{a}_n \bar{\mathbf{Q}}}{\mathbf{v}(\mathbf{A} + d\mathbf{a}_n)\bar{\mathbf{Q}}} \neq \frac{\Pi^{(A+)}\mathbf{p}(\mathbf{A} + d\mathbf{a}_n)\bar{\mathbf{Q}}}{\mathbf{p}(\mathbf{A} + d\mathbf{a}_n)\bar{\mathbf{Q}}}. \tag{5.5.4}$$

Thirdly, total surplus value will be different from total profits; that is, in general,

$$\sigma \mathbf{v} d\mathbf{a}_n \bar{\mathbf{Q}} \neq \Pi^{(A+)}\mathbf{p}(\mathbf{A} + d\mathbf{a}_n)\bar{\mathbf{Q}}. \tag{5.5.5}$$

As is well known, Marx thought (incorrectly) that these three expressions would all be equalities.[13] That cannot be so, except in special cases or under certain particular conditions.[14] It may well be interesting to examine all these special cases or conditions.

6 The 'Standard System' as a Special Case

Before proceeding further, it may be of interest to open a digression and consider the special case of a hypothetical economic system which happens to realise the proportions of Sraffa's standard system. We must, however, distinguish between a standard system defined with respect to the matrix **A** and a standard system defined with respect to the matrix $\mathbf{A}^{(+)}$, since these two matrices are here explicitly distinguished from each other.

Consider first the standard system defined with reference to matrix **A**. As we know, a standard system of this kind is defined by the vector of quantities $\mathbf{Q}^*$ which is the solution of the system of equations

$$[\mathbf{I} - (1 + R)\mathbf{A}]\mathbf{Q}^* = 0, \tag{4.12.4}$$

$$\mathbf{a}_n\mathbf{Q}^* = 1, \tag{4.12.5}$$

13 See, e.g., Marx (1959, pp. 42, 157, 164).

14 Of course, one can always take advantage of the degree of freedom in the price system and explicitly choose the *numéraire* in such a way as to reduce one (but not more than one) of these three inequalities to an equality.

where

$$\det[\mathbf{I} - (1 + R)\mathbf{A}] = 0.$$

Taking the standard net product as the *numéraire*, the 'prices-of-production system' for such an economic system will be given by

$$\mathbf{p}[\mathbf{I} - (1 + \Pi^{(A+)})(\mathbf{A} + \mathbf{d}^*\mathbf{a}_n)] = 0, \tag{5.6.1}$$

$$\mathbf{p}(\mathbf{I} - \mathbf{A})\mathbf{Q}^* = 1, \tag{5.6.2}$$

where we explicitly assume that $\mathbf{d}^*$, the actual wage rate in physical terms, has the same composition as the standard commodity. The corresponding system of 'values' will of course be different:

$$\mathbf{vA} + \mathbf{vd}^*\mathbf{a}_n(1 + \sigma) = \mathbf{v}. \tag{5.6.3}$$

It will be noted that the total quantity of labour having been set equal to unity (4.12.5) can be rewritten as:

$$\mathbf{a}_n(\mathbf{I} - \mathbf{A})^{-1}(\mathbf{I} - \mathbf{A})\mathbf{Q}^* = 1, \tag{5.6.4}$$

which, from (5.2.5), becomes

$$\mathbf{v}(\mathbf{I} - \mathbf{A})\mathbf{Q}^* = 1. \tag{5.6.5}$$

That is, the quantity of labour embodied in the net product of the system is equal to unity. Thus, owing to the normalisation adopted, the net product comes to be equal to unity, whether it is evaluated at prices of production – equation (5.6.2) – or at 'Marxian values' – equation (5.6.5).

It also follows that thinking of fractions of the *standard* net product in terms of prices always comes to be the same as thinking of them in terms of 'Marxian values' (i.e. of quantities of embodied labour). Hence, if wages were actually paid in standard commodity, that is, in fractions of the standard net product, as we have here assumed, the wage rate w, which in the normalised standard system also represents the fraction of the net product which goes to wages, comes to represent also the fraction of the total labour which is embodied in wages (or the fraction of the working 'year' in which the worker works for himself), which we previously called δ (Section 3). This implies that w can be replaced by δ in the remarkable relation (4.12.9) derived by Sraffa for the standard system.

However, this cannot be done here. The 'prices-of-production system' (5.6.1) of Marx's analysis is different from Sraffa's price system, since profits are also reckoned on wages. (That is, Marx assumes that wages are advanced to the workers at the beginning of the production

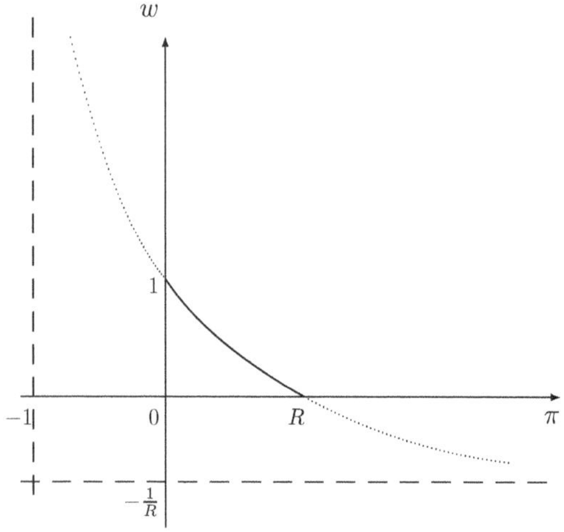

Figure 5.1 Standard system relation between π and w when wages are advanced.

period, while Sraffa assumes them to be paid at the end.) We must therefore derive the relation between π and w, which is analogous to Sraffa's relation (4.12.9), for the case in which wages are paid at the beginning of the year. By going through the steps of our earlier argument, (4.12.2)–(4.12.9), with the sole difference that the vector of wages $\mathbf{a}_n w$ is now multiplied by $(1 + \pi)$, we arrive at the new relation

$$\pi = \frac{R}{1 + Rw}(1 - w), \tag{5.6.6}$$

in place of Sraffa's (4.12.9). As will be seen, we still obtain a relation between π and w which is very simple, is independent of prices, and has intercepts: $\pi = R$ and $w = 1$. However, (5.6.6) is no longer a linear function, but a hyperbolic one, with asymptotes $w = -1/R$ and $\pi = -1$. (See Figure 5.1.)

Thus, returning to the preceding argument, it may be concluded that in a standard system in which wages actually consisted of a standard commodity, (5.6.6) could be rewritten

$$\pi = \frac{R}{1 + R\delta}(1 - \delta), \tag{5.6.7}$$

from which, using (5.3.5), one can also derive the relation between the rate of profit and the rate of surplus value:

$$\pi = R\frac{\sigma}{1 + \sigma + R}, \tag{5.6.8}$$

$$\sigma = \pi \frac{1+R}{R-\pi}. \tag{5.6.9}$$

These two expressions, incidentally, provide a confirmation of the three propositions concerning the relations between π and σ[15] stated in Section 5.

It is now interesting to check what happens to the three inequalities (5.5.3)–(5.5.5). First of all, total gross output, given by the vector $\mathbf{Q}^*$, is a scalar multiple of the standard net product, that is, of the vector $(\mathbf{I}-\mathbf{A})\mathbf{Q}^*$. And, since $\mathbf{p}(\mathbf{I}-\mathbf{A})\mathbf{Q}^* = \mathbf{v}(\mathbf{I}-\mathbf{A})\mathbf{Q}^*$, it must also be true that $\mathbf{p}\mathbf{Q}^* = \mathbf{v}\mathbf{Q}^*$. Secondly, with wages being paid in standard commodity, all that remains after the payment of wages – surplus value, if evaluated at 'Marxian values'; or profits, if evaluated at prices – will also consist of standard commodity and will therefore be a scalar multiple of the net product. This means that total surplus value will be equal to total profits. Finally, the rate of profit, by being a ratio between two scalar multiples of the same standard net product, will remain the

[15] In the hypothetical case of wages being paid at the end of the production period (as in Sraffa's model), the three relations (5.6.7)–(5.6.9) would become much simpler; i.e., in the same order,

$$\pi = R(1-\delta), \tag{5.6.7 bis}$$

$$\pi = R\frac{\sigma}{\sigma+1}, \tag{5.6.8 bis}$$

$$\sigma = \frac{\pi}{R-\pi}. \tag{5.6.9 bis}$$

Notice the elegance, besides the simplicity, of (5.6.7 bis), which here would replace Sraffa's (4.12.9).

From the standpoint of Marxian analysis, these expressions have the drawback of not making the rate of profit necessarily smaller than the rate of surplus value, the reason being that in Sraffa's prices the rate of profit is proportional to 'constant capital' only, and not to the sum of 'constant' plus 'variable' capital, as in Marx's 'prices-of-production system'.

John Eatwell (1975), who proposed expressions (5.6.7 bis)–(5.6.9 bis), also claimed that these expressions are valid in general, and not only with reference to the 'standard system', with the one proviso that the wage rate be expressed in terms of the standard commodity – in the same way as Sraffa's (4.12.9) is valid in general, if the wage rate is expressed in standard commodity. This claim, however, seems to me a rather weak point to make in a Marxian context. For, in Marx's analysis, the wage rate is not something that can indifferently be expressed in terms of *any numéraire*. What matters to any worker is a well-defined set of commodities making up his/her wage. And the labour embodied in such a set of commodities would obey relations (5.6.7 bis)–(5.6.9 bis) only if the wage rate were actually paid in standard commodity.

same, whether evaluated at 'values' or at prices. In other words, all three inequalities (5.5.3)–(5.5.5) become equalities in the present case.

But let us now consider the standard system defined with respect to the matrix $\mathbf{A}^{(+)} = \mathbf{A} + \mathbf{d}\mathbf{a}_n$. Its solution will here be denoted by $\mathbf{Q}^{**}$. In formal terms, this new standard system is represented by the same equations as considered in (4.12.4) and (4.12.5) – except that the matrix **A** must be replaced by the matrix $\mathbf{A}^{(+)}$. However, we have to distinguish two cases: (i) the case in which the real wage **d** is of the same composition as the standard commodity, so that $\mathbf{d} = \mathbf{d}^*$, and (ii) the case in which the real wage **d** has a composition different from that of the standard commodity. In case (i), it will be clear that $\mathbf{Q}^* = \mathbf{Q}^{**}$, and hence that one returns to the standard commodity defined with respect to the matrix **A** (i.e. the two standard systems come to coincide). In case (ii), by contrast, $\mathbf{Q}^* \neq \mathbf{Q}^{**}$. The standard system defined with respect to the matrix **A** differs from that defined with respect to matrix $\mathbf{A}^{(+)}$. With this new standard system it is no longer possible to use the normalisation of the price system suggested by Sraffa. For (4.12.5), which now becomes $\mathbf{a}_n\mathbf{Q}^{**} = 1$, always implies that the net product of the system, wages plus profits, is equal to unity when evaluated at 'Marxian values'. But the expression $\mathbf{p}(\mathbf{I} - \mathbf{A}^{(+)})\mathbf{Q}^{**}$ no longer represents the net product of the system but rather a 'net product' which does not include wages; that is, it represents only profits. (This is the Classical notion of 'net product'.) If one wishes to maintain direct comparability between 'Marxian values' and 'prices-of-production system', this 'net product', evaluated at 'prices-of-production system', must be set equal to the quantity of labour embodied in it; hence, the price system must be closed, not by equation $\mathbf{p}(\mathbf{I} - \mathbf{A}^{(+)})\mathbf{Q}^{**} = 1$, but rather by equation

$$\mathbf{p}(\mathbf{I} - \mathbf{A}^{(+)})\mathbf{Q}^{**} = \mathbf{v}(\mathbf{I} - \mathbf{A}^{(+)})\mathbf{Q}^{**}, \tag{5.6.10}$$

in which both sides will, of course, be *less than* unity. (It also follows that the sum of wages and profits, which has a 'value' equal to unity, will no longer necessarily be equal to unity if evaluated at 'prices-of-production system'.)

Nevertheless, even with this normalisation, the three inequalities (5.5.3)–(5.5.5) become equalities in the new standard system. Total surplus value and total profits are equal to each other owing to (5.6.10). Moreover, $\mathbf{p}\mathbf{Q}^{**} = \mathbf{v}\mathbf{Q}^{**}$, because each side of this equality is the same scalar multiple of the corresponding term in (5.6.10). Finally, as in all standard systems, the rate of profit is a physical notion and is therefore independent of both 'values' and prices.

Sraffa's concept of 'standard system' (and 'standard commodity') therefore yields further contributions also in the field of 'Marxian-value' analysis. It confirms that, even in the case in which the wage rate is paid at the beginning of the production period, the distribution of income (i.e. the relation between π and w) remains independent of the price system. By simply being converted from a straight to a hyperbolic line, it shows absolutely no dependence on prices. Moreover, the three inequalities specified at the end of Section 5 are all transformed into equalities. Of course, all this is for the special case in which production is actually carried out in the proportions of the Sraffa 'standard system'.

7 The 'Transformation of Marxian Values into Prices of Production'

But what happens in the general case?

As is well known, Marx held the strong conviction that the institutions of the capitalist economies, by driving the rates of profits towards equalisation in all industries, carry out a process of 'transformation' of all 'values' into corresponding 'prices of production'. This process of 'transformation' is not immediately evident, because 'values' are not observable in a capitalist economy – only 'prices of production' are.

It becomes necessary at this point to explore explicitly what this process of 'transformation' consists of.

By defining $\hat{\mathbf{v}}$ to be a diagonal matrix of order $(n-1)$, which has the $n-1$ 'values' as its principal diagonal elements, we can post-multiply the 'Marxian-value system' (5.3.7) throughout by $\hat{\mathbf{v}}^{-1}$ and rewrite it as

$$\mathbf{1}(\hat{\mathbf{v}}\mathbf{A}\hat{\mathbf{v}}^{-1}) + \mathbf{1}(\hat{\mathbf{v}}\mathbf{d}\mathbf{a}_n\hat{\mathbf{v}}^{-1})(1+\sigma) = \mathbf{1}, \tag{5.7.1}$$

where $\mathbf{1}$ is a row vector with every element equal to unity. This system is, of course, closed by the same equation as before, namely by

$$\mathbf{vd}(1+\sigma) = w^* = 1, \tag{5.3.8}$$

which sets a unit of embodied labour to be the unit of measurement for the 'Marxian values'.

Written in this way, system (5.7.1) is a 'Marxian-value system' which has, so to speak, been transformed with respect to the physical quantities. The physical quantities of commodities are no longer expressed in their conventional units of measurement (tonnes, metres, litres, etc.) but have instead been re-expressed in terms of physical quantities of embodied labour. As will be realised, the term $\hat{\mathbf{v}}\mathbf{A}$ re-expresses all the inter-industry coefficients in terms of embodied labour, while the post-multiplication by $\hat{\mathbf{v}}^{-1}$ (i.e. the division of each column of the matrix by the quantity of labour embodied in each unit of the corresponding commodity produced) means that each inter-industry coefficient is now referred to the corresponding commodity output measured in units of embodied labour. In the same way, $\hat{\mathbf{v}}\mathbf{d}$ re-expresses the physical wage rate in terms of quantities of embodied labour, while the vector $\mathbf{a}_n\hat{\mathbf{v}}^{-1}$ re-expresses the direct labour coefficients so that each of them refers to an output embodying one unit of labour. And since the 'value' of each physical unit of embodied labour is unity, by definition, the new transformed vector of 'values' is simply the vector $\mathbf{1}$ (a vector with every component equal to unity). From another point of view, we could say that we have re-defined each physical unit of measurement of *any* commodity in such a way as to fix its 'Marxian value' (i.e. its content of labour) equal to unity.

Reconsider now the system of 'prices of production':

$$(\mathbf{pA} + \mathbf{pda}_n)(1+\pi) = \mathbf{p}, \tag{5.4.1}$$

to which must be added an equation defining the *numéraire* for the system. To preserve symmetry with (5.3.8), the logical step seems to be to set

$$\mathbf{pd}(1+\sigma) = 1. \tag{5.7.2}$$

Thus, the 'complete' wage rate, or per-worker net product in terms of wage goods, is set equal to unity, when evaluated in terms of 'prices of production', in the same way as it is set equal to unity when evaluated at 'Marxian values'.

We now define a new row vector $\mathbf{x}$, which shows the ratios of the 'prices of production system' to the corresponding 'Marxian values':

$$\mathbf{x} = \mathbf{p}\hat{\mathbf{v}}^{-1}, \tag{5.7.3}$$

and, conversely,

$$\mathbf{p} = \mathbf{x}\hat{\mathbf{v}}. \tag{5.7.4}$$

Post-multiplying (5.4.1) by $\hat{\mathbf{v}}^{-1}$ and substituting from (5.7.4), we obtain

$$\mathbf{x}(\hat{\mathbf{v}}\mathbf{A}\hat{\mathbf{v}}^{-1} + \hat{\mathbf{v}}\mathbf{da}_n\hat{\mathbf{v}}^{-1})(1+\pi) = \mathbf{x}, \tag{5.7.5}$$

where $\mathbf{x}$ is itself a vector of 'prices of production', these prices being expressed, however, relative to the 'Marxian values'.

This system of equations is the same as the 'prices-of-production system' in Section 4, except that it is now so written as to single out explicitly the 'Marxian values' as the magnitudes from which to start. Hence, its 'solution' is equivalent to a 'transformation' of the 'transformed values' $\mathbf{1}$ into the 'transformed prices' $\mathbf{x}$. This is precisely the 'transformation' of the 'Marxian values' $\mathbf{v}$ into the 'prices of production' $\mathbf{p}$.

It goes without saying that, in general, $\mathbf{x} \neq \mathbf{1}$ and hence $\mathbf{p} \neq \mathbf{v}$. Prices and 'Marxian values' will diverge. These divergences will depend *mainly* on the 'organic composition of capital' in each industry as compared with that in the industry producing the commodity which is taken as the *numéraire*, but also on the intricate network of relations between rate of profit and prices in the whole economic system. We have examined this problem in Section 5.7 of Chapter 4, with reference to the divergences between any two sets of prices. 'Marxian values' and 'prices-of-production system' are clearly a particular case of such a problem. And we know we cannot state a general rule, that is, a rule valid for absolutely all cases. We can say that *in most cases* those ratios, in $\mathbf{x}$, referring to commodities with an 'organic composition of capital' greater than that of the composite commodity $\mathbf{d}$, will turn out to be greater than unity (and hence the respective prices greater than the corresponding 'Marxian values'); and those ratios relating to commodities with an 'organic composition of capital' smaller than that of the composite commodity $\mathbf{d}$ will turn out to be less than unity (and hence the respective prices smaller than the corresponding 'values'). There may always be some prices, however, which do not follow this rule.

The choice of the composite commodity $\mathbf{d}(1+\sigma)$ as *numéraire* (and hence of its price as the 'watershed' between prices which are greater and prices which are smaller than the corresponding 'Marxian values') is, of course, an arbitrary choice. Other choices could equally well be made. And, indeed, in the economic literature on the transformation problem, various alternative suggestions have been made in this connection,[16] all of which reduce to the choice of a particular commodity,

[16] The following alternative suggestions may be mentioned: $\mathbf{vQ} = \mathbf{pQ}$, total value equal to total prices; $\mathbf{vda}_n\mathbf{Q}\sigma = \mathbf{pA}^{(+)}\mathbf{Q}\Pi^{(A+)}$, total surplus value equal

or composite commodity, the 'value' of which remains invariant when it is transformed into a 'price of production'.[17] In our example, this choice has just been made in (5.7.2) and is equivalent to setting

$$\mathbf{vd} = \mathbf{pd}, \tag{5.7.6}$$

that is, to choosing the composite wage commodity as the commodity whose 'value' and 'price of production' remain invariant in the transformation process. It is to be noted that the criterion used in this choice is simply one of logical symmetry.[18] Definition (5.7.2), for the unit of measurement of 'prices-of-production system', is logically symmetrical to definition (5.3.8) for the unit of measurement of 'Marxian values'.

In any event, whatever may be the commodity, or composite commodity, whose 'value' and 'price of production' are chosen to remain invariant, it can be concluded that what Marx called the 'transformation of values into prices of production' consists in a perfectly logical analytical process, expressed by the solution of a system of linear equations. It consists in the search for a linear operator which will 'transform' a certain vector $\mathbf{v}$ into another vector $\mathbf{p}$ (or into some scalar multiple thereof).

It may be worth pausing for a moment at this point to consider one of Marx's most ingenious devices.

to total profits; $\mathbf{v}(\mathbf{I} - \mathbf{A}^{(+)})\mathbf{Q}^{**} = \mathbf{p}(\mathbf{I} - \mathbf{A}^{(+)})\mathbf{Q}^{**}$, standard commodity, with reference to matrix $\mathbf{A}^{(+)}$, evaluated at the 'values', equal to the same, evaluated at the 'prices of production'. The first and the third of these alternative suggestions have been justified with reference to Marx's idea of a commodity with organic composition of capital equal to the 'social average'. The second, on the other hand, has been justified with reference to Marx's argument that capitalists redistribute surplus values among themselves under the form of profits (see Winternitz 1948, Meek 1956, Seton 1956–1957, Medio 1972). In all these attempts to be faithful to Marx the difficulty is, of course, that Marx's own arguments are not always logically consistent and thus would seem to justify different postulates at different places.

17 The 'transformation problem' therefore also entails the choice of an 'invariance postulate', as it has been called by Seton (1956–1957).

18 Yet it is interesting to find that Marx himself thought of the wage-goods industries as those with an 'organic composition of capital' which is near to the average for the whole economy. See Dobb (1940, pp. 46, 72–73) and Meek (1956, p. 96). In fact, the choice of the composite commodity $\mathbf{d}$ is not without a justification, as will be revealed by the analysis of Section 10.

8 Uniform 'Organic Composition of Capital' – Marx's Special Case

As the reader may realise, the above-mentioned problem of the 'transformation of values into prices of production' is not after all such an analytically simple problem at all. Marx found it convenient to leave it to the end of his analysis (without then ever managing to solving it correctly). However, he devised a very simple, but effective, short-cut. In Volumes I and II of *Capital*, he carried out his analysis *as if* the 'organic composition of capital' were the same for all industries.[19] This device allowed him to avoid the 'transformation' problem altogether. Our notation of Section 7, where all the physical quantities are expressed in terms of embodied labour, turns out to be particularly useful to reconsider this Marxian device.

Consider an economic system in which the 'constant capital' in each industry is exactly the same proportion, γ, of the 'variable capital' (both kinds of capital being expressed in terms of quantities of embodied labour), so that

$$\mathbf{1}\hat{\mathbf{v}}\mathbf{A}\hat{\mathbf{v}}^{-1} = \gamma \mathbf{1}\hat{\mathbf{v}}\mathbf{da}_n\hat{\mathbf{v}}^{-1},$$

where $\gamma \geq 0$ denotes the 'organic composition of capital' (which is the same for all industries).

Note now that, for the definition of uniform 'organic composition of capital' to be consistent with all possible income distributions, it must in fact also be true that

$$\hat{\mathbf{v}}\mathbf{A}\hat{\mathbf{v}}^{-1} = \gamma\hat{\mathbf{v}}\mathbf{da}_n\hat{\mathbf{v}}^{-1}. \tag{5.8.1}$$

Substituting into (5.7.5), we obtain

$$\mathbf{x}\hat{\mathbf{v}}\mathbf{A}\hat{\mathbf{v}}^{-1} + \pi\gamma\mathbf{x}\hat{\mathbf{v}}\mathbf{da}_n\hat{\mathbf{v}}^{-1} + \mathbf{x}\hat{\mathbf{v}}\mathbf{da}_n\hat{\mathbf{v}}^{-1}(1+\pi) = \mathbf{x},$$

or:

$$\mathbf{x}(\hat{\mathbf{v}}\mathbf{A}\hat{\mathbf{v}}^{-1}) + \mathbf{x}(\hat{\mathbf{v}}\mathbf{da}_n\hat{\mathbf{v}}^{-1})(1+\pi\gamma+\pi) - \mathbf{x}, \tag{5.8.2}$$

from which, by calling

$$\sigma = \gamma\pi + \pi, \tag{5.8.3}$$

which implies:

$$\pi = \frac{\sigma}{1+\gamma}, \tag{5.8.4}$$

[19] For details, see Pasinetti (1977a, pp. 21–22).

it can be seen that the equation system (5.8.2) comes to coincide exactly with equation system (5.7.1). Hence, the solutions of the two systems must be the same; that is, it must be true that, in the present case,

$$\mathbf{x} = \mathbf{1}, \tag{5.8.5}$$

which implies[20]

$$\mathbf{p} = \mathbf{v}. \tag{5.8.6}$$

We obtain thereby a confirmation of the proposition that, in the special case of a uniform 'organic composition of capital' throughout the economic system, (relative) 'Marxian values' and (relative) 'prices of production' coincide: there is no need for a transformation.[21]

[20] An alternative proof may be given in the following way. Start from

$$\hat{\mathbf{v}}\mathbf{A}\hat{\mathbf{v}}^{-1} = \gamma\hat{\mathbf{v}}\mathbf{d}\mathbf{a}_n\hat{\mathbf{v}}^{-1}, \tag{5.8.1}$$

and pre-multiply by $\mathbf{a}_n\hat{\mathbf{v}}^{-1}$. We obtain:

$$\mathbf{a}_n\hat{\mathbf{v}}^{-1}\hat{\mathbf{v}}\mathbf{A}\hat{\mathbf{v}}^{-1} = (\gamma\mathbf{a}_n\hat{\mathbf{v}}^{-1}\hat{\mathbf{v}}\mathbf{d})\mathbf{a}_n\hat{\mathbf{v}}^{-1}.$$

We may note now that the whole expression within brackets is a scalar. Call it $\lambda = (\gamma\mathbf{a}_n\hat{\mathbf{v}}^{-1}\hat{\mathbf{v}}\mathbf{d})$, and we have

$$(\mathbf{a}_n\hat{\mathbf{v}}^{-1})(\hat{\mathbf{v}}\mathbf{A}\hat{\mathbf{v}}^{-1}) = \lambda\mathbf{a}_n\hat{\mathbf{v}}^{-1}.$$

Thus, $\mathbf{a}_n\hat{\mathbf{v}}^{-1}$ turns out to be an eigenvector of matrix $\hat{\mathbf{v}}\mathbf{A}\hat{\mathbf{v}}^{-1}$. Since $\mathbf{a}_n\hat{\mathbf{v}}^{-1}$ is a vector of direct labour coefficients, and $\hat{\mathbf{v}}\mathbf{A}\hat{\mathbf{v}}^{-1}$ is an inter-industry coefficient matrix, expressed in terms of physical units of embodied labour, it follows that all prices will always remain the same at all possible levels of the rate of profit (see footnote 9 p.125 and footnote 17 p. 133). In the present context this means that the 'prices-of-production system' always coincide with the 'Marxian values'.

[21] The argument carried out in the text can also be reversed. Call

$$\gamma_i = \frac{\sum_i v_i a_{ij}}{a_{nj}\sum_i v_i d_i}, \qquad j = 1, 2, \ldots, n-1,$$

('organic composition of capital' in each industry), and

$$\pi_j = \frac{\sigma a_{nj}\sum_i C_i d_i}{\sum_i v_i a_{ij} + a_{nj}\sum_i v_i d_i} \qquad j = 1, 2, \ldots, n-1,$$

(rate of profit in each industry if exchanges took place according to 'values'). Following the same formulation and the same steps as in the text yields:

$$\sigma = \gamma_j\pi_j + \pi_j,$$

and thus:

$$\pi_j = \frac{\sigma}{1+\gamma_j}, \qquad j = 1, 2, \ldots, n-1.$$

Together with the hypothetical case of a production system in Sraffa's 'standard' proportions, this is another special case in which the three inequalities, mentioned at the end of Section 5, are all turned into equalities.

9 The Linear Operator Which Effects the 'Transformation' in the General Case

But let us now return to the, more complex, general case.

The linear operator which, in general, 'transforms' the vector of 'Marxian values' **v** into the vector of 'prices of production' **p** is already implicit in the expressions we have considered in Section 7, as has there been pointed out. But there are many alternative ways of expressing such linear operator, depending on the convention chosen to close the degree of freedom of each of our equation systems. For our purposes, it may be useful to consider at least two of them.

The way that emerges as the most natural one, from the point of view of the present analysis, is that of proceeding straight from the formulations of Section 7, where the 'prices-of-production system' was closed with the equation

$$\mathbf{pd}(1+\sigma)=1, \qquad (5.7.2)$$

which is symmetrical to the equation

$$\mathbf{vd}(1+\sigma)=1, \qquad (5.3.8)$$

with which we had earlier (in Section 3) closed the 'Marxian-value system'. This amounts to expressing both the 'prices of production' and the 'Marxian values' in terms of the per-worker net product, as composed by the wage goods, specified in vector **d** – see (5.3.1). Thanks to (5.7.2), the price of each commodity is being expressed in terms of what we called the 'ideal', or 'complete', wage rate, a wage rate which – if realised – *could* purchase (i.e. *command*) a quantity of labour exactly equal to the labour embodied in it.

It necessarily follows that rates of surplus value and rates of profit can simultaneously be uniform in the whole economic system (this also implies surplus values equal to profits and 'value' equal to 'price of production' in each single industry) if and only if the 'organic composition of capital' is exactly the same in all industries.

By adding (5.7.2), as the equation defining the *numéraire*, into the equations system (5.4.1)–(5.4.4), and setting the rate of profit at its maximum, $\Pi^{(A+)}$, we obtain the new expression:

$$\mathbf{p} = \mathbf{v}[\mathbf{I} - \Pi^{(A+)}\mathbf{A}(\mathbf{I} - \mathbf{A})^{-1}]^{-1}\frac{1 + \Pi^{(A+)}}{1 + \sigma}, \tag{5.9.1}$$

where $\Pi^{(A+)}$ is the economically meaningful solution, for π, of the characteristic equation:

$$\det[\mathbf{I} - (1 + \pi)(\mathbf{A} + \mathbf{da}_n)] = 0, \tag{5.4.7 bis}$$

and σ is the solution of the algebraic equation:

$$\det[\mathbf{I} - \mathbf{A} - (1 + \sigma)\mathbf{da}_n] = 0. \tag{5.3.9}$$

Expression (5.9.1) now gives us explicitly the linear operator which we have been looking for – and hence an explicit solution to the Marxian problem of 'transformation of values into prices of production'. The matrix

$$[\mathbf{I} - \Pi^{(A+)}\mathbf{A}(\mathbf{I} - \mathbf{A})^{-1}]^{-1}\frac{1 + \Pi^{(A+)}}{1 + \sigma}, \tag{5.9.2}$$

emerges as the linear operator which transforms the 'values' $\mathbf{v}$ into the 'prices of production' $\mathbf{p}$, both being expressed in terms of the same 'complete' real wage rate $\mathbf{d}(1 + \sigma)$, or per-worker net product, fixed in terms of the composite wage good. This being a one-to-one transformation, the inverse of the matrix in Solution 5.9.2, that is,

$$[\mathbf{I} - \Pi^{(A+)}\mathbf{A}(\mathbf{I} - \mathbf{A})^{-1}]\frac{1 + \sigma}{1 + \Pi^{(A+)}}, \tag{5.9.3}$$

is the linear operator which effects the inverse transformation of the 'prices of production', $\mathbf{p}$, into the 'Marxian values' $\mathbf{v}$.

There is another (alternative) way of looking at the same 'transformation', which is generally considered to be more congenial to Marxian economists. It consists in keeping (5.3.8) as the *numéraire* of the 'Marxian-value system', but adopting, as *numéraire* of the price system, not the 'ideal', or 'complete', wage, but the wage rate which is actually paid; a procedure frequently used also by us in Chapter 4. If, in the price system, we set:

$$w = \mathbf{pd} = 1, \tag{5.9.4}$$

(instead of (5.7.2)), all prices come to be expressed in terms of the quantity of labour which any particular commodity can purchase in the economic system (i.e. in terms of 'labour commanded'). Relation (5.4.1) in this case becomes:

$$\mathbf{pA}(1+\pi)+\mathbf{a}_n(1+\pi)=\mathbf{p}, \tag{5.9.5}$$

and can be rewritten in the following ways:

$$\mathbf{p}(\mathbf{I}-\mathbf{A})=\pi\mathbf{pA}+(1+\pi)\mathbf{a}_n,$$
$$\mathbf{p}=\pi\mathbf{pA}(\mathbf{I}-\mathbf{A})^{-1}+(1+\pi)\mathbf{a}_n(\mathbf{I}-\mathbf{A})^{-1},$$

$$\mathbf{p}[\mathbf{I}-\pi\mathbf{A}(\mathbf{I}-\mathbf{A})^{-1}]=(1+\pi)\mathbf{a}_n(\mathbf{I}-\mathbf{A})^{-1}. \tag{5.9.6}$$

As may be seen from (5.2.5), the right side of (5.9.6) is simply $(1+\pi)\mathbf{v}$, so that (5.9.6) can be rewritten as

$$\mathbf{p}=\mathbf{v}[\mathbf{I}-\pi\mathbf{A}(\mathbf{I}-\mathbf{A})^{-1}]^{-1}(1+\pi). \tag{5.9.7}$$

Again our 'transformation' problem is solved. The matrix

$$[\mathbf{I}-\pi\mathbf{A}(\mathbf{I}-\mathbf{A})^{-1}]^{-1}(1+\pi),$$

emerges, in (5.9.7), as the linear operator which transforms the 'Marxian values' $\mathbf{v}$ into the 'prices of production' $\mathbf{p}$. Again, of course, in the present context, $\pi = \Pi^{(A+)}$, where $\Pi^{(A+)}$ denotes the economically meaningful solution of the characteristic equation (5.4.7 bis).

What are the different implications – we may ask – of these two *numéraires*, which may alternatively be chosen for the same 'prices-of-production system'?

In (5.9.7), as may be verified by inspection, the 'prices of production' will *always* turn out to be greater than the corresponding 'values', except in the limiting case in which $\pi = 0$, and thus $\mathbf{p} = \mathbf{v}$. The reason for this is that, whereas the 'Marxian values' are by definition expressed in terms of 'embodied labour', the 'prices of production' are expressed here – owing to (5.9.4) – in terms of 'labour commanded'. These two types of quantities of labour only coincide in the limiting case in which the rate of profit is zero. But, as long as the rate of profit is positive, each commodity will be able to purchase, in the economic system, a quantity of labour ('labour commanded') which is greater than the quantity of labour embodied in it.[22] This may also explain

[22] Whereas 'labour embodied' is physically determined by the technique of production, the amount of labour which any commodity can 'command' varies with the level of the rate of profit (it increases as the rate of profit increases or – which is the same – as the *real* wage rate decreases). This can be seen from 5.9.7 where, owing to $\mathbf{A}$ and $(\mathbf{I}-\mathbf{A})^{-1}$ and consequently to

why this way of fixing the *numéraire* is generally the one considered by Marxian economists: it evinces explicitly the gap between each 'price' and its labour content, owing to the presence of a profit component, which obviously disappears only when the profit rate is squeezed to zero. Analytically, this procedure has the drawback of having the 'Marxian values' and the 'prices of production' expressed in terms of two different kinds of quantities of labour and therefore of not making immediate the comparison between the two (having to be made via the relation between 'labour commanded' and 'labour embodied').

This drawback is avoided by the first *numéraire*, which relies on exactly the same physical (composite) commodity for both 'Marxian values' and 'prices of production'. By contrast with (5.9.7), prices (5.9.1) are not, unilaterally, greater than the corresponding 'values'. Some prices, as we have seen, will prove to be greater than, while others will prove to be smaller than, the corresponding 'values', the borderline case being provided by the composite commodity $\mathbf{d}(1+\sigma)$, which, *ex-hypothesis*, has been set with both its 'price' and its 'value' equal to unity.

10 Price System and Rate of Surplus Value (after Sraffa)

Expressions (5.9.1) and (5.9.7) are worth being looked into more carefully and closely. Many of their properties are by now well known to us.

In the particular case in which the rate of profit (and thus the rate of surplus value) is zero, prices (5.9.1) and prices (5.9.7) coincide with each other. Moreover, both of them coincide with 'Marxian values' (5.2.5). Yet, as soon as the rate of profit is positive (i.e. $\pi > 0$ and thus also $\sigma > 0$), they all become different from one another. 'Prices' and 'values' will in general differ in a very complicated way, as we have seen. On the other hand, within the price system, the two alternative formulations (5.9.1) and (5.9.7) – since they express exactly the same

$\mathbf{A}(\mathbf{I}-\mathbf{A})^{-1}$ all being non-negative matrices – each of the non-zero elements of the inverse matrix within square brackets increases as π increases (see also Pasinetti 1977a, pp. 272, 275). All prices are therefore an increasing, monotonic function of π.

It may also be of interest to point out that the columns of matrix $\mathbf{A}(\mathbf{I}-\mathbf{A})^{-1}$ have a well-defined economic meaning. They represent the vertically integrated units of productive capacity. See Pasinetti (1973).

relative prices (the same price structure), their only difference being the different chosen *numéraire*- will obviously differ only by a scalar multiple. The interesting thing to note is that this scalar multiple (by which they differ) happens to be $(1+\sigma)$, that is, the same scalar multiple by which 'necessary labour' differs from total labour (i.e. the sum of 'necessary labour' plus 'surplus labour').[23] This circumstance carries a crucial consequence.

Prices (5.9.7), by being in terms of the actual wage rate, represent 'labour commanded' as we know. Prices (5.9.1), on the other hand, are in terms of the 'ideal' wage rate, which coincides with the per-worker net product. From the way we have constructed prices (5.9.1), the assumption underlying their *numéraire* is that of a composition equal to that of the actual wage. Considered singly, these prices do not, of course, represent labour embodied in the corresponding commodities (for, by definition, it is the 'Marxian values' that represent labour embodied). However, we know that, in the aggregate, the amount of labour embodied in the *total* net product of an economic system is always the same, irrespective of its composition. This allows us to start directly from expression (5.7.2), defining the *numéraire*, which, for prices (5.9.1), implies the remarkable relation:

$$w(1+\sigma) = w^* = 1, \tag{5.10.1}$$

or

$$\sigma = \frac{1}{w} - 1. \tag{5.10.2}$$

Notice now that this expression reproduces exactly the same relation between σ and δ given by (5.3.5), that is, a relation in terms of physical quantities of embodied labour, although w is here the wage rate that emerges from the 'prices-of-production system'. In other words, the particular *numéraire* (5.7.2) is allowing us, in this context, to obtain the relation between rate of surplus value and labour embodied in the real wage (or 'necessary labour') by simply using the wage rate as it emerges from the 'prices-of-production system'. In this price system, w and δ have become interchangeable, precisely as they are in Sraffa's standard system (see Section 6, p. 181.) But the crucial difference, with respect to the Sraffa case (and the analysis of Section 6), is that in

[23] See p. 174.

Sraffa's it was necessary to assume a real wage $\mathbf{d}^*$ having the same composition as the standard commodity. Nothing of this sort is required here. Expression (5.10.2) is a relation which is valid in general. How can this be?

What generates this remarkable result is that the rate of surplus value is in terms of labour. As may now be realised, it does not therefore depend on the composition of that part of the net product that goes to the capitalists. It only depends on the physical composition and on the magnitude of the real wage. This is what confers upon the composite commodity (5.3.1), that is, on the actual real wage, a relevance that goes beyond and has nothing to do with the circumstance of whether it is or it is not an 'average' commodity.[24] Relation (5.10.2) does indeed hold for the general case![25]

To conclude, in any actual economic system (and not only in an economic system in which the net product is all expended on wage goods), it is the particular composition of the real wage – kept constant in the process of blowing it up to the point of absorbing the whole net product – that confers on the per-worker *net product* the property, if used as the *numéraire* of the price system, to make the wage rate w acquire the meaning of fraction of 'necessary labour' out of total labour. This was denoted by δ in Section 3, but here we have a context in which it coincides with w. It follows that, in such a price system, the rate of surplus value (or 'rate of exploitation', in Marxian terminology) can be obtained directly from the 'prices-of-production system' as the reciprocal of the wage rate minus one, as is revealed by expression (5.10.2).

The analytical importance of this result needs hardly be stressed. Quite apart from the disputes about inequalities (5.5.3)–(5.5.5) that raged through the literature on Marxian economics, our upshot is that the rate of surplus value is already and quite clearly contained in the system of the 'prices of production' of a capitalist economy (intended as an economy in which total profits are distributed in proportion to the amount of total capital evaluated at the current 'prices of

[24] Marx obviously sensed the importance of the wage commodity in value-price relations but did so only intuitively. See footnote 18 on p. 188.

[25] To be more specific, just in the same way as in Sraffa's case (5.10.2) depends on the wage rate being of exactly the standard composition $\mathbf{d}^*$, here too the same relation depends on the wage rate being of the composition of vector $\mathbf{d}$. However, here it is precisely the composition of vector $\mathbf{d}$ that determines the magnitude of the rate of surplus.

production'). The only requirement to see this explicitly is that the price system be expressed in terms of the per-capita net product, or 'complete' wage rate, obtained by blowing up – but keeping its composition constant – the actual wage rate to absorb the whole per-worker net product, which in this way is capturing the relation between total labour and 'necessary' labour. The crucial analytical point is that the composition of the commodities on which profits are expended is irrelevant to obtain the basic relation (5.10.2), which is framed in terms of physical labour.

Notice that, to obtain this relation, it is not even necessary to compute the 'Marxian-value system'. The rate of surplus value σ emerges from the relation (5.10.2) directly from the wage rate w, which emerges as having a physical meaning, and yet entering the 'prices-of-production system'.

11 Concluding Remarks

The analysis allows us to conclude that the Marxian problem of the 'transformation of values into prices of production', which has generated so much controversy in the economic literature, is expressed, in analytical terms, by an algebraic operation of linear transformation. A certain vector, representing the 'values', is transformed into another vector, representing the 'prices of production', on being multiplied by a matrix which represents the logical process of solving a system of equations. And the inverse of this matrix effects the opposite transformation of 'prices of production' into 'values'. There is therefore a one-to-one correspondence between Marxian 'values' and 'prices of production'. This is a conclusion which should no longer be open to dispute.

Discussions of course are bound to continue over the interpretation and most of all the *social meaning* of such 'transformations'.

In Marx's conception, the 'transformation of values into prices of production' is not merely an analytical, algebraic operation; it also reflects a real historical process. In his conviction, it is the system of 'values' which correctly represents the relations between the people taking part into the productive process.[26] The system of prices of

[26] In Marx's own words: '. . . it is quite appropriate to regard the values of commodities as not only theoretically but also historically *prius* to the prices of production' (Marx 1959, p. 177).

production by contrast is conceived as an institutional superstructure imposed by the *capitalist* societies, which *distorts* the original genuine exchange ratios and makes them conform to the capitalists' own inner (institutional) need of rendering the rates of profit uniform all over the economic system.

Most critics of Marx reject this interpretation in favour of the following opposing view. They consider Marxian accounting in terms of 'values' as a useless duplication of market accounting in terms of prices. The point which is stressed is that, *on a strictly analytical ground*, there is no justification for giving logical priority to either 'values' over prices or to prices over 'values'. It is by now accepted that each of them can be derived from the other and both of them can be obtained from the inter-industry relations expressed in terms of physical quantities of commodities. But the argument which is generally taken as conclusive by them is that, of the two systems of exchange ratios, the only one which can be observed empirically is the system of prices. The 'value' system is invisible in practice and is therefore regarded by them as something which, so to speak, belongs to Marxist ideology and is deprived of empirical evidence.

However, we may simply add, at this point, that these arguments would seem to have been substantially weakened by the results of Section 10, where it is shown that the surplus value can be directly obtained from the prices of production, subject only to an accounting operation of relying on a particular *numéraire* of the price system (and we know that the choice of the *numéraire* is arbitrary).

For us, at this stage of our analysis, the most appropriate attitude seems to be that of avoiding taking any definite stand on this type of controversy and waiting until we have completed our investigations concerning the more substantial problem of the relations that become relevant between the 'natural' economic system and the *institutional* framework of the kind of society that we want to investigate.

6 *The Notion of Vertical Integration in Economic Analysis*

1 Introduction

Very few notions in economic analysis are so seldom explicitly mentioned as the notion of vertical integration and are at the same time so widely used, implicitly or without awareness.[1] I came to this conviction during the discussions on a multi-sector model of economic growth which I presented in Pasinetti (1965). The synthetic notion of a 'vertically integrated sector' is used explicitly in that model, but within a simplified context, and I have always been faced with questions.[2]

An explicit and more general investigation of the meaning and relevance of vertical integration in economic analysis may therefore prove of some usefulness. Instead of starting from the synthetic notions and going back to their elementary components, I shall start here from these elementary components – that is, from the now familiar schemes of inter-industry analysis – and go on to the synthetic notions. The crucial role played by vertical integration in the theories of value, income distribution and economic growth should emerge clearly as the

[1] The notion of vertical integration is implicit in all discussions on the theory of value of the Classical economists, and in fact, given its fundamental character, also of those marginalist economists who did perceive the importance of production. The same thing can be said of the marginalist economists. When, e.g., Léon Walras adopted the device of eliminating intermediate commodities from his analysis of production, he was making use of the logical process of vertical integration (Davar 2014, Walras 1874). Keynesian macroeconomic analysis is also generally carried out in terms of vertically integrated magnitudes (net national income, net savings, new investments, consumption and so on). Very rarely, however, is the logical process of vertical integration explicitly discussed. Generally it is simply taken for granted.

[2] These questions have normally been concerned with the problem of how to construct the vertically integrated Sectors in the general case. The indications given in Pasinetti (1965, ch. 6) are too brief and incomplete. Now the time has come to face them explicitly, which is what we are now beginning to do in this chapter.

investigation develops. The whole analysis will be carried out with reference to the general case of production of all commodities by means of commodities. [The simplified case of capital goods produced by means of labour alone will be shown at the end as a particular case.]

2 Production of Commodities by Means of Commodities

An economic system will be considered in which all commodities are produced by means of commodities, used as capital goods. Commodities enter the process of production at the beginning of each 'year' as inputs, jointly with labour services, and commodities come out at the end of the year as outputs. The economic system is supposed to be *viable*, in the sense that it is capable of producing larger quantities of commodities than those required to replace used-up capital goods.

The following notation will be used throughout.[3]

(i) Column vector $\mathbf{Q}(t) \equiv [Q_i(t)]$, $i = 1, 2, \ldots, m$, to denote the physical quantities of the m commodities that are produced in year t.

(ii) Column vector $\mathbf{Y}(t) \equiv [Y_i(t)]$, $i = 1, 2, \ldots, m$, to denote the net product of the economic system, that is, what is available for consumption and new investments after deducting replacements from $\mathbf{Q}(t)$. Of course, $\mathbf{Y}(t)$ may further be regarded as a sum of commodities devoted to consumption and of commodities devoted to investments, to be denoted by column vectors $\mathbf{C}(t) \equiv [C_i(t)]$ and $\mathbf{J}^{(d)}(t) \equiv [J_i^{(d)}(t)]$, $i = 1, 2, \ldots, m$, respectively. By definition, $\mathbf{C}(t) + \mathbf{J}^{(d)}(t) \equiv \mathbf{Y}(t)$.

(iii) Column vectors $\mathbf{S}(t) \equiv [S_i(t)]$, $i = 1, 2, \ldots, m$, to denote the physical quantities of commodities that are required as capital goods (capital stocks), at the beginning of year t, in order to obtain quantities $\mathbf{Q}(t)$ at the end of year t.

(iv) Row vector $\mathbf{p}(t) \equiv [p_i(t)]$, $i = 1, 2, \ldots, m$, to denote prices of commodities $i = 1, 2, \ldots, m$.

(v) Scalar $L(t)$, to denote the labour force required by the economic system in year t, measured, let us say, in men years.

[3] Symbol $\equiv$ will be used to denote a definitional equality and, in particular, as in all cases in this chapter, an equality of two different notations for the same thing.

(vi) Scalar π, to denote the (uniform) rate of profit.
(vii) Scalar $w(t)$, to denote the (uniform) wage rate.

As far as technology is concerned, two successive analytical stages will be taken – a procedure which is by now customary in this type of analysis. Usually, as is well known, one begins by considering, first, production with circulating capital goods; then one goes on to production with fixed capital goods. The advantage of this procedure is that almost all basic concepts can be singled out at the first stage, where relatively few analytical complications arise. The second stage can then be devoted to pointing out which conclusions still hold and which conclusions are affected by generalisation. A slightly more general approach is taken in the present work. Fixed capital goods are introduced immediately at the first stage, but with a simplifying assumption on how they depreciate. The case of production with fixed capital goods in general will, of course, be considered as a second stage.

3 Fixed Capital Goods with a Simplifying Assumption

We shall begin by considering a technology which requires both circulating capital goods (which are used up within one year) and fixed capital goods (which last for more than one year). The simplifying assumption will be made that in each industry j a constant proportion δ_j of all fixed capital goods drops out of the production process each year ($j = 1, 2, \ldots, m$). Moreover, for the time being, all technical coefficients will be supposed to be constant through time.

The technique of the whole economic system will be represented by

(i) a row vector $\mathbf{a}_n = [a_{nj}]$, $n = m + 1$, $j = 1, 2, \ldots, m$, all $a_{nj} \geq 0$, where each a_{nj} denotes the annual input of labour required by one physical unit of the commodity produced in industry j;
(ii) a square matrix $\mathbf{A} \equiv [a_{ij}]$; $i, j = 1, 2, \ldots, m$, all $a_{ij} \geq 0$, in which each column j represents the physical stocks of capital goods (both circulating and fixed) required for the production of one physical unit of the commodity produced in industry j. Square matrix $\mathbf{A}$ may be regarded as the sum of two non-negative square matrices: $\mathbf{A}^{(C)} \equiv [a_{ij}^{(C)}]$ and $\mathbf{A}^{(F)} \equiv [a_{ij}^{(F)}]$; $i, j = 1, 2, \ldots, m$, as representing the stocks of circulating capital goods and the stocks of fixed capital goods, respectively. Therefore, $\mathbf{A} \equiv \mathbf{A}^{(C)} + \mathbf{A}^{(F)}$, by definition. Of course, each year in each industry j, the economic system has

to replace all circulating capital goods and a fraction δ_j of the fixed capital goods; $j = 1, 2, \ldots, m$. If we call $\hat{\boldsymbol{\delta}}$ a diagonal matrix with all the δ_js on the main diagonal, we may therefore define another square matrix $\mathbf{A}^{\ominus} \equiv [a_{ij}^{\ominus}] \equiv \mathbf{A}^{(C)} + \mathbf{A}^{(F)}\hat{\delta}$, as representing that part of the initial stocks of capital goods that are actually used up each year by the production process. By definition, $\mathbf{A}^{\ominus} + \mathbf{A}^{(F)}(\mathbf{I} - \hat{\delta}) \equiv \mathbf{A}$. The particular case in which all capital goods are circulating capital goods is represented by $\mathbf{A}^{(F)} = \mathbf{O}$, where $\mathbf{O}$ is the zero matrix, and, therefore, $\mathbf{A}^{\ominus} = \mathbf{A}$.

With this notation, the physical economic system may be represented by the following system of equations:

$$(\mathbf{I} - \mathbf{A}^{\ominus})\mathbf{Q}(t) = \mathbf{Y}(t), \qquad (6.3.1)$$

$$\mathbf{a}_n\mathbf{Q}(t) = L(t), \qquad (6.3.2)$$

$$\mathbf{A}\mathbf{Q}(t) = \mathbf{S}(t), \qquad (6.3.3)$$

where (6.3.1) and (6.3.2) represent the flow of commodities and labour services required in year t to produce net product $\mathbf{Y}(t)$, and (6.3.3) represents the stocks of capital goods required at the beginning of year t for production to be effected. At the same time, equilibrium prices are represented by the following system of equations:

$$\mathbf{p} = \mathbf{a}_n w + \mathbf{p}\mathbf{A}^{\ominus} + \mathbf{p}\mathbf{A}\pi, \qquad (6.3.4)$$

which determines all prices if one of these and the wage rate (or alternatively the rate of profit) are fixed exogenously.

4 An 'Industry'

On the assumption just made concerning fixed capital goods, each industry j ($j = 1, 2, \ldots, m$) produces only one good: commodity j; and in order to produce one physical unit of such a commodity, it needs a quantity of labour represented by the jth coefficient of vector $\mathbf{a}_n$ and a series of heterogeneous stocks of capital goods, represented by the jth column of matrix $\mathbf{A}$. Industry j may therefore be synthetically represented by a 'direct labour coefficient, – the jth component of vector $\mathbf{a}_n$ – and by what may be called a 'unit of direct productive capacity' – a composite commodity defined by the jth column of matrix $\mathbf{A}$.

In equations (6.3.1–6.3.3), the physical quantities of an economic system are classified precisely in this way, that is, according to the criterion of the 'industry'. This classification has the advantage of being immediately observable, but it maintains our attention at a rather superficial level. A reclassification of the same physical quantities may be obtained on the basis of a conceptually more complex, but analytically far more powerful, criterion, which we shall now consider.

5 A 'Vertically Integrated Sector'

We may define a new vector $\mathbf{Y}_i(t)$ as a column vector the components of which are all zeros except the *i*th one, defined here as $Y_i(t)$ – that is, the *i*th component of vector $\mathbf{Y}(t)$. Moreover, we shall use scalar $L^{(i)}(t)$ to denote the quantity of labour required, column vector $\mathbf{Q}^{(i)}(t)$ to denote the physical quantities of commodities to be produced, and column vector $\mathbf{S}^{(i)}(t)$ to denote the stocks of capital goods required, in the whole economic system, in order to obtain physical quantity $Y_i(t)$ of final good i $(i = 1, 2, \ldots, m)$.

For each particular net product $Y_i(t)$, we obtain from (6.3.1) to (6.3.3)

$$\mathbf{Q}^{(i)}(t) = (\mathbf{I} - \mathbf{A}^{\ominus})^{-1}\mathbf{Y}_i(t), \tag{6.5.1}$$

$$L^{(i)}(t) = \mathbf{a}_n(\mathbf{I} - \mathbf{A}^{\ominus})^{-1}\mathbf{Y}_i(t), \tag{6.5.2}$$

$$\mathbf{S}^{(i)}(t) = \mathbf{A}(\mathbf{I} - \mathbf{A}^{\ominus})^{-1}\mathbf{Y}_i(t), \qquad i = 1, 2, \ldots, m, \tag{6.5.3}$$

that is, in fact, m sub-systems (as Piero Sraffa has called them, Sraffa (1960, p. 89)). From 6.5.1 to 6.5.3 and the definition of $\mathbf{Y}_i(t)$ it follows that

$$\sum_i^m \mathbf{Y}_i(t) = \mathbf{Y}(t), \qquad \sum_i^m \mathbf{Q}^{(i)}(t) = \mathbf{Q}(t), \tag{6.5.4}$$

$$\sum_i^m \mathbf{L}^{(i)}(t) = L(t), \qquad \sum_i^m \mathbf{S}^{(i)}(t) = \mathbf{S}(t). \tag{6.5.5}$$

The m sub-systems add up to the original complete economic system.

The economic meaning of the coefficients appearing on the right-hand side of (6.5.1) had been widely illustrated in the economic literature. Matrix $(\mathbf{I} - \mathbf{A}^{\ominus})^{-1}$ is known as the Leontief inverse matrix; after Leontief (1951), its *i*th column $(i = 1, 2, \ldots, m)$ contains the series of heterogeneous commodities that are directly and indirectly required in the whole economic system to obtain one physical unit of commodity i as a final good. On the other hand, less attention has been paid to the economic meaning of the coefficients that appear on the right-hand side of (6.5.2) and (6.5.3). (It is again Leontief (1953b, 1956), who first applied these concepts.) More synthetically, we may define,

$$\mathbf{a}_n(\mathbf{I} - \mathbf{A}^{\ominus})^{-1} \equiv \mathbf{v} \equiv [v_i], \tag{6.5.6}$$

$$\mathbf{A}(\mathbf{I} - \mathbf{A}^{\ominus})^{-1} \equiv \mathbf{H} \equiv [\mathbf{h}_i], \qquad i = 1, 2, \ldots, m, \tag{6.5.7}$$

where each $\mathbf{h}_i$ is a column vector, and thus rewrite (6.5.2) and (6.5.3) in a more compact way:

$$L^{(i)}(t) = \mathbf{v}\mathbf{Y}_i(t) \equiv v_i Y_i, \tag{6.5.2a}$$

$$\mathbf{S}^{(i)}(t) = \mathbf{H}\mathbf{Y}_i(t) \equiv \mathbf{h}_i Y_i, \qquad i = 1, 2, \ldots, m. \tag{6.5.3a}$$

Each coefficient v_i in (6.5.3a) expresses in a consolidated way the quantity of labour directly and indirectly required in the whole economic system to obtain one physical unit of commodity i as a final good. We shall call it the *vertically integrated labour coefficient* for commodity i ($i = 1, 2, \ldots, m$). Likewise, each column vector $\mathbf{h}_i$ in (6.5.3a) expresses in a consolidated way the series of heterogeneous physical quantities of commodities $1, 2, \ldots, m$ which are directly and indirectly required as stocks, in the whole economic system, in order to obtain one physical unit of commodity i as a final good ($i = 1, 2, \ldots, m$). This is another particular composite commodity, which we shall call *a unit of vertically integrated productive capacity* for commodity i ($i = 1, 2, \ldots, m$).

Scalar v_i and column vector $\mathbf{h}_i$, together, represent what we may call the *vertically integrated sector* for the production of commodity i as a final good (whether for consumption or for investment); $i = 1, 2, \ldots, m - 1$. A vertically integrated sector is therefore a compact way of representing a sub-system, as it synthesises each sub-system into a single labour coefficient v_i and a single composite commodity $\mathbf{h}_i$. For an economic system with m commodities, we obviously obtain m labour coefficients (the m components of row vector $\mathbf{v}$) and m units of productive capacity (the m columns of matrix $\mathbf{H}$), that is, m vertically integrated Sectors for the production of the m commodities as final goods.

In comparison with Section 4, we may say that vector $\mathbf{a}_n$ and matrix $\mathbf{A}$ classify the total quantity of labour $L(t)$ and total quantities of stocks of capital goods $\mathbf{S}(t)$ according to the criterion of the industry in which they are required:

$$L(t) = \mathbf{a}_n\mathbf{Q}(t), \qquad \mathbf{S}(t) = \mathbf{A}\mathbf{Q}(t). \tag{6.5.8}$$

All these quantities are directly observable and directly quantifiable. Vector $\mathbf{v}$ and matrix $\mathbf{H}$ reclassify the same physical quantities according to the criterion of the vertically integrated sector for which they are directly and indirectly required:

$$L^{(i)}(t) = \mathbf{a}_n(\mathbf{I} - \mathbf{A}^{\ominus})^{-1}\mathbf{Y}_i(t) = \mathbf{v}\mathbf{Y}_i(t), \qquad (6.5.2b)$$

$$\mathbf{S}^{(i)}(t) = \mathbf{A}(\mathbf{I} - \mathbf{A}^{\ominus})^{-1}\mathbf{Y}_i(t) = \mathbf{H}\mathbf{Y}_i(t), \qquad i = 1, 2, \ldots, m, \qquad (6.5.3b)$$

$$L(t) = \sum_i^m L^{(i)}(t), \qquad \mathbf{S}(t) = \sum_i^m \mathbf{S}^{(i)}(t). \qquad (6.5.9)$$

Neither $\mathbf{v}$ nor $\mathbf{H}$ is directly observable, but they can be obtained through post-multiplication by $(\mathbf{I} - \mathbf{A}^{\ominus})^{-1}$ from quantities $\mathbf{a}_n$ and $\mathbf{A}$, which are directly observable. They are therefore quantifiable in an indirect way.

To conclude, precisely the same physical quantities $L(t)$ and $\mathbf{S}(t)$ appear in both (6.5.8) and (6.5.9), but they are classified according to two different criteria – the more immediate criterion of the 'industry' in the former and the conceptually more complex criterion of the 'vertically integrated sector' in the latter. Both classifications are empirically quantifiable – the former directly and the latter through the indirect logical process of vertical integration.

6 Vertical Integration in the Theory of Value and Income Distribution

When Adam Smith (1904, pp. 49 and 52) put forward the proposition that every commodity finally resolves itself into wages, profits and rents, he rightly sensed that he had reached an important conclusion: he had (implicitly) grasped the basic concept of vertical integration.

In our analysis, neither the price system written in Section 3 on the basis of directly observable magnitudes

$$\mathbf{p} = \mathbf{a}_n w + \mathbf{p}\mathbf{A}^{\ominus} + \mathbf{p}\mathbf{A}\pi, \qquad (6.3.4)$$

nor what may be called its 'solution'

$$\mathbf{p} = \mathbf{a}_n(\mathbf{I} - \mathbf{A}^{\ominus} - \mathbf{A}\pi)^{-1}w, \qquad (6.6.1)$$

can give us a clear idea of Adam Smith's theoretical insight.

But if we perform a few logical operations and rewrite (6.3.4) as

$$\mathbf{p}(\mathbf{I} - \mathbf{A}^{\ominus}) = \mathbf{a}_n w + \mathbf{p}\mathbf{A}\pi, \qquad (6.6.2)$$

$$\mathbf{p} = \mathbf{a}_n(\mathbf{I} - \mathbf{A}^{\ominus})^{-1}w + \mathbf{p}\mathbf{A}(\mathbf{I} - \mathbf{A}^{\ominus})^{-1}\pi, \qquad (6.6.3)$$

we can see the two notions characterising a vertically integrated sector reappear. After substitution from definitions (6.5.6) and (6.5.7), (6.6.3) may be written

$$\mathbf{p} = \mathbf{v}w + \mathbf{pH}\pi. \tag{6.6.4}$$

This is a remarkable expression, as it explicitly shows that each price is ultimately made up of only two components: wages and profits.[4] It is precisely the logical operation of vertical integration that makes this evident, by consolidating the complex intermediate stages into one single labour coefficient and one single unit of productive capacity – the former being multiplied by the wage rate, and the latter (after being evaluated at the current prices) by the rate of profit. It may be noticed that vector **pH** is nothing but a vector of the m vertically integrated capital/output ratios evaluated at the prices of the commodities of which they are made up. Hence, one alternative way of representing the m vertically integrated Sectors might be that of using vector **v** (the m vertically integrated labour coefficients) and vector **pH** (the m vertically integrated capital-per-unit-of-output ratios).[5]

Another property of (6.6.4) is that it exposes the antagonism of wages and profits in income distribution. When $\pi = 0$, the second addendum vanishes and prices become

$$\mathbf{p} = \mathbf{v}w. \tag{6.6.5}$$

Wages are obviously at their maximum, as they absorb the whole purchasing power deriving from prices.

Conversely, when $w = 0$, profits are at their maximum, and (6.6.4) becomes a linear and homogeneous system of equations

$$\mathbf{p}(\mathbf{I} - \Pi\mathbf{H}) = 0, \tag{6.6.6}$$

where Π stands for the rate of profit corresponding to $w = 0$, or maximum rate of profit. Since the economic system is viable *ex-hypothesis*, Π must be positive. Maximum rate of profit Π also emerges, from (6.6.6), as the reciprocal of the eigenvalues – which we may call λ – of matrix **H**. Non-trivial solutions require, of course,

$$\det(\lambda\mathbf{I} - \mathbf{H}) = 0, \tag{6.6.7}$$

4 No rents are considered in the present scheme.

5 This is in fact the way suggested in Pasinetti (1965, ch. 6), where the procedure to obtain them is also given (multiplication of direct labour coefficients and direct capital/output ratios by the inverse Leontief matrix).

an algebraic equation that yields m roots for λ. However, since $\mathbf{H}$ is a non-negative matrix,[6] we know on the basis of the Perron–Frobenius theorem that its maximum eigenvalue, λ_{max}, (i) is a real and positive number; (ii) has a non-negative eigenvector; and (iii) is also the eigenvalue which is maximum in modulus (i.e. $\lambda_{max} = |\lambda|_{max}$). This is the only root of (6.6.7) that is economically relevant[7] and we shall therefore straight away define

$$\Pi = \frac{1}{\lambda_{max}}. \tag{6.6.8}$$

For any positive π lower than Π, we also know on the basis of the Perron–Frobenius theorem that $(\mathbf{I} - \pi\mathbf{H})^{-1}$ is non-negative, so that the general solution of (6.6.4),

$$\mathbf{p} = \mathbf{v}(\mathbf{I} - \pi\mathbf{H})^{-1}w, \tag{6.6.9}$$

yields non-negative prices and an inverse monotonic relation between π and w, whatever the standard in terms of which w is measured.[8]

The same problems may be looked at in a more 'classical' way if the wage rate itself is used as the *numéraire* of the price system, that is, if we put $w = 1$, In this case, all prices come to be expressed in terms of the wage rate, that is, in terms of 'labour commanded'. But the components of $\mathbf{v}$, the vertically integrated labour coefficients, express what classical economists called 'labour embodied' (and Marx simply called 'values'). Therefore, wages – by being distributed in proportion to 'labour embodied', as appears from (6.6.4) – can 'command' only part of the purchasing power deriving from prices. The difference

$$\mathbf{p} - \mathbf{v} = \mathbf{pH}\pi \tag{6.6.10}$$

is absorbed by profits. 'Solution' (6.6.9) becomes

$$\mathbf{p} = \mathbf{v}(\mathbf{I} - \pi\mathbf{H})^{-1} \tag{6.6.11}$$

[6] Both $\mathbf{A}^{\ominus}$ and $\mathbf{A}$ are non-negative *ex-hypothesis*; and, moreover, the technique is supposed to be viable, which implies that $(\mathbf{I} - \mathbf{A}^{\ominus})^{-1}$ is non-negative. It follows that $\mathbf{H}$ is also non-negative.

[7] The assumption is made, following Sraffa, that the internal rate of reproduction of non-basic commodities (if there are any) is higher than the internal rate of reproduction of basic commodities.

[8] Since no price can become negative in terms of *any* standard (within the interval, $0 \leq \pi \leq \Pi$), no price can fall faster than w as π is increased. It follows that π and w (in terms of *any* standard) must be inversely and monotonically related to each other. See the detailed proof given by Sraffa (1960, pp. 39–40).

and may also be regarded as expressing the 'transformation' of $\mathbf{v}$ into $\mathbf{p}$, that is, of Marxian values into prices. The linear operator $(\mathbf{I}-\pi\mathbf{H})^{-1}$, where the m units of vertically integrated productive capacity are shown to play a crucial role, represents such 'transformation' in logical terms. Only when $\pi = 0$ does 'labour commanded' become equal to classical 'labour embodied' (and prices to Marxian values), that is,

$$\mathbf{p} = \mathbf{v}, \tag{6.6.12}$$

while matrix $\mathbf{H}$ drops out the picture altogether.

7 A Newly Discovered Unit of Measurement of Capital Goods (Vertically Integrated Productive Capacity)

We may go back to the physical quantity system. So far in this analysis, all commodities have been measured in terms of the physical units that are commonly used to measure them (e.g. tonnes, bushels, numbers etc.). But expressions (6.5.7) and (6.5.3a) suggest the possibility of an alternative physical unit of measurement of capital goods. More precisely, they suggest the possibility of measuring capital goods in terms of a particular composite commodity which we may call 'physical unit of vertically integrated productive capacity'.

There clearly exists one such physical unit for each final good that is produced. If there are m final goods, there exist m physical units of vertically integrated productive capacity, represented by the columns of matrix $\mathbf{H}$, that is, by

$$\mathbf{h}_i = \mathbf{A}(\mathbf{I} - \mathbf{A}^{\ominus})^{-1}\mathbf{e}_i, \qquad i = 1, 2, \ldots, m, \tag{6.7.1}$$

where $\mathbf{e}_i$ is the ith unit column vector.

For the purpose of our analysis, a composite commodity does not present any conceptual difficulty. (As a matter of fact, any commodity – for instance, a pair of shoes – can always be considered as composed of various elementary commodities – such as leather, strings, rubber – put together in fixed proportions.) Therefore, when such units are used, the existing stocks of capital goods may be represented by an m component column vector

$$\mathbf{K}(t) \equiv [K_j(t)], \qquad j = 1, 2, \ldots, m. \tag{6.7.2}$$

It follows by definition that, in equilibrium,

$$K_i(t) = Y_i(t), \qquad i = 1, 2, \ldots, m. \tag{6.7.3}$$

It is always possible to 'translate' capital goods expressed in terms of vertically integrated productive capacities into capital goods expressed in ordinary physical units by the transformation

$$\mathbf{S}(t) = \mathbf{H}\mathbf{K}(t). \tag{6.7.4}$$

Matrix $\mathbf{H}$ thereby appears as a linear operator which – when applied to a vector of physical quantities measured in terms of vertically integrated productive capacities – reclassifies them in terms of ordinary physical units. When $\mathbf{H}$ is a non-singular matrix, there even exists a unique inverse transformation

$$\mathbf{K}(t) = \mathbf{H}^{-1}\mathbf{S}(t). \tag{6.7.5}$$

But, of course, $\mathbf{H}^{-1}$ need not necessarily exist (i.e. there may be more than one way, or there may be no exhaustive way, of forming vertically integrated units of productive capacity from arbitrarily given existing stocks of ordinary capital goods).

8 Vertically Integrated Sectors for Investment Goods Expressed in Physical Units of Vertically Integrated Productive Capacity

When capital goods are measured in physical units of vertically integrated productive capacity, new investments (which are additions to the existing stocks of capital goods) must be measured in the same units. But new investments are considered to be final goods, and we know that it is possible to construct conceptually a vertically integrated sector in correspondence to each final good. Such a logical construction has been obtained in Section 5 for final goods measured in ordinary physical units. It now becomes possible to obtain similar logical constructions for investment goods measured in physical units of vertically integrated productive capacity.

We may denote by $\mathbf{J}^{(v)}(t) \equiv [J_i^{(v)}(t)]$, $i = 1, 2, \ldots, m$, the column vector of new investments measured in units of vertically integrated productive capacity for the corresponding final goods $1, 2, \ldots, m$; and by $\mathbf{J}_i^{(v)}(t), i = 1, 2, \ldots, m$, a column vector the components of which are all zeros excepting the ith one, which is equal to $J_i^{(v)}(t)$. Obviously, $\sum_i^m \mathbf{J}_i^v(t) = \mathbf{J}^{(v)}(t)$. It follows from (6.7.4) that $\mathbf{J}^{(v)}(t)$ – new investments expressed in physical units of vertically integrated productive capacity – and $\mathbf{J}^{(d)}(t)$ – new investments expressed in ordinary (direct) physical units – are related by

$$\mathbf{J}^{(d)}(t) = \mathbf{H}\mathbf{J}^{(v)}(t). \tag{6.8.1}$$

Similarly to what has been done in Section 5, we may denote by $L^{(k_i)}(t)$ the labour services and by $\mathbf{Q}^{(k_i)}(t)$ and $\mathbf{S}^{(k_i)}(t)$, respectively, the column vectors of the physical quantities produced and of the stocks of capital goods required, in the whole economic system, for the production of final good $\mathrm{J}_i^{(v)}(t)$. Of course, $i = 1, 2, \ldots, m$.

For each physical quantity $\mathrm{J}_i^{(v)}(t)$, we may now write the corresponding sub-system,

$$\mathbf{Q}^{(k_i)}(t) = (\mathbf{I} - \mathbf{A}^{\ominus})^{-1}\mathbf{H}\mathrm{J}_i^{(v)}(t), \tag{6.8.2}$$

from which, after substitution into (6.3.2) and (6.3.3), we obtain

$$L^{(k_i)}(t) = \mathbf{a}_n(\mathbf{I} - \mathbf{A}^{\ominus})^{-1}\mathbf{H}\mathrm{J}_i^{(v)}(t) \equiv \mathbf{v}\mathbf{H}\mathrm{J}_i^{(v)}(t), \tag{6.8.3}$$

$$\mathbf{S}^{(k_i)}(t) = \mathbf{A}(\mathbf{I} - \mathbf{A}^{\ominus})^{-1}\mathbf{H}\mathrm{J}_i^{(v)}(t) \equiv \mathbf{H}^2\mathrm{J}_i^{(v)}(t), \qquad i = 1, 2, \ldots, m. \tag{6.8.4}$$

Here again scalar $L^{(k_i)}(t)$ is the quantity of labour and vector $\mathbf{S}^{(k_i)}(t)$ is the series of stocks of capital goods directly and indirectly required in the whole economic system in order to produce quantity $J_i^{(v)}(t)$ of the investment good (measured in units of vertically integrated productive capacity) required for final good i. Therefore vector $\mathbf{vH}$ in (6.8.3), which we may call $\mathbf{v}_k$, that is,

$$\mathbf{v}_k \equiv \mathbf{v}\mathbf{H} \equiv \mathbf{a}_n(\mathbf{I} - \mathbf{A}^{\ominus})^{-1}\mathbf{A}(\mathbf{I} - \mathbf{A}^{\ominus})^{-1}, \tag{6.8.5}$$

is a vector of vertically integrated labour coefficients and matrix

$$\mathbf{H}^2 \equiv \mathbf{A}(\mathbf{I} - \mathbf{A}^{\ominus})^{-1}\mathbf{H} \equiv \mathbf{A}(\mathbf{I} - \mathbf{A}^{\ominus})^{-1}\mathbf{A}(\mathbf{I} - \mathbf{A}^{\ominus})^{-1}, \tag{6.8.6}$$

in (6.8.4) is a matrix the columns of which represent units of vertically integrated productive capacity. Vector $\mathbf{v}_k$ and matrix $\mathbf{H}^2$ together represent the m vertically integrated sectors for the m investment goods expressed in units of vertically integrated productive capacity. As was to be expected, the vertically integrated sectors for investment goods, expressed in physical units of vertically integrated productive capacity, have been obtained through a logical operation of vertical integration performed twice.

9 Prices of Investment Goods Expressed in Units of Vertically Integrated Productive Capacity

When investment goods are expressed in ordinary physical units, their prices are those found in Section 6 (i.e. the prices of the commodities of system (6.3.1)–(6.3.4), whether they are used for consumption or for investment). But, when investment goods are expressed in physical units of vertically integrated productive capacity, their prices – which we may denote by row vector $\mathbf{p}_k \equiv [p_{k_i}]$, $i = 1, 2, \ldots, m$ – are weighted average of the prices $\mathbf{p}$ of their elementary components, namely

$$\mathbf{p}_k = \mathbf{pH}. \qquad (6.9.1)$$

After substitution from (6.6.4) to (6.8.5), we obtain

$$\mathbf{p}_k = \mathbf{v}_k w + \mathbf{p}_k \mathbf{H}\pi. \qquad (6.9.2)$$

This is a new price system in which prices, instead of being referred to the m ordinary commodities as in system (6.6.4), are referred to m composite commodities obtained by reclassifying the m ordinary commodities of system (6.6.4) by the operation of vertical integration (i.e. by multiplication by $\mathbf{H}$). Of course, the price system (6.6.4) and the price system (6.9.2) are equivalent. They yield the same maximum rate of profit. (As may be seen, Π emerges here, as in (6.6.4), as the reciprocal of the maximum eigenvalue of $\mathbf{H}$). And they yield the same maximum wage rate in terms of pre-assigned standard. If we put $\pi = 0$ and $w = 1$, the components of $\mathbf{p}_k$ again turn out to be equal to the corresponding vertically integrated labour coefficients ($\mathbf{v}_k$ in this case). For all intermediate cases in which $0 < \pi < \Pi$,

$$\mathbf{p}_k = \mathbf{v}_k(\mathbf{I} - \pi\mathbf{H})^{-1} w, \qquad (6.9.3)$$

which gives for $\mathbf{p}_k$ precisely the same general expression that (6.6.9) gives for $\mathbf{p}$. All remarks and elaborations made for $\mathbf{p}$ in Section 6 could therefore be repeated here for $\mathbf{p}_k$.

10 Vertically Integrated Sectors of Higher Order

After performing the logical operation of vertical integration twice, it is natural to ask oneself whether there is any meaning in performing it a third time. The answer is straightforward. The units of vertically integrated productive capacity for investment goods, expressed in units of vertically integrated productive capacity, are themselves composite commodities. We may therefore conceptually construct the vertically hyper-integrated Sectors for these newly found composite commodities. Such vertically integrated Sectors clearly require a logical process of vertical integration to be performed three times. For analytical convenience, we may call such sectors 'vertically integrated Sectors of the third order', and therefore we may now call vertically integrated Sectors of the second order and vertically integrated Sectors of the first order, respectively, the logical constructions obtained in Sections 8 and 5.

After using subscribe k to denote the vertically integrated labour coefficients of the second order, we shall for consistency use subscript k^2 to denote the vertically integrated labour coefficients of the third order, to be obtained from the second-order vertically integrated labour coefficients through post-multiplication by $\mathbf{H}$, that is,

$$\mathbf{v}_{k^2} \equiv \mathbf{v}_k\mathbf{H} \equiv \mathbf{a}_n(\mathbf{I} - \mathbf{A}^{\ominus})^{-1}\mathbf{H}\mathbf{H}. \tag{6.10.1}$$

No new notation is needed for the matrix of the vertically integrated productive capacities of the third order, which clearly is $\mathbf{H}^3$.

These definitions now allow us to generalise the logical process of vertical integration to any higher order we may like. We can proceed from the vertically integrated Sectors of the third order to the vertically integrated Sectors of the fourth order, and from those of the fourth order to those of the fifth order, of the sixth order, and so on, step by step to the vertically integrated Sectors of the sth order, where s is any natural number, as high as we may choose. Analytically, each step in this process to a higher and higher order of vertical integration is simply represented by post-multiplication by matrix $\mathbf{H}$. The m units of vertically integrated productive capacity thus play a crucial role in the whole process.

In other terms, we may characterise the m vertically integrated Sectors of the sth order by (i) a vector,

$$\mathbf{v}_{k^{s-1}} \equiv \mathbf{a}_n(\mathbf{I} - \mathbf{A}^{\ominus})^{-1}\underbrace{\mathbf{H}\ \cdots\ \mathbf{H}}_{(s-1)\text{times}} \equiv \mathbf{v}\mathbf{H}^{s-1} = \mathbf{v}_{k^{s-2}}\mathbf{H}, \tag{6.10.2}$$

the components of which are the m sth order vertically integrated labour coefficients and by (ii) a matrix,

$$\mathbf{A}(\mathbf{I} - \mathbf{A}^{\ominus})^{-1}\underbrace{\mathbf{H}\ \cdots\ \mathbf{H}}_{(s-1)\text{ times}} \equiv \mathbf{H}\mathbf{H}^{s-1} \equiv \mathbf{H}^s, \tag{6.10.3}$$

the columns of which represent the m sth order vertically integrated physical units of productive capacity.

Each series of m physical units of the sth order vertically integrated productive capacity has of course (associated with it) its own series of m prices, which for consistency we shall denote by row vector $\mathbf{p}_{k^{s-1}}$. We clearly have:

$$\mathbf{p}_{k^{s-1}} = \mathbf{p}_{k^{s-2}}\mathbf{H} = (\mathbf{v}_{k^{s-2}}w + \mathbf{p}_{k^{s-2}}\mathbf{H}\pi)\mathbf{H} = \mathbf{v}_{k^{s-1}}w + \mathbf{p}_{k^{s-1}}\mathbf{H}\pi, \tag{6.10.4}$$

from which we obtain:

$$\mathbf{p}_{k^{s-1}} = \mathbf{v}_{k^{s-1}}(\mathbf{I} - \pi\mathbf{H})^{-1}w, \qquad (6.10.5)$$

a remarkable general expression, of which (6.9.3) and (6.6.9) may be regarded as particular cases. All the theoretical remarks and elaborations made for prices $\mathbf{p}$ in Section 6 could now be referred to prices $\mathbf{p}_{k^{s-1}}$ in general.

11 Higher-Order Vertical Integration and Reduction of Prices to a Sum of Weighted Quantities of Labour

The notion of higher-order vertical integration may at first appear to be a very highly abstract notion indeed, and one may wonder whether any application of it can be found at all. But let us analyse the price system more deeply.

By using first-order vertical integration, we have been able in Section 6 to split up each price into its two basic components – wages and profits. When the wage rate itself is used as the *numéraire* – that is, when w is put equal to unity – (6.6.4) actually becomes

$$\mathbf{p} = \mathbf{v} + \mathbf{p}\mathbf{H}\pi, \qquad (6.11.1)$$

which shows the two components of prices in yet another light. The total purchasing power of prices, in terms of 'labour commanded', is shown to be equal to 'labour embodied' plus a residual absorbed by profits. A solution for $\mathbf{p}$ may of course be obtained immediately:

$$\mathbf{p} = \mathbf{v}(\mathbf{I} - \pi\mathbf{H})^{-1}, \qquad (6.11.2)$$

as was done in Section 6. But an alternative procedure may also be followed – a procedure of successive approximations, which is conceptually far more interesting from a theoretical point of view.

Residual $\mathbf{p}\mathbf{H}\pi$ contains the same prices as appear on the left-hand side of (6.11.1). It may therefore itself be further split up into two components. After substitution from (6.9.1) to (6.9.2) we obtain

$$\mathbf{p}\mathbf{H}\pi \equiv \mathbf{p}_k\pi \equiv \mathbf{v}_k\pi + \mathbf{p}_k\mathbf{H}\pi^2. \qquad (6.11.3)$$

Second-order vertical integration has thereby come onto scene. The two components of $\mathbf{p}\mathbf{H}\pi$ are shown to be (i) profits on the second-order vertically integrated labour coefficients and (ii) a second-order residual, itself containing $\mathbf{p}_k$. A chain argument has been started. Residual $\mathbf{p}_k\mathbf{H}\pi^2$ may itself be split up into two further components by using the notion of third-order vertical integration. After substitution from (6.10.4) we obtain

$$\mathbf{p}_k\mathbf{H}\pi^2 \equiv \mathbf{p}_{k2}\pi^2 \equiv \mathbf{v}_{k2}\pi^2 + \mathbf{p}_{k2}\mathbf{H}\pi^3, \qquad (6.11.4)$$

which in turn shows the second-order residual as a sum of the rate of profit (at the second power) on third-order vertically integrated labour coefficients plus a third-order residual containing prices, and itself liable to be split up into two further components. This logical chain may be pursued, step by step, to whatever degree we may choose. By using the same recurring formula (6.10.4), we obtain

$$\begin{aligned} \mathbf{p}_{k2}\mathbf{H}\pi^3 &\equiv \mathbf{p}_{k3}\pi^3 \equiv \mathbf{v}_{k3}\pi^3 + \mathbf{p}_{k3}\mathbf{H}\pi^4, \\ &\vdots \qquad\quad \vdots \\ \mathbf{p}_{k^{s-1}}\mathbf{H}\pi^s &\equiv \mathbf{p}_{k^s}\pi^s \equiv \mathbf{v}_{k^s}\pi^s + \mathbf{p}_{k^s}\mathbf{H}\pi^{s+1}, \end{aligned} \qquad (6.11.5)$$

where s is a natural real number as high as we may choose. Each step may now be substituted back into the previous one, in (6.11.5), and then in (6.11.4), (6.11.3), and (6.11.1), so as to obtain

$$\mathbf{p} = \mathbf{v} + \mathbf{v}_k\pi + \mathbf{v}_{k2}\pi^2 + \cdots + \mathbf{v}_{k^s}\pi^s + \mathbf{p}_{k^s}\mathbf{H}\pi^{s+1}. \qquad (6.11.6)$$

There still remains a $(s+1)$th order residual, but this residual can be made as small as may suit one's purpose by making s as great as is necessary. In the limit, as $s \to \infty$, the residual vanishes[9] and prices entirely resolve themselves into an infinite sum of weighted quantities of labour:

$$\mathbf{p} = \mathbf{v} + \mathbf{v}_k\pi + \mathbf{v}_{k2}\pi^2 + \mathbf{v}_{k3}\pi^3 + \cdots. \qquad (6.11.8)$$

The remarkable upshot of this succession is that at the first round of approximation we find the first-order vertically integrated labour

[9] The $(s+1)$ order residual, after substitution from recurring formula (6.10.4), may be written as

$$\mathbf{p}_{k^s}\mathbf{H}\pi^{s+1} = \mathbf{p}(\pi\mathbf{H})^{s+1}. \qquad (6.11.7)$$

Supposing $\mathbf{p} > 0$, a necessary and sufficient condition for this expression to vanish, as $s \to \infty$, is $\lim_{s\to\infty}(\pi\mathbf{H})^s = 0$. This is precisely the case if $\pi < 1/|\lambda_{\max}|$. A proof can be given by using the similarity transformation of matrix $\mathbf{H}$ called its *Jordan canonical form*, that is, $\mathbf{F} = \mathbf{V}\mathbf{H}\mathbf{V}^{-1}$, where $\mathbf{V}$ is a square non-singular matrix and $\mathbf{F}$ is a matrix with all eigenvalues of $\mathbf{H}$ on its main diagonal and zero elsewhere, except some ones on the next diagonal. Clearly $\mathbf{F}^s = \mathbf{V}\mathbf{H}^s\mathbf{V}^{-1}$. It can now be seen that if $\pi < 1/|\lambda_{\max}|$, all the elements of $(\pi\mathbf{F})^s$ tend to zero as s tends to infinity. This ensures the tendency of $(\pi\mathbf{H})^s$ to $\mathbf{O}$ as s tends to infinity.

coefficients, at the second round of approximation we find the second-order vertically integrated labour coefficients, at the third round the third-order vertically integrated labour coefficients, and so on. Since these rounds go on to infinity, *all* higher-order vertically integrated labour coefficients contribute to the logical process of finding the final solution.

The condition under which the infinite series (6.11.8) is convergent can be seen immediately upon substitution from (6.10.2). We obtain

$$\mathbf{p} = \mathbf{v}[\mathbf{I} + \pi\mathbf{H} + \pi^2\mathbf{H}^2 + \pi^3\mathbf{H}^3 + \cdots], \qquad (6.11.9)$$

where within square brackets appear in succession all the higher-order units of vertically integrated productive capacity, appropriately weighted with the powers of the rate of profit. It is not difficult to see that the series is convergent provided that $\pi < 1/|\lambda_{\max}| = \Pi$.[10] Only when $\pi = \Pi$, that is, when all the purchasing power of prices is absorbed by profits, is the series not convergent, and prices can 'command' an infinite quantity of labour. To the opposite extreme is the case in which $\pi = 0$, which makes all profit-weighted addenda vanish, and prices (in terms of 'labour commanded') become equal to the only unweighted addendum in the series – classical 'labour embodied'. In between these two extremes, that is, for $0 < \pi < \Pi$, the series is infinite and convergent. As may be noticed, the series actually corresponds to the well-known iterative numerical method for obtaining the inverse of matrix $(\mathbf{I} - \pi\mathbf{H})$, which appears in (6.6.11). In other words, the sum of the infinite series converges to inverse matrix

$$(\mathbf{I} - \pi\mathbf{H})^{-1}, \qquad (6.11.10)$$

which means that step-by-step solution (6.11.8) converges to 'exact solution' (6.6.11).

The notions of higher-order vertically integrated labour coefficients have therefore the remarkable property of conferring an economic meaning of high theoretical relevance on each round of approximation to be carried out in the search for the price solution. They resolve

[10] This result is an immediate consequence of what is shown in the previous footnote, the series being a geometric one. The convergence of the infinite series (6.11.9), when $\pi < 1/|\lambda_{\max}|$, is a particular case of a more general theorem concerning functions of matrices. For a rigorous proof of this more general theorem, see, e.g., Pasinetti (1977a, *Mathematical Appendix*, Section 9.11).

the price of every commodity into a sum of profit-weighted quantities of labour.[11]

12 A 'Dual' Exercise

Matrix $\mathbf{H}$ and all its powers have a dual counterpart which, though not essential to the arguments of the present book, will here be evinced explicitly, for the sake of completeness. The analytical framework of the previous pages enables us to proceed very quickly at this stage, as we can start directly with an application that brings out all the dual notions at once.

Suppose that in the economic system considered so far the labour force is growing in time at the steady percentage rate $g > 0$ per annum, that is,

$$L(t) = L(0)(1+g)^t. \qquad (6.12.1)$$

And suppose that average consumption per head is also constant through time, so that we may write $\mathbf{c}$ for the column vector of average per-capita consumption coefficient. We have

$$\mathbf{C}(t) = \mathbf{c}\mu^{-1}L(t), \qquad (6.12.2)$$

where μ is the (constant) proportion of active to total population.

We shall consider the problem of finding a solution for the equilibrium (full employment) composition of total production $\mathbf{Q}(t)$ in each year t. Of course, $\mathbf{Q}(t)$ must include commodities for consumption, commodities for new investments (i.e. for the expansion at rate g of all fixed and circulating capital goods, whether used for the production of consumption or of investment goods), and commodities for the replacement of all used-up capital goods (whether used up by production of consumption or of investment goods), that is,

$$\mathbf{Q}(t) = \mathbf{C}(t) + g\mathbf{A}\mathbf{Q}(t) + \mathbf{A}^{\ominus}\mathbf{Q}(t). \qquad (6.12.3)$$

[11] As may be realised, expression (6.11.8), by being the iterative solution of (6.6.11), also represents an iterative solution of Marx's 'transformation problem'. So Marx was not off the track, after all, when he sensed he could start from 'values' and calculate profits directly on them. But he tried to settle the problem in one step, while what is needed is a long iterative process.

This system of equations may of course be solved immediately for $\mathbf{Q}(t)$. If we follow a slightly roundabout way, we obtain

$$\mathbf{Q}(t) = (\mathbf{I} - \mathbf{A}^{\ominus})^{-1}\mathbf{C}(t) + g(\mathbf{I} - \mathbf{A}^{\ominus})^{-1}\mathbf{A}\mathbf{Q}(t),$$

$$\mathbf{Q}(t) = [\mathbf{I} - g(\mathbf{I} - \mathbf{A}^{\ominus})^{-1}\mathbf{A}]^{-1}(\mathbf{I} - \mathbf{A}^{\ominus})^{-1}\mathbf{C}(t). \tag{6.12.4}$$

We may now define a new matrix $\mathbf{G}$, that is,

$$\mathbf{G} \equiv (\mathbf{I} - \mathbf{A}^{\ominus})^{-1}\mathbf{A}, \tag{6.12.5}$$

which immediately appears as dual to $\mathbf{H}$. After substitution into (6.12.4) we may write

$$\mathbf{Q}(t) = (\mathbf{I} - g\mathbf{G})^{-1}(\mathbf{I} - \mathbf{A}^{\ominus})^{-1}\mathbf{C}(t). \tag{6.12.6}$$

This expression concerning physical quantities is clearly dual to expression (6.6.11) concerning prices. In general, of course,

$$\mathbf{G} \equiv (\mathbf{I} - \mathbf{A}^{\ominus})^{-1}\mathbf{A} \neq \mathbf{A}(\mathbf{I} - \mathbf{A}^{\ominus})^{-1} \equiv \mathbf{H}. \tag{6.12.7}$$

But $\mathbf{G}$ and $\mathbf{H}$ have exactly the same eigenvalues. In particular, $\lambda_{\max} = |\lambda|_{\max}$ is the maximum eigenvalue of both of them.

We may now proceed, as in Section 11, to finding the solution of (6.12.3) through the alternative procedure of successive approximations. Total production $\mathbf{Q}(t)$ must certainly contain a batch of commodities, which we may call $\mathbf{Q}^{I}(t)$, that provide for consumption goods $\mathbf{C}(t)$ and for all commodities that go to replace the used-up means of production for producing $\mathbf{C}(t)$, that is,

$$\mathbf{Q}^{I}(t) = \mathbf{C}(t) + \mathbf{A}^{\ominus}\mathbf{Q}^{I}(t),$$

$$\mathbf{Q}^{I}(t) = (\mathbf{I} - \mathbf{A}^{\ominus})^{-1}\mathbf{C}(t). \tag{6.12.8}$$

If the economic system were stationary (i.e. if $g = 0$), that would be all that is needed; $\mathbf{Q}^{I}(t)$ would simply coincide with $\mathbf{Q}(t)$ and that would be the end of the story. But we are supposing $g > 0$. Therefore, another batch of commodities, which we may call $\mathbf{Q}^{II}(t)$, is needed for *expansion* of the capital goods needed for the production of $\mathbf{Q}^{I}(t)$ and also for replacement of the capital goods to be used up for $\mathbf{Q}^{II}(t)$, that is,

$$\mathbf{Q}^{II}(t) = g\mathbf{A}\mathbf{Q}^{I}(t) + \mathbf{A}^{\ominus}\mathbf{Q}^{II}(t),$$

$$\mathbf{Q}^{II}(t) = g(\mathbf{I} - \mathbf{A}^{\ominus})^{-1}\mathbf{A}\mathbf{Q}^{I}(t) \equiv g\mathbf{G}\mathbf{Q}^{I}(t). \tag{6.12.9}$$

A chain argument has now been started. What has been said for $\mathbf{Q}^{I}(t)$ must be repeated for $\mathbf{Q}^{II}(t)$. A third batch of commodities, $\mathbf{Q}^{III}(t)$, is needed for expansion at growth rate g of $\mathbf{Q}^{II}(t)$ and replacement of the corresponding capital goods, that is,

$$\mathbf{Q}^{III}(t) = g\mathbf{G}\mathbf{Q}^{II}(t) = g^2\mathbf{G}^2\mathbf{Q}^{I}(t). \qquad (6.12.10)$$

And so the chain argument goes on. A fourth batch of commodities, $\mathbf{Q}^{IV}(t)$, is needed for the next round, and then a fifth batch of commodities, a sixth batch, a seventh, and so on to infinity:

$$\begin{aligned} \mathbf{Q}^{IV}(t) &= \quad g\mathbf{G}\mathbf{Q}^{III}(t) \equiv g^3\mathbf{G}^3\mathbf{Q}^{I}(t), \\ &\vdots \\ \mathbf{Q}^{s}(t) &= g\mathbf{G}\mathbf{Q}^{s-1}(t) \equiv g^{s-1}\mathbf{G}^{s-1}\mathbf{Q}^{I}(t) \\ &\vdots \end{aligned} \qquad (6.12.11)$$

Total production $\mathbf{Q}(t)$ clearly consists of the conceptual sum of the infinite series

$$\mathbf{Q}(t) = \mathbf{Q}^{I}(t) + \mathbf{Q}^{II}(t) + \mathbf{Q}^{III}(t) + \cdots, \qquad (6.12.12)$$

or, after substitution from (6.12.8)–(6.12.11),

$$\mathbf{Q}(t) = [\mathbf{I} + g\mathbf{G} + g^2\mathbf{G}^2 + \cdots](\mathbf{I} - \mathbf{A}^{\ominus})^{-1}\mathbf{C}(t), \qquad (6.12.13)$$

where in square brackets appears the series of all the powers of matrix $\mathbf{G}$, appropriately weighted with the powers of g. This series is clearly dual to the series in (6.11.9), while expression $(\mathbf{I} - \mathbf{A}^{\ominus})^{-1}\mathbf{C}(t)$ is dual to expression $\mathbf{a}_n(\mathbf{I} - \mathbf{A}^{\ominus})^{-1} \equiv \mathbf{v}$. Again, it is not difficult to see that the present series converges to inverse matrix

$$(\mathbf{I} - g\mathbf{G})^{-1}, \qquad (6.12.14)$$

provided only that $g < 1/|\lambda_{\max}|$,[12] which is exactly the same condition required required for convergence of the series in (6.11.9). As was to be expected, step-by-step solution (6.12.13) converges to the exact solution (6.12.6).

The problem remains of giving matrix $\mathbf{G}$ an explicit economic interpretation. We have seen in the previous pages that the columns m of matrix $\mathbf{H}$ represent the m units of vertically integrated productive capacity – that is, each column i of $\mathbf{H}$ represents the series of heterogeneous commodities directly and indirectly required as *capital goods stocks* in the whole economic system in order to produce one physical unit of final good i ($i = 1, 2, \ldots, m$). The economic meaning of $\mathbf{G}$ is the exact dual analytical counterpart. Each column j of matrix $\mathbf{G}$ represents the series of heterogeneous commodities directly and indirectly

[12] The proof may be given along the same lines as those indicated with reference to $\pi < 1/|\lambda_{\max}|$ and matrix $\mathbf{H}$ in footnotes 9 and 10.

required as *flows* in the whole economic system in order to produce all the stocks of capital goods necessary for one physical unit of commodity j ($j = 1, 2, \dots, m$). While **H** is a matrix of stocks for the production of flows, **G** is a matrix of flows for the production of stocks.[13]

And, of course, the logical process that leads to matrix **G** can be applied all over again, in the same way as the logical process leading to matrix **H** has been applied all over again in Section 10. The flows represented by **G** themselves require stocks of capital goods, and the production of these stocks requires (directly and indirectly) the flows represented by $(\mathbf{I} - \mathbf{A}^{\ominus})^{-1}\mathbf{A}(\mathbf{I} - \mathbf{A}^{\ominus})^{-1}\mathbf{A} \equiv \mathbf{G}^2$. A further step back yields $\mathbf{G}^3$ and a still further step back yields $\mathbf{G}^4$, and so on. This logical process may be pursued to any higher order as we may choose, each step requiring pre-multiplication by **G**. All these higher-order notions represented by the powers of matrix **G**, appropriately weighted with the powers of g, then appear in the infinite series (6.12.13), where they confer a specific economic meaning on the successive rounds of approximation to be carried out in the search for the equilibrium growth solution.

13 Production with Fixed Capital Goods in General

The whole analysis has been carried out so far on the simplifying assumption that a constant proportion of all fixed capital goods drops out of the production process each year. This assumption may now be relaxed. In general, the way in which fixed capital goods wear out may vary widely from one industry to another and from one type of equipment to another. But in principle there is no difficulty in representing analytically any pattern of capital-good wear and tear. All capital goods may be considered, at the beginning of each year, to be entering the production process as particular inputs. Then, when, at the end of the year, they come out of the production process one

[13] As on other occasions, the economic relevance of each part of the same analytical dual exercise does not necessarily lead to equally relevant conceptions, from an economic theory point of view. Our case is itself an interesting example. While the economic meaning of the columns of **H** are indeed extremely relevant, as we shall see more specifically in the following analysis, various attempts to find equally important meanings for the columns of matrix **G** have not led, at least so far, to any comparable result. See, e.g., Steedman (1989).

year older, they may be considered as different commodities jointly produced with the commodities they contribute to produce.

This procedure requires each industry to be decomposed into as many 'activities' as there are 'years' in which the capital goods are used, each activity representing the same process of production but with a fixed capital good of a different age. Since each activity except one (the final one in which the capital good concerned drops out of the production process) produces jointly with the good that is produced also a capital good of a different age (which is considered as a different commodity), equality is maintained between the number of activities and the number of commodities.

Analytically, if technical coefficients remain constant through time, the technique for the whole economic system may be represented by

(i) a non-negative row vector of direct labour coefficients $\mathbf{a}_n \equiv [a_{nj}]$, $n = m + 1; j = 1, 2, \ldots, m$, where j stands now for the jth activity and m for the number of activities (and of commodities);
(ii) a non-negative square matrix of commodity–input coefficients $\mathbf{A} \equiv [a_{ij}]; i, j = 1, 2, \ldots, m$ (this matrix includes all capital goods, both circulating and fixed, since all of them are considered as entering the production process as inputs at the beginning of the 'year');
(iii) a non-negative square matrix of commodity–output coefficients $\mathbf{B} \equiv [b_{ij}]; i, j = 1, 2, \ldots, m$ (this matrix represents all commodities existing at the end of each year – consumption goods and capital goods of all types, new and old).

To complete the notation a convention must be chosen regarding the normalisation of all technical coefficients (i.e. regarding the scale to which each unit activity is referred). And the choice made here is to refer all the coefficients in each column (activity) j of $\mathbf{a}_n, \mathbf{A}, \mathbf{B}$, to the physical unit produced of commodity $i = j$ $(i, j = 1, 2, \ldots, m)$. This procedure has the convenient property of making all elements on the main diagonal of $\mathbf{B}$ equal to unity (after suitable rearrangements of rows and columns) and therefore of allowing us to make use of all notation defined in Section 3.

When production takes place with fixed capital goods in general, the physical economic system is thus represented by the system of equations

$$(\mathbf{B}-\mathbf{A})\mathbf{Q}(t) = \mathbf{Y}(t), \tag{6.13.1}$$
$$\mathbf{a}_n\mathbf{Q}(t) = L(t), \tag{6.13.2}$$
$$\mathbf{A}\mathbf{Q}(t) = \mathbf{S}(t), \tag{6.13.3}$$

and prices by the system of equations

$$\mathbf{p}\mathbf{B} = \mathbf{a}_n w + \mathbf{p}\mathbf{A} + \mathbf{p}\mathbf{A}\pi. \tag{6.13.4}$$

In the particular case of constant proportion depreciation, the number of activities reduces to one in each industry; output matrix **B** reduces to identity matrix **I**; and input matrix **A**, which appears both in (6.13.1) and in the second addendum of (6.13.4), reduces to $\mathbf{A}^{\ominus}$. General system of production with fixed capital goods (6.13.1)–(6.13.4) reduces to the previously considered particular system (6.3.1)–(6.3.4).

14 Generalisations and Restrictions

The complications of production with fixed capital goods in general make it no longer possible to give an unambiguous meaning to the notion of 'industry' (each industry may be made up of many activities, each of which has its own labour coefficient and its own unit of direct productive capacity), but the notion of vertically integrated sector remains unaffected by complications. The whole economic system remains susceptible to being conceptually decomposed into m sub-systems precisely in the same way as has been done in Section 5. The only formal difference is that matrix $(\mathbf{B}-\mathbf{A})^{-1}$ takes the place of matrix $(\mathbf{I}-\mathbf{A}^{\ominus})^{-1}$ in expressions (6.5.1–6.5.3). Therefore, for production with fixed capital goods in general, the vertically integrated labour coefficients and the physical units of vertically integrated productive capacity come to be defined respectively by the components and by the columns of

$$\mathbf{v} \equiv \mathbf{a}_n(\mathbf{B}-\mathbf{A})^{-1}, \tag{6.14.1}$$
$$\mathbf{H} \equiv \mathbf{A}(\mathbf{B}-\mathbf{A})^{-1}, \tag{6.14.2}$$

which represent a generalisation of (6.5.6) and (6.5.7). Similarly, the vertically integrated Sectors of higher order come to be defined by

$$\mathbf{v}_{k^{s-1}} \equiv \mathbf{a}_n(\mathbf{B}-\mathbf{A})^{-1}\mathbf{H}^{s-1}, \tag{6.14.3}$$
$$\mathbf{H}^{s} \equiv [\mathbf{A}(\mathbf{B}-\mathbf{A})^{-1}]^{s}, \tag{6.14.4}$$

(where s is any positive natural number), which represents a generalisation of (6.10.2) and (6.10.3).

What becomes more difficult to do, in the case of production with fixed capital goods in general, is to devise a neat way of discriminating between the cases in which 6.13.3 and 6.13.4 have and the cases in which they do not have an economic meaning. In the simplified case of the previous pages the procedure is clear. Non-negativity of $\mathbf{A}^{\ominus}$ is sufficient to ensure non-negativity of $(\mathbf{I} - \mathbf{A}^{\ominus})^{-1}$. But here the fact that both $\mathbf{B}$ and $\mathbf{A}$ are non-negative *ex-hypothesis* does not necessarily imply that $(\mathbf{B} - \mathbf{A})^{-1}$, and as a consequence $\mathbf{v}$, $\mathbf{H}$ and $\mathbf{G}$, should also be non-negative. Actually $\mathbf{v}$, $\mathbf{H}$ and $\mathbf{G}$ might indeed contain some negative elements and still make good economic sense. What we can say is that, since prices cannot be negative, $\mathbf{v}$ cannot be accepted as economically meaningful if it contains negative components when the rate of profit is zero. But there is nothing to prevent prices from all being positive, even if some components of $\mathbf{v}$ are negative, when the rate of profit is positive. And in this case a vector $\mathbf{v}$ with some negative components would make perfectly good economic sense. Similarly, we can say that if a particular column k of matrix $\mathbf{H}$ contains some negative components, the production of commodity k alone as a final good would require some activities to be run in reverse, and this would be impossible (and thus would have no economic sense). But commodity k might not be produced as a final good at all, or there might be no necessity to produce it alone (the sub-systems are only conceptual, not real, constructions). And in this case too a matrix $\mathbf{H}$ with some negative components would make perfectly good economic sense. A similar (but dual) argument can be developed for matrix $\mathbf{G}$.

In any case, the prices of the m commodities, expressed in ordinary physical units, continue to be given by the formulations of Section 6, again with the only difference that more general matrix $(\mathbf{B} - \mathbf{A})$ is to replace $(\mathbf{I} - \mathbf{A}^{\ominus})$, and more general matrix $\mathbf{A}$ to replace $\mathbf{A}^{\ominus}$. Similarly, the prices of the m composite commodities, representing the physical units of vertically integrated productive capacity of any order, continue to be expressed by (6.10.4) and (6.10.5), with the more general definition of $\mathbf{v}$ and $\mathbf{H}$ given by (6.14.1) and (6.14.2). Actually, if both $\mathbf{v}$ and $\mathbf{H}$ happen to be non-negative, all remarks made in Section 6 hold good in their entirety. In the case in which $\mathbf{v}$ and/or $\mathbf{H}$ do happen to contain some negative elements, what is no longer certain is that prices should remain all non-negative (i.e. economically meaningful) at *all* levels of the rate of profit and, as a consequence, that the relation between w and π should always be inverse and monotonic in terms of *all* commodities. However, the remarks made in Section 6 on the relationship between the classical notions of 'labour commanded' and 'labour embodied' continue to hold.

But the most interesting results of all refer to the elaborations of Sections 11 and 12, which do continue to hold. The step-by-step solution for prices $\mathbf{p}$ continues to be represented by infinite series (6.11.8) or (6.11.9), with the vertically integrated units of productive capacity of all orders $\mathbf{H}, \mathbf{H}^2, \mathbf{H}^3, \ldots$, and with the vertically integrated labour coefficients of all orders, $\mathbf{v}, \mathbf{v}_k, \mathbf{v}_{k^2}, \ldots$, being defined by more general expressions (6.14.1)–(6.14.4). The condition of convergence of the series is again the same, that is, $\pi < 1/|\lambda_{\max}|$.[14] Similarly, the step-by-step solution for total production $\mathbf{Q}(t)$ continues to be expressed by the infinite series (6.12.13), with more general matrix $(\mathbf{B} - \mathbf{A})^{-1}$ in the place of $(\mathbf{I} - \mathbf{A}^{\ominus})^{-1}$. The series is again convergent for $|\lambda_{\max}|$.

What must be added here is that we can no longer be certain that the eigenvalue of $\mathbf{H}$ and $\mathbf{G}$ which is maximum in modulus – that is, $\lambda_{\max}$ – is also the eigenvalue which is economically relevant. If there exists a $\lambda_{\max} > \lambda_e$, where λ_e represents the economically relevant eigenvalue, the series (6.11.9) and (6.12.13) converge for all π and g smaller than $1/\lambda_{\max}$ but do not converge for π and $g \geq 1/\lambda_{\max}$. In other words (and with reference to π, for the sake of brevity, since the same thing can be repeated for g), if we define $\pi^* = 1/\lambda_{\max}$, the series (6.11.9) converges for all rates of profit within the range $0 < \pi < \pi^*$. In those cases in which λ in $\lambda_{\max}$ is a real positive number, π^* coincides with Π, and (6.11.9) converges, as before, for all economically significant rates of profit up to Π (but at at, or beyond, Π). In other, more complicated, cases in which $\pi^* < \pi_e$, where $\pi_e = 1/\lambda_e$, π^* becomes the new critical level of the rate of profit. The series (6.11.9) converges for all rates of profit up to π^*, but not at or beyond π^*. It is, however, important to realise that $|\lambda_{max}|$ is finite. Therefore π^* is in any case positive. This means that, from zero upwards (even in the most complicated cases for joint production!), there always exists a range of positive rates of profit within which the series (6.11.9) is convergent.

[14] See footnotes 9 and 10.

The reduction of prices to a sum of weighted quantities of labour is thereby revealed to be a result of great generality. The series

$$\mathbf{p} = \mathbf{v} + \mathbf{v}_k\pi + \mathbf{v}_{k2}\pi^2 + \mathbf{v}_{k3}\pi^3 + \cdots, \qquad (6.14.5)$$

where $\mathbf{v}_{k^s} \equiv \mathbf{v}[\mathbf{A}(\mathbf{B}-\mathbf{A})^{-1}]^s$, clearly represents a generalisation of Piero Sraffa's reduction of prices to *dated* quantities of labour (which is only possible in the case of single-product industries). The logical process of infinite successive vertical integration is thus revealed to be more general and to go much deeper than the logical process of infinite chronological decomposition. A generalisation of this type, with all its theoretical implications, is no doubt one of the most remarkable results of the present analysis.

15 Technical Progress

So far in our analysis, all technical coefficients have been assumed to be absolutely constant through time, simply because this has been imposed by the concept of 'industry' as defined in both Leontief's and Sraffa's analyses. But this is no longer necessary in an analytical framework in which we consider vertical integration! The notion of a vertically integrated sector is not only unaffected by technical change; it has actually been conceived in order to remain relevant precisely when there is technical change! In particular, the notion of a physical unit of productive capacity, by being defined with reference to the commodity that is produced, continues to make sense, as a physical unit, whatever complications technical change may cause to its composition in terms of ordinary commodities. This is in fact one of the most remarkable results of the analysis of vertical integration.

If there is technical progress in the economic system, we may suppose for consistency with our previous analysis that changes take place at discontinuous points in time. Technical coefficients may be supposed to change at the beginning of each year and then remain constant during the year. With this convention, the whole previous analysis may simply be reinterpreted as referring to a particular year t. This means that all magnitudes considered in the previous pages must be *dated*. Not only physical quantities $\mathbf{Q}(t)$, $\mathbf{Y}(t)$, $\mathbf{S}(t)$, and so on, but also prices $\mathbf{p}(t)$, techniques $\mathbf{a}_n(t)$, $\mathbf{A}(t)$, $\mathbf{B}(t)$, and, as a consequence, vertically integrated Sectors, $\mathbf{v}(t)$, $\mathbf{H}(t)$; $\mathbf{v}_k(t)$, $\mathbf{H}^2(t)$; $\mathbf{v}_{k2}(t)$, $\mathbf{H}^3(t)$, and so on, must be written with a time suffix.

A distinction, however, has to be made at this point between two types of technical progress.

(i) *Disembodied technical progress.* We may call 'disembodied' technical progress those improvements that do not affect the physical characteristics of capital goods and simply enable production of larger physical quantities of commodities out of existing capital goods. Analytically this type of technical progress is expressed by the diminution of some technical coefficients and presents no difficulty. Capital goods, measured in ordinary physical units, remain the same, but their relations to capital goods, measured in terms of vertically integrated productive capacities, change as time goes on. This means that a particular matrix $\mathbf{H}(t)$ expressing the relation between the two types of units comes into existence for each particular year t; so that an appropriate $\mathbf{H}(t)$ has to be used in each year in order to transform the vertically integrated units of capital goods (and thus the units of productive capacity) into ordinary units [of capital goods].

(ii) *Embodied technical progress.* We may call 'embodied' technical progress those improvements that need to be embodied into specific (new) capital goods. In particular, these improvements are supposed to be embodied in such new capital goods that render the old ones either entirely or partially obsolete, in the sense that the old capital goods, even if they continue to be used for the time being, will never be replaced by physical capital goods of the same type when they are actually replaced. It must therefore be specified that notation $\mathbf{a}_n(t)$, $\mathbf{A}(t)$, $\mathbf{B}(t)$ is to be understood as denoting the latest technique for the whole economic system, as this is known at the beginning of year t, so that $\mathbf{v}(t) \equiv \mathbf{a}_n(t)[\mathbf{B}(t) - \mathbf{A}(t)]^{-1}$, $\mathbf{H}(t) \equiv \mathbf{A}(t)[\mathbf{B}(t) - \mathbf{A}(t)]^{-1}$ represent the corresponding vertically hyper-integrated Sectors *as they would be* if the technique of time t had been known in the past and the composition of the capital goods had thereby become evenly balanced. This means that technique $\mathbf{a}_n(t)$, $\mathbf{A}(t)$, $\mathbf{B}(t)$, and corresponding vertically integrated Sectors $\mathbf{v}(t)$, $\mathbf{H}(t)$ represent *hypothetical* magnitudes in this case. The *actual* economic system, if it is to be represented in the same way, requires a different notation; for example, we may write $\bar{\mathbf{a}}_n(t)$, $\bar{\mathbf{A}}(t)$, $\bar{\mathbf{B}}(t)$, to denote the technique which is actually in operation in year t (a mixture of activities of different 'vintages'). Then $\bar{\mathbf{v}}(t) \equiv \bar{\mathbf{a}}_n(t)[\mathbf{B}(t) - \mathbf{A}(t)]^{-1}$, $\bar{\mathbf{H}}(t) \equiv \bar{\mathbf{A}}(t)[\mathbf{B}(t) - \mathbf{A}(t)]^{-1}$ will represent the corresponding *actual* vertically integrated Sectors. It goes without saying that all cases considered so far, including that of embodied technical progress, may be regarded as particular cases in which hypothetical and actual vertically integrated Sectors happen to coincide.

Of course, both the hypothetical and the actual vertically integrated Sectors are relevant – when they are distinct from each other – but for different purposes. The *hypothetically* vertically integrated Sectors are crucial to the determination of prices, as they express the latest technique. The *actual* vertically integrated Sectors become relevant for the purpose of representing the physical economic system as it has been inherited from the past.

16 The Rationale of Framing a Dynamic Analysis in Terms of Vertically Integrated Sectors

At this point, the reader may like a more explicit comparison of the purposes for which each of the two types of classification discussed so far is suited and a more explicit explanation of the reasons why the vertically integrated Sectors have been preferred to input–output industries in the present dynamic analysis.

Let me begin by recalling that both the inter-industry and the vertically integrated ways of looking at the production processes of an economic system are by no means new in economic analysis; they can be found quite extensively used at different stages in the history of economic thought. It is very significant, however, that they have normally been used for different purposes and independently of each other: the inter-industry approach has mostly been associated with analyses at the micro-level and of a static nature, while the vertically integrated approach has mostly been associated with dynamic and macro-economic types of works. As a result, a sort of gap has gradually appeared between the two approaches; a gap which the foregoing discussion now puts us in a position to investigate.

At a given point of time, the two models make the connections between the two approaches quite obvious and well defined. Leontief has provided, for the inter-industry approach, a much more aggregated framework than the one usually used. The analysis which has been discussed here gives, on the other hand, a much more disaggregated framework for the vertically integrated approach. Between the two, the inverse matrix mentioned in Section 5 in value and income distr provides the analytical bridge. As a matter of fact, once we possess the inverse matrix, all relations between the two approaches at a given point of time take the form of one-to-one correspondences. No gap really exists in this case: the two ways of looking at the productive activities meet half-way, through the above-mentioned inverse matrix, which represents the analytical tool for re-classifying the same transactions according to two different criteria and points of view.

Of course, at any given point in time, the input–output model gives us more information. If we were simply interested in what happens at a specific point of time, the input–output model would be the obvious one to use because it provides a more complete picture. But, over time, the input–output coefficients change and the inter-industry system breaks down. The connections described above begin to vanish. Then, it is only the vertically integrated model that allows us to follow the vicissitudes of the economic system through time.

Let us consider briefly how this happens. Technical change, at the level of the single units of production, usually manifests itself in a continuous way, as has been remarked earlier. Even when new technical methods or new products are invented, their introduction into the economic system very rarely takes the form of a sudden change. In most cases, the new methods or the new products are operated uneconomically for a period, until experience and slow improvements put them on a competitive footing and prepare the ground for further improvement and development. To an external observer, looking for the 'best-known technique', the methods of production may sometimes look like being introduced at a certain point and then remaining stable for long periods of time; but when a reckoning of the inputs and outputs of an industry is carried out, widely varying shifts are found from one moment to the next. Even at a given point of time, there are many directions from which the inputs may come and to which the outputs may go.

These are well-known problems which have always caused difficulties to all builders of input–output tables and which sometimes cast serious doubts on the meaning to be attributed to the coefficients of very disaggregated input–output systems. Of course these doubts diminish the more the industries are aggregated, but in this direction the meaning of an input–output framework diminishes too. Hence, input–output experts have always tried to find a sort of optimum point at which to stop the process of aggregation-disaggregation, so as to take advantage of the usefulness of an input–output table without making its coefficients too unstable.

What has not been sufficiently realised is that the property of eliminating these shortcomings belongs to the completely aggregated quantities, not because they are aggregated, but because – by being completely aggregated – they necessarily are vertically integrated. The property extends to all vertically integrated magnitudes as well. By resolving all varieties of products into the same constituent elements – a flow of labour and a stock of capital goods both expressed in physical terms – the vertically integrated approach leads to relations whose permanence over time is independent of specific technical possibilities. For example, two equivalent methods that, at a given point of time, entail the same cost for the same output are represented, in an inter-industry equations system, by *two different* technical functions. But in a vertically integrated equations system they are expressed by exactly the *same* function. Their being equivalent means that they require the same amounts of inputs, and these inputs are expressed in the same terms (quantities of labour) independently of the industry in which they are used. Similarly, a sudden shift taking place at the level of a particular technical process in the origin of one of the inputs (e.g. a shift in the provenance of a fibre from the textile industry to the chemical industry) means that less labour (or labour equivalents) than before is required to produce it through the new channel. A shift of this type changes an inter-industry relation by causing the disappearance of a commodity–input coefficient (and of the corresponding variable) and the appearance of another, *different*, commodity–input coefficient (and of the corresponding variable). In the vertically integrated relation, it only causes a small diminution of *the same* coefficient. If we imagine many of these shifts taking place over time and, along with them, corresponding changes in the consumption coefficients – which is, after all, the normal path that technical progress takes – the input–output table is continuously upset and all relations change from one moment to the next. On the other hand, the vertically integrated relations remain unaffected. The only consequence for them is that their coefficients gradually diminish through time in a movement which, for analytical purposes, has been approximated in the present work by a smooth trend developing at a certain rate of change.

Concluding and summarising, we may say that, at any given point of time, between the static input–output model and the analysis presented in the previous pages there exists a very definite relation through a fully specifiable matrix of coefficients. Considered at a given point in time, the input–output model is more analytical – it has much more to say about the structure of an economic system. However, over time, and as the conditions of production and of consumption change (owing to technical progress, economies and diseconomies of scale, etc.), the inter-industry relations break down and become different from one moment to the next, so that a particular input–output table is needed for each stage in the evolution of the economy under consideration. These tables can be compared (comparative statics analysis), but they cannot be analytically linked to one another – no theory of any generality can be provided for passing from the one to the other. The continuity in time is kept, on the other hand, at the vertically integrated level, where the relations which can be set up possess – to use the Frisch-Haavelmo terminology[15] – a higher degree of *autonomy*. This means that the permanence of these relations in time is independent of technical change. In this context, the vertically integrated technical coefficients acquire a meaning of their own, independent of the origin of the single parts which compose them. The movements of these coefficients through time, and the various consequences thereof, can be investigated and followed as such. When more information is needed about the industrial structure at a particular point of time, the vertically integrated coefficients can be split and analysed into inter-industry coefficients particular to that point in time.

In this way, static input–output analysis and dynamic vertically integrated analysis appear as mutually complementary and completing

[15] Trygve Haavelmo, 'The Probability Approach in Econometric', in *Econometrica*, supplement, July 1944, Chapter II. 'In scientific research', Haavelmo writes on p. 38, 'our search for explanations consists of digging down to more, fundamental relations than those that appear before us when we merely *stand and look*. Each of these fundamental relations we conceive of as invariant with respect to a much wider class of variations than those particular ones that are displayed before us in the natural course of events'. The process of going over from inter-industry to vertically integrated relations, for the purpose of dynamic analysis, seems to be a typical example of this 'digging down to more fundamental relations'.

each other. Inter-industry relations, referring to any particular point of time, represent a cross-section of the vertically integrated magnitudes, whose movements through time express the structural dynamics of the economic system.

17 A Dramatic Opening Up of the Circular Production Approach (Towards Dynamic Analysis)

The reader may have realised already that the notion of vertical integration is at this point opening up new horizons precisely in the field of the dynamic analysis of capital goods. This is a dramatic breakthrough.

In the general case of production of all commodities by means of fixed capital goods with the existence of technical progress of the most general type, the relation between ordinary physical capital goods and capital goods measured in units of productive capacity breaks down at the end of each period, and the problem arises of what meaning can one give to the physical operation of replacement of the capital goods. Clearly, 'replacement' ceases to have any meaningful sense in terms of ordinary physical units. But on the other hand, 'replacement' does continue to make sense in terms of physical units of productive capacity. Even in the midst of a maze of physical and qualitative changes, we may indeed continue to say that replacement of used-up capital goods has taken place if, at the end of each period, the economic system has recovered the same productive capacities as it had at the beginning.

The analytical consequences of these remarks are far-reaching. With technical progress, any relation in which capital goods are expressed in ordinary physical units becomes useless for dynamic analysis. But we are now in possession of an entirely new analytical tool: namely, a newly conceived, physical unit in terms of which to express the units of productive capacity. With this, relations expressed in physical units of productive capacity continue to hold through time and actually acquire an autonomy of their own, quite independently of their changing composition. At the same time, the elaborations of the previous pages provide the way for a return to the ordinary physical units any time that this is necessary, within each specific period of time t. Of course, different results will be obtained for each single period.

This property seems to me to confer on the logical process of vertical integration an analytical relevance for dynamic investigations which has not been realised in the past. The vertically integrated Sectors seem to belong to that category of synthetic notions which, once obtained, contribute to reduce in many directions the very order of magnitude of the analytical difficulties.

It may not be too much to hope that a better understanding, and a more explicit utilisation, of the logical process of vertical integration will help to overcome the widely recognised failure of modern economic theory to come to grip with the analytical difficulties entailed by the introduction of technical change.

It is important to realise at this point the true richness of the whole framework of the vertically integrated Sectors. Without taking anything away from inter-industry analysis and in fact allowing us to get back to inter-industry relations at any given point of time – the vertically integrated approach is really plunging us into an investigation which is now truly dynamic. Essentially, there is complementarity (not incompatibility!) between vertically integrated sectoral analysis and inter-industry analysis. The appropriate analytical direction becomes that of a logical combination of the two approaches, or, more specifically, of finding the correct way of switching back and forth – from one approach to the other. In this, one can pave the way for a truly modern version of the basic principles of Classical economic analysis: an economic framework that may encompass, at the same time, the circular process of production and the evolution over time of the whole economic system.

These concepts will be further expanded in Chapter 10. Meanwhile, however, an Appendix seems to be useful here to stress the empirical significance of the vertically integrated analysis, as against the well known, more traditional, inter-industry elaborations pioneered by Leontief and Sraffa.

Appendix to Section 6
The Empirical Significance of Vertically Integrated Analysis

1 Vertically Integrated Sectoral Analysis vs. Input–Output Analysis

The analysis which has been developed in this part (Part II) of the present book has ended up with the new concepts of vertically integrated Sectors. But the reader may wonder at this point: what is the relation with inter-industry analysis? It will be remembered that with the Chapter 5, all inter-industry connections and intermediate commodities, at a given point of time, have been deliberately left aside. Our aim was to arrive at a dynamic investigation as quickly as possible. Yet, we may now go back for a moment to the earlier stage. There is no need to reintroduce intermediate commodities. These have been extensively developed already in Part II. The task can here be limited to showing how they relate to the vertically integrated analysis used in the previous pages.

In particular, the two theoretical schemata developed by Wassily Leontief and Piero Sraffa are quite sufficient for our purposes. In fact, Piero Sraffa corresponds better than the former to the theoretical approach taken in the present work, but the former has had wider empirical applications. Therefore, it will be convenient to take Leontief's system as the static term of our comparisons.

First of all, let me point out the similarity of approach, from an empirical point of view, of the previous dynamic (vertically integrated) analysis and the static input–output analysis. Both of them share the characteristic of being built on coefficients which are intended to represent actual outcomes and which can therefore, at least in principle, be given an empirical content, simply by recording the actual performance of the economic system. Of course, the technical and the consumption coefficients, by which this actual performance is represented, come from a choice, made from among a larger set of possibilities. But all the alternative possibilities that might have, but have not, been chosen have become irrelevant. (We shall come back to this point in further detail later on.) The coefficients that appear both in the input–output analysis and in the present (vertically integrated) analysis must, therefore, be interpreted as representing those physical quantities which can actually be observed.

Notice, moreover, that input–output analysis and vertically integrated analysis also coincide in the way they look at the final sector of the economy – the last column of the coefficient matrix is the same in the two schemes (with the only difference that, in the present analysis, consumption goods and investment goods have been listed separately). However, they differ profoundly in the way they consider the production processes. The same production structure of the economy is looked at from two different points of view – one is very close to it and to what is immediately observable and the other is placed much further away, at the final stage of the consumption and investment goods. The input–output approach can certainly be more immediately grasped. One of the things by which one is most impressed, when looking at the real transactions which take place in an economic system, is the great number of inter-relations among productive units. One's first instinct is, therefore, to inquire into these inter-industry connections and try to reproduce them analytically. This is the idea which originally underlay Quesnay's *Tableau Économique* and which has been developed and given a full empirical content by Leontief.

A different approach is taken in the present work. Not 'industries', in the input–output sense, but 'sectors' have been taken as the basis of the whole investigation. And sectors have been defined in such a way as to be vertically integrated. All inter-relations which can be observed in the real world are looked at as parts of a process which has not yet come to an end. Any process reaches its completion only when the product which comes out is a final commodity (consumption or investment good). A vertically integrated sector is, therefore, from an interindustry point of view, a very complex 'sector' as it repeatedly goes through the whole intricate pattern of inter-industry connections. However, from the point of view of the homogeneity of the inputs, it becomes a very simple one, as it eliminates all intermediate goods and resolves each final commodity into its ultimate constituent elements: a (flow) quantity of labour and a (stock) quantity of capital goods. [It may be interesting to recall that this procedure was used by Leon Walras himself in his *Elements*, although in a more rudimentary way.][16]

At a given point in time, between the two ways of looking at the economic system there really is no logical difference. Both models represent the same thing, looked at in a different way. The difference, in other words, lies only in the classification, and we can pass from the one to the other simply by an algebraical re-arrangement, corresponding to a process of solving a system of linear equations: the production coefficients of a vertically integrated model turn out to be a linear combination of the production coefficients of the corresponding input–output model.

This can be shown immediately, if goods are expressed in physical terms. If we take an input–output equations system and isolate the inter-industry transactions, by opening it with respect to the final sector, and if we further drop from the equations system the last row: representing the inputs of direct labour into each industry, that is, the row $a_{n1}, a_{n2}, \ldots, a_{n1,n-1}$, we obtain

$$\begin{bmatrix} 1-a_{11} & -a_{12} & \cdots & -a_{1,n-1} \\ -a_{21} & 1-a_{22} & \cdots & -a_{2,n-1} \\ & & \ddots & \\ -a_{n-1,1} & -a_{n-1,2} & \cdots & 1-a_{n-1,n-1} \end{bmatrix} \cdot \begin{bmatrix} Z_1 \\ Z_2 \\ \vdots \\ Z_{n-1} \end{bmatrix} = \begin{bmatrix} U_1 \\ U_2 \\ \vdots \\ U_{n-1} \end{bmatrix}, \tag{6-A.1.1}$$

where the a_{ij}s stand here for the inter-industry technical coefficients, the Z_is for the total outputs of the various commodities, and the U_is for the final demands for the various commodities $(i, j = 1, 2, \ldots, n-1)$. By solving (6-A.1.1), we arrive at

$$\begin{bmatrix} Z_1 \\ Z_2 \\ \vdots \\ Z_{n-1} \end{bmatrix} = \begin{bmatrix} 1-a_{11} & -a_{12} & \cdots & -a_{1,n-1} \\ -a_{21} & 1-a_{22} & \cdots & -a_{2,n-1} \\ & & \ddots & \\ -a_{n-1,1} & -a_{n-1,2} & \cdots & 1-a_{n-1,n-1} \end{bmatrix}^{-1} \cdot \begin{bmatrix} U_1 \\ U_2 \\ \vdots \\ U_{n-1} \end{bmatrix}, \tag{6-A.1.2}$$

where the exponent -1 indicates the operation of matrix inversion. Now each column of the inverted matrix represents the amounts of

[16] Walras (1954, p. 241).

all intermediate goods which directly and indirectly are going into one unit of the final commodity. This means that, by multiplying each column of the inverted matrix by the row vector of the input–output direct labour coefficients, which has been excluded from (6-A.1.1), we arrive at the labour coefficients of vertically integrated sectoral analysis.

In algebraic terms, if we denote by $v - i$ $(i = 1, 2, \ldots, n - 1)$ the vertically integrated labour coefficients, we obtain

$$\begin{bmatrix} v_1 \\ v_2 \\ \vdots \\ v_{n-1} \end{bmatrix} = \left\{ \begin{bmatrix} 1 - a_{11} & -a_{12} & \cdots & -a_{1,n-1} \\ -a_{21} & 1 - a_{22} & \cdots & -a_{2,n-1} \\ & & \ddots & \\ -a_{n-1,1} & -a_{n-1,2} & \cdots & 1 - a_{n-1,n-1} \end{bmatrix}^{-1} \right\}' \cdot \begin{bmatrix} a_{n1} \\ a_{n2} \\ \vdots \\ a_{n,n-1} \end{bmatrix}, \tag{6-A.1.3}$$

where the mark $'$ denotes the operation of matrix transposition. Equation (6-A.1.3) now give the algebraic relation, existing in a given period of time, between the direct labour coefficients of an input–output model and the vertically integrated labour coefficients to be used in vertically integrated sectoral analysis. The ones may be obtained from the others, as the (6-A.1.3) directly show, by a straightforward algebraic operation.

2 Fitting Empirical Data into a Vertically Integrated Sectoral Model

The algebraic relation which has just been obtained and which links the input–output technical coefficients with the vertically integrated labour coefficients is of course of crucial importance for the purpose of giving a vertically integrated sectoral model an empirical content. Of course, since each coefficient or variable appearing in both input–output analysis and sectoral (vertically integrated) analysis refers to actually observable magnitudes, the problem of fitting empirical data into these models is in principle very straightforward for both of them. But the criterion of classification is different. In the input–output model, the criterion is the industry producing a certain commodity, intermediate or final, as it may be, and the problem is to reckon where its inputs come from and where its outputs go to. In a vertically integrated model, the criterion is the process of production of a final commodity, and the problem is to build conceptually behind each final commodity a vertically integrated sector which, by passing through all the intermediate commodities, goes right back to the original inputs.

The procedures for collecting and ordering data for input–output analysis purposes are well known. On the other hand, collecting data for the purposes of a vertically integrated model may seem a rather laborious task. But the difficulties are only apparent. It is true that to classify production processes in a vertically integrated way would be almost an impossible task, if attempted directly. But this task need not be attempted directly. The algebraical procedure which has been shown by (6-A.1.1 to 6-A.1.3) allows us to go over to a vertically integrated type of classification by starting from a classification of the input–output type.

All this means that, in order to give a vertically integrated sectoral model an empirical content, one must first of all collect data and fit them into an input–output table in the usual inter-industry way. Moreover, data must be collected about physical capital goods (or about capital/output ratios) in each single industry of the input–output classification. Then the resulting system of input–output linear equations can be opened with respect to the final goods and solved by computing the inverse of the coefficient matrix. This inverse matrix, or more precisely the transpose of this inverse matrix, as shown in Section 1, provides both the logical and the empirical link between the input–output type of classification and the one which is needed in a vertically integrated model. This means that to go over from one classification to the other is simply a matter of computation. The procedure, which has been shown by (6-A.1.3) with reference to the labour coefficients, remains exactly the same for the physical stocks of capital goods (or for the series of capital-output ratios). In other words, after multiplying the transposed inverse matrix by the vector of the stocks of physical capital goods (or of the capital/output ratios) of each input–output industry, we obtain the vector of the stocks of physical capital goods (or of the capital–output ratios) of each vertically integrated sector. And since each vertically integrated sector is constructed with reference to a specific final commodity, each vector of the stocks of physical capital goods thereby obtained may be regarded as a particular composite commodity representing a unit of (vertically integrated) production capacity for the corresponding final commodity. The transposed inverse matrix appears, therefore, as the linear operator which may be applied to an inter-industry classification of labour and capital goods, in order to reclassify them according to the new type of (vertically integrated) sectors.[17]

In this way, each vertically integrated sector is reduced to one flow-input of labour and to one stock-quantity of capital goods; or, more specifically, to one vertically integrated labour coefficient and to one vertically integrated unit of productive capacity. These magnitudes do not correspond to labour or capital goods employed in any particular firm or industry, since the whole framework of intermediate relations has been consolidated; but they do represent all the labour and capital goods, in whatever remote corner of the economic system they may have been applied, which are necessary to produce the final commodity under consideration. Formally, the new coefficients are, therefore, derived concepts (derived from the consolidation of the inter-industry coefficients) but they have a deeper economic meaning and possess, as will be stressed in a moment, much more favourable characteristics for dynamic analysis.

3 The Rationale of Framing a Dynamic Analysis in Terms of Vertically integrated Sectors

At this point, the reader may like a more explicit comparison of the purposes for which each of the two types of classification discussed above is suited, and a more explicit explanation of the reasons why the vertically hyper-integrated Sectors have been preferred to input–output industries in the present dynamic analysis.

Let me begin by recalling that both the inter-industry and the vertically integrated ways of looking at the production processes of an economic system are by no means new in economic analysis; they can be found quite extensively used at different stages in the history of economic thought. It is very significant, however, that they have normally been used for different purposes and independently of each other: the inter-industry approach has mostly been associated with analyses at the micro-level and of a static nature, while the vertically integrated approach has mostly been associated with dynamic and macro-economic types of works. As a result, a sort of gap has

[17] These algebraic transformations have been worked out in detail in my *Metroeconomica* article, see Pasinetti (1973); they have also been substantially reproduced in Sections 13 and 14 of Chapter 6.

gradually appeared between the two approaches; a gap which the foregoing discussion now puts us in a position to investigate.

At a given point of time, the two models which have been confronted above make the connections between the two approaches quite obvious and well-defined. Leontief has provided, for the inter-industry approach, a much more aggregated framework than the one usually used. The analysis which has been discussed here gives, on the other hand, a much more disaggregated framework for the vertically integrated approach. Between the two, the inverse matrix mentioned above provides the analytical bridge. As a matter of fact, once we possess the inverse matrix, all relations between the two approaches at a given point of time take the form of one-to-one correspondences. No gap really exists in this case: the two ways of looking at the productive activities meet half-way, through the above mentioned inverse matrix, which represents the analytical tool for re-classifying the same transactions according to two different criteria and points of view.[18]

Of course, at any given point in time, the input–output model gives us more information. If we were simply interested in what happens at a specific point of time, the input–output model would be the obvious one to use because it provides a more complete picture. But, over time, the input–output coefficients change and the inter-industry system breaks down. The connections described above begin to vanish. Then it is only the vertically integrated model that allows us to follow the vicissitudes of the economic system through time.

Let us consider briefly how this happens. Technical change, at the level of the single units of production, usually manifests itself in a continuous way, as has been remarked earlier. Even when new technical methods or new products are invented, their introduction into the economic system very rarely takes the form of a sudden change. In most cases, the new methods or the new products are operated uneconomically for a period, until experience and slow improvements put them on a competitive footing and prepare the ground for further improvement and development. To an external observer, looking for the 'best-known technique', the methods of production may sometimes look like being introduced at a certain point and then remaining stable

18 Further elaborations on this point are given in my already mentioned *Metroeconomica* Pasinetti (1973) article.

for long periods of time; but when a reckoning of the inputs and outputs of an industry is carried out, widely varying shifts are found from one moment to the next. Even at a given point of time, there are many directions from which any of the inputs may come, and to which the outputs may go.

These are well-known problems which have always caused difficulties to all builders of input–output tables and which sometimes cast serious doubts on the meaning to be attributed to the coefficients of very disaggregated input–output systems. Of course these doubts diminish the more the industries are aggregated, but in this direction the meaning of an input–output framework diminishes too. Hence input–output experts have always tried to find a sort of optimum point at which to stop the process of aggregation-disaggregation, so as to take advantage of the usefulness of an input–output table without making its coefficients too unstable.

What has not been sufficiently realised is that the property of eliminating these shortcomings belongs to the completely aggregated quantities, not because they are aggregated but because – by being completely aggregated – they necessarily are vertically integrated. The property extends to all vertically integrated magnitudes as well. By resolving all varieties of products into the same constituent elements – a flow of labour and a stock of capital goods both expressed in physical terms – the vertically integrated approach leads to relations whose permanence over time is independent of specific technical possibilities. For example, two equivalent methods that, at a given point of time, entail the same cost for the same output, are represented, in an inter-industry equations system, by two different technical functions. But in a vertically integrated equations system they are expressed by exactly the same function. Their being equivalent means that they require the same amounts of inputs, and these inputs are expressed in the same terms (quantities of labour) independently of the industry in which they are used. Similarly, a sudden shift taking place at the level of a particular technical process in the origin of one of the inputs (e.g. a shift in the provenance of a fibre from the textile industry to the chemical industry) means that less labour (or labour equivalents) than before is required to produce it through the new channel. A shift of this type changes an inter-industry relation by causing the disappearance of a commodity–input coefficient (and of the corresponding variable) and the appearance of another, different, commodity–input coefficient (and of the corresponding variable). In the vertically integrated relation, it only causes a small diminution of the same coefficient. If we imagine many of these shifts taking place over time and, along with them, corresponding changes in the consumption coefficients – which is, after all, the normal path that technical progress takes – the input–output table is continuously upset and all relations change from one moment to the next. On the other hand, the vertically integrated relations remain unaffected. The only consequence for them is that their coefficients gradually diminish through time in a movement which, for analytical purposes, has been approximated in the present work by a smooth trend developing at a certain rate of change.

Concluding and summarising, we may say that, at any given point of time, between the static input–output model and the analysis presented in the previous pages there exists a very definite relation through a fully specifiable matrix of coefficients. Considered at a given point in time, the input–output model is more analytical – it has much more to say about the structure of an economic system. However, over time, and as the conditions of production and of consumption change (owing to technical progress, economies and diseconomies of scale etc.) the inter-industry relations break down and become different from one moment to the next, so that a particular input–output table is needed for each stage in the evolution of the economy under consideration. These tables can be compared (comparative statics analysis), but they cannot be analytically linked to one another – no theory of any generality can be provided for passing from the one to the other. The continuity in time is kept, on the other hand, at the vertically integrated level, where the relations which can be set up possess – to use the Frisch–Haavelmo terminology[19] – a higher degree of autonomy. This means that the permanence of these relations in time is independent of technical change. In this context, the vertically integrated technical coefficients acquire

[19] Haavelmo (1944) 'In scientific research', Haavelmo writes on p. 38, 'our search for explanations consists of digging down to more fundamental relations than those that appear before us when we merely stand and look. Each of these fundamental relations we conceive of as invariant with respect to a much wider class of variations than those particular ones that are displayed before us in the natural course of events'. The process of going over from inter-industry to vertically integrated relations, for the purpose of dynamic analysis, seems to be a typical example of this 'digging down to more fundamental relations'.

a meaning of their own, independent of the origin of the single parts which compose them. The movements of these coefficients through time, and the various consequences thereof, can be investigated and followed as such. When more information is needed about the industrial structure at a particular point of time, the vertically integrated coefficients can be split and analysed into inter-industry coefficients particular to that point in time.

In this way, static input–output analysis and dynamic vertically integrated analysis appear as mutually complementary and completing each other. Inter-industry relations, referring to any particular point of time, represent a cross-section of the vertically integrated magnitudes, whose movements through time express the structural dynamics of the economic system.

PART III

Structural Economic Dynamics: A Step-by-Step Approach

7 Production in the Short Run

1 Introduction

to explain the change of attitude which the present investigation has achieved with the introduction of structural economic dynamics

The change of approach, introduced by vertically integrated analysis, with respect to the more well-known inter-industry analysis approach, is carrying with it – as already explained – a dramatic change of analytical possibilities of which we can, and must, now take advantage.

We shall now try to proceed, in our investigation, to adhere to this new (vertically integrated) approach which, far from being incompatible with the more traditional inter-industry approach, comes to complement it, while at the same time allowing us to pursue newly, earlier unknown perspectives.

Precisely for this purpose, it appears useful to go back and resume our investigation within the 'production paradigm', as it was originally sketched out and presented in Chapter 1.[1]

2 A Well-Diversified Economic System [Carried Out Thanks to the Simplicity Allowed by Vertical Economic Integration]

Let us begin here by considering the process of production in an economic system at a given point in time or, to be more realistic, within a *short period of time*, defined in such a way that, within it, changes in

[1] This may entail some repetition with what we saw in the inter-industry analysis, but at the same time, it will also induce us to apply, where necessary, quite different criteria in deciding which are the really relevant simplifications to be adopted and, in this way, to allow us to proceed to frame the whole analysis to the characteristics suitable for a required jump towards a dynamic investigation.

population, productive capacity, technical knowledge and consumers' preferences are negligible.

The economic system we are considering is *closed* and consists of a society of individuals whose purpose is to produce goods in order to derive enjoyment (or relief from pain) by consuming them. Two types of activities are therefore performed: a production activity and a consumption activity. At the beginning of the time period considered, the production processes are programmed in the best way that is technically known, and, at the end of the production processes, the production goods are ready to be consumed. The technical knowledge is however supposed to be quite advanced so that each process of production requires division of labour and market specialisation. Therefore, each individual consumes only a very small part of the commodities he (or she) produces (or contributes to the production of producing) and obtains all the others through exchange. Total production (and therefore consumption) is well diversified: the economic system produces many types of commodities, according to the needs and preferences of its individual members.

In order to keep the analysis in as simple terms as possible, we begin by considering only *final* commodities. To begin with, no intermediate stage, and thus no intermediate commodity, will be explicitly represented. All production processes will be considered as vertically integrated, in the sense that all their inputs are reduced to inputs of labour and to services from stocks of capital goods. It is important to stress that, for our purpose, this entails no loss of generality. For it is always possible, when needed, to re-introduce intermediate stages and intermediate commodities by linear algebraic transformations.

3 Production by Means of Labour Alone: A Very Simple, but Significant Case

It will be useful to begin by taking a very simple step. In this section and in the following one, we shall adopt the expository device of developing a theoretical model where production is carried out exclusively by labour. Capital goods, as complementary to labour, will be introduced only later, from Section 6 onwards.

Even in an economic system as simple as this, there is a whole series of flows – or rather two different series of flows – which take place inside the period of time considered: flows of labour services from the individuals as labourers to the production processes and flows of commodities from the production processes to the individuals as consumers. Suppose that the number of final commodities produced is $(n-1)$. Then, since we consider no intermediate stage, there is a production process behind each commodity, which goes right back to what have traditionally been called its 'factors of production': labour alone in our present simple case. We have, therefore, $(n-1)$ production processes or *sectors*, each of which consists of one labour input and of one product output. Finally, all the individuals may be considered as grouped into a final sector, which may be called household – sector n – which receives all outputs for consumption and provides all labour services from production.

All these flows may be framed into a usual input–output table, which in our case becomes extremely simple. As is well known and has seen earlier, the table may be looked at from two different points of view and accordingly represented by two systems of identities. From a *physical* point of view, the production of each commodity is identically equal to the sum of all quantities of that commodity which are delivered as inputs to the other sectors. (In our simple case this sum is reduced to one term: the amount delivered to the household sector.) Moreover, the sum of all labour services is identically equal to total labour employed. Similarly, at *current prices*, the production of each commodity must be equal to the sum of its total inputs, and the sum of all productions must be equal to the sum of the total income which is distributed to the members of the community (all labourers in our case).

We therefore have

$$\left\{\begin{array}{lllll} X_1 & & & -x_{1n} & = 0, \\ & X_2 & & -x_{2n} & = 0, \\ & & & \cdots & \\ & & & \cdots & \\ & & & \cdots & \\ & & & -x_{n-1,n} & = 0, \\ -x_{n1} & -x_{n2} & -x_{n,n-1} & X_n & = 0, \end{array}\right. \tag{7.3.1}$$

and

$$\begin{cases} X_1p_1 & & -x_{n1}p_n = 0, \\ & X_2p_2 & -x_{n2}p_n = 0, \\ & & \dots \\ & & \dots \\ & & \dots \\ -x_{1n}p_1 & -x_{2n}p_2 & +X_np_n = 0, \end{cases} \tag{7.3.2}$$

where X_j represents the physical quantity produced of commodity j; $j = 1,2,\dots,(n-1)$; p_i represents the price of commodity i; $i = 1,2,\dots,n$; X_n represents the quantity of labour used in all production activities; x_{ij} represents the physical flow from sector i to sector j. All these magnitudes are supposed to be non-negative.

It appears now very useful, for reasons of symmetry, to put

$$a_{ij} = \frac{x_{ij}}{X_j}, \tag{7.3.3}$$

$$a_{ij} \geq 0, \qquad i,\ j = 1,2,\dots,n. \tag{7.3.4}$$

Then, systems (7.3.1) and (7.3.2) may be expressed in matrix notation[2]:

$$\begin{bmatrix} -1 & 0 & \dots & 0 & a_{1n} \\ 0 & -1 & \dots & 0 & a_{2n} \\ & & \ddots & & \vdots \\ 0 & 0 & \dots & -1 & a_{n-1,n} \\ a_{n1} & a_{n2} & \dots & a_{n,n-1} & -1 \end{bmatrix} \cdot \begin{bmatrix} X_1 \\ X_2 \\ \vdots \\ X_{n-1} \\ X_n \end{bmatrix} = \begin{bmatrix} 0 \\ 0 \\ \vdots \\ 0 \\ 0 \end{bmatrix}, \tag{7.3.5}$$

$$\begin{bmatrix} -1 & 0 & \dots & 0 & a_{n1} \\ 0 & -1 & \dots & 0 & a_{n2} \\ & & \ddots & & \vdots \\ 0 & 0 & \dots & -1 & a_{n,n-1} \\ a_{1n} & a_{2n} & \dots & a_{n-1,n} & -1 \end{bmatrix}, \begin{bmatrix} p_1 \\ p_2 \\ \vdots \\ p_{n-1} \\ p_n \end{bmatrix} = \begin{bmatrix} 0 \\ 0 \\ \vdots \\ 0 \\ 0 \end{bmatrix}. \tag{7.3.6}$$

The $(a_{n1}, a_{n2}, \dots, a_{n,n-1})$ represent technical coefficients of production, and the $(a_{1n}, a_{2n}, \dots, a_{n-1,n})$ represent demand coefficients of consumption. An evident property of these two systems is that they

[2] Here and in all subsequent analysis, I shall be using matrices to represent the systems of linear equations (in order to evince immediately all symmetrical properties). Any compact notation will be avoided, however, and matrices will always be written in full. In this way, the whole following analysis will remain understandable also to the readers who have no specific acquaintance with matrix algebra.

have the same, but transposed, coefficient matrix. As they have been defined, they are nothing but an algebraic representation of the flows which take place in the economic system under examination. However, they can be looked at in a different way. If we consider the a_{ij}s as parameters, then (7.3.5) and (7.3.6) form two systems of equations, and we can inquire into the nature of their solutions. These two systems are of a particular kind – they are linear and homogeneous. Therefore, in order that they may have non-trivial solutions (i.e. solutions which are not all equal to zero), the coefficient matrix must be singular; namely, it must satisfy the following condition (which is the same for both systems)[3]:

$$\begin{vmatrix} -1 & & & & a_{1n} \\ & -1 & & & a_{2n} \\ & & & & \vdots \\ & & & -1 & a_{n-1,n} \\ a_{n1} & a_{n2} & \dots & a_{n,n-1} & -1 \end{vmatrix} = 0. \tag{7.3.7}$$

By developing this determinant, the condition may be stated more simply as

$$a_{n1}a_{1n} + a_{n2}a_{2n} + \cdots + a_{n,n-1}a_{n-1,n} - 1 = 0. \tag{7.3.8}$$

If this condition is satisfied, then each of the two systems gives solutions for $(n-1)$ variables, while the nth variable can be fixed arbitrarily. In our case, there is evidently, for system (7.3.5), a magnitude which is fixed, namely $\bar{X}_n$: the total quantity of labour available. By contrast, no similar magnitude can be considered as fixed in (7.3.6). This expresses the well-known property that any economic system, considered in real terms, can give solutions for *relative* prices only, but not for their absolute level. Therefore, the choice being arbitrary, let us put, for the time being, $p_n = \bar{p}_n$. Hence

$$\begin{cases} X_1 \quad = a_{1n}\bar{X}_n, \\ X_2 \quad = a_{2n}\bar{X}_n, \\ \vdots \\ X_{n-1} = a_{n-1,n}\bar{X}_n, \end{cases} \tag{7.3.9}$$

[3] For the sake of simplicity, as already done earlier, the zeros will not be explicitly written, so that all entries in the matrices which are left blank are to be interpreted as zeros.

$$\begin{cases} p_1 &= a_{n1}\bar{p}_n, \\ p_2 &= a_{n2}\bar{p}_n, \\ \vdots \\ p_{n-1} &= a_{n,n-1}\bar{p}_n, \end{cases} \tag{7.3.10}$$

which present, respectively, the solutions of the system for physical quantities, relative to total labour available, and the solutions of the system for prices, relative to the price of labour. The meanings of expressions (7.3.9) and (7.3.10) are fairly straightforward. Each of the coefficients $(a_{1n}, a_{2n}, \ldots, a_{n-1,n})$ expresses average per-capita demand for each commodity, so that (7.3.9) means that production of each commodity depends exclusively on demand. If there were no demand, there would be no production. On the other hand, each of the coefficients $(a_{n1}, a_{n2}, \ldots, a_{n,n-1})$ expresses the labour input in each physical unit of output, so that (7.3.10) means that the price of each commodity is directly proportional to the quantity of labour required to produce it.

4 A Smithian Pure Labour Theory of Value and the Keynesian Principle of Effective Demand

An interesting aspect of the solutions (7.3.9) and (7.3.10) is that, in their amazing simplicity, they immediately call to mind the fundamentals of Smith's pure labour theory of value and also of Keynes's principle of effective demand.[4]

We may notice that the separation of the physical quantity system and the price system is complete. These two systems of equations can be solved independently of each other – a characteristic that should be further investigated.

Looking at solution (7.3.10), concerning the price system, one sees that prices turn out to be proportional to labour coefficients: quantities of labour are multiplied by the wage rate. One can immediately feel here an unmistakable classical flavour; a result after all quite obvious. In a system in which the only factor of production is labour, prices cannot but be proportional to quantities of labour. There is not even any reason to distinguish between 'embodied' labour and 'commanded'

[4] These characteristics were of course already revealed by inter-industry analysis (see Chapter 3).

labour (a distinction that caused so many complications to the classical economists). In a pure labour economy, the two notions necessarily coincide: the quantity of labour that each commodity can command is always exactly equal to the quantity of labour embodied in it. Precisely in this very connection, the meaning of prices emerges as typically classical: they do not express *market* prices (that would inevitably depend on the temporary whims of market supply and demand). They express those prices which the classical economists called 'natural prices' – a more fundamental notion of price, which reflects permanent and fundamental determinants. And, in our case, the permanent determinants are the production costs, expressed as quantities of necessary labour.[5]

Going on to consider solution (7.3.9) for the system of physical quantities, we see that the quantities turn out to be proportional to the consumption coefficients. Per-capita quantities of demand for consumption goods are multiplied by total population. And here we can unmistakably feel a Keynesian flavour. The solution (7.3.9) brings to the surface a production theory dominated by effective demand. Independently of the way decisions are made, solution (7.3.9) tell us that the physical quantities produced are determined by the effective demand that is actually being exerted for the various commodities. It could be said that the principle of effective demand emerges from the solutions of this system of physical quantities in a pure way, and in fact in a way which is clearer than in the elaborations of Keynes himself. As a direct result of the hypothetical absence of capital goods, the overall productive capacity in this model is represented by the multiform productive capacities of labour. And it is, therefore, a productive capacity, so to speak, widespread and undifferentiated, that makes itself available right there where demand so requires. The production is, in this sense, activated, or, as is also said, generated by effective demand. And

[5] The distinction between 'natural' and 'market' prices goes back to Smith (1904, book I, chapter 7). More accurate definitions can be found in Ricardo (1821, chapter 4), where the market prices are said to be 'disturbed by any temporary and accidental cause', due to the inevitable non-correspondence, at every instant, between the possibilities of production and the temporary whims of market demand. The 'natural' prices, on the other hand, are said to reflect the 'primary and natural' elements, that, being fundamental, are independent from demand Ricardo (1951, vol. 1. pp. 88–92). It is to the 'natural prices' that all classical economists, and more specifically Ricardo, always referred their basic formulations.

it is in this way that the Keynesian principle of effective demand here emerges, we might say, in its pure form.

There is only one constraint, not sectoral, but global, or macro-economic. This is the constraint which is set by the overall existing productive capacity, that is, in the present scheme, by the overall availability of total labour, namely, by its full employment. Here we come up precisely against the problems raised by Keynes (1936), concerning the importance of a particular macro-economic condition, which in the present scheme is expressed by necessary condition (7.3.8).

5 A Necessary (Overall) Condition for Full Employment

Condition (7.3.8) will recur time and again in the subsequent analysis, and we may well investigate its economic meaning immediately.

From a mathematical point of view, fulfilment of (7.3.8) is a necessary condition for each of the systems (7.3.5) and (7.3.6) to have non-trivial solutions. However, non-fulfilment does not imply no meaningful solution. The coefficient matrix of (7.3.5) and (7.3.6) has a particular form (all its entries are zeros, except those in the last row, in the last column, and along the main diagonal), which means that the solutions of the systems can be derived directly, without substitution, from the first $(n-1)$ equations of (7.3.5) and from the first $(n-1)$ of (7.3.6), respectively. Therefore, relative prices and relative quantities are determined independently of condition (7.3.8), whose binding restrictions fall entirely on the last equation of each of the two systems. Let us see what this means. Suppose, for example, that

$$\sum_{i=1}^{n-1} a_{ni}a_{in} < 1. \tag{7.5.1}$$

This inequality implies two things. In the context of the system (7.3.6) it implies[6] that $\sum a_{in}p_i < \bar{p}_n$, namely that average per-capita expenditure is less than the income that each worker receives: a situation of under-consumption. In the context of the system (7.3.5), it implies that $\sum a_{ni}X_i < \bar{X}_n$, namely that total labour employed is less than total labour available: a situation of under-employment.

[6] From now on, for the sake of simplicity, the limits of the summations will also be omitted. In other words, all summations that will appear in our analysis have to be interpreted as running from 1 to $(n-1)$, unless otherwise specified.

Conversely, the fulfilment of (7.3.8) implies both full expenditure of national income and full employment.

Looking at condition (7.3.8) more analytically, we may notice that it is a sum of binomials $a_{ni}a_{in}$ $(i = 1, 2, \ldots, n-1)$, where each of these binomials has the property of being composed of one technical coefficient and one consumption coefficient, both referring to the same commodity. Therefore, each $a_{ni}a_{in}$ expresses the *proportion* of total labour which is employed in that sector, or – which is the same – the proportion of full employment national income which is spent in that sector (sector i). Evidently, the sum of these proportions, for $i = 1, 2, \ldots, n-1$, must be equal to unity in order to achieve full employment. In those cases in which average per-capita expenditure turns out to be less than the income each worker receives, prices and quantities are determined all the same, but total production turns out to be less than potential production, and there will be unemployment in the economic system. This situation is expressed by condition (7.3.8) being under-satisfied, that is, by the summation of (7.3.8) being less than unity. The gap between $\sum a_{ni}a_{in}$ and unity expresses the proportion of labour that remains unemployed.

It is important to note immediately the overall (today we also say *macro-economic*) character of condition (7.3.8): it does not depend on the number of sectors that exist in the economy. Condition (7.3.8) is just one referring to the economic system as a whole, no matter how many (or how few) sectors may be considered. We may express it by simply saying that total expenditure must equal potential national income if full employment is to be achieved.

When put in these terms, condition (7.3.8) sounds familiar. It expresses a conclusion which has become well known in economic theory since Keynes brought it out explicitly.[7] The novelty here is that this macro-economic result emerges immediately from a pure production model of the type we are dealing with; and moreover that it emerges from a model which has been developed on a *multi-sector* basis, thereby revealing its truly macro-economic nature.[8]

7 Keynes (1936).

8 There are relations, in economic analysis, which take up a macro-economic form only when the analysis itself is carried out at a macro-economic level. These relations are macro-economic only artificially. They cease to be macro-economic as soon as the analysis is carried out at a more disaggregated

It must be added that, with the particular hypotheses of the present simple case (where no capital goods are needed), the condition that all income must be spent also means something more specific, namely that all income must be *consumed*. By adopting a Keynesian definition of savings, that is, by defining savings as the part of personal incomes that is not spent, macro-economic condition (7.3.8) may also be expressed by saying that there can be *no savings in this economic system* as a necessary condition for full employment. Single individuals, of course, may save, but there must be other individuals who dissave by the same amount so that savings and dissavings, in the aggregate, cancel each other out. The only form of savings which is possible for the economic system as a whole is in *real* terms, that is, by carrying over durable (produced) commodities from one period to another. But, within each period, total demand must be such as to induce the full utilisation of the production potential if full employment has to be reached. This is another important property of a production system. There must be demand – and in our simple case demand for consumption goods, whether durables or non-durables – for such an amount as to generate that quantity of production that requires the full employment of the existing labour force.

6 Production by Means of Labour and Capital Goods

We may now consider a more complex economic system which has all the properties of the system analysed in Sections 1 to 5, with one difference. The production processes, in order to be carried on, also require, besides labour, capital goods. Each production process is characterised, as in the previous case, by a flow-input of labour and a flow-output of final commodity, but now also requires the existence of a stock of capital goods, on which the labour services have to be performed, in order to produce the final output.

Capital goods are themselves commodities which have been produced in the economy, so that the final outputs of the economic system

level. But there are other relations which maintain a macro-economic form quite irrespective of the degree of disaggregation at which the analysis is carried out. It is these relations only that may be termed as *truly* macro-economic. Expression (7.3.8) is one of them.

are now of two types: consumption goods, which are consumed, as in the previous case, and capital goods, which are invested in the process of production. Capital goods are *durable* and, therefore, once produced, they go to increase the existing stock of capital goods. However, although durable, they are not eternal. As a result of being used by labour, they wear out and must be continually replaced if production is to go on. This means that each production process leading to a final commodity needs a further item. Besides a flow-input of labour and an existing stock of capital goods, each process also needs a further flow-input of capital goods to keep the initial capital stock intact. Hence, total production of capital goods, which represents total gross investment of the economic system, must be distinguished into two parts. A first part of it (replacement) simply goes to replace worn-out capital: in fact it is nothing but a cost of production, since it is needed in order that the production processes may end up with the same stocks of capital goods with which they began. The rest of the total production of capital goods, namely the excess over replacement, represents a net addition to the existing stocks of capital goods (*new investments*).

Capital goods may be grouped among themselves and measured in many different ways. How are we going to measure them here? In our analysis, all commodities have been measured so far in two ways: in terms of physical units – whatever the physical unit may be – and in terms of current prices – physical quantities multiplied by prices. The same procedure will be used for capital goods, but a particular physical unit will be adopted here, namely the unit of *vertically integrated productive capacity*. A physical unit of vertically integrated productive capacity (for the sake of simplicity, we shall simply say 'productive capacity', except where the omission of the term 'vertically integrated' may generate ambiguities) is defined with reference to the final commodity for which it is intended. There is therefore a specific physical unit of productive capacity for each final good which is produced in the economic system. Of course a unit of productive capacity is, in an ordinary sense, a very composite physical commodity: it is made up of different types of physical goods in different proportions. The reason why such a unit of measure is here used is the same that prompted the use of the concept of a final commodity. These concepts permit useful simplifications of exposition; they will actually become necessary in the dynamic analysis of the chapters that will follow.[9]

7 The Physical Stocks and Flows of the Economic System

Let us begin by considering the physical aspect of our economic system in a given period of time. We are faced with a series of flows and a series of stocks.

At the beginning of the time period, there exists a series of stocks of capital goods which have been inherited from previous periods. We may represent them by a vector

$$[K_1, K_2, \ldots, K_j, \ldots, K_{n-1}], \tag{7.7.1}$$

where each K_j stands for the stock of capital goods, measured in terms of physical units of productive capacity, in sector j ($j = 1, 2, \ldots, n.1$). When our analysis begins, the K_js are obviously given. However, they are not given by 'nature'. They are the result of a production activity in earlier periods of time, each K_j being the sum of all net investments made in the past in sector j.

We might say that, in the economic system, there is also another stock at the beginning of the time period we are considering, a really major stock, namely population. However, for economic purposes, this stock is not relevant as such, that is, as a stock (except in a slave society, which is outside our interests). Its economic relevance is connected only with the flows it calls into being.

Let us come, therefore, to consider these flows. As in the previous case, all the members of the community are grouped into a final sector n. This final sector provides the labour services to all productive processes and owns the stocks of capital goods. Moreover, it exerts the demand for all the final goods, which are now of two types – consumption goods and capital (or investment) goods.

The flows of consumption goods, as before, come from $(n-1)$ consumption goods sectors. In addition to these, we now have a whole series of flows of investment goods, which will be denoted with the suffix k. As a first major step to the more general formulation of Section 9,

[9] The notion of a physical unit of vertically integrated productive capacity was discussed at length, for the general case, first in Pasinetti (1965), then in Pasinetti (1973) – reprinted in Pasinetti (1980) – The 1973 Essay is in fact here reproduced as Chapter 6.

we shall assume that capital goods are required only for the production of consumption goods, while capital goods can be produced from labour alone. Since the physical units of measurement of capital goods (units of productive capacity) are specific to each consumption goods sector, the process for the production of capital goods must itself be expanded into $(n-1)$ sectors. Our system thereby acquires $(n-1)$ new variables: $X_{k_1}, X_{k_2}, \ldots, X_{k_{n-1}}$, each of which represents the production of capital goods for the corresponding consumption goods sector. This production of capital goods is devoted partly to new investment (expressed by demand coefficients in the final sectors: $a_{k_1 n}, a_{k_2 n}, \ldots, a_{k_{n-1} n}$) and partly to replacement of worn-out capacity (expressed by replacement coefficients: $a_{k_1 1}, a_{k_2 2}, \ldots, a_{k_{n-1} n-1}$). Hence, the whole structure of physical flows can be represented by the following linear and homogeneous system of equations, which here takes the place of (7.3.5):

$$\begin{bmatrix} -1 & & & & & & a_{1n} \\ & \ddots & & & & & \vdots \\ & & -1 & & & & a_{n-1,n} \\ a_{k_1 1} & & & -1 & & & a_{k_1 n} \\ & \ddots & & & \ddots & & \vdots \\ & & a_{k_{n-1} n-1} & & & -1 & a_{k_{n-1} n} \\ a_{n1} & \ldots & a_{n,n-1} & a_{nk_1} & & a_{nk_{n-1}} & -1 \end{bmatrix} \cdot \begin{bmatrix} X_1 \\ \vdots \\ X_{n-1} \\ X_{k_1} \\ \vdots \\ X_{k_{n-1}} \\ X_n \end{bmatrix} = \begin{bmatrix} 0 \\ \vdots \\ 0 \\ 0 \\ \vdots \\ 0 \\ 0 \end{bmatrix}. \tag{7.7.2}$$

A few words may be added about the replacement coefficients. Each $a_{k_1 i}$ $(i = 1, 2, \ldots, n-1)$ represents the amount of capital, in physical terms, which is required in each period of time in order to keep productive capacity intact. This is the general definition of the $a_{k_1 i}$s. However, as an expository device, we shall find it useful in the subsequent analysis to adopt a simplification, because of its immediately apparent meaning. We may assume that, in each period of time and in each sector, a *constant* proportion of the productive capacity vanishes owing to wear and tear, so that by writing $a_{k_1 i} = (1/T_i)$, the T_i may be interpreted as a quantity which is very near (though, depending on the sectoral rate of growth, not exactly coincident with) the average life-time of physical capital goods in sector i $(i = 1, 2, \ldots, n-1)$.

By now following exactly the same steps as in Section 3, the condition to be satisfied in order that the system of equations may have non-trivial solutions emerges as

$$\sum a_{ni}a_{in} + \sum (1/T_i)a_{nk_i}a_{in} + \sum a_{nk_i}a_{k_in} = 1, \tag{7.7.3}$$

and the solutions for the physical quantities take the form

$$\begin{cases} X_1 &= a_{1n}\bar{X}_n, \\ &\vdots \\ X_{n-1} &= a_{n-1,n}\bar{X}_n, \\ X_{k_1} &= [a_{k_1n} + (1/T_1)a_{1n}]\bar{X}_n, \\ &\vdots \\ X_{k_{n-1}} &= [a_{k_{n-1,n}} + (1/T_{n-1})a_{n-1,n}]\bar{X}_n. \end{cases} \tag{7.7.4}$$

As can be seen, the first $(n-1)$ solutions, referring to consumption goods, are again of the simple type of the previous case: they actually coincide with the (7.3.9). But the following $(n-1)$ solutions, referring to investment goods, now contain two addenda, expressing the fact that production of these goods is generated by two distinct types of demand: demand for new investments and demand for replacement of worn-out capacity.

8 The Structure of Prices

From the physical flows which have just been considered, another (dual) system of equations may be derived for prices. At first, one might think that one should write the same matrix entering (7.7.2) (but transposed) and multiply it by prices. This procedure, however, is no longer sufficient because the production processes now require capital goods, besides labour, and therefore the total income which flows to sector n has two components: a wage component proportional to physical labour and a profit component, proportional to the value of capital goods. In each (vertically integrated) sector, the value of output must be equal to the amount of wages due the labourers plus the amount of profits due the owners of the capital goods used in the production processes (in terms of productive capacity: $X_1, X_2, \ldots, X_{n-1}$). By calling w the wage rate and π the rate of profit, equation system (7.3.6) is replaced by

$$
\begin{bmatrix}
-1 & & & a_{k_1 1} & & a_{n1} \\
& \ddots & & & \ddots & \\
& & -1 & & a_{k_{n-1},n-1} & a_{n,n-1} \\
& & & -1 & & a_{nk_1} \\
& & & & \ddots & \vdots \\
& & & & -1 & a_{nk_{n-1}} \\
a_{1n} \; \cdots & a_{n-1,n} & a_{k_1 n} & \cdots & a_{k_{n-1} n} & -1
\end{bmatrix}
\cdot
\begin{bmatrix}
p_1 \\ \vdots \\ p_{n-1} \\ p_{k_1} \\ \vdots \\ p_{k_{n-1}} \\ w
\end{bmatrix}
+ \tag{7.8.1}
$$

$$
+ \begin{bmatrix}
\dfrac{\pi X_1 p k_1}{X_1} \\ \vdots \\ \dfrac{\pi X_{n-1} p_{k_{n-1}}}{X_{n-1}} \\ 0 \\ \vdots \\ 0 \\ \left(-\dfrac{\pi}{X_n}\right) \sum X_i p_{k_i}
\end{bmatrix}
=
\begin{bmatrix}
0 \\ \vdots \\ 0 \\ 0 \\ \vdots \\ 0 \\ 0
\end{bmatrix}.
$$

Here we are faced with a complication. Comparing (7.8.1) with (7.3.6), we can see that the unknown, p_n, has been eliminated, but only in order to be replaced by *two* new unknowns, w and π. This means that, if we want to keep determinate solutions for relative prices, we must assume that either w or π to be given, or alternatively, we must introduce a new explanatory relation.

This is an old dilemma in economic analysis. When the Classical economists (Ricardo in particular) faced it, they thought they could take the wage rate as given from outside the sphere of economics. Ever since, economists have been looking for other explanatory relations. The neo-classical economists, as is well known, introduced a series of new hypotheses and built up a whole theory behind the technical coefficients – the theory of marginal productivity.

In the present work, I am in a sense going back to the approach of the Classical economists, but with a reversal of their hypothesis. At this stage, I shall take as given, not the wage rate, but the rate of profit. It must be made clear, however, that this step does not have, in the present analysis, the same meaning that taking a given wage rate had for Classical economists. The rate of profit is not an *exogenous* magnitude in our theoretical scheme (as technology and consumers' preferences are). What taking the rate of profit as given here means is a simple assertion that the rate of profit is not determined by the elements of the model so far considered. Of course, the determinants of the rate of profit come within the scope of our economic investigation, and indeed they must (and shall) be examined. But, this will be done later, in Chapter 11, where the basic determinants of the rate of profit will be discussed in a dynamic context. For the time being, we only need to add here the assumption that the rate of profit is given exogenously *with respect to the theoretical scheme considered so far*. And there is of course no necessity to assume that the rate of profit is the same in all sectors. There may well be a particular rate of profit for each specific sector.

This allows us to express the new vector appearing in (7.8.1) in terms of prices and to incorporate the rates of profit and all exogenous elements into the coefficient matrix. Thus, system (7.8.1) becomes

$$\begin{bmatrix} -1 & & & \left(\pi_1 + \frac{1}{T_1}\right) & & a_{n1} \\ & \ddots & & & \ddots & \vdots \\ & & -1 & & \left(\pi_m + \frac{1}{T_m}\right) & a_{n,m} \\ & & & -1 & & a_{nk_1} \\ & & & & \ddots & \vdots \\ & & & & -1 & a_{nk_m} \\ a_{1n} & \dots & a_{m,n} & (a_{k_1 n} - \pi_1 a_{1n}) & \dots\ (a_{k_m n} - \pi_m a_{m,n}) & -1 \end{bmatrix} \cdot \begin{bmatrix} p_1 \\ \vdots \\ p_m \\ p_{k_1} \\ \vdots \\ p_{k_m} \\ w \end{bmatrix} = \begin{bmatrix} 0 \\ \vdots \\ 0 \\ 0 \\ \vdots \\ 0 \\ 0 \end{bmatrix}. \tag{7.8.2}$$

Here again we have obtained a system which is linear and homogeneous. Note that the coefficient matrix is different from the one entering (7.7.2). However, it is a remarkable property of these two matrices that their determinants are exactly the same, as can easily be demonstrated.[10] The necessary condition for (7.8.2) to yield non-trivial

[10] The determinant of the matrix entering (7.7.2), after substituting the $(1/T_i)$s for the $a_{k_i i}$s, emerges as

$$\sum a_{ni}a_{in} + \sum a_{nk_i}a_{k_i n} + \sum (1/T_i)a_{in}a_{nk_i} - 1, \tag{7.8.3}$$

and the determinant of the matrix entering (7.8.2) emerges as

$$\sum a_{ni}a_{in} + \sum (a_{k_i n} - \pi_i a_{in})a_{k_i n} + \sum (\pi_i + 1/T_i)a_{nk_i}a_{in} - 1. \tag{7.8.4}$$

This second expression can easily be reduced to the first, by expansion. We obtain solutions is therefore exactly the same as that which has been found already for (7.7.2), namely (7.7.3). Then, the solutions for prices (relative prices) come out as

$$\begin{cases} p_1 &= [a_{n1} + (\pi_1 + 1/T_1)a_{nk_1}]w, \\ &\vdots \\ p_{n-1} &= [a_{n,n-1} + (\pi_{n-1} + 1/T_{n-1})a_{nk_{n-1}}]w, \\ p_{k_1} &= a_{nk_1}w, \\ &\vdots \\ p_{k_{n-1}} &= a_{nk_{n-1}}w. \end{cases} \tag{7.8.6}$$

As the reader can see, the last $(n-1)$ prices are still of the simple type, as they appear in Section 7. But this is only because of the simplifying assumption that capital goods require no capital goods to be produced. The formulation for the $(n-1)$ prices of consumption goods is more general and more interesting. Each price is expressed as a sum of two addenda which we may call: the prime cost a_{ni} (i.e. the quantity of labour required to produce one unit of the corresponding capacity) and the gross profit mark-up $(\pi_i + 1/T_i)a_{nk_i}$. The latter is in turn composed of the rate of profit (π_i) and of the depreciation allowance $(1/T_i)$, both of them being proportional to a_{nk_i}, which represents the quantity of labour required to produce one unit of productive capacity for sector i; $i = 1, 2, \ldots, n-1$.

At this stage already, it would appear that a pure labour theory of value is no longer discernible in our formulations (or, at least at a first look, is discernible only for particular cases, such as the case in which $\pi_i = 0$, for all $i = 1, 2, \ldots, n-1$ – a zero rate of profit – or the case in which $(a_{ni}/a_{nk_i}) = (a_{nj}/a_{nk_j})$ for all $i, j = 1, 2, \ldots, n-1$ – that is, a uniform capital intensity of the production processes). But, in general, if the rates of profit are positive and the capital intensity is different from one production process to another, relative prices will depend

$$\sum a_{ni}a_{in} + \sum a_{nk_i}a_{k_in} + \sum (1/T_i)a_{in}a_{nk_i} - \sum \pi_i a_{in}a_{nk_i} + \sum \pi_i a_{in}a_{nk_i} - 1, \tag{7.8.5}$$

where it can be seen that the last and the last but one summations cancel each other out. What remains coincides with (7.8.3).

Thus, the introduction of a whole series of rates of profit does not make any difference to the formulation of the macro-economic equilibrium condition, which continues to be given by physical magnitudes alone.

both on wages on the labour inputs and on the rate of profit on the value of capital goods.

It is important to notice, however, from (7.8.6), that our approach has made it possible to express *all* price components in such a way as to allow the wage rate to be factored out. This means that what appears in the square brackets, by being multiplied by the wage rate, must obviously be either a physical quantity of labour or something which is made to be equivalent to a physical quantity of labour. We shall examine in Chapter 11 the conditions under which the magnitude here appearing in square brackets can actually be reduced to physical quantities of labour. For the time being, let us notice that – whatever the way in which the rates of profit are determined – (7.8.6) imply a theory of value which is based on quantities of physical labour and moreover on quantities which are made to be equivalent to physical quantities of labour. As can be seen, the indirect physical labour is weighted more than the direct physical labour when the (exogenously given) rate of profit is positive. The prices thereby express a theory of value which (at least for the time being) is no longer in terms of strictly physical labour but in terms of what we shall provisionally call *labour equivalents*.

9 A More Comprehensive Model Involving Capital Goods for the Production of Capital Goods

We have assumed so far that no capital goods are needed for the production of capital goods, but the simplification has been made only in order to keep the formulations as short as possible.

Dropping this assumption does not entail any conceptual difficulty; it only requires some further algebraic manipulations. We may assume, for example, in order not to go on *ad infinitum*, that each of the capital goods sectors makes capital goods for itself and for the corresponding consumption goods sector, and we may denote by γ_i, in each sector i $(i = 1, 2, \ldots, n-1)$, the ratio of one physical unit of capital goods expressed in terms of productive capacity for the consumption goods sector to one unit of capital goods expressed in terms of productive capacity for the capital goods sector:

$$\gamma_i = \frac{X_i}{X_{k_i}}, \qquad i = 1, 2, \ldots, n-1. \tag{7.9.1}$$

In other words we might say that the physical machinery is supposed to be the same in both sectors and can produce either X_i physical units of consumption good i or $(1/\gamma_i)X_{k_i}$ units of capital goods for consumption good i (i.e. its productive capacity itself).

Then, a new series of $(n-1)$ replacement coefficients for the capital goods sectors has to be introduced into the matrix (7.7.2), in addition to those already considered for the consumption goods sectors. Similarly, a new series of $(n-1)$ profit and depreciation mark-ups, for the prices of investment goods, has to be introduced in matrix (7.8.2), in addition to those already considered for the prices of consumption goods.

In both matrices, the new $(n-1)$ elements fall along the second half of the main diagonal.[11] Again the two matrices are different from each other. Yet their determinants coincide, as can easily be checked. The condition under which the two matrices are singular (a necessary condition for non-trivial solutions) is therefore again the same for both of them and emerges as

[11] The coefficient matrix for the quantity system is

$$\begin{bmatrix} -1 & \dots & 0 & 0 & \dots & 0 & a_{1n} \\ \vdots & \ddots & \vdots & \vdots & \ddots & \vdots & \vdots \\ 0 & \dots & -1 & 0 & \dots & 0 & a_{m,n} \\ \frac{1}{T_1} & \dots & 0 & -\left(1-\frac{\gamma_1}{T_{k_1}}\right) & \dots & 0 & a_{k_1 n} \\ \vdots & \ddots & \vdots & \vdots & \ddots & \vdots & \vdots \\ 0 & \dots & \frac{1}{T_m} & 0 & \dots & -\left(1-\frac{\gamma_m}{T_{km}}\right) & a_{k_{n-1}n} \\ a_{n1} & \dots & a_{n,m} & a_{nk_1} & & a_{nk_m} & \bar{X}_n \end{bmatrix},$$

while the coefficient matrix for the price system is

$$\begin{bmatrix} -1 & \dots & 0 & \pi_1+\frac{1}{T_1} & \dots & 0 & a_{n1} \\ \vdots & \ddots & \vdots & \vdots & \ddots & \vdots & \vdots \\ 0 & \dots & -1 & 0 & \dots & T_m+\frac{1}{T_{n-1}} & a_{nm} \\ 0 & \dots & 0 & -\left(1-\frac{\gamma_1}{T_{k_1}}-\gamma_1\pi_{k_1}\right) & \dots & 0 & a_{nk_1} \\ \vdots & \ddots & \vdots & \vdots & \ddots & \vdots & \vdots \\ 0 & \dots & 0 & 0 & \dots & -\left(1-\frac{\gamma_m}{T_{k_{n-1}}}-\gamma_m\pi_{k_{n-1}}\right) & a_{nk_m} \\ a_{1n} & \dots & a_{mn} & a_{k_1 n}-(\pi_1+\pi_{k_1}\gamma_1) & \dots & a_{k_m n}-(\pi_m+\pi k_m\gamma_m) & w \end{bmatrix}.$$

$$\sum a_{ni}a_{in} + \sum (1/T_i)\frac{T_{k_i}}{T_{k_i} - \gamma_i}a_{nk_i}a_{in} + \sum \frac{T_{k_i}}{T_{k_i} - \gamma_i}a_{nk_i}a_{k_in} = 1. \tag{7.9.2}$$

When this condition is satisfied, the solutions for relative quantities and relative prices are again easily found and come out as follows:

$$\begin{cases} X_1 &= a_{1n}\bar{X}_n, \\ \vdots & \\ X_m &= a_{n-1,n}\bar{X}_n, \\ X_{k_1} &= \frac{T_{k_1}}{T_{k_1}-\gamma_1}[a_{k_1n} + (1/T_1)a_{1n}]\bar{X}_n, \\ \vdots & \\ X_{k_m} &= \frac{T_{k_{n-1}}}{T_{k_m}-\gamma_m}[a_{k_mn} + (1/T_m)a_{m,n}]\bar{X}_n, \end{cases} \tag{7.9.3}$$

$$\begin{cases} p_1 &= \left[(\pi_1 + 1/T_1)\frac{T_{k_1}}{T_{k_1}-\gamma_1-\pi_{k_1}\gamma_1T_{k_1}}a_{nk_1} + a_{n1}\right]w, \\ \vdots & \\ p_m &= \left[(\pi_m + 1/T_m)\frac{T_{km}}{T_{km}-\gamma_m-\pi_{km}\gamma_mT_{km}}a_{nk_m} + a_{n,m}\right]w, \\ p_{k_1} &= \frac{T_{k_1}}{T_{k_1}-\gamma_1-\pi_{k_1}\gamma_1T_{k_1}}a_{nk_1}w, \\ \vdots & \\ p_{k_m} &= \frac{T_{km}}{T_{km}-\gamma_m-\pi_{km}\gamma_mT_{km}}a_{nk_m}w. \end{cases} \tag{7.9.4}$$

These two new series of solutions are basically similar to (7.8.6), although they are a little more complicated. Each production of capital goods now satisfies not only the demand for replacement and new investments in the corresponding consumption goods sector but also the demand for replacement and new investment in the capital goods sector itself. Similarly, each of the prices now covers not only the profit and depreciation allowance for the consumption good to which it refers but also the profit and depreciation allowance for the corresponding capital goods.

Since, in this case, the production processes of capital goods are explicitly assumed to require as inputs a part of their own outputs, there is a further necessary condition that must be satisfied to ensure positive solutions for the physical quantities, or rather, there is a series of $(n-1)$ necessary conditions – one necessary condition for each (vertically integrated) sector.[12] This series of conditions emerges clearly from expression (7.9.3) and can be stated algebraically as

$$T_{k_i} > \gamma_i, \qquad i = 1, 2, \ldots, n-1, \tag{7.9.5}$$

meaning that the total output from the employment of each set of machines, in the whole course of its life, must be more than one set of the same type. If it were not so (i.e. if any process of production for capital goods were to require more as inputs than can be given as outputs), production would be impossible. As will be realised, these are conditions that have become known in the economic literature as *viability conditions*. Their counterparts for the price system again emerge immediately from (7.9.4) and can be expressed as:

$$\pi_i < \frac{T_{k_i} - \gamma_i}{\gamma_i T_{k_i}}, \qquad i = 1, 2, \ldots, n-1. \tag{7.9.6}$$

In other words, for each (vertically integrated) sector, there is a finite maximum rate of profit that cannot be exceeded if prices are to remain positive.[13]

Yet, in spite of these algebraic complications, the reader will notice that the theory of value implied by (7.9.4) has exactly the same features as the theory of value implied by (7.8.6). More specifically, all components of prices are expressed in terms of labour, or labour equivalents, multiplied by the wage rate.

[12] No condition of this type emerges from the theoretical scheme of Sections 7 and 8 (at least as long as our formulations are not re-interpreted with reference to inter-industry systems, the explanation being that, in the scheme considered in Sections 7 and 8), no commodity is supposed to require itself for its own production; hence, the maximum eigenvalue of the coefficient matrix entering (7.7.2) and (7.8.2) is zero.

[13] The viability condition (7.9.6), when it is written as

$$T_{k_i} > \gamma_i + \pi_i \gamma_i T_{k_i}, \tag{7.9.7}$$

immediately appears as more restrictive than the corresponding viability condition (7.9.5) for the physical quantity system. The reason is that we are here considering production with reference to a single period of time. We shall see later on that, when exponential economic growth is introduced into the analysis, the formulations for physical new investments will become more complete. From these more complete formulations, the viability conditions for the physical quantity system will emerge as perfectly symmetrical (or rather, mathematically 'dual') to the viability conditions for the price system, the rates of growth taking the place of the rates of profit; see also footnotes 3 and 9.

This will allow us, for most of the subsequent analysis, to continue to use formulations (7.7.3), (7.7.4) and (7.8.6), instead of the corresponding (more laborious) formulations (7.9.2)–(7.9.4), without any loss of generality, because conceptually they do not differ from one another.

10 Simplifications

A further simplification becomes possible in the analysis of the following three chapters, besides those just mentioned and concerning the use of expressions (7.7.3), (7.7.4), and (7.8.6), instead of (7.9.2)–(7.9.4). As a purely expository device, the same rate of wear and tear $(1/T)$ will be used for the capital goods of all sectors. This will cut down the number of suffixes in our formulations, without at the same time losing the possibility of reintroducing them on any occasion in which they may become relevant.

Similarly, for the time being, we shall use the same rate of profit (π) for all sectors. Here the assumption of uniformity may appear to have a more important economic content, since the equalisation of the rates of profit in all sectors is a tendency normally associated with the institutions of capitalist systems. However, whatever interpretation one normally attaches to this hypothesis, in the following analysis it will simply stand as a provisional step that allows us to deal with one problem at a time. We shall come back to non-uniformity of rates of profit in Chapter 11, where we turn to a specific examination of the determinants of the rates of profit in the different sectors.

11 The Equilibrium Conditions

No comment has yet been made on the new form taken by the full employment condition. Expression (7.7.3) – or for that matter (7.9.2) – represents, in mathematical terms, a condition that must be satisfied in order that the corresponding two linear and homogeneous systems may have non-trivial solutions. It clearly takes the place of (7.3.8) of the previous case and has exactly the same economic meaning – a necessary condition for achieving full employment. Unlike (7.3.8), expression (7.7.3) now makes a distinction among three different types of demand: demand for consumption goods, demand for replacing worn-out capital goods and demand for new investments. However, the importance of this distinction will only be seen in the dynamic analysis which will follow, since differing compositions of demand in a given period of time evidently have different consequences on the stocks of capital goods in the ensuing period. For the time being, and as far as a short-run analysis is concerned, the composition of demand does not matter. To fulfil (7.7.3), that is to achieve full employment, the only requirement that is imposed is that the *sum* of all types of demand be such as to imply a total overall expenditure equal to total potential national income.[14]

What must be added, however, is that the fulfilment of (7.7.3) is no longer enough, because it only refers to the flow aspect of the economic system and thereby implies only potential full employment. Some other conditions must be fulfilled with regard to the stocks. First of all, there must be enough productive capacities in the economic system to make it possible to produce what is required by potential demand, that is,

$$K_i \geq X_i, \qquad i = 1, 2, \ldots, n-1. \tag{7.11.1}$$

Yet this could not be defined as a satisfactory situation if some strict inequality were to hold, that is, if some productive capacity were far beyond what is required by full employment. We have to impose also the conditions of full capacity utilisation, namely:

$$K_i \leq X_i, \qquad i = 1, 2, \ldots, n-1. \tag{7.11.2}$$

It follows that, for the (7.11.1) and (7.11.2) to be both satisfied, all the K_is must be equal to the X_is.

To sum up, two types of conditions are now necessary for the systems (7.7.2) and (7.8.2) to hold, namely

$$\sum a_{ni}a_{in} + \sum a_{nk_i}a_{k_in} + \sum (1/T_i)a_{nk_i}a_{in} = 1, \tag{7.11.3}$$

and

$$K_i = X_i, \qquad i = 1, 2, \ldots, n-1. \tag{7.11.4}$$

[14] It must be pointed out, however, that the introduction of an exogenously given rate of profit has now made values at current prices no longer proportional to physical quantities of labour. This means that each binomial under the summations (7.7.3), while still keeping the meaning of proportion of total labour that is employed in the corresponding sector, loses the meaning of proportion of total final national income, at current prices, that is accounted for the same sector. We shall see later on Chapter 11 that this second meaning may be regained, under certain conditions.

We may notice that (7.11.3), like (7.3.8), is a macro-economic condition: there must be a total amount of demand equal to potential national income if full employment is to be reached. On the other hand, (7.11.4) represents *a series* of sectoral conditions: one condition for each sector. Each sector i must be endowed with that stock of productive capacity which is necessary to produce the amount of commodity i which is demanded ($i = 1, 2, \ldots, n-1$).

At this point, one may wonder what would happen if (7.11.3) and (7.11.4) were not satisfied. And the answer is that this clearly depends on how the non-fulfilment comes about. A few interesting cases may usefully be considered. Inequalities of type (7.11.1), plus the left-hand side of (7.11.3) being lower than its right-hand side, mean idle capacity and less than full employment: a situation which we may call of Keynesian under-employment,[15] for is due to lack of effective demand. On the other hand, inequalities of type (7.11.2), again plus the left-hand side of (7.11.3) lower than its right-hand side, correspond to a situation in which the capital structure is smaller than the one which would make full employment possible: a situation which may be called one of Marxian under-employment. The two opposite cases as to condition (7.11.3) represent situations of inflation of different types, due respectively to lack of labour and to lack of productive capacity.

But a further question that may arise at this point is the following: if any of these cases, or if any other situation takes place, in which (7.11.3) and (7.11.4) are not satisfied, how is the system going to react? The answer clearly depends on the particular institutional set-up that the economic system has adopted. But it is not my purpose, as already

[15] Of course, Keynes had a *behavioural* theory about this situation, with reference to a capitalist economy. In terms of the present terminology, Keynes's theory was that, for psychological reasons,

$$\sum a_{ni} a_{in} < 1,$$

namely that total demand for consumer goods on the whole tends to be smaller than full employment national income. Of course, demand for investment goods might be such a proportion of total national income as to make up for the difference from unity in the inequality stated above. But Keynes pointed out that there is no reason necessarily to expect this, because the two types of demand depend on different factors. He thought that the most likely situation to arise in practice would be one in which there is lack of effective demand and excess of productive capacity, as is the case characterised by the inequalities referred to in the text.

said, to go into any inquiry of problems of this type for the time being. At this stage, no *behavioural* theory implying any particular institutional set-up will be introduced. The purpose here is simply to find and to specify the conditions that *must* be satisfied, in any case, if full employment is to be reached. We shall return to the problems of disequilibrium later.

To conclude, when both (7.11.3) and (7.11.4) are fulfilled, the two systems of equations (7.7.2) and (7.8.2) hold in their entirety. This means that the economic system they represent has achieved full employment of labour and full utilisation of existing productive capacity. From now on, for the sake of simplicity, we shall simply refer to such a situation as one of *equilibrium*. It should perhaps be stressed that no connotation of automaticity and no association with any particular adjustment mechanism is intended to be implied by such an expression. A *situation of equilibrium* will simply be taken to mean a situation in which there is full employment of the labour force and full utilisation of the existing productive capacity. It is with these assumptions that our analysis will proceed.

12 The Step towards a Dynamic Analysis

The foregoing analysis, after the introduction of capital goods, has acquired an important characteristic: although still a short-term analysis, it is no longer a static analysis. Even if we suppose that equilibrium conditions (7.11.3) and (7.11.4) are satisfied, we cannot say that we are at the end of our analysis. These conditions refer to a certain period of time, but, in order to be fulfilled in that time period, they may (and normally will) contain some elements (investments) whose mere existence means modifying, in the following time period, those magnitudes (the stocks of capital goods) on which the previous equilibrium situation was based.

In this theoretical framework, therefore, the attainment of equilibrium in a given period of time does not mean at all that all economic problems have been solved.

On the contrary, a whole new field of analysis has been opened: we are inevitably led, by our own analysis, from the investigation of equilibrium conditions in a given period of time to the investigation of equilibrium conditions through time.

8 *Population Growth at Constant Returns to Scale as the Simplest Case of Economic Expansion*

1 A Simple Dynamic Model

Our inquiry will now venture into what happens *after* the single period so far considered has elapsed and into what happens in general as time goes by. From an analytical point of view, there are two notions of time which may be adopted. Time may be conceived of as a succession of finite periods, with the supposition that changes take place only between one period and another. Or time may be conceived of as bringing along changes in a continuous way, so that the finite periods of the previous procedure become so short as to be infinitesimal. For our purposes, it is immaterial whether the first or the second procedure is adopted. But since the second procedure makes things analytically simpler, from our point of view, it will normally be followed in the following dynamic analysis. However, the arguments will also be re-cast now and then in terms of the first procedure when that appears useful and illuminating.

If we look beyond a single period of time, all magnitudes considered so far must be *dated*. The previous short-run analysis remains valid within each time period, but from one time period to another, those quantities which have hitherto been taken as given may undergo important changes.

Our procedure will now be to make some hypotheses about the movements through time of those magnitudes (population, technical progress and consumption patterns) which we accept as given from outside economic investigation, and then to inquire into the equilibrium movements of the economic variables. For analytical purposes, in this chapter, we shall consider the simplest of all cases of dynamic change by supposing that, over time, the only *exogenous* factor which is changing is population. This simple case has been extensively dealt with already in the economic literature, and the purpose of the present chapter is not, therefore, to obtain new result. The purpose is to evince the connections with the already known growth models and, at the same time, to develop formulations which will be needed in the following analysis.

Our hypotheses may now be listed schematically as follows:

(i) First of all, the *initial conditions* are such that, when our analysis begins, at a time defined as zero, there is full employment of the labour force and full utilisation of productive capacity. In our terminology, the economic system is in a situation of equilibrium.

(ii) Over time, population increases at a steady percentage rate g, so that

$$X_n(t) = X_n(0)e^{gt}, \tag{8.1.1}$$

where t denotes time, and e is the basis of the natural logarithms.[1]

(iii) Technical condition remain absolutely fixed over time; expansion takes place at constant returns to scale. In other words, all technical coefficients (the a_{ni}s, the a_{nk_i}s and the T_is; $i = 1, 2, \ldots, n-1$) remain unchanged in time.

(iv) Consumers' tastes also remain constant, which means that, if individuals continue to receive the same income, their consumption – that is, all the coefficients $a_{in}s$; $i = 1, 2, \ldots, n-1$ – remain constant through time.

These are all the hypotheses that are needed in this case, besides of course the convention (discussed in Chapter 7, Section 7) of taking the rate of profit as given. The reader may have noticed that there is a series of coefficients which have not been mentioned: the $a_{k_in}s$, namely the demand coefficients for new investments. The reason is that these coefficients cannot be specified in advance; in a dynamic analysis, they are themselves unknown, they must be determined in such a way as to be consistent with the growing productive potential of the economic system.

Our task is now to find, first of all, the condition under which the initial equilibrium situation may be maintained through time and then to investigate the time paths of the economic variables.

1 The letter g thus denotes a *percentage* rate of growth per period of time. For brevity's sake, however, we shall simply refer to it as a 'rate of growth', except in those cases where omission of the adjective 'percentage' and of the reference to the period of time might generate misunderstanding.

2 The Conditions for a Dynamic Equilibrium

We might begin by saying that, in order to maintain equilibrium over time, conditions (7.11.3) and (7.11.4), which are satisfied *ex-hypothesis* at time zero, must also and constantly be kept satisfied as time goes on. A statement of this kind, however, now becomes uninteresting and superficial, because those two conditions cease to be independent of one another as soon as time is allowed to elapse.

If population is growing, both the availability of labour services and the demand for each product increase over time. In order that the new labour force may find employment and the growing potential demand may become effective, productive capacity must also increase. Thus, in time, the equilibrium conditions for productive capacity become

$$\frac{d}{dt}[K_i(t)] = \frac{d}{dt}[X_i(t)], \qquad i = 1, 2, \ldots, n-1, \tag{8.2.1}$$

which simply means that there must be an increase in the productive capacity of each commodity, parallel to the increase in its demand.

The formulation may be expressed in a more helpful way by making use of a few definitions. We know from (7.7.4) that each demand for capital goods ($X_{k_i}; i = 1, 2, \ldots, n-1$) is composed of two parts: replacement of worn-out capacity $[(1/T_i)a_{in} = \frac{1}{T_i}a_{in}\bar{X}_n]$ and new investment ($a_{k_in}X_n$). Denoting these two parts respectively by X'_{k_i} and X''_{k_i}, so that

$$X_{k_i}(t) = X'_{k_i}(t) + X''_{k_i}(t), \tag{8.2.2}$$

we have

$$X''_{k_i}(t) = \frac{d}{dt}[K_i(t)], \qquad i = 1, 2, \ldots, (n-1). \tag{8.2.3}$$

By substituting (8.2.3) into (8.2.1), we obtain

$$X''_{k_i}(t) = \frac{d}{dt}[X_i(t)], \qquad i = 1, 2, \ldots, (n-1), \tag{8.2.4}$$

which amounts to expressing the productive capacity equilibrium conditions in the form of equilibrium relations between the demand for new capital goods in each period of time and the *rate of change* of demand for the corresponding consumption goods. Using (7.7.4) and (8.1.1)

$$a_{k_in}X_n(0)e^{gt} = \frac{d}{dt}\left[a_{in}X_n(0)e^{gt}\right],$$

or

$$a_{k_in}X_n(0)e^{gt} = ga_{in}X_n(0)e^{gt},$$

and finally[2]

$$a_{k_in} = ga_{in}, \qquad i = 1, 2, \ldots, n-1. \tag{8.2.7}$$

This is a remarkable formulation. It states the series of sectoral productive capacity conditions in terms of flows (and no longer in terms of stocks) by specifying a very definite relation which must hold between each demand coefficient for new investments and the corresponding demand coefficient for consumption goods. Hence, as a condition to endow the economic system with equilibrium productive capacity, each sectoral new investment, in physical terms, must be equal to the corresponding sectoral final demand multiplied by the rate of growth of population. This determines sectoral equilibrium new investment in the whole economic system:

$$X''_{k_i}(t) = ga_{in}X_n(t), \qquad i = 1, 2, \ldots, n-1. \tag{8.2.8}$$

We shall call these conditions *the capital accumulation conditions* for keeping full employment over time (or capital accumulation equilibrium conditions).

If we like, the expression (8.2.8) may also be expressed in terms of ratios between physical quantities evaluated at current prices. After multiplying both sides of (8.2.8) by p_{k_i} and dividing by p_iX_i, we obtain

$$\frac{p_{k_i}X''_{k_i}}{p_iX_i} = g\frac{p_{k_i}X_i}{p_iX_i}, \qquad i = 1, 2, \ldots, n-1. \tag{8.2.9}$$

2 In the more complex case considered in Section 9 of Chapter 7, these formulations become slightly more complex. Expression (8.2.4) becomes

$$X''_{k_i}(t) = \frac{\mathrm{d}}{\mathrm{d}t}\left[X_i(t) + \gamma_i X_{k_i}(t)\right], \qquad i = 1, 2, \ldots, n-1, \tag{8.2.5}$$

and therefore expression (8.2.7), that is, the capital accumulation equilibrium conditions, becomes

$$a_{k_in} = g\frac{T_{k_i}}{T_{K_i} - \gamma_i - g\gamma_i T_{k_i}}a_{in}. \tag{8.2.6}$$

Notice also that the replacements of worn-out capacity will have to be modified accordingly. They emerge as

$$X'_{k_i}(t) = (1/T_i)\frac{T_{k_i}}{T_{K_i} - \gamma_i - g\gamma_i T_{k_i}}a_{in}X_n(t).$$

which means that, in equilibrium, each sectoral ratio of new investment to output, evaluated at current prices, must be equal to the corresponding sectoral capital/output ratio multiplied by the rate of population growth. As the reader will realise, the expression (8.2.9) represents a multi-sector version of what has become known, in the economic literature, as the 'Harrod-Domar equation'.[3] Our 'capital accumulation equilibrium conditions' are in fact nothing but a series of 'Harrod–Domar equations'; there is a particular Harrod–Domar equation that must be satisfied in each particular sector.

When these conditions are kept satisfied through time, the economic system as being constantly endowed with exactly those stocks of productive capacity which are necessary to provide full employment for all the workers. This however does not, *per se*, ensure full employment and full utilisation of productive capacity. In order that equilibrium be reached, the other necessary condition – the macro-economic relation referring to demand in the economic system as a whole – must also be satisfied. After substituting

$$\sum a_{ni}a_{in} + (g + 1/T)\sum a_{nk_i}a_{in} = 1. \qquad (8.2.10)$$

The economic meaning is again that total expenditure must be equal to total potential gross national income if full employment and full capacity utilisation are to be attained. However, (8.2.10) now also requires a very definite division of total expenditure between new investments, replacements and consumption. The effect of substituting into these capital accumulation equilibrium conditions has been to specify the magnitude of the term $(g + 1/T)\sum a_{nk_i}a_{in}$, which is nothing but an analytical break down of the proportion of total labour required by equilibrium gross investments. This equilibrium proportion, as can be seen, is exclusively determined by the three exogenous forces of the economic system. Population growth, technology and consumers' preferences. Therefore, if (8.2.10) is to be satisfied (i.e. if full employment is to be kept), it is the effective demand for consumption goods that must absorb the whole remaining proportion of total labour – represented by the first expression of (8.2.10). Condition (8.2.10), since it thereby determines the size of total effective demand, may be called the *effective demand condition* for keeping full employment.

[3] See Harrod (1939), Harrod (1948) and Domar (1946).

To conclude, two kinds of necessary conditions must be satisfied in order to keep equilibrium over time. First of all, there is a series of capital accumulation conditions (8.2.7), ensuring that each sector be endowed all the time with precisely that amount of additional productive capacity which is required by the expanding demand. These conditions state that the ratio of new investments to the level of production must be equal, in each sector, to the technologically determined capital/output ratio multiplied by the rate of population growth. Secondly, in order to ensure the full utilisation of the available productive capacity and the full employment of the available labour force, a further macro-economic effective demand condition (8.2.10) must also be satisfied. This condition states that, given (by the first series of conditions and by replacement requirements) the total amount of equilibrium gross investment, total demand for consumption goods must be such as to absorb the whole remaining part of potential gross national income.

It is important to notice that these conditions, in the case we are considering here, present no problem *through time*. Since all coefficients are constant, once conditions (8.2.7) and (8.2.10) are satisfied at time zero, they will remain satisfied for all time.

3 A More Complex Formulation of the Effective Demand Condition

It may be useful to take a further step, at this point, to complete formulation (8.2.10). Population has been referred to in general terms so far, both with respect to demand for commodities and with respect to supply for labour. This has meant assuming implicitly that population and labour force are the same thing. In practice, this is not so. All people do contribute to demand for commodities, but only a fraction of them (representing active population) actually take part in the process of production. Moreover, a further complication arises in connection with the fact that our coefficients have a time dimension. The point may be made clearer by supposing a finite period, for example a year, as the unit of time. In this case, the consumption coefficients refer to yearly per-capita consumption, but, normally, the technical coefficients refer to that fraction of the unit of time which corresponds to actual working time. When this is done, the a_{in}s and the a_{in}s come no longer to be expressed in terms of the same number of people and not even to refer to the same unit of time.

To be consistent, a correction must be made to the technical coefficients in order to make them comparable with the demand coefficients, and the simplest way to do this is to divide each technical coefficient by two parameters, the first of which – let us call it μ – represents the proportion of active to total population and the second – let us call it ν – the ratio of, let us say, working hours to the total number of hours forming the unit of time considered.

Evidently,

$$1 > \mu > 0, \tag{8.3.1}$$

$$1 > \nu > 0. \tag{8.3.2}$$

These corrections do not affect the expression we found for prices, which contains the technical coefficients, provided of course that the wage rate refers to a unit of actual working time (as it usually does). They do affect, on the other hand, the expression for the effective demand condition for equilibrium, where both demand coefficients and technical coefficients appear together. (This is after all intuitive: the conditions for reaching full employment are different, according to the ratio of active to total population and to the length of the working week.) Hence, after introducing μ and ν, (8.2.10) becomes

$$(1/\mu\nu)\sum a_{ni}a_{in} + (g + 1/T)(1/\mu\nu)\sum a_{nk_i}a_{in} = 1, \tag{8.3.3}$$

which must be considered as a more complete formulation of the effective demand condition for a dynamic equilibrium.

4 The Dynamic Movements of the Economic Variables

To find out how prices and physical quantities move, as time goes by, is now a relatively easy task. As to prices, it can immediately be seen from the expression (7.8.6) that, under the present hypotheses, all their components are constant over time, so that *all relative prices remain constant over time.*

The expression (7.7.4) for physical quantities, on the other and, all contain one component, namely population, which is increasing at a percentage rate g. This component, however, is the same for all of them, so that *all physical quantities increase in time at the same percentage rate of growth g*. We might also say that *relative* physical quantities remain constant over time.

As a consequence, sectoral outputs at current prices, which we shall denote by $V_i(t)$, that is,

$$V_i(t) = p_i(t)X_i(t), \qquad i = 1, 2, \ldots, n-1, k_1, k_2, \ldots, k_{n-1}, \qquad (8.4.1)$$

will all grow through time at the same percentage growth rate g, as can easily be checked after substitution from (7.7.4) and (7.8.6).

Besides prices and quantities, there are other magnitudes in the economic system which are of economic interest and which are worth considering. To begin with, the time-path of the amount of employment in each sector can be derived immediately from the movements of physical quantities. Denoting sectoral employment by $E_i(t)$, we have

$$E_i(t) = a_{ni}(t)X_i(t), \qquad i = 1, 2, \ldots, n-1, k_1, k_2, \ldots, k_{n-1}. \qquad (8.4.2)$$

And again, after substitution from (7.7.4), it can be seen that, under the present hypotheses, *all* E_is increase in time at the same percentage rate of growth of population (g). In other words, the *structure* of employment remains invariant.[4]

Further, we may consider the capital/output ratios and the capital/labour ratios in each sector and in the economy as a whole. Denoting the sectoral capital/output ratios by $\kappa_i, i = 1, 2, \ldots, n-1$ and the overall capital/output ratio by Γ, and using, for simplicity, formulations (7.7.4) and (7.8.6), that is, considering an economic

[4] All the conclusions drawn in this section on the dynamic movements of prices, physical quantities, sectoral outputs and sectoral employment remain the same, as can easily be checked, in the case of the more complex model considered in Section 8 of Chapter 8.

We are in fact in a position, at this stage, to specify in more detail the physical quantity solutions. By inserting the new expressions for replacement and for the capital accumulation conditions (8.2.6) – see footnote 2 – the physical quantity solutions (7.9.3) become

$$\begin{cases} X_i(t) = a_{in}X_n(0)e^{gt}, \\ X_{k_i}(t) = (g + 1/T_i)\frac{T_{k_i}}{T_{k_i} - \gamma_i - g\gamma_i T_{k_i}} a_{in}X_n(0)e^{gt}, \qquad i = 1, 2, \ldots, n-1. \end{cases} \qquad (8.4.3)$$

A novelty of these formulations is that the viability conditions for the physical quantities now emerge as

$$T_{k_i} > \gamma_i + g\gamma_i T_{k_i}, \qquad i = 1, 2, \ldots, n-1, \qquad (8.4.4)$$

that is, as perfectly 'dual' to the expression (7.9.7), referring to prices.

system where capital goods are required only for the production of consumption goods, we may write them as:[5]

$$\kappa_i(t) = \frac{p_{k_i}K_i}{p_iX_i} = \frac{a_{nk_i}(t)}{a_{ni}(t) + (\pi + 1/T)a_{nk_i}(t)}, \qquad i = 1, 2, \ldots, n-1, \tag{8.4.6}$$

and[6]

$$\Gamma(t) = \frac{\sum a_{in}(t)a_{nk_i}(t)}{\sum a_{in}(t)a_{ni}(t) + (g + \pi + 1/T)\sum a_{in}(t)a_{nk_i}(t)}. \tag{8.4.7}$$

As can be seen, the components of (8.4.6) and (8.4.7) are nothing but coefficients. And since, under the present hypotheses, all coefficients remain constant through time, it follows that all sectoral capital/output ratios and also the overall capital/output ratio remain absolutely constant over time.

[5] In each sector, the capital/output ratio is

$$\kappa_i = \frac{p_{k_i}K_i}{p_iX_i}.$$

Remembering that, in equilibrium, K_i and X_i coincide, and using (7.7.4) and (7.8.6), we obtain

$$\kappa_i = \frac{a_{nk_i}w}{[a_{ni} + (\pi + 1/T)a_{nk_i}]w} = \frac{a_{nk_i}}{a_{ni} + (\pi + 1/T)a_{nk_i}},$$

which is the expression in the text.

When the more complex formulations (7.9.3) and (7.9.4) are used, the result is

$$\kappa_i = \frac{a_{nk_i}}{a_{ni}(T_{k_i} - T_{k_i}\gamma_i\pi_{k_i} - \gamma_i)(1/T_{k_i}) + (\pi_i + 1/T_i)a_{nk_i}}. \tag{8.4.5}$$

[6] The overall capital/output ratio is, in our notation,

$$\Gamma = \frac{\sum p_{k_i}K_i}{\sum p_iX_i + \sum p_{k_i}X''_{k_i}}.$$

Taking (7.7.4) and (7.8.6), and again remembering that, in equilibrium, K_i and X_i coincide, we obtain

$$\Gamma = \frac{\sum a_{in}a_{nk_i}wX_n}{\sum a_{in}[a_{ni} + (\pi + 1/T)a_{nk_i}]wX_n + \sum g a_{in}a_{nk_i}wX_n} = \frac{\sum a_{in}a_{nk_i}}{\sum a_{in}a_{ni} + (g + \pi + 1/T)\sum a_{in}a_{nk_i}},$$

which is the expression used in the text.

Denoting now the sectoral capital/labour ratios by $\chi_i(i = 1.2,\ldots,n-1)$ and the overall capital/labour ratio by Λ, and again using, for simplicity, formulations (7.7.4) and (7.8.6), we may write them as[7]

$$\chi_i(t) = \frac{p_{k_i}K_i}{a_{in}X_i}\frac{a_{nk_i}(t)}{a_{ni}(t)}w(t), \qquad i = 1,2,\ldots,n-1, \tag{8.4.9}$$

and

$$\Lambda(t) = \sum a_{in}(t)a_{nk_i}(t)w(t). \tag{8.4.10}$$

These ratios, beside depending on the coefficients, also depend on the wage rate. But since, under the present hypotheses, both the coefficients and the wage rate (in terms of any physical commodity) remain constant, it follows that all sectoral capital/labour ratios and also the overall capital/labour ratio remain absolutely constant over time.

It goes without saying that, as a straightforward corollary of the previously discussed results, all aggregate quantities – such as gross and net national income, total consumption, total investment, and total aggregate capital – increase in real terms at the same rate of growth (g) as population over time.

5 The Elegant Features of the Present Case of Economic Growth

The dynamic features of the economic system considered here, as they emerge from the foregoing sections, are of extreme simplicity. The merits of this simplicity are entirely attributable to the assumption of a fixed technology and constant returns to scale, which confers upon this

[7] In each sector, the capital/labour ratio is

$$\chi_i = \frac{p_{k_i}K_i}{a_{ni}X_i}.$$

Remembering again that, in equilibrium, K_i and X_i coincide, and using (7.7.4) and (7.8.6), we obtain

$$\chi_i = \frac{a_{nk_i}}{a_{ni}}w,$$

which is the expression used in the text.

When the more complex formulations (7.9.3) and (7.9.4) are used, the result is

$$\Lambda = \frac{\sum p_{k_i}K_i}{X_n}. \tag{8.4.8}$$

case all the elegant properties it possesses. With an invariant technology and constant returns to scale, the growth of the economic system is entirely determined by the rate of growth of population (and thus of the labour force). This growth does not affect the position of any single individual: per-capita income remains constant over time, and economic growth simply means that the economic system expands all its sections at the same percentage rate, while the structure of the economic system (its relative composition) remains constant over time.

This case of growth is well known in the economic literature. A clear though rudimentary picture of it can be found already in Cassel.[8] More recently, the attempts to get into dynamics are due to Von Neumann and Leontief. Although in different ways, they have both based their elaborations precisely on this same case. But, most interesting of all, this is the case to which all the macro-economic models of growth can be correctly applied. Since the economic system expands while keeping its proportions constant, there is in fact no loss of generality in framing the whole analysis in macro-economic terms. The usual convention that the variables must be considered as measured in terms of a composite commodity, made up of a fixed 'basket of goods', is in this case perfectly legitimate and logically unobjectionable. As all our results have shown, all single coefficients remain constant through time, so that the composition, or *structure*, of the economic system, once specified at time zero, remains invariant for all times.

[8] Cassel (1918, pp. 27 and ff.).

9 *The Explosive Forces of Technical Change: The Twin Aspects of Production Expansion and Evolution of Demand*

1 Technical Progress in Macro-economic Models

The case of Chapter 8, despite its popularity among theoretical economists, remains a very special – and we must indeed say unrealistic – case of economic growth. In practice, as soon as we look beyond a single period of time, a whole series of changes take place in the technical methods of production and in the evolution of demand. For any analytical investigation, these changes are clearly much more complex and problematic than those in the size of the population.

Technical change has been the great neglected factor in economic analysis. It is only in the last few decades that economists have begun to consider it, through the elaboration of models of economic growth. But in the literature, all the models of economic growth with technical progress have been developed in *macro-economic* terms, that is, with the implicit assumption that one single commodity (or a composite commodity of invariable composition) is being produced in the economic system. And technical change has been introduced in the form of an overall 'rate of technical progress', which has been treated exactly like, and symmetrically to, the rate of population growth.[1]

Unfortunately, this approach has been accepted rather uncritically in the economic literature. My purpose is now to show that this approach is unacceptable, but in order to do so, I must invite the reader to take

[1] The pioneering work has been that, already mentioned, of Harrod. After Harrod, and the similar contribution by Domar, the models of economic growth with technical progress have followed two distinctly different theoretical paths. One has been in the direction of pursuing the Keynesian approach of Harrod and Domar (Robinson (1956) and Kaldor (1961) are perhaps the best examples). The other has been in the direction of trying to re-absorb Harrod–Domar ideas into traditional marginal theory (e.g. Solow (1956) and Meade (1961)). All these efforts, however, have been framed in macro-economic terms, or at most in terms of a two-sector (i.e. consumption and investment) economy.

a closer look at all the implications that this approach entails. Our disaggregated analysis will turn now to be very useful for this task.[2]

As said earlier, any macro-economic analysis implies that all variables considered are measured in terms of a composite commodity or 'basket of goods' of fixed and invariable composition through time. Therefore, unless the macro-economic framework is given up altogether, the introduction of an overall rate of technical progress in such an analysis necessarily implies two further and much more specific assumptions: (i) that technical progress is going on at the same rate in all sectors of the economic system and (ii) that demand for *each* product is expanding at the same rate.

In this chapter, we shall carefully consider a hypothetical case of economic growth, in which productivity movements and demand expansion conform to this hypothetical uniform pattern.

2 A Hypothetical Economy with Uniform Technical Progress and Uniform Expansion of Demand

After dealing with the case of population expansion with constant returns to scale, the hypothetical case of economic growth taking place with uniform technical progress and uniform expansion of demand can be treated more summarily.

[2] Disaggregated analysis will also be a way of showing the limitations inherent in a (for many purposes interesting) line of thought that has recently made its appearance in the economic literature (see as a meaningful example Romer 1990). It concerns economic growth models that, even if moving within the area of aggregate neo-classical models, take the crucial step of introducing learning and technical change. They may well make a turning point, as their inspiration seems to go back to the earlier works of Haavelmo (1944) on the role of education, of Kaldor (1961) on the technical progress function and of Arrow (1962) on learning by doing – all works that tried to 'endogenise' technical change in the earlier economic growth literature. A non-linear 'endogenous' growth is now made up to emerge by various features – increasing returns to scale, externalities, diffusion of non-rival goods and so on. Unfortunately, the explicit references – sometimes brilliant – to concrete facts of industrial reality are most of the time translated into analytic expressions – generally based on neo-classical production functions – which are aggregate and risk acting as a sort of straightjacket. Besides hiding noted, well known – but unsaid and unresolved – analytical problems, they do not leave any space for structural dynamics, which is proposed here as one of the most characteristic features of industrial reality.

The hypotheses are now as follows:

(i) the initial conditions, as in the previous case, are such that at time zero there is full employment and full capacity utilisation;

(ii) over time, population remains constant;

(iii) technical progress is the same in all sectors of the economic system. This means that, over time, all technical coefficients of production decrease at a steady percentage rate ϱ, that is,[3]

$$a_{nj}(t) = a_{nj}(0)e^{-\varrho t}, \qquad j = 1, 2, \ldots, (n-1),\ k_1,\ k_2, \ldots, k_{n-1}; - \tag{9.2.1}$$

(iv) consumers' tastes are such that *the composition* of consumption is invariant to changes in income. In other words, when income increases, each individual expands demand for *all* the commodities consumed *in the same proportion*. This means that, if per-capita income increases at a percentage rate ϱ through time (as in equilibrium it must do), all coefficients of consumption will also increase at the rate ϱ, that is,

$$a_{in}(t) = a_{in}(0)e^{\varrho t}, \qquad i = 1, 2, \ldots, n-1. \tag{9.2.2}$$

Under these hypotheses, the two conditions for a dynamic equilibrium come out rather straightforwardly. By following exactly the same procedure as in Section 2 of Chapter 8, the capital accumulation equilibrium conditions emerge as

$$a_{ni}(t) = a_{in}(0)e^{\varrho t}, \tag{9.2.3}$$

which are similar to expression (8.2.7), the only difference being that now the rate of technical progress has replaced the rate of population growth. Of course, in expression (9.2.3), all coefficients are moving, but they are moving at the same percentage rate of change so that all relations among them remain constant through time. The effective demand condition also emerges as very similar to (8.2.10), or rather to (8.3.3), namely:

$$(1/\mu v)\sum a_{ni}(t)a_{in}(t) + (\varrho + 1/T)(1/\mu v)\sum a_{nk_i}(t)a_{in}(t) = 1, \tag{9.2.4}$$

[3] As in the case of g (see footnote 1 on p. 271), ϱ represents a *proportional* or *percentage* rate of change per period of time. But again, for the sake of simplicity, we shall simply refer to it as a 'rate of technical progress' or 'rate of growth of productivity', the adjectives 'proportional' or 'percentage', and the reference to the period of time, being omitted, except in those cases where omission might generate misunderstanding.

where again the rate of technical progress has taken the place of the rate of population growth. The (mathematically) interesting feature of this case of growth is that all coefficients of production and all coefficients of consumption, although moving in time, are moving in an opposite direction and at exactly the same rate. As a result, in (9.2.4), *each single binary product* of coefficients under the two summations *remains constant* over time – the movements of the two components exactly cancelling each other out. This means that the contribution to total employment (and to total national income) of each single sector remains constant. As in the previous case, condition (9.2.4) does not raise any problem through time. Once it is satisfied at time zero, it will remain satisfied for ever, because, in all sectors, productivity and demand are increasing at the same rate.

The time paths of all economic magnitudes can be found immediately by substituting (9.2.1) and (9.2.2) into (7.7.4), (7.8.6) and (8.4.1)–(8.4.10). As can easily be checked, if the rate of profit remains constant, the results are as follows:

(i) physical production of each commodity increases in time at the rate ϱ; therefore, all relative quantities remain constant;
(ii) all commodity prices – if w is taken as the arbitrarily fixed *numéraire* – decrease in time at the rate ϱ. Alternatively – if any commodity instead of w is taken as the *numéraire* – then all commodity prices remain constant over time, while the wage rate increases at the rate ϱ. Another way of stating this result is to say that the commodity price structure (the relative prices of all commodities) remains constant through time, while the real wage rate increases at the rate ϱ;
(iii) employment in each sector remains invariant over time;
(iv) production of each commodity, evaluated at the current prices, remains constant in time (if w is taken as the arbitrarily fixed *numéraire*) or increases at the rate ϱ (if any one of the commodity prices, instead of w, is taken as given);
(v) all sectoral capital/output ratios, as well as the overall capital/output ratio, remain absolutely constant over time. The time paths of the (sectoral and overall) capital/labour ratios, on the other hand, depend on the choice of the *numéraire* of the price system. They also remain absolutely constant if the wage rate is taken as the arbitrarily fixed *numéraire*, or else they increase at the rate ϱ, if any one of the commodity prices, instead of w, is taken as given.

3 Analytical Properties of the Two Cases of Economic Growth Considered Thus Far

The most attractive property of the case of economic growth just examined is that it still retains the most elegant features of the previous case, namely the constancy in time of all proportions of the economic system. By the device of uniformity, both in technical change and in demand expansion, all movements of coefficients cancel out *inside* each sector, and the structure of commodity prices remains unchanged. Thus, again, the economic system expands by multiplying all its sections in the same proportion, while its relative composition is invariant with respect to growth and time.

From an analytical point of view, there is a remarkable symmetrical correspondence between the two cases of economic growth considered so far. In the case of population growth, the wage rate was constant and the economic system was growing at the same rate as population; in the case of uniform technical progress just examined, population remains constant and the wage rate is growing at the same rate as technical progress. The two cases may easily be combined, and the results of such a combination are so straightforward that it is of no use to spell them out in detail. We may, however, explicitly state the conditions of dynamic equilibrium, which emerge as follows:

$$a_{k_in}(t) = (g + \varrho)a_{in}(t), \qquad i = 1, 2, \ldots, n-1 \tag{9.3.1}$$

and

$$\frac{1}{\mu v}\sum a_{ni}(t)a_{in}(t) + \frac{1}{\mu v T}\sum a_{nk_i}(t)a_{in}(t)(g+\varrho)\frac{1}{\mu v}\sum a_{nk_i}(t)a_{in}(t) = 1. \tag{9.3.2}$$

The economic meaning is immediate. Each single sector and the economic system as a whole expand at a rate which is the sum of the rate of population growth and the rate of technical progress, a sum which has become known in the economic literature by Harrod's term of *natural rate of growth*.

At this point, however, after admiring the symmetry and the analytical beauty of the two cases of economic growth considered so far, we must also draw from the results we have obtained at least two logically inescapable conclusions.

The first one refers to the method of analysis. If the hypotheses embodied in the two cases of economic growth considered were acceptable, then there really would not be much insight gained into the working of an economic system by using a disaggregated formulation. The merit of such a formulation would only be to show the structure of the economic system at a given point of time. But since this structure remains the same forever, the dynamics of the economic system would always be uniform, which means that no extra information could be obtained by disaggregation. In other words, a macro-economic formulation would be quite sufficient and entirely satisfactory.

The second conclusion is of much more practical relevance. If the hypotheses embodied in the two cases of economic growth considered were to correspond, even roughly, to what in the long run is happening in the real world, then any preoccupation with problems of economic growth would be entirely unjustified. The model considered amounts in fact to saying that economic growth *as such* would present no problem at all. The only thing that, in any growing economic system, would have to be done is the setting up of that particular structure which is most desired – the only constraint being that it must satisfy relations (9.3.1) and (9.3.2). This is a *once for all problem.* Once this structure has been set up, no problem would exist any more. Thereafter, the economic system could expand forever, its proportions remaining constant.

Attractive though the first conclusion may be, the second one is so much in striking contrast with everyday experience and with the economic policies of all governments, that it should immediately lead one to infer that there must be something wrong somewhere. And it is not difficult to see that the flaw is to be found precisely in the hypothetical case of economic growth considered in the foregoing section. For the hypotheses behind the case considered in Chapter 8 (no technical progress and constant returns to scale) are unlikely, but at least they are theoretically and logically possible. On the other hand, the hypotheses behind the case just considered (uniform technical progress accompanied by uniform expansion of demand) are not only unlikely; they are impossible. And we know that they will always be impossible, as long as the world in which we live is inhabited by human beings.

To substantiate and expand these assertions will require all the rest of the present chapter.

4 The Production Aspect of Technical Change

We must embark on a careful examination of the economic meaning and implications of technical change. When the technical coefficients of production change over time, there are two distinctly different sets of effects which are called into being. On the one side (let us say, on the production side), technical change means a variation in the methods of production and, therefore, a change in the physical quantities and qualities of goods which may be produced out of a given amount of physical inputs. On the other side (let us say, on the demand side), it means a change in the amount of per-capita real income at the disposal of consumers in general, and therefore a change in their potential demand.

Let us consider the production aspect first. Here the causes of change may be manifold. For a long time, economists have been mainly impressed by those changes which are connected with the fact that natural resources are limited. To Malthus and Ricardo, for example, it appeared as a matter of logical necessity that the continuation and expansion of the process of production, on natural resources which are given, should inevitably lead to decreasing returns, that is, to an increasing trend in the technical coefficients of production. But the economic history of the industrial countries has by now persistently brought to the fore another, more important and widespread, process of change continuously at work in any modern society: technical progress.

Technical progress is a very complex phenomenon. In the sense in which it is relevant for economic activity, it includes not only, and not so much, the great scientific discoveries (which by their own nature come about in a discontinuous and irregular way), as their practical application on an industrial scale, which takes place through a much longer and continuous process. Furthermore, it includes all the innumerable series of expedients and devices, small if considered individually but of great relevance if jointly gauged, which are the daily upshot of experience, experiment, research and rethinking of the organisation of production. This is indeed a very complicated process, emerging from the learning activity of human beings and the application of this learning to production. By its nature, this process is therefore a slow, but persistent, one. It consists of long and repeated attempts not only to reorganise the old methods of production, produce new products, find new resources and discover new sources of energy.

It would certainly be out of place to develop a theory of technical progress here. If such a theory should ever be developed, it would pertain to a much wider field than economics, because it could not avoid some definite conceptions about the aims and ends of human society. Therefore, as far as the present work is concerned, the usual procedure will be followed of taking technology as given, not fixed technology but the *movements* of the technical coefficients, in general, through time.

The concept of technical change which is thereby adopted remains a very general one, as it includes all possible types of change, from technical improvements to increasing or decreasing returns to scale. But in order to reach practically relevant conclusions, the analysis which follows will be carried out with reference to those movements of technology which empirical evidence has shown by now to be everywhere the most typical ones in modern societies. These movements may be briefly stated in three proportions:

(i) In the long run, the effects of technical progress are, on a (weighted) average, by far more important and more widespread than the effects of decreasing returns to scale. This means that, over time the coefficients of production decrease (i.e. productivity increases) in most sectors, although in a few sectors the coefficients might increase (i.e. productivity decrease).

(ii) As a net effect of decreasing returns and technical progress, production coefficients are persistently moving through time. Yet, each of them may be moving at a different speed. In other words, there normally is a wide dispersion amongst the rates of change of productivity in the different branches of the economic system.

(iii) Technical progress consists not only of increases in productivity but also of continuous additions of new sectors producing new and better goods and machines.

5 The Demand Aspect of Technical Change

Let us now consider the effects of technical change on demand. If, on the whole, technical change is in the direction of a persistently increasing trend of productivity, it means a higher and higher amount of wages and profits, or, more generally, an increasing trend in per-capita incomes at the disposal of the members of the community. It follows that, in each period of time, technical progress compels the members of the community to make new decisions; they must decide on which commodities they are going to spend the increments to their incomes. And here, clearly, their preferences as consumers come to play a crucial role.

Consumers' preferences may of course be widely manipulated, but they ultimately depend on human nature, which represents, in the same way as the technical conditions of production do, a fundamental external datum for any meaningful economic investigation. No commodity, whatever ingenious technique it may require, can be successfully produced if its (real or imagined) utility for the consumers is not sufficient to justify its cost: it would remain unsold. The relevance of technical progress itself depends on potential demand: an increase in productivity, however large it may be, loses much or even all of its meaning if it takes place in the productive process of a commodity for which demand can only be small or negligible. This means that any investigation into technical progress must necessarily imply some hypotheses (and if not explicitly, it necessarily does so implicitly) about the evolution of consumers' preferences as income increases. Not to make such hypotheses and to pretend to discuss technical progress without considering the evolution of demand would make it impossible to evaluate the very relevance of technical progress and would render the investigation itself meaningless. Increases in productivity and increases in income are two facets of the same phenomenon. Since the first implies the second, and the composition of the second determines the relevance of the first, the one cannot be considered if the other is ignored.

Unfortunately, the economic theory which has been developed so far is hardly able to give us any help on this problem. The consumers' demand theory that we know today is a highly sophisticated logical framework, built on entirely static premises. It relies on the existence of a perfectly known and consistent set of preferences defined at a given level of per-capita income. Such a theory, however admirable it may be on formal grounds, and whether it is useful or not in showing the consequences of price changes at a given level of income, is clearly unable to offer us any guide to the investigation of changes in demand following successive and persistent *increments* to income.

The regrettable consequence of this state of affairs has been that, when, recently, the elaboration of growth models with technical progress has compelled their authors to make definite hypotheses about the expansion of demand, they have made, in the absence of any guiding principle, those assumptions that best suited the mathematical properties of their models. As pointed out already, they have invariably postulated, either explicitly or implicitly, a uniform and proportional expansion of per-capita demand.[4]

Now, if there is something that we do positively know about the expansion of per-capita demand when income increases, it is that per-capita demand for each commodity *does not expand proportionally*. All the empirical investigators who in the last 100 years have looked into this matter have invariably and without exception found and stressed this tendency.

As is well known, the first empirical generalisation on the evolving pattern of demand in response to increases in incomes comes from an old discovery in economics which goes back to Ernst Engel[5] in the 1850s. Engel, after studying the conditions of consumption of workers in the kingdom of Saxony, stated what has since become known as the Engel law. This 'law' says that the proportion of income spent on food declines as income increases. A more general formulation of this empirical law, stating that the proportion of income spent *on any type of good* changes as per-capita income increases, has been confirmed ever since and evinced by all the econometricians who have been concerned with empirical work on demand.

These results come in fact as no surprise. It should not take long to realise that what they reveal is a basic tendency inherent in the human nature of the consumers. We shall go into this matter in more detail in Sections 6–8. Meanwhile we can safely draw the conclusion that the hypothesis of a uniform expansion of per-capita demand, which has been put so far at the basis of almost all theories of economic growth with technical progress, is incompatible with one of the most fundamental empirical 'laws' of economics. Since increases in per-capita

[4] The effect of all this is that all recent models of economic growth share a defect which was characteristic of classical economic analysis. They have concentrated their emphasis exclusively on the technological side of economic reality and have entirely forgotten the other side, related to demand.

[5] Engel (1857).

income necessarily imply non-proportional expansion of demand, and since technical progress leads to increases in per-capita incomes, the introduction of technical progress in any dynamic economic investigation necessarily implies a non-proportional expansion of demand. The hypothesis of proportional growth, adopted in practically all current models of economic growth, is therefore unacceptable.

6 Minimum Modifications that Appear to be Needed for the current Theory of Demand

It is no doubt very significant, as an indication of practical relevance, that all empirical works on demand, even long before the elaboration of any theory of consumer's behaviour, have always and without any exception made of 'Engel's law' one of their major themes, if not their only major theme.[6] And it seems to me very unfortunate that the demand theory that has been developed in the economics treatises and which is contained in our textbooks today should have concentrated almost exclusively on behaviour at given levels of per-capita income. This has practically amounted to giving up all attempts to incorporate the information obtainable from Engel's law into our theory of consumer's demand. Only the econometricians,[7] so far – by being faced with facts – have gone into this field. But their attitude has generally been rather accommodating. They have normally paid formal tribute to existing theory and have gone on to make a few piece meal theoretical adjustments that suited their empirical purposes. As a result, Engel's discovery has remained until our own day at the state of an empirical law, almost entirely isolated from the main body of the theory of consumer's demand.

It is not my purpose, of course, to engage in a comprehensive theoretical investigation of demand here. Yet it is necessary at this point to face this matter explicitly, albeit very briefly, because the evolution

6 See the interesting survey by George Stigler (1954). Stigler points out that empirical studies on the effect of income on consumer's demand began seventy years before the elaboration of any theory of consumer's behaviour, while empirical studies on the effect of prices on consumer's demand did not start until forty years after.

7 See, e.g., Allen and Bowley (1935); Prais and Houthakker (1955); Wold and Juren (1953); Stone (1954); Gilbert and Kravis (1954); and Houthakker (1957).

of demand, in response to increases in income, is going to play a crucial role in all subsequent analysis.[8] More specifically, I shall take into account at least two theoretical aspects of consumer's behaviour, in order to make a few essential modifications and additions to current demand theory, otherwise insufficient for our purposes.

The first point I should like to make refers to the information we do have on the shape of consumers' preferences at different levels of real income. Although possibilities of substitution among commodities are of course relevant at any given level of real income, there exists a hierarchy of needs. More precisely, there exists a very definite *order of priority* in consumer's wants, and therefore among groups of goods and services, which manifests itself as real incomes increase. This order of priority is particularly clear-cut at low levels of income, where satisfaction of some wants is a *conditio sine qua non*, even to the appearance of all others. But the order persists at higher levels as well, where the decision process becomes more complicated only because the order itself may no longer be so obvious and needs first to be discovered.

The second point of modification to current demand theory which I should like to make refers to the nature of the whole consumers' *activity*, which is behind the structural evolution of demand described Section 5. Here again, traditional theory has been constrained, by its static approach, to dealing with only one component (the rational component) of the consumer's activity. But in an evolving society, there is another component that becomes relevant – a component which is actually more basic than, and preliminary to, rational behaviour, namely learning.

We know that, at low levels or real incomes – let us say at near-subsistence levels – consumers can have very little hesitation in expressing their consumption preferences. Their demand is dominated entirely by physiological urges. But, as per-capita incomes grow higher and higher, choices grow wider and wider. Consumers' demand becomes dependent less and less on their instincts and more and more on their

[8] However, a few hints at a dynamic theory of demand in which the major factor influencing the evolution of demand in time is the growth of per-capita national income have already been given. Although they are not reproduced here, the reader is referred to them. (see Pasinetti 1981, pp. 71–75).

knowledge. This means that each consumer is increasingly bound to carry out a preliminary process of discovering his preferences before he (or she) can express them. Knowledge, as we know, can be acquired both from external information and from experience. Obviously, the amount of external information a consumer can obtain depends very much on the institutional set-up of the society in which he (or she) lives. But to the extent that information is imperfect and, even if it were perfect, to the extent that personal tastes are relevant, preferences can only be discovered through experience, that is, through actual consumption. This is, after all, the usual way in which human beings learn when faced with situations which are new: they learn through experiment. And if real per-capita incomes are continually rising, and consumers are enjoying extra amounts of income over time, they are indeed continually facing new situations. Even if they are reasonably aware of their preferences at the old levels because they have never experienced such levels before – they must learn their new preferences. This is not all. Over time, the quality of old goods may change, and the price structure may also change, while old needs may be satisfied with better (superior) goods. The consumers' learning activity is thus required over the whole range of their preferences. We may add that some consumers may try to educate themselves to make better choices in consumption, and others may simply be prone to imitate those consumers who are in the immediately higher income brackets or may easily become the prey for deceptive advertising.

And this means that, at each point of time, we can never expect each consumer to make the best possible consumption decision. Even if he (she) were to act according to perfect rationality, any of his (her) decisions could be 'rational' only relative to the amount of knowledge he (she) has been able to collect and which he (she) knows himself (herself) not to be entirely reliable. He (she) will always be in a position to improvise his (her) absolute levels of utility by carrying on a more basic process than that of acting rationally: that is, by learning. Thus, in any society where incomes are increasing, consumers' activity becomes more complexly motivated. Even if we wanted to preserve the traditional concepts of consumers' maximisation of satisfaction, we would clearly have to put behind them the much more basic and solid process of consumers' learning; a process which cannot but be preliminary to any rational choice.

7 The Evolution of Demand in Time

The discussion carried out in the foregoing sections is sufficient for our present purposes. To synthesise those results which are relevant for the analysis that follows, we may simply state them in three propositions:

(i) At any given level of per-capita income and at any given price structure, the proportion of income spent by each consumer on any specific commodity may be very different from one commodity to another.

(ii) As per-capita real income increases, whatever the price structure may be, each *increment* of consumers' demand tends to concentrate on a particular group of goods and services. This group of goods and services gradually changes from one level of income to another. In other words, whatever the process through which consumers' preferences are reached, they are such as to set up a definite order in the consumption of the various goods, that is, to saturate higher priority wants before passing to considering the satisfaction of further wants. Hence, as income increases, the tendency is not to increase proportionately the consumption of already bought goods and services but rather to buy new goods and services or to satisfy old needs with different (and hopefully better) goods.

(iii) There is no commodity for which any individual's consumption can be increased indefinitely. An upper saturation level exists for all types of goods and services, although at different levels of real income: it may be reached sharply – in the case of goods satisfying physiological needs – or only through a slow and long process as income increases – in the case of services yielding a very sophisticated kind of satisfaction – but its attainment is eventually inevitable. Demand for some particular goods (inferior goods) may even decrease, after reaching saturation, if better (superior) goods exist and if real income persistently goes on growing.[9]

[9] A more variegated expression of the evolution of demand in time can be found in Pasinetti (1981, Chapter IV).

10 A General Multi-sector Dynamic Model

1 The Hypotheses

We are by now in a position to expound a very general multi-sector dynamic model. By taking advantage of the analytical tools of vertical integration, all relations become extremely simple, even though concerning movements of surprisingly wide generality and complexity. After the foregoing analysis, the exposition need not be long, and we may proceed in a schematic way to a really general multi-sectoral structural dynamic model.

The hypotheses which are going to be made will be listed here under two headings, referring to initial conditions and to movements through time:

A. *Initial conditions.* At the time when our analysis begins, which we may denote as time zero, the economic system we are considering is defined by the following:

(i) The human population $X_n(0)$, which is taken as the really major exogenous magnitude. The flow of labour services which this population can provide in each unit of time is equal to $X_n(t)$ divided by the product of two coefficients – $\mu(t)\nu(t)$ – standing for the proportion of active to total population and the proportion of actual working time to the total time composing the time unit respectively. The subscript t has been added to both coefficients because they may be moving on a long run trend.

(ii) A series of $n-1$ stocks of capital

$$K_1(0),\ K_2(0),\ \ldots, K_{n-1}(0), \tag{10.1.1}$$

which are the result of past productive activity. The assumption will be kept, for simplicity,[1] that capital goods require no capital goods to be produced.

[1] I have myself been stunned by the richness of analysis that this assumption is allowing us. Later on, we shall be able to proceed to complete generalisation,

(iii) A series of $2(n-1)$ technical coefficients,

$$a_{n1}(0), \ldots, a_{n,n-1}(0), a_{nk_1}(0), \ldots, a_{nk_{n-1}}(0), \tag{10.1.2}$$

each expressing the input of labour, required in the unit of time to produce one physical unit of final commodity. There is moreover a series of $n-1$ technical coefficients,

$$T_1, \ldots, T_{n-1}, \tag{10.1.3}$$

expressing the reciprocal of the coefficients of wear and tear of the capital goods[2] in each sector where capital goods are required.

(iv) A series of $n-1$ consumption goods coefficients,[3]

$$a_{1n}(0), \ldots, a_{n-1,n}(0), \tag{10.1.4}$$

expressing per-capita demand for each consumption good (or service) per unit of time.

(v) A series of $(n-1)$ investment coefficients,

$$a_{k_1n}(0), \ldots, a_{k_{n-1}n}(0), \tag{10.1.5}$$

expressing per-capita demand for each investment good per unit of time.

All these magnitudes, at time zero, are assumed to be such as to satisfy the relations defining *equilibrium* in the economic system. This means that

(i) the series of $n-1$ stocks of productive capacity mentioned under (ii) are exactly of the size required by demand;

(ii) the series of $n-1$ investment coefficients mentioned under (v) are such as to satisfy, at time zero, the dynamic requirements of the economic system (which will be discussed in detail in Section 4);

without losing the synthetic conclusions that the assumptions here made allow us to reach.

2 This is a simplification which, as pointed out in Section 7 of Chapter 7, is made because of the immediately apparent meaning of the T_is. No modification to our conclusions would come from adopting the more general coefficients: $a_{k_1 1}, a_{k_2 2}, \ldots, a_{k_{n-1} n-1}$, in the place of the T_is.

3 It may be useful to point out explicitly that, although the technical coefficients and the per-capita demand coefficients occupy a symmetrical place in the two equation systems, they are not of the same nature. Technical coefficients represent *sectoral* concepts. Each of them is given by the state of technology in each particular sector. Per-capita demand coefficients represent *macro-economic* concepts. Each of them is an average taken over the whole economic system.

(iii) the technical coefficients and the demand coefficients – that is, (iii)–(v) – taken all together, are such as to satisfy the macroeconomic effective demand condition (7.11.3).

Conditions (i)–(iii) (i.e. *dynamic equilibrium*) simply represent, in our formulations, a way of saying that, at time zero, there is, *ex-hypothesis*, full employment of the labour force and full utilisation of the existing productive capacity.

B. *Movements through time*. Over time, the following movements take place:

(i) population increases at a steady percentage rate g, so that

$$X_n(t) = X_n(0)e^{gt}; \qquad (10.1.6)$$

(ii) productivity changes at a particular percentage rate of change in each sector. It will be assumed that these rates of change (ϱ_j, given by advancing technology) are in general different from one sector to another, but that they are steady through time in each (hyper-integrated) sector.[4] This means that

$$a_{nk_j}(t) = a_{nk_j}(0)e^{-\varrho_{k_j}t}, \qquad j = 1, 2, \ldots, n-1. \qquad (10.1.7)$$

Most ϱ_js and ϱ_{k_j}s are positive, but a few of them (referring to those sectors where, let us say, the exploitation of natural resources is becoming more and more difficult) might be negative;

(iii) per-capita demand changes at a particular percentage rate for each commodity. We shall denote these rates of change as r_i, ($i = 1, 2, \ldots, n-1$). The r_is *are not constant over time*; they change as a result of a very complex process, as has been hinted at in Chapter 9. The r_is as such are not exogenous magnitudes in our analysis. What has been assumed as an exogenous datum is the process of formation of consumers' preferences. Thus, over time, the movements of technical coefficients postulated by (10.1.7) determine the time movements of the r_is. We may write

[4] This is only a simplifying assumption, not at all necessary to our results. Non-steady rates of change in productivity can be dealt with by using the same procedure adopted below for the rates of change of per-capita demand. This will actually be done, in the following pages, whenever it becomes useful.

$$r_i(t) = f_i\{a_{n1}, \ldots, a_{n,n-1}, a_{n_k1}, \ldots, a_{nk_{n-1}}; \frac{\mathrm{d}}{\mathrm{d}t}[a_{n1}, \ldots, a_{n,n-1}, a_{n_k1}, \ldots, a_{nk_{n-1}}]\ t\}, \quad i = 1, 2, \ldots, n-1; \tag{10.1.8}$$

where the f_is depend on consumers' preferences and on how they evolve through time – a process which is defined in such a way as to satisfy propositions (i)–(iii) of Chapter 9, Section 7. The technical coefficients that appear in (10.1.8) influence the r_is through the medium of two channels: the level and rate of change of real per-capita incomes and the variations in the structure of prices.

Here, for purposes of simplicity and symmetry, the assumption will be made that the movements of per-capita demand may approximately be broken down (if we represent them on a logarithmic scale) into stretches of straight lines. In other words, we assume that time can be divided into finite stretches of length z (larger than the unit of time we are adopting) within which, for each commodity i, the percentage rate of change of demand r_i remains constant. Then, passing from one stretch of time of length z to the next, r_i changes, remaining then constant again for another stretch of time z. And so on.

Therefore, by defining now a new variable θ as

$$\theta = t - \eta z, \tag{10.1.9}$$

where η is the greatest integer that, multiplied by z and subtracted from t, leaves a positive remainder (θ), the movements through time of demand coefficients may be synthesised as[5]

$$a_{in}(t) = a_{in}(t - \theta)e^{r_i\theta}, \qquad i = 1, 2, \ldots, n-1, \tag{10.1.10}$$

where each r_i is an f_i function of the technical coefficients and now also of $(t - \theta)$. In order not to complicate the notation excessively, this

[5] As explained in footnote 3, consumption coefficients represent *average* per-capita consumption. No complication is here discussed in connection with a possible changing relative distribution of income among individuals or a changing composition of population as regards sex and age. The simplest way of interpreting our procedure is to suppose that both these features remain invariant over time. However, introducing complications of this type would not affect our conclusions, the only effect being that of anticipating or postponing turning points, without altering the nature of the trends through time.

functional dependence is not explicitly written in (10.1.10), nor will it be written hereafter, but it must always be taken as understood.

Of course, the same notation in terms of θ could be used also in formulations (10.1.6) and (10.1.7), and this will be done[6] in the following analysis, any time it is required by reasons of convenience or symmetry.

2 Restrictions

It is necessary to impose a few restrictions on the coefficients of our economic system in order to limit our mathematical formulation to the range in which they have an economic meaning.

To begin with, all technical coefficients, whether referring to the production of consumption goods or of investment goods, and all consumption demand coefficients can never be negative, that is,

$$\begin{cases} a_{nj}(t) \geq 0, & \\ a_{nk_j}(t) \geq 0, & j = 1, 2, \ldots, n-1, \\ a_{in}(t) \geq 0, & \\ T_i \geq 0, & i = 1, 2, \ldots, n-1, \end{cases} \tag{10.2.1}$$

which have a quite straightforward meaning. A negative amount of labour or of consumption or of wear and tear would make no economic sense.

On the other hand, the coefficients of demand for new investment might become negative, although only to a certain extent, that is, up to that point that still preserves gross investment as non-negative. The non-negativity restriction applies however to total gross investment. It need not necessarily apply to gross investment in each single sector, if capital is flexible enough to allow some transfers of capital goods from some sectors to others, when needed. In other words, taking first the most restrictive of all cases,

$$a_{k_i n}(t) + (1 + T_i) a_{in}(t) \geq 0, \qquad i = 1, 2, \ldots, n-1. \tag{10.2.2}$$

Should a situation arise in which the equilibrium conditions (which will be discussed in a moment) require some of the inequalities (10.2.2) to be reversed, then some further information about existing capital stocks would be needed in order to tell what can happen. If, in those

6 See footnote 4.

sectors where inequalities (10.2.2) need to be reversed, capital goods are specialised and cannot be transferred anywhere else, then idle capacity (which, in our model, means a discontinuity) will appear. If, on the other hand, capital goods are adaptable and can be transferred to other processes of production, then even negative gross investments can take place in some sectors.

In no case, however, as said above, can total gross investment become negative. Even if there were perfect mobility and adaptability of all capital goods, a fall of demand below the level at which total gross investments are zero would simply cause idle capacity. In other words, the inequality

$$\sum [a_{k_i n}(t) + (1 + T_i) a_{in}(t)] \geq 0, \qquad (10.2.3)$$

cannot but always and in any case be satisfied. The opposite inequality has no economic sense.

3 The Flows of the Economic System

Within each single period of time (finite or infinitesimal as it may be), there are flows of commodities from the final sector to the production processes. These flows have been examined already in our short-run analysis of Chapter 7, and need not be further discussed here. Within each single period of time, the structure of the economic system is represented by a system of equations (7.7.2) and (7.8.2), and we may well consider these two systems as rewritten here. The only difference is that a time subscript must now be added to each single coefficient and to each single variable so as to obtain a pair of those systems of equations for each unit of time we are considering. And since a very specific set of hypotheses has been made (in Section 1, heading B) about how the production and demand coefficients change over time, we shall now at last be able to look into the whole dynamics of the economic system. In other words, after finding the solutions of the equations in each particular period of time, we shall be in a position to look at the *movements* of these solutions through time.

For the same reasons discussed in Chapter 7 (Section 10), both the rate of wear and tear ($1/T$) and the rate of profit (π) which appear in equation system (7.8.2) will here be taken for convenience as uniform and constant. There is no difficulty in introducing non-uniformity. In any case, the relevant discussion on the determinants of (non-uniform) rates of profit will be carried out in detail later on, in Chapter 11.

A further point is that the hypotheses made in Section 1, heading B, do not provide us with the dynamics of all coefficients that appear in systems (7.7.2) and (7.8.2). The movements through time of one series of coefficients – the demand coefficients for new investments – have not been specified. (We have only accepted them as given at time zero.) This series of structural coefficients is the only one that affects the stocks of the economic system, that is, productive capacity in each sector; hence, it cannot be taken as given from outside. These coefficients must be such as to be compatible with the process of economic growth and will therefore themselves be determined as a part of the equilibrium conditions. We shall examine their movements [in time] in Section 9.

4 The Conditions for a Dynamic Equilibrium

According to our initial hypotheses, when our analysis begins (time zero), the economic system we are considering is in *equilibrium* – there is full employment of the labour force and full utilisation of productive capacity. We know already that, if this equilibrium situation is to be kept through time, two types of conditions must be satisfied.

First of all, since both population and technology are changing, the economic system must continually enlarge its productive capacity so as to keep up both with the increasing per-capita demand and with the increasing labour force. This means that, in each sector, a very definite relation must be satisfied between new investment and the rate of change of the corresponding final demand for consumption goods. The problem has been discussed already in Section 2 of Chapter 8. By following here the same procedure and by inserting the dynamic movements of per-capita demand and population which have been postulated in Section 1, the mentioned relations emerge as

$$a_{k_i n}(t) = (g + r_i) a_{in}(t - \theta) e^{r_i \theta}, \qquad (10.4.1)$$

or, more compactly,

$$a_{k_i n}(t) = (g + r_i) a_{in}(t), \qquad i = 1, 2, \ldots, n \quad 1, \qquad (10.4.2)$$

which represent the *capital accumulation conditions* for keeping full employment over time (or capital accumulation equilibrium conditions).

If we refer (10.4.2) to total new investment in each sector, instead of referring them to per-capita investment, they may also be written as

$$X''_{k_i} = (g + r_i)X_i(t), \qquad i = 1, 2, \ldots, n-1, \tag{10.4.3}$$

which specify equilibrium new investment in each single sector. Their sum represents total equilibrium new investments in the economic system as a whole. As can be seen, equilibrium new investments, in physical terms, are exclusively determined by the expansion of demand. Secondly, since the actual undertaking of all these investments only provides the required productive capacity, a further (macro-economic) condition concerning total effective demand must be satisfied in order to ensure the attainment of full employment in the economic system as a whole.

In mathematical terms, all this is expressed by the fact that conditions (10.4.1) only come to complete the two systems of equations (7.7.2) and (7.8.2) by providing us, at any point of time, with the series of coefficients (demand coefficients for new investments) which was still missing. But the two systems of equations, thus completed, are of the linear and homogeneous type. In mathematical terms, their coefficient matrix must be singular if they are to yield non-trivial solutions. This condition of singularity, which was earlier expressed by (7.11.3) with reference to a particular period of time, may now be written – after substitution from (10.4.1) and the completions carried out in Section 3 of Chapter 8 – as follows:

$$\begin{aligned} 1 = {} & (1/\mu v) \sum a_{ni}(t-\theta) a_{in}(t-\theta) e^{(r_i - \varrho_i)\theta} \\ & + (1/\mu v) \sum (g + r_i + 1/T_i) a_{nk_i}(t-\theta) a_{in}(t-\theta) e^{(r_i - \varrho_{k_i})\theta}. \end{aligned} \tag{10.4.4}$$

This expression finally represents the *effective demand condition* for keeping full employment through time.

It is important to point out immediately that, owing to our present hypotheses, condition (10.4.4) poses a whole series of *new* problems, in the sense that it poses problems which did not exist in the cases previously analysed. As opposed to what happened in the two simpler cases of (proportional) economic growth considered in Chapter 8 and in the first part of Chapter 9, respectively, the fulfilment of conditions (10.4.4), at any given point of time, no longer automatically entails that it will remain fulfilled through time.

5 Impossibility of Automatically Maintaining Full Employment through Time

We may begin at last to assess the relevance of the disaggregated type of analysis which has been developed in the previous pages.

The two simpler cases of economic growth discussed in Chapter 8 and in the first part of Chapter 9, respectively, have been conceived of in such a way as to exclude any process of structural dynamics.

As the reader will remember, both the capital accumulation equilibrium conditions and the effective demand equilibrium condition, in those two cases, have been assumed to be such as to be independent of time and of the stage of development the economic system has reached. Once fulfilled at a certain point in time, they remain fulfilled forever. This means that the situation of a precisely adequate productive capacity and of full employment of the labour force, once achieved at a given point in time, is such as to be automatically maintained for all time.

Our analytical possibilities have become radically different with the present analytical scheme. Concentrating our attention on macroeconomic condition (10.4.4), we may notice immediately that each one of its components is changing over time. It appears quite clear that there is no simple way in which condition (10.4.4) may be kept satisfied through time, *even if* all percentage rates of change were to remain absolutely constant. In this case, if we take all higher-order derivatives with respect to time, it appears immediately that all derivatives of the left-hand side of (10.4.4) vanish, while all even-order derivatives of its right-hand side remain necessarily positive (except in a very special case to which we come back in a moment).

The conclusion is straightforward. Even if we start from an equilibrium position (i.e. even if full employment of the labour force and full productive capacity utilisation are realised at a given point time), the structural dynamics of the economic system cause that position to change and therefore make it impossible in general to automatically maintain full employment through time.

6 A Hypothetical (Third) Case of Proportional Economic Dynamics (that Clearly Shows the Necessity of a Structural Equilibrium Dynamics)

The two special cases of economic growth considered in Chapter 8 and in the first part of Chapter 9, respectively (both entailing proportional economic growth), may now be looked at as the two obvious, but very special, cases in which all higher-order derivatives of the right-hand side of (10.4.4) are zero. Clearly, when the technical and consumption coefficients are all constant (the case considered in Chapter 8) and when all technical coefficients and all consumption coefficients move in time at precisely the same rate of change, but in opposite directions (the case considered at the beginning of Chapter 9), both expressions on the right-hand side of (10.4.4) remain constant with respect to time; hence, all their derivatives vanish.

When the problem is put in these terms, it becomes evident that there also exists a third particular case, already hinted at before, but to be specified now, owing to its analytical properties, which will turn out to be exceptionally relevant – a very particular, but analytically interesting case – in which the same thing happens. This third case is the one in which:

$$r_i = \varrho_i = \varrho_{k_i}, \qquad i = 1, 2, \ldots, n-1, \tag{10.6.1}$$

namely the case in which the rates of change, though different from any sector to another, yet are such that, *in each single sector*, demand grows at exactly the same percentage rate of change as that of the growth of labour productivity, which incidentally, in (10.6.1), is supposed to be moving, for simplicity, at the same percentage rate both in the consumption good sector and in the sector producing capital goods for it.

This further case of proportional economic growth, on the face of it, appears equally special as the two previously considered. For, in this case, all time movements are different from sector to sector, and yet they are such as to cancel out *inside* each sector, so as to leave the proportions among all sectors exactly constant (in terms of both employment and their contributions to total national income).

It goes without saying that this further case of proportional dynamics, for the same basic reasons stated in Chapter 9, can only be looked at as an analytical curiosity. Nevertheless, this particular case of proportional dynamics possesses analytical properties that make it singularly useful in the development of formulations which will become useful for the general case. This is because, granted that the assumptions behind the first equality in (10.6.1) are realistically unacceptable, on the basis of our previous arguments, the assumptions behind the second equality are not essential at all. (In fact, it will be seen later on that they correspond to the case of 'neutral technical progress in the sense of Harrod'. See Chapter 12, Section 10.) To be specific, our analysis reveals that the very crucial step to render structural dynamic analysis necessary lies in the contrasting evolution of technology on the one side and demand on the other, which means that it lies at the very point of going over from (10.6.1) to

$$r_i \neq \varrho_i, \qquad i = 1, 2, \ldots, n-1, \tag{10.6.2}$$

where all rates of change are taken to be different from any sector i to another.

Whether then also the equalities ($\varrho_i = \varrho_{k_i}$)'s hold or not is immaterial to our arguments, because these latter equalities refer to the sphere of technology within itself and not to the contrast between technology and demand. In fact we may well suppose, for convenience, that these equalities, ($\varrho_i = \varrho_{k_i}$)'s, hold, without creating any analytically relevant consequence for our basic arguments. In fact these assumptions will shortly turn out to be extremely interesting for our analysis as a first step to considering the sector making each consumption good i and the corresponding sector k_i which makes capital goods for it as vertically integrated (we shall say 'hyper-integrated') with each other. Analytically, this means that, in our earlier stated 'hypotheses B, *movements through time*', listed in Section 1, we may take the hypothesis (ii), that is, expressions (10.4.4), as including the simplification $\varrho_i = \varrho_{k_i}$ ($i = 1, 2, \ldots, n-1$), which we shall denote with the new symbol ϱ'_i, where

$$\varrho'_i \equiv \varrho_i = \varrho_{k_i}, \qquad i = 1, 2, \ldots, n-1, \tag{10.6.3}$$

stands for the *vertically hyper-integrated* rate of change of productivity of the consumption good sector i and of sector k_i (that makes capital goods for it), taken together.

Notice that, when we make such hypotheses, we obtain a series of (vertically hyper-integrated) rates of change of productivity:

$$\varrho'_1, \varrho'_2, \ldots, \varrho'_{n-1}, \qquad i = 1, 2, \ldots, n-1, \tag{10.6.4}$$

which have the formal property of standing in symmetry to the rates of change of per-capita demand:

$$r_1, r_2, \ldots, r_{n-1}, \qquad i = 1, 2, \ldots, n-1, \tag{10.6.5}$$

arising from hypothesis (10.1.8), while, of course, in general, technology and demand, in each sector, will move through time at a different rate, that is,

$$r_i \neq \varrho_i', \qquad i = 1, 2, \ldots, n-1. \tag{10.6.6}$$

The crucial step is precisely here, and it is crucial because it compels us to face the contrast between the dynamics of technology and the dynamics of demand. The opening up to structural dynamics that such hypotheses render necessary will be seen in a moment. For the time being let us keep to the most general case.

7 Full Employment as an Actively Pursued Target of Macro-economic Policy

The specific hypotheses that have been made since Chapter 9 allow us to go far beyond the general result of Section 5. By going deeper into what happens to the components of (10.4.4), we can in fact trace out the basic tendencies at work.

If almost all technical coefficients are decreasing in time, as we have assumed, then macro-economic condition (10.4.4) is bound to become under-satisfied as time goes on, unless the demand coefficients increase in the same proportion. But we know already that no demand coefficient can increase indefinitely, because per-capita demand for any commodity eventually reaches a saturation level. Therefore, we must conclude that condition (10.4.4) inevitably manifests a tendency to become *under-satisfied*, that is, to generate unemployment, as time goes on.

Fortunately there are two factors, operating in the long run, which can counter-balance the above-mentioned tendency. One of them is the same one which causes the whole trouble: technical progress. So far in this chapter, technical progress has been considered in the form of increases in productivity. But it has been pointed out earlier that technical progress also takes the form of introducing new goods. Our theoretical scheme must therefore be completed by opening it up to the possibility of the introduction of new sectors. This can be done by taking the number of sectors as running no longer from 1 to a fixed $n-1$, but from 1 to, let us say, $[n(t)-1]$, where $n(t)$ becomes a number which itself increases as an effect of technical progress. This means that, as time goes on, new equations keep on being added to our two systems of equations so that condition (10.4.4) becomes

$$\sum_{1}^{n(t)-1} a_{ni}(t-\theta)a_{in}(t-\theta)e^{(r_i-\varrho_i)\theta}+$$
$$+\sum_{1}^{n(t)-1}(g+r_i+1/T_i)a_{nk_i}(t-\theta)a_{in}(t-\theta)e^{(r_i-\varrho_{k_i})\theta}=\mu(t)v(t). \qquad (10.7.1)$$

The effects of technical progress on the effective demand condition are thus twofold. On the one hand, technical progress brings about a reduction through time of most of the $a_{ni}a_{in}$'s, referring to the commodities so far produced, and on the other hand, it keeps on *adding* new coefficients (referring to new commodities). The second tendency may succeed in counter-balancing the first.

However, even if this counter-balance were not to come about, there still is a second way in which condition (10.7.1) may be brought towards fulfilment. That is through a decreasing trend in its right-hand side – the coefficients μ and v – that is, a decreasing trend in working time (or, what amounts to the same, an increasing trend in leisure time), to be achieved by a decrease either in the proportion of active to total population or of the length of the working week or of both.

All these conclusions may seem, after all, to boil down to the commonsense proposition that technical progress gives society a choice between producing *more* (or new) goods and enjoying more leisure. Our analytical formulation, however, just because of its macro economic implications, reveals something more than that: something which is, in fact, crucially important. It evinces the fixed framework within which the choice has to be made. It shows that there is a macroeconomic constraint to the problem – represented by the requirement of keeping full employment – which restricts the choice to those combinations of goods and leisure which, in terms of time required, add up to that fixed amount determined by the existing working population and technical knowledge.

To express the same thing in a more effective way, we might say that the choice between more (or better) commodities and leisure is not merely a possibility, but a *necessity*, if full employment is to be maintained. There does not exist the alternative of not choosing! Technical progress, which characterises our societies and which brings with it that choice, does not come – so to speak – under the form of a free gift which, by being always susceptible of being refused, could only add to, and never diminish, the pre-existing wealth. It comes under the form of a flow which cannot be stopped and has to be continually channelled in new directions, which themselves have to be discovered anew because the old ones saturate. This entails an ever-standing problem of utilisation under a fixed restriction represented by condition (10.7.1); a problem for which the failure to find solutions may cause damage to the situation carried over from the previous period. We shall return to these problems any time that our analysis gives us the opportunity to dwell upon them.

For the time being, we may draw the important conclusion that the structural dynamics of the economic system inevitably tend to generate what has rightly been called *technological* unemployment. At the same time, the very same structural dynamics produce counterbalancing movements which are capable of bringing macro-economic condition (10.7.1) towards fulfilment, *but not automatically*. There is nothing in the structural evolution of technical coefficients on the one side and of per-capita demand on the other, as such, that will automatically ensure fulfilment of macro-economic condition (10.7.1), that is, the maintenance of full employment. Therefore, if full employment is to be kept through time, it will have to be actively pursued as an explicit aim of (overall) economic policy.

8 A Central Institutional Agency Entrusted with the Task of Achieving and Maintaining Full Employment

From the conclusion of Section 7, it follows that, if full employment is to be kept through time, a central institutional organisation – let us call it for simplicity, the government – must be entrusted with the specific task of achieving and maintaining full employment.[7] This is by no means an easy task; for the problems to be solved will always be different from one period of time to the next.

[7] In theory, of course, one might alternatively conceive of a hypothetical institutional mechanism that automatically leads the economic system towards the full employment dynamic path. Yet, even in such a hypothetical case – and apart from whether such an institutional mechanism is or is not possible – the Government would clearly have to be in charge of a general supervision and of intervening any time that such an institutional mechanism failed to work, or were disrupted.

In very general terms, this necessity emerges both as long run strategy and a series of short run expedients.

In the long run, a sort of permanent surveillance becomes necessary on the evolution of the counterbalancing forces mentioned in Section 7 so as to make it sure – when necessary, and with appropriate interventions – that, at least tendentially, those forces do move in the direction of counterbalancing one another. And even when this task is fulfilled, further surveillance becomes necessary on the process of the actual carrying out of the required investments.

In the short run, given the difficulty of exercising an influence on technical coefficients, it is the rates of change in demand that afford the widest possibility of being influenced. For, although governed by basic tendencies, most r_is are indeed open, at least in the short run, to external influence. Some of them may not even reflect consumers' demands at all but actually be under the direct control of the government.

We shall assume here that a government is in fact actively vigilant so as to influence total effective demand, as may be necessary, to keep macro-economic condition (10.7.1) at least approximately and tendentially satisfied. This assumption will be kept until we shall be able to face explicitly the questions and problems of the role to be played by the institutions in industrial societies.

9 The Structural Dynamics of Physical Quantities and of Relative Prices

We shall now proceed to examine, one by one, the constituent components of our whole newly sketched-out economic system, supposed to be kept in constant equilibrium-growth through time.

When condition (10.7.1) is (at least tendentially) satisfied, each of the two linear and homogeneous systems of equations representing the flows of the economy – that is, (7.7.2) and (7.8.2) – yield solutions, as we well know, for all their unknowns, except one, which can be fixed arbitrarily. But, since all coefficients and unknowns are now dated, these solutions no longer take the form of single values but of *movements through time*. It is evidently *one of these movements* which, in each of the two equation systems, can be arbitrarily fixed. Now, in the case of (7.7.2) one of the X's – namely X_n (population) – is a variable whose movement through time has always been considered as given from outside our economic analysis. There is no choice in this case.

On the other hand, in the case of equation system (7.8.2), the one concerning prices, the case is strikingly different. We can only say that the system determines the dynamic movements of *relative* prices. This means that the choice of one of the prices is entirely open. Suppose, as a matter of convenience, that we begin by choosing the wage rate as the basis of our price system and take it as given at $\bar{w}$, both at a given point of time and through time, which means setting $w(t) = \bar{w}$.

Then, the dynamic overall movement of physical quantities and relative prices may be represented as follows:

$$\begin{cases} X_i(t) = Ae^{(g+r_i)\theta}, \\ X_{k_i}(t) = (g + r_i + 1/T)Ae^{(g+r_i)\theta}, \end{cases} \tag{10.9.1}$$

$$\begin{cases} p_i(t) = Be^{-\varrho_i\theta} + (\pi + 1/T)Ce^{-\varrho_{k_i}\theta}, \\ p_{k_i}(t) = Ce^{-\varrho_{k_i}\theta}, \qquad i = 1, 2, \ldots, [n(t) - 1], \end{cases} \tag{10.9.2}$$

where A, B, C are constants which stand for the initial conditions, namely

$$A = a_{in}(t - \theta)X_n(t - \theta),$$
$$B = a_{ni}(t - \theta)\bar{w},$$
$$C = a_{nk_i}(t - \theta)\bar{w}.$$

The economic meaning of (10.9.1) and (10.9.2) at a given point of time has been discussed already in Section 7 of Chapter 7, and there is no need for repetition here. But now, besides the determination of quantities and prices at a given point of time, expressions (10.9.1) and (10.9.2) also bring out their *movements through time*. And here is the point where the symmetry between the two systems of equations breaks down.

On the one hand, each physical quantity follows a time path of its own, expanding at a particular rate $(g + r_i)$, which is the sum of two rates of growth: the rate of growth of population and the rate of change of per-capita demand. The first of these two rates is the same for all goods, while the second is different from one commodity to another. Therefore, in general, *the whole production structure in physical terms is changing over time*. This means that, in its process of growth, the economic system is continually changing the proportions in which it produces the various commodities. This is what we have called so far the structural dynamics of production.

But, at this point we face a substantial difference between the two equation systems. They have always been considered in a symmetric way to each other, but now, a difference emerges between them. Each relative price, as appears from (10.9.2), is also changing over time. By contrast, however, as was already hinted at above, a choice must now be made. With the convention of adopting, to begin with, a given $\bar{w}$, the wage rate, as the basis of the price system through time, each price will be decreasing at a rate resulting from a weighted average of the pace at which productivity changes are taking place in the sector to which it refers and in the sector which produces capital goods for it. But since the choice of *numéraire* is here arbitrary, any one of the commodity prices, and not necessarily the wage rate, might alternatively be chosen as the basis for the price system through time. This means that all analytical possibilities are here enormously extended. It means that the price system is no longer symmetrical to the case of physical quantities, and the consequences of such an asymmetry are no doubt substantial. For example, if we set $p_h(t) = \bar{p}_h$, then each one of the other commodity prices would increase or decrease according to whether the rate of growth of productivity in the corresponding sector is lower or higher than the rate of growth of productivity in the sector producing the commodity chosen as *numéraire*. And the wage rate itself would increase through time at a rate of growth equal to the rate of productivity growth in the sector producing the *numéraire* commodity.

Whatever the *numéraire* that has been chosen, since all rates of change of technical coefficients are in general different from one another, *the whole price structure will change as time goes on* in a way which is specific to the newly chosen *numéraire*.

The time paths of sectoral productions, evaluated at current prices – the $V_i(t) = p_i(t)X_i(t)$ and the $V_{k_i} = p_{k_i}X_{k_i}$; $i = 1,,2,\ldots,[n(t)-1]$ – will be entirely specific to the chosen *numéraire*. This means that a specific choice must be made. By multiplying each of the (10.9.1), for example, when $w(t) = \bar{w}$, by any of the corresponding (10.9.2), we would obtain

$$\begin{cases} V_i(t) = De^{(g+r_i-\varrho_i)\theta} + (\pi + 1/T)Ge^{(g+r_i-r_{k_i})\theta}, \\ V_{k_i}(t) = (g + r_i + 1/T)Ge^{(g+r_i-\varrho_{k_i})\theta}, \\ \qquad i = 1,2,\ldots,[n(t)-1], \end{cases} \tag{10.9.3}$$

where the constants D and G stand for the initial conditions, namely

$$\begin{cases} D = a_{ni}(t-\theta)a_{in}(t-\theta)\bar{w}X_n(t-\theta), \\ G = a_{nk_i}(t-\theta)a_{in}(t-\theta)\bar{w}X_n(t-\theta). \end{cases} \tag{10.9.3 bis}$$

As can be now seen directly, each of the V_is and V_{k_i}s, in general, will move through time in its own way, for two reasons: because the physical quantity concerned is changing and because the corresponding price is changing. Each $V_i(t)$ is the sum of two addenda (and each V_{k_i}, for simplicity, of only one), each of which is moving through time, $i = 1, 2, \ldots, [n(t)-1]$, according to an algebraic sum of rates of change: the rate of population growth plus the rate of change of per-capita demand, minus the rate of growth of productivity in the corresponding sector.[8]

[8] It may be interesting to point out explicitly that the conclusions about the dynamic movements through time remain exactly the same if the more complex case considered in Section 9 of Chapter 7 were to be adopted. More precisely, as may easily be checked, from (7.9.3), (7.9.4) and (8.2.6) and from the fact that the rates of growth are now $(g + r_i)$ the expressions (10.9.1)–(10.9.3) of this section would remain:

$$\begin{cases} X_i(t) = A'e^{(g+r_i)\theta}, \\ X_{k_i}(t) = (g + r_i + 1/T)A''e^{(g+r_i)\theta}, \end{cases} \tag{10.9.1 an}$$

$$\begin{cases} p_i(t) = B'e^{-\varrho_i\theta} + (\pi + 1/T)C'e^{-\varrho_{k_i}\theta}, \\ p_{k_i}(t) = C'e^{-\varrho_{k_i}\theta}, \end{cases} \tag{10.9.2 an}$$

$$\begin{cases} V_i(t) = D'e^{(g+r_i-\varrho_i)\theta} + (\pi + 1/T)G'e^{(g+r_i-r_{k_i})\theta}, \\ V_{k_i}(t) = (g + r_i + 1/T)G'e^{(g+r_i-\varrho_{k_i})\theta}, \end{cases} \tag{10.9.3 an}$$

$$i = 1, 2, \ldots, [n(t)-1],$$

where *only the constants* take up a more complex formulation, namely,

$$A' = A,$$

$$A'' = \frac{T_{k_i}}{T_{k_i} - \gamma_i - (g + r_i)\gamma_i T_{k_i}} A,$$

$$B' = B,$$

$$C' = \frac{T_{k_i}}{T_{k_i} - \gamma_i - \pi_{k_i}\gamma_i T_{k_i}} a_{nk_i}(t-\theta)\bar{w},$$

$$D' = D,$$

$$G' = \frac{T_{k_i}}{T_{k_i} - \gamma_i - \pi_{k_i}\gamma_i T_{k_i}} a_{nk_i}(t-\theta)a_{in}(t-\theta)\bar{w}X_n(t-\theta),$$

$$G'' = \frac{T_{k_i}}{T_{k_i} - \gamma_i - (g + r_i)\gamma_i T_{k_i}} G', \qquad i = 1, 2, \ldots, [n(t)-1].$$

The structural dynamics behind the components of all these movements through time would thereby be changed in its own way.

All this may not always lead to different results, but only if some homogenising devices could be found, or thought up, able to induce comparable results. This would itself open up specific, and not quite simple, problems of comparability. We shall face these types of problems in the following pages.

This conclusion may well be dramatic. The effects of the structural dynamics of the price system added on, or not to be added to, the structural dynamics of the physical quantities, can most probably be defined as one of the major consequences that have been brought about by the advent of the industrial revolution.

10 The Structural Dynamics of Employment

Before proceeding further, it may be useful to stop for a moment and stress the particular interest and importance for the community as a whole of the dynamic movement of employment in each single sector. Having denoted them by $E_i(t)$ and $E_{k_i}(t)$, respectively, we obtain

$$\begin{cases} E_i(t) = Me^{(g+r_i-\varrho_i)\theta}, \\ E_{k_i}(t) = \left(g + r_i + \frac{1}{T}\right) Ne^{(g+r_i-\varrho_{k_i})\theta}, \\ \qquad i = 1, 2, \ldots, [n(t) - 1], \end{cases} \tag{10.10.1}$$

where the constants M and N stand for the initial conditions, namely,[9]

$$\begin{cases} M = a_{ni}(t-\theta)a_{in}(t-\theta)v^{-1}X_n(t-\theta) \\ N = a_{nk_i}(t-\theta)a_{in}(t-\theta)v^{-1}X_n(t-\theta) \end{cases}$$

An interesting feature that emerges from these formulations is that the solutions, in order to be non-negative, now require fulfilment of the viability conditions:

$$T_{k_i} > \gamma_i + (g + r_i)\gamma_i T_{k_i},$$

$$T_{k_i} > \gamma_i + \pi_i \gamma_i T_{k_i}, \qquad i = 1, 2, \ldots, [n(t) - 1],$$

which are 'dual' to each other.

[9] The $E_i(t)$ and $E_{k_i}(t)$ have been expressed here in terms of men per unit of time. For example, if the unit of time is one year, they would be expressed in terms of man-years; so that

$$\sum [E_i(t) + E_{k_i}(t)] = \mu x_n(t).$$

As is seen, employment in each sector i or k_i, $i = 1,2,\ldots,n-1$, moves through time at a rate of change equal to the rate of population growth plus the rate of increase of per-capita demand for commodity i or k_i, minus the sectoral rate of increase of productivity.

Here new problems arise immediately because the E_is and E_{k_i}s, although representing flow variables (services from labour in the unit of time), come from, and are inseparably linked to, a stock variable (the labour force), that may not be perfectly mobile. As appears from (10.10.1), when population is constant (i.e. $g = 0$), employment in each sector i increases through time if

$$r_i > \varrho_i, \tag{10.10.2}$$

and decreases through time if

$$r_i < \varrho_i, \quad i = 1,2,\ldots,n-1, \ k_1, \ k_2,\ldots,k_{n-1}. \tag{10.10.3}$$

This means that, even if macro-economic condition (10.7.1) is constantly being kept satisfied, that is, even if full employment is maintained in the economic system *as a whole*, half of the sectors, on (a weighted) average, are generating technological unemployment, over time, while the other half of the sectors, on average, will be offering jobs and will thus reabsorb the technological unemployment generated by the former sectors. The important point to stress is that sectoral employment will *have* to change – workers will have to be shifted from sector to sector in order to keep macro-economic condition (10.7.1) satisfied, that is, in order to maintain full employment through time. Clearly, this might create a very serious state of affairs – especially in economic systems with large ϱ_is – if labour were highly specialised and not susceptible of being transferred from one sector to another except at creating social losses in productivity.

Fortunately, the natural movements of population come in to help here in the right direction, and in two ways. First of all, the natural process of people ageing through time permits a redistribution of employment among sectors by directing young workers towards expanding sectors and by not replacing retiring people in the contracting sectors. This may be a slow process, but it is one which is going on even when population is stationary. Secondly, when population is growing, its rate of increase is a net positive addition to the rate of change of demand (and therefore of employment) in *all* sectors.

It follows that the sectors which will actually lose employment, in absolute terms, are those in which

$$(g + r_i - \varrho_i) < 0, \qquad (10.10.4)$$

and the sectors which will be compelled to actually dismiss workers are those in which

$$(g + \delta_i + r_i - \varrho_i) < 0 \quad i = 1, 2, \ldots, n-1, \qquad (10.10.5)$$

where δ_i denotes the rate at which workers retire from productive activity in sector i. That is, those sectors will actually be compelled to dismiss workers (in spite of full employment being kept in the economic system as a whole) where the rate of growth of productivity is so high and the rate of increase of per-capita demand so low that the difference between the two is not only negative, but negative to such an extent as to more than offset the positive effects of both population growth and people's retirement from work. Agricultural sectors seem to be amongst the most typical sectors that have experienced such feature. But there are signs, in some advanced countries (such as the U.K.) that some manufacturing sectors may begin to fall into this category (a phenomenon improperly called 'de-industrialisation').[10]

To sum up, we may say that over time, the whole structure of employment changes in the sense that the *proportions* in which total employment is distributed among the different sectors of the economic system are all changing. A complex process of structural dynamics of employment is therefore required, behind macro-economic condition

[10] At this point restrictions (5.2.2), discussed in Section 2, may be rewritten with reference both to the stocks of capital and to employment of labour in each single sector, in terms of rates of change:

$$g + r_i + \frac{1}{T} \geq 0, \qquad (10.10.6)$$

$$g + r_i - \varrho_i + \delta_i \geq 0, \qquad i = 1, 2, \ldots, [n(t) - 1]. \qquad (10.10.7)$$

We may say that, when all (10.10.6) and (10.10.7) are satisfied, our theoretical scheme retains all its properties. But if some of these inequalities were to be reversed, then, in order to find out what would happen, one would need more information about the degree of flexibility of capital – in the case of (10.10.6) – and about the degree of mobility of labour – in the case of (10.10.7). If no mobility of capital or of labour is possible between any one sector and the others, then some idle productive capacity – in the case of a reversal of (10.10.6) – and some technological unemployment – in the case of a reversal of (10.10.7) – becomes unavoidable.

(10.7.1) in order to maintain full employment in the economic system as a whole. Half of the sectors, on average, will need to absorb an expanding proportion of total employment, and the other half, on average, will need to decrease their proportion of total employment. Fortunately, the actual expulsion of workers from the (relatively) declining sectors will not be so sharp as might appear at first from the changes in the proportions. It will be mitigated by the expansionary effects of population growth, when $g > 0$, and by the counterbalancing (though slow) effect of not replacing people going into retirement. Nevertheless, especially in economic systems with particularly strong technical change, the necessity of moving some labour out of certain sectors and into others might pose very serious social problems.

11 The Structural Dynamics of the Sectoral Capital/Output and Capital/Labour Ratios

One further important consequence of the movements of the price system through time concerns the dynamic movements of the capital/output and of the capital/labour ratios. The movements through time of these ratios follow straightforwardly from the previous analysis. They will actually become relevant later on in our analysis of Chapter 12, Section 10, but it may well be useful to bring them out explicitly here, where they are first emerging.

After substituting (10.9.1) and (10.9.2) into (8.4.6) and (8.4.9), we precisely obtain the sectoral capital/output ratios (κ_is), and the sectoral capital/labour ratios (χ_is):

$$\kappa_i(t) = \frac{a_{nk_i}(0)e^{-\varrho_{k_i}t}}{a_{ni}(0)e^{-\varrho_i t} + (\pi_i + 1/T_i)a_{nk_i}(0)e^{-\varrho_{k_i}t}}, \tag{10.11.1}$$

$$\chi_i(t) = \frac{a_{nk_i}(0)e^{-\varrho_{k_i}t}}{a_{ni}(0)e^{-\varrho_i t}} w(t), \qquad i = 1, 2, \ldots, n-1. \tag{10.11.2}$$

As may be seen, the dynamic movement of each capital/output ratio $\kappa_i(t)$ depends exclusively on technical change in sector i and in sector k_i, $(i = 1, 2, \ldots, n-1)$. Over time, each $\kappa_i(t)$ will increase, decrease or remain constant according to whether the rate of growth of productivity in the sector i is greater than, lower than, or equal to, the rate of growth of productivity in the corresponding capital good sector k_i.

On the other hand, the dynamic movement of each capital/labour ratio $\chi_i(t)$ depends not only on technological change, in sectors i and k_i, but also on the movement through time of the wage rate, and therefore on the *numéraire* of the price system.

And it is here that the necessity emerges of a specific choice of *numéraire* for the price system, otherwise any comparison through time would remain indeterminate. At this stage the obvious point of reference appears to be the adoption of some notion of *real* wage rate, so as to make the increase of the wage rate express the increase of physical production per man. There is a simple way of doing this, which consists in allowing the wage rate to grow exponentially through time at a percentage rate ϱ^* – that is, $w(t) = w(0)e^{\varrho^* t}$ – where ϱ^* is defined as the weighted average of all rates of growth of productivity (the precise expression for ϱ^* will be obtained in Section 13). Then (10.11.2) becomes

$$\chi_i(t) = \frac{a_{nk_i}(0)}{a_{ni}(0)} w(0) e^{(\varrho_i + \varrho^* - \varrho_{k_i})t}. \tag{10.11.3}$$

We are now in a position to say that the dynamic movement of each capital/labour ratio $\chi_i(t)$, besides depending on the rate of growth of productivity in sectors i and $k_i, i = 1, 2, \ldots, n-1$, also depends on the overall (or, as it will be called in a moment, the 'standard') rate of growth of productivity in the economic system as a whole. Expressions (10.11.3) and (10.11.1) will actually be used in Chapter 12 (Section 10) in connection with a classification of technical change.

12 The Price System through Time – A Degree of Freedom at Time Zero and a Degree of Freedom among the Rates of Change

The analysis of Section 11 brings to the centre of our attention the question of the choice of *numéraire* for the price system, and at this point it becomes necessary to face the problem explicitly.

We began by repeatedly stressing that in each of the equation systems (10.9.1) and (10.9.2), the whole movement through time of one of the unknowns is to be determined exogenously. And we have seen that as far as the physical quantities are concerned, there arises no particular problem. In (10.9.1), there is one physical quantity, namely population, the absolute value of which at a given point of time and its rate of change through time are indeed determined from outside economic analysis.

But the problem, as we have seen, is dramatically different for the price system. In (10.9.2), there is no specific price that can obviously be said to be determined exogenously. At least in principle, the choice of *numéraire* is indeed open to any exogenous choice.

It is important to realise that this arbitrary choice concerns *a whole movement* of one of the prices through time. This means, in an analysis like the present one, where we have chosen to express movements through time by exponential functions, the magnitudes to be determined exogenously are in fact not one, but two: an absolute value at the initial point in time and a rate of change over time.

More specifically, if we choose to reckon prices in terms of the wage rate, as we have done to begin with, and close the price system (10.9.2) by the equation:

$$w(t) = \bar{w}, \tag{10.12.1}$$

or, even more specifically, if we chose to reckon prices in terms of Classical 'labour commanded' and write

$$w(t) = 1, \tag{10.12.2}$$

what in fact we do is fix two magnitudes, namely the level of the wage rate at any supposedly given initial point in time and its rate of change through time. In general, we may well say that we take the wage rate $w(t)$ as an exponential function of time:

$$w(t) = w(0)e^{\sigma_w t}, \tag{10.12.3}$$

where $w(0)$ is the wage rate as fixed at time zero, and σ_w is the percentage rate of change of the wage rate through time. We may well assume that both are exogenously and externally assigned as particularly given values. Thus, when we choose equation (10.12.2), it is as if we take equation (10.12.3) and insert into it two particular values, namely

$$\begin{cases} w(0) = 1, \\ \sigma_w = 0. \end{cases} \tag{10.12.4}$$

Similarly and alternatively, if we choose any particular physical commodity (or composite commodity) h as *numéraire*, and close the price system (10.9.2) by the equation:

$$p_h(t) = 1, \tag{10.12.5}$$

we may say that we assume, in general, $p_h(t)$ to be an exponential function of time:

$$p_h(t) = p_h(0)e^{\sigma_h t}, \qquad (10.12.6)$$

where $p_h(0)$ is the price of commodity h at time zero, and σ_h is the (percentage) rate of change of the price through time, which means that they are assigned the particular values:

$$\begin{cases} p(0) = 1, \\ \sigma_h = 0. \end{cases} \qquad (10.12.7)$$

Note that, since h may be any one of the $(n-1)$ goods or services of our economic system, we are in fact introducing, at this point, in our system of equations, an auxiliary series of new variables – namely, after introducing the rate of change:

$$\sigma_w,$$

for the wage rate, we are also introducing a whole new series of auxiliary variables, namely:

$$\sigma_1, \sigma_2, \ldots, \sigma_{n-1}, \qquad (10.12.8)$$

these being the rates of change of the prices of all our commodities $(i = 1, 2, \ldots, n-1)$.

Essentially, as our choice to close the price system through time, we are introducing the exponential function (10.12.3) with the particular values (10.12.4), or alternatively we are introducing any one of the exponential functions (10.12.6), with the corresponding particular values (10.12.7).[11]

Expression (10.12.3), with (10.12.4), may appear at first as a more complicated way of writing (10.12.2), and, similarly, expression (10.12.6), with (10.12.7), may appear as a more complicated way of writing (10.12.5). But, as we shall shortly see, the new expressions have important analytical properties.

First of all, they make it explicit that the price system, when considered over time, contains two – not one – degrees of freedom: namely, a degree of freedom at the initial point in time (choice of the 'standard of

[11] These propositions are in fact valid in general, but they may give rise to analytical complications (which however do not affect our basic arguments), when technical progress is not 'neutral'. For convenience, we suggest the reader to consider our following elaborations with the explicit assumption (10.6.3), by which all complications are immediately avoided.

value' at a specific point of time) and also a degree of freedom through time (choice of one of the rates of change of prices).[12]

Secondly, since *all* movements of prices through time come to be represented by exponential functions, we can see immediately from these functions that – provided our analysis is kept within the 'natural' economic system[13] – once the rate of change through time of one of them is fixed exogenously, then the rates of change of all other exponential functions are determined.

The important analytical consequence is that any one of these exponential functions – and not necessarily the specific exponential function representing the movement of the *numéraire* – can be used to close the price system, provided that its two parameters (initial condition and rate of change) are fixed in the appropriate relation to those of the *numéraire*.

To be more specific, we have seen previously that choosing any particular commodity h as *numéraire* of the price system through time, that is, setting $p_h(t) = 1$, is equivalent to writing exponential function (10.12.6) with particular values (10.12.7). But, once all our equations have been converted to exponential functions, an alternative way of obtaining exactly the same result is to write the exponential function (10.12.3), concerning the movement of the wage rate, as our basic equation of reference, and then insert into it the particular values:

$$\begin{cases} w(0) = \bar{w}_h(0), \\ \sigma_w = \varrho'_h, \end{cases} \qquad (10.12.9)$$

where $\bar{w}_h(0)$ – the wage rate at time zero – is fixed in terms of commodity h, and σ_w – the rate of growth of the wage rate – is fixed at $\sigma_w = \varrho'_h$ – the rate of growth of productivity in (vertically hyper-integrated) sector h.

12 Of course these two degrees of freedom are not always used independently of each other. For example, choosing to measure prices in terms of labour implies *both* $w(0) = 1$ *and* $\sigma_w = 0$; and similarly choosing to measure prices in terms of any specific physical commodity h implies both $p_h = 1$ and $\sigma_h = 0$. But there is no inherent necessity in the price system for couplings of this type. The degrees of freedom are indeed two and they can be used independently of each other. This will appear more evidently in the next section.

13 A term which will slowly emerge to be properly defined as essential to our analysis.

Since this holds with reference to *any* commodity i ($i = 1, 2, \ldots, n-1$), it follows that – within the natural economic system – all the rates of change of prices are linked to the respective rates of change of productivity, the ϱ_i''s (if we take the vertically hyper-integrated version of these rates of productivity growth), and to the rate of change of the wage rate σ_w, through the relations[14]

$$\sigma_j = \sigma_w - \varrho_j', \qquad j = 1, 2, \ldots, n-1. \qquad (10.12.10)$$

The fascinating result that emerges, for our purposes, is that exponential function (10.12.3), concerning the wage rate, can be used *in general* as the equation that closes the price system (10.9.2). In other words (provided of course we move within the natural price system), the choice of *numéraire*, whatever this *numéraire* may be, can simply be made by fixing the two appropriate particular values of $w(0)$ and σ_w – that is (10.12.9) – in the exponential function that expresses the movement of the wage rate through time, that is, in (10.12.3). All the rates of change of prices of the whole system then follow therefrom, according to expression (10.12.10). We shall take advantage immediately of this remarkable analytical property.

13 The 'Standard' (Physical) Rate of Growth of Productivity

As we have seen in Section 12, the evolution of the price system through time contains two degrees of freedom. These degrees of freedom may be closed, in general, by taking exponential function (10.12.3) and exogenously inserting into it the initial wage rate and its rate of change.

Since the choice is free, we may insert the following particular values:

$$\begin{cases} w(0) = \bar{w}, \\ \sigma_w = \varrho^*, \end{cases} \qquad (10.13.1)$$

where $\bar{w}$ is the wage rate at time zero, measured in terms of whatever unit of account may be chosen, and ϱ^* is defined as the weighted average of the rates of change of productivity in the whole economic system. We shall denote this remarkable magnitude:

$$\varrho^*, \qquad (10.13.2)$$

and call it the 'standard rate of growth of productivity'.

[14] Let us be careful: this is an extremely important relation.

To clarify our procedure, it may be useful to follow three simplifying stages (or problems).

The first problem to face is of course of how to compute ϱ^*. An average of uneven magnitudes, such as the rates of increased productivity ϱ_is in our case, calls for a search of the appropriate weights. But, fortunately, these weights are implicitly contained already in our theoretical scheme! In order to make them emerge clearly, it will be useful and in fact convenient to proceed step by step by beginning to consider each of the three simplified cases of our previous analysis, in which the sectoral composition of the economic system remains constant through time. In these three simple cases, the computation of ϱ^* is immediate and straightforward, as it leads to a zero result.

The first simplified case is the one considered in Chapter 8, where all technical and consumption coefficients are supposed to remain absolutely constant (i.e. all rates of change are supposed to be zero). Clearly this yields $\varrho^* = 0$.

The next simplified case is the one considered in Section 2 of Chapter 9, in which all technical coefficients are supposed to decrease at the uniform rate ϱ, and all consumption coefficients are supposed to grow at the same uniform rate, $r = \varrho$. Also, this second case equally yields $\varrho^* = \varrho = r$, this being the uniform rate of growth of both productivity and demand.

A little more complex, but at the same time much more interesting, is the third case, which has been considered in Section 6. In this case, the rates of growth of productivity are all supposed to be different from one another, and yet each of them is supposed to be exactly equal to the growth rate of demand of the corresponding consumption good so as to keep the composition (i.e. the 'weights') unchanged. The interest of this case is that it requires us to look for the weights explicitly. In order to do so, we may go back to the effective demand equilibrium condition (10.4.4), which – for our present purposes – may be written as

$$\frac{1}{\mu v} \sum a_{in}(t)[a_{ni}(t) + (g + r_i + 1/T_i)a_{nk_i}(t)] = 1. \qquad (10.13.3)$$

This is indeed the interesting expression! We know that $a_{in}(t)$ is the coefficient of per-capita demand for consumption good i, while $[a_{ni}(t) + (g + r_i + 1/T_i)a_{nk_i}(t)]$ is what may be called *the vertically hyper-integrated labour coefficient* for consumption good i, as it includes all labour inputs for good i (both in the sector directly producing it and in the sector producing capital goods for it). This means that each addendum under summation (10.13.3) represents the *proportion* of total labour required by the (vertically hyper-integrated) production of consumption good i, $i = 1, 2, \ldots, n-1$. As may easily be realised, this is precisely the 'weight' which is appropriate to the corresponding consumption good. We can therefore now specify the 'weights' we have been looking for. Denoting them by λ_i, they clearly are

$$\lambda_i(t) = \frac{1}{\mu v} a_{in}(t)[a_{ni}(t) + (g + r_i + 1/T_i)a_{nk_i}(t)], \qquad i = 1, 2, \ldots, n(t) - 1. \tag{10.13.4}$$

Note that (10.13.4) is a perfectly general formulation, as it has been derived from the formulae of the general case.

The elegant formal property of the particular case we are considering here is that $a_{in}(t)$ increases through time at the rate $r_i = \varrho_i$, while the whole expression in square brackets (since $\varrho_i = \varrho_{k_i}$ *ex-hypothesis*) decreases through time at exactly the same rate ϱ_i, so that each $\lambda_i(t)$ remains absolutely constant, while $n(t) = \bar{n}$, that is, the number of goods remains constant, $i = 1, 2, \ldots, (\bar{n} - 1)$. Hence, the standard rate of growth of productivity precisely emerges, in this case, as

$$\varrho^* = \sum \varrho_i \lambda_i, \tag{10.13.5}$$

where each ϱ_i and each λ_i, though different between one commodity and the other, are – according to our assumptions – absolutely constant. A *fortiori* the overall standard rate ϱ^* will remain constant.

Now we can face at last the general case. It has been pointed out previously that (10.13.4), as such, refers already to the general case, as it has been obtained from the general case formulations. Our problem, therefore, has been solved already by the formulation (10.13.4), which, for the general case, will retain the time subscript. The only modification we might introduce is to split up each weight $\lambda_i(t)$, by expansion of the square brackets, into two separate weights, for consumption good i and for the corresponding capital good k_i, any time that $\varrho_i \neq \varrho_{k_i}$. But in fact, for many purposes, and especially for present purposes, it turns out to be more convenient to refer the rates of growth of productivity to the corresponding vertically hyper-integrated labour coefficients.[15] In other words, it turns out more convenient to call, let us say, ϱ_i' the percentage rate at which the whole magnitude contained

[15] This is what has been already anticipated in footnote 11.

in square brackets of (10.13.4) decreases through time. This means that we come to define (as has been done already in the initial section (10.1.7))

$$\varrho_1', \quad \varrho_2', \ldots, \quad \varrho_{n-1}', \tag{10.6.4}$$

as the rates of change (with negative signs) of the vertically hyper-integrated labour coefficients for commodities $i = 1, 2, \ldots, n-1$. Then, we can use (10.13.4) as it is for the general case. The standard rate of growth of productivity therefore emerges, in general, as

$$\varrho^*(t) = \sum \varrho_i' \lambda_i(t), \tag{10.13.6}$$

where the ϱ_i' is meant to incorporate both the consumption goods sectors and the sectors that make capital goods for them (i.e. their hyper-integrated productivity coefficients).

Note that, when effective demand condition (10.13.3) is under-satisfied, the proportion of the total labour force that remains unemployed is, by (10.13.6), attributed a zero rate of productivity growth, which is precisely what is wanted.

Of course, formulation (10.13.6), concerning the economic system as a whole, may present various complexities. As opposed to what happens in the simplified case of Section 6, the weights $\lambda_i(t)$ are all changing, and moreover $n(t)$ is increasing, that is, new sectors, for new goods, are continually being added. Yet, for the economic system as a whole, many of the changes will no doubt compensate for each other. To the extent that, in spite of the ever-changing composition of its components, the standard rate of productivity may be considered as roughly steady through time, the usefulness of closing the price system by exponential function (10.12.3) with the particular values (10.13.1) – as is suggested at the beginning of this section – should now appear very clearly.

The computation of the 'standard' rate of growth of productivity provides us with a concept of the *real* wage rate which possesses extraordinarily interesting properties, as it avoids all the ambiguities entailed by reference to any particular commodity. As will be seen in further detail in a moment, all prices and the wage rate come to be expressed in terms of a *physical* 'average commodity' for the economic system as a whole.

14 A 'Dynamic' Standard Commodity

The implications of using the 'standard' rate of growth of productivity in expression (10.12.3) are manifold. In an economic system in which, as is normally the case today, the *numéraire* of the price system is a conventional unit of account (i.e. inconvertible paper money, as will be described in a moment), rather than any actual physical commodity, there is no difficulty in accepting any number as expressing the wage rate $\bar{w}$ at time zero. Then, to let the wage rate $w(t)$ increase at the standard rate ϱ^* simply means letting it grow exactly in step with the average *physical* growth of per-capita production; that is, it means letting it grow at the rate of growth of its 'average' purchasing power, in physical terms. This has straight-forward effects on the price level.

Obviously, to close the price system by exponential function (10.12.3) with particular values (10.13.1) is equivalent to measuring all the prices, and the wage rate, in terms of a particular composite commodity for which productivity is growing through time at the 'average' growth of productivity of the economic system as a whole. In terms of such a commodity, therefore, half of the prices, on (a weighted) average, will increase, and the other half, on (a weighted) average, will decrease, so that the general level of prices neither increases nor decreases. This is its remarkable property.

Note that no other physical commodity, if chosen as *numéraire*, would keep the general price level constant. For, in an economic system with structural change, in general, no single price can remain constant, and so also no average of prices can remain constant in terms of *any* commodity *numéraire*. Actually any average of prices would move differently over time according to the physical commodity that is chosen as *numéraire*. But we have found a particular 'composite' commodity that eliminates these ambiguities. The prices of its components move in time at rates of change the average of which is zero by definition. In terms of such a commodity, and only in terms of such a commodity, can we talk of stability of the general price level.

It may be useful to look more in detail into the features of such a commodity. Actually, it is easier to state the properties of such a commodity than to state precisely what it is physically made of. First of all, such a commodity is defined no longer in terms of its composition (in fact its composition is changing all the time), but in terms of the weighted rates of change of labour requirements of its components. We may say that it is a composite commodity for which the labour requirements decrease through time at the 'standard' rate ϱ^*, which is the weighted average of all rates of productivity change. In the present theoretical framework, in which technical progress is typically 'labour-potential augmenting', such a commodity appears to be a sort of physical *dynamic* counterpart of Ricardo's 'invariable standard of value'. I shall therefore call it the 'dynamic standard commodity'.[16]

As a justification of this terminology, let me stress that what characterises the dynamic standard commodity is not its physical composition (which, in the general case, is ever changing), but its *dynamic properties*. In the two particular cases of Chapter 8 and of Chapter 9, Section 2, *any* commodity fulfils the requirements of a dynamic standard commodity, while in the hypothetical case of Section 6 an overall average is necessary, but the composition (at current prices) remains invariant. In the general case, the composition (both in physical terms and at current price) is changing all the time. And yet something, lying much deeper, remains constant, in spite of all the complex structural dynamics change. This something is precisely what has been called 'augmented' labour. As time goes on, technical progress renders labour more and more productive, but in a different way from one commodity to another. The dynamic standard commodity is that particular commodity for which the growth of labour productivity is exactly equal to the overall average. It is a commodity, therefore, that always embodies the same amount of overall 'augmented' labour.

[16] As is well known, Ricardo's 'invariable standard of value' was a particular commodity which was supposed to satisfy two requisites: (i) a commodity which 'now and at all times requires precisely the same quantity of labour to produce it' Ricardo (1951, vol. 1, p. 17); and (ii) a commodity the value of which is invariant to changes in income distribution.

Piero Sraffa (1960, *Production of Commodities*) focused on the second of these requisites. By 'freezing', so to speak, the economic system at a given technique, Sraffa has constructed a composite commodity (his 'standard commodity') whose value is invariant to changes in income distribution. In the present analysis, I am following a symmetrical approach. I have focussed on the first of Ricardo's requisites, interpreted in dynamic terms. The economic system is again 'frozen', so to speak, at a given income distribution, and a commodity has been constructed (the 'dynamic standard commodity') which through time always requires the same quantity of 'augmented' labour.

15 Price Changes and the Rate of Inflation

We have seen in Chapter 7 that all the (relative) 'natural' prices and the wage rate are linked to one another according to expression (7.8.6), and we have seen in Section 12 that their relative movements through time are linked to one another by relations (10.12.10), within a standard 'natural' economic system. These relative movements through time, by using the convenient assumption (10.6.3), can even more simply be written in terms of the (percentage) rates of change of consumption goods prices, which have been denoted by

$$\sigma_1, \quad \sigma_2, \ldots, \quad \sigma_{n-1}, \tag{10.12.8}$$

and of the (percentage) rate of change of the wage rate, σ_w. We have already in fact simply obtained in Section 12:

$$\sigma_j = \sigma_w - \varrho_j', \qquad j = 1, 2, \ldots, n-1. \tag{10.12.10}$$

If the economic system keeps to the evolution of its 'natural' structure, as we are supposing here, it is the *relative* prices that are linked to one another, both at any initial point of time and through time. The absolute level of prices – that is, one of the prices in (7.8.6) – and the speed of the overall movement of prices through time – that is, one of the rates of change in (10.9.2), or more simply, in (10.12.10) – are to be fixed from outside the price system.

These are the two degrees of freedom that, according to what has been seen in Section 12, need to be closed exogenously from outside the price system.

We have seen in the same Section 12 that this can be done, in general, by simply fixing the initial wage rate and its rate of change through time in exponential function (10.12.3), in terms of any arbitrarily chosen *numéraire*.

When the *numéraire* of the price system is a conventional monetary unit of account – let's say, paper money – we may fix:

$$w(0) = \bar{w}^{(M)}(0), \tag{10.15.1}$$

at time zero, where $\bar{w}^{(M)}$ is the wage rate in terms of the conventional monetary unit of account. Then, through the (7.8.6), all prices are determined in terms of money at time zero. Moreover, we may fix:

$$\sigma_w = \bar{\sigma}_w^M, \tag{10.15.2}$$

that is, the rate of change of the wage rate in terms of the nominal unit of account. The rates of change of all ('natural') prices, in terms of money, are then determined by (10.12.10).

But what are now the relations between monetary and 'real' magnitudes? It is here that a profound difference comes to light between a price system in which a physical commodity is used as *numéraire* and one in which prices are measured in terms of a conventional unit of account (paper money). In the former case, the unit of reference is a well-defined physical magnitude (e.g. an ounce of gold). Its price is equal to unity, by definition, and remains unity through time (its rate of change cannot but be zero). More specifically, in this case, the two degrees of freedom contained in the price system are inherently coupled to each other and in fact compacted into the same unit. On the other hand, in the case of prices expressed in terms of a conventional monetary unit of account (paper money), even after fixing one of the prices, in terms of money, at time zero (or alternatively after fixing the wage rate, in terms of money), complete freedom still remains as to its movement through time. The degrees of freedom of the price system, as was pointed out above, remain two. A further equation is needed, besides the initial one, and this is precisely what is provided by equation (10.15.2).

Note that, in (10.15.2), $\bar{\sigma}_w^M$ can be given *any* value. In other words, the wage rate, in terms of money (a nominal unit), can grow at *any* rate. But of course an arbitrary growth of the wage rate would be a purely nominal growth. What becomes important is to find its relation to the movements of the 'real' magnitudes. It is precisely for this purpose, as we may now realise, that the 'dynamic standard commodity', defined in Section 14, shows its real relevance.

The dynamic standard commodity is an ideal commodity for which productivity changes through time at the 'standard' rate ϱ^*, that is, at the weighted average of the rates of change of productivity in the whole economic system. It may therefore be taken as the 'real' standard of reference. We know that, if the wage rate, in terms of any conventional monetary unit, were to move through time precisely at the 'standard' rate of growth ϱ^*, that is, if it were to happen that

$$\bar{\sigma}_w^M = \varrho^*, \tag{10.15.3}$$

then all 'natural' prices would *ipso facto* turn out to be measured in terms of the dynamic standard commodity. Each price $p_j(t)$ would change through time at very specific rate:

$$(\varrho^* - \varrho_j), \qquad j = 1, 2, \ldots, n-1. \tag{10.15.4}$$

This means that half of the prices, on average, would decrease (those referring to commodities with above-average increases in productivity), and the other half of the prices, on average, would increase (those referring to commodities with below-average growths of productivity), while the weighted average of all their rates of change would be exactly zero.

We may indeed refer to a situation of this type as a situation of perfect (average) price stability.

It is this ideal situation that represents the basic point of reference.

Clearly any time that

$$\bar{\sigma}_w^M > \varrho^*, \tag{10.15.5}$$

that is, any time that the money wage rate increases at a rate of growth higher than ϱ^*, the overall level of prices is increasing, even though some prices might still be decreasing. This is the situation which in common parlance is generally referred to as one of *price inflation.* Conversely, any time that:

$$\bar{\sigma}_w^M < \varrho^*, \tag{10.15.6}$$

the overall level of prices is decreasing, though some of the prices might still be increasing – a situation of price deflation.

Therefore, the difference $(\bar{\sigma}_w^M - \varrho^*)$, which we may denote by σ^M, that is,

$$\bar{\sigma}_w^M \equiv \bar{\sigma}_w - \varrho^*, \tag{10.15.7}$$

becomes of crucial importance in any monetary economy. By expressing the rate of change through time of the price of the 'dynamic standard commodity' in terms of the monetary unit, it comes to represent the rate of change of the overall level of prices. It comes to represent what may indeed be called 'the general rate of price inflation'.[17]

[17] Note that no other physical commodity, when chosen as *numéraire*, would enable us to use unambiguously the concept of price inflation. The choice of *numéraire* must therefore be made with care if the movement of the price level is of any concern. This is what was hinted at in Section 14. Even if we were to choose as the *numéraire* a physical commodity, the movement through time of the average price level will indeed turn out to be different depending on the (physical) *numéraire* that is chosen. For example, choosing as *numéraire* the physical commodity with the fastest growing productivity would yield an overall level of price which is constantly increasing, and conversely, choosing

We may look at the same concepts in another way. When $(\sigma_w - \varrho^*)$ is different from zero, *all* prices are undergoing the same change through time, over and above whatever change each of them may be undergoing owing to the relative changes of productivity, as expressed by (10.15.4). As opposed to changes (10.15.4), which are specific to each price, change (10.15.7) affects all prices in the same way. Each one of the rates of change (10.12.10) may in fact now be rewritten in the following way:

$$\sigma_j = (\bar{\sigma}_w - \varrho^*) + (\varrho^* - \varrho_j), \qquad j = 1, 2, \ldots, n-1. \qquad (10.15.8)$$

This is the very general formulation of central interest.

It evinces explicitly the two components that make up the total rate of change of each price. There is a *particular* component $(\varrho^* - \varrho_j)$, which is specific to each price, and there is a *general* component $(\bar{\sigma}_w - \varrho^*)$, which is common to all prices.

The general component $\bar{\sigma}^M = (\sigma_w - \varrho^*)$ is precisely the 'general rate of price inflation' or, as we may elliptically, but more simply, say, the 'rate of inflation'.

There is of course also a reciprocal way of looking at these movements. Rate of change σ_j, with a negative sign, also represents the rate of fall of the purchasing power of the monetary unit in terms of each specific commodity j, $(j = 1, 2, \ldots, n-1)$. And the rate of change σ^M, with a negative sign (i.e. the opposite of the rate of increase of the money price of the dynamic standard commodity), represents the weighted average rate of fall of the purchasing power of the monetary unit – what may simply be called the rate of fall (through inflation) of the purchasing power of money.

16 A Second Institutional Goal: Stability of the General Price Level

The practical relevance of breaking down the general dynamics of the price system into its two components – the structural component and the inflationary component – should appear quite evident,

as *numéraire* the physical commodity with the slowest growing productivity would yield an overall level of price which is constantly decreasing. Only measurement in terms of the *dynamic standard commodity* can keep the overall level of prices constant, thus providing the basic point of reference for using the concept of price inflation.

in fact dramatic, at this point. Both components have important and pervasive implications, but of a very different nature. The structural component is tied up with problems of attainment of efficiency in each single branch of production. The inflationary component concerns the economic system as a whole. The first component poses questions, at a sectoral and micro-economic level, that recall investigations rather familiar in economic analysis. The second component brings to light the involvement of the economic system as a whole – [a field of investigation which has not been nearly so well explored].

Incidentally, the reader will not miss the implications that the changeover from monetary regimes with physical *numéraires* to monetary regimes with purely nominal *numéraires* must have had on the, necessary, appearance of a central banking institution, as has happened. Although we do not aim here, as has been repeatedly pointed out, at entering into any discussion of the institutional set-ups of the various economic systems, it is important to underline how clearly, at the present stage of analysis, one can see emerging the necessity, with regard to the economic system considered as a whole, of stating an objective concerning the movement through time of the general price level.

The obvious objective would appear to be precisely that of achieving stability of the general price level, or at least, when the pursuit of rigorous stability generates too many difficulties, that of not going beyond a moderate deviation of the general price level, provided that it is at a steady rate of variation.

What seems important to point out here is that such an objective concerns the whole economic system. Within the framework of nominal *numéraires*, one cannot see how it could be pursued by single individuals or by single groups. It seems indeed to require a central banking institution.

This is the second time that, from the present analytic scheme, there emerges the existence of a macro-economic task – that is, a task which cannot be pursued by single individuals but necessarily involves the economic system as a whole. In Section 4 there emerged the macro-economic task of pursuing and achieving (and maintaining) full employment. Now there emerges the task, again typically macro-economic, of pursuing the stability of the general price level.

17 The 'Monetary' Production Economy (Imposing the Necessity of a Central Monetary Institution)

From the analysis just carried out in the foregoing sections, the step is short to realise that a modern production economy cannot come into existence except by taking the shape of a 'monetary' production economy, in the sense that John Maynard Keynes had the intuition to anticipate.

In a modern industrial economy there is no possibility of achieving a solid and sensible price system, in the sense of following its stability in distributing and holding the whole purchasing power of the economic system, except through the setting up of a standard of reference that involves the whole *general level of prices* and its evolution through time, as we have seen.

No given physical commodity can assure through time a solid, stable purchasing power to the system of prices considered as a whole. Wishes and imagination may well go back to the symbolic role of *gold* (which by the way still nowadays is kept as a reserve in the safes of the Central Banks). For centuries past, it provided the symbol of solidity of money and wealth at large. *Aura sacra famis*, Keynes reminded us, stirred up for millennia the idea and ambitions of *wealth*, both for individuals and for societies, groping for a standard of value of a non-diminishing purchasing power over goods and services. It is a fact that gold, or any other physical commodity, cannot any longer fulfil the function that it used to be attributed to it in the past. It certainly can no longer at present; even less in the future.

Central banking institutions have since long been established by now. Our analysis of a modern production system shows that they have become a necessary feature in industrial societies.

It has become a fact that the traditional defective characteristics of a gold-based monetary unit are no longer so much a consequence of any inability to ease the management of any monetary price system relying on any particular physical commodity, whatever reasonable real commodity standard in the system may have been chosen as *numéraire*, as rather a consequence of a more basic feature, namely, the *structural dynamics* inherent in modern production systems.

Central banking institutions have, since long, discovered the efficiency and flexibility of purely *nominal* monetary units of accounts, but they have at the same time experienced the risks, and then quite often the reality, of abuses following from the compulsions of external events that have made nominal sums of money evaporate in the nothingness of monetary hyper-inflation. To keep the monetary price system on a solid basis – even if it stands on nothing that is real – one must first of all have a clear theoretical framework that allows to single out some solid point, or path of reference, that may be set up behind the whole system of values.

What does the logical framework of a 'natural economic system' provide us on this respect?

Although not entering into any analysis of what are the appropriate institutions – which may evolve in time and change – our investigation gives indeed the basic lines of requirements as emerging from the features of the 'natural economic system'. And certainly it offers the basic concepts.

The natural economic system certainly offers two *physical* standards on which we may rely, namely physical labour, and thus the wage rate, which is the counterpart within all the moving features of the price system. And secondly, it provides us with the *dynamic standard commodity*, which has emerged from the foregoing pages as the new physical expression of the instruments to achieve the stability of the whole system of prices.

In between the dynamic movements of these two magnitudes – the wage rate and the dynamic standard commodity – there lies the standard rate of growth of labour productivity, which relates the movement of the wage rate to the monetary expression of the movement of the dynamic standard commodity. The link between the two is not subject to any physical constraint; it may well go beyond the movements through time of each of them. And it can indeed go beyond them, according to a well-defined 'rate of monetary inflation', σ_A, of the general level of prices, which is made to emerge from the whole price system in the very well-defined form of a steady rate of change through time. This calls for an explicit appropriate management of the whole price system through an overall monetary institution, external to the 'natural economic system'.

Within this framework, the most reasonable (and efficient) of all the standards of reference for the price system does emerge as a purely *nominal* standard of reference (a monetary unit of measurement of prices, call it the dollar, the euro, or any other), since after all, the industrial economic systems have long discovered – provided it is managed with a very precise set of relations among all the relevant rates of change of the variables that constitute it through time – the dynamics of the price system.

Within the framework of steady rates of change, as per hypothesis depicted in Section 1, the important result that has emerged is to have set up an analytical framework – within a purely *nominal* monetary economic system – for referring to, and linking together, the 'natural' movements of all the single prices, to the rates of change of labour productivity of the corresponding commodities, that is, to the rate of monetary inflation (expressed by the excess of the nominal rate of change of the wage rate over the standard rate of change of labour productivity), whatever the nominal unit of account for the price system that may have been chosen.

This is the essence of the setup that emerges from the 'natural economic production system' that has been presented in the foregoing analysis.

18 Macro-economic Variables through Time

A few final remarks may be added about the dynamics of the aggregate magnitudes normally used in macro-economic investigations and comparisons (i.e. national income, total capital, consumption, investment etc.). From (10.9.1) and (10.9.2), it follows that all these aggregate magnitudes move in time in a very (structurally) composite way. Each of them results from a sum of physical quantities, whose proportions are changing, multiplied by prices, whose structure is also changing over time. Moreover, new and better goods are continually coming into being.

From these features, it is normally concluded that all macro-economic magnitudes have a well-defined physical meaning at any specific point in time in relation to the technical and demand conditions prevailing at that point in time, but, at the same time, that any comparison through time inevitably introduces some degree of arbitrariness. For, the simultaneous change of both component structures (physical quantities and relative prices) makes it impossible to reduce the macro-economic magnitudes to a strictly comparable physical basis. The same collections of physical quantities turn out to be expressed by different macro-economic figure according to the physical commodity (or composite commodity of fixed physical composition) in terms of which they are measured. But most of all, given any specific physical (single or composite) commodity, to be used as standard of measurement, the same collections of physical quantities turn out to be expressed by different macro-economic figures according to whether the relative prices used are those of the initial, the final, or any intermediate, period of time. These remarks express what has been called the 'index-number problem' – very well known to all statisticians. The index-number problem does not mean that comparisons cannot be made; but it does mean that there is a margin of indeterminateness in all comparisons of macro-economic magnitudes through time, when the macro-economic magnitudes are expressed in terms of any physical (single or composite) commodity, facing a movement of changing relative prices. This is a margin of indeterminateness which, though small, or even negligible, when short periods of time are considered, becomes wider and wider the longer the period of time involved.

The foregoing analysis does not contradict (in fact, it confirms) these conclusions, but at the same time it does provide an entirely new basis for comparisons through time; it provides an alternative standard of measurement that allows us to escape from the ambiguities of index numbers. By going much deeper into the determinants of the evolution of an economic system, and by singling out the ultimate constituent of all production, namely (vertically hyper-integrated) embodied labour, the foregoing analysis has put us in a position to give a physical content to the continually increasing productivity of labour. A dynamic relation has been found between labour and its changing physical productivity, in terms of the average physical commodity which the consumers have chosen to demand. Such a dynamic relation is synthesised by the standard rate of growth of labour productivity and is governed, as was to be expected, by the joint operation of the two determinants of the evolution of the economic system: the evolution of technology on the one side and the changing composition of demand on the other.[18]

[18] In the present work, the whole analysis is carried out on the basis of per-capita consumption coefficients, which are averaged over the whole economic system. Of course, the composition of individual consumption may be different from one consumer to another. This means that if a society were very markedly non-egalitarian, that is, the personal distribution of income were rather uneven, then the overall 'average' per-capita consumption, though significant for the economic system as a whole, would become less significant for those individuals (or classes of individuals) whose per-capita income, and

19 Short-run Flexibilities

Before closing the chapter, it may be useful to point out explicitly that the relations between the equilibrium conditions of the economic system and equilibrium time paths of the variables which have been considered are never to be taken as absolutely rigid. Any given structure of productive capacity and of the labour force, defining the production potential of an economic system, is, in the short run, always susceptible to some flexible adjustments, which – at least temporarily – may allow increases in production out of the same existing physical capital and population. In our formulation, these possibilities of adaptation are connected with the degree of flexibility of the parameters μ, v, T.

The magnitudes of μ, v, T which have been used in our analysis represent the long-run normal values of these parameters, which may be constant or may be showing mild trends over time. But, in the short run, these parameters are always susceptible of being influenced, sometimes quite substantially. At least up to a certain degree, they can, so to speak, be stretched, thereby affecting the size of the *stocks* that the economic system can use. In other words, at any given point of time, productive capacities and available labour are never related to existing physical equipment and existing population by rigid one-to-one relations. Between these last physical quantities, which at any point in time are given, and the parts of them that are relevant for production, the flexibility of the mentioned parameters provides a sort of cushion. Temporary variations of μ and T mean temporary variations in the

thus composition, were very far away from the average, that is, in practice for the very poor and the very rich. However, there is nothing in our analysis that prevents, at least in principle, the breakdown of consumers into as many groups as one may find useful. In practice, it might be reasonable to construct, besides the overall average 'standard' rate of growth of productivity, at least two other auxiliary standard rates: a 'lower-third' standard rate and an 'upper-third' standard rate. Each of them would differ from the overall 'average' one but would be more significant for the individuals in the lower-third and upper-third income brackets, respectively. To the extent that these two auxiliary standard rates are substantially different from the overall standard rate, they come to express a very real phenomenon, namely the different quantitative expression that technical progress takes for the different income classes. Labour is in fact being 'augmented' by technical progress in a different manner for each group of consumers depending on the composition of their per-capita consumption.

productive capacities of existing physical equipments, which may be attained by utilising them more intensively or by keeping in operation some machines which were due to be scrapped. Similarly, variations of μ and v mean variations of working hours out of a given population, which may be obtained by lengthening (or shortening) the working week or by varying the proportion of active to total population – more (or fewer) working women; later (or earlier) retirement ages.

The degree of flexibility of parameters μ, v, T, therefore, represents very important characteristics of any specific economic system. They express the extent to which the system is capable of short-run adaptations and adjustments in the face of disturbances of any kind.

20 Crying out for Decisions Concerning the Economic Institutions

Before closing the elaborations of the present chapter, it may be useful to remember that there have been *two points* in our analysis at which the logic of the model of a natural economic system, which we have been setting up, has been crying out for the necessity of decisions to be taken at the institutional level for the economic system as a whole.

The first point was in Section 7, where we have seen that the necessity of reaching and keeping the overall equilibrium condition, which means full employment of labour and full utilisation of productive capacity through time, is crying out for the setting up of a central institution which must take care of the purpose of carrying out such task. No specific type of institution is indicated, but the task that must be performed has emerged very clearly.

The second point was in Section 12, where two degrees of freedom have been shown to emerge concerning the closure of the price system as it is moving through time. They concern the choice of the monetary unit of account and the choice of the movement in time of the general level of prices. See also Section 16 for hints concerning the problem of (relative) price stability in time. Here again, no specific institution is indicated, but what has clearly emerged is that there is an important task of making decisions on how to govern the evolution of the price system.

The model is thus intrinsically crying out for the setting up of *institutions* aimed on the one side at carrying out an activity for keeping full employment and full capacity utilisation over time and on the other side at managing and governing the evolution in time of the whole system of the levels of prices.

It certainly will be noticed that both tasks have behind them motivations that cannot be solved at the level of the behaviour of the single individuals, since they concern the economic system as a whole.

PART IV

A General (Objective) Pure Labour Theory of Value

11 *The Natural Features of a Growing Economic System*

1 Introduction

Empowered by the dynamic analysis developed in Chapter 10 and taking advantage of its simplification devices, we are ready to proceed to sketching out and completing the overall basic features of what we may well call a 'natural' growing economic system.

2 Two Basic Properties

To begin with, there are two properties of our theoretical scheme, which must be explicitly stressed before proceeding.

The first property is that it has been developed for the purpose of detecting the 'permanent' forces moving a production economic system, irrespective of transitory, or unduly imposed, deviations which may temporarily occur. Essentially, the aim pursued is the one that was perceived by the Classical economists. It was most clearly expressed particularly by Ricardo, when he stated that he aimed to detect the 'primary and natural' determinants of the variables he considered, and, therefore, we may now add in a dynamic context, their basic movements through time.[1]

The second property is that the analysis has been developed independently of the institutional set-up of society, that is, independently of the particular institutional mechanisms which may in practice be put into operation in order to bring those 'primary and natural' features

[1] These 'natural and primary' determinants are those that should and ought to be allowed to make themselves felt in the long run, whatever (transitory) short-run deviations there may be or may be imposed. This is something more than saying that the present analysis is a long-run analysis. We have been, and we are, concerned with the norm, and the norm is always there – even if it is not so much apparent – in the *short* no less than in the long run, whatever amount of disturbances, or unduly imposed deviations, there may be.

into being. This does not mean paying no attention to the institutional requirements that the natural economic system may from time to time make evident. The investigation has started directly from a growing population, an evolving pattern of technical knowledge, and an evolving pattern of consumers' preferences. From these natural forces, and from nothing else, a series of structural movements have been derived which may indeed be called the *natural features* of a growing, evolving and learning production, economic system.

3 The 'Natural' Features of an Industrial Economic System

Before proceeding, let me recall and state – on the basis of the analysis developed so far – a list of the *natural* features that have emerged:

(i) an evolving structure of physical production of goods and services;
(ii) an evolving structure of corresponding commodity (and service) prices;
(iii) the time path of the wage rate and, at a given rate, or rates, of profit (to be precise, the rate, or rates, of profit have not in fact been explicitly examined as yet; they have simply been taken as given: see Chapter 7, Sections 8 and 9). But, they are going to be immediately and explicitly examined in a moment; and
(iv) in the background, the existence of a series of capital goods stocks, shaped by the natural forces that acted in the past;

Moreover, as requirements for all these structural movements to take place in 'equilibrium' – by which is simply meant full employment and full productive capacity utilisation – two types of necessary conditions have emerged, namely:

(v) a series of *sectoral* new investment conditions, defining the evolving structure of the accumulation of the stocks of capital goods;
(vi) a *macro-economic* effective demand condition, referring to total demand in the economic system as a whole.

Structural features (i), (ii), (iii), (iv), and equilibrium conditions (v) and (vi) – duly supplemented (when more details are needed with reference to a given period in time) by the inter-industry relations which have been examined in Part II of the present work – form a theoretical scheme representing what may be called a *natural*, growing and evolving economic system.

In the economic analysis which has been developed above and will continue to be developed in the following pages, we shall suppose that these natural features have been shaped in the past, and they are in time all evolving in 'equilibrium' (which means with full employment of the labour force and full utilisation of the existing productive capacity).

4 The Natural' Rate(s) of Profit as the Most Basic, Striking Emerging Feature of the New World

As the reader may easily have noticed, there still is one crucial problem which has been left open hitherto and which must now be settled before proceeding. As just mentioned in Chapter 10, one of the economic magnitudes of our theory – indeed a crucial one, namely the rate of profit in each sector, has not been explicitly examined nor has been explained so far. It has simply been taken as given (Chapter 7, Sections 8 and 9). But at this stage, it is quite natural to advance a precise question: does the previous theoretical framework, besides evincing the factors determining the natural prices and physical quantities, also logically imply a *natural* rate, or rates, of profit? The answer is: Yes. A *natural* rate of profit is already logically implied in the previous theoretical framework because the economic system considered is a growing one. For clearness of arguments, it may be useful, for this purpose, to consider separately the two basic cases of economic growth: population growth and technical progress.

Suppose first of all an economic system characterised by constant returns to scale (no technical progress) and by a population increasing at a steady proportional rate g. In this case, the productivity of labour is constant over time *ex-hypothesis*. But since the population is increasing, the conditions of dynamic equilibrium require that the present population cannot consume the whole fruit of its productivity. In order to maintain a constant production per head over time, a part of the productive capacity must be devoted to producing intermediate capital goods. This means that, since technology requires the use of capital goods in the production processes, an increasing population causes the amount of goods that the present generation can afford to consume – that is, the amount of enjoyable reward that the present generations obtain for their productive activity – to be less than it would be if population were constant. The proportion by which it is less is given by the rate of population growth multiplied by the overall capital/output ratio. Another way of putting the problem is to say that since technology requires the use of capital goods in the production processes, an increasing population forces down in each period the productivity of labour in terms of the commodities that the community can actually consume. This means that if there are, for example, two commodities, A and B, of which the first is produced by labour alone and the second is produced by the same amount of labour, except that it is partly direct labour and partly labour first embodied into a machine, the second commodity is dearer for the community to produce when population is increasing because, in order to produce it at constant productivity through time, an extra amount of labour must be devoted to make *additions* to productive capacity. Thus, an increasing population causes the productivity of labour in terms of B to be lower than the productivity of labour in terms of A. As a consequence, the price of B will have to be higher than the price of A by the same proportion as the corresponding labour productivity is lower. All this means that a rate of profit on the value of capital goods must be charged equal to the rate of growth of population. Therefore, in an economic system with increasing population and no technical progress, there is a *natural* rate of profit, which turns out to be equal to the percentage rate of growth of population.

Suppose now an economic system in which population is stationary but technical knowledge is continually improving. Average per capita incomes will increase, and therefore demand for consumption goods will have to increase, if dynamic equilibrium is to be maintained. The rates of per capita demand for each consumption good, $r_1, r_2, \ldots, r_{n-1}$, will normally be different from one another, as has been argued in Chapter 9.

Consider a particular commodity i and compare the two alternative cases in which $r_i > 0$ and $r_i = 0$. Clearly, we may now repeat the same arguments developed previously with reference to the two alternative cases of a positive and of a zero rate of population growth. In the case in which $r_i > 0$, commodity i is, for the economic system as a whole, more expensive to produce (in terms of final consumption goods) than in the case in which $r_i = 0$. For, in the former case, sector i will require not only direct wages and replacement of used-up capital goods (indirect wages) but also an extra amount of capital goods (an extra amount of indirect wages: we may say 'hyper-indirect' wages) to expand its productive capacity. The value of these extra capital goods which are required will be precisely given by the sectoral rate of growth r_i multiplied by the sectoral capital/output ratio. In this case again, an increasing demand for commodity *i* forces down in each period the productivity of labour in terms of the commodities the community can afford to consume. Or, to put the matter in another way, if there are two commodities, *i* and *j*, both of which are expanding at the same per capita rate of growth ($r_i = r_j$), both of which require exactly the same amount of labour to be produced, but such that the labour required by the first commodity is all direct, while the labour required by the second commodity is partly direct and partly first embodied into a machine, then for the community as a whole, when $r_i = r_j > 0$, the second commodity is more expensive to produce than the first. For, in order to produce it, an extra amount of labour must be devoted to make additions to productive capacity. Thus, the productivity of labour in terms of consumption good *i* and the productivity of labour in terms of consumption good *j* are exactly the same when $r_i = r_j = 0$; but the former is higher than the latter when $r_i = r_j > 0$. As a consequence, the price of *j* will have to be higher than the price of *i* by the same proportion – given by the new investment requirement (10.4.2) – as the corresponding productivity is lower. All this means that a rate of profit on the value of capital goods must be charged equal to the rate of growth of demand for commodity *j*. Therefore, in an economic system with technical progress and a constant population, there is a particular *natural* rate of profit for each particular sector of the economy. This natural rate of profit is equal to the sectoral rate of growth of per capita demand (and production).

By now combining this result with the previous one, we may conclude that a growing economic system logically implies a *natural* rate of profit. This natural rate of profit is uniform only in the case of population growth at constant technical coefficients. When there is both population growth and technical progress, there are as many natural rates of profit as there are rates of expansion of demand (and production) of the various consumption goods. Each natural rate of profit is given by the sum of two components: the rate of population growth, common to all of them, and the rate of increase of per capita demand for each consumption good (equal to the rate of increase of per capita production, as we are considering dynamic equilibrium situations). In formal terms, we may write:

$$\pi_i^* = g + r_i, \qquad i = 1, 2, \ldots, n-1, \tag{11.4.1}$$

where π_i^* represent the *natural rate of profit* for sector i. The (11.4.1) define $(n-1)$ natural rates of profit which, without recourse any longer to any exogenously given economic magnitude, now come to complete and close the whole relative-price system of our theoretical scheme.

Hence, this expression emerges as the most striking feature of the new world!

5 A Labour Theory of the 'Natural' Rate(s) of Profit

The interpretation of the 'natural' rate of profit outlined in Section 4 follows directly and logically from the approach to economic reality which has been adopted in the present work. In contrast with the scarce resource approach of traditional marginal economic theory, which would have amounted to reducing labour to one of many natural resources (each of which is treated on the same footing, as if it had a kind of personality of its own), the theory developed in the present work has put the whole economic system immediately into relation with what is its only source and *raison d'être*: the activity and the wants of Man. Nothing in the present theoretical price scheme has any economic relevance – that is, value – other than in relation to the activity and wants of the members of the community. What nature offers is a datum – it is taken for granted. Any commodity, by itself, has no personality: it has no right or claim. Of course, commodities do physically produce other commodities – machines produce machines, animals reproduce animals – but this 'physical' productivity must be correctly interpreted. Commodities cannot appropriate the commodities that come out of them. Only Man can. The physical productivity of commodities simply is a part of their technical or biological properties, which for Man is a datum. What becomes relevant for economic purposes, which means for the process of pricing, is only the amount of human activity which is required, whether directly or indirectly (or hyper-indirectly, as we shall state in a moment), to make a technological or a biological process work. The fact, for example, that machine

A can produce 1 unit of commodity a per day and machine B can produce 100 units of commodity b per day is a technical characteristic. For pricing purposes, what matters is the amount of human activity which has been and has to be used in the production. If the two machines have been made from the same inputs, and if they are operated by the same amount of labour, the value of their daily product – however, different their *physical* productivity may be – will be the same. The price of b will be 1/100 the price of a. It is in this sense that what becomes economically relevant is only and exclusively the productivity of Labour.

The theoretical consequences are far-reaching. As long as the rate of profitindex[subidx]Natural rates of profit@'Natural' rate(s) of profit was simply taken as exogenously given, the theory of value implied in the previous analysis, as pointed out in Chapter 7, Sections 8 and 9), was a theory of value in terms of labour equivalents (the quantities of labour being weighted differently according as to whether they were applied directly or indirectly). But now that a natural rate of profit is introduced, all relations become more straightforward. The theory of value implied by the present theoretical scheme becomes a theory in terms of simple labour – *a pure labour theory of value.*

To make this apparent, we may insert (11.4.1) into the expression for prices discussed in Chapters 7, 8 and 10, and write[2]

$$p_i(t) = [a_{ni}(t) + (\pi_i^* + 1/T_i)a_{nk_i}(t)]w(t), \qquad i = 1, 2, \ldots, n-1. \tag{11.5.1}$$

When all prices are expressed in terms of the wage rate, that is, when we put $w(t) = 1$, and growth rates are inserted explicitly, we have

$$p_i(t) = [a_{ni}(t) + (1/T_i)a_{nk_i}(t) + (g + r_i)a_{nk_i}(t)], \qquad i = 1, 2, \ldots, n-1. \tag{11.5.2}$$

The reader will realise that what appears in square brackets is precisely what has already been called (Chapter 10, Section 13) the vertically hyper-integrated labour coefficient for consumption good i. It now appears clearly that the price of each consumption good i

[2] The expression (11.5.1) refers to the simplest of all models we have considered. Using the more complicated model of Section 9 of Chapter 7 would simply make the formulae more complex, but would not alter our arguments and conclusions. Note that it is the simplest symbol of the present work which has the extraordinary property of being both simple and valid in general.

$(i = 1, 2, \ldots, n-1)$ is the sum of three *unweighted* physical quantities of *labour*: labour required directly in sector i (*direct labour* $a_{ni}(t)$) labour required to replace the worn-out productive capacity (*indirect labour* $(1/T_i)a_{nk_i}(t)$), and labour required to expand equilibrium productive capacity (what we have called *hyper-indirect labour* $(g + r_i)a_{nk_i}(t)$).[3] In each price $p_i(t)$, the replacement component and the profit component thereby appear as perfectly symmetrical and as fulfilling the same function of computing amounts of labour indirectly required elsewhere in the economic system for the equilibrium production of consumption good i. They both represent charges made in order not to violate the basic principle of equal rewards for equal amounts of homogeneous labour.

All this may appear at first as very striking. But short reflection should evince that it follows logically and inevitably from the very approach to economic reality taken in the present work. Labour emerges from the very logic of the present analysis as the only ultimate factor of production. And it is interesting that, in a growing economic system, this does imply a rate of profit. Contrary to what traditional economics has maintained for a long time, it is not the 'productivity of capital', or of any commodity, that turns out to be the *raison d'être* of a rate of profit. It is the additional capital required by the increasing productivity of labour![4]

[3] See Chapter 10, Section 13.

[4] To illustrate further, the contrast between this interpretation and the traditional one, consider the much exploited example, taken from the biological, of rabbits reproducing themselves, so often used to evince Böhm-Bawerk's third ground – namely the physical productivity of goods through time – for the existence of a rate of profit. This physical productivity is a biological property which, along with all other technical properties, will set constraints. In the present case, the activity of producing rabbits (or any other commodity) is obviously incompatible with a rate of profit higher than the physical own-rate of reproduction of rabbits. But this has nothing to do with any process of determination of the rate of profit. To set a constraint is something quite different from determining an economic magnitude. In a modern society, rabbits reproduce themselves because Man provides the favourable conditions (suitable place, fodder, organisation) for them to do so. The number of rabbits which can be taken for consumption in each unit of time is, for the economic purposes of pricing, the product of the direct, indirect and hyper-indirect labour put into this activity. It is the hyper-indirect labour (which depends on the growth of production) that determines the

6 Recalling the Two Basic Functions of the Price System

It may be useful to ponder a little further in our analysis on these problems by adding a few reflections on the equations of the price system. At any given point of time, the variables that emerge are a whole set of commodity prices, the wage rate and the rate (or rates) of profit.

We may well say that, in any economy, the price system basically performs two quite distinct and separate functions: a 'decentralised-decision-process' function and an 'income-distribution' function.

The 'decentralised-decision-process' function is performed at the intermediate stages of production. With reference to this function, the wage rate and the rates of profit are often referred to, in the economic literature, as 'factor prices'. But this terminology is misleading, though for reasons quite different from those that might be inferred from traditional economics. At the intermediate stages of the production process, *all* prices of the commodities used as inputs, and not only the wage rate and rate(s) of profit, are 'factor prices', in the sense that they fulfil the same basic function of providing an appropriate evaluation of the corresponding inputs in the process of production.

In order to visualise this important 'factor price' function of the whole price system, it is useful to revert to the inter-industry relations discussed in Part II of the book. In any advanced economic system, characterised by a very complex network of inter-industry relations, each producer is called upon, every day, to make decision about inputs which, before coming to him (her), have passed through a huge number of previous intermediate stages, sometimes in the most remote corners of the economic system. If, in order to take any single decision, one were required to know everything which has gone on in all those remote corners of the inter-industry network, the working of any economy would become practically impossible. But, if, with each input, whatever the stage at which it has arrived, an index can be associated summarising all operations which have been performed on it, and therefore expressing the relative importance of that input as against any other, then decisions can be taken very quickly and efficiently, in a decentralised way.

natural rate of profit, quite independently of (though physically constrained by) rabbits' own biological productivity.

It is precisely this remarkable decentralised decision-making process that the price system as a whole makes possible at the intermediate stages of production. From this point of view, there is no difference whatsoever between the prices of commodities, the wages to be paid to workers and the profits to be computed on the values of capital goods for the single producer, faced with a production decision. They are costs, or, if we like, they are all intermediate 'factor prices'. So that, for the economic system as a whole, the problem that arises is that of ensuring that the set of indexes that are used for production decisions (commodity prices, wage rate and rate(s) of profit) are not distorted. And it is not difficult to realise that the non-distorted set of indexes is precisely represented by the 'natural' price system. For, this particular price system has the property of ultimately reducing all inputs to physical quantities of labour, no matter where and when they have been applied in the production process. And this is precisely what is required.

We may conclude, therefore, that, as far as the 'decentralised-decision-process' function, or 'factor price' function, of the price system is concerned, commodity prices, wage rate and rate(s) of profit all play exactly the same role of providing appropriate indexes for efficient decentralised decisions.

But if we were to restrict our attention to how things appear at the level of any single intermediate stage of production, we would remain at the surface of economic problems. The price system also fulfils another, most important, function, which we may call the 'income distribution' function of the price system. Separately from, and in a reverse direction to, the process of production, any economic system inherently and inevitably carries out a process of distribution of claims to share in the final national product. And as far as this function is concerned, commodity prices on the one side and the wage rate and rate(s) of profit on the other do set themselves in opposition to each other. While the former maintain their role of intermediate devices, the latter acquire the character of final 'distributive variables'. More specifically, wages and profits, which represent the starting stage of the process of production, appear, in reverse, as the final stage of the process of income distribution. We have seen that, at the final stage of the process of production, the final national product of an economic system is represented by a series of physical quantities with which our equations have associated a series of corresponding commodity prices. When the physical quantities are multiplied by the corresponding commodity prices, these prices fulfil the remarkable function of distributing all through the economic system an amount of purchasing power, which is equal in the end to the sum of wages and profits. In this way, all commodity prices disappear eventually, and the whole purchasing power corresponding to the final national product finds itself distributed either in the form of wages or in the form of profits.

It is with reference to this 'income distribution function' that commodity prices on the one hand and the wage rate and rate of profit on the other hand evince their profoundly different nature. To be more specific, the intermediate role played by commodity prices remain 'intermediate' in either direction – in one direction they carry with them the precise indication (they represent indexes) of the costs that have occurred in the previous stages of production; in the opposite direction, they channel a corresponding amount of purchasing power towards those earlier stages of production. By contrast, the wage rate and the rate of profit (irrespective of what they may look like to the single producer) precisely do not let the corresponding purchasing power go back to any previous stage. They refer to something (inputs of labour) that takes place *at that* production stage and thus directly channel purchasing power to final beneficiaries of the production process. Their basic nature therefore is that of claims to shares in final national income.

Looking at the same contrast in another way, we may say that, in the process of income distribution, any time we find a commodity price, we know we are at an intermediate stage of the distribution process: a certain amount of purchasing power is channelled back to the previous stages of production. Any time we find profits and wages, we know that the income distribution process has come to an end.

We may also look at these concepts in the context of the national income accounts, where we see them appearing on the two opposite sides of the balance sheet. The physical quantities of all final commodities which are produced, evaluated at their prices, appear on one side. The sum of total wages and total profits appears on the opposite side. And the sums of the two sides are identically equal to each other. They provide two different ways of looking at the same thing: the final national income – as it is produced on the one side, and as it is distributed on the other.

7 The Conceptual *Macro-economic* Nature of the Real Wage Rate

We shall continue our reflections on the price system by pointing out the basically different nature of the wage as opposed to the commodity prices. Here again we may contrast the foregoing analysis with the interpretation which is given by traditional economic theory.

As will be realised, traditional economic theory, by looking at the wage rate through the filter of a scarce-resource economic world, has inevitably concentrated on its decentralised-decision-process function, while almost entirely neglecting its income-distribution function. Within such a theoretical framework, it becomes inevitable to look at the wage rate as a micro-economic concept, along with any other commodity price. More specifically, traditional economic theory has related the wage rate to its corresponding 'marginal productivity', which is a physical concept referring to marginal variations of production in the specific firm where labour is applied. From the point of view of the present analysis, such an approach appears very primitive. To concentrate attention on physical productivities within a single sector, or firm, might in fact have had a lot of heuristic merit in an economic system of the pre-industrial type, where each labourer normally produces directly the major part of the goods which his family consumes. But in a modern economic system, such an approach becomes patently irrelevant – not only owing to, and quite apart from, the difficulties and ambiguities inherent in the concepts of 'marginal productivities',[5] but more fundamentally because of the fact that, in a highly specialised society, the physical productivity of any single worker (whether marginal or average) can only have a negligible influence on claims that refer to the economic system as a whole. Fundamentally, in a modern economic system (at least in the institutional forms that have taken shape so far), the distributive variables are *macro-economic concepts.*

In Sections 4 and 5 of this chapter, it was pointed out in detail how irrelevant the physical productivity of any single commodity is to the determination of the natural rates of profit. A similar (much stronger) point can be stressed immediately here, with reference to the wage rate. On this problem, in fact, the limits of a static approach appear even

[5] For details on the criticism of the concepts of marginal productivities, we refer to Pasinetti (1981, Chapter IX, pp. 201–205).

more striking. In a hypothetical world, such as the one considered by traditional economic theory, where technology is supposed to be absolutely constant, one is led too easily to neglect what happens anywhere else in the economic system by concentrating one's attention on what happens in the sector under consideration. But in a dynamic context, in which technology is changing in all sectors, it becomes evident that it is precisely *what happens in the other sectors* that is of paramount importance in determining the real content of the wage rate and not the changes in productivity in the sector under consideration, whether at the margin or on the average.

The reader will notice that we are concerned here with the *real* wage rate, that is, with the wage rate in terms of physical commodities. Here again, the contrast with the current theory is striking. The 'real wage rate' of traditional economic theory is related to the 'marginal productivity' of labour. It is a single number – a number of physical units of the commodity which is produced in the sector where the worker is actually working. But this is not the concept of the real wage rate which is emerging from the present model, and indeed not the one that is relevant in a modern economic system. When the degree of specialisation in production is very marked, the concept of the 'real wage rate' that becomes relevant is represented, not by a single number, but by a whole series of numbers (a vector), indicating the physical basket of goods on which the wage rate is actually spent, and, as such, depending on the physical productivity of *the economic system as a whole.*

A short example may be useful to illustrate this important point. A worker who tightens screws on the assembly line of a car factory produces tightened screws, but he is not paid in terms of the number of screws tightened. He is paid with an amount of abstract purchasing power over *all* commodities. And when, as it is usually the case, an entirely negligible proportion of this purchasing power is spent on tightened screws, concentrating all economic analysis of wages on the worker's physical productivity in terms of tightened screws means magnifying out of proportion one tiny and negligible side of the whole problem. The real meaning of that worker's wage rate cannot but be sought in the basket of goods and services which the screws he has tightened can buy in the whole economic system. And the size of such a basket of goods and services depends on the absolute levels, and on the rates of change, of productivity in *all* the sectors that produce them. It depends, in practice, on the degree of productivity of the whole economic system. The reader has no doubt understood how important it is to realise the macro-economic nature of the concept of real wage rate.

To conclude, traditional economic theory has concentrated on one aspect of the real wage rate, which has become more and more negligible, and more and more remote from its physical content. It has concentrated on the physical productivity of each single individual, at a time when, between the physical productivity of any single worker and his (her) *real* wage rate, there has grown the entire and complex technological structure of the whole economic system. It is also useful to point out how more meaningful the concept of a wage rate becomes when re-expressed in terms of units of a 'dynamic standard commodity'.

8 A History-of-Economic-Thought Digression on the Determination of Relative Prices and Physical Quantities in a Dynamic Context

We may now open a digression here and go on briefly to investigate more specifically these movements through time. We shall begin with the evolution of the commodity prices together with the evolution of the corresponding physical quantities. Our dynamic analysis has put us in the enviable position of being able to take a fresh look at an old economic problem – the problem of singling out the basic determinants, through time, of the relative prices and physical quantities of the commodities produced in an economic system.

Some readers may look surprised at this statement and think that this is something which no longer needs any discussion, since the answer can be found in any elementary economics textbook, under the chapter (or chapters) devoted to the theory of value. But it is precisely this conviction that I should like to dispute, because the theory of value refers to one half of the whole problem. So far it has been impossible even to realise that there exists another half, because the static limitations imposed on economic theory have left the other half in the shade. Since the issue has kept a central place in economic analysis, it is almost impossible to deal with it without opening a digression and retracing the story from the beginning, by going back, albeit very briefly, to the standard works of the Classical, the Marginalist, and the Neoclasical economists.

The position of the Classical economists is masterly expressed by Ricardo in the first two pages of his *Principles*. He makes first of all the distinction between *produced commodities* and *scarce commodities* (Ricardo 1951, vol. 1, p. 12). Then, on grounds of economic irrelevance, he leaves the commodities of the *scarce type* out of consideration and exclusively concentrates on those commodities which are the outcome of a process of production. 'Utility', says Ricardo, 'is not the measure of [their] exchangeable value, although it is absolutely essential to it'.[6] Their value – he claims – is determined by their cost of production, which he mainly conceives of in terms of labour.

Fifty years later, as is well known, the Marginalists reacted violently against this statement. They objected that the Classical economists had neglected demand. They were right. Unfortunately, however, instead of correcting the Classical economists, they went in a completely different direction. They turned their attention to the other types of goods – the goods of the scarcity type – that the Classical economists did not consider at all and, by taking them as representative of *all* goods, they claimed that *utility*, and not the cost of production, is the fundamental determinant of value. 'Repeated reflection and inquiry had led me to the somewhat novel opinion that *value depends entirely upon utility*'.[7] This was the starting point, and the central tenet, of all works of Jevons, one of the first leading and most vigorous proponents of the utility theory. It was really unfortunate that the Ricardian distinction between commodities which are scarce and commodities which are produced had not been kept in mind: it would have shown so clearly how the Classical economists and the Marginalists were talking about different things.

When, at the turn of the century, Marshall tackled the problem, he was taken up by the Marginalist arguments, but he was concerned with explaining what happens in 'industry', and he was confronted with the puzzle of whether the cost of production or utility determines the value of commodities. To solve it, he proposed a famous compromise, which is still nowadays considered to be the standard answer to the problem, though it has been slightly modified by the monopolistic and imperfect competition theories.

[6] Ricardo (1951, vol. 1, p. 11).

[7] Jevons (1871), p. 1 (italics in the original), see also Chapter 2, Section 5.

Marshall's argument is very ingenious, and it is worth recalling it in detail. Both the cost of production and utility – Marshall claims – contribute to determining prices, in the same way as both blades of a pair of scissors contribute to cutting a piece of paper. He carries on this analogy very effectively by explaining that 'when one blade is held still, and the cutting is effected by moving the other, we may say with careless brevity that the cutting is done by the second'.[8] Similarly in the market, when the structure of production is given and held still – which happens in the short run – we may say that demand is the main factor responsible for the determination of prices. On the other hand, in the long run, when there is time for the structure of production to be adapted, it is the cost of production which will determine prices. Therefore, in the long run, 'if a person chooses to neglect market fluctuations. . .he may be excused for ignoring the influence of demand and speaking of (normal) price as governed by cost of production'.[9]

This is all right but, if we consider it carefully, it only reconciles the Marginalists' difficulties in understanding the Classical economists. *It does not* solve the problem that Ricardo (and the Classical economists) left unsolved. Marshall has the merit of grasping two important features of the Ricardian analysis, which the utility theorists had missed. The first is that the commodities under discussion are those ones which are important in an industrial type of society, namely the commodities of the reproducible type, and Marshall refers his analysis to them. The second feature is that the Ricardian theory is concerned with the long run (or rather, with fundamental determinants, which make themselves felt in the long run).

Now, what Marshall's arguments amount to is simply saying that in a market economy the commodities of the reproducible type are, in the short run, assimilated to the goods of the scarce type, because the adaptation of production to the unforeseen circumstances requires time. Therefore, in the short run, the market demand will influence their prices. On the other hand, in the long run, when 'adjustment of the flow of the appliances' can take place, the cost of production will eventually come out as the determinant of price.

[8] Marshall (1920, p. 348).

[9] Ibid., p. 349.

This is a statement that perhaps Ricardo would even had accepted. Only he would have pointed out that he was not terribly interested in the first part of it, because his purpose was to bring out the fundamental determinants of economic variables, independently of any temporary and short-lived deviations due to any market fluctuation.[10]

But, in this way, we are back to where Ricardo was. Marshall – apart from beginning to explore the effects of short run and temporary difficulties within a certain institutional system (the market economy) – does not bring that analysis ahead a single jot. In particular, Marshall's formulation leads one to conclude – in the same way as Ricardo did – that demand has no role to play in the long run. This is incorrect.

With the help of a dynamic scheme representing the evolution of both technology and demand, we can see the whole problem much more clearly. We may return, for a check, to the solutions of our systems of equations in this chapter. By expression (10.9.2) we are told that natural prices at a certain point in time and through time depend exclusively on technical factors: labour and capital goods required in the production of each unit of output. In other words, we are told that, in the long run, the cost of production determines prices, as both Ricardo and Marshall stated. But this is only half of the story. There is another (dual) series of solutions which has been forgotten – expression (10.9.1). This other series of solutions says that the quantities to be produced depend on demand factors, namely on the per-capita evolution in time of consumers' preferences and on population. In other words, in the long run, demand determines the *quantity* of each commodity which has to be produced. This is the half of the problem which Ricardo did not see,[11] and which Marshall then himself failed to bring out.

[10] Incidentally, we can clearly see here that Marshall's analysis, in spite of its apparent symmetry, is in fact a very hybrid one. For it puts on exactly the same footing elements belonging to the 'natural' economic system, which are objectively given for all types of economic systems, and elements which are temporary and specific to a particular institution (the market economy).

[11] Now that we have discovered it, we may go back for a moment to Ricardo's original statement. Indeed he was right in saying that cost of production, and not utility, determines the *natural* price of (produced) commodities but he added: 'although utility is absolutely essential to it'. This is misleading. That 'it' must be referred to the production of the commodity and not – as in Ricardo's context – to the prices. Those (reproducible) commodities that have no utility will simply not be produced (zero quantity), although they may have positive costs and, therefore, positive 'natural' prices. The only thing we can

The conclusions that follow are very simple and at the same time rather stringent. It is not true – as both Ricardo and Marshall implied – that demand has no role in to play in the long run. Both technology and demand are indeed relevant; both of them have their own role to play. But they determine two different things. Cost of production, that is, technology, determines *relative prices*; consumer's decisions, that is, their demand, determine *relative quantities*. In dynamic terms, the process emerges at its clearest – the pattern of productivity increases determines the evolution over time of the structure of prices, and the pattern of consumer's decisions determines the evolution over time of the structure of production.

This conclusion needs perhaps a few words of elaboration because the determining process, while conceptually straightforward in the case of relative prices, is more complex in the case of physical quantities, where the consumption coefficients that appear in our analysis change as a result both of the variation of the price structure and of the increase in per capita incomes. The whole process may be viewed as a succession of asymmetrical relations, which evince a definite causation chain. The first exogenous factor of our scheme, technology, which is at the origin of the whole process, directly determines the structure of natural (relative) prices, independently of anything else. But technology also determines the height of potential per capita income. At this point, when the price structure has been (conceptually) determined already, the consumers' decision and the population size (other two exogenous factors in our scheme) come in to determine the physical quantities to be produced.

This process is so fundamental that one can follow it even if we used the extreme approach of looking at it from a strictly traditional (marginal utility) point of view. By using traditional terminology, one may say that, at any given level of technology – that is, at any given price structure and level of real income – each consumer acting rationally will push demand for each commodity to that point at which his (her) marginal utility equals the given price. This is indeed a typically traditional conclusion, but the reader will notice that the chain of causation emerges as exactly reversed. It is the relative prices that determine what the individual marginal utilities are going to be and not

say is that natural price, although positive, will never have a chance of coming into being because production is zero.

vice versa! Yet this static outlook still conceals the process which has been and is going on. It is only by considering the movements of per capita incomes and of the price structure through time that the way in which demand shapes the structure of physical quantities emerges in its entirety. As per-capita incomes increase, consumers' preferences will determine the order of succession in which the various commodities are wanted, while the rate at which the 'marginal utility' of each commodity falls, as more and more of it is consumed, will determine the speed of variation of the structure of per capita consumption, as has been explained in Chapter 9, Sections 5 and 6. The rate of population growth is then the final additive element for the determination for each commodity of the rate of expansion of its total production through time.

9 The Dynamic Paths of the Wage Rate and of the Rate(s) of Profit

It becomes important to point out and stress, at this point, the fundamentally different movements through time of the wage rate, on the one side, and of the rates of profit, on the other, so often coupled in the literature with income distribution.

We have seen in our previous analysis that the very same basic principle underlying income distribution implies two different distribution criteria: profits related to rates of change and wages related to absolute levels of production. As a consequence, precisely the same principle also entails two basically different types of dynamic movement. If rates of profit are related to rates of change, while the real wage rate is related to the absolute level of overall productivity, then clearly the two cannot follow the same type of dynamic path. Changes in rates of change and changes in absolute levels belong to two entirely different orders of magnitude.

The real wage rate, by reflecting the absolute level of average per capita productivity, is bound to exhibit a continually and persistently rising trend over time. The longer the time, the larger the real wage rate is bound to be. On the other hand, the rates of profit, and *a fortiori* their average, by reflecting rates of change of per capita demand and of population, are bound to show no monotonic trend in either direction. There may well be periods in which the rates of growth of per capita demand and population slowly increase and periods in which they slowly decrease. But the effect will remain different in a fundamental way: to increases (or decreases) in the rate(s) of profit, there will correspond accelerations (or decelerations) in the growth of the real wage rate. In the long run, therefore, while the real wage rate will *persistently* grow, the rate(s) of profit cannot but roughly remain at the same level. For, all the changes in the rates of change cannot but be of a temporary and reversible character: the rate of growth of population cannot go beyond certain strict limits, owing to simple biological reasons, and similarly the overall rate of growth of per capita demand is bound to remain within strict physical limits, owing to the limited amount of knowledge that human beings can acquire within each period of time.

The consequences are important. The very same hypothesis on population growth and on technological change, whatever this hypothesis may be, entails two basically different dynamic paths for the rate(s) of profit and the wage rate. In our case, the simplest of all hypotheses – namely the hypothesis that population grows exponentially and that, on average, people are born over time with roughly the same ability to learn – entails a stable (roughly constant) trend for the overall average of the rates of profit and a monotonically increasing trend for the real wage rate.

10 The Asymmetric Relation between Total Profits and Total Wages

A straightforward macro-economic implication follows immediately. Within any period of time, the division of the final national product between profits and wages emerges through a chain of typically asymmetrical relations. The total amount of profits at (natural) prices is determined first of all, independently of anything else. If we call it Π^* we have

$$\Pi^* = \sum \pi_i^* p_{k_i} K_i. \qquad (11.10.1)$$

The total wages follow, absorbing all that is left over, after profits have been paid.

What happens to relative shares, over time, that is, to the share of total profits, and as a consequence to the share of total wages in the final national income, will obviously depend on the movements of all the rates of profits and of all the capital/output ratios. If it were to happen, for example, that the (weighted) average of all rates of profit and the (weighted) average of all capital/output ratios remained roughly constant over time, then, as can be seen by dividing both sides of (11.10.1) by the final national income, the share of total profits (and thus the share of total wages) would also remain constant over time. In general, of course, relative shares will change, but there is no reason to expect any persistent trend in either direction.

In any case, within the 'natural' economic system, whether we look at profits and wages at the macro-economic level, in terms of absolute amounts, or in terms of shares, the asymmetrical nature of the determining process emerges very clearly. Total profits emerge as a kind of prior claim to share in the final national income, while total wages – by being (conceptually) determined after profits have been determined already – emerge as a kind of residual, or, looking at it from a different point of view, as a 'surplus' that remains over and above what has been charged for profits. Of course, wages represent a very big and essential 'residual' – a very important 'surplus'. To produce and to continually increase the 'surplus' through technical progress is precisely the purpose of the whole production process.

At the end of all these elaborations on profits and wages, the results may appear to be quite simple and common sense, and of course they are. The reader will realise, however, that they are in sharp contrast with the interpretation of wages and profits and of their movements through time that the whole of economic theory (both Classical and Neoclassical) has given up till now.

11 New Investments

The same role which is played by the rate(s) of profit and the wage rate in the price equations is played by the rates of growth of productive capacity and by consumption, respectively, in the physical quantity equations system. But here, the dynamic movement of population is taken as exogenously given and the various relations emerge in the form of necessary conditions imposed by the requirement of full employment of the labour force.

There is first of all the series of new investment equilibrium conditions, defined by (5.4.3), which specify the amounts of additional productive capacity that must be built in each single sector if full employment is to be maintained over time.[12]

As a straightforward consequence, the total amount of new investment in the economic system as a whole, which we may call I, can be derived by a simple sum:

$$I = \sum (g + r_i) p_{k_i} X_i. \tag{11.11.1}$$

The importance of this expression is that, by determining total equilibrium investment, it also *ipso facto* determines the equilibrium amount of total new savings for the economic system as a whole. By dividing both sides of (11.11.1) by aggregate final national income, we also obtain the equilibrium proportion of final national income that must be saved and devoted to new investment, if full employment is to be maintained. It is important to realise that this equilibrium ratio (the overall savings ratio) emerges as being determined directly by the exogenous factors of our analysis. As may be seen immediately by expanding its components, it is determined by consumers' consumption coefficients, population, technology, and their movements through time.

12 Total Consumption

The set of capital accumulation equilibrium conditions just examined are sectoral conditions and have a macro-economic consequence only as a result of their sum. But we know that they must be inserted into the other equilibrium condition, expressed by (10.4.4) and concerning total effective demand. As already pointed out, this is a genuinely

[12] Of course, more than one technical possibility may be available, and hence, it might seem that to determine investments in terms of productive capacity, as done by the (5.4.3), is not yet to determine them in terms of actual machines and therefore in terms of current values. Since, in each sector, the rate of profit is determined exogenously by the same factors that enter expression (5.4.3), the whole problem of choice of technique can be solved independently of expression (5.4.3), and has a unique solution, except in the very particular case in which, with a discrete technology, the rate of profit happens to settle precisely at a switch point between two techniques (for details, see Pasinetti 1981, Chapter IX Sections 8–12). We shall assume, for simplicity, that this is not the case. This means that the capital accumulation equilibrium conditions (5.4.3) will normally determine investments in each particular sector, not only in terms of productive capacity but also in terms of actual machines.

macro-economic condition: it is just one condition embracing the economic system as a whole. And since a part of total demand – the sum of all demands for new investments – has been determined already by (10.4.4), this condition comes down to imposing that the whole remaining part of equilibrium total demand must be devoted entirely to absorbing consumption goods.

We therefore find here another asymmetrical chain of relations, parallel and similar to, but distinct from, the one determining the division of the final national income between profits and wages. This new asymmetrical chain of relations governs the equilibrium division of final national income between new investment (and thus savings) and consumption.

To conclude, the exogenous magnitudes of our theoretical scheme determine equilibrium new investment (and thus the equilibrium amount of total savings), first of all and independently of anything else. Then, condition (10.4.4) determines how big total demand for consumption goods can, or rather must, be. Total consumption is, therefore, another macro-economic magnitude that (conceptually) emerges as a kind of residual, or 'surplus'. It must absorb all what is left over after providing for the necessary additions to productive capacity, as a requirement for full employment growth. Again we may say, of course, that total consumption represents a very big and essential 'residual' or 'surplus', and that to produce such a surplus and to continually increase it through technical progress is the whole purpose of the production process.

13 Profits and Savings, Wages and Consumption in the 'Natural' Economic System

It now becomes strikingly evident – after the introduction of the 'natural' rates of profit – that the two systems of equations (for prices and physical quantities, respectively) representing our theoretical scheme have again become at this stage 'dual' to each other. Out of all possibilities of completing these two systems of equations, that one which is associated with the particular features of the 'natural' production system has remarkable properties of coherence, symmetry and simplicity.

Each of our two equations systems is closed by a set of sectoral relations.

The price equations system is closed by sectoral expression (10.9.2), synthesised by their sum (11.10.1), which defines total 'natural' profits (and, as a residual, total wages), and the physical quantity system is closed by sectoral expressions (10.9.1), synthesised by their sum (11.11.1), which determines equilibrium savings (and, as a residual, total equilibrium consumption).

Notice that these two sets of sectoral expressions have been obtained independently of each other, as two different requirements of logical consistency (equal weight for equal quantities of labour in the first case, full employment and full capacity utilisation in the second case). They express in fact two different economic phenomena altogether. But the remarkable result is that, in the 'natural' economic system, they exactly coincide. Total profits turn out to be equal to total savings, and total wages turn out to be equal to total consumption.

It is important to realise that this is not a mere overall averaging-out result, but the consequence of a whole series of equalities realised at each single sectoral stage. The best way of making this clear is again to go back to the macro-economic effective demand equilibrium condition (10.4.4) and analyse its components. We have seen that, when this condition is written in the form (10.13.3), each expression i under the summation represents the *proportions* of total available labour that is employed in the 'vertically hyper-integrated sector' i, ($i = 1, 2, \ldots, n-1$). Earlier in our analysis, we had seen that, in a pure labour economy, the same expression also represents the proportion of final national income, at the current prices, accounted for by the same sector i.[13] But then, we had also seen that, in general, this coincidence ceases to hold when capital goods are introduced.[14] Now, however, a new result emerges. When the rates of profit are at their 'natural' level, a further really remarkable property of theirs is that they re-establish that coincidence. In each single (vertically hyper-integrated) sector, 'natural' prices become proportional to physical quantities of labour, and the two proportions again come to coincide. The relevant extension, with respect to the case of a pure labour economy, is that here the economic system, by having to produce a whole series of (intermediate) capital goods (for replacement and for new investment), also

[13] See Chapter 7, Section 5.
[14] See Chapter 7, Section 11.

re-absorbs them, so to speak, within each (vertically hyper-integrated) sector, so that the coincident proportions refer to labour on the one side and to final production of consumption goods on the other.

To conclude, in the 'natural' economic production system, profits turn out to be equal to new investments; and wages turn out to be equal to consumption; hence, values of consumption goods turn out to be proportional to quantities of labour – not only in the economic system as a whole but also (and most importantly) in each single (vertically hyper-integrated) sector.

14 The Consumption Goods Basis of a Pure Labour Theory of Value

The remarkable property of the 'natural' production economic system, which has just emerged, deserves a some further attention. When 'natural' prices are expressed in terms of the wage rate, the value of the production of each consumption good i turns out to be equal to the sum of the physical quantities of labour employed in the vertically hyper-integrated sector which is producing it: that is, in the consumption goods sector i and in the investment goods sector k_i (the sector which produces capital goods for sector i); $i = 1, 2, \ldots, n-1$. To put the consequence in a classical way, the physical quantity of labour which consumption good i can 'command' turns out to be equal to: the physical quantity of direct labour embodied in consumption good i, plus the physical quantity of labour embodied in the required replacement of the corresponding capital goods and plus the physical quantity of labour embodied in the new investment goods necessary to the expansion of production of the consumption good i concerned.

The 'natural' features of the economic system, when realised, thus make it regain all the properties of a pure labour economy, provided that all relations are referred to the final commodities used as consumption goods. The apparently astonishing but really basic equality that emerges is between labour and consumption, both in each single sector – where value at natural prices becomes equal to the physical quantity of labour – and in the economic system as a whole – where the total value of all consumption goods becomes equal to the total wages (equal to the total labour force if $w = 1$).

As the reader will realise, this is indeed a complete generalisation of the pure labour theory of value.

15 'Labour Embodied' versus 'Labour Commanded' – Adam Smith's Early Intuition Fulfilled

It may be interesting to note, by using the simplified version of our previous analysis as set out in Chapter 10, that it is possible to arrive at the same conclusions reached here by giving an overall historical synthesis of the process through which these conclusions have been reached.

By raising our eyes above and beyond our formulae, we are able to give a comprehensive close-up of the evolution of the (objectively conceived) theory of value, through a compacted history of economic thought since the Classical economists.

The analytical framework developed in the foregoing sections shows how Adam Smith's (objectively conceived) pure labour theory of value contained the seeds of a surprising and unexpected generalisation: from the stage of a primitive economy, as originally it was natural to think of it, to the analysis of a really full-fledged advanced, industrial, economic system.

The crucial notion to go back to is right at the beginning and is represented by the equality of 'labour embodied' and 'labour commanded', taken as the basic features of the natural price of each single, produced commodity, thus evincing 'natural' value in an objective, unambiguous sense.

When facing such equality, it was spontaneous to think, at the beginning, of a primitive economy, where production is carried out by labour alone, land is free and the tools of production are so minimal as to justify considering them as negligible. Within such a context, labour unquestionably emerges as the only 'factor of production' and it becomes natural to consider it – and nothing else – as the objective constituent of relative prices, and thus of values.

Such a picture – quite naturally – was the first one to be considered also in the present work. It emerged as the case of a strictly pure labour economy; the very first step (see Section 4 of Chapter 7), in our step-by-step approach to a production economy.

By looking back to the general theoretical framework which has been sketched out in the very first chapter of the present work, when we examined the origin and historical development of a general (objective) theory of value, such particular case is clearly the one in which (in the notation we have adopted there, with respect to the one adopted here),

$$\ell_i(t) = a_{ni}(t), \qquad i = 1, 2, \ldots, n-1. \qquad (11.15.1)$$

'Labour embodied' and 'labour commanded' coincide, in a strictly pure labour economy, in the most obvious way.

But this was only the beginning. Very few minds could have imagined the possibility of any extension of such a simple equality.

Yet, from the analysis we have carried out, the whole history of economic thought, since Adam Smith, could now be looked at as a slow, though tormented, journey towards the fulfilment of what might have appeared, at the beginning, as the 'dream' of a complete generalisation of such (apparently naïve) simple idea.

Significantly, one realises that the characteristics of that very primitive stage were in fact never abandoned by Adam Smith himself, even at the cost of facing puzzling ambiguities. He obviously investigated a fully advanced – and not merely a primitive – economy. Hence, his interpreters were compelled to try to make sense of his arguments by attributing to him, indeed, an objective theory of value, but a theory relying on a sort of adding-up principle (costs, and thus natural prices, as the sum of wages plus profits plus rent). This generated the ambiguities in his writings which all his readers continued to stress and which he himself endorsed when compelled to specify. All this being said, it is a fact that, when making general, foundational, statements, Adam Smith basically kept on referring to 'the fund' of 'annual labour of every nation' as the basic source of 'all the necessaries and conveniences of life'.[15]

Ricardo, fifty years later, had an easy task in picking up Adam Smith's ambiguities. As is well known, he abandoned Adam Smith's apparent contradictions by shifting his analysis to what he considered the 'principal problem of political economy' (Ricardo 1821, p. 5), namely the *distribution of income* among what Smith himself had to consider as the three factors of production – land, capital and labour. Ricardo had a most brilliant idea: he focussed on the 'marginal' piece of land – that is, on the land that by definition yields no rent. This allowed him to eliminate rent altogether from his investigation on

[15] Here is the very opening sentence of the *Wealth of Nations*: 'The annual labour of every nation is the fund which originally supplies it with all the necessaries and conveniences of life, which it annually consumes and which consists always either in the immediate produce of that labour, or in what is purchased with that produce from other nations' (Smith 1776, p. 1)

value. But he still remained with the task of explaining income distribution between wages and profits. We all know the difficulties he faced, but, again, *significantly*, we also know that it is basically on a *labour* theory of value – no matter how imperfect – that he himself relied on. While following Adam Smith's 'adding-up principle', that everybody could obviously accept, and by narrowing down the partition of the net product to two categories – wages and profits (rent being relevant on intra-marginal land, but not on the marginal land where it is zero) – Ricardo returned to address his attention to *labour* as the fundamental determinant of value. He relied on a beautifully helpful but unrealistic assumption; namely that of a homogeneous proportion of labour to capital in all production processes. Or at least, he tried to argue that deviations from such a rule could be considered as negligible (whereby came George Stigler (1958) witty expression of 'a 93% Ricardo labour theory of value'!).

Fifty years after Ricardo came Marx. He followed Ricardo, even in the analytical device of assuming a homogeneous proportion of labour to capital in all sectors of production. But he had no patience to bother about details and analytical technicalities. For Marx value was *labour*, by definition. Whatever else there could be in any price (never mind whether under the form of profit or of rent) was for him *un*-paid labour. And there, within the production paradigm, the question remained for another century.

It is a fact, however, that both Ricardo and Marx, with respect to Smith, had taken a remarkable analytical step forward. In their view of how labour would contribute to make up the total cost of production, what they termed 'embodied' labour was no longer the 'direct' labour. It was extended also to include 'indirect' labour, that is, the labour first embodied into the material means of production.

This analytical step, following that of a primitive economy, has been expressed in our foregoing analysis by the stage of our investigation (Chapter 7) where production is supposed to be carried out by means of labour and capital goods. At first, the simplified step was taken of considering capital goods only in the production of consumption goods. But, in fact, this has emerged not only as the most immediate but also as the clearest of all cases, allowing us to concentrate on it, thanks to its simplicity.

The consumption goods prices – see (7.8.6) – appear as the sum of wages on 'direct' labour – the a_{ni}'s – wages on 'indirect' labour – the

$1/T_{ni}a_{nk_i}$'s – and moreover wages on a third, more complex, term, which includes both indirect labour and profits (the $\pi_i a_{nk_i}$'s). It is the presence of this, more complex, term which, at that stage, suggested the using of the expression 'value in terms of labour equivalents' (made in Chapter 7, Section 9).

I should like to draw attention on this expression, that is, on (7.8.6), because, *conceptually*, it persists in all subsequent stages of our approach. By introducing further and further complications (specifically the assumption of capital goods to make capital goods in the most varied way), the algebraic expressions have become more and more complicated, but the substance of their economic meaning never varied; it has always remained the same. Even in the most general case, which shall be investigated in a moment (Chapter 13), these basic concepts persist unchanged. Clarity and simplicity thus suggest to keep our analysis in terms of the three-addenda price expression given in (7.8.6).

The real problem however consists, at this point, precisely in dealing with the third addendum, in which the rate of profit enters as an external, unexplained, magnitude.

A glimpse at the way to the general solution which we have indeed been able to achieve might be perceived more easily with the help of an analogy. Think of a procedure analogous to the one invented by Ricardo for overcoming the difficulties inherent in the complications connected with the presence of rent. Ricardo solved his problem by concentrating on the case in which there is no rent. Similarly, we may here begin by concentrating, first, on a stage in which the economic system is in a perfectly stationary state. At this stage, at least ideally, it is reasonable to envisage a situation in which the rate of profit is zero. But, if profits are zero, the third terms, in each of the expressions (7.8.6), drop out; they fall to nought. Those price expressions simply become

$$p_i(t) = [a_{ni} + (1/T_i)a_{nk_i}]w(t), \qquad i = 1, 2, \ldots, n-1. \qquad (11.15.2)$$

This means that, in this case, consumption goods prices emerge as made up of wages on 'direct' labour plus wages on 'indirect' labour. It is important to point out that this happens also in all more complicated cases envisaged either by expressions (7.9.4) of Chapter 7 or in the still more complex expressions that will be examined in a moment (in Chapter 13), as long as we remain within a stationary economic system, that is, as long as $\pi = 0$. With such hypotheses, we can simply stick to (11.15.2), with no loss of generality.

The expression in square brackets, in (11.15.2), is what we earlier called the vertically hyper-integrated labour coefficient for consumption good i. We are, therefore, entitled to re-express it simply as

$$p_i(t) = \ell_i(t)w(t), \qquad i = 1, 2, \ldots, n-1, \tag{11.15.3}$$

where the meaning of the $\ell_i(t)$s is now extended (from 'direct' labour) to labour 'embodied directly and indirectly' in each unit of consumption good i. Interestingly enough, expressions (11.15.3) exactly remain the same price expressions from which we started in Chapter 1. However, each coefficient $\ell_i(t)$ is now explicitly covering a more complex concept, since it has to be re-interpreted as the 'vertically hyper-integrated' labour coefficient. It now represents the sum of direct plus indirect labour embodied in each unit of consumption good i ($i = 1, 2, \ldots, n-1$). And, what is more, in the (now more complex) sense, 'labour embodied' remains exactly equal to 'labour commanded'. Notice that this result would emerge already from Ricardo and Marx – or for that matter also from Sraffa – if we simply were to put $\pi = 0$.

The astonishing thing to notice now rather is that the basic concept of 'labour embodied' has not made further progress ever since. As already mentioned previously, it was so in Ricardo and Marx, and it has also remained so in Sraffa. In the present work, this has been reflected by our formulations up to the end of Part II. To be more specific, the concept of 'labour embodied' has been kept at the stage of 'quantity of labour directly and indirectly embodied' for more than a century! In this context, it is of course easy to see that as soon as we introduce non-zero profits, we introduce as a consequence a kind of wedge between 'labour embodied' and 'labour commanded'. These become separated from each other since profits have come to absorb that part of the net product which does not go to wages.

It is precisely at this point that the real novelty of the present work appears. Starting from Chapter 7, the third addendum, in the natural price formulations, has begun to express a novel concept: the concept of 'hyper-indirect labour'. Thus, no longer have we come to face an externally given, unexplained, addendum, but we have uncovered a very specific magnitude and a very basic magnitude indeed – a physical quantity of labour!

At this point, we have also finally come to the conclusion of our chain of arguments. The upshot is complex but liberating and astonishing. It has entailed the crucial step not only of going over (from a stationary) to a growing economic system, not only of explicitly accepting profits as a part of the third component of each consumption good price, as is shown by expression (7.8.6) of Chapter 7, but of actually accepting a whole set of very specific rates of profit: those rates of profit which in the present chapter have finally emerged as the 'natural' rates of profit; that is,

$$\pi_i^* = g + r_i, \qquad i = 1, 2, \ldots, n-1. \tag{11.4.1}$$

Following this procedure, the third terms of expression (7.8.6), or more specifically, in a dynamic context, the corresponding term in expression (10.9.2), are indeed turned into non-zero magnitudes, but magnitudes which take up very definite (normally positive) signs. These formulations finally become

$$p_i(t) = [a_{ni} + (1/T_i)a_{nk_i} + (g + r_i)a_{nk_i}]w(t), \qquad i = 1, 2, \ldots, n-1. \tag{11.5.1}$$

As we may notice, the expressions within square brackets have now become sums of *purely physical magnitudes*. This is the crucial result. This sum is what (since Chapter 10, Section 13) we have called the *vertically hyper-integrated labour coefficient* for consumption good i $(i = 1, 2, \ldots, n-1)$.

We may well return at this point to the very beginning of our analysis (i.e. straight back to Chapter 1). The expressions under square brackets in (11.5.1) are nothing but the $\ell_i(t)$ of our original analysis – that is, 'labour embodied' – generalised however to cover *all* sorts of 'embodied labour' – direct, indirect and hyper-indirect in each specific commodity – now re-expressed in the simplest of all configurations, namely

$$p_i(t) = \ell_i(t)w(t), \qquad i = 1, 2, \ldots, n-1. \tag{11.15.4}$$

This is the really relevant conclusion of our history-of-economic-thought journey. Expression (11.15.4) reproduce formally the same, simplest, expressions of Chapter 1, but with the most complex of all the specifications we have reached so far in our analysis. The $\ell_i(t)$s represent at this stage the amounts of physical labour directly, indirectly and hyper-indirectly embodied in each unit of any specific consumption good i.

The result may well be termed surprising and remarkable. The expressions from which we started in Chapter 1 have formally remained unchanged, all throughout the analytical procedure that has accompanied our long journey. At the end of it, the contents of the labour coefficients $\ell_i(t)$s have been generalised to a complete coverage of the notion of 'embodied labour' in each specific commodity, in the widest of all its conceptual generalisations.

And what is more, the concept of 'embodied labour' in each consumption good i, in this widest, expanded sense, remains exactly equal to the amount of labour it can 'command'. 'Labour embodied' and 'labour commanded' remain equal to each other in the most general of all senses.

The 'natural production economic system' has made Adam Smith original 'dream' come true. If it was originally a 'dream', it is now a dream no longer. At this final stage of generalisation, it emerges as one of the most fertile intuitions generated by the prolific mind of Adam Smith.

16 A More Compact Definition of the 'Natural Rates of Profit'

The procedure followed so far to reach the concept of a sectoral 'natural rate of profit' may well be looked at the other way round. The same result may be arrived at in a more compact (and elegant) way.

Going back, for a moment, to the expressions of Chapter 7, where we appeared to have arrived at a theory of value in terms of *labour equivalents* – see (7.8.6) – we are now able to see more clearly that the crucial analytical step which was taken was that of going over to considering an economic system that is undergoing a process of *structural dynamics*. This is what has come out of Chapter 10.

Compare expression (10.9.1) for physical quantities and expression (10.9.2) for commodity prices. The former are in physical terms, as is all too obvious. The latter are not – they contain a rate of profit. This was the feature that earlier compelled us to look at them in terms of 'labour equivalents', as they were depending on whichever externally given rate of profit was hypothetically introduced.

But now we are in a position to formulate our propositions by reversing the question: *Which* rate (or rates) of profit could we insert into expression (10.9.2), such as to transform them into expressions in which the quantities of labour have become *strictly physical* magnitudes?

The answer is straightforward. There is only one rate of profit, for each consumption good i, that can transform the corresponding price into a summation of addenda, all expressing labour in physical terms. And this is the specific rate of profit

$$\pi_i^* = g + r_i, \qquad (11.16.1)$$

for each

$$i = 1, 2, \ldots, n - 1, \qquad (11.16.2)$$

that is to say, the 'natural' rate of profit. This is the rate of profit, specific to each final consumption good i, that transforms the sum of all labour coefficients into *vertically hyper-integrated labour coefficients.*

More explicitly, from all possible externally given rates of profit, the specific rate of profit π_i^* for consumption good i ($i = 1, 2, \ldots, n - 1$), when appropriately inserted into the price expression (10.9.2), represents that rate of profit which makes 'labour embodied' (in the most general sense) exactly equal to the amount of labour which that final consumption good i can 'command'.

This is the most compact definition of the 'natural' rate of profit that can be formulated.

To repeat it in slightly different words, the 'natural' rate of profit is that particular rate of profit that makes (hyper-integrated) labour, 'embodied' in each specific consumption good i exactly equal to the amount of labour it can 'command'.

This property can be evinced, even more revealingly, if we look at the economic system as a whole, that is, if we go over, from the expressions for each of the 'natural' prices to the macro-economic equilibrium condition (10.4.4). If, for simplicity's sake, but without any loss of generality, we leave aside all complications – connected with the variations of rates of change (i.e. non-steadiness) through time, and of the proportion of active to non-active population in time – and concentrate on the strictly relevant concepts we are here considering, we may write (10.4.4) simply, but most effectively, as

$$\sum [a_{ni}(t) + (1/T_i)ank_i(t) + (g + r_i)a_{nk_i}(t)]a_{in}(t) = 1. \qquad (11.16.3)$$

What does, from this, emerge? Precisely the three components of vertically hyper-integrated labour (direct, indirect, hyper-indirect) are multiplied by the corresponding consumption goods coefficients (the a_{in}'s), summed up for the economic system as a whole.

We can indeed hark back to the origin of our whole elaboration (i.e. to Chapter 1) and rewrite condition (11.16.3) in the simplest of all forms, namely:

$$\sum \ell_i(t)c_i(t) = 1, \qquad i = 1, 2, \ldots, n-1, \tag{11.16.4}$$

where the contents and meanings of the ℓ_is have become

$$\ell_i(t) = a_{ni}(t) + (1/T_i)a_{nk_i}(t) + (g + r_i)a_{nk_i}(t), \qquad i = 1, 2, \ldots, n-1. \tag{11.16.5}$$

They have indeed become those of the vertically hyper-integrated labour coefficients for each consumption good in the whole economic system (while the original c_i's are simply the earliest notation for the $a_{in}(t)$'s of our full-fledged analysis).

The equality of the quantities of (hyper-integrated) 'labour embodied', and of 'labour commanded' emerges as the corner-stone of an (objective), fully general, pure labour theory of value.

Adam Smith original, intuitive conception has been fully vindicated.

12 *The Accumulation of Capital and the Progress of Technical Knowledge*

1 The Two Most Immediately Conspicuous Features of Industrial Societies

In this chapter, I want to deal (all too briefly, I am afraid) with some problems concerning two of the most conspicuously striking features of all modern industrial societies: capital accumulation and technical progress.

In the previous chapter, our investigations have mainly been carried out at the level of macro-economic variables, and rightly so. We know – as was pointed out at the beginning of Chapter 6 – that macro-economic analysis *ipso facto* is vertically hyper-integrated. But we also know that vertically hyper-integrated magnitudes are complex and compact analytical tools, and may sometimes not allow us immediately to perceive the further rich, more detailed inter-industry relations that are behind them. At the same time, we must admit that the phenomena behind the two major features we want to investigate (technical progress and capital accumulation) may apparently look like being nearer the level of inter-industry analysis rather than that of vertical integration. Yet we also know that both levels of analysis are necessary (and complementary, as already pointed out in Chapter 6 and its Appendix).

Our task here may be said to be that of showing how we may take advantage of the analysis of vertical hyper-integration in order to more correctly understand the essential implications following from the combination of both inter-industry and vertically hyper-integrated analysis considered together. These implications in many cases cannot be seen separately. Some of them have in fact remained so far unperceived in all traditional economic investigations. More specifically, by forcibly remaining constrained exclusively to the first level of investigation (the inter-industry one) the nature and meaning of a dynamic approach could not be seen and some conclusions may traditionally even have been proposed that are in contrast with the more appropriate and true one, as they are bound to emerge from a more complete (dynamic) enquiry.

In this chapter, I shall examine a few problems which are precisely related to the investigation of the two above mentioned most conspicuous features of industrial societies and have remained either hidden or bound to be interpreted incorrectly. I shall begin with the problems related to capital accumulation and then slowly slide into the technicalities concerning the economic meaning of technical progress.

2 Capital Accumulation as a Condition for Equilibrium Economic Growth

Capital accumulation, in our previous analysis, has been shown to come into existence as a requirement of the sectoral equilibrium conditions which represent the new investment (see Chapter 10, Section 4). These conditions precisely require the coming into existence of a whole set of stocks of capital goods – works, buildings, plants, equipment and appliances of all sorts, partially new and partially inherited from the past – which are set aside for production and have then to be maintained (replaced and/or renewed) ever after. They represent the most apparent feature of modern economies, the tangible expression of our modern world. Their *raison d'être* is technical. The technical methods of production, in order to be implemented, normally require that some commodities are set aside, kept in existence, and used as means of production.

These commodities – generally called capital goods – are *produced* goods, which are used as intermediate commodities in the production process. They are produced by the economic system itself. As far as the technical processes are concerned, they are in no physical way different from consumption goods. Many commodities may in fact be used as consumption goods as well as capital goods. But there is a profound difference on the side of their demand. Consumption goods are demanded for their own sake, for consumption by the consumers. Such demand is autonomous: it is whatever consumers like it to be. Demand for capital goods, on the other hand, is not autonomous. It is (logically) determined as intermediate means for producing consumption (or other) goods. As we have seen (see expression 10.4.3) they have emerged in the form of *conditions* for equilibrium growth of the whole economic system.

It is this *derived demand* aspect of investment goods, due to their being used as *means of production*, that is new and typical of production systems. There was nothing of the sort, or there was only a rudimentary shade of them, in more primitive economies.

But in industrial societies, the production process requires the bringing into existence, and the maintenance, of a whole series of capital goods; it requires *a process of capital accumulation*, as a condition for equilibrium growth. In this chapter, we shall begin by concentrating on some of these problems.

3 Four Quantitative Notions of 'Capital'

It is of course understandable – and for many purposes useful – that, at any given point in time, the whole complex structure of existing capital goods should be referred to by an all inclusive collective noun: Capital.

It is less understandable that to such a medley of heterogeneous things economists should have tried so often to give a single quantitative expression valid for all purposes. Not surprisingly, this has turned out to be misleading, and in most cases even impossible, except by making a series of almost absurd assumptions (such as those of a one-commodity type of capital, which is also a consumption good, which is malleable and adaptable to all purposes, which can absorb, instantaneously and without cost, any possible type of technical change, etc.).

But there is no reason for disappointment or dismay. One must simply realise that it is in the very nature of 'capital' to be heterogeneous. Capital goods are economically relevant in too many different ways. Hence, to turn upside down a widespread complaint about the measurement of capital, I might say that the difficulty with capital is not that it is impossible to measure, the difficulty is that it is measurable in too many different ways. But one must specify, first of all, the purpose for which measurement is made. What is of course impossible is to find a type of measurement that can be used for all purposes.

On various occasions, even in the course of the present analysis, we have already used, implicitly or explicitly, at least for different quantitative notions of 'capital':

(i) First of all, we have talked of capital goods in terms of, let us say, *physical machines*. In these terms, capital goods are a series of heterogeneous commodities, each having a specific technical characteristics. There is no way of expressing all the machines and plants as a single physical entity, except when they are of the same type. In other words, we can add up the numbers of turning-lathes of the same type, but not the number of turning-lathes and the number of cranes.

(ii) Secondly, we have been measuring capital goods at *current* prices (in our case, 'natural' prices). That is: the physical units of capital goods have been multiplied by the corresponding prices, expressed in terms of a particular commodity – single or composite – which has been chosen as *numéraire*. This type of measurement provides a standard in terms of which any commodity can be compared with any other. A turning-lathe and a crane can be added up, if each of them is first weighted by its price, expressed in terms of a third commodity, which is used as the common standard. This type of measurement is the most widespread in economic analysis; yet it has turned out to be more limited than was thought. It depends not only on technology, but also on income distribution at any point in time. Current relative prices change, even with a constant technique, when income distribution changes.

(iii) A third way in which we have measured capital goods is again in physical terms, but in terms of *units of vertically hyper-integrated productive capacity*. A unit of vertically hyper-integrated productive capacity is, conceptually, a rather complex unit. It is defined with reference to a physical unit of the final commodity which is going to be produced. Yet, when this commodity can be specified, the useful property of this concept is that it has an unambiguous meaning through time, no matter which type of technical change, and how much of it, may occur.[1]

[1] This property becomes particularly useful, e.g., for the problems of the replacement of worn-out equipment, as has been pointed out in Chapter 6, Section 7. With technical change going on, each machine is never replaced by an exactly similar physical machine, and this makes it impossible to say what it is that is replaced and kept intact. Measurement in terms of units of productive capacity overcomes this impossibility.

(iv) Fourthly, and finally, we have been measuring capital goods in terms of *physical quantities of labour* required to produce them ('embodied labour'). This type of measurement might simply appear to be a particular case of the one mentioned under (ii), and of course it is, namely the particular case in which all prices are natural prices and the chosen *numéraire* is the wage rate. It possesses however an individuality of its own, as it expresses something physically well defined and quite independent of any *numéraire*. What must be realised is that this is not an easy type of measurement to obtain, as it requires evaluation at natural prices with the inclusion of natural rates of profit.

An approximate method of measuring capital goods in these terms consists in taking current values (whatever the rate of profit may be) and dividing them by the wage rate. This approximate type of measurement has been used, among others, by Keynes, who called it measurement in terms of wage units, and by Joan Robinson, who has taken it to express what she has called 'real capital'. It has also been used in our previous analysis, since the very beginning, when pointing out that, by taking physical units of productive capacity multiplied by their prices and dividing them by the wage rate, one obtains quantities of what have there been called 'labour equivalents' (see Chapter 7, Section 9).

It should not be difficult to realise at this point that a distinction between these four quantitative concepts of 'capital' becomes essential in the context of a dynamic analysis. There is no ground for concentrating on any particular one of them, or for calling any one of them 'superior' to any other. Each one is relevant, but for quite different purposes.[2]

4 Essential Distinctions for Dynamic Analysis

We may immediately note that, in a hypothetical world without technical progress, concepts (iii) and (iv), as defined in Section 3, would

[2] It may also be worth pointing out explicitly that the four quantitative notions of capital listed above must not be considered as exhaustive. For example, for some purposes, it might well become relevant to measure 'capital' in terms of the employment which it can provide. And in the present work itself (see Chapter 14) we shall come across another important configuration of 'capital' that concerns the 'financial' capital.

be superfluous. Method of measurement (i) would coincide, or rather would have a one-to-one correspondence, with method (iii), since more physical machines would mean more physical productive capacity in the same proportion. And method (ii) would have a one-to-one correspondence with method (iv), since more capital in terms of any given commodity-*numéraire* would mean more quantities of labour in the same proportion.

In fact, this may help to explain why traditional economic analysis has never made use of concepts (iii) and (iv); or rather, it has always taken concept (i) also to mean concept (iii), and concept (ii) also to mean concept (iv). The association does not matter when the analysis refers to a stationary economic system or concerns comparisons of magnitudes at the same point in time. But the same association breaks down in comparisons through time.

Over time, technical coefficients change, and if technical coefficients change, more productive capacity – concept (iii) – does not necessarily entail more machines – concept (i) – and more capital in terms of any given commodity-*numéraire* – concept (ii) – does not necessarily entail more physical quantities of 'embodied labour' – concept (iv).

Over time, therefore, each one of the four quantitative concepts of capital defined above follows its own path and must carefully be kept distinct from all the others.

5 Ambiguities in the Concept of 'Roundaboutness': Capital Intensity versus Degree of Mechanisation (or, More Specifically, Capital/Output Ratio versus Capital/Labour Ratio)

What has just been said carries profound theoretical consequences.

When Böhm–Bawerk and then Wicksell developed their famous theories of capital, they thought – as is well known – that they could present capitalistic production in roughly the following way. It pays for society as a whole to devote its efforts (its 'factors of production') to producing 'capital' first, and then, in subsequent periods of time, to using 'capital', together with further labour, to produce the final commodities which are wanted. By this indirect process, the final commodities can often be obtained from smaller quantities of original 'factors of production' than would be the case by using direct methods. Thereby, the process of capitalistic, as opposed to primitive, production is presented as more efficient by being more *indirect* or *roundabout*.

But there is a serious ambiguity in this conception of 'indirectness' of capitalistic production – an ambiguity which does not reveal itself when one deals with a stationary economy (as both Böhm-Bawerk and Wicksell did) but breaks out strikingly as soon as one goes on to dynamics.

Indirectness or roundaboutness of a production process clearly refers to a relation between stocks and flows. A production method α is said to be 'more indirect' than a production method β if it requires a higher stock of capital goods for given flows. But here is where the ambiguity lies. Which flows are we to consider? The input flows of labour or the output flows of production? We clearly obtain two entirely different concepts altogether according to whether we express the relation between stocks and flows in terms of capital per flow of labour services (the capital/labour ratio) or in terms of capital per flow of output (the capital/output ratio). Let us examine these two concepts in turn, taking the latter first.

The capital/output ratio is the ratio of a stock of capital goods to the flow of output that in each period of time comes out of the production process. Since both stocks and flows are expressed at current prices, the wage rate appears in both of them, that is, both in the numerator and in the denominator, and therefore cancels out. This means that it does not matter whether capital and output are expressed at current prices or as physical quantities of labour.[3] It expresses the physical quantity of labour that, so to speak, has to be kept 'locked up' in the stock of capital goods per unit of physical quantity of labour that in each period of time is required by the current production process. The capital/output ratio may therefore be taken to express that type of 'indirectness' or 'roundaboutness' that has been called the 'degree of capital intensity' of a production process.

It is important to be clear about the economic problems for which the concept of 'capital intensity' is relevant. There are at least two such problems, both of which are of crucial economic importance.

[3] The proposition refers strictly to the case of natural prices. In the case in which prices contain a uniform rate of profit, instead of the corresponding *natural* rates of profit, 'physical quantity of labour' must be of course intended as physical quantity of labour-equivalents (see Chapter 7, Section 9).

First of all, the capital/output ratio is relevant in evaluating the effects of investment on production. That is: for any given production process, the capital/output ratio characterising it expresses the amount of investment that has to be undertaken, that is, the amount of resources of the economic system has to give up, in order to increase by one unit the flow of production. Secondly, and much more importantly, the capital/output ratio is relevant for the problem of price formation. As appears from our formulation, the incidence of capital in each commodity price, that is, the component of each price which has to be charged for the use of capital, is proportional to the capital/output ratio required in that production process, quite independently of the number or the value of the machines operated by each worker. The lower the capital/output ratio, the lower the charge for capital in each price, no matter whether and how much the capital/labour ratio may be changing. This is so much the case that an alternative definition of the concept of capital intensity might well be given in terms of the components of prices. We may indeed say that a process of production α is more 'capital intensive' than a process of production β, if α entails for the price of the commodity being produced a higher proportion of charges for capital (replacements plus profits) to charges for labour (wages). The definition is perfectly general and is equivalent to the one in terms of the capital/output ratio.

The concept expressed by the capital/labour ratio is quite different. As can be seen immediately from our formulations (10.11.1)–(10.11.3), the stock of capital that appears in the numerator is expressed at current prices, while the flow of labour that appears in the denominator is expressed in physical quantities. There is no cancelling out of the wage rate, so that the capital/labour ratio will change for two quite distinct reasons: (i) because of changes in the quantities of labour embodied in the capital goods (for given current labour and wage rate) and (ii) because of changes in the wage rate (for given quantities of embodied and current labour). There is a further difficulty, represented by the fact that the wage rate depends on the *numéraire* – a difficulty that can, however, be overcome immediately by adopting formulation (5.11.3) of our analysis, where the wage rate is specifically expressed in terms of the 'dynamic standard commodity', which means in terms of a constant (average) level of prices.

Now, changes of type (i) affect both the capital/labour ratio and the capital/output ratio, but changes of type (ii) are specific to the capital/labour ratio. Hence, changes in the wage rate will indeed affect the capital/labour ratio while leaving the capital/output ratio entirely unaffected. To put the problem the other way round, only in the particular case in which the wage rate remains constant will the changes in the capital/labour ratio go in the same direction as the changes in the capital/output ratio (i.e. in capital intensity). But when the wage rate is increasing – which is the typical case of an economy with technical progress – that will no longer be the case. Changes of type (i) and changes of type (ii) will not necessarily go in the same direction; they might well go in opposite directions and partially or totally, or more than totally, compensate and offset each other. This leads us to a first, very important, conclusion – the capital/labour ratio cannot in general be taken as an index of capital intensity. As a consequence, the type of 'indirectness' expressed by the capital/labour ratio is irrelevant for the two crucial problems mentioned above, namely, the determination of new investment and the formation of prices.

To single out the type of 'indirectness' which the capital/labour ratio may be an expression of (as distinct from the type of 'indirectness' expressed by the capital/output ratio), one must look for what is associated with a change in the wage rate when the proportion of 'locked-up' labour and current labour (i.e. capital intensity) remains constant. Now, an increase in the wage rate at a constant price level reflects an increase in overall productivity, and an increase in productivity will keep the sectoral capital/output ratio constant only if there is an increase in the degree of mechanisation. We may well say, therefore, that the type of 'indirectness' or 'roundaboutness' that is represented by the capital/labour ratio is an expression of the 'degree of mechanisation' of the production process to which it is referred.

It is easy to realise, at this point, that the economic problems for which the concept of degree of mechanisation is relevant must be looked for in the sphere of employment. Indeed, the capital/labour ratio indicates the number of extra workers that will be required (the number of jobs that will be created) by an addition of one unit of investment evaluated at current prices. It follows that changes in the degree of mechanisation, as expressed by the capital/labour ratio, mean changes in the size of employment associated with any given amount of capital goods, expressed at (average) constant prices.

To conclude, the notion of 'indirectness' or 'roundaboutness' of the capitalistic process of production, which has come to us from traditional capital theory, becomes ambiguous, and hence must be abandoned, in a dynamic context. One must carefully distinguish among at least two different concepts: the concept of 'capital intensity', as expressed by the capital/output ratio, and the concept of 'degree of mechanisation', as expressed by the capital/labour ratio. Both concepts are relevant, but for different problems. The concept of capital intensity (the capital/output ratio) is relevant for the problems concerning investment and price formation; the concept of degree of mechanisation (the capital/labour ratio) is relevant for the problems concerning employment. It clearly is essential to use each one of the two concepts strictly with reference to the problems for which it is appropriate.

6 Capital Intensity and Degree of Mechanisation in Comparisons through Time

It may be useful to point out straight-away how the distinction between the concepts of 'capital intensity' and 'degree of mechanisation' becomes particularly important in a dynamic context.

In a hypothetical world in which there were no technical progress, the movements of the capital/output ratio and the movements of the capital/labour ratio would have a one-to-one correspondence with each other. A distinction between the two would be unnecessary. Incidentally, this again may help to explain why in traditional economic analysis, which has normally relied on the assumption that technical progress is either non-existent or unimportant, the necessity for a distinction between the two concepts has never been felt.

But in a dynamic context, when comparisons are to be made through time, the distinction is crucial. Consider a simple example. Suppose a case in which technical progress brings about an increase in the number of physical machines operated by each worker, but in such a way as to keep the quantity of labour embodied in the increasing number of physical machines absolutely constant. An evaluation of this invariant amount of embodied labour, at current prices (supposing that the average level of prices remains constant), would yield an increasing value of the capital stock per worker, over time, because the overall wage rate is increasing as a result of the overall growth of productivity. This means that the ratio of physical machines to men and the ratio of capital, at current prices, to men will be increasing. In other words, the 'degree of mechanisation' will be increasing all the time. Yet, if we divide the value of capital thus obtained by the value of production coming from it, the increasing wage rate (by appearing both in the numerator and in the denominator) cancels out. The capital/output ratio (i.e. the capital intensity of the production process) remains constant, thereby representing the constant proportion of the quantity of labour which must be kept 'locked up' in the capital stock to the amount of labour employed in direct production.[4]

We thereby have a simple example where the capital/labour ratio (i.e. the degree of mechanisation) is continually increasing through time, while the capital/output ratio (i.e. the capital intensity of the production process) remains constant. A distinction between the two concepts has become absolutely essential.[5]

7 Capital Intensity and Degree of Mechanisation of Different Economic Systems

The distinction considered above also becomes essential in any comparison of different economic systems.

The machines and equipment which are purchased on the international market are characterised by certain technical relations, that

[4] Later on we shall see that this is a case of 'capital-intensity neutral' technical progress – a technical progress which, in the economic literature, has been called 'neutral' in the sense of Harrod.

[5] An example of the contradictions into which one may fall when one fails to distinguish between the two concepts may be seen in a well-known article by R. M. Solow ('Technical Change and the Aggregate production Function', in the *Review of Economics and Statistics*, 1957). Solow tried to estimate technical change in the United States economy from 1909 to 1949 and, after finding that capital per man increased in that period, came to the conclusion that the overall growth of productivity could be attributed to technical progress by 87.5% and to 'increased capital intensity' by 12.5%. I had myself the opportunity of pointing out that, by using the same data and computing the overall capital/output ratio, one finds that this ratio *decreased* from 2.75 in 1909 to 2.20 in 1949! (See my paper: 'On Concepts and Measures of Changes in Productivity' in the *Review of Economics and Statistics*, 1959, p. 274.) Solow's conclusions are therefore ambiguous and contradictory. What one can simply say is that the technical change that took place in the U.S. economy, from 1909 to 1949, was accompanied by an increase in the degree of mechanisation (and not in capital intensity), and by a decrease (not an increase!) in capital intensity.

is, by certain degrees of mechanisation, as expressed by capital/labour ratios, which are technically given and therefore remain the same for all countries. However, the very same physical machines will in general represent different capital intensities (i.e. will entail different capital/output ratios) for different countries.

To be more specific, if a certain set of machinery is imported into a country because, for example, it cannot be made in the country itself, it must be paid for by using the proceeds coming from other goods which are exported. This means that the amount of embodied labour which imported machinery represents for the importing country is given by the amount of labour required in the importing country to produce those commodities which are given in exchange, and not by the amount of labour which has actually been embodied in the machinery in the country of origin. Therefore, the same technical production processes (the very same machines) have for the two countries a different *economic* meaning. In fact, they will usually entail higher capital/output ratios, that is, more capital-intensive processes of production, in the importing country than in the exporting country, and therefore also a higher proportion of charges for capital to charges for labour in the final prices.

To give a simple example, suppose that India imports from the USA a certain set of machinery for an integrated chemical production process which is set up in India with exactly the same technical characteristics as it has in the US. The physical capital per man will obviously be exactly the same in both countries, and so will be its current value, evaluated at international prices, for example, in dollars. But suppose that the Indian industrial wage rate (at comparable efficiency and in dollars) is 1/4 of the wage rate in the US: then the capital/output ratio entailed by this production process will be much greater (up to four times greater) in India than in the US, despite the fact that the capital/labour ratio is exactly the same. The explanation is that the lower Indian wage rate will influence the price of final output but not the price of the machinery (which is bought on the international market). In other words, the lower Indian wage rate will influence that part of the price of the final goods which is the charge for labour but not that part which is the charge for capital. The very same technical equipment, that is, the very same degree of mechanisation (the same capital per man, whether in physical terms or at current prices), will entail a much greater degree of capital intensity for India than for the US.

8 The So-called Leontief Paradox, No Longer a Paradox in the Present Theoretical Context

The importance of the conclusions reached in the foregoing pages is bound to emerge on any occasion in which comparisons are made through time for the same country or between countries that are at different stages of technological development. Any failure, in such comparisons, to draw a distinction between capital intensity and degree of mechanisation will inevitably lead to contradiction. In this section, as a striking example, a well-known 'paradox' will be considered that arose some years ago from comparisons of international trade carried out by Wassily Leontief.

Leontief adopted an interpretation of international trade consisting in extending to 'capital' the given-resource-endowment approach (the so-called Heckscher-Ohlin model) of marginal economic theory. The traditional position is in fact very well summarised by Leontief himself at the beginning of his inquiry:

> Our economic relationships with other countries are supposed to be based mainly on the export of such 'capital intensive' goods in exchange for foreign products which – if we were to make them at home – would require little capital but large quantities of American labour. Since the United States possesses a relatively large amount of capital [...] and a comparatively small amount of labour, direct domestic production of such 'labour intensive' products would be uneconomical; we can much more advantageously obtain them from abroad in exchange for our capital intensive products. (Leontief 1953a, p. 333)

Leontief then carried out an empirical study on the composition of imports and exports in the USA and arrived at an 'unexpected result'. He found that the proportion of labour to capital required by one million dollars of US exports is higher than the proportion of labour to capital that would be required by one million dollars of US competitive imports if these imports were made at home. Leontief was baffled: he had expected the opposite, since he had taken for granted – from the fact that in the United States the amount of capital per man was higher than anywhere else – that the US was the most capital-intensive economy in the world. This 'Leontief paradox', as it as been called, has then, for a good many years, become the subject of many complicated explanations and interpretations.[6]

The foregoing analysis allows us to realise that the 'Leontief paradox' is in fact no paradox at all, but precisely what should have been expected. The error which has caused the surprise lies precisely in having taken the capital/labour ratio as an index of capital intensity.

Now, it is certainly indisputable that the capital/labour ratios (either for the economy as a whole or for single processes) are generally higher in the United States than in the rest of the world. This simply means that the US economy has a higher degree of mechanisation than the outside world. But the degrees of mechanisation (the capital/labour ratios) have no relevance for the problems of price formation, and therefore of comparative costs, and therefore of international trade!

To find whether the US economy is more or less capital intensive than other economies, one must look at capital/output ratios. And there is no reason why capital/output ratios should be higher in the United States than in the rest of the world, while there are many reasons that make us expect the capital/output ratios to be higher in the outside world than in the US. (Consider on this problem the arguments carried out in Section 7.[7]) And if capital/output ratios are lower in the

[6] The explanation given by Leontief himself (and many others) must have sounded very pleasing to American readers: 'Let us reject the simple but tenuous postulate of comparative technological parity and make the plausible alternative assumption that in any combination with a given quantity of capital, one man-year of American labor is equivalent to, say, three man-years of foreign labor' (Leontief 1953a, p. 344). See the following footnote.

[7] Production processes outside the United States are generally less mechanised than in the United States. But to the extent that certain machines are imported, let us say in India, and are operated in the same way they are operated in the US, there will indeed be 'technological parity' – the same degree of mechanisation. Hence, contrary to what Leontief says, the Indian worker operating the same physical machine is exactly as productive or as efficient as his American counterpart. However, he receives a much lower wage rate, reflecting the lower productivity of the Indian economy as a whole, as compared with the American economy as a whole. It is, therefore, the productivity of the economy as a whole that is lower in India, *not* the productivity of the worker operating the same identical machine, which is obviously the same as in the US. This lower overall productivity, by rendering

US than elsewhere, then we must conclude that production processes in the US are less capital intensive (not more capital intensive!), than in the rest of the world, in spite of the fact that they entail a higher degree of mechanisation (higher capital/labour ratios). It is therefore quite natural that the United States should import goods that – if made at home – would require production processes that would be more capital intensive than the processes employed to make the corresponding exported goods.

It may perhaps be useful to underline the fact that the association of the capital/output ratio with the concept of capital intensity and of the capital/labour ratio with the concept of degree of mechanisation, from which the above conclusions have been drawn, is not a mere question of definition. If it were a question of definition, one could of course choose whichever definition one preferred. But the important point to stress is that, in drawing conclusions on the composition of international trade, it is *the relative prices* of commodities that matter, and in the determination of relative prices, it is the capital/output ratio which is relevant and not the capital/labour ratio. Leontief, as so many other economic theorists, has simply fallen into the trap of taking the capital/labour ratio as an index of capital intensity and then proceeding to draw conclusions *as if* the definition of capital intensity had been taken on the basis of the capital/output ratio. We should not be surprised to find paradoxes and contradictions.[8]

the Indian wage rate lower, renders the capital intensity of the very same physical machines (imported from the United States) much higher in India than in the US.

[8] It is important to stress these results because misunderstandings due to a confusion of the two different concepts expressed by capital/output and capital/labour ratios have been only too frequent in economic analysis. Let me mention two illustrious examples taken respectively from Ricardo and Marx.

In Ricardo's analysis, the concept of capital intensity plays a crucial role in his discussions on the theories of value and distribution. His labour theory of value holds only in the particular case of uniform capital intensity in all production processes. It is clear that, for this problem (price formation), it is the concept of capital intensity (i.e. the capital/output ratio) that is relevant. But Ricardo never realised that this was something different from the concept of degree of mechanisation, as expressed by the capital/labour ratio; and when, in the controversial chapter XXXI, 'On Machinery', of his *Principles* (3rd Edition), he came to be concerned with employment (or more precisely with the unemployment generated by technical change) for which it is the concept of degree of mechanisation (i.e. the capital/labour ratio) that is relevant, he fell into well-known contradictions.

9 The Economic Meaning of Technical Progress

We may now turn to technical progress, the other major feature of industrial societies. 'Technical change' is a very general term. But we may ask more specifically: when is it that technical 'change' actually means technical 'progress'?

First of all, there obviously is 'progress' when technical change takes the form of invention of entirely new, previously unknown, goods.

But we are here concerned with that type of technical change which consists of improvements in the production of *already known* goods. In this case, the answer to the above question is no longer so straightforward. To begin with, we may say that there is 'progress' when, for the production of any given unit of output, a reduction takes place in the amounts of required inputs. This definition, however, is not very helpful. Or rather, it may be helpful only in those particular cases in which not one of the inputs has increased. But, in general, some inputs decrease and others increase over time, and a standard is needed on the basis of which to assess, and set against one other, positive and negative changes of heterogeneous inputs.

It is for this purpose that, by going over to the vertically hyper-integrated level, our formulations come to help. By taking the earliest of our price formulation (from 7) and by using the wage rate as the *numéraire*; that is, $w(t) = 1$, as we have seen, the unit price of each commodity i, may be written as:

Similarly, in Marx's analysis, it is the concept of capital intensity, i.e. the capital/output ratio – or as Marx calls it, the 'organic composition of capital' – that is relevant for his discussions on value and related problems (such as the problem of the 'transformation of values into prices'). But when Marx went on to discuss the consequences of technical change on unemployment (in his terms, on generating the 'reserve army of labour'), he should have used concepts associated with the capital/labour ratio. By failing to do so he too fell into the error of thinking that the introduction of new machinery would be associated with an increase in the degree of capital intensity, or organic composition of capital (i.e. of the capital/output ratio, thereby causing a fall of the rate of profit). But this may not be so at all. New machinery may well entail an increase in the degree of mechanisation (and therefore of unemployment, at constant output), but at the same time may well be associated with a constant (or even a decreasing) organic composition of capital. The effects on the rate of profit, in Marx's own scheme, are therefore unpredictable.

There are many further implications of the capital accumulation process which are not reported here. The reader may find many of them in Pasinetti (1981, Chapter IX, Sections 8–12).

$$p_i(t) = a_{ni}(t) + (\pi_i + 1/T)a_{nk_i}(t) \qquad i = 1, 2, \ldots, n-1. \qquad (12.9.1)$$

At this stage, we may say that, for any given rate of profit $\bar{\pi}_i$, there is technical progress in the production of commodity i when, through time,

$$\frac{\mathrm{d}p_i(t)}{\mathrm{d}t} < 0, \qquad i = 1, 2, \ldots, n-1. \qquad (12.9.2)$$

Note that the qualification 'for any given rate of profit' is absolutely necessary. Having used the general formulation for p_i, the diminution of inputs (technical progress) implied by (12.9.2) still remains assessed in terms of 'labour equivalents' and therefore has a sense only *relative* to a given rate of profit. This means that in these terms, it is not yet completely unambiguous. In general, cases cannot be excluded in which $\mathrm{d}p_i(t)/\mathrm{d}t < 0$ for certain rates of profit and $\mathrm{d}p_i(t)/\mathrm{d}t > 0$ for others rates of profit. This is as far as one can go in the context of an externally given rate of profit, where costs emerge as evaluated in terms of 'labour equivalents'.

But we have gone beyond that stage, precisely by going over to the 'natural' price system, where all ambiguities disappear and things remarkably simplify. When the rate of profit is fixed at its 'natural' level, $\pi_i^* = g + r_i$, $i = 1, 2, \ldots, n-1$, then, thanks to the elaborations of Chapter 11, (12.9.1) becomes

$$p_i(t) = a_{ni}(t) + (1/T)a_{nk_i}(t) + (g_i + r_i)a_{nk_i}, \quad i = 1, 2, \ldots, n-1, \qquad (12.9.3)$$

which has now been turned into a purely technical formulation. Expressions (12.9.3) have become sums of purely physical quantities of labour: direct labour plus indirect labour, plus hyper-indirect labour. So much so that we have been able to write them:

$$\ell_i(t) = a_{ni}(t) + (1/T)a_{nk_i}(t) + (g_i + r_i)a_{nk_i}(t), \quad i = 1, 2, \ldots, n-1, \qquad (12.9.4)$$

where $\ell_i(t)$ defines what we have called (in Chapter 10) the vertically hyper-integrated labour coefficient for commodity i ($i = 1, 2, \ldots, n-1$).

At this point we are indeed in a position to make unambiguous statements. When, through time, there is a diminution of $\ell_i(t)$, and thus of $p_i(t)$, as expressed by (12.9.3), we know that, somewhere in the economic system, there has been a saving of labour requirements. More precisely, when, through time,

$$\frac{\mathrm{d}\ell_i(t)}{\mathrm{d}t} < 0 \qquad i = 1, 2, \ldots, n-1, \tag{12.9.5}$$

we can say, without any sort of ambiguity, that there is technical progress in the production of commodity i.

This is a remarkable conclusion. It represents yet another aspect of the pure labour character of the natural prices. It precisely allows us to look at their efficiency property in terms of a process of minimisation of physical quantities of labour.

The major implication is clear. Ultimately, technical progress is revealed to be a diminution of labour inputs. To put it in another way, all technical progress is, in the end, labour saving.

In a production economic system, it is the reduction of labour that emerges as the ultimate economic meaning of technical progress.

10 A Classification of Technical Progress

The consequences of the conclusions just reached are of paramount importance. On the surface of it, progress in production will always appear as a heterogeneous mixture of saving of direct and indirect inputs, that is, both of labour and of intermediate commodities (i.e. of capital goods). The economic literature has devoted considerable space to classify the various types of technical progress according to the degree and stage of indirectness at which they take place.

The novelties on this problem that emerges from the present analysis consist in allowing us to go down to essentials. And the results are really striking.

All technical progress is ultimately labour saving, as we have just concluded, but according as to whether it takes place in the production of straight consumption goods or in the production of capital goods, its effects on the production structure are quite different. By using the two concepts of degree of capital intensity and degree of mechanisation developed earlier in this chapter, a classification of the various types of technical progress can now be made by looking precisely at their effects on the capital/output ratios and on the capital/labour ratios. For clarity, the 'natural' price system will be used throughout; and thus the particular 'natural' rate of profit appropriate to each sector will be inserted into the corresponding ratio. But the results can obviously be extended to all other cases as well, provided only that they are considered *relative* to any externally given rate of profit.[9]

Let us first resume, therefore, our formulations for the sectoral capital/output ratios, the (κ_i)'s, and the sectoral capital/labour ratios, the (χ_i)'s.

By making the rates of change explicit and by inserting the 'natural' rates of profit from Chapter 10, Section 11, we obtain

$$\kappa_i(t) = \frac{a_{nk_i}(0)e^{-\varrho_{k_i}t}}{a_{ni}(0)e^{-\varrho_i t} + (g_i + r_i + 1/T_i)a_{nk_i}(0)e^{-\varrho_{k_i}t}}, \tag{12.10.1}$$

and

$$\chi_i(t) = \frac{a_{nk_i}(0)}{a_{ni}(0)} w(0)e^{(\varrho_i+\varrho^*-\varrho_{k_i})t},$$

$$i = 1, 2, \ldots, n-1, \tag{12.10.2}$$

where the symbols are those defined in Chapter 10; and where, as we can see, ϱ^* – the standard rate of productivity growth, that is, the (weighted average) rate of growth of productivity in the economic system as a whole – only appears in the capital/labour ratios. This means expressing the wage rate in terms of a constant (weighted average) price level, according to the insertion into (10.12.3) of the *numéraire* defined by (10.13.1). It also amounts to expressing all prices in terms of the 'dynamic standard commodity'.

Supposing, of course, that expression (12.9.5) is satisfied in each sector i which we are considering, we may now distinguish first of all three basic cases of technical progress, to be indicated under headings (a)–(c) (please follow also Figure 12.1).

(a) 'Capital-intensity neutral' technical progress

When technical progress takes place at exactly the same percentage rate in the production of commodity i and in the production of capital goods for commodity i that is, when:

[9] Notice that we could formally perform the same elaborations also in all other cases, where the rates of profit are *not* at their natural level. However, when extended in this way, the meanings of such elaborations would become more restricted, because minimisation of costs would result as evaluated in terms of 'labour equivalents' (instead of pure physical labour) and would therefore not necessarily lead to the choice of efficient (i.e. labour-input minimising) techniques for the economic system as a whole.

$$\varrho_i = \varrho_{k_i}, \qquad (12.10.3)$$

the numerator and the denominator of (12.10.1) change through time at exactly the same rate. The sectoral capital/output, $\kappa_i(t)$, remains constant, although the technical coefficients are changing all the time. This is the type of technical progress which, in the economic literature, has been called 'neutral' in the sense of Harrod.[10] Technical progress is 'neutral' with reference to the *degree of capital intensity* of the production process. The quantity of labour to be used directly and the quantity of labour to be kept locked up in capital goods maintain the same proportion to each other in time. Note now, from (12.10.2), that the capital/labour ratio is, on the other hand, increasing all the time at the rate ϱ^*, since the wage rate is increasing, in real terms, as a reflection of the growth of productivity in the economic system as a whole. Each worker, so to speak, will be using more and more expensive machines. Assuming – as it is reasonable to assume – that more capital per man, at (on average) constant prices, also means more *physical* capital per man, that is, more mechanised machinery, the *degree of mechanisation* in the production of commodity i is increasing all the time. 'Capital-intensity neutral' technical progress thus always entails the use of more physical capital per man: it always is '*physical*-capital using'.

(b) 'Capital-intensity increasing' technical progress

When productivity is increasing both in sector i and in sector k_i, but:

$$\varrho_i > \varrho_{k_i}, \qquad (12.10.4)$$

then both the capital/output ratio (i.e. the degree of capital intensity) and the capital/labour ratio (i.e. the degree of mechanisation) are increasing through time. Labour productivity is clearly increasing in the whole hyper-integrated sector, but in a way as to shift the proportions of labour inputs towards the indirect stages of production. 'Capital-intensity increasing' technical progress is always *a fortiori* 'physical-capital using'.

[10] See Harrod (1948).

(c) 'Capital-intensity decreasing' technical progress

When:

$$\varrho_i < \varrho_{k_i}, \tag{12.10.5}$$

the capital/output ratio (i.e. the degree of capital intensity) is decreasing. However, the capital/labour ratio (i.e. the degree of mechanisation) may be increasing or may be decreasing. As we can see from (12.10.2), that part of the ratio which refers to the technical coefficients is decreasing through time – as is the case for (12.10.1). However, unlike what happens to the capital/output ratio, the capital/labour ratio also contains the wage rate (at constant average prices), and this is increasing through time at the overall rate of growth of productivity. In this case, various possibilities are open as to the movements of *physical capital*. To sort them out, we must further distinguish three sub-cases; to be listed under headings (c,i)–(c,iii)

(c,i) 'Physical-capital-neutral' technical progress

If it were to happen that productivity growth in the capital good sector were to exceed the productivity growth in the corresponding consumption good sector by a difference (in the rates of change) exactly equal to the 'standard' rate of change of labour productivity, that is, if:

$$\varrho_{k_i} - \varrho_i = \varrho^*, \tag{12.10.6}$$

then, as may be seen from (12.10.2), the capital/labour ratio would remain constant through time, although the capital/output ratio would continue to be decreasing. A technical change that leaves the capital/labour ratio constant was called 'neutral' by Hicks.[11] As we may now see clearly, technical progress is, in this case, 'neutral' with respect to the degree of mechanisation of the production process. It is 'neutral'

[11] To be precise, Hicks's (1932, pp. 121–122) definition is in terms of a constancy of the capital/labour ratio and also of an increase of the 'marginal productivities' of capital and labour in the same proportions. In our context, the concepts of 'marginal productivities' make no sense (for further details, see Pasinetti 1821, p. 201). In their place, one might refer to constancy of the income shares. But it is clear that (12.10.6) does not necessarily keep income shares constant. Therefore, physical-capital neutral technical progress, as defined by (12.10.6), does not exactly coincide with Hicks' definition of neutrality. It takes, however, the same bench-mark for neutrality (constancy of the capital/labour ratio).

with respect to the use of *physical* capital per man (to the extent that changes in capital goods at constant – average – prices reflect changes in *physical* capital, as we have assumed). However, it is not neutral with respect to the degree of capital intensity, which continues to be decreasing in time.

(c,ii) 'Physical-capital using' technical progress

When

$$\varrho_{k_i} - \varrho_i < \varrho^*, \tag{12.10.7}$$

the capital/labour ratio (i.e. the degree of mechanisation) is increasing, even though the capital/output ratio (i.e. the degree of capital intensity) continues to be decreasing. Technical progress is physical-capital using, but at the same time it continues to be capital-intensity decreasing.

(c,iii) 'Physical-capital saving' technical progress

When

$$\varrho_{k_i} - \varrho_i > \varrho^*, \tag{12.10.8}$$

technical progress is so strong in the capital goods producing sector as to overcome the effects of productivity growth both in the consumption goods sector and in the economic system as a whole. Hence, the capital/labour ratio too, and not only the capital/output ratio, is decreasing through time. Technical progress is both capital-intensity decreasing *and* physical-capital saving.

To complete the classification, with reference to the terminology that has been used in the economic literature, it may be useful to mention that Robert Solow has shown special concern precisely with this last type of technical progress, which clearly causes an increasing efficiency of the physical capital goods. He has called it 'capital-augmenting' technical progress.[12] Thereby yet another criterion of 'neutrality' has emerged. To cover this criterion as well, we may sub-distinguish this case, that is, case (c,iii), into three further sub-cases, to be indicated by sub-headings (c,iiia)–(c,iiic).

[12] Solow (1963, p. 59).

(c,iiia) 'Direct-labour neutral' technical progress

When the (12.10.8) is satisfied, and, of course, $\varrho_{k_i} > 0$, but

$$\varrho_i = 0, \qquad (12.10.9)$$

both the capital/output ratio and the capital/labour ratio are decreasing, but the ratio of (physical) output in sector i to its direct labour inputs remains absolutely constant. A technical progress that leaves the output/labour ratio constant has been called 'neutral' in the sense of Solow.[13] (It is 'neutral' with respect to the output/labour ratio). This simply means that all improvements in productivity take place in the capital goods sector (with no technical progress in the consumption goods sector). It becomes particularly clear, from our analysis, that Solow's 'capital-augmenting' technical progress – as he called it – is in fact a '*physical*-capital saving' technical progress. Ultimately, it expresses an increase of labour productivity (i.e. a saving of labour) in *the capital goods* producing sector.

(c,iiib) 'Direct-labour saving' technical progress

When, (in addition to $\varrho_{k_i} > 0$) also:

$$\varrho_i > 0, \qquad (12.10.10)$$

then there is an increasing labour productivity both in sector i and in sector k_i, but the latter is so prevalent as to maintain $\varrho_{k_i} - \varrho_i > \varrho^*$, which causes the ratio of output to labour increase through time, as after all always happens in all cases (a), (b), (c,i) and (c,ii).

(c,iiic) 'Direct-labour using' technical progress

Finally, when:

$$\varrho_i < 0, \qquad (12.10.11)$$

13 See, e.g., Hahn and Matthews (1964, pp. 830); Allen (1967, p. 239). Here again one must repeat the same *caveat* expressed in footnote 10 with reference to Hicks. Direct-labour neutral technical progress, as expressed by (12.10.9), does not keep the income shares constant. Hence, it does not exactly coincide with the definition of Solow neutrality given by Hahn-Matthews and by Allen. However, it takes the same neutrality bench-mark (constancy of the output/labour ratio).

and yet, from (12.10.8), $\varrho_{k_i} - \varrho_i > \varrho^*$, to such an extent as to ensure $(d\ell_i(t)/dt) < 0$ (for otherwise there would not be technical progress), then the ratio of (vertically hyper-integrated) labour to output continues to be decreasing through time; though, in fact, in this case, there is technical *regress* in the strictly final consumption goods producing sector, but technical progress in the capital goods producing sector is so strong as to more than compensate for it.

Our classification is now complete. Figure 12.1 summarises the results.

It should also be noted that the whole of our classification of technical change has been made *at the vertically-hyper-integrated sectoral level* simply because it is only at the sectoral level that capital/output ratios and capital/labour ratios have a purely technical meaning. The overall capital/output ratio and the overall capital/labour ratio are more composite concepts, as they depend not only on technology but also on the composition of (overall) consumption (and output, except in the trivial case of a one-commodity world).

It seems important to stress in any case that – in spite of all the variegated forms of technical change, and independently of the sectors in which they are taking place – *all* cases we have come to consider in our classification – namely cases (a), (b), (c,i), (c,ii), (c,iii,a), (c,iii,b) and (c,iii,c), as specified above and summarised in Figure 12.1 – *always* emerge, ultimately, as being 'labour saving' in the most general and complete sense of the term (i.e. in the sense of encompassing direct plus indirect plus hyper-indirect labour).

The conclusion stated at the end of Section 9 is thus confirmed in a definitive manner. The persistent reduction of labour inputs (i.e. essentially the overall saving of labour) emerges as being the ultimate meaning (and purpose) of technical progress.

11 Alternative Criteria of 'Neutrality' of Technical Progress and Their Information Contents

We may begin by noting that the three alternative criteria of 'neutrality' of technical progress mentioned above, by referring to constancy of, respectively, the capital/output ratio, the capital/labour ratio and the output/labour ratio, carry quite different information contents.

Capital-intensity *neutral*, i.e. ‘neutral in the sense of Harrod, when:

$$\varrho_i = \varrho_{k_i}$$

Capital-intensity increasing when:

$$\varrho_i > \varrho_{k_i}$$

} *always* physical capital-using

Capital-intensity decreasing when:

$$\varrho_i < \varrho_{k_i}$$

Physical-capital *neutral* when:

$$\varrho_{k_i} - \varrho_i = \varrho^*$$

Physical-capital using when:

$$\varrho_{k_i} - \varrho_i > \varrho^*$$

} *always* direct labour saving

Physical-capital saving when:

$$\varrho_{k_i} - \varrho_i < \varrho^*$$

Direct-labour *neutral* when:

$$\varrho_i = 0$$

Direct-labour saving when:

$$\varrho_i > 0$$

Direct-labour using when:

$$\varrho_i < 0$$

[and yet $(\mathrm{d}l_i/\mathrm{d}t) < 0$]

} *always* overall (*i.e.* hyper-integrated) labour saving

Figure 12.1 Classification of technical progress.

The first of these criteria of 'neutrality' – which takes constancy of the capital/output ratio as the benchmark of neutrality – seems to be the richest one in terms of information content. In fact, this criterion is the one originally proposed by Roy Harrod. It is basically purported to convey useful information when the purpose of the investigation concerns problems that depend on the proportion between that labour, which must be kept locked up in the means of production, and the labour which is currently required for production purposes. Owing to this feature, Harrod's criterion of 'neutrality' – out of the three criteria – is the one that emerges as the most relevant for the major problems of our analysis, to wit: value, income distribution and international trade.[14] Neutrality in the sense of Harrod would also seem to be, in practice, the most widespread to have taken place, when – as is reasonable to expect – the improvements in technical knowledge are evenly spread over the whole range of the vertical hyper-integrated technological process of production. No surprise, therefore, if Harrod's criterion has been the most usually used in macro-economic growth theory, that is, when the models are supposed to refer to the average of what happens in the economic system as a whole.

The other two criteria of neutrality of technical progress, however – proposed by Hicks and by Solow respectively – should not by any means be considered as useless. Their usefulness clearly depends on the purposes to which they may be applied.

For instance, Hicks's criterion – which takes constancy of the capital/labour ratio as the benchmark of neutrality – does convey a relevant piece of information in macro-economic models any time that problems arise concerning the size of employment (or unemployment) associated with the given stock of capital goods.

Solow's criterion of neutrality on its turn – though superficially appearing a poor criterion, in terms of information content – might not always be so irrelevant, even if the only information it conveys is about the tendency of technical progress to take place mainly in the capital goods producing sector. By concentrating on the capital goods industries as the source of productivity growth, this criterion might become interestingly relevant in order to illustrate the consequences of

[14] For the latter problem (international trade), I should like to refer to Pasinetti (1981, Chapter XI, pp. 245–276) and moreover to Pasinetti (1993, Chapter IX).

cases where the increasing productivity of human activity and ingenuity is particularly active in the techniques concerning the intermediate commodities. The recent bewildering growth of knowledge and discoveries in the computer producing and communication sectors might well be indicated as a case in point. To reflect on it, the amazingly high speed with which such technological development has recently taken place is inviting us to imagine what would happen in the limit as a consequence of a development of technologies of such type. If strongly pursued, they would seem to reduce to the minimum, almost to eliminate, the *physicality* of capital goods while concentrating progress mainly on the increase of human knowledge (quite a contrast with the once traditional idea of the heavy industries as the basis of industrialisation!). They might indeed point attention in the direction of what has also been called the 'weightless economies'. Could it not happen that a drive towards economies lighter and lighter in terms of physical capital might make the economic system approach many of the features of the 'pure labour economy' we considered at the beginning? It is a paradox to realise that the original reason that induced Solow to propose his criterion was the purpose of stressing the importance of *capital* as 'a factor of production', and therefore as exactly symmetrical to, and at *par* with, labour. But curiously enough, the use of Solow's concepts would seem to acquire relevance precisely when technical change is eventually pointing in the opposite direction, that is, in the direction of causing a decreasing use of the intermediate physical means of production, coupled with an increasing use of the intellectual power of the human mind.[15]

12 Increase in the Degree of Mechanisation, Falsely Appearing as a Process of 'Substitution' of Capital for Labour

There is an interesting question that is difficult to avoid at this point, namely: which type of technical change is more likely to take place in the real world, and is, therefore, more relevant in economic investigations dealing with the accumulation of capital? One cannot of course fully answer this question except by empirical research. Yet one can make a few definite and important remarks besides venturing some guesses.

[15] See especially the last chapter of Pasinetti (1993).

Clearly, *all* types of technical change will be observed in practice, sometimes and somewhere. Yet experience seems to indicate that, by and large, in the industrial world in which we live, most technical progress – though of course *not* each single technical change – takes the external form of an increase in the degree of mechanisation or of substitutes to mechanisation. We have seen that this does not necessarily mean an increase in capital intensity. In fact, in spite of the continually increasing degree of mechanisation, the *proportion* of labour embodied in the capital goods to immediate current labour has not shown anywhere any definite tendency to increase. This would seem to make neutrality in the sense of Harrod appear to be, from among the three types of neutrality, also the one that comes nearest on average to the actual processes that are taking place all the time.

To the extent that this is so, it is important to notice that a process of continual increase of the capital/labour ratio (at roughly constant, or sometimes even increasing, capital/output ratios) will appear as the normal pattern of technical change in industrial systems. If this were in fact the pattern of technical change, each worker would be operating more, and more complex, and more expensive, machinery – that is, would actually be using more and more 'capital', both in physical terms and at current (constant) prices – in spite of the fact that the labour directly and indirectly embodied in such machinery remains roughly constant, or may at times even decrease. Note now that this is precisely that usual pattern of technical change, which in common parlance and in most textbooks is usually, but wrongly, referred to as 'substitution of capital for labour'.

It is important to stress this point, as we can see most clearly here, that the usual process of increasing mechanisation, which to any external observer *appears* as one of 'substitution' of capital for labour, first of all has nothing to do with the 'substitution process', which has been presented by traditional economic theory, as if it were 'a movement along' a production function; secondly, it has nothing to do with an increase in the wage rate, a decrease in the rate of profit and a move to more 'roundabout' (more capital intensive) processes of production.

The analysis carried out here shows that there is nothing of the sort in what emerges as the usual pattern of technical change. 'Roundaboutness', if we take it correctly, in the sense of a degree of capital intensity, need not change at all (it may actually decrease). The rate of profit need not change either and yet the degree of mechanisation (what is falsely presented as a 'substitution of physical capital for labour') may be increasing all the time! The wage rate will appear always to increase, but as an effect, not a cause (!), of technical change.[16]

An important implication of this analysis, explicitly worth underlining, is that – contrary to what traditional economics has always maintained – the process of substitution of physical capital for labour, and thus the problems related to changes in the degree of capital intensity of the production processes, cannot in any relevant way be linked to changes on the rate of profit.

In an industrial production system – we may conclude – the process of continually increasing the degree of mechanisation, which for all practical purposes is presented as one of 'substitution of physical capital for labour', emerges as the normal expression of the process of change of techniques – the normal pattern of technical progress.[17]

13 The Determinants of Capital Intensity

What is it then that determines the degree of capital intensity? Rigorously speaking, this question has been implicitly answered already in the course of our previous analysis. It may be useful to provide a more explicit answer here.

At the sectoral level, each capital/output ratio is essentially determined by *technology*. In more practical terms, if at any given point in time, the capital/output ratio in a sector such as 'house renting' is of the order of, let us say, 100 times larger than in a sector such as 'clothing', the reason simply is that *technology* is such that the minimum cost

[16] It is quite easy to be mislead on these matters. If we notice, e.g., that in a certain branch of industry the process of increasing wages – which reflects the general increase of productivity – causes at a certain point the replacement of some workers by a machinery (whose price has remained constant or has increased less than the wage rate) this does not mean at all that the shift of technique has been caused by the fact that the higher wage rate has made 'labour relatively more expensive than capital'. The wage rate has increased for the process of making the machines as well! What the substitution simply means is that improvements in productivity must have taken place in the machine producing industry so that the cost of the machines has increased less than the wage rate. In this way, in the new situation, it takes a lower total (direct and indirect) amount of labour inputs per unit of output to make the new machines and then to operate them with fewer workers than to employ the replaced workers with the old machines.

[17] See on this Pasinetti (1977c) and Pasinetti (2007).

of production processes requires in the house renting sector a capital/output ratio which is 100 times larger than in the clothing sector![18] Clearly, no change in the rate of profit will appreciably change this proportion. Similarly if, in any production process, at a certain point of time, machines are substituted for labour, the reason simply is that productivity in the machine producing sector is increasing faster than the overall wage rate. Most of all and most decisively for our arguments, this process, again, is entirely independent of any change in the rate of profit.

At the level of the economic system as a whole, the picture becomes more complex, because the aggregate capital/output ratio also contains the demand coefficients. This means that both technology and demand contribute to determining the degree of capital intensity of the economic system as a whole, and both the evolution of technology and the evolution of demand govern its movement through time. But (and this is the important point), no relevant role on these matters can be attributed to the changes in the rate of profit.

14 Again Underlining the Asymmetry between the Profit Rate and Wage Rate Mirroring the Deeper Asymmetry between Capital and Labour

It may seem rather otiose at this point to further stress, in spite of what has been already stated, the asymmetrical roles played by the rate of profit and the wage rate, once it is understood that this asymmetry, here as elsewhere, reflects the more fundamental asymmetry that exists between capital and labour in the production process.

Note that the present analysis by now clearly shows how the reduction of all capital goods to physical quantities of labour is complete. No profit residual remains in our analysis thanks to the concept of a 'natural' rate of profit; nor is there a commodity residual thanks to our technical progress approach to capital accumulation.

[18] This proportion is taken from Grosse (1953). The statements made in the text are so plain that they would not even require mentioning were it not for the fact that traditional economic theory, by its emphasis on changes in the rate of profit, has led us to overlook them – namely to neglect the role played by factors accounting for differences of the order of 1 to 100 – and to concentrate on factors of uncertain influence and in any case of negligible importance.

It is important to realise the extent to which these features, far from being mere analytical devices, are in fact further steps towards modelling the theory to reflect essential characteristics of the real world.

In the economic literature, the reduction of prices to physical quantities of labour has usually been shown so far with the help of infinite series going backwards in time, within the context of given technical coefficients.[19] In such time series the intermediate commodities never disappear altogether (except in the limit). But such infinite series must be correctly interpreted; they can only have a conceptual, not a real, meaning, that is, no empirical or historical sense.

Our previous analysis, by making technical change play a role at each stage in time, provides a much more direct reflection of the actual process. In the real world, there can never be an *infinite* series. Today's turning-lathe was made yesterday with a less perfect turning-lathe, which was made earlier with an even less perfect turning-lathe, which was made with no turning-lathe at all, but with more primitive tools. And so on backwards in time. No machine ever has an infinite series of intermediate commodities behind it, but only a chain of successive evolving sets of more primitive tools and machinery, which in time reduce to nothing, provided that one goes sufficiently far back. In any actual (as against any conceptual) time series, we arrive, in *finite* time, at labour alone.

To realise that this is the case, one may look at the production process in yet another way. A moment's reflection will suffice to make anyone realise that the whole structure of capital goods would not exist if labourers did not exist, while the contrary is not true. If we were to imagine, for a moment, that all capital goods were somehow to suddenly vanish, a terrible crisis would of course ensue. But the lucky human beings who survived the crisis would start the whole process of capital accumulation all over again: from primitive tools to atomic reactors! (And faster than it took the first time.) Labour alone can eventually make all the capital goods. If we were to imagine the opposite catastrophe – the disappearance of all human beings – we can very well realise what would follow: absolutely nothing. Human beings can make capital goods, but capital goods alone can make nothing.

[19] This is after all what has been shown above in Chapter 4 regarding Sraffa's analysis.

13 *Growing Sub-systems, Vertically Hyper-integrated Sectors and the Pure Labour Theory of Value: Generalisation Completed*

1 Introduction

The concept of 'sub-system' was originally presented by Piero Sraffa in a brief non-mathematical 3/4 page appendix to his book (Sraffa 1960, p. 89). His purpose was that of providing an 'alternative if less intuitive line of approach' to evaluate the quantities of labour that directly and indirectly enter the production of each commodity (Sraffa 1960, p. 56). To this effect he had used, in the text of his book, the more intuitive method of 'reduction to dated quantities of labour'. But this method, while unexceptionable in the case of single products, does not work for joint production. Sraffa was proud to find that the sub-system approach works in all cases.

The concept of sub-system, however, has turned out to be of much wider relevance than Sraffa himself could have imagined. In a previous Essay (Pasinetti 1973), here reproduced as Chapter 6, I linked up Sraffa's direct and indirect quantities of labour with the 'direct and indirect requirements' emerging from Leontief's inverse matrix (Leontief 1951), and I proceeded therefrom to develop the two symmetrical concepts of vertical integrated labour coefficient and vertically integrated unit of productive capacity.

The present chapter goes one step further in the direction of a complete generalisation of the concepts of sub-system and vertically integrated sector. It will be shown that the analytical device of partitioning an economic system into sub-systems (and correspondingly of constructing vertically hyper-integrated Sectors) can indeed be taken into dynamic analysis not only with remarkable implications but with further results to be achieved.

In fact, if one looks carefully at the physical quantity side, as against the price side, of the usual system of equations representing a production economic system, one may notice a formal asymmetry. In the physical quantity system, the means of production are specific to each particular sub-system; there is a specific vector of means of production for each particular sub-system. In a sense, the physical quantities of the means of production appear as playing a sort of ancillary role with respect to the physical quantities of final demand; the former being, so to speak, 'at the service' of the latter.

By contrast, in the price system, a similar feature does not emerge. There is absolutely no difference, in the scheme earlier proposed, between the prices of the means of production and the prices of the final goods. The vector of prices is exactly the same for all sub-systems.

It is shown in the following pages that this asymmetry disappears when the analytical scheme is further generalised.

2 Growing or Hyper-subsystems

Consider an economic system of the type sketched out in Pasinetti (1973) and here reproduced in Chapter 6. In each particular unit of time, m commodities are produced by means of commodities and labour. The physical quantity system at time t may be represented by

$$\mathbf{A}\mathbf{Q}(t) + g\mathbf{A}\mathbf{Q}(t) + \mathbf{C}(t) = \mathbf{B}\mathbf{Q}(t), \qquad (13.2.1)$$

$$\mathbf{a}_n\mathbf{Q}(t) = L(t), \qquad (13.2.2)$$

$$\mathbf{A}\mathbf{Q}(t) = \mathbf{S}(t), \qquad (13.2.3)$$

where $\mathbf{A}$ and $\mathbf{B}$ are the input and output inter-industry matrices respectively, $\mathbf{a}_n$ is the input direct-labour coefficient (row) vector, $\mathbf{Q}(t)$ is the physical quantity (column) vector, $\mathbf{C}(t)$ is the consumption goods (column) vector, $\mathbf{S}(t)$ is the means of production (column) vector, $L(t)$ is the (scalar) quantity of labour and g is the (scalar) percentage rate of growth of the labour force (for simplicity no distinction is made between labour force and population). All matrices are m order matrices and all vectors have m components. The physical units are chosen so as to make the main diagonal of $\mathbf{B}$ a list of ones. The technical coefficients are such as to be economically meaningful at all levels of the population percentage rate of growth, g, from zero to its maximum, that is, in the interval $0 \leq g \leq G$, where G is the maximum rate of growth allowed by existing technology.

Suppose, to begin with, constant technical coefficients and population growth. It is also convenient to assume immigration. Immigrant labour is assumed to be available in a practically unlimited amount. When the growth of demand is very strong, workers are allowed to come in, and when the growth of demand slackens the foreign workers leave the country, so that there always is full employment, as a result of adapting the labour force to the requirements of production (rather than the other way round).[1] It is also convenient to assume that the consumption tastes of the immigrants are different from those of the indigenous population, so that the per capita rates of growth of demand for commodities $1, 2, \ldots, m$ are all different from one another. This means that, if g, defined previously, is the proportional rate of growth of the labour force (whether by natural growth or by immigration) and if r_i (which may be positive or negative) is defined as the per capita rate of growth of consumption demand for each commodity i, then the rate of growth of consumption demand for each commodity i will be $(g + r_i)$, and in general will be different from one consumption good to another (i.e. $r_i \neq r_j$ in general).

Let us now partition the economic system into as many such newly defined sub-systems as there are consumption goods. Since the economic system is growing, these 'newly defined sub-systems' are more comprehensive than those considered in Chapter 6, because they include not only the labour and the means of production for the reproduction of each sub-system, but *also* the labour and the means of production necessary to its *expansion* at its particular rate of growth $(g + r_i)$. We call these newly defined sub-systems, the (m) *growing hyper-subsystems* or, more compactly, the (m) *hyper-subsystems* of the economic system under consideration.

We denote by $C_1(t), C_2(t), \ldots, C_m(t)$ the m consumption goods produced in period t, making up the (m) components of the already defined consumption goods (column) vector $\mathbf{C}(t)$. Each $C_i(t)$ is expanding through time at its particular rate of growth $(g + r_i)$, which we assume to be steady for the time being:

$$C_i(t) = c_i(0)e^{(g+r_i)t}, \qquad i = 1, 2, \ldots, m. \tag{13.2.4}$$

We now proceed in a way perfectly analogous to the one used in defining the earlier sub-systems in Chapter 6, but with the essential difference here of including in each hyper-subsystem *all* gross

[1] This is simply an analytical device to avoid inconsistencies in assuming differentiated growth rates for different consumption goods, in the presence of constant technical coefficients.

investments (both replacements *and* net investments). We thereby obtain:

$$\mathbf{X}^{(i)}(t) = [\mathbf{B} - (1+g+r_i)\mathbf{A}]^{-1}\mathbf{C}^{(i)}(t), \qquad (13.2.5)$$

$$\mathrm{L}_i(t) = \mathbf{a}_n[\mathbf{B} - (1+g+r_i)\mathbf{A}]^{-1}\mathbf{C}^{(i)}(t), \qquad (13.2.6)$$

$$\mathbf{S}^{(i)}(t) = \mathbf{A}[\mathbf{B} - (1+g+r_i)\mathbf{A}]^{-1}\mathbf{C}^{(i)}(t), \qquad (13.2.7)$$

$$\sum \mathbf{C}^{(i)}(t) = \mathbf{C}(t), \quad \sum \mathbf{X}^{(i)}(t) = \mathbf{Q}(t), \qquad (13.2.8)$$

$$\sum \mathbf{S}^{(i)}(t) = \mathbf{S}(t), \quad \sum \mathrm{L}_i(t) = L(t), \quad i = 1, 2, \ldots, m, \qquad (13.2.9)$$

where $\mathbf{C}^{(i)}(t)$ is a (column) vector, the components of which are all zeros except the ith one, which is the scalar C_i, that is, the ith component of vector $\mathbf{C}(t)$; and $\mathbf{X}^{(i)}(t)$, $\mathbf{S}^{(i)}(t)$, $L_i(t)$ are those particular corresponding magnitudes, that, in a self-contained expanding economic system, are necessary to produce through time that physical (expanding) quantity $C_i(t)$, and at the same time to produce all the means of production necessary both to maintain in operation such an economic system and to expand it at the required rate of growth $(g + r_i)$.

In this way, each hyper-subsystem i is characterised by

(i) production of one single consumption good i, expanding through time at its particular rate of growth $(g + r_i)$;
(ii) absorption of a physical quantity of labour $L_i(t)$, expanding in time at whatever rate is required by the technical coefficients (in our case, clearly, at rate $(g + r_i)$);
(iii) maintenance of a circular production process that *both* reproduces all the means of production which are absorbed by the production process for consumption good $C_i(t)$, *and* also produces those means of production that are strictly necessary to expand such a circular process at a rate of growth $(g + r_i)$.

Since $i = 1, 2, \ldots, m$, there are (m) such hyper-subsystems, and the sums of the physical magnitudes of these m hyper-subsystems – see (13.2.8) – add up to the physical magnitudes of the actual economic system.

For convenience, we may define the following vectors and matrices:

$$\boldsymbol{\ell}^{(i)} = \mathbf{a}_n[\mathbf{B} - (1+g+r_i)\mathbf{A}]^{-1}, \qquad (13.2.10)$$

$$\mathbf{M}^{(i)} = \mathbf{A}[\mathbf{B} - (1+g+r_i)\mathbf{A}]^{-1}, \quad i = 1, 2, \ldots, m. \qquad (13.2.11)$$

Unlike what happened in Sraffa's sub-systems, each hyper-subsystem i is now characterised by a particular vector $\boldsymbol{\ell}^{(i)}$ and by a particular matrix $\mathbf{M}^{(i)}$, $i = 1, 2, \ldots, m$.

It should be noticed, however, that not all columns of matrix $\mathbf{M}^{(i)}$ are relevant, but only the ith column, which we may denote by a star:

$$\mathbf{m}_i^{(i)} = \mathbf{m}_i^*. \tag{13.2.12}$$

This is a vector which defines a particular composite commodity that may be called *a unit of vertically hyper-integrated productive capacity* for commodity i. Similarly, not all components of vector $\boldsymbol{\ell}^{(i)}$ are relevant, but only the ith component, which we may equally denote by a star:

$$\ell_i^{(i)} = \ell_i^*. \tag{13.2.13}$$

This scalar defines what may be called the *vertically hyper-integrated labour coefficient* for commodity i.

We may now ask: What then is the meaning of any other column $\mathbf{m}_j^{(i)}$ of each matrix $\mathbf{M}^{(i)}$ and of any other component $\ell_j^{(i)}$ of each vector $\boldsymbol{\ell}^{(i)}$; $i \neq j$; $i, j = 1, 2, \ldots, m$? The answer is that their meaning takes a *hypothetical* connotation. Each vector $\mathbf{m}_j^{(i)}$ (each component $\ell_j^{(i)}$) in matrix $\mathbf{M}^{(i)}$ (in vector $\boldsymbol{\ell}^{(i)}$), where $j \neq i$, has the meaning of a unit of vertically hyper-integrated productive capacity (of a vertically hyper-integrated labour coefficient), *if* commodity j were to be produced as a consumption good (though it is not) in hyper-subsystem i.

Therefore, in each matrix $\mathbf{M}^{(i)}$, we may call the relevant column $\mathbf{m}_i^*$ the *actual* unit of vertically hyper-integrated productive capacity and all the other columns $\mathbf{m}_j^{(i)}$ the *hypothetical* units of vertically hyper-integrated productive capacity in the hyper-subsystem i. Similarly, in each vector $\boldsymbol{\ell}^{(i)}$, we may call the relevant component ℓ_i^* the *actual* vertically hyper-integrated labour coefficient and all the other components $\ell_j^{(i)}$, the *hypothetical* vertically hyper-integrated labour coefficients; $j, i = 1, 2, \ldots, m$; $j \neq i$.

The generalising features of this analytical construction should now be evident. In the very particular case in which all $g + r_i = 0$, $i = 1, 2, \ldots, m$, that is, in the particular case of a perfectly stationary economic system, all matrices $\mathbf{M}^{(i)}$ coincide with one another and with matrix $\mathbf{H}$ as defined in Chapter 6. And similarly all vectors $\boldsymbol{\ell}^{(i)}$ coincide with one another and with vector $\mathbf{v}$ of Chapter 6. In other words, when $g + r_i = 0$, the m hyper-subsystems reduce to the simpler sub-systems previously defined. The latter thereby emerge as particular cases of the former. Or, to put it in the other way round, the growing or hyper-subsystems represent a truly general notion, of which Sraffa's sub-systems are particular cases.

3 The Natural Price Sub-systems

We may now turn to the system of prices. Here the general attitude (which was also followed by Sraffa) has been that of accepting a uniform exogenously given rate of profits. In this case, we should be back to the usual price system:

$$\mathbf{pB} = \mathbf{a}_n w + \mathbf{pA} + \mathbf{pA}\pi, \tag{13.3.1}$$

where $\mathbf{p}$ is the (m)-components row price vector, and w and π are scalars for the wage rate and the rate of profits respectively. Equation system (13.3.1) contains two degrees of freedom, which may be closed by choosing a particular *numéraire* of prices, for example, by fixing

$$w = 1, \tag{13.3.2}$$

which means expressing all prices in terms of 'labour commanded', and by considering the (uniform) rate of profits π as determined from outside. Thereby we should indeed be back to the usual price system, but at the same time we should be back to the asymmetry pointed out at the end of Section 1.

The relevant, and significant, alternative is to depart from the traditional assumption of a uniform rate of profit. Following the approach of Pasinetti (1981), here reproduced and expanded in Chapter 11, I shall therefore now resume the notion of a natural rate of profit. A *natural* rate of profit, denoted by a star, π^*, is defined as a rate of profit which is equal to the rate of growth of demand for the corresponding consumption good. This means that in general we shall have, in the whole economic system, (m) different *natural rates of profit*, as we have seen before:

$$\pi_i^* = g + r_i, \qquad i = 1, 2, \ldots, m. \tag{13.3.3}$$

More specifically, this means that there will be a particular natural rate of profit for each hyper-subsystem.

It follows that there will also be a specific set of *natural prices* for each particular hyper-subsystem. In total, there will be (m) sets of natural prices, each one referring to the corresponding hyper-subsystem.

A crucial distinction emerges at this point which did not arise before. The distinction is between the natural prices of the consumption goods and the natural prices of the means of production.

In each hyper-subsystem i, we can see that its specific set of natural prices refers, to begin with, to the means of production (which may well include the particular good i, which is also used as a consumption good). Calling $\mathbf{p}^{(i)}$ this specific set of natural prices, we have the particular price vector:

$$\mathbf{p}^{(i)} = \mathbf{a}_n[\mathbf{B} - (1 + \pi_i^*)\mathbf{A}]^{-1}w, \tag{13.3.4}$$

or, from definitions (13.2.10) and (13.3.3)

$$\mathbf{p}^{(i)} = \boldsymbol{\ell}^{(i)}w. \tag{13.3.4 bis}$$

But $i = 1, 2, \ldots, m$, that is, there are (m) hyper-subsystems. It follows that there exist (m) sets of natural prices for the same means of production, each set of natural prices being specific to a particular hyper-subsystem.

The situation is remarkably different for the (m) consumption goods. Each consumption good *only* appears in one hyper-subsystem and therefore has only *one* natural price. The consumption good natural price is the ith price in each price system (13.3.4). By calling it p_i^*, it clearly emerges as

$$p_i^*(t) = \mathbf{a}_n[\mathbf{B} - (1 + \pi_i^*)\mathbf{A}]^{-1}\mathbf{e}_i w = \ell_i^*(t)w, \qquad i = 1, 2, \ldots, m, \tag{13.3.5}$$

where $\mathbf{e}_i$ is the unit (column) vector and $\ell_i^*(t)$ is the corresponding actual vertically hyper-integrated labour coefficient, defined by (13.2.13)

In all hyper-subsystems taken together, that is, in the whole economic system, each good therefore has only one natural price as a consumption good, although it may have up to (m) different natural prices as a capital good.

Notice, from (13.3.5) to (13.2.6) that, since $\pi_i^* = g + r_i$, when we put $w = 1$, the price p_i^* of commodity i; $i = 1, 2, \ldots, m$, (i.e. its price as a consumption good), is simply equal to $L_i(t)/C_i(t)$, which means that $p_i^* C_i(t)$, the value of $C_i(t)$, is simply equal to $L_i(t)$. The value of the physical quantity of each consumption good that is produced turns out to be equal to the physical quantity of labour which has directly, indirectly and – as I have called it here in Chapter 11 – hyper-indirectly been required by its production. Because of linearity, the consumption goods and the quantities of labour allocated to the (m) hyper-subsystems exhaust all the produced consumption goods, while the quantities of labour allocated to the (m) hyper-subsystems exhaust all the available labour.

This is a complete generalisation of the pure labour theory of value. Each physical quantity of any consumption good is unambiguously related to a physical quantity of labour, and the two have, in between them, a physically defined self-replacing, and expanding, circular process.

In terms of the compact notation defined by (13.2.10), each p_i^* is simply proportional – and in the case in which w is used as *numéraire* it is exactly equal – to the corresponding actual vertically hyper-integrated labour coefficient ℓ_i^*, which precisely represents the quantity of labour which is necessary directly, indirectly and hyper-indirectly to its production.

But the interesting result that follows immediately from this compact notation is that the natural prices $\mathbf{p}^{(i)}$ of the corresponding means of production have exactly the same meaning, although assuming a *hypothetical* connotation. As emerges from (13.3.4) and (13.3.4 bis), these prices are proportional (or actually equal, in the case in which w is used as *numéraire*), to the quantity of labour that *would* be necessary – directly, indirectly and hyper-indirectly – to produce them as consumption goods, *if* they were produced as consumption goods in the corresponding hyper-subsystems (though in fact they are produced as capital goods and not as consumption gods). In other words, they are proportional to the corresponding *hypothetical* vertically hyper-integrated labour coefficient s, as defined in Section 2.

At this point, the whole set of natural prices of the means of production appear as performing in each hyper-subsystem a sort of ancillary role with respect to the corresponding price of the consumption good. Formal symmetry has been re-established perfectly between all aspects concerning physical quantities and all aspects concerning prices.

4 The General, Pure Labour, Theory of Value Considered from a Different Viewpoint

The elaborations of Section 3, which provide a complete generalisation of the pure labour theory of value, may be further illustrated by taking an alternative route which allows to link them up with the elaborations of Chapter 5.

Let us start from the general price system (13.3.1) and suppose that there is a *uniform* rate of profit, $\bar{\pi}$, which is actually imposed from outside. We can always rewrite (13.3.1) as

$$\mathbf{pB} = \mathbf{a}_n w + \mathbf{pA} + (g + r_i)\mathbf{pA} + (\bar{\pi} - g - r_i)\mathbf{pA}, \qquad (13.4.1)$$

where $(g + r_i)$ is the rate of growth of demand for any one of the consumption goods. Of course, since $i = 1, 2, \ldots, m$, there are (m) *different* ways, expressed by (13.4.1), of rewriting *the same* general price system (13.3.1), each one of them with reference to the particular consumption good i, $i = 1, 2, \ldots, m$, whose rate of growth $(g + r_i)$ is explicitly introduced. Let us proceed with one of them – which we call i. By re-arranging, and by using the previous notation, we obtain

$$\mathbf{p}[\mathbf{B} - (1 + g + r_i)\mathbf{A}]^{-1} = \mathbf{a}_n w + (\bar{\pi} - g - r_i)\mathbf{pA}, \qquad (13.4.2)$$

$$\mathbf{p} = \mathbf{a}_n[\mathbf{B}-(1+g+r_i)\mathbf{A}]^{-1}w+(\bar{\pi}-g-r_i)\mathbf{pA}[\mathbf{B}-(1+g+r_i)\mathbf{A}]^{-1}. \qquad (13.4.3)$$

To consider it carefully, this is a remarkable expression. On the right-hand side, the first addendum contains the vector of the vertically hyper-integrated labour coefficients for hyper-subsystem i, and similarly the second addendum contains the matrix of the vertically hyper-integrated units of productive capacity for the same hyper-subsystem i. Using definitions (13.2.10) and (13.2.11), expression (13.4.3) may now be rewritten

$$\mathbf{p} = \boldsymbol{\ell}^{(i)} w + (\bar{\pi} - g - r_i)\mathbf{pM}^{(i)}. \qquad (13.4.3 \text{ bis})$$

Clearly, in the very particular case in which

$$\bar{\pi} = g + r_i, \qquad (13.4.4)$$

the second addendum, on the right-hand side of (13.4.3 bis), vanishes and the expression comes to coincide with $\mathbf{p}^{(i)}$ in (13.3.4 bis) – the natural prices for hyper-subsystem i.

It is important to stress that, since we can write expression (13.4.1) in (m) different ways, with reference to each specific r_i – that is, to the rate of growth of per capita demand for consumption good i; and in general $r_i \neq r_j$, for $i, j = 1, 2, \ldots, m$ – then it follows that if it were to happen that (13.4.4) were satisfied for a specific consumption good i, it would *not* in general be satisfied for any of the other $[(m - 1)]$ consumption goods.

In general, therefore, when $\bar{\pi}$ is uniform, the second addendum on the right-hand side of (13.4.3 bis) does not vanish, and we will be able to rewrite (13.4.3 bis) as

$$\mathbf{p} = \boldsymbol{\ell}^{(i)}[\mathbf{I} - (\bar{\pi} - g - r_i)\mathbf{M}^{(i)}]^{-1}w; \qquad i = 1, 2, \ldots, m, \qquad (13.4.5)$$

(which of course reduces to

$$\mathbf{p} = \boldsymbol{\ell}^{(i)}w, \qquad i = 1, 2, \ldots, m, \qquad (13.4.6)$$

coinciding with the natural prices for hyper-subsystem i, *only in the very particular case* in which $\bar{\pi} = g + r_i$).

We can see now, in another way (i.e. from the point of view of the solution of the price system) that there are (m) different ways, expressed by (13.4.5) – each one with reference to each of the consumption goods and therefore to each of the particular hyper-subsystems – of writing the *same* general price system (13.3.1), when one takes a uniform rate of profits as given from outside.

It also emerges very clearly at this point that expression (13.4.5), when $w = 1$, can also be regarded as providing a complete generalisation of Marx's 'transformation problem'.[2] It 'transforms' the physical quantities of vertically hyper-integrated labour $\boldsymbol{\ell}^{(i)}$ into the prices $\mathbf{p}$ of an economic system in which there is a uniform rate of profit $\bar{\pi}$.

There are (m) expressions (13.4.5), for any given uniform rate of profit $\bar{\pi}$, which means that there is a particular 'transformation', carried out by the corresponding hyper-subsystem, with reference to each particular consumption good produced in the economic system. This transformation concerns *both* the price of the consumption good *and* the prices of the corresponding means of production.

It is at this point that we should be able to look from yet another point of view at the meaning of the complete generalisation of the labour theory of value emerging from the foregoing elaborations.

In a hypothetical economic system in which we were able *actually to separate* the various hyper-subsystems, it would be possible at least in principle to envisage (m) different natural price sub-systems, which would embody a perfectly general pure labour theory of value. Such a labour theory of value would be general in the sense that it

[2] This complete generalisation concerns the version of Marx's transformation problem as presented in Pasinetti (1973, pp. 9, 16, 17n), and here reproduced in Chapter 5, pp. 171–198.

would realise, for an advanced society, the fundamental characteristic of the pure labour theory of value originally proposed by Adam Smith with reference to a primitive society: namely a set of values that realise a universal equality of 'labour commanded' and 'labour embodied'. The analytical step that allows the achievement of this result is of course a re-definition of the concept of 'labour embodied', which must be intended as the quantity of labour required directly, indirectly *and* hyper-indirectly to obtain the corresponding commodity as a consumption good.

In any economic system in which the analytical process of deriving the various hyper-subsystems is to be taken as a *conceptual* (and not as a real) process, any rule of price determination that starts from a uniform rate of profit inevitably entails a 'transformation' process, no matter whether the economic system itself is organisationally centralised or decentralised. In such a context, the general pure labour theory of value that has emerged from the foregoing elaborations is providing a logical frame of reference – a conceptual construction which defines a series (for the consumption goods), and actually a family of series (for the capital goods), of ideal *natural* prices, which possess an extraordinarily high number of remarkable, analytical and normative properties.

5 Choice of Efficient Techniques

There is a further normative property of the natural prices that emerges with reference to the problem of choice of techniques.

In the previous sections, all analysis has been carried out with reference to an economic system with a *given* technique, represented by the technical triple $[\mathbf{a}_n, \mathbf{A}, \mathbf{B}]$. In general, however, many alternative techniques of production, which we may call α, β, ω, may be available. More specifically, alternative technical triples:

$$[\mathbf{a}_n, \mathbf{A}, \mathbf{B}]^{(\alpha)}, [\mathbf{a}_n, \mathbf{A}, \mathbf{B}]^{(\beta)}, \ldots, [\mathbf{a}_n, \mathbf{A}, \mathbf{B}]^{(\omega)}, \tag{13.5.1}$$

may be open to choice. A criterion of choice becomes necessary. Now, if the criterion of choice to be adopted is the usual one of minimisation of costs, then it follows that the natural system of prices, by virtue of expressing physical quantities of labour (directly, indirectly and hyper-indirectly required), possesses the normative property of leading to the choice of that technique which entails the minimisation of labour inputs. This means that natural prices possess the normative property of being *efficient prices*.

But in a growing economic system, as has been shown, the quantities of labour that are required directly, indirectly and hyper-indirectly for the corresponding commodities are *different* (for the same commodities) in the various hyper-subsystems, just in the same ways as the corresponding natural prices are different in the various hyper-subsystems.

It follows that the efficient technique – that is, that technique the choice of which entails the minimisation of labour inputs – may turn out to be different from one hyper-subsystem to another. If it is technique α that minimises labour inputs for hyper-subsystem 1, it may well be that another technique, let us say technique β, is the technique that minimises labour inputs for hyper-subsystem 2, and so on.

A further consequence will now be noticed. The actual choice of different techniques in different hyper-subsystems will *a fortiori* entail different natural prices systems. In other words, the natural prices, in general, will turn out to be different from one hyper-subsystem to another, not only because of the differences in the natural rates of profit, which would be the case even if the efficient technique were to remain the same for all hyper-subsystems, as has been considered up to this section, but also, and more fundamentally, because of differences in the efficient techniques themselves. For, as a consequence of minimisation, the efficient technique may well turn out to be different from one hyper-subsystem to another.

Notice, again, that the differences in the natural prices concern the prices of the means of production, *not* the prices of consumption goods. Each consumption good continues to have one single natural price – the one that emerges as reflecting the physical quantity of labour directly, indirectly and hyper-indirectly required in the corresponding hyper-subsystem. Of course the same physical good, to the extent that it is also used as capital good in other hyper-subsystems, may also have other natural prices *as a capital good*. But its natural price as a consumption good is unique.

This property further enhances *the ancillary role*, already pointed out, of the natural prices of capital goods, with respect to the natural prices of consumption goods.

But of course, at this point, it becomes necessary to go back to consider the meaning to be attributed to the logical construction of the hyper-subsystems. The partitioning of the whole economic system into (m) hyper-subsystems has been presented, since the beginning, as a *logical* operation *not* as a *factual* one.

In practice, that is the way in which hyper-subsystems will have to be considered, that is, as *logical* constructions. Thus, the foregoing analysis allows us to state that, if it were actually possible to separate the various hyper-subsystems from each other, then a whole series of families of natural prices could actually come into existence, with the normative properties that have been brought into evidence by the foregoing analysis. It goes without saying that, when actual separation is not possible, the choice of technique induced by current prices (which may deviate from natural prices) will entail deviations from efficient positions. An interesting point to stress is that this will be so in any economic system, whether market oriented (i.e. decentralised) or centrally planned.

More specifically, there are two distinct obstacles to the full achievement of efficient positions through the choice of efficient techniques, as has emerged from the foregoing analysis. The first obstacle is represented by the difficulty of applying differentiated rates of profit in the various hyper-subsystems. The second obstacle is represented by all those factors that prevent the possibility of actually carrying on a particular choice of technique in each growing hyper-subsystem. While the first obstacle is typical and specific to decentralised (i.e. market oriented) economies, the second obstacle is common to both decentralised and centralised economic systems.

6 The Analytical Achievements, for Value Theory, of the Concept of Vertically Hyper-integrated Sectors

There remains one further aspect to be explored, and that is the relation of the hyper-subsystems to the concept of vertically hyper-integrated sectors defined in Chapter 6.

The effects of the generalisation of the analysis of Chapter 6 to the present analysis concerning the vertically hyper-integrated sectors becomes obvious and immediate at this stage. If we return, for clarity of exposition, to the case of a single technique $[\mathbf{a}_n(t), \mathbf{A}(t), \mathbf{B}(t)]$ in the whole economic system at time t, and thus common to all hyper-subsystems, we may see very clearly the distinction and at the same time the relations between the two points of view, from which any production economic system may be looked at as described in the previous literature: the point of view of the circularity of the production process and the point of view of final (consumption) demand.

The former point of view is evinced by the construction of the sub-systems, which now achieve completeness by becoming hyper-subsystems owing to the inclusion of the relations concerning the expansion of the means of production, besides those concerning their replacement.

The other point of view – that is, the point of view of final demand – is evinced in an even sharper way. In a growing economic system, *consumption* appears at one extreme of the production process (the output extreme) and labour appears at the other (the input) extreme, and the two are directly and immediately put into relation with each other. The complex circular (but expanding) production process, which is in between, is on the other hand taken for granted, as it is closed onto itself and thus fulfils an intermediate and ancillary function. From the point of view of final demand, this ancillary role of all intermediate circular processes emerges at its clearest. At the same time, these two points of view stand up as perfectly complementary. For the economic system appears as being made up of as many vertically hyper-integrated sectors as there are consumption goods. It is the compactness of these vertically hyper-integrated sectors that confers remarkable properties on the whole elaboration.

Each vertically hyper-integrated sector i, when operating at unit activity, may compactly be represented by the elementary vector:

$$[1, 1, \ell_i, (g + r_i)], \qquad i = 1, 2, \ldots, m, \qquad (13.6.1)$$

where the first component refers to one unit of consumption good i, the second component to one unit of vertically hyper-integrated productive capacity for consumption good i, the third to the physical quantity of (vertically hyper-integrated) labour for consumption good i and the fourth to the growth rate of demand for consumption good i (in the hyper-sector i). The corresponding magnitudes in the price system continue to be represented by the simple vector:

$$[p_i, p_{k_i}, w, \pi_i], \qquad i = 1, 2, \ldots, m, \qquad (13.6.2)$$

where p_i is the price of one physical unit of consumption good i, and p_{k_i} is the price of one unit of vertically hyper-integrated productive capacity for consumption good i (while w and π_i are, as usual, the overall wage rate and the sectoral rate of profit). All asymmetries have now disappeared: vectors (13.6.1) and (13.6.2) are perfectly symmetrical.

One should notice the extreme simplicity with which the *unit of vertically hyper-integrated productive capacity* in (13.6.1), and the corresponding price p_{k_i} in (13.6.2), have emerged. They have been introduced without the need of any specification of the composition (in terms of ordinary physical commodities) of the (conceptually so complex) unit concerned. Remarkably enough, at any point in time, t, given $\mathbf{A}(t)$, $\mathbf{B}(t)$, $\mathbf{a}_n(t)$, the relation of each unit of vertically hyper-integrated productive capacity to the ordinary physical commodities of which it is composed, and correspondingly the relation of the natural prices $\mathbf{p}_{k_i}$ of each unit of vertically hyper-integrated productive capacity to the natural prices $\mathbf{p}_i$ of the various commodities, measured in physical ordinary units, are conceptually very complex but analytically clear. The latter are obtained directly from (13.2.7) while the former are obtained by multiplying (13.3.4) by (13.2.11), that is,

$$\mathbf{p}_{k_i}(t) = \mathbf{p}^{(i)}(t)\mathbf{M}^{(i)}(t) = \boldsymbol{\ell}^{(i)}(t)\mathbf{M}^{(i)}(t)w(t),$$

or, by expansion,

$$\mathbf{p}_{k_i}(t) = \mathbf{a}_n(t)[\mathbf{B}(t) - (1+\pi^*)\mathbf{A}(t)]^{-1}\mathbf{A}(t)[\mathbf{B}(t) - (1-\pi^*)\mathbf{A}(t)]w(t), \quad i = 1, 2, \ldots, m. \tag{13.6.3}$$

The crucial point to notice is that these relations will continually be upset, as time goes on, because of technical change.

Yet, essential though these complex relations are for any analysis concerning the interrelations of the circular (expanding) process at any given point of time, they become consolidated (by the conceptual process of vertical hyper-integration) for all those dynamic analyses that concern the movements through time of the final consumption goods and of the corresponding physical quantities of (vertically hyper-integrated) labour, as well as for all those relations that follow there from – think, for example, of the analyses concerning the evolution of sectoral employment and of income distribution.

As may now appear, the two simple series of vectors (13.6.1) and (13.6.2) carry with them a remarkable overall synthesis of the relations that are at the basis of the whole comprehensive structural dynamics of the economic system, as picked up by the resulting structural evolution of the final consumption goods at the one extreme and of the labour inputs compactly entering into them at the other extreme.

That is what, after all, had already emerged from our essential, but much simpler, model developed in Part Three of this book – see the synthetic list of the 'natural' features of a growing production system with which we have opened Part Four of this book.

Essentially, vertical hyper-integration has led us to a complete emancipation from the constraints of fixed technical coefficients. The synthetic series of vectors (13.6.1) and (13.6.2) renders our analysis open to the absorption and compact expression of the effects of technical progress in whatever form it may take place.

14 *Beyond Production: The 'Natural' Rate of Interest*

1 Personal Savings as Distinct from Overall Savings

With the closing of the Chapter 13, we have achieved completion of the 'natural' *production* economic system, but not yet of the *entire* 'natural' economic system itself. There still is one further, important, in fact by now crucial, economic variable that has not been dealt with so far: the 'natural' rate of interest.

Surely the reader must have well thought of it before. In any society, since time immemorial, long before the Industrial Revolution, the rate of interest has been a most typical magnitude that has characterised economic inter-personal relations, particularly with reference to personal savings and personal indebtedness. How is it that, so far, it has not emerged from our theoretical scheme?

The answer to this question is inherent in the concentration and stress that, in the foregoing analysis, has been laid on the process of *production* in an *industrial* society, where – in connection with capital and savings – the crucial role is played by the 'natural rate (or rates) of profit', *not* by the rate of interest which has been, surprisingly perhaps but accurately, kept out. It will be noticed, incidentally, that this characteristic has at the same time rendered the whole production structure, as we have investigated it, entirely closed onto itself, independently of any inter-personal relation that may be undertaken among the various individuals, or groups of individuals, especially with reference to their final needs of consumption.

But, at this point, we must obviously go *beyond* the strict sphere of production. We must open our analysis up also to the whole series of *personal relations*, which logically *follow* the process of production, though still preceding actual, effective, consumption.

In order to understand why this is so, it may be useful to recall in synthesis what has been done so far, with reference to individual consumption and savings.

We have actually seen that, in a *production* natural economic system considered as a whole, *total* (equilibrium) savings are physically determined by the amount of total investments. Within the natural features of any *production* economic system, as we have seen, there is a series of sectoral new investment conditions (see Chapter 9, Section 2, and 11, which determine the total overall amount of the new investments, whose sum *ipso facto* determine the total amount of *savings necessary for the economic system considered as a whole* (see Chapter 12, Section 10). Within this framework, it is the configuration of the 'natural rate of profit' which ensures that all single ('hyper-integrated') sectors (and then as an aggregate consequence the economic system as a whole) receive – as re-invested profits – exactly those flows of savings in terms of sectoral purchasing power that are exactly sufficient (no more and no less) to meet the requirements of all the new investments. Within such a logical framework, our analysis has shown that the whole process of production is such as to be complete in itself. It takes place within the (vertically hyper-integrated) production structure of the 'natural economic system'. And this process is logically quite apart, and independent, of any inter-personal relation concerning consumption.

This being so, our major concentration up till now on investments (and on total profits), as determining the total amount of required savings, was necessary in order to mark the distinction between the level of investigation concerning the production economic system as a whole and the level of investigation concerning personal savings of single individuals or groups of individuals, which is what we are now going to concentrate on.

And now, for this purpose, we must go *beyond* the strict field of production. The whole network of the production processes, and with it of overall savings, does not exclude, even less eliminate, the equally complex network of debt/credit relations that always grow up in connection with the phenomena of *personal* savings.

It is however important to realise that this is something *distinct* from what we have investigated so far. And, in order make this distinction in a clear and unmistakable way, it actually becomes fruitful at this point to take advantage of the *analytical* properties of the present analysis and go back to – in a sense re-start from – the very beginning, namely from the initial hypothetical case in which *total overall savings are* (in the equilibrium of the production process) *required to be zero*, without, however, giving up the introduction of growth of technical knowledge. The analytical advantage of doing this is that a great deal of relations, which we have investigated already for the economic system as a whole, do not arise in this case and thus give us no new further problems with which to deal. Nevertheless, we should immediately be able to realise how *personal* savings remain entirely open to being carried out by individuals or groups of individuals, or indeed by the Public Authorities, and thus clearly perceive how vast the zone is, which is opening up between the end of the production process (which we have investigated so far) and the point in time where the various individuals, or public authorities, may choose their preferred times at which to reach the fulfilment of their final consumption.

The initial (analytical) case we are going back to, is that of a hypothetical economic system as considered in Chapter 7, Sections 2 and 3, where goods are supposed to be made by labour alone, that is the case of a strictly 'pure and direct labour' economy. We shall, however, reverse our previous procedures and immediately introduce technical progress, leaving capital accumulation aside for the time being. In this way we shall have the possibility of taking advantage of the specific *analytical* properties of our procedures. For, in the case of a pure labour economy, it becomes absolutely clear that no savings whatsoever *for production purposes* are required in *the economic system considered as a whole*[1]; and yet, for single individuals, the possibilities of *personal* savings remain entirely open, as always, to a really broad and huge extent indeed!

While it may at first appear paradoxical, we shall be able in the following pages to concentrate on the possibilities of personal savings, quite independently of the whole production process. Once the inter-personal saving relations have been clarified for this crystal clear, marvellously simple case, it will become easy to show the conditions under which they remain the same (or how they might be modified) in the more general case of production with physical capital goods, thus confirming the appropriateness of the *virtual* analytical separation (as followed in the present analysis) of the sphere of production on the one side – on which we have concentrated in this section – and the sphere

[1] In such a case, the only way to carry purchasing power over time is *to embody it in physical goods*, confining it to the hoarding of physical *durable consumption goods*. See footnote 2.

of inter-personal debt/credit relations on the other side – which is the subject on which we are now going to concentrate.

2 Impossibility of Shifting Total *Equilibrium* Consumption in Time; Yet Huge Possibilities of *Personal* Savings, through the Cumulation of Financial Assets and Liabilities

As just anticipated, in order to stress the distinction between the two fields of analysis just mentioned (the field of physical production on one side, and the field of *personal* savings on the other), we may begin our investigation of personal savings by going back to the analysis of Chapter 7, where we investigated the case of an economy in which there are *no capital goods* and thus there can be *no equilibrium savings for the economic system as a whole.* Let me recall that these *null* overall savings are a straightforward macro-economic consequence of the effective demand equilibrium condition (8.2.10). Since, in the case considered, the whole productive capacity of the economic system must be devoted to the production of consumption goods, one can strictly and clearly see here an expression of the original *Keynesian principle of effective demand.* It implies that, if total *demand for consumption goods* were to fall short of total potential national income, the difference would not go to any saving for the future. It would simply represent lost consumption, that is, consumption goods that are lost *because of idle productive capacity.* This also means that, for the economic system as a whole, in such a situation of lack of effective demand, consumption foregone[2] is lost forever!

[2] The possibility is always open, of course, of *physically* storing up *non-perishable* consumption goods and carrying them over in time. The most obvious case of this phenomenon is represented by all houses, dwellings, palaces and works of art, which are all *consumption* – not production – goods from the point of view of our analysis. This physical hoarding is not only possible, but actually necessary for a complete fulfilment of consumers' aspirations, though it is subject to strict physical limits. Yet in order to make our relations emerge in an absolutely clear way, and without complications, we shall make, for the time being, the *heroic* assumption that all consumption goods are perishable, and therefore that there is no physical hoarding of consumption goods. The introduction of physical hoarding of non-perishable consumption goods presents no analytical problem and can always be introduced at a second analytical stage of investigation, without affecting the conclusions which will be reached at the end of the present elaborations.

Yet again, impossibility for the economic system as a whole of transferring physical consumption over time does not entail impossibility for *single individuals* of postponing or of forward anticipating, their consumption, that is it does not entail any impossibility of *personal* savings or dissavings. Any single individual may indeed abstain from consuming part of his (her) current income, and postpone its consumption, in time, *provided that* he (she), or the economic system as a whole, can find some other individual, or individuals, or Public Agencies willing to do the opposite.

Operations of this type may be carried out to a very large extent indeed. Individuals have natural lives that are longer than their active lives; moreover they normally have families whose components vary in age, requirements and number, in each particular time period. This means that the time profile of each family's consumption needs will normally differ from the time profile of the family's incoming income, even when their total sums coincide. Hence, there may be periods in which a particular family needs to save (income exceeding consumption) and periods in which the same family needs to dissave (consumption exceeding income). Normally these needs for savings and dissavings will arise at different times for different families, so that – within each period of time – those people whose incomes are in excess of their consumption needs may lend their excess purchasing power to those people whose incomes fall short of their consumption needs and then have it back when the personal situations have reversed.[3]

It is quite evident that, in an economic system with millions of individuals, inter-personal lending and borrowing may take place with very little complications. In theory, in each single period of time, any individual may lend to others an amount of purchasing power up to the whole amount of his (her) current income; and, at other times, may even borrow multiples of the amount of purchasing power corresponding to his (her) current income. There is no practical limit to this lending and borrowing.[4] The only constraint is of a different type: it is *a macro-economic constraint*; imposed by the overall effective demand

[3] As the reader will realise, this is the phenomenon that has been at the basis of the 'life-cycle hypothesis' theories of savings, of the type proposed, e.g., by Modigliani and Brumberg (1955) and then extensively developed in the economic literature.

[4] Note the contrast with physical hoarding, which meets strict *physical* limits.

equilibrium condition. In any closed economic system, all personal lending and borrowing must cancel each other out. There can be no net savings or dissavings for the economic system as a whole, however large personal savings and dis-savings may be.

Here and now we arrive at a consequence of crucial importance. The coming into being of inter-personal lending and borrowing relations, in any economic system, entails the formation of *stocks of financial assets and liabilities*. This means that even when no physical stocks of goods are carried through time (as is the case we are hypothetically considering) the economic system may normally carry *financial* stocks through time, representing claims to future purchasing power, and thus to future consumption by some individuals as against others. Overall, positive and negative claims – that is financial assets and liabilities – necessarily cancel each other out. Yet they may grow to very large amounts indeed and, through them, single individuals, or indeed large parts of the community as a whole, have the possibility of making their annual consumption go well beyond, or restrict it much below, the (physically determined) amounts of their annual incomes.[5]

The consequence is precisely what we are now going to investigate: namely the cumulation of financial assets and liabilities.

3 The Emerging of a Rate of Interest and with it, of a Social Function to be Performed by the *Numéraire* of the Financial Assets

The relations of debts and credits, among the various individuals and/or, as we may also add, between private citizens and Public Authorities (and therefore the coming into existence of financial assets and liabilities) have immediately crucial implications.

[5] This is also the point, in our analytical scheme, at which the investigation of *financial transactions* appears in our analysis, and/or could be introduced with all their variety and complications (a field which, however, is not our purpose to pursue here). The crucial difference of financial assets (and liabilities) with respect to physical capital stocks, generated by the production process is that, while the durable capital goods brought into being by the production process are physically constrained, *the financial stocks are not*. Virtually, financial stocks can increase to any amount (even to high multiples of national income!). They can grow to almost infinity without any *physical* constraint (though they come to face – and of course will have to face – other constraints, mainly of *institutional* character).

Essentially, for each single individual, they insert, so to speak, a wedge, they open up a gap, between the process of reception of incomes and the actual outflows of expenditure for consumption. We can see very clearly now that the connections remain committed to the choice of the *numéraire* (of the price system). The existence of financial assets and liabilities necessarily requires the choice of a specific *numéraire* in terms of which they are denominated. We have implicitly assumed (and we shall continue to assume) that debt/credit relations are denominated in terms of the same *numéraire* chosen for the commodity prices. Though there is no necessity that it should be so, this is the most logical and simple assumption to make in our analysis. But, in any case, this analytical step is sufficient to uncover an extension of the *social function* which is inherent in the choice of the *numéraire* of the price system and now also of the debt/credit relations. In Chapter 10 we considered the social function of the *numéraire* that emerged from the decision which must be made in order to fix the level (and the evolution of the level) of all commodity prices. Now we come across the realisation that this social function is much wider than what would be necessary to consider if our analysis were to stop – as it has been so far – at the stage of the prices of production. Now it comes to include a further function, namely, at any given point in time and through time, also that of fixing the purchasing power of all the *financial* assets and liabilities. Notice, incidentally, that in the case we are considering here, there is, *ex-hypothesis*, absolute absence of any *physical* assets. Our relations all refer to *financial assets* only.

Let us therefore immediately be aware of the important implications that these relations are carrying with them. This becomes now an absolute novelty, but at the same time a necessity, in our whole analysis. Once the *numéraire* of the debt/credit relations has been fixed, all financial assets and liabilities are bound to remain constant through time only in terms of the chosen *numéraire*. But if all the 'natural prices' are varying through time, as we have been supposing in our analysis, it follows that the purchasing power of all financial assets and liabilities will vary through time in terms of *all* commodities (and, what is more, in a different manner from one commodity to another!), with the only exception of the commodity which has been chosen as the *numéraire*. This is another reason for which, in the presence of structural dynamics, the choice of the *numéraire* of the price system (and now, by our choice, also of the debt/credit relations), far from being an arbitrary, or irrelevant, decision, becomes a very important decision, in fact a crucial decision, indeed. It is a decision that entails full and heavy *social* implications. In fact it now emerges very clearly that the decision confers on the choice of *numéraire* a further *social* function that goes beyond the one which emerged in Chapter 10 in connection with the production price system.[6]

To show this in detail, let us go a little bit more in detail. If the percentage rates of growth of productivity in the $n-1$ (vertically integrated) sectors are $\varrho_1, \varrho_2, \ldots, \varrho_h, \ldots, \varrho_{n-1}$, ranked in a decreasing order, and if commodity h (call it 'gold') is the one that is used as *numéraire*, which means that all debts and credits are stipulated in terms of commodity h, then all debts and credits will clearly remain constant through time only in terms of commodity h. In terms of any other commodity, the purchasing power of all debts and credits will change. More precisely, over time, all debts and credits will revalue at rate $(\varrho_1 - \varrho_h)$ in terms of commodity 1, at rate $(\varrho_2 - \varrho_h)$ in terms of commodity 2, ..., at rate $(\varrho_{n-1} - \varrho_h)$ in terms of commodity $(h-1)$. And they will devalue at rate $(\varrho_h - \varrho_{h+1})$ in terms of commodity $(h+1), \ldots$, at rate $(\varrho_h - \varrho_{n-1})$ in terms of commodity $n-1$.

In order to show the crucial implications, in *real* terms, of this structural dynamics on the purchasing power of financial assets and liabilities, suppose that, at a certain moment, we wanted to change the *numéraire* of the price system. Clearly, if we did so, the evolution through time, in real terms, of all debt/credit relations would be altered. To express the problem more cogently, suppose that we wanted to change the *numéraire* but at the same time we wanted to keep inter-personal relations unaltered through time in real terms. Then, we would have to introduce a correction – precisely in the form of a *rate of interest*,[7] even if no rate of interest had originally been stipulated on debts and credits in terms of commodity h. For example, if a change of *numéraire* were to be made from commodity h to commodity 1, in

6 Or, if we like, we might say that the choice of the *numéraire* performs two *distinct* and different functions, or carries with it two aspects, which through the choice of the *same numéraire* both for the price system and for the debt/credit relations, comes to merge together, without however losing their respective and different social functions, connected with the prices of production on the one side and the financial assets on the other.

7 For simplicity's sake, as before, we shall talk of a 'rate of interest' to mean a *percentage* rate of interest per period of time.

order that all debt and credit relations remain unaltered in real terms through time, a rate of interest equal to $(\varrho_1 - \varrho_h)$ would have to be introduced on all debts reckoned in terms of the new *numéraire* (on top of whatever rate of interest might have been stipulated originally when debts were reckoned in terms of the old *numéraire*).

The conclusion is of crucial importance. In a *structurally dynamic context*, the coming into being of financial assets and liabilities, reflecting inter-personal or private-public debt/credit relations, implies *inevitably* (i.e. even if nothing had been stipulated on the matter), the emerging of a rate of interest.

4 A Whole Set of Own-Rates of Interest Implied by the Structural Dynamics of Prices

In fact, the existence of financial assets and liabilities, *when coupled with a structural dynamics of natural prices*, implies the existence – not just of one rate of interest – but of a whole set of (implicit) rates of interest. More specifically, it implies the existence of a particular own-rate of interest for each commodity.

To illustrate the point, suppose that the wage rate is chosen as the *numéraire* through time, that is $w(t) = 1$, and suppose that loans, in terms of the wage rate, are stipulated at a rate of interest equal to zero. Thus, when a loan expires, the lender simply receives back from the borrower an amount of purchasing power (in terms of labour) equal to the amount that was lent at the beginning, without receiving any interest in the meantime. However, the natural price of each commodity j, in terms of labour, has been decreasing in the meantime at the percentage rate ϱ_j, $(j = 1, 2, \ldots, n-1)$. Hence, the amount of the loan repaid, at time t, although unchanged in terms of labour, could purchase a quantity of each commodity j equal to $q_j(0)e^{\varrho_j t}$, where $q_j(0)$ is the quantity of commodity j which the amount that is repaid could have purchased at time zero. This means that the amount of the loan, though unchanged in terms of labour, has grown, in terms of each specific commodity j, at a compound rate of interest equal to ϱ_j, $(j = 1, 2, \ldots, n-1)$ Percentage rate ϱ_j therefore represents, in this case, what may be called the own-rate of interest for commodity j. There are $n - 1$ such own-rates of interest, namely:

$$\varrho_1, \varrho_2, \ldots, \varrho_{n-1}, \tag{14.4.1}$$

for commodities $1, 2, \ldots, n-1$, respectively; all implied by an actual rate of interest equal to zero in terms of the wage rate.

If the actual rate of interest, stipulated on loans in terms of the wage rate, instead of being zero, were $i_w > 0$, then the set of own-rates of interest implied by i_w would be:

$$(i_w + \varrho_1),\ (i_w + \varrho_2), \ldots, (i_w + \varrho_{n-1}), \qquad (14.4.2)$$

for commodities $1, 2, n-1$ respectively.

The same concepts may alternatively be illustrated with reference to the case in which a particular commodity (instead of the wage rate) – let us say commodity h (our 'gold') – is chosen as *numéraire* in terms of which loans are reckoned through time, that is the case in which $p_h(t) = 1$. In this case, if an actual rate of interest i_h is stipulated, to be paid on loans reckoned in terms of commodity h, then this actual rate of interest i_h clearly implies a set of own-rates of interest:

$$\begin{aligned}&[i_h + (\varrho_1 - \varrho_h)], [i_h + (\varrho_2 - \varrho_h)], \ldots, [i_h + (\varrho_{h-1} - \varrho_h)],\\ i_h &= [i_h + (\varrho_h - \varrho_h)], [i_h + (\varrho_{h+1} - \varrho_h)], \ldots, [i_h + (\varrho_{h-1} - \varrho_h)],\end{aligned} \qquad (14.4.3)$$

for commodities $1, 2, \ldots, h-1, h, h+1, \ldots, n-1$, respectively; and also an own-rate of interest

$$i_h + 0 - \varrho_h = i_h - \varrho_h, \qquad (14.4.4)$$

for 'labour commanded'.

A particularly interesting case is that one in which the chosen *numéraire* is the 'dynamic standard commodity', which has been denoted by h^* (see Chapter 10, Section 14). In this case, if i_{h^*} is the actual rate of interest, stipulated on loans denominated in terms of the dynamic standard commodity, such rate of interest implies a set of own-rates of interest

$$i_{h^*} - (\varrho^* - \varrho_j), \qquad j = 1, 2, \ldots, n-1, \qquad (14.4.5)$$

for the $n-1$ commodities, and an own-rate of interest

$$i_{h^*} - \varrho^*, \qquad (14.4.6)$$

for 'labour commanded'.

As one may see, the own-rate of interest for each commodity j ($j = 1, 2, n-1$) is given by the difference between the actual rate of interest and the (positive or negative) excess of the standard rate of growth of productivity over the rate of growth of productivity in the specific jth sector, while the own-rate of interest for labour commanded is simply, in this case, the difference between the actual rate of interest and the standard rate of growth of productivity.

5 The 'Nominal' or 'Money' Rate of Interest

The rates of interest considered in Section 4 (though only one of them is explicit, and the other $n-1$ own-rates are implicit) are all 'real' rates of interest, in the sense that each of them refers to purchasing power in terms of a specific physical commodity (simple or composite as it may be).

But in modern economic systems, as we know well, the chosen *numéraire* normally is a nominal unit of account (a paper-money unit). And when it is this nominal unit of account (which we shall simply call the money unit) to be adopted in the stipulation of debt and credit relations, the rate of interest will be expressed in the same terms, that is it will be a nominal, or, as we shall call it, a 'money' rate of interest, normally to be fixed exogenously by a *Central Monetary Authority*.

If we denote such a nominal or money rate of interest by i_M, that is a rate of interest stipulated on loans denominated in terms of the nominal (money) unit of account, it is evident that such a rate of interest – in order to acquire meaning – must be put into relation with the movement over time of the general level of prices, as it has been investigated in Chapter 10, Section 12. And it is here that we clearly come to realise that the two aspects of the social function of the choice of the *numéraire* described Section 3[8] merge together while maintaining their specific nature.

A few further elaborations may be carried out.

When the inter-personal debt/credit relations are denominated in terms of a nominal unit of account (a paper-money unit), and the actual rate of interest on the loans so denominated has been stipulated at level i_M (also a money, or nominal, rate of interest), it becomes necessary to resume our analysis behind the time movement of all prices in order to find the corresponding real own-rates of interest.[9]

Resuming notation σ_j, $(j = 1, 2, n-1)$ and σ_W of Chapter 10, Section 12 for the rates of change of the commodity prices and of the wage

[8] See also what was said already in footnote 6.

[9] Note here the crucial *institutional* decision to be taken by the Central Monetary Authority to fix the central value of the σ_W variable.

rate, respectively (all expressed in terms of the nominal or 'money' unit of account), we may express, first of all, the (real) own-rate of interest for each commodity j by the difference:

$$i_M - \sigma_i, \qquad i = 1, 2, \ldots, n-1, \tag{14.5.1}$$

and the (real) own-rate of interest for 'labour commanded' by the difference:

$$i_M - \sigma_w. \tag{14.5.2}$$

But in order to compare these expressions with the previous ones, we must go much deeper. We can take advantage of expression (10.12.8) of Chapter 10, Section 12 and rewrite (14.5.1) and (14.5.2) as

$$i_M - (\sigma_w - \varrho^*) - (\varrho^* - \varrho_j), \tag{14.5.3}$$

and

$$i_M - (\sigma_w - \varrho^*) - \varrho^*. \tag{14.5.4}$$

respectively.

As may be seen, these expressions, when compared with the corresponding (14.4.5) and (14.4.6), reveal the algebraic addition of a new addendum, namely $(\sigma_w - \varrho^*)$ which – as we know – represents the rate of monetary inflation, and which we have called σ_M (see Chapter 10, Section 15). Therefore, (14.5.3) and (14.5.4) may also be rewritten:

$$i_M - \sigma_M - (\varrho^* - \varrho_j), \tag{14.5.5}$$

and

$$i_M - \sigma_M - \varrho^*, \tag{14.5.6}$$

respectively.

This means that, when the unit of account is the nominal (money) unit, in order to obtain the (real) own-rates of interest, it is necessary to deduct, from the nominal rate of interest i_M, the rate of monetary inflation σ_M. Then, we are back to the formulations of Section 4 – compare (14.5.5) and (14.5.6) with (14.4.5) and (14.4.6), respectively.

Notice that, for the dynamic standard commodity, expression (14.5.6) simply reduces to

$$i_M - \sigma_M, \tag{14.5.7}$$

that is to say: the own-rate of interest for the dynamic standard commodity is simply given by the difference of the nominal, or money, rate of interest, and the rate of increase of the general level of prices (i.e. the rate of monetary inflation).

Expression (14.5.7) represents a crucial overall magnitude: it essentially expresses a sort of *average 'real' rate of interest for the economic system* as a whole.

We shall call it the *'standard' (real) rate of interest.*

6 Closing the Rate of Interest's Degree of Freedom

The foregoing analysis has already yielded a very important result indeed. It would make no sense to posit the question of whether there should or should not be a rate of interest. A whole structure of rates of interest exists in any case, whatever the actual 'nominal' rate of interest (even if it were equal to zero), and whatever the *numéraire* chosen as the basis of the price system. In other words, a whole structure of own-rates of interest – all of them 'real' – is inevitably inherent in the *structural dynamics of relative prices*, as soon as this structural dynamics is accompanied by inter-personal debt/credit relations.

The problem now to be posited, however, is another but central one, namely the problem of fixing the appropriate level at which to peg the whole structure of the own-rates of interest. More specifically, the problem is that of singling out which (money) rate of interest is the appropriate one to apply to all debt/credit relations, stipulated in terms of the money unit. This is in fact the only variable that still has remained indeterminate in the present theoretical scheme, since we have introduced the inter-personal debt/credit relations.

It has been pointed out already in Section 3 that the coming into existence of debt/credit relations has opened up a gap, for each single individual, between the reception of personal incomes and the outflow of expenditures. Now we can say, in more precise analytical terms, that it has opened up a new degree of freedom in the price system. The closure of this degree of freedom requires the determination of the actual rate of interest.[10]

[10] In more detail, each wage earner has the possibility, through debt/credit undertakings, of decoupling his or her current personal consumption from personal current wage. He or she can carry through time a personal (positive or negative) stock of *financial* wealth, which, at the end of each time unit, will be the algebraic sum of: wages minus consumption, initial financial assets minus initial financial liabilities, interest received minus interest paid on financial stocks. Although all these items cancel out in the aggregate, as the economic system we are considering can carry as a whole no net wealth

Indeed, the basic question is: which rate of interest?

Here we must go back to fundamentals. If a new variable has entered the whole price system, this variable must obviously be determined in a way which is logically consistent with the rest of the theory. Now, from among all possible price systems, the present theoretical scheme has adopted the 'natural' price system, that is prices proportional to physical quantities of labour ('embodied' or 'commanded'). The determination of the rate of interest must be consistent with this theoretical scheme.

The basic question, which has emerged and must now be answered, may therefore be re-stated in the following terms. From all possible levels of the actual rate of interest (and by implication of the whole structure of the own-rates of interest), *which* specific rate of interest may legitimately be claimed to be the 'natural' level of the rate of interest? (And, by implication, the 'natural' structure of the own rates of interest?)

7 The 'Natural' Rate of Interest (at Last!) to Complete the Natural Economic System

The question just stated, in order to be answered, requires the specification of a well-defined criterion. And the criterion to be adopted here cannot but be the one of logical consistency with the whole previous analysis.

7.1 Definition of the 'Natural Rate of Interest'

In an economic system in which all contributions to, and benefits from, the production process are regulated on the basis of physical quantities

through time (total wages being always equal to total consumption, that is to total production), yet a very articulated structural dynamics takes place in the amounts of personal purchasing power. We know that, given the *numéraire* in terms of which the debt/credit relations have been denominated – let us say a conventional money unit – and given the rate of change of the money wage rate (or alternatively the rate of change of any one of the commodity prices), there exist well-defined relations between the evolution of the money prices and the evolution of the purchasing power of the money unit, in terms of each single physical commodity. This means that the evolution of the actual distribution of real purchasing power among all individuals is not determined until the current (actual) rate of interest is fixed.

of labour ('natural' prices being proportional to labour, both 'embodied' and 'commanded'), the natural rate of interest is obviously that rate of interest which maintains constant through time all existing purchasing power relations in terms of labour. It obviously and logically means a zero rate of interest *in terms of labour*.

We have seen already, in Section 4, that a zero rate of interest in terms of labour implies a rate of interest equal to ϱ_1 in terms of commodity 1, a rate of interest equal to ϱ_2 in terms of commodity 2, ..., a rate of interest equal to ϱ_{n-1} in terms of commodity $n-1$, and, we may now add, a rate of interest equal to ϱ^* in terms of that physical commodity, which we have called the *dynamic standard commodity*. We shall therefore call this the *'natural' structure of the own-rates of interest*.

Clearly, given this structure of own-rates of interest, what the *actual* rate of interest will have to be, in order to bring such structure into being, depends on the *numéraire* in terms of which debts and credits are denominated. Hence, the (actual) natural rate of interest does depend on the *numéraire* of the price system. If we denote the natural rate of interest by an asterisk, that is if we represent it by i^*, we should normally have to add a subscript to this symbol in order to specify the *numéraire* in terms of which all debt/credit relations are reckoned.

When the *numéraire* chosen is the wage rate (i.e. when $w(t) = 1$) and all debt/credit relations are reckoned in terms of labour, then the natural rate of interest, to be denoted by i^*_w, turns out to be:

$$i^*_w = 0. \tag{14.7.1}$$

When the *numéraire* chosen is any commodity h (i.e. when $p_h(t) = 1$), and all debt/credit relations are stipulated in terms of commodity h, then the natural rate of interest i^*_h turns out to be:

$$i^*_h = \varrho_h, \qquad h = 1, 2, \ldots, n-1. \tag{14.7.2}$$

And when, as a particular case, the *numéraire* chosen is that singularly interesting composite commodity which we have called the 'dynamic standard commodity', then the 'natural rate of interest' (which we may denote in this case by i^*_{h*}) turns out to be equal to the *'standard' rate of growth of productivity*:

$$i^*_{h*} = \varrho^*. \tag{14.7.3}$$

The usual case, however, will be one in which the *numéraire* chosen is a conventional money unit of account and all debt/credit relations are stipulated in terms of such a money unit. In this case, the natural rate of interest (in terms of money) is expressed by the average movement through time of all prices. We know that such movement coincides with the movement through time of the price of the 'dynamic standard commodity'. Hence, we only need to take (14.7.3) and add to it the rate of change, σ_M, of the (unique) price of the dynamic standard commodity in terms of the adopted money unit of account. We obtain:

$$i^*_M = \varrho * + \sigma_M. \qquad (14.7.4)$$

This is the natural, *money*, rate of interest. As we can see, it is simply equal to the sum of two overall magnitudes: the standard rate of growth of productivity and the rate of change of the general level of prices. We may note that all these expressions are equivalent in real terms. They simply represent different ways, in relation to the particular choice of *numéraire*, of making the price system produce the same 'real' effects, that is of making it produce the same structure of (natural) own-rates of interest and thus of preserving intact through time the original purchasing power of all loans in terms of labour.

Notice now that there is a particularly interesting expression that emerges from all these elaborations. Since:

$$\varrho^* + \sigma_M = \varrho^* + \sigma_w - \varrho^* = \sigma_w, \qquad (14.7.5)$$

then (14.7.5) may simply be written:

$$i^*_M = \sigma_w. \qquad (14.7.4a)$$

The consequences are amazing: what we have just stated may also be said of (14.7.3), of (14.7.2), of (14.7.1)! In other words, these three expressions may also be written, respectively, as:

$$i^*_{h*} = \sigma_w, \qquad (14.7.3a)$$

$$i^*_h = \sigma_w, \qquad (14.7.2a)$$

$$i^*_w = \sigma_w, \qquad (14.7.1a)$$

where, in each expression, the wage rate is measured in terms of the corresponding *numéraire*. Thus, in general, *whatever may be the numéraire* that is chosen, the natural rate of interest possesses the remarkable property of always being equal to the rate of growth of the wage rate.

We may well write, without the trouble of any need of any subscript:

$$i^* = \sigma_w, \qquad (14.7.6)$$

where σ_w is the percentage rate of change of the wage rate, expressed in whatever *numéraire* has been chosen as the basis of the price system and of the debt/credit relations. This is the simplest of all expressions of the 'natural rate of interest'!

The definition stated at the beginning of this section may therefore simply and compactly be re-expressed by stating expression (14.7.6). Whatever be the *numéraire* in terms of which debts and credits relations are stipulated, *the 'natural' rate of interest is equal to the rate of growth of the wage rate.*

This is the rate of interest that preserves intact through time the purchasing power of all relations in terms of labour: it is also the final magnitude that completes the *Natural Economic System.*

8 A 'Labour Principle of (Inter-temporal) Income Distribution'

The definition of the natural rate of interest, which has just been given, has practical implications of extraordinary relevance. Let us look at it in very practical but extremely simple terms. In an industrial economy, on average, labour productivity normally grows at a positive rate. This implies that the (actual) natural rate of interest will normally be positive, at least with reference to the *numéraires* so far considered (the only exception occurring when the *numéraire* chosen is the wage rate, which implies by definition $\sigma_w = 0$, and thus a natural rate of interest equal to zero). This means that, when a natural rate of interest is adopted, positive interests will normally have to be paid on loans, at the end of each time period. And it may not be immediately evident what implications this may have for income distribution, in an economic system in which income is to be distributed in proportion to labour contributed to the production processes.

To investigate this question – in an economic system with natural prices, as it has been assumed throughout the present analysis – let us begin by considering first the case in which the *numéraire* chosen is the wage rate and all debt/credit relations are reckoned in terms of labour. One can see clearly, in this case, that in each time period the whole national income is distributed to people in proportion to labour contributed. Then, side by side to the income distribution process carried out by natural prices, at the end of each production period, a whole series of debt/credit relations may come into being, owing to the needs of single individuals to transfer personal consumption through time.

Some people may save and other people may dissave by exchanging positive and negative purchasing power among themselves, while all financial transactions cancel out for the economic system as a whole. Since all debts and credits are in terms of the wage rate, and the natural rate of interest is therefore equal to zero, each creditor will receive, at maturity, an amount of purchasing power, *in terms of labour*, which is exactly equal to the amount originally lent. It appears absolutely clear, in this case, that *the income distribution process, which is in operation, distributes income through time as well as at any given point in time, on the basis of quantities of labour*. All national income, whether at any given point of time or through time, is distributed to all people in proportion to the labour that each one of them has contributed to the production process. We may well say that income is distributed through time according to a *labour principle of income distribution*.

But we can also easily see that the situation remains exactly the same, in real terms, with any other *numéraire* of the price system and of inter-personal debit/credit relations, provided that the *natural rate of interest is charged*. Suppose, for example, that a particular (single or composite) commodity h is taken as the *numéraire* of the price system and that all debt/credit relations are reckoned in terms of commodity h. Then, the natural rate of interest on loans is $i_h^* = \varrho_h$. At the end of each time period, the national income, measured in terms of commodity h, is distributed in proportion to labour contributed to the production process. But now loans are stipulated in terms of commodity h, and since labour productivity in sector h is increasing at rate ϱ_h, the wage rate, in terms of commodity h, will increase through time at rate ϱ_h. This means that, *in terms of the wage rate*, all financial assets are devaluing through time at rate ϱ_h. It is precisely in order to compensate for this devaluation that the (natural) rate of interest $i_h^* = \varrho_h$ has to be paid on all loans. If interests were in fact not paid but accumulated at the end of each period with the amounts of the loans, all financial assets and liabilities would grow in time at rate ϱ_h, in terms of commodity h, but would remain constant in terms of labour. In real terms, the situation would be exactly the same as in the previous case, in which $w(t) = 1$. If, on the other hand, as is more usually the case, interest is actually paid at the end of each time period, then the illusion might be created that some income is distributed to rentiers. But this is not the case. When interest is computed at the natural rate, all paid interests correctly compensate for the devaluation of loans in terms of labour.

The payment of natural interest is therefore revealed to be, in most cases, a partial reimbursement of debt.

Exactly the same arguments could be restated for the case in which a conventional monetary unit of account (paper money) is used as *numéraire* in terms of which all debt/credit relations are stipulated. We have seen that, in this case, the natural rate of interest is $i^*_M = \sigma_M + \varrho^*$ – see (14.7.4) – which is also equal to σ_W, that is, to the rate of increase of the money wage rate. And this is precisely the rate at which all financial assets and liabilities devalue through time in terms of labour. Therefore, the payment of the natural rate of interest – a rate of interest in this case equal to σ_W – again takes the character of a correct compensation of creditors for the devaluation of all their financial assets in terms of labour.

Thus, whatever the *numéraire* in terms of which loans are stipulated, the definition of a natural rate of interest, given in Section 7, allows us to say that the actual payments of natural interest on financial assets have the character of partial repayments of debts, since the debts themselves – when they are stipulated in terms of a *numéraire* other than the wage rate – normally devalue in terms of labour precisely by the amount that is paid as natural interest. Only the payment of *natural* interest correctly compensates for the devaluation of financial assets through time, thereby ensuring that their purchasing power remains unchanged in terms of labour.[11]

We can in fact go on and draw a further important conclusion. Any actual rate of interest, when it differs from the natural rate of interest, inevitably *distorts over time* the distribution of income from taking place in proportion to labour contributed to the production process. A higher than natural rate of interest distorts the distribution of income in favour of creditors (who would be able through time to 'command' more labour than they have 'lent'). And similarly, a lower than natural

[11] Note that the notion of 'natural' rate of interest, as a compensation for a loss of purchasing power, recovers the original etymological meaning of the term 'interest', as distinct from 'usury'. Let me give a couple of references. Noonan (1957) points out that in Roman law, the term 'interest' arose 'In discussing applications for damages because of the non-fulfilment of contractual obligations [...] *Quod interest*, the difference, is what the delinquent party is held to pay the damaged party' (p. 106). Homer (1963) notices that 'The latin verb *intereo* means "to be lost"; a substantive term "*interisse*" developed into the modern term "interest." Interest was not profit but loss' (p. 73).

rate of interest distorts the distribution of income in favour of debtors, for the opposite reasons. Only a natural rate of interest (provided of course that *natural prices* prevail) ensures that no distortion takes place in income distribution.

An alternative way of defining the 'natural' rate of interest is, therefore, simply to say that the natural rate of interest is that particular rate of interest which ensures no distortion from 'the labour principle of (inter-temporal) income distribution'; that is to say from the principle that national income be distributed both at any given point of time and through time, in proportion to labour contributed to the production process.

9 Capitalistic Production, or by Now, the General Case of Production with Labour and Capital Goods

We have reached, at this point, a crucial stage in our investigation. The analysis of the previous pages has led us to the really final stage of our enquiry: namely at the stage of production with capital goods, a stage at which production takes place with labour *and* already produced commodities. This is the stage of *capitalistic* production, which is the basic feature of the modern era – the era that was opened to us by the Industrial Revolution.

But the extraordinarily novel feature of our whole previous analysis is that this novel era has finally landed us with an extremely powerful analytical framework, of extreme simplicity and generality, provided that it is followed up to the end.

We began by carrying out the whole analysis, in this chapter, for the sake of simplicity and clearness, with reference to a pure labour economy. Yet, after the elaborations developed in the *previous* chapters – and more explicitly and openly in Chapter 9 – an extension to the more general case in which production requires not only pure labour, but also capital goods, may be considered at this stage in a surprisingly very expeditious way.

When production takes place with both direct labour and capital goods, *the equilibrium conditions* for the economic system as a whole, as we have seen, entail an amount of overall savings which is equal to the overall amount of new investments. These savings, however, do not concern single individuals! If natural prices prevail and therefore include accumulations gathered with the appropriate 'natural' rates of profit, each vertically hyper-integrated sector of the economy will receive an amount of profits precisely equal to the amount of its required new equilibrium investments. In a 'natural' economic system – *provided of course* that a natural economic system is actually brought into existence (!) – *the production units* would have no need for any borrowing or lending!

All savings that are needed for production purposes automatically accrue to the appropriate sectors, in the appropriate amounts, as an effect of the overall operation of the natural price system (which includes, let us remember, physical accumulation through the 'natural' profits). This also means that production units (the whole production section of the economy) will never need to be involved in paying any interest, simply because they will never need to undertake any loan!

At the same time, however, and of course separately – that is through a (virtually separate) *financial system* – all borrowing and lending possibilities remain entirely open to single individuals, *precisely in the same way*, as was examined in the previous simplified case, of a pure labour economy!

Note that, from the very conception of a 'natural' production system, total consumption has to be equal to total wages, exactly as in the previous case of a pure labour economy. The only difference with respect to the previous, simpler, case is that total consumption, for the economic system as a whole, is now represented no longer by total national income, but by total national income minus the amount of equilibrium new investments: more explicitly by total gross national income minus *both replacements and also new investments*. The major conclusion of the previous, simpler, case therefore remains unaltered: if we abstract from *durable consumption goods*, which for simplicity we have left aside – but could easily be dealt with separately at this stage – *the equilibrium total amount of consumption cannot be transferred through time* (as was underlined in Section 2). Within each single time period, it is either produced and consumed, *or it is lost*, through idle productive capacity. And when it is lost, it is lost for ever; it cannot be recovered![12]

12 As suggested above in §2, completing the model with the existence of durable consumption goods can be carried out separately at this stage. What is needed, from an analytical point of view, is not difficult to imagine and carried out (Graziani 1989, p. 3).

But again, as we may notice *and repeat at this stage*, what is impossible to the economic system as a whole (owing to the requirements of the production side of the natural economic system) remains indeed possible to any single individual, or groups of individuals. Each single individual – and his/her family – are in a position to consume more or to consume less than their incoming incomes, to any extent, *provided that* some other individuals (and their families, or more likely, some public institutions) are prepared to do the opposite. The only constraint that is in operation is therefore the same macro-economic constraint that has emerged from our analysis of the previous, simpler, case. For the economic system as a whole, all personal lending and personal borrowing exactly compensate each other, and, overall, are cancelling out.

The problems previously considered thus continue to arise here, as before, concerning the *coming into being of financial assets and liabilities*, due to interpersonal credit/debts relations. And the related problem arises – exactly as in the simpler case considered above – of finding which rate of interest is the appropriate one to apply to all these inter-personal loans. But after our elaborations concerning the concepts of vertical hyper-integration, the conclusion of the previous analysis can simply be extended in a straightforward manner. We may in fact go straight to the conclusion drawn before, at the end of Section 7 and begin by simply repeating that there exists a 'natural' rate of interest which is that particular rate of interest that *preserves intact over time the original purchasing power of all loans in terms of labour*. In other words, in general, and quite independently of whether we consider a production economic system that does or does not need capital goods, the natural rate of interest is indeed equal to the percentage rate of growth of the wage rate, in terms of whatever *numéraire* has been chosen for all transactions.

As far as the natural rate of interest is concerned, very little needs in fact to be added here to show the general validity of these remarkable propositions. All that is required is a re-interpretation of the symbols used to represent the structure of the own-rates of interest. To make this point clear, let us use the same expedient adopted before and suppose, for simplicity, that we choose the *numéraire* that makes the rate of growth of the wage rate exactly zero. More specifically, in this case, we may begin by supposing, for simplicity, that the wage rate is fixed at unity for all time (i.e. $w(t) = 1$). The actual 'natural' rate of interest, in this case, turns out to be equal to zero. But, at the same time, the price of each single commodity j, in terms of the wage rate, as appears from (10.9.2), will decrease in time at a percentage rate which is a weighted average of the rate of growth of productivity in sector j and the rate of growth of productivity in sector k_i (the sector that produces capital goods for sector j). As we have seen, this (weighted average) rate of growth of productivity is a rate of growth which is vertically integrated one further, or one forward (according to how we look at it) stage back, or forward, that is vertically hyper-integrated, so as to include also the making of all the capital goods necessary to produce each consumption good j, $(j = 1, 2, \dots, n-1)$. We have come across this rate of change, since the beginning, in Chapter 10 of Section 16 and we have denoted it by the symbol ϱ_i'. This represents the rate of growth of productivity in the vertically hyper-integrated sector for consumption good j. It clearly follows that, when $w(t) = 1$, the (implicit) own-rates of interest for all the $(n-1)$ consumption goods will be:

$$\varrho_1',\ \varrho_2', \dots, \varrho_{n-1}'. \tag{14.9.1}$$

Thus, all that we need to do is to replace the $\varrho_1, \varrho_2, \dots, \varrho_{n-1}$ of our analysis in this whole chapter, that is in Sections 3–8, with the $\varrho_1', \varrho_2', \dots, \varrho_{n-1}'$ specified above, which represent the rates of growth of productivity in the $(n-1)$ vertically hyper-integrated sectors of our economic system. These are also the 'natural' (implicit) own-rates of interest for the $(n-1)$ final consumption goods.

We may well go over, now as before if we like, to alternatively consider the cases of all other possible alternative *numéraire*. And we may indeed simply refer to the corresponding expressions which have been obtained in our previous analysis. Again these expressions remain the same for the general case of production with capital goods, provided only that the simple rates of growth of productivity ϱ_1, $\varrho_2, \dots,$ ϱ_{n-1}, indicated before, are replaced by the corresponding, more general (and comprehensive), rates of growth of productivity ϱ_1', $\varrho_2', \dots,$ ϱ_{n-1}', referring to the vertically hyper-integrated sectors for consumption goods 1, 2,…, $n-1$, respectively. These latter rates of growth of productivity include the former as special cases. We need not repeat, therefore, but simply confirm, the analysis of Sections 3 and 8), and of Section 18 of Chapter 10 (which refers to the money inflation rates).

The conclusion is that – after the development of the concepts of vertical integration and, then, of vertical hyper-integration – the introduction of capital goods (single or many period-lasting) into our analysis carries no *logical* complication into our previously considered relations.

As to the final analysis of Section 8, there is not even any need to replace any symbol. The 'natural' structure of the own-rates of interest, as expressed here by (14.9.1), is precisely the structure which is produced, in real terms, by the actual 'natural' rate of interest:

$$i^* = \sigma_w, \tag{14.9.2}$$

where σ_w is the rate of increase of the wage rate in terms of whatever *numéraire* has been chosen, be it a single or a composite physical commodity, or labour, or indeed any conventional monetary unit of account (paper money or else).

The definition stated by a relation as simple as (14.9.2) – namely a rate of interest that is equal to the rate of increase of the wage rate, in terms of whatever *numéraire* has been chosen, for both the whole production price system and for the financial assets evaluations – is therefore confirmed as *a completely general definition of the natural rate of interest.*

10 Necessity of an Institutionally created Central Agency (or Agencies) for the Management, Control and Supervision of all Financial Activities

At this point, what emerges quite strikingly is the absolute necessity in a modern industrial system to be equipped with a Central institutionally conceived Agency (or more likely Agencies!), to be in charge of the management, supervision and control of the whole of the national financial activities. This is the third time in our analysis of the *Natural Economic System* that the need emerges of a centrally conceived Institution. But, in the present case, this need emerges in an exceptionally stronger and even major way. This point is so important as to compel us not to forget but to draw back to the problem more than once in our analysis.

For the time being, let me simply recall the previous occasions when similar institutional needs were signalled to arise. The first time was in the case, which emerged immediately in our investigation on production, of the physical necessity of ensuring the tendency to full employment of labour (and full utilisation of production capacity), jointly with the actual realisation of new equilibrium investments required for economic growth (see Chapter 10, Section 8). We called these necessities, respectively, overall (macro-economic) equilibrium condition and sectoral equilibrium investment conditions for the economic growth of the whole economic system.

The second time was in the almost parallel analytical connection of the necessity of choosing the *numéraire* of the price system and the subsequent decision of its evolution through time by the fixing of the rate of increase of the level of prices (i.e. the monetary – or price – inflation). Practically, this meant the beginning of the institutional requirements and needs of Central Banking (see Chapter 10, Sections 17 and 20).

The third time is the present one. In the literature, this case is usually almost too easily confused with the second (the Central Banking case) – even though the choice of the same *numéraire* is normally jointly made for both monetary purposes and financial purposes, (though this does not necessarily need to be so – see Section 3). But the present, third, case is by far so much wider as in fact to be something historically new. As it has emerged quite promptly from the present chapter, this new social function of the Central Bank is considerably more comprehensive and extremely more variegated (than the one concerned with the much earlier, but simpler, function of the monetary activity of a Central Bank) as to require it being singled out as such. It is time that we consider it more appropriately here as a very specific institutional necessity emerging from the particular characteristics of the capitalistic era. It is so variegated as to emerge quite strikingly, only at this stage, on our proceeding *beyond* the analysis of the process of production and as to require the setting up, not merely of a unique Central Agency, but presumably and more extensively, of a plurality of inter-related Financial Institutions, owing to the complexity of the financial activities, as they have been evolving in the modern industrial structure. It would only appear superfluous to state that all these modern financial activities immediately entail the necessity of being centrally coordinated. Their multiform evolution is clearly an absolute characteristic of modern Finance in the industrial age.

In any case, by now it must be emphasised that all three of the just listed circumstances, even if they originally emerged separately from one another – not merely in economic investigations, but in the evolving practices of an industrial society – share the common characteristic that they cannot be left to the spontaneous behaviour of single individuals. They all require the creation of highly complex social coordination and thus of highly (complex) institutional organisations: sometimes not merely at the national, but in fact also at the international level.

As usual in our present analysis, we shall abstain from entering into the further details and complications concerning the workings of the *Institutions* behind the major field of Modern Finance, unless where it may become absolutely necessary. It is already quite clear from our investigation that the task of fixing the overall rate of interest cannot but be an *institutional* task. But the process of determining its natural level comes from the whole structure of the production economic system. This is what we have achieved in the present chapter.

11 The Natural Rate of Interest (as against the 'Natural' Rate of Profit)

It may be useful and interesting to stop for a moment at this point and briefly reflect on what paradoxically emerges at a distance as an entirely new variable in our analytical framework; namely, the rate of interest. The paradox is that – as we all know – the rate of interest is perhaps one of the oldest of all the economic variables that appear in economic investigations!

Yet, what is really impressive is how detached the rate of interest has emerged in our analysis with respect to the rate of profit. This may well be one of the most striking aspects of our entire investigation.

Note that this detachment is sharp and drastic and goes against tradition.

Historically, the rate of interest appeared millennia ago – it even pops up in the Gospels' parables. On the other hand, the rate of profit, at least the 'natural' rate of profit, which is what concerns us in the present investigation, is a recent phenomenon: the concept is inherent to the industrial age.

Let us briefly retrace our analysis on this matter.

To begin with, it is important to stress that the 'natural rate of interest' has emerged from a purely *financial*, inter-personal analysis, in the present chapter. The 'natural rate of profit', on the other hand, emerged from the analysis, in earlier in this book, of the *physical production* framework of the Natural Economic System. Logically, the two concepts, as they have been coming out in our analysis, are quite distinct.

This might seem strange, since in our analysis they originate from the very same theoretical scheme. But, nonetheless, they are two entirely different concepts and magnitudes, and they *must not be confused* with each other.[13]

To substantiate this claim, let's take a step by step look at their simple algebra.

We had seen in the previous three Chapters 11–13 that, in any 'natural' economic system, there is a whole series of (explicit) 'natural' *rates of profit*:

$$\pi_j^* = g + r_j, \qquad j = 1, 2, \ldots, n-1, \tag{14.11.1}$$

which – through the working of all hyper-integrated sectors – allow the required expansion of the production of all consumption goods.

Next, we have seen in the present chapter, that by considering what is bound to happen *after the process of production* has taken place, situations may come into existence of personal debt and credit interrelations, from which there also emerges a parallel series of (in this case) *implicit* 'natural' (yet real) own-*rates of interest*, connected with the various rates of growth of the labour productivities, namely with the series:

$$\varrho_i', \qquad i = 1, 2, \ldots, n-1, \tag{14.11.2}$$

in a way that would maintain, constant through time, in terms of labour, the purchasing power of all financial assets expressed on the basis of any arbitrarily chosen *numéraire*.

We can immediately see at this point, from the above analytical expressions, that since g is a rate of growth of the labour force, r_j is a rate of growth of per-capita demand for each consumption good j, and ϱ_i' is a (vertically hyper-integrated) rate of growth of productivity for each single sector i, then the natural rates of profit, as expressed by (14.11.1), cannot but be different in general from the natural *own* rates of interest as expressed by (14.11.2).

In fact, the entire previous analysis has been deliberately carried out in such a way as to make this contrast emerge sharply. The notion

[13] Of course, the confusion is generally made and has persisted for centuries in the economic literature, due to the coming into being of the *particular institutions* of the capitalist economies, as we shall more specifically bring to new evidence in the following pages.

of a 'natural own-rate of interest' has emerged, in the central part of the present chapter, from a theoretical scheme in which *ex-hypothesis* (as for the sake of simplicity and clarity we have supposed) there is no production of physical capital goods and therefore there cannot be any rate of profit. Similarly, in Chapter 12, the notion of a natural rate of profit emerged from a theoretical scheme in which there are no inter-personal debt/credit relations, and therefore there cannot be any rate of interest.

These relations show most clearly that a 'natural rate of interest', as we have defined it, may indeed exist without the necessary existence of any rate of profit, and conversely a 'natural rate of profit' may indeed exist without the necessary existence of any rate of interest.

Yet, both these concepts emerge from precisely the same approach to economic reality! The 'natural rate of profit' stems from the principle that – within the process of production – all prices be proportional to the physical quantities of labour that have been required by them in a dynamic context, and this expresses an *entirely generalised labour theory of value*. On the other hand, the 'natural rate of interest' stems from the principle that, within the financial system, all individuals, when they undertake debt/credit inter-relations, should be able to maintain through time their holding of an amount of purchasing power that remains constant in terms of labour. This symmetrically represents an *entirely generalised labour theory of inter-temporal income re-distribution*. The two aspects of these entirely generalised labour theories of value and of income re-distribution imply, and complete, each other.

The (apparent) difference between the two theories comes from their expressing the same basic principles within two separate spheres of economic activity. The 'natural' rate of profit pertains to the *sphere of production*, which, in a 'natural economic system', is complete in itself and does not *necessarily need external financial transactions* to achieve its 'natural' self-sustained growth. The rate of interest, on the other hand, pertains to the sphere of deferred (or anticipated) consumption, that is to the needs that individual consumers (or group of consumers) have to transfer (individually chosen parts of) personal income to actual consumption at some (individually chosen) point of time in the future (or in the past in anticipation of present needs). This sphere too is complete in itself, while all inter-personal borrowing and lending cancel each other out for the economic system as a whole, quite independently of what is meanwhile emerging from the sphere of production.

To conclude, there is no *logical* reason, to associate the concept of a natural rate of profit to the concept of a *natural* rate of interest. Theoretically and conceptually, they are distinct from each other. *They represent two entirely different concepts altogether*, and they are aimed at performing two different, though complementary and essential, social functions: namely, the determination of those 'natural' values of the produced goods and services that concern equilibrium investments for economic growth; and the maintenance, through time, of a 'natural personal distribution of income' in terms of labour content (embodied and commanded): not merely at the strict stage of production, but also at any other time in the future (and past).

12 The *Macro-economic* Nature of the Actual, Unique (and Explicit) 'Natural' Rate of Interest

The counter-position, and confrontation, just made, of the two concepts (of the 'natural' rates of profit and of the 'natural' rates of interest) has not yet arrived at the completion of our investigation. There is still one final step that must be taken.

The $(n-1)$ 'natural' rates of profit (each one of them for every corresponding vertically hyper-integrated sector) are all real and explicit, as each of them is expressed in terms of the finally produced commodity which it has contributed to produce.

At the same time, the $(n - 1)$ 'natural' own-rates of interest (one for each produced consumption good) are also 'real' – each one of them concerning the specific commodity to which it refers. But they cannot be seen explicitly because they are *implicitly* and inherently built into the whole network of the 'structural dynamics of prices and quantities' of the whole economic system.

Yet, there is one major way in which the 'natural rate of interest' can be seen explicitly with reference to the economic system considered as a whole. We arrived at it already in Section 7! Following from expressions (14.7.4)–(14.7.6), we obtained:

$$i^* = \sigma_w = \varrho^* + \sigma_M. \tag{14.12.1}$$

This is indeed one of the most remarkable outcomes of the present analysis.

We can see here that the 'natural' rate of interest, i^*, emerges *explicitly* from its composition as the sum of the 'standard' rate of growth of productivity, ϱ^*, and of the rate of monetary inflation, σ_M. Both these magnitudes are *macro-economic*: they concern the entire economic system.

As we have seen, their definition implies two preliminary operations:

(i) the computation of the 'standard' (weighted average) rate of growth of productivity ϱ^* (see Chapter 10, Section 13);
(ii) the choice of the *numéraire* in terms of which debt/credit relations, that is all financial assets, are denominated, where-from emerges σ_M, the evolution in time of the general level of prices, or rate of monetary inflation.

Notice the crucial property of both ϱ^* and σ_M, appearing on the right-hand side of (14.12.1): they are both macro-economic concepts. They emerge from the economic system taken as a whole. This implies that the (unique) *explicit* expression of the 'natural' rate of interest, that is of (14.12.1) (in striking contrast with the rate(s) of profit!) is a *macro-economic* magnitude. Curiously, yet significantly enough, we may also note that this is a basic property that, in the now complete *Natural Economic System*, the 'natural' rate of interest (14.12.1) shares with the wage rate! (see Section 9).

In other words – and let me repeat it, in order to stress the importance of these properties – the '*natural* rate of interest' and the 'natural wage rate' are both *macro-economic* concepts. Hence, each is unique and specific to the overall economic system to which it refers.[14]

13 Production versus Finance, or Else Value versus Inter-temporal Income Re-distribution

We may well proceed to the final, concluding, logical steps of our whole analytical and theoretical framework.

The most unexpected – and perhaps, dare I say, – astonishing implication of the elaborations that have just come to completion is the

[14] By contrast, the natural rates of profit (in the plural!) are sectoral magnitudes. In each economic system there exist as many 'natural' rates of profit as there are vertically hyper-integrated sectors. Nonetheless, there is one single macro-economic, natural rate of interest!

sharp distinction that has emerged – within the *natural economic system* – between (i) the sphere of industrial production and (ii) the sphere of income distribution (which more appropriately has emerged from our analysis as a sphere of inter-temporal income *re-distribution*!). The first refers to *physical* concepts and magnitudes, the second to *financial* concepts. In more simple terms, the first refers to what has happened in the past, and the second refers to what may happen in the future.

As we have seen, the sphere of production starts from the original labour inputs – through the whole complex inter-industry, or more compactly, hyper-integrated framework – and proceeds to the production of goods and services devoted to consumption. It ideally ends with the distribution of *all* the produced national income, under the form of wages, to the active part of the population, [strikingly and] wholly, for [their] consumption.

But, in any advanced stage of an industrial society, this is not the end of the *natural economic system*. Precisely at this point, the sphere of debt/credit relations – in comprehensive terms, that is the sphere of what may be called the *Finance* of an industrial economic system – opens up. Production has been completed, but, the *natural economic system* proceeds beyond production, through a complex, vast network of debt/credit relations, which constitute an intricate panoply of *financial stocks* of assets and liabilities, into which the industrial society has recently, more specifically, immersed us. Let us note again: these financial stocks (inserted in between the sphere of production and the sphere of consumption) have nothing specifically *physical* behind them, they are strictly financial, we might even add *immaterial*. They play a double and crucial role by being partly positive and partly negative, in such a precise way as to cancel out in the aggregate – their algebraic sum, at any time, adding up to zero. But in this way, while zero in the aggregate, they are extraordinarily effective in their singularity. Far from being irrelevant, they have the possibility of piling up, simultaneously, in the positive and in the negative directions, with different and variegated structures and distributions, to really huge amounts, nowdays well beyond the size of the system's yearly national income itself. Their division in two lots (one positive and the other negative), even if matching up and cancelling out in the aggregate, is conferring to our modern societies possibilities and characteristics that had been unimaginable in the past. A whole literature has recently spread on what has been called, with (undue but myopic) admiration, the well-diffused so-called *financialisation* of our 'capitalist' economies, even to induce the (false) suggestion that it may generate *additional* incomes!

This is of course an illusion! Yet, we may wonder: where have the two traditional aspects of value and of income distribution – about which so much has been written in the past two centuries – gone into hiding? No surprise of course: the problem of value and the problem of income distribution are inevitably intertwined. But, our analysis of the *natural economic system* shows that the substantial process is taking place in a radically different manner than what has been taken for granted so far. This illusion has been mainly caused by the development of the *financial institutions*, which have recently been extensively created, especially in the particular 'capitalist' societies of recent times. Quite simply, if we accept that income becomes effective only through the final fulfilment of real consumption, then, as we have seen, consumers may choose to shift and distribute the satisfaction of their incomes far away (forward and/or backward in time) from the strict accomplishment of the production process. And this may be taking place with the help of a fantastic collection of *purely financial* (immaterial) assets and liabilities, which almost unbelievably have recently been invented and have become so prominent as to characterise the whole financial world, even if essentially in the end they add up (or should add up) to zero![15]

It might be tempting to ask: what happened? Have the earlier aspects of production and distribution now been turned into the two novel aspects of production and finance? (Let's reflect on what this would mean: wages and interest as being turned into distributive variables?)

Obviously not! The natural rate of interest can never be a *distributive* variable in this context. At most, we might call it an *ancillary*, or *auxiliary*, variable, whose purpose is (or should be) that of avoiding any *distortions* from the basic principle – always to be kept intact – of assuring constancy through time, as well as at any time, of all *evaluations of assets* in terms of that unique physical magnitude, which is dominating from the centre the whole *Natural Economic System*: namely human labour, or more comprehensively, if we like, the whole human anthropological activity.

[15] [Specification needed of the simplifying assumptions analytically used in order to obtain these amazingly clear and neat results?]

14 The Auxiliary Role of Financial Capital – Out of Nothing and Yet Needing an Appropriate, Perhaps Even a Radical Re-Thinking of Our Financial Institutions

The conclusions just reached are so important as to deserve some further reflections, which will be made here for the purpose of clarifying basic concepts – even at the risk of some repetitions and of a few temporary, non-realistic assumptions. To do this, I shall again refer to two analytically useful expedients (two logical, hypothetical models), which in fact have been used since the beginning of the present investigation: namely the model of a pure labour economy (which we may take here as our analytic *phase one*) and then the novel and central case of capitalistic accumulation (analytic phase two; to be resumed in Section 15).

These two schemes have the peculiar, but extremely useful and interesting, property of allowing us to analyse the concepts concerning the rate of interest separately into two quite distinct situations: one without and the other with the presence of physical Capital. This allows us to place the two situations in stark contrast with each other.

Let's first consider the case of a hypothetical pure labour economic system in which – let me stress! – there are *no physical capital goods*, but in which nevertheless, technology is consistently supposed to be improving all the time: every good or service being produced by labour alone. Let us assume, for analytical purposes only (soon to be dropped), that each consumption good or service is such as to require to be totally consumed at the end of each production period. In this logical framework (analytic *phase one*), all goods are strictly *consumption* goods. There are no physical capital goods simply because, according to the hypotheses made, they are not technologically necessary for the production process. Moreover, let's assume that the whole National Product (it does not matter whether net or gross, as the two would coincide in this case) at the end of each production period is entirely consumed. The reader should not be alarmed by the non-realism of these assumptions (which are only made temporarily): these suppositions are only set as a logical expedient to highlight, in a clear and simple manner, certain concepts important for our purposes. Their *raison d'être* is simply to create a net and clear distinction between the *stocks* of *physical* capital goods and the monetary stocks of *financial* assets, which can be created out of nothing in our logical *phase one* (having supposed that there are no physical capital goods). But, evidently this does not at all exclude that there may be *monetary* and *financial stocks* (as indeed we are supposing). People, or associations of people, can very well exchange securities with which to undertake credit and debt relations, denominated in terms of a conventional unit of purchasing power. These debt/credit securities may have coordinated dates of expiration, based upon pre-established agreements (with debt and credit contracts), so that the loans can return to those who set their desired deadlines with various agreed inter-temporal configurations. The *relevant aspect to stress* here is that there can be *stocks of debts and credits*, which represent purchasing power to be exerted at specific points in time, *even if no corresponding physical stocks exist in nature*. The relevant analytic characteristic is precisely that we are hypothesising an economic system which, while having *no stocks of real physical goods*, has created a variety of financial stocks that are set up out of nothing, that is financial *stocks* (positive and negative), which cancel themselves out overall. This means *financial wealth* for the creditors, but nonetheless, at the same time, cancelling out in the system as a whole, they equivalently set up financial liabilities (a negative wealth) of those who are indebted. Hence, overall, in this pure labour model in equilibrium growth, *net* wealth in financial terms does *not* exist: the sum of credits and debts cancel out. For the community as a whole its worth is zero. Naturally, as we have seen already, there may be multiple justifications for the existence of such (positive and negative) financial stocks. The most obvious, already mentioned one, is that each economic agent can benefit from the flow of positive buying power (typically originated by wages for one's work) and from the cumulation of *negative* buying power of a accumulation of already enjoyed consumer goods. When the wage flows do not coincide in time with the desired consumption flows, the need arises for money and credit securities of various types to be circulated (let us notice!) with the help of *monetary and financial institutions* – *external* to production – which act as intermediaries, to facilitate the smooth acquisition of wages, on the one side, and then on the other side, smooth flowing expenditures on consumer goods. [giving rise to inter-temporal networks of debts and credits relations, which correspond to various desires and preferences of when to undertake their actual consumption]

[Notice that one could well introduce in this financially conceived model all the complexities one would like to consider on credit and debt securities, issued by *institutionally created agencies*, and stipulating contracts which include debtors paying interest to creditors in the most varied and sophisticated ways imaginable.]

The relevant feature to stress for our purposes is that a simple hypothetical pure labour economic system – in other words, an economic system in which *there are no real physical capital stocks* – can create debt/credit relations to no end, even if, they cancel out on the whole.

Thus, purely financial stocks can be created out of nothing and without limits, to the personal satisfaction of people who are acting to shift their actual consumption through time according to their preferences.

It is important to stress that this is precisely the relevant and basic characteristic of the financial means which have been invented and developed, especially recently. In fact, this is the strikingly extraordinary feature of all financialised monetary economies, even those of zero overall net wealth, while a pure labour model, as used here, emerges perhaps as the most logically consistent scheme that brings forth their characteristics.

There is no doubt, therefore, that these characteristics – limitless possibilities of purely financial stocks – open up a whole *new* field of investigation, which concerns, however, the realm of *institutions* (specifically the *financial* institutions), not the realm of the *Natural Economic System*, which in itself is already complete and remains entirely independent of institutions.

There is nothing, therefore, that the analysis of these financial institutions can add to our analyses and properties of the *Natural Economic System*, except at most the minor costs of their intermediation services (if and when their costs are justified). On the other hand, there really is a whole lot that the framework of an ideal *Natural Economic System* is going to give us in terms of concepts and relations concerning the actual financial institutions (!), whose ideal function is thereby basically and strikingly revealed to be an *auxiliary* one, aimed at achieving a more sensible, inter-temporal re-distribution of desired consumption, as well as at eliminating – through the charging of a *natural* rate of interest – any *deviation* from the *natural* course of a distribution of income, always corresponding to embodied quantities of labour (i.e. in essence the prevention of any deviations from what we earlier called (see Section 8) the *labour principle of income distribution*). The problem would exist, of course, of searching for the appropriate institutions in order to achieve the *Natural Economic System*! But, this is quite a different and further matter: we will have to come back to it in the following pages.

[To this purpose nevertheless, it is not difficult to realise that the financial institutions that are at present operating in the economic systems in which we live, the so-called capitalist societies, clearly appear to be in need of considerable (in fact of a rather revolutionary) process of rethinking.]

15 Introduction of *physical* Capital Accumulation (Our Analytical Stage Two) [Immediately Generating Stark Contrasts with the Pure Labour Analytical Model]

We may well proceed to our second analytically logical stage, with the introduction of physical capital goods. This is obviously the really relevant and crucial phase of our analysis, as it plunges us precisely into the investigations of the economic features of the *novel* epoch of our times – the era of the mode of production with capital goods (the 'capitalistic' stage).

We know already, from our previous analysis, that all capital goods essentially come from labour inputs, even if in different ways (whether in direct, indirect or hyper-indirect form).

Hence, the immediate question that arises is whether the analysis just carried out with reference to a pure labour production model is strictly extendable to a more complete stage in which there is capital accumulation. We may recall, that we have already faced this problem, though in a different context, in Section 9. There, we gave it a straight, logical answer. Here the question may deserve some further reflections, but the *logical* answer remains the same.

Yes indeed: the logical answer to the stated question remains the same as given in Section 9. The properties of the analysis we have already carried out there, namely the central property of the limitless possibilities of carrying out *purely financial* debt/credit transactions, and the consequent effect of a *re-distribution in time* of individually chosen (positive or negative) amounts of purchasing power, all remain exactly the same, in spite of our having accessed analytical stage two – the one concerning capital accumulation.

This unequivocally means that when we *extend* to 'capitalistic' production the whole analysis concerning the *purely financial* operations examined in Sections 1–14, with regard to both the determination of the natural rate of interest and the re-distribution of the *consumption* purchasing power *over time*, the answers that we have obtained remain exactly the same.

But of course the extension must be made in the correct way!

And it is here that a major problem immediately appears. In analytical terms, when we make such an extension, a clash emerges against a most important and huge proviso, which – to be precise – has been already implied throughout our entire analysis. This is the proviso of operating in a *Natural Economic System.*

I am making this proviso re-emerge explicitly now, owing to the hunch that the great majority of my readers may still be reasoning in terms of our existing and pervasive institutions, that is according to the 'capitalist' economies[16]; and they may easily tend to forget it. Not to mention that in the 'capitalist' societies in which most of us live, the inducement to forego the mentioned proviso is quite diffuse.

However, the proviso is so basic to the whole of our analysis as to place the case of production *with* capital in stark *physical* contrast with the case of production with labour alone (with no capital). Essentially, the relevant proviso is that the whole production system we are considering should satisfy the configuration of the *Natural Economic System*. And a *Natural Economic System*, as we know, requires a series of strict physical (not financial!) *equilibrium conditions.* The list of these conditions was given at the beginning of Chapter 10, and has never been abandoned. (They are also mentioned in Section 2 of the present chapter though for a different purpose.)

Such equilibrium conditions, in the previous case of a pure labour economy, essentially and simply concern and come down to the fulfilment of the usual macro-economic effective demand condition. This condition was so obvious as to be taken for granted above. But, in any case, the reader may now have already noticed or realised that it is precisely the process of *physical* capital accumulation that conducts the *equilibrium conditions* forward in relevance and importance. Perhaps it may be useful to compactly re-express the gist of the *equilibrium conditions* of the *Natural Economic System* in the case of

[16] Please keep in mind the crucially different meanings of the two terms: 'capitalist' and 'capitalistic', which have been here adopted and used, explicitly since the *Prologue.*

capitalistic production. They must concern the following two propositions. First, deploying all possible efforts to achieve and maintain full employment of the labour force while, at the same time, deepening the level and structure of human knowledge. (This condition was of course already present in the pure labour model considered in Section 14. But, in that context, it was made irrelevant due to the assumption of the non-existence of capital goods). Second (now the crucially relevant proposition), the physical requirements must include the concrete carrying out of all those *physical* investments that are newly required by the economic growth of the novel *industrial* branches of the economy. Essentially, this means the actual bringing into being of all the *new investments* specified in the vertically hyper-integrated part of the economic system. These are precisely the *physical* conditions that express the actual carrying out of the specific innovative branches of a developed industrial economic system. This is what should have been quite evident since the beginning, when the *Natural Economic System* was effectively brought into being, through the flows of the natural rates of profit, which provide the required savings in the correct amounts to every hyper-integrated growing sub-sector of the whole economic system. Notice that no problem of finance arises in the economic system at this stage. This is nothing but the physical expression of the structural dynamics that so deeply characterises the modern capitalistic system of production, with all financial needs exactly being met by the emerging *internal natural* amounts of profits, according to the requirements of the new investment equilibrium conditions (see Chapter 10, Section 4).

It may well appear paradoxical that while the characteristics revealed by the hypothetical model of pure labour, that is, the model with no capital goods, are quite simple and explicit in helping us understand the meanings of the extraordinary magnitudes and sizes of modern Finance (so large as to allow reaching huge, almost infinite possibilities, even if in the aggregate they come out to nothing!), the characteristics revealed, on the other hand, by the undertaking of the sectoral equilibrium investments and thus of the equilibrium accumulation of *physical* capital, impose such specific and definite quantitative constraints on the whole framework of the capitalistic mode of production, as to bring about precisely those whole and major structural dynamic constructions, which are the unmistakably evident feature of all up-to-date modern economic systems. And all this, as we may now realise, in strikingly *physical* magnitudes and forms, and not only in the broad field of finance, however complex it might be, but most of all in the tangibly physical aspects and shapes of the complex constructions characterising the whole modern industrial world!

The contrasts between the two analytical stages (the first with pure labour alone and the second – here being resumed – with labour and capital goods) are in this way conspicuously revealed.

Institutionally considered, this is the crucial passage that must be adopted – in fact, imposed – in order to finally arrive at the actual, effective, realisation of the *Natural Economic System*.

16 The Relevance of Durable Consumption Goods [besides that of Durable Capital Goods]

An opening must now be made in another direction. Up to here we have practically examined two separate analytical stages: one with pure labour and no capital goods (analytical stage 1), and the other with both labour and capital goods, that is, full capitalistic production (analytical stage 2).

But we should not forget that these two analytical stages, interesting and useful as they may have been, do not exhaust the enormous possibilities of our modern economic systems. For convenience, in both analytical stages, we have made the assumption that all produced consumption goods are immediately consumed. But, we are now able to drop this assumption. This means that in what we originally called analytical stage 1, we must now also add the possibility of the production of durable consumption goods. Moreover and symmetrically, in analytical stage 2, besides the durable capital goods, we must now also add the production of durable consumption goods. Essentially, we now come to have a new, more comprehensive stage (shall we call it analytical stage 3?), containing both durable consumption goods and *durable* capital goods. What are the consequences of this change?

We might well say that there is almost nothing that we can add to what we said for our analytical stage 2, where there could now be the production of both durable consumption goods and durable capital goods. But there is so much more that can happen when we add durable consumption goods to analytical stage 1. Of course, this change should not come as a surprise. Think of the typically representative durable good – namely gold – which since time immemorial has been a commodity that fulfils the durability function both as an exchangeable good (able to be converted into other desired commodities at any chosen point in time) and as money itself.

Lets reflect on this. The introduction of a more comprehensive analytical stage 3, which allows both consumers and producers to undertake inter-temporal transactions, is very far from being a minor change! The addition of durable goods, most particularly when considered within a production 'capitalist' institutional economic system, introduces in our analysis another dramatic turning point in our industrial history. This will become much clearer in the following pages.

17 An Apparent Terminological Squabble (Capitalist vs Capitalistic), Absconding, and Thus Confusing, a Most Strategic Epochal Change of Our Time

At this stage, our analysis seems to have led us to a dramatic showdown. The whole of our investigation had the purpose of setting together a logically consistent framework, which we have called the *natural* economic system. But, a *Natural Economic System*, as we already stated from the beginning and will be further expanded in the following chapter, does not come into existence by itself. It needs a set of *institutions* in charge of bringing it into existence. If this is so – we might well ask – where could we find an example (or an explicit attempt to achieve an example) of a *Natural Economic System* in the real world of today?

The extraordinary, unbelievable, surprising thing is that this question is doomed to remain unanswered.

No actual economic system on the face of the earth is at present conceived with the *explicit* aim of achieving a *natural* economic system; not even conceptually in the minds of its bureaucrats, or politicians, or ideologues, or indeed economists. Yet this problem is crucial; it is only in the direction of a *Natural Economic System* that our analysis can take steps towards a consistent, final, logical framework.

Of course, as we all know, we must admit that something entirely new has recently happened. An entirely novel economic category – what we have called *Capital* – in all its many forms, features, shapes and consequences, has conspicuously and most dramatically characterised the recent surging of our anthropological new age.

This has not been a hidden, or unperceived, change in the economic systems in which we live. It has been a major change affecting the production structure of the economic systems, which have been altering their anthropological shapes.

But, after the initial enthusiastic discovery of this novelty (think of the vibrating enthusiasm among the Physiocrats in the eighteenth century!), a tragic, collective overall change seems to have taken place in the profession of the Political Economists themselves! Widespread misconception seems to have been infused in almost all analytical elaborations, which have percolated through our economics textbooks, through the whole of economic literature and even into our common parlance. Almost the entire profession and most of our famous fellow-economists seem to have got the observable ('capitalistic') industrial structure and its institutions mixed up in a most unbelievable confusion.[17] They have, all too quickly, called our economies *capitalist* (not 'capitalistic'), but this has happened in a very queer sense.

What, in fact, has come to be called *capitalist* is a sort of particular *institutional* construction and setup of society, characterised by a re-shaping of old-fashioned *institutional* relations, especially with reference to the role of private property and of the appearance of *capital goods*. All too easily and quickly, what has been attempted is to assimilate the novel problems, that have come into existence with the help of capital goods, to other features that had once characterised *earlier* societies, especially with reference to land and natural resources. And the whole profession seems to have been collectively misled. It has come to miss the very important fact that it is *capital* itself that is the real *novel feature* – not merely as something to be investigated as inherited from the past, but rather as a strikingly novel category of the new structure of our society, even when it takes advantage of old objects and concepts.

All this has become, in various forms, radically new in the very objective and technical sense that production is carried out with the use of goods which are themselves part of the goods that already exist or are an adaptation of newly invented and *produced* goods. In

[17] In what sense? I am glad to have been able to present, in the foregoing pages, the two crucial analytical schemes (one with the hypothetical absence, and the other with the insertion of *produced* capital goods) that can give the idea of what has been mixed up and confused!

this way, since production with (new) technologies necessarily needs already produced goods, this has undeniably become *capitalistic* in the proper sense of the term – that is in the sense that it is using *produced* capital goods. But this, *ipso facto*, does not mean that they have been made *institutionally* capitalist!

The term *capitalist*, as it began to be used, came to mean something else. It has come to mean a whole series of particular *institutions* – normally old, or sometimes entirely new – re-adapted in an apparently attractive way, yet imposed from *external* sources on top of the technically *capitalistic* features of the modern new age. This difference is important, and we should not confuse the two sources nor the specific essence of each of the two different conceptions!

In other words, we should not confuse the analytical and physical properties of the new way of carrying out production – which is typical of the novel industrial age and which implies that *commodities are produced by means of commodities*, as Piero Sraffa was keen to specify – with the features of a complex comprehensive social and *institutional* setup, invented and developed with the purpose of constructing a framework of particular *organisational* arrangements of economic, legal, inter-individual, relations that more generally and more commonly have (attractively, but misleadingly) been called the *capitalism* – or, even, various sorts of *capitalisms* – of our time!

In this way, the whole profession of mainstream economists has in fact *smuggled* into economic analysis exactly the opposite of what should have been done. Instead of starting from the features of an ideal, possibly largely accepted, *normatively conceived* economic framework – namely, what we have called the *Natural Economic System* – they seem to have been caught into the trap of the hypothetical properties of an *imaginary* ultra-rational individualistic type – or of various types – of Agents' behaviours, institutionally framed (normally in an unconstrained artificial vision of perfect market *institutions*)[18] and unwarrantedly tried to attribute to them properties and privileges of a mythical mechanism, supposedly able to drive and lead, *alone by itself*, the actual economic systems to automatically generate optimality results.

[18] Which by the way might themselves possess their own merits.

But these are entirely unwarranted claims! In some cases, they might even be called a *fraud*, however 'innocent' it might be, or could be![19]

What should have been done instead, as stated in the previous sentence, is something entirely different and more sensible. Namely, first: the singling out of a largely, and ideally widely accepted, normatively conceived, economic framework actually aimed to be achieved, in our anthropologically governed society. Then, *from such a normative framework*, go back and examine and confront it, in practice, with the actual world, and check and test how and whether the *existing* institutions – that is the ones *actually* built and in operation – satisfy, or fail to satisfy, that normatively conceived *Natural Economic System*, which the newly formed industrial institutions should have been meant to achieve. And, if not, press ahead for its achievement.

But it is here, quite clearly, that we arrive at the dramatically sad and unfortunate clash. This clash comes from the confrontation of the actually realised 'capitalist' *institutions* of our times, with the analytically clearer model of a *Natural Economic System*, containing the essence of a truly *capitalistic* (not 'capitalist') society.

From the whole of our analysis, one is forced to conclude that the prospects for re-addressing the scientific state of Political Economy in vogue today (in most *institutionally* prevailing so-called capitalist societies) could be (or have become) largely unfavourable to taking those required simple, but crucial, steps in the true direction that our economies would, and desperately should, need to pursue!

The currently prevailing conception of the 'capitalist' structure of our industrial society unbelievingly indicates too many features that are exactly the opposite of what they should be. A dramatic, yet clear, confusion seems to have taken place between major capitalistic events and (even laudable) institutions (we shall come back to these aspects in the following final pages of the present investigation). It seems even paradoxical that the present situation should remind us of that famous historical accusation made in the 1870s by William Stanley Jevons, at the beginning of the so-called *Marginal Revolution* and addressed against David Ricardo. Unbelievably, for Jevons, it was Ricardo who

[19] This is actually how John Kenneth Galbraith described them in the last book he was able to write Galbraith (2004).

had 'shunted the car of Economic science on to the wrong line'.[20] What a striking, sentence, delivered no doubt with a laudable sense of urgency and yet, entirely wrong! We can see now, from our analysis, that it was Jevons, not Ricardo, who dramatically had shunted the car of economics onto a line that was irretrievably 'wrong'! And unfortunately, in the whole mainstream economic literature, it has remained there ever since!

[20] Jevons' *Preface* to his Second Edition (1879) of *The Theory of Political Economy* (Jevons 1871).

15 Concluding Notes on the Social Implications of an Evolving, Learning Economy

This chapter has been assembled by Enrico Bellino, Nadia Garbellini, Giovanni Pasinetti, Roberto Scazzieri and Ariel Wirkierman on the basis of the provisional notes left by Luigi Pasinetti. We have limited our intervention to eliminating repetitions and standardising the text, trying to remain as faithful as possible to Luigi Pasinetti's original draft.

We sincerely thank Alberto Quadrio Curzio and Mauro Baranzini for their encouragement on this stage of the work.

The whole logical framework of the *Natural Economic System* is now complete.

The analysis carried out in Chapter 14, devoted to the natural rate of interest, gives us a perfect connection to introduce the discussion of some crucial aspects of what we called the Natural Economic System and to explicitly deal with a set of issues of crucial importance.

1 Introduction[1]

The step-by-step approach to the definition of the natural rate of interest brings to the fore a first, fundamental distinction: that between the rate of interest and the rate of profit. Whereas a rate of interest may emerge even in a pure labour economy, which we might call a pre-capitalistic society, the concept of the rate of profit is strictly related to capitalist systems (see later), since profits are the form in which capitalists acquire surplus value.

[1] By Nadia Garbellini and Enrico Bellino.

A rate of interest does emerge anytime people, or associations of people, want to exchange securities with which to undertake credit and debt relations, denominated in terms of a conventional unit of purchasing power. These debt/credit securities may have coordinated dates of expiration, based upon pre-established agreements (with debt and credit contracts) so that the loans can return to those who set their desired deadlines with various agreed inter-temporal configurations. In this case, the need arises for money and credit securities of various types to be circulated with the help of monetary and financial institutions – external to production – which act as intermediaries.

In the same way, as stated in the previous paragraph, the term profits is associated to a particular institutional setting, that of capitalist societies, in which the owners of the means of production appropriate the social product which is over and above what is required for the producers to reproduce.

And yet, the purpose of the present analysis is to develop a theory which remains neutral with respect to the institutional organisation of society, my preoccupation being that of singling out, to resume Ricardo's terminology, the 'primary and natural' features of a pure production system, a system in which commodities are produced by means of commodities. This is the meaning of the term capitalistic, as opposed to capitalist: the former simply refers to industrial societies, where goods and services are produced by means of labour and capital, and growth is led by capital accumulation; the latter is a capitalistic system whose institutions have been shaped in a very specific way.

Singling out the 'primary and natural' features of a capitalistic system requires acknowledging the sharp separation existing between those economic problems that have to be solved on the ground of logic alone – for which economic theory is entirely autonomous – and those economic problems that arise in connection with particular institutions, or with particular groups' or individuals' behaviour – for which economic theory is no longer autonomous and needs to be integrated with further hypotheses, which may well come from other social sciences. It is with the first type of problems that the present work is basically concerned.

The separation is evident and can be found in some economists.[2] In my earlier works, I have talked of this aspect by calling it a 'separation theorem'. In fact, the latter relations may vary from time to time or be suggested by pressing circumstances; by contrast, the former are inherent to the characteristics of the Natural Economic System.

In the light of this, then, how can two concepts such as the interest rate and the rate of profit, generally associated with specific institutional settings, be part of the Natural Economic System?

Reasoning in these terms might appear as counterintuitive, when coming to the issue of the distribution of income. In fact, the way in which income is distributed depends on social relations of production, on cultural, ethic, legal considerations. In short, precisely on the institutional setup of society. How can a theory of the rate of profit be conceived that is independent of it?

The 'natural' economic system deals with logical relations, objectively based on measurable magnitudes, and emerging from the physical growth requirements of the system itself. The question to be asked, therefore, is the following: is there a natural rate of profit, already logically implied in the previous theoretical framework, because the economic system considered is a growing one?

At a pre-institutional stage of the analysis, a theory of the rate of profit cannot be a theory of income distribution among income recipients, since we miss the very categories among which the purchasing

[2] I have earlier given an account of how David Ricardo was aware of this distinction. I have also given two citations that reveal this awareness respectively in Marx and Sraffa. I may now add another interesting citation, even more explicit, that comes from Sraffa's *Unpublished Papers*: 'Cost is means not inducement. The *possibility* to produce depends upon the absolute real size of the remuneration: there is no trick possible, it is a physical material necessity. [The *willingness* to produce depends upon the way in which payment is made: time wages or piece wages, premiums etc. (which can be deducted from initial wage, so as to make the total wage equal to physical necessaries), payment conditional upon delivery of the goods (Robertson, in Economica) etc. it is a psychological necessity only, and can be overcome by tricks, cheating, etc. Cost in the sense of means belong to *natural economics*, i.e. they are equal in all forms of society, and are *independent of institutions*.] Cost in the sense of *inducements* belong to *institutional* economics, they vary according to 'social standard', examples, envy, desire for equality, for rising in social standing etc'.

power generated in the process of production is to be distributed. However, while on the one side industrial systems are characterised by a clearcut distinction between the means of production that enter a circular process, and the set of commodities which are consumed, on the other hand in a growing system new investments are required to expand the means of production.

We can therefore consider profits and wages as establishing the amount of purchasing power to be devoted to producing the means of production – those commodities that re-enter the circular flow as circulating capital, or accumulated fixed capital – and to the purchase of final consumption commodities, respectively. The different economic functions arise from the conditions of production of physical quantities, in particular, from the need to separate what enters the circular flow (and is used as means of production) from what does not (and is consumed).

Natural profits, therefore, exactly correspond to the surplus which each vertically hyper-integrated sector must generate in order for capital accumulation conditions to be satisfied.

And what about the natural rate of interest?

As we have seen, the sphere of production starts from the original labour inputs – through the whole complex inter-industry, or more compactly, hyper-integrated framework – and proceeds to the production of goods and services devoted to consumption. It ideally ends with the distribution of all the produced national income, under the form of wages, to the active part of the population. Precisely at this point, the sphere of debt/credit relations – in comprehensive terms, that is, the sphere of what may be called the Finance of an industrial economic system – opens up. Production has been completed, but the natural economic system proceeds beyond production, through a complex, vast network of debt/credit relations, which constitute an intricate panoply of financial stocks of assets and liabilities. These financial stocks have nothing specifically physical behind them. They cancel out in the aggregate, their algebraic sum, at any time, adding up to zero.

Again, defining the natural rate of interest means answering the following question: is there a natural rate of interest, already logically implied in the previous theoretical framework? Also in this case, the answer is yes.

In this framework, value is given by quantities of direct, indirect and hyper-indirect embodied labour. Hence, anytime inter-temporal debt/-credit relations are set up, the natural function of the rate of interest is that of keeping the quantity of exchanged labour unaltered, according to the labour principle of income distribution. Therefore, the natural rate of interest has to counterbalance changes in productivity occurred during the time span covered by loans. That is the rationale at the basis of the elaborations of Chapter 14, and this is the only role a rate of interest might perform within the Natural Economic System.

2 The 'Institutional Problem'

Max Planck is quoted as saying that he had considered studying economics but found the subject too complicated and opted for physics instead. Alas, economic analysis lost a most beautiful mind, but the justification that Max Planck is supposed to have given is not a joke. Social Sciences must deal with relations put into existence by human beings[3] and not, as in the case of physics, to be found as given from an external environment.

This means that the *Natural Economic System* does not automatically come into existence by itself; it must be brought into existence. Hence, for any actual economic system, the problem arises of inventing and setting up those organisational devices – in other words, those human 'institutions' – which are able to bring the *Natural Economic System* into existence.

This in itself is not an all-or-nothing undertaking. If not in an absolutely accurate and precise way, the *Natural Economic System* may be aimed at with a tolerable degree of approximation. Moreover, it is not a once-for-all undertaking either, as it must take place continually as time goes on. It is an overall moving operation. Ex-hypothesis, if we were to imagine a hypothetically perfect stationary (or proportionally growing) economic system, the setting up of certain institutions rather than others would not make much difference, except at the outset. The natural features would sooner or later be discovered. Then, once singled out and achieved, they would remain forever. But this is not the

[3] See Pasinetti (2002).

type of world which we are investigating. Our world is one in which all coefficients of production and of demand vary continuously; natural positions, even if achieved at a given point in time, may no longer be so as time goes on. It therefore becomes necessary and important to single out those organisational devices that may continually search for, and lead to, the natural positions.

This is what I have called 'the institutional problem'.

The hints that I have found most interesting on this problem have been made only by those economists who have recognised and admitted that in the social sciences there essentially is a *separation* of concepts, or rather of conceptions, that must be made.[4]

This *separation* is between those relations that are fundamental to what I have called the *Natural Economic System* or, as they have also been called, the *economic relations of 'pure theory'* and those relations that – in any particular circumstance in history – refer to temporary human events that are not so essential, or fundamental, or natural.

The natural relations are permanent, while the 'institutional relations' may change with time or circumstances, with the achievements of new forms of organisation. The former are so fundamental as indeed to be part of the 'pure economic theory' of the *Natural Economic System*. The institutional relations are pressing, experimental and changing over time. Understandably, there have always been attempts at enhancing the merits of the institutional relations and also efforts to define some of them as *natural* institutions. But, this has always ended up in useless sorts of attempts.

By and large my basic contention is that, in economics, 'natural' institutions do not exist.

To be more specific, the institutional problem does not need to have a unique solution, nor does it emerge once and for all. By being a problem of construction of organisational devices (the *institutions*) in order to achieve certain results (and these are those of the *Natural Economic System*), it is obviously susceptible of being faced in different ways, from time to time, from place to place, and at the variation of many external circumstances, without mentioning that the organisational field itself is subject to continuous evolution and innovation.

[4] See Note 2.

We must be aware that an economic system does not come about in a vacuum. It presupposes a complex network of political, juridical, and legal institutions. Some, which we may call 'civic', institutions may come to be shaped through historical processes, according to different traditions in different countries, sometimes even with stronger requirements than those behind economic institutions. Within this wider institutional framework, the strictly *economic* institutions come to intermingle and merge with others while carrying out the task entrusted to them.

One should be careful not to confuse the two levels of investigation just specified. The important aspect to stress is that the first of these two levels of investigation (the 'Natural') is independent of the second (the 'Institutional'). This independence is in fact another remarkable property of the *Natural Economic System*. However and moreover, the opposite is not the case!

One may admit that the idea of a *natural* institution has always been attractive, but at the same time misleading. So attractive and complex that historically, it has been attempted and faced many times. Yet, it has never been satisfactorily achieved.

Indeed, the problem of constructing supposed natural economic institutions in an industrial economy is so attractive as to have led economists, philosophers and politicians towards the temptation to conceive some of their preferred institutional conceptions as part of the framework of what I call the Natural Economic System, without however being able to provide a satisfactory solution.

In the field of economic analysis as such – to which our investigations are confined – we may well state, or rather confirm that supposedly 'natural' *economic* institutions do not exist. There have undoubtedly been some principles, mainly behind 'juridical institutions', that have come to predominate certain stages of history, but these attempts have nothing to do with the *normatively binding* concepts of the *Natural Economic System*.

In general, we cannot find any economic institutions that are ready-made for our investigation. The existing institutions have all been the result of human invention and ingenuity, and as such, they do not deserve the appellation of 'natural', which would imply an exclusiveness that institutions do not and cannot have.

On the contrary, the Natural Economic System expresses the basic overall equilibrium and objective framework of an evolving industrial society as it should be, independently of whether, how, or which, economic institutions society has decided to adopt. For practical purposes, it may well become useful to take it in conjunction with all those normative rules, or conditions, or regulations that society may decide to adopt, even from outside the sphere of economic activity, in order to have a complete framework of normative rules.

In Section 1, I said that the *Natural Economic System* is independent of economic institutions, but also that the opposite proposition is not the case. Once the *Natural Economic System* has been spotted out and ideally configured, it becomes paramount in pressing ahead and leading society to choose from among possible (alternative) institutions. Of course only those economic institutions that can drive the actual economic system towards its *'natural'* configuration become eligible and should be considered for choice, not those that would divert the economy in directions far away from it!

3 The Difficulties of Grasping the Requirements of an Epochal Change

After stressing objectivity and independence from institutions as two abstract, basic properties of the *Natural Economic System*, it becomes inevitable at this point to reflect explicitly, for a while, on their connections with the epochal events that have emerged in our very recent history. We have of course dealt with these major events already at the beginning of this book (Chapters 1 and 2); yet we are now in a position to take advantage of a few further really basic elaborations that have emerged.

There are two major questions we need to answer. The first has become obvious: the necessity of the choice of one of the alternative analytical paradigms developed by economic theorists – the objective (or pure production) and the subjective (or pure exchange) paradigm, as explained in Chapter 1.

It would be difficult to deny that the objective paradigm is the one that has become relevant since the Physiocratic School of François Quesnay and his followers in France, and the Classical School of Adam Smith, Robert Malthus, David Ricardo and followers in Great Britain.

The idea that something really fundamental had taken place was markedly clear to all of them. Not by chance, but by inherent conviction, the economists' intellectual movement in France was called Physiocracy (the 'government of nature').

The second basic question that is less obvious and still remains problematic: where and indeed when did our predecessor fellow economists realise that they had to sharply separate the two fields of economic investigation – the 'natural' from the 'institutional' – as we have examined in Section 2?

Here we find ourselves in deep waters. It looks as if no economist, or intellectual scholar of high standard, could clearly realise, at the beginning of the Industrial Revolution, what was going to be the appropriate framework and evolution of the institutions of the industrial systems and, most of all, what in our terms was to be considered as 'natural' and what was to be framed as the appropriate and fair 'institutional' evolution of things that were in motion.

There was perhaps an exception, namely David Ricardo. As was pointed out in Chapter 2, he did realise that an important distinction was to be made between *natural* magnitudes and *institutionally* determined magnitudes. But David Ricardo was, as just said, an exception, his brilliance not fully appreciated or understood, not even by his pupils.

On the whole, Classical economist as a group were far from being clear in realising the consequences of the major events at hand. Adam Smith himself gives us, perhaps, the best example. On the one hand, in what became a famous citation, in the first chapter of the *Wealth of Nations*, he unequivocally and very clearly stated a labour theory of value.[5] At the same time, however, immediately in the following (second) chapter of the same work, he developed that famous example on the wonders of market competition among shopkeepers that was later taken to be an embryonic perception of an all too obvious institutional feature (i.e. of the supposed efficiency of well self-regulated, competitive markets).[6] Most economists, even Adam Smith, failed to openly make the crucial distinction between the two types of investigation mentioned previously. Realistically, we must of course accept that for two centuries after the outbreak of the Industrial Revolution,

[5] See Chapter 2, footnotes 15–17.

[6] With a famous, no more than intuitive hunch, he used the famous expression of an 'invisible hand' operating in the commercial transactions to determine prices and quantities.

the attitudes of major economists were mixed and open to various interpretations.

We may simply concede that it would have been unreasonable to expect, on the part of the Classical economists or of their immediate followers, a quick clear realisation of the relevance of the distinctions.

However, we must at the same time realise that the consequences of such a lack of awareness turned out to be dramatically serious. What happened in fact is that – immediately after Ricardo – owing to the political and social conditions that came into existence at the time, almost the whole attention of the major economists was driven *away* from the too intricate theoretical problems that had emerged, and which they had failed to solve.

They concentrated their efforts on the pressing attempts of trying to envisage ways to face the *institutional* consequences of the technical and economic changes that were taking place. The relevant aspect of this historical circumstance is that insistence and pressures on the ways and extent to which the social *institutions* were to be organised, brought the economic profession to a dramatic split, essentially between what became the *mainstream* economics of John Stuart Mill – as the acknowledged leader of what was (mistakenly) supposed to be a continuation of the Classical School – and those economists who – under the powerful influence of Karl Marx – emerged as opposed to an entirely established 'capitalist society' that was in the process of being formed.

At the middle of the nineteenth century, this bifurcation constituted (sometimes even in a ferocious way) the strikingly major characteristics of the general opinions of the whole economics profession. It allowed no compromise: one had to be either on the one side or on the other.

It is clearly dramatic to realise today how this bifurcation, with its inherent split, remained the dominating force, not only for the remaining part of the nineteenth century, but also for the whole of the following twentieth century, in which it had to act across major historical events: two world wars, a series of political (communist) take-overs in Eastern Europe and, in the West, a remarkable attempt to redress the effects of a major depression (1929–1940 and after), which remained incomplete. Nevertheless, this bifurcation remained standing until, on the one side, the dramatic collapse of the whole (institutional) system that had been imposed on Eastern European (communist) countries and, on the other side, a still nowadays unexplained economic and financial crisis that has characterised the beginning of the Third Millennium.

If we pause for a moment and calmly look at the unusual consequence of this controversy, we will realise that it was not so much because it was relevant for the discussions and controversies engendered by the leading works of John Stuart Mill, and thus on the side of some form of liberal, socially inspired, 'capitalism', but it was basically because it was relevant for the discussions (and controversies) stimulated by Karl Marx and the various forms of socialism.

The interesting and major aspect of these events, especially if considered from today's standpoint, is that rather suddenly it became evident that at the very origin (in the 1870s, immediately after the publication of Marx's major work, *Das Kapital*) the real force behind the two sides of the bifurcation was *a dramatic change in the basic substance of the confrontation*. The difference between the two sides of the discussion shifted to the framing of a new *economic theory* which immediately became the theory behind the whole *mainstream economics*.

Paradoxically, this appeared as a striking jump forward in theoretical research (see the details already given in Chapter 2), so much so that it came to be called – at first almost unbelievably – the marginal economics 'revolution'. Its force turned out to be that it was presented, not so much as an innovation, but as a really major 'scientific' progress of exactly the same previous (anti-Marxist) stand. In fact, it did turn out to be a real (*counter-*) *revolution*. Quite extraordinarily, this is an aspect to which very little attention has been paid thus far in the discussions on economic theory. Yet, it has turned out to be of immense importance.

The enormously impressive flourishing of analytical economic theory at the end of the nineteenth century was presented as an outgrowth of the 'liberal'-minded part of 'economic science'. One must stress that, to this surprising shift of emphasis on the *mainstream* side of the controversy, there was no corresponding shift on the more *classical* side of economic theory. One may object, of course, that analytical developments – mainly behind the scenes and by a few scholars – did take place, especially with reference to Ricardo-Marx's economic theory. Indeed this is what Part II and Part III of the present work have been devoted to.

Nonetheless, one must admit that there is no comparison that may be made with the extremely vast bulk of development of what became *mainstream* economics. Essentially, the most important and real difference is that, quite suddenly, before the end of the nineteenth century, an entirely new branch of economic theory was born.[7] It was expressed in terms of elegant analytical tools, based on entirely new foundations (see them as expressed in Section 7 of Chapter 2). In essence, this turned out to be the more analytical development 'exchange paradigm' in alternative to the 'Classical' production one. The extraordinary paradox is that the world historical period to which such a paradigm would have been appropriately relevant had already been overtaken by history! With all this, the apparently new paradigm was so well presented, and most of all, so well in line with the general expectations on how economic theory should be – namely on lines similar to those of all the other scientific branches (especially physics) – as to conquer the whole profession of economists of the Western world!

Very little, in fact almost nothing that could compete in analytical terms with this new economic theoretical development, was presented as an alternative, or within any other competing paradigm, even if there was indeed another paradigm, and one that was standing, that is the one that was in continuation of 'Classical' economic theory![8]

Notably enough, there was a respite and in fact only a glimmer of hope of a return to common sense! But it came as a consequence of

[7] There is only one economist who understood the tragedy of this change of economic theory that took place in the 1870s; this economist is Piero Sraffa. Here is what he states in an extract which I found in his unpublished papers: 'It is terrific to contemplate the abysmal gulf of incomprehension that has opened itself between us and the classical economists. Only one century separates us from them: [then the following sentence, here reproduced in italics, is added as a footnote] *I say a century; but even 1/2 a century after, in 1870, they did not understand it. And during the preceding century an obscure process of 'disunderstanding' [sic] had been going on.* How can we imagine to understand the Greeks and the Romans? [then the following sentence, again here reproduced in italics, is added as a footnote] *Or rather, the extraordinary thing is that we do understand, since we find them perfect, Roman law and Greek philosophy.* The classical economists said things which were perfectly true, even according to our standards of truth: they expressed them very clearly, in terse and unambiguous language, as is proved by the fact that they perfectly understood each other. We don't understand a word of what they said: has their language been lost? Obviously not, as the English of Adam Smith is what people talk today in this country. What has happened then?' (*Sraffa Papers* D 3/12/4, f.14.). See also my 'Preface' to the Catalogue of the Library of Piero Sraffa (Pasinetti 2014).

[8] See on this Chapter 2, Section 7.

a major economic disaster in the middle of the twentieth century – namely the Great Depression of 1929 – a phenomenon which, to be overcome, required the development of the well-known economic theories of J. M. Keynes, after World War II. It is dutiful to record that, on the other side, a major historical event also took place in the late 1980s, namely the unexpected dramatic collapse of the economies of the Eastern European bloc, that is of those countries that, after World War II, had been taken over by the socialist spread of enthusiasm for economy nationalisations.

But after all this, it is even more astonishing to realise what has been happening since! At the end of the twentieth century and at the beginning of the new millennium, a second terrific economic disaster, quite surprisingly parallel to that of 1929, has taken place. The so-called capitalist world has again plunged into major economic and financial crises from which, up to the present day, it seems unable to recover. What is even more peculiar is that the new disaster clearly appears extraordinarily similar, in fact strikingly and essentially of the same type, as the one of 1929! But, unfortunately, there is an incredible reluctance in the economics profession to admit this.

We may well ask: have we really lost our ability to learn the most elementary lessons of our recent history?

4 The Snares of Subjectivism and of Methodological Individualism

It may be of some interest to add a few further reflections on what we must acknowledge as the persistent and tenacious tendency of the prevailing economic theorists to develop their present scientific contributions within a paradigm that, by our time, should be considered surpassed and obsolete.

From a careful analysis, one can spot out not simply a single, but a whole list of oddities behind the defence of the present mainstream economics, based on the 'pure exchange' paradigm. It would seem almost unbelievable to find such an instance by the present leaders of the current stream of Political Economy, to oppose the rejection of what is by now an obsolete mainstream economics.

Let me mention a few of these oddities.

To begin with, it seems odd that the present Political Economy should so persistently concentrate on a scheme based on individuals aiming at selfishly maximising their own individual 'utility'. The idea of an *homo oeconomicus* behind human behaviour is an old one but appears quite primitive and rudimentary, even more so when the attempt is made of extending such behaviour not only to the economic field of personal utility but – as the latest most sophisticated defenders do – to *any* aspect of human life itself.[9]

Secondly, even more odd is to see the insistence of mainstream economists to deny scientific status to any theoretical model that departs from their traditional hypotheses – heuristically called 'micro-foundations' of human behaviour. This claim is plainly tantamount to assuming that there should be only one way to engage in economic theory (namely the traditional process of utility maximisation under constraints), thus *a-priory* relegating to non-acceptability all other approaches – a very queer way, as it should appear – of defining a *scientific* approach.

Thirdly, this 'micro-founded' way of investigation is generally inserted into a framework of perfect atomistic markets, with ideally perfect competition, perfect information, perfect forecasts. In this way, the 'micro-foundations' appear to be inserted into an extraordinary mixing-up of the two earlier mentioned aspects, that is: the

[9] Let me end with a short, but significant quotation from Evandro Agazzi, a major author of the claim that *objectivity* is the modern conception in science that must come to replace the older concept of *truth* in scientific investigations. In his critique of the negativity of subjectivity, Agazzi states: 'while subjectivity seems to be the first mark of our knowledge, it is also considered as its worst defect, a defect with which humankind has struggled for centuries, our ideal being a form of knowledge which, though inevitably acquired by various subjects, is nevertheless independent of them in its validity', (2014, p. 50).

When I specifically asked Evandro Agazzi to express his own criticism of the *subjectivity* criterion, I received the following answer: 'The negative characteristic of subjectivity is *privacy*; it retains the doubt that our representation of the object we wish to know is unfaithful. Dreams, hallucinations, the errors of our senses are experiences which we all have and induce us to search for some form of guarantee that we are not in error. The most spontaneous response is to search for confirmation in others of what we say we know. This can take place both by communicating concretely with other persons, or by consulting, written or printed works, but also by our repeating, when possible, the same cognitive situation. Certainly, this is not a simple problem, the fact that the debate on scepticism is still open indicates that the question is not yet entirely solved' (email from Agazzi received on 25 February 2016).

fundamental and the *institutional* relations – a conceptual muddle from our (and perhaps anybody's) point of view.[10]

In fact, one could go on to list further *oddities*.

Mainstream economics considers the existing world as totally given to us from an external, exogenously given, source. In such a world, economic theorising would be conceived as an autonomous intellectual exercise in which the economic theorists have the ambition of performing in the social sciences the same role that physics has performed in the natural sciences. That is, the economic behaviours that are studied today would be conceived as those that have always existed before, in all previous periods of time, updated if one likes, but substantially immutable, the same as they prevailed in the past. Within this conception, economic theory should progress not because the investigated world is changing – as our whole experience suggests – but only because new analytical tools or methods have become available[11] to be applied to exactly the same, invariant, problems.

Since Alfred Marshall, at the beginning of the twentieth century, successfully coined the epithet of 'neoclassical' economics, one might say that he deployed all his efforts to frame an apparently reasonable claim of a sort of continuity (even where it does not exist!) of marginal economic theory following from Classical economic theory.

Along these lines, all sorts of counter positions would be eliminated between the Classical economists of the eighteenth (and beginning of the nineteenth) century, and the Marginalist economists of the end of the nineteenth (and beginning of twentieth) century, thus also appearing to overcome that sort of 'dis-understanding', which Piero Sraffa unveiled and complained about![12]

There is only one way to escape from the too easy danger of falling into the all too common contradictions amply in the previous sentences, so widespread in the mainstream economics of the present times: give up the pretence to follow the exclusively *individualistic behaviour* of the consumers and of the so-called economic 'agents'.

[10] See S. Abu Turab Rizvi's critiques in Rizvi (1994, 2006).

[11] According to this line, we are supposed to have been witnessing for the past two centuries an application of a series of successive analytical tools: from arithmetic and geometric maps to infinitesimal calculus, to game theories, to set theories, to rational expectation probabilities, all giving successive application of similar, or even more sophisticated analytical tools etc.

[12] See footnote 7.

For too long, too many economic theorists (of all tendencies) have been dreaming to discover 'natural' mechanisms or rules of *individualistic* behaviour that could automatically lead to the best of all economic results. We must stop entertaining such dreams.

The present work of course has concentrated on the discovery, description, enquiry of the fundamental *economic* relations that constitute the foundations of the *Natural Economic System* in which all the *basic normative features* of an industrial society should ideally be found to be included.

This is the really radical methodological turn in economic theory of our own time that is now becoming necessary. It is, of course, a radical change of methodology as it has been hinted at already since the beginning of the present work.

As we may now see more clearly, this is in effect a radical change which again is an aspect behind what I have earlier called the 'Separation Theorem'; that is the separation of those investigations that refer to the foundations of the *Natural Economic System* and those investigations that refer to the setting-up of those economic institutions which must be devised in order to bring the *Natural Economic System* into existence.

5 Openness Needed in Order to Face the Crucial Challenge of Choosing the Institutional Framework of a Modern Industrial Society

The present analysis does not aim at all at an exclusion, nor at a lack of concern, for the importance of the 'institutions' of the economic system. On the contrary, we have in fact seen that the achievement of the configuration of the *Natural Economic System* brings us precisely to the search and discovery of those features that are behind the economic 'institutions' necessary to bring the *Natural Economic System* into being.

The Natural Economic System implies the construction of social institutions – that is of bodies, or mechanisms, or apparatuses – that supervise, or bring about, or facilitates, or actually bring into effect a coordination which goes beyond simple individualistic behaviour, thus necessarily requiring social cooperation, simply because, in a structural dynamics context, it would be impossible to carry it out through the initiatives or behaviour of single atomistically considered individuals.

To conclude, we can thus clearly see emerging here other basic characteristics of the *Natural Economic System*, which are independent of the economic institutions, without meaning and even less implying that the opposite should be the case. A major characteristic of the *Natural Economic System* is indeed the spotting out and indicating where, with which functions and for which purposes, some economic need emerges for the satisfaction of which social (as opposed to individually based) institutions must be constructed or must be newly invented, if they do not already exist. It is in this way that we come to identify and underline the *social* functions of those *economic* institutions that become not only appropriate, but *necessary* to the actual achievement of the 'natural' features of an industrial society (of course in its process to shape a *Natural Economic System*).

And here we arrive at what for two centuries by now has been a real major problem for all economists: namely the configuration of the economic institutions of an industrial society. A perfectly general institutional framework, really appropriate for the industrial society as such, has not been found, in spite of many (false) pretences, thus far. Most probably it does not exist. Or, if at all, it still needs to be invented, or is still in needs to be *continuously* invented, which means that perhaps it will never be entirely completed.

The crucial point here is that one cannot exclude that there always may well be other, perhaps even more successful, ways to examine and understand the actual workings of particular, and sometimes developing, new kinds of institutions (e.g. not only markets, but actual organisations, or new types of individual, or collective, institutions) that may be different from those traditionally investigated with the usual assumptions of maximisation, under constraints, or of the utility of single individuals, or other similar concepts. To give an example, some Italian economists[13] have recently gone back to investigate the writings of economists (like Cesare Beccaria and Pietro *cum* Alessandro Verri), who in the eighteenth century did carry out their research in parallel to, but on different lines from the French and Scottish economists. And their research may well have been too quickly left aside. They worked out an economic framework which they called

[13] See on this Bruni and Zamagni (2015), *L'economia civile. Un'altra idea di mercato*.

'economia civica' (of 'civil economics') which was based on postulates more complex than those of selfishness, or of utility maximisation, while relying on the existence of relations among the traders that were based on personal trust and reciprocity of contacts. Their approach was strikingly different from those that were, later on and elsewhere, developed by the more successful champions of methodological individualism (e.g. Weber, Hayek, and more recently, Friedman and Lucas). For these purposes, our previous analysis is quite open to consider all these wider perspectives and attempts.

Within the *Natural Economic System* of an industrial society, there is much more than straight individual demand and supply schedules. Think of the multiplicity of the degrees of freedom that have emerged from our analysis (in the price system, in the composition of consumer demand, in the decisions of an inter-temporal fruition of the produced commodities and services). Equilibria among these variables should of course be sought, in order to obtain, in an overall *natural* economic system, overall macro-economic conditions that depend on overall effective demand, which includes both consumers' needs and investment needs, within hyper-integrated growing sub-systems as we have seen, for the expansion of the economic system.

We should especially be careful not to miss – within the ideal visions of what in our analysis appears as the components of the *Natural Economic System* – the possible presence of specifiable series of quantitative singularities. As we have seen, the overall magnitudes of the *Natural Economic System* contain many extraordinarily important degrees of freedom, as we have seen at various points. In many cases, the important aspects emerge precisely in the relations between the centrality of the *Natural Economic System* as a whole and the structural dynamics of many of its sectoral magnitudes, within various inter-related movements that may take place inside the structural evolution of what misleadingly appear and so often are presented as impossibly homogeneous macro-economic magnitudes.

The essential aspects here lay in how the varied (sometimes quite curious) evolutions of the most important inside parts, versus the outside, appear macro-economic magnitudes that come to influence the perception of single individuals, or of groups of individuals, so as to change completely – outside the most obvious expectations – the performance of the whole aggregate economic system.[14]

In these cases, there is no need and no purpose to go into the analysis of single typical or atypical cases. The inter-relations of all sectors may well lead to seeming contradictions between the realm of the obvious behaviour of the single individuals and the realm of the economic system as a whole. The degrees of indirectness of all the physical production links may cause unexpected and unavoidable inter-dependencies that are not immediately perceivable at the level of either the single individuals or their groups, as they transcend the behaviour of the single individual and affect uncertain and unprecedented overall reactions that become of crucial importance for the community as a whole. Sometimes they may even appear mysterious in their evolution, yet effective in their results.

Essentially, however, the frame and structure of the Natural Economic System must never be lost from sight; it must always represent the central framework – we might say in a sense the scientific objective – of all our economic investigations!

6 The Cause and Beauty of a Socially Upsetting Mixture of Events and Institutions

But, what is it – one might ask – that makes it necessary to go back to investigate so intensely and in depth, the degree of structural interdependence within the structural dynamics of the process of production? This is a question that plunges us down into the roots of the coming into existence and the accumulation of capital in our post-Industrial Revolution economies. A more detailed and specific analysis may be helpful at this point.

For millennia, mankind had produced the goods it needed by means of labour and natural resources (essentially through the cultivation of land, the domestication of animals and the discovery of new uses of material objects, to carry out their various activities). But in the last

[14] See the contrast that has been brought to light through the confrontation between the macroeconomics stand propounded by the U.S. so-called Keynesian macro-economists (in particular the exchange on *structural dynamics* between R.M. Solow and L.L. Pasinetti in part III of Arena and Porta (2012)).

few centuries, something new, in fact something dramatically new, has happened first, in a circumscribed part of the world, and then slowly spreading to the whole planet. The factual evidence made us perceive at first, what appeared to be a sort of new factor of production, which had almost suddenly emerged on the economic scene. People called it: *Capital*. As we all know, physical capital (which is what is relevant at this stage, but not exclusively, as we shall see in a moment) is a collective name that stands for a set of material goods which are made, not for their own sake, but because they are instrumentally used – together with natural resources and direct labour – to obtain final consumption goods and services, besides the capital goods themselves (since these need to be constantly and periodically replaced). This *capitalistic* transformation of production, in the correct sense of the word – that is in the sense already mentioned in Section 1 of man's production of commodities by means of commodities[15] – was generated, as we know, by a combination of inventions and progressive use of machines, operated no longer by human or animal energy but by a whole series of new sources of energy that had been, and still are, cumulatively developing. The crucial point is that all this did bring about an enormous increase of overall production and wealth – however unequally as it may have been distributed originally and more disturbingly subsequently.

This has no doubt been one of the most terrific and fascinating phases of our whole history. If we try to look at it in a somewhat detached way, we face a sort of enigma, concerning at least two markedly novel features that characterise it and have become more and more apparent as time has elapsed. From our analysis they have both been emerging quite elegantly, apparently in a separate way, but in fact inter-dependently, as has appeared in Part II and in Part III of the present work, respectively.

Let us pay some attention to them.

From Part II of our investigation, which has relied essentially on inter-industry analysis (what Leontief called input–output and Piero Sraffa called 'production of commodities by means of commodities') the clear feature that has emerged is that *all* commodities, consumption goods as well as capital goods, are not normally distinguishable

[15] And not in the looser, inappropriate and misleading, sense criticised in the Sections 1 and 3.

from one another at their physical-technological level. The very same physical commodity might well be used indifferently, for different purposes, as consumption goods or as capital goods. Thus, consumption goods, which may disappear after fulfilling the task for which they have been produced, and capital goods, which may also disappear after being used up, with the difference however that they must be *replaced* in order that the process of production may go on, may not reveal the necessity of making any distinction from each other, nor may they have to be treated analytically in a different way from each other. But, what introduces a crucial difference between the two is the use to which they are set to task.

Consumption goods are enjoyed as such by the people who have come directly or indirectly to possess them. They mark the ultimate final stage and fulfilment of the production process that was meant to generate them. On *purely physical appearance*, capital goods may well undergo the same fate. They are used up, and in general they slowly disappear, in the production of other goods and of themselves. But there is a crucial difference: at the same time, they are (they *must* be) replaced by other physical goods that are put in their place, not necessarily with exactly the same technical characteristics, but with the same *productive capacity*. They are expanded, if enlargement of productive capacity is required, or they may be shrunk, if disinvestments are required because of diminutions or changes in their demand that may come through events quite external to the existing production or demand structures. Capital goods therefore are something that, so to speak, once they come into being, last forever, though in different forms. This is the peculiar characteristic of accumulated capital goods: they must be kept forever *with the required adaptations* in terms of their *productive capacities*.

There has been slowness in grasping the really upsetting implications of these novelties (most of all in terms of the *Institutions* that should have been induced, or even required). I have myself stressed elsewhere, in an analytical way, how different the impact of capital goods is compared with that of consumption goods on an economic system considered as a whole[16] Briefly, in the case of consumption

[16] See Pasinetti (1963), Pasinetti (1983), Pasinetti (2007), and Chapter 11, Section 4.

goods, the economic system suffers no consequences from decisions concerning the way these goods are used. The owners of consumption goods are entirely free from constraints – either physical or from duties to the society in which they live. They are free, on the consumption goods which they possess, to make any decision they like. A consumption good may be entirely consumed, it can be hoarded for future use, if it is durable, it can be sold, or given away to the external world, it could even be destroyed, with no consequences whatever on the actual working of the production economic system. This is not the case for the capital goods. Capital goods must be kept in existence in terms of *their productive capacities*. They must be used for the production they have been made for, but then, as they wear out, they *must* be replaced with other, similar, or rather similarly functioning, means of production; otherwise, the whole production process would come to a halt. It is important to realise that the existence, and then the renewal, of physical capital is an absolute necessity in the production process of the industrialised economies.

7 The Social Function of 'Capital'

All that has been said means that the physical capital goods – unlike consumption goods – perform what we might call a function which is relevant for society as a whole. They procure employment for the labourers. We may well say at this point that capital goods – independently of who owns them – have an overall social function to fulfil. For this reason (and others), capital and labour cannot be put on the same plane. In any economic system, quite independently of its institutional setup, labour and capital, though complementary and placed side by side in the production process, do not play a symmetrical role.

Another equally novel and equally basic feature may appear when one comes to realise the existence of the sharp consequential differences between the indirect (and hyper-indirect) and the more direct production processes. As we have seen, directness, plus indirectness, plus hyper-indirectness of the production processes make them add up, through the complex inter-industry relations, to the total amount of pure labour that comes to determine the 'natural' value of the corresponding final consumption good (or goods). From this stance, there is no difference in the total value of the corresponding final consumption good, whether the corresponding labour piles up directly, indirectly or hyper-indirectly.

This implies that the natural price of each consumption good incorporates *all* the quantities of labour that have accumulated in the whole, complex, vertically hyper-integrated process of making up the corresponding unit of consumption good. In other words, to trace out the value of each unit of consumption good, one must go back, all through the inter-industry and structural relations behind it. This constitutes a process that reconstructs backwards (and in reverse order exhausts) all the value of the final consumption goods; or, to put it more crudely, that pays for all the labour (direct, indirect, hyper-indirect) which has made it up (as explained in various places of this work; more specifically in Chapters 10, 12, and then, even more compactly, in Chapter 13).

But directness or indirectness (and hyper-indirectness) of the various parts of the production process, while having the same effect on cumulating the physical quantities of labour (and the corresponding wages) that come to determine the natural final price, have a dramatically different effect on the material expression of the physical quantities of the 'non-direct' labour concerned!

Quite conspicuously, direct labour, after being exerted, leaves no trace. It materialises in the final consumption good which it brings into being. On the other hand, the indirect plus hyper-indirect labour bestowed in the successive stages of the production of each consumption good (besides entering, together with direct labour, the final consumption good into which it is incorporated), leaves behind, so to speak, an external *material trail*, in the form of actual, physical capital goods. These are normally material objects, separate and in excess with respect to the final consumption good into which their contents of labour have come to be incorporated! They are not autonomous; they have been made (and they will have to be kept into existence) in order to maintain the running flow of final consumption goods. But they have a materiality of their own, separate from that of the consumption goods into which their content of labour has already been incorporated.

The nature of this materiality of the intermediate goods constitutes, without any sort of doubt, one of the most extraordinary and fascinating features – perhaps the most fascinating feature, but at the same time the strikingly most upsetting, socially profound, revolutionary feature – of all the complex set of physical, material things and of the whole process of capital accumulation, which the industrial era has brought into existence.[17]

By way of example, it would be interesting to compare the way in which, let us imagine an alien coming from outer space in two separate periods of time – let us say at the inception of the 'Agricultural Revolution' (eighth-fifth millennia BC), and again later on, during our own time – would describe the major changes that could be observed on our planet. Surely the most conspicuous novel features that would be noticed are precisely those associated with what we may indeed call the physically impressive capital infrastructures (the *capitalistic* framework of the new economic system) that have come into existence.

Curiously enough, if (of course a big *counter-factual if*) the whole world economic system had meanwhile evolved in strict accordance to its 'natural' path which we examined in our previous analysis, our outer-space guest would find it difficult to make any distinction between the physically independent (for us) external natural environment and the 'natural' anthropologically made capital infra-structures. Remember that the accumulation of the latter in time would have taken place by allotting all the costs of indirect labour to the replacements of worn-out, previously existing but discarded, capital goods, plus all the costs of hyper-indirect labour to the new equilibrium investments, that have become necessary in order to remain on the 'natural' equilibrium growth path of the *Natural Economic System.*

Indeed, our imaginary outer space guest would find no distinction between the 'natural' capitalistic infrastructure and any other natural resource or element of the natural environment. It would come to it as most natural to consider the whole material and even immaterial structure of production – of physical capital infrastructures, as well as of all natural resources and natural environment alike – as a *free external endowment* (like water or air), being given to us, or having made to come about for, the human community as a whole!

[17] The content of this section was in fact anticipated in my earlier works. I shall especially mention my works of Pasinetti (1981), Pasinetti (1983), Pasinetti (2005), Pasinetti (2007) and most specifically, see ultimately Pasinetti ((2012a), p. 86). In all these works, I pointed out that, in the previous literature, this puzzling problem has never been given a convincing solution.

8 The Strategic Role of *Financial* Capital

Continuing with our fiction, our imaginary outer-space guests would also soon realise that there is another aspect that is extraordinarily important and binding for the human inhabitants of our planet, which at first would have appeared invisible to them. From observing human behaviour, they would clearly perceive that a strikingly large amount of invisible complexity of positive and negative magnitudes indeed exists in our earthly society, in spite of adding up to nothing in total (specifically, these would be the amounts of purely *financial* debts and credits among individuals, or groups of individuals). These would not be immediately seen because their total sum is zero – overall, purely *financial* debts and credits cancel out. And yet, if we were to point them out, these debts and credits could amount to huge figures!

It may be useful to briefly resume the distinction we have repeatedly taken advantage of between the two analytical roles concerning either the *absence* of capital or the *presence* of durable capital goods. We may well now take them as highlighting the background of the two quite distinct, but important, roles of *Finance* in the process of production of an industrial economic system (as already considered in Chapter 14, Section 14). Let us begin with the first role in which production is supposed to be carried out by labour alone (with no capital goods). We may assume as usual, for analytical purposes only, that each consumption good or service is such as to require to be consumed by the end of each production period. In this logical framework, which we have called analytical stage one, all goods are strictly *consumption* goods. This means that the whole National Product (it does not matter whether net or gross, as the two coincide in this case) is consumed at the end of each production period.[18]

Clearly, having supposed that there are no physical capital goods, there also are no physical real stocks in the model. However, this does not at all exclude the fact that there may be *monetary* and *financial stocks*. The various economic agents can very well exchange securities with which to undertake credit and debit relations denominated in terms of a conventional unit of buying power. These debt/credit securities may have coordinated dates of expiration, based upon

[18] Of course this too is an assumption only made for analytical purposes which will be dropped later.

pre-established agreements (with debt and credit contracts), so that the loans can return to those who set the desired deadlines with various agreed inter-temporal configurations. The relevant aspect to underline here is that there can be stocks of debts and credits, which can be stipulated for purchasing power in time, even if no corresponding physical stocks exist in nature. Evidently, these financial *stocks* cancel themselves out overall. They constitute financial wealth for creditors, but at the same time, they cancel out by an equivalent financial liability of those who are indebted.

Overall, in a pure labour model, such as the one we are considering here, even when its productivity is increasing *net*, overall purely financial wealth does not exist. For the community as a whole, the sum of credits and debts equals zero. The relevant characteristic for our purposes is that a simple pure labour economic system in which there are absolutely no physical capital goods – in other words, where there are no real physical stocks – can create debt/credit relations to no end, even if (and perhaps because of), in the whole system, they overall cancel out. Financial stocks can be created without physical limits!

This is precisely the relevant extraordinary feature of a modern monetary economy. Differently from what happens with *physical* capital goods, there are no physical limits to purely financial operations; the only limits are those that may (and in fact should, as we may immediately realise) be imposed by the existing monetary and financial *institutions*, to be set up by the community as a whole, which are in any case subject to modifications, in ways and forms always open to innovation, invention, and whatnot in financial relations.

We are ready to proceed at this point to consider the really crucial stage of the introduction of *physical* capital goods. Thus, we come to consider the analytically more complex economic system, where production is the outcome of employment not only of direct labour, but also of indirect and hyper-indirect labour, that is, of capital goods. We thus are at last considering the full stage of our industrial economic systems. At this stage, each unit of production must necessarily be endowed with specific physical capital goods which are characterised by a *corresponding* size of productive capacity for the goods to be produced. It is important to underline that, at this stage, it is the whole of the *real* stocks of physical capital goods that become relevant. This means the imposition of *physical* magnitudes, and these also create physical limits to the magnitudes of productive capacity of the existing (equilibrium) capital goods (exactly as we have investigated in Chapters 11–14).

Most of all, it is important to stress that at this stage, it is capital in terms of physical productive capacity and in terms of physical employment of labour that becomes crucially relevant. But of course in this case, physical capital goods, measured in terms of productive capacity, cannot go beyond the physical limits which are exactly appropriate to absorb the full employment of available labour. If they were to go beyond such limits, they would necessarily generate idle productive capacity and therefore entail inefficiencies. More specifically – and looked at from a different point of view – the size of the *real stocks* of physical capital goods comes to impose physical limits which correspond to the equilibrium amounts of investments arising from the various growing sub-systems composing the *Natural Economic System*.

Now we may indeed note how crucial the difference is with respect to the previous case. The present procedure would *not* be the case for the purely *financial stocks* of the previous case, which could be created *ad libitum*!

Paradoxically considered, an insertion, or an extension of financial stocks to the present case – and this is the crucial point – could indeed be made as well, independently and quite beyond the whole process of physical capital accumulation!

9 The Historical Intellectual Difficulties of Grasping the Centrality of the (industrial) Rate of Profit

From the way and process through which the rate of profit has emerged from our analysis, we must acknowledge that this has been the substantially *new variable* that has typically come to characterise the industrial economic systems. It is so new that not only has it not been perceived as 'new', but it has immediately been confused with another variable that had emerged on its own and had been already dominant on the economic scene for centuries before: namely the *rate of interest*.

As has clearly appeared from the comparison and confrontation of the rate of profit and the rate of interest (see Chapter 14, Sections 11–13), these two magnitudes are essentially two *different* variables. We analysed, in detail and in an explicit fashion, their logical and analytical properties in Chapter 14.

The rate of profit emerged as the new, typically central, variable in the industrial society, while the rate of interest had emerged long before in any society where a reasonable degree of organisation had been set up to manage personal relations of debts and credits among individuals and/or institutions.

What has happened recently in the economies in which we live (which for most of us are 'capitalist' economies) is that, although the two variables are essentially different, they have been set up and made use of together. Each of the two variables has either found an application next to the other, or has been easily, but strikingly confused with the other, or even taken to be the same thing.

To understand how this could have happened, one needs to review both their specific essential origin, which we have done before, and additionally, a few historical facts. Let us begin with the historical facts. Both the rate of interest and the rate of profit are expressed by a magnitude in percentage form, though applied to a *different* object: a sum of borrowed purchasing power (usually money) in one case and an amount of physical investments in the other. But in history, the magnitude to which the percentage figure is applied has, without much hesitation and quite often, been referred to by using the same name ('Capital').

One might think that to add the specification *monetary* in one case and *physical* in the other could help. But history has repeatedly demonstrated that it does not help and has actually increased the confusion, because the *physical* and the *financial* specifications are, all too often and too easily, quickly or even inadvertently, exchanged with one another.

How did this happen? It is at this point that the historical-institutional aspect may be of help, as it prevented a clear distinction between the rate of interest and the rate of profit. Curiously, but once again, the phenomena are connected, since they have both been brought together by roughly the same historical events of the Industrial Revolution.

With the advent of industrial production, the rate of profit emerged as associated with production in physical terms, that is it was associated with 'capital', in terms of physical *machinery*. But machinery is not an autonomous or independent resource (like air or water), it is an object that itself needs to be produced.

Then, in economic systems with institutions of the liberal-capitalist type, as historically has happened, it seemed normal to ask people in particular positions of ownership – who came to be called the *capitalists* – to provide, through *loanable* funds, the necessary financial means (not for consumption, but) for building the machines with which to produce the physical means of production (the needed machinery and the physical places of work themselves; i.e. the factories).

In other words, in basic terms, the 'capital goods' constructed with the use of the *financial* means supplied by the 'capitalists', seemed to be the appropriate channel to use for the construction of works and machines and all physical means of production in an *institutional* environment (which came to be) called *capitalist.*

This entire process – so evident with the advent of industrialisation – clearly indicated that the industrial society was in dire need of a qualitative conceptual jump.

Now history indicates that this qualitative jump, with all its dramatic consequences, has in fact been made. Not, however, as a spontaneous evolution of the appropriate institutions, as could and should have been envisaged by the economics profession. It simply took place – and history now shows us how it happened – through what we might call a true *revolution.* It was a revolution that occurred slowly, silently, at times with abrupt events, even though the mainstream economics profession has always refused to acknowledge (or look dispassionately at) it.

Let us look into some of the relevant events. They were first the hints of (socialist) new-Ricardian economists; then the most fruitful part of Ricardo's analysis (as even re-interpreted in the first volume of Marx's *Geschichte*); then the most vital part of what Keynes called *his* revolution; and today as a turnaround, as we might hope, of an explicit change of the scientific paradigms – which could mean a change from a *pure exchange paradigm* to a *pure production paradigm*!

All these events provide the clearest historical premise to the real outbreak of the latest results, which were themselves complicated and not entirely understood or absorbed. One might even dare to call the whole process the Anthropogenic revolution of the industrial age.

Essentially, we should not try to up-turn the history of economic thought and pretend to go back to any form of individualism, as unfortunately the recent mainstream economists are so persistently and stubbornly trying to do.

What is described above is in fact a true 'revolution'.[19] It happened slowly, silently, we might even say*abscondedly*, but in reality, effectively, in our societies.

10 How Did the *Absconded* Revolution Take Place?

It has taken time, a long time, even in the dynamic era of industrialisation, for the profession of economists to reflect and eventually realise the technical and economic processes that were taking place. After the long succession of historical events mentioned in Section 9, which we might call it our *premise*, and against the wishful tradition of a well-established profession of economists – always on the whole, instinctively averse to it – it was the reaction of a younger generation of post-Keynesians (such as Domar, Harrod, Kaldor) that essentially realised – even if without stating it explicitly, or perhaps even not entirely realising it – that a novel variable of crucial importance had come to dominate the new horizon of the industrial economies.

This variable was the *rate of profit*, which in its true form emerged as the really novel variable in the processes of industrialisation and capital accumulation, as has been shown in Section 9.

What happened? We may begin by starting to recall a very simple formulation in a famous article devoted to a review of the theories of income distribution.

Nicholas Kaldor defined the above-mentioned re-elaboration as the Keynesian theory of economic growth and income distribution (Kaldor 1955), even if such a theory does not appear anywhere in Keynes's work. In fact, we arrive here at a crucial stage, which began to emerge from the article by Nicholas Kaldor, that concerns both the theories of income distribution and of economic growth.

Kaldor's arguments were nevertheless rather clear in their purpose, although their analytical formulations were convoluted. They turned out to emerge as obvious and immediate only if one assumed that workers' savings are zero (by the way a typically Classical assumption). In such a case, the profit share in the net national product and the equilibrium rate of profit, respectively, emerge from the extremely simple formulae:

[19] Or a counter-revolution, if we prefer to keep the term revolution attached to aspects in favour of labourers.

$$P/Y = (1/s_c)(I/Y), \tag{15.10.1}$$

$$P/K = (1/s_c)(I/K), \tag{15.10.2a}$$

where Y = net national product, K = total stock of capital, I = investments required by the economic system in order to expand in dynamic equilibrium, P = total profits in the economic system, s_c = 'capitalist' propensity to save.

More concisely, equation (15.10.2a) could well be written as

$$\pi = (1/s_c)g_n, \tag{15.10.2b}$$

where π = equilibrium rate of profit and g_n = *natural* rate of growth of the economic system (deriving from the sum of the rate of population growth and the rate of growth in productivity).

Note that with such an assumption (i.e. with $s_w = 0$), equation (15.10.2b), in its simplicity, entails consequences that are immediately of crucial relevance in dynamic equilibrium. The rate of profit of the economic system emerges simply as equal to the natural rate of growth of the whole economy, divided by the capitalists' propensity to save. In these extremely simple but suggestive terms, equation (15.10.2b) was christened by the term: the 'Cambridge equation'.

This equation was immediately criticised arguing that the assumption $s_w = 0$, while justified within the arguments which were set forth by Classical economists (in the early 1800s), had no justification in formulations that referred to our present day.

In truth, this objection was reasonable and valid.

However, imagine now the general surprise when, in preparing his Ph.D. dissertation, the present author discovered that the 'Cambridge equation' – the (15.10.2b) – in fact remains valid not only in the particular case when $s_w = 0$, but *in general*, that is when $s_w > 0$! This emerges as an asymptotic tendential result of the re-distribution of the stocks of capital which, due to the act of saving, come to be owned also by the workers and not only by the capitalists.[20] The only condition required to obtain this result, in fact by no means restrictive but

20 The result is not easily perceived and in fact slipped through or passed unnoticed in all of the preceding economic literature. The general validity of the 'Cambridge Equation' (15.10.2b) derives from the discovery, and highlighting of a fundamental relation which links profits to savings through ownership (direct or indirect) of the capital accumulated through savings (see the details in Pasinetti 1963, or more particularly Pasinetti 1974, p. 174).

rather obvious, is that the proportion of the workers' total savings – presumably then lent to the capitalists – must be less than (and in any case not more than) the share that would be necessary for financing entire amount of equilibrium investments (otherwise the economic system would fall into an economic slump due to lack of effective demand). In other terms, the condition simply is

$$s_w < I/Y \qquad (15.10.3)$$

But as it is obvious, equation (15.10.3) can never be inverted, if the system is to remain in full employment equilibrium.

The result of this discovery inevitably had a devastating effect on the discussions concerning growth and income distribution. Its insertion into the ongoing debates was equivalent to formulating a genuinely new theory of income distribution, a 'Keynesian' theory that, if accepted, as it had to be, would supplant the traditional Neoclassical theory of income distribution, the theory which had dominated mainstream economics for almost a century.

Especially at M.I.T., in Cambridge, Massachusetts, this result created much discomfort. Paul Samuelson and Franco Modigliani took up the challenge and reacted. By working jointly, they accurately scrutinised the result, and after finding it correct, they called it the *Pasinetti Theorem*; a too dangerous result, however, for traditional mainstream economic theory. Four years later (in Samuelson and Modigliani (1966) and in the same *Journal*), Samuelson and Modigliani published a joint article, where they presented a mathematical model which finally appeared to have generalising prerogatives. Samuelson and Modigliani acknowledged, to begin with, the correctness of the 'primal' theorem (the *Pasinetti Theorem*, as they called it), and hence, the 'Keynesian' elaborations which were derived from it; but at the same time, they also presented another counter-posed theorem which was presented as logically 'dual' and symmetrical to the first, and which they called the *Anti-Pasinetti Theorem*.[21] This theorem,

[21] These expressions are those used by Samuelson-Modigliani. My objection to Samuelson-Modigliani has always been based on the fact that the 'dual' theorem is only formally, and therefore only in appearance, symmetrical to the 'primal' one. In its *substantial* significance, it is not symmetrical at all because it requires an enormous sequel of supplementary assumptions which are absent in the case of the 'primal' theorem (see Pasinetti 1966, p. 305). It is significant to note that, at the Lincei Academy's Conference on Modigliani,

however, would become effective only if the share of savings of the workers in total income surged to the point where it provides the entire amount of savings necessary for the equilibrium growth of the whole economic system. In this case, it was shown that the share of capital owned by the 'capitalists' would decrease, till it tended towards zero. That is to say, the class of 'pure capitalists' was doomed continuously to decrease, until it would asymptotically disappear. I called this provocatively 'A "euthanasia" of the capitalists'. It may sound surprising, but this is precisely what Samuelson and Modigliani were forced to argue. They even cited proportions of 'saved' income by workers which they defined as 'econometrically reasonable' (yet unseemingly high, as they would have to cover *all* required savings!). And all this in order to justify their *Anti-Pasinetti Theorem*.[22] What had happened? The strange occurrence lies precisely here. Initially, Nicholas Kaldor had presented his formulation by beginning with the supposition that workers' savings were zero. This was considered to be econometrically *unreasonable*, at least for our times (no matter what justification it may have had in Ricardo's time). Later, it was discovered and highlighted that the above mentioned relation between savings and profits – the *Pasinetti Theorem* – proved that workers' savings had no effect in determining profits, thereby implying that the much criticised assumption that workers' savings were equal to zero ($s_w = 0$) was unnecessary! At this point, Samuelson and Modigliani literally invented a formally dual theorem that required the extreme and opposite assumption that workers would be able to generate *all* the required savings while the 'capitalists' were asymptotically doomed to disappear. This assumption, opposite and extreme as it was, but favourable to mainstream theory, was at this stage argued to be econometrically *reasonable*.[23]

Samuelson once again was compelled to resume the same attitude, insisting on the (formal) symmetry of the two theorems (see Paul Samuelson 'The variety and originality of Franco Modigliani's many contributions to economics', in 'Franco Modigliani tra teoria economica e impegno sociale', *Atti dei Convegni Lincei*, p. 9) (Conference held in Rome on 17–18 February 2005).

22 See Samuelson and Modigliani (1966), Samuelson–Modigliani (1966, p. 329).

23 It may be interesting to mention this absurd claim in defence of mainstream economics, especially now days when, in the U.S., the low-income classes have been encouraged to buy their houses by borrowing, i.e., to generate negative savings to an extremely unreasonable degree.

In fact, the Samuelson-Modigliani dual theorem (i.e. their Anti-Pasinetti Theorem) – apart from original skirmishes; see Meade (1966) – never attracted serious attention. It has never been considered relevant for any practical purposes.[24] Its sole function was that of protecting mainstream economics from a debacle by giving the impression that it could provide an alternative to the 'Cambridge Equation'. More substantially, the real purpose was to relegate the entire earlier discussion to oblivion.[25]

The aspect which was really terribly difficult for mainstream economists to accept was precisely what lies at the core of the 'Keynesian' theory of income distribution proposed by Kaldor. This economic theory would be in perfect continuity with Classical economic theory, but it would reverse its causal direction by inverting the contrasting roles of the workers and the capitalists. There is in any case an immediate recognition of the 'natural' function which is performed by the profits. This function is identified and justified by providing the equilibrium investments; that is exactly those investments that are necessary to fulfil the requirements of technical progress and population growth, so as to maintain full employment. That part of national income which then emerges as the 'surplus' – the result of the growth in productivity of the economic system – is meant to be devolved to the whole working population. This is precisely and essentially the gist of Kaldor's original contribution.

[24] Quite different, turned out to be the development that followed the 'primal' theorem (the Pasinetti Theorem). The Keynesian approach to the relationship between profits and income, savings and investments, income flows and the distribution of wealth continued to stimulate a proliferation of contributions, which were generally excluded from mainstream journals and textbooks. They found their place in numerous other journals, anthologies and textbooks. Without attempting a summary, which in any case would become too long, one can simply refer to the over 500 references listed in Baranzini (2005) and Baranzini and Mari (2011) to realise the richness of the problems considered, the variety of the contributions obtained, the developments stimulated by the theorem (especially with reference to multiple classes of workers' savings – i.e. whose savings come from their wages as well as from profits), juxtaposed to the compact class of 'pure capitalists', and the possible coexistence of different rates of interest set against a single rate of profit, as well as the possibility of introducing issues regarding income and tax expenditure, etc.

[25] This expedient had already been applied, as mentioned above, to the 'capital theory controversy'.

The importance of this outcome goes well beyond Kaldor's attempt at applying it to the working of a capitalist economy. The principle of income distribution that emerges from this theory really becomes much more important than Kaldor himself thought. It belongs to that level of investigation which I have called 'natural' (i.e. normative). At such a, more basic, level of investigation, the 'Cambridge Equation' becomes independent even of the institutional setup of the society which is considered.

Obviously, at this point, the time would come for going into an investigation of its implications for the specific institutional framework which is considered. And this would belong not so much to the 'critique' part of the Sraffian scientific project, but at last to its 'constructive' part. I shall try to come back to these aspects with at least some hints later. For the time being, let me return to the debate between the two Cambridges.[26]

11 The False Myth of the *Modigliani-Miller* Theorem of Perfect Financial Markets

It is a crude and at the same time an extraordinary fact that, from that point of time onwards, the dominant theory on savings, investment and growth was abruptly made to sharply change track. The prevailing attention of the economic profession, especially in the United States, was re-addressed, and turned to a radically different direction.[27]

The mainstream – that is the majority of the – economic profession unexpectedly stopped sharing any interest in continuing the discussion

[26] See Pasinetti (2012b, pp. 1437–1440).

[27] For the sake of completeness, I must mention that there also was another development of the savings theory, due mostly to Franco Modigliani, based on the 'life cycle' (i.e. on the assumption that each individual rationally distributes his/her disposable income along his/her entire life). This hypothesis is interesting. It works in a perfectly logical manner when each individual's wealth is strictly constituted by the flow of income that is received over a lifetime and devoted to consumption, so as to accumulate savings during the active life and to then spend it entirely afterwards up to the point of having none of it left at death. This hypothetical behaviour holds less and less, in this inter-temporal distribution, when one also introduces both a stock of wealth inherited from the preceding generation and a planned accumulation of another stock destined to following generations. These aspects have recently been further illustrated in Baranzini (2005).

with the Cambridge-England economists with whom they had before conducted such strong and animated discussions. They behaved as if they literally wished to forget any discussion that had earlier taken place and turned their attention to an entirely different sort of investigation. This shift, which had quietly started even before, began to attract extraordinary attention following the publication of a set of theorems that, considered all together, have become known by the name of the *Modigliani-Miller Theorem* (They were elaborated by Merton Miller and Franco Modigliani, in part separately and in part jointly, but, in the economic literature, they subsequently came to be known jointly as the *Modigliani-Miller Theorem*). The emphasis and insistence, as well as the thrust, with which the *Modigliani-Miller Theorem* was adopted, elaborated and presented in such numerous articles, books and textbooks of mainstream economic theory, contributed to generating a dramatic shift in the whole economic, monetary and financial policies over the following decades.[28]

I have thought it significant to reproduce here the initial paragraphs (each representing a synthesis of the item to which they refer) that appear in the New Palgrave Dictionary of Economics (Newman et al. 1987) and in the New Palgrave Dictionary of Money and Finance (Newman et al. 1992): that means in the texts most widely used for the teaching and diffusion of mainstream economic theories and imposed on students whose future is most likely to be in the management of corporations, monetary and financial institutions or in holding important academic posts in the economically and financially advanced Western world.

> In 1961, scientific inquiry into the motives and consequences of corporate dividend policy *shifted dramatically* with the publication of a classic paper by Miller and Modigliani. Perhaps the most significant contribution of the Modigliani-Miller paper was to spell out in careful detail the assumptions under which their analysis was to be conducted. The most important of these include the assumption that
>
> (i) the firm's investment policy is fixed and known by investors;
> (ii) there are no taxes on dividends or capital gains;
> (iii) individuals can costlessly buy and sell securities;

[28] I personally carried out a strong criticism of the *Modigliani-Miller Theorem* in an article of mine published in Pasinetti (2012b, pp. 1433–1453).

(iv) all investors have the same information;
(v) investors have the same information as the managers of the firm;
(vi) there are no contracting or agency costs associated with stock ownership.

With this set of assumptions, Modigliani and Miller demonstrated that a firm's dividend policy is a matter of indifference to stockholders. That is, the value of the firm is independent of the dividend policy adopted by management.

(*The New Palgrave Dictionary of Economics* 1987, vol. 1, p. 896)

The Modigliani-Miller (MM) Theorem is a collection of results showing, under ideal market assumptions *often taken for granted* by economic theorists, that the financial policy of a corporation is irrelevant. Based on a series of papers by Modigliani and Miller beginning in 1958, this theory has been cited for separate Nobel prizes in Economics awarded to Franco Modigliani and Merton Miller. While it is widely conceded that corporate financial policy is indeed important, the Modigliani-Miller theory is nevertheless the core of modern corporate finance since 'showing what *doesn't* matter can also show, by implication, what does' (Miller, M., Fall 1988, 'The Modigliani-Miller Propositions after Thirty Years', *Journal of Economic Perspectives*, vol. 2, n. 4, pp. 99–120)

(*The New Palgrave Dictionary of Money and Finance* 1992, vol. 2, p. 715)

Note the particularly long list of assumptions listed in the footnote to the first citation, and note moreover the last statement in the second citation, which to me seems quite misleading. How can the showing of what doesn't matter [italics in original], contain by implication what is important, especially if what is important is not stated? Yet, this phrase of Miller's has been widely used as a supposedly persuasive proposition in the ample literature on the *Modigliani-Miller Theorem* (as if it were Gospel truth!). If we want to interpret it benevolently, as suggested, for example by T. Cozzi at the Conference on Modigliani (*Accademia dei Lincei 2005*), the sentence may be interpreted as an invitation to accurately consider the importance and realism that the stated assumptions have, in order to evaluate the relevance of the proof of any theorem. But, if the assumptions are untrue, not even in largely approximate terms, then the theorem cannot be accepted, even if many economists (and economic agents!) have persisted all the same in believing them (or are obdurately insisting in saying that they believe in them, even now)!

But let me try to re-express in simpler words, without the pretence of being complete or exhaustive, the essential content of this famous theorem. One could say that the *Modigliani-Miller Theorem* demonstrates, under certain, specific, ideal conditions – essentially, by making all the necessary assumptions for defining a market of intermediary agents which is absolutely perfect[29] – that the market value of a corporation does not depend on its financial structure: in short, it does not depend on its debts to assets ratio. The theorem has in this way led theorists (and financial operators!) to believe that increasing indebtedness has no counter-indications, without considering that an absolutely necessary assumption for reaching such a conclusion is that corporations must always remain in the same category of risk, which of course is impossible if the corporation's indebtedness increases. In even simpler, immediate and practical words, the theorem has led to the belief that there is no difference between the two traditionally considered alternatives regarding the allocation of each single firm's profits, that is: (i) that of using them internally by adding them to the existing capital stock, or (ii) that of immediately distributing the dividends to the shareholders. However, one must note that, for these two alternatives to be equivalent, the second option needs the assumptions, '*often taken for granted by economic theorists*' (to resume the wording of the second citation quoted earlier), of perfect freedom for corporation managers on the one side and owner-shareholders on the other to have complete and total freedom to rely, with rational decisions, on supposedly perfect financial markets, in order to obtain externally the necessary financial means to undertake the new investments, or else to use them in any other direction. From still another viewpoint, the investment decisions and the possibilities of financing these decisions are supposed to be entirely separate and independent of each other, whatever their size (which in reality can never be the case).

The adherence to this way of thinking evidently led to a sharp contrast between the 'Classical' way of considering the accumulation of capital, and a new methodology based on the supposedly rational behaviour of economic agents, within the context of ideally perfect

[29] This means in terms of the micro-economic behaviour of the economic agents involved, in terms of the circulation of the necessary information (technical, institutional, legal) and in terms of market competitiveness.

markets. The former method (the 'Classical' method – and by implication also the 'Keynesian' one) is considered rough and primitive, while the second method is crowned with analytical beauty and exalted as the *only* possible way of achieving a rational and efficient management of economics and finance.

We can basically say that until the formulation of the *Modigliani-Miller Theorem*, the prevailing view was that the traditional role of the 'capitalists' – deserving praise, in Ricardo's opinion, condemned by history in Marx's view – was that of not distributing profits, but of keeping them within the firms and adding them to the pre-existing stock of capital, thereby generating that process of capital accumulation which characterises our capitalist economies. The *Modigliani-Miller Theorem* came to introduce a sharp break with the whole Classical – and by implication Keynesian – approach. It channelled all economic arguments to a supposedly micro-economic process relying on the rational behaviour of the single economic agents, in the search of efficiency for the corporation's investments, internal or external, in the strong belief that efficiency was associated, not so much with the traditional maximisation of profits, since this could generate complications in regimes of uncertainties, but with the maximisation of the corporations' market value (i.e. of the value of the corporations' shares, as evaluated on the stock exchange market).

This view reached its apex with a famous paper by Jensen and Meckling (1976), which became the most cited academic article, especially in business schools, claiming that the corporation managers should simply concentrate on maximising the value of the corporations for their shareholders. In practice, the idea was a very simple one, namely that of considering the firm as a commodity, to be bought and sold on the market like any other commodity. On this striking idea, see also Putterman (1988).[30]

[30] It may be interesting to mention that only after one recent stock exchange colossal crash, have the leading personalities of the business world shown, at last, an inclination to a dramatic turnaround by going back to common sense. One can read in *The Economist* (April 24, 2010): 'in a recent article of the Harvard Business Review, Roger Martin, dean of the University of Toronto's Rotman School of Management, charts the rise of what he calls the "tragically flawed premise" that firms should focus on maximising shareholder values, and argues that "it is time we abandoned it"'. To mention another case, the former General Manger of General Electric, Jack Welch, in a widely reported

12 Recalling Again Some Notes of Historical Background Containing the Absconded Revolution

But, how could all this have happened? How could one have arrived at such a set of unbelievable convictions? It seems dutiful to ask. But, the answer is not easy to give.

One must at least, even if briefly, recall a cumulative intellectual process that has occurred over an entire century in the history of economic thought and on which we have drawn attention since the beginning of the present investigation, but it becomes here necessary to recall.

It must be reminded that the dominant economic theory – heir to what was also called the marginalist revolution (at the end of the eighteenth and the beginning of the nineteenth centuries) – had elaborated an extremely elegant, logical-mathematical model (the model of *general economic equilibrium*) founded on a conception of economic analysis which was counter-posed to the one developed by Classical economics. The Political Economy of Adam Smith and of the Classics, aimed at 'investigating the nature and causes of the wealth of nations', had been set aside and replaced by the Economics of Marshall and the Neoclassical economists, who considered Economics as a science basically concerned with the optimal allocation of the given available resources. The works to be considered as symbols of this new conception of Economics are probably indicated in Samuelson (1947) *Foundations of Economic Analysis* and in Debreu (1959) 'Theory of value' – see Section 1 of Chapter 2.

These works essentially dealt with prices and *real* physical quantities, within a context of constrained maximisation of microeconomic functions of consumers' utility and of firms' profits. It must perhaps be stressed that behind this approach, there is the conviction that the maximising analytical tool was to be identified as the unique universal principle of all economic analysis, within a dominant context of

interview, after having been in the past a strong supporter of the maximisation of value for the share-holders, has also come himself to change his view by coming to recognise the same 'flaw', and in fact by arriving to define 'the idea of maximising shareholder value as insane' (*Financial Times*, 12 March 2009). All this of course, in a cultural context of supposedly perfect knowledge, generating the perfect communication of information, and within an institutional framework of perfectly automatic self-regulating free markets.

methodological individualism.[31] Initially, monetary phenomena were left out of the model. But, it then became the task of the 'monetarist' economists (among whom, the prominent leadership was taken by Milton Friedman) to introduce them later, thereby closing the only degree of freedom that had still been left in the theoretical model. This logical operation could hold together the logical framework of the model, provided that the assumption was introduced of a perfect neutrality of money (i.e. the assumption that money acted only as a 'veil' and had no impact on real phenomena). At this point, it was the turn of the *Modigliani-Miller Theorem* to take the further crucial and final logical step. The idea, considered brilliant (and which I personally presume has turned out to be folly), was that of extending the very same theoretical model concerning the optimal allocation of given resources (with the addition of all those numerous assumptions which became necessary) not only to the monetary phenomena, but also (and most of all) to those concerning the whole sphere of finance. The landslide of these types of 'extensions' could no longer be stopped. It moved on to new configurations, with the so-called innovative finance, and with the continual invention of new financial instruments and devices of all sorts with absolute freedom and independence from any necessary institutional control: a hyper-liberalism that has led to a truly new phenomenon – the 'financialisation' of the economy both nationally and internationally to a degree that could never have been imagined before.

One must admit that this was a true 'revolution', or rather a counter revolution, both at the analytical and at the institutional level. At the analytical level, the theorists proceeded to accurately scrutinise the numerous assumptions which needed to be made in order to obtain formally unassailable models. But, the consequences of non-fulfilment – always possible after all – of the implied necessary conditions were not sufficiently evaluated, or more clearly, they were simply ignored. At the institutional level – and here I come to an aspect which in my view is extremely important – it seems to me that they did not consider the basically relevant fact that introducing assumptions in a theoretically

[31] To be accurate, Paul Samuelson, in the course of updating his textbooks, has always shown a reasonably eclectic and flexible attitude. See his last article Samuelson (2008) 'Farewell to Friedman-Hayek Libertarian Capitalism', Tribune Media Services, posted 10/15/2008 at 7:00 pm EST.

(unrealistic) ideal model was equivalent to closing the whole logical system to any alternative. More specifically, the procedure was leading to losing freedom of choice with reference to which institutional setup to adopt – a crucially important aspect which was inexplicably underestimated. The main concern was that the model should theoretically lead to situations of optimisation, but there was no concern with the fact that this procedure implied a unique institutional configuration on which one was compelled to rely. More specifically, the only admissible institutional setup was that of absolutely perfect markets; however, without specifying how these markets could come into being, or rather by simply assuming them to be self-creating and self-regulating. What was performed was basically an act of faith in all those conditions supposed to be automatic that are necessary for the realisation of an ideal (entirely hypothetical) institutional context – a context, by the way, which in the analysis of the present investigation was characteristic of a historical phase that belonged to the past.[32] Most importantly, the procedure implied a process of exclusion of any type of institutional alternative. One had to have perfectly free markets or nothing else. The path of research and examination of alternative solutions was automatically barred.

13 A New Form of 'Corporate' Capitalism?

I should like to draw the attention of the reader to the fact that 'with the publication of the Classic paper by Miller and Modigliani'... 'the motives and consequences of the corporate dividend policy shifted dramatically'; and again (by recalling the second citation) 'the MM theory [has by now become]... the core of modern corporate finance'. This is where we have been led. Leaving aside the 'motives' and trying to concentrate on the consequences, I shall try to list a few of the most evident characteristics which have recently appeared in our economies:

(i) A wild rush towards short-term profits and a rapid distribution of dividends. In fact it is the announcement of the level of the corporations' dividends, which immediately affects the stock market share quotations (classified as expressing the community's 'wealth').

[32] See Chapter 2 of the present work and also Pasinetti (2007), pp. 250–255.

(ii) An anxious race by corporations to recruit *managers* with ability in these types of operations (essentially short term), remunerated with fabulous salaries, and further privileges, preferably tax free, such as: *bonuses, stock-options*, as well as a paraphernalia of benefits of all sorts.

(iii) (On a strictly social level), a decreasing interest in all types of research, either undertaken or stimulated or recommended, on the phenomenon of income distribution, not only with reference to the amount of distributed shares at the macroeconomic level, but also and more importantly with reference to personal income distribution. It seems generally recognised that the inequalities in the levels of personal income distribution have widened almost everywhere – among categories, among different jobs and tasks, as well as among geographical regions.[33] The disparities are usually justified with meritocratic motivations, but not always are these assertions explicitly demonstrated.

(iv) At the same time, over the last few decades, it seems to me that among economists and politicians there has been a decreasing preoccupation over unemployment. According to the authors of the so-called real business cycle theory – economists such as Edward Prescott or Robert Lucas, just to mention two Nobel laureates in economic science – it is argued that involuntary unemployment in fact does not exist. In other words, it is argued that, if one examines the decisions and motivations of each single individual, one can show that workers rationally choose not to work and thus to remain unemployed. As outlandish as this affirmation may appear, the arguments are elaborated in such a logical manner as to make the workers' choices appear rational, while usually taking as given the institutional framework of perfect markets.

(v) It is in any case generally accepted that there has been a significant increase in the process of financiarisation of our economies. According to the U.S. Department of Commerce, the 'financial sector', which in the forty years from 1950 to '90 represented on average 10% of corporate profits, went up dramatically in the Nineties by more than doubling to 22%. In the five years that then

[33] For more detailed explanations, refer to the data presented and elaborated, e.g., in Galbraith and Garcilazo (2009), Galbraith and Garcilazo (2004).

followed (i.e. the first five of the new millennium), total corporate profits went up even further to 34%.[34] It seems to me that it is hard not to see these figures as anything but pathological.

It is more than natural to ask oneself: what are we witnessing? Is this a supposed genetic mutation of capitalism?[35] It seems generally recognised that phenomena of *real* instability were perceived even before those of financial instability.[36] But *further* elements of financial instability, on which Keynes was never tried to insist upon, are entrenched in capitalist market economies. Empirical analysis has confirmed that the history of capitalism abounds with cases of financial instability, even acute ones, also when *real* economic instability was avoided. Yet, the recent overflow of an abnormally financialised capitalism in our economies appears to me as too evidently pathological. It seems clear and generally accepted from this current crisis that the institutions and structures which must be re-examined and re-structured in depth are precisely and above all those in the (institutional) financial field.

In light of these recent events, it must be said that it would be very difficult to accept that all these consequences should bear no relation with the diffusion and the conviction of the actual relevance probably even much beyond the original intention of the authors of the *Modigliani-Miller Theorem*. If this is the case, it seems to be as most necessary to deduce that such statements (as the one in the second citation in Section 12) which defines the MM theorem as 'the core of modern corporate finance' should cause very serious concern and should generate strong preoccupations, or in any case, should undergo profound and serious scrutiny, re-examination and almost entire revision.[37]

[34] These figures are given by Friedman (2009), 'The Failure of the Economy and of the Economists'.

[35] Zygmunt Bauman has recently used the expression of 'parasitic capitalism' (see his book in Italian, Bauman 2009).

[36] I have also recently insisted on the origin of this instability (Pasinetti 2007, pp. 229–231).

[37] Re-examination, however, presupposes openness of mind and readiness to raise questions even on the very basic propositions and on the most entrenched beliefs which have been taught to us. No doubt, this is not easy.

To give an example, it is extraordinary for me to find that even now, at this stage of the economic crisis as it has been developing, an eminent personality such as Paul Volcker, former Governor of the Federal Reserve and then

14 The Simplest of All Economic Growth Models

At this point, one cannot avoid a sort of final but crucial question: what should we state as the result of the investigations we are pursuing here, all explicitly based on the novel 'paradigm of production', which was after all so clearly perceived at the beginning of the *Political Economy* of the Classical economists and then, instead of being developed, so unwisely set aside and submerged by the *Marginal Counter-revolution*)?

One immediate aspect of the contrast would be to realise how the economic policies and especially the financialisation theories which have widely dominated the recent decades (think of their symbol: the *Modigliani-Miller Theorem*, which most probably emerged from the attempt, presumably by Modigliani, to neutralise the more objective Cambridge Pasinetti-Kaldor theory of growth and income distribution) all require, specifically and exclusively, an *institutional* framework strictly based on supposed micro-behaved markets, rationally guided, with perfect knowledge and perfect forecasts – that is an institutional framework that in reality simply does not exist!

In contrast to this, the rationality of the *Natural Economic System* that we have investigated is so much simpler and much wider! It is rich of degrees of freedom, that may be used and guided in various directions, within various circumstances, and susceptible to respond to external influence, through new methods of analysis and innovations.[38] Due to this characteristic, it does not even exclude the

Chairman of the Economic Recovery Advisory Board to President Obama, after giving an astonishingly dramatic review of the major failures that have emerged in the course of the present crisis – in an article commissioned to him by the *New York Review of Books* by the title 'The Time We Have Is Growing Short' – should be unable to get away from the very basic Neoclassical conviction that the exclusive central role of economics is the optimum allocation of resources. He explicitly writes: '[. . .] I suspect we all would support [that] "Economics is fundamentally about efficiently allocating resources so as to maximise the welfare of individuals"'(Volcker 2010).

[38] This is exactly the opposite of what we find in the mainstream approach which provides no freedom whatsoever. In it, in fact, the concept of methodological individualism rules supreme. And, there is no way of escaping it. The model of rational, individualistic behaviour leaves no room for escape. It is closed in itself. One is either 'inside' and remains there, or one is 'outside' (see critiques of this mainstream theoretical aspect in Pasinetti 2007, pp. 263–269 and also here in pp. 478–485). When alternatives are proposed

possibility of taking advantage of many of the existing institutions, or indeed even of other institutions (when the conditions of the real world happen to be useful, and most of all with the exclusion of absurd suppositions necessary for any reliance on perfect markets, which – as are supposed – do not and cannot even exist). At the same time, it is perfectly compatible with other institutions, even with those which are at the opposite extreme from an institutional standpoint, such as the centralised systems. And this is besides all the other alternative intermediate configurations, in their varying methodological shades and degrees.

The contrast with the dominant approach is, therefore, extensive and in some sense diametrically opposite, on a sheer methodological plane!

To clearly understand this aspect, I thought it could be useful to briefly consider, at least as an example, one of the alternative configurations which show the implications that emerge, thereby giving a more immediate idea of the sharply contrasting methodology. To this effect, the simplest approach seems to be exactly the opposite extreme with respect to the supposed market economies relying on methodological individualism. Furthermore, and in a sense most of all, it is useful to remember that the extreme case which we are here considering is – as an important point of reference – the case in which precisely the need for making suppositions regarding the institutional aspects are at their minimum!

With this objective in mind, we may go back and consider the very original attempt which I made in Pasinetti (1962). In it, I presented the case of what I called a 'social economy': explicitly treated – let me clearly point out – *not at all* in order to support any particular type of institutional setup, but only in order to give an *example* of the simplest dynamic model which lies at the opposite extreme and in which, on the contrary, institutional requirements and suppositions are

outside the mainstream model, one must be prepared to be submerged by a shower of undue criticism. As noted in Section 11, one can answer critiques in a positive and appropriate manner. What is discouraging and difficult to accept is being forced out of the discussions with the systematic technique of neglect and oblivion as has happened all too often – see as examples what has happened to the capital controversy, or to the Solowian attempts to equip the major novelty of the industrial age (i.e. the coming into existence of *Capital*) for the earlier examination of the characteristics and properties of *Land*.

minimised, especially regarding the behavioural relations of individuals and groups.

In all its simplicity, the case envisioned in the previous paragraph may simply be presented as follows.[39]

In an ideally 'social' economy all the members of the community belong to the category of 'workers'. The responsibility for organising the production process and the *direct ownership* of the means of production (in the most appropriate way that may be invented by human ingenuity) belong to the State. However, the State as such cannot consume: consumption is undertaken only by individuals. Consequently (disregarding transfers), if any amount of national product is not distributed to the members of the community in the form of wages, or in the form of interest on their loans to the State, that amount becomes *ipso facto* saved. This means that, as an inherent characteristic of this institutional setup, even the single parameter, that is (s_c), used in the original versions of the (see Section 10) discussions (with reference to Kaldor's theory of distribution as s_c becomes unity ($s_c = 1$) – which means that even *the only behavioural parameter that remained in the last formulae disappears*). It may actually be surprising to devote attention to the simplicity of these results.

Equations (15.14.1) and (15.14.2), presented in Pasinetti (1962) respectively become extraordinarily simple, namely:

$$P/Y = I/Y \tag{15.14.1}$$

$$P/K = I/K \tag{15.14.2}$$

In these equations *all behavioural parameters have disappeared* with the obvious result that, in equilibrium, total profits are equal to total investments, and the rate of profit (which for simplicity and exceptionally, but according to the current capitalist institutions, may simply be made as equal to the rate of interest on government bonds) is equal to the economic system's natural growth rate. Consequently, total wages are always equal to total consumption, and total profits are always equal to total savings. This does not mean, however, that total wages would be spent and that total profits would be saved! Equations

[39] This paragraph follows the steps taken in Pasinetti (1962, pp. 277–278). It does not entirely follow all the prescriptions associated to the configurations of a *Natural Economic System*, but it is certainly the nearest to it without the necessity of any deviation.

(15.14.1) and (15.14.2) are obtained without introducing any type of assumption on individual choices regarding savings. In dynamic equilibrium, each individual is supposed to be completely free to decide which portion of her/his income (wages and interests) he/she intends to save, without this decision affecting equations (15.14.1) and (15.14.2) in any way. This conclusion, for a 'socialist system' at this point, is simply equivalent to what was considered the most surprising result of the so-called *Pasinetti Theorem* (as denoted by Samuelson and Modigliani 1966).

In this way, the procedure indicated in Pasinetti (1962, Section 3) becomes extremely simple: since $s_c = 1$, in a dynamic equilibrium, individual savings from wages are exactly equal to individual consumption from interests, so that total consumption (from wages and interests) is equal to total wages.

An important corollary follows: it is not necessary for a State, with the simple characteristics considered previously, to interfere in the decisions regarding individual consumption and savings. There is just one constraint which must be fulfilled (which in this case is shared by the corresponding capitalist system) expressed by equation (15.10.1). The community as a whole cannot remain in dynamic equilibrium if it insists on saving more than what is required by the natural growth rate of the economic system. If it were to persist, the system would slump into a chronic state of under-employment due to a lack of effective demand.[40] If the saving's limit is not surpassed, there is no need to place any restriction on individual savings. The only effect of these savings is to require from the State the issuing of a national debt for a part of the stock of accumulated capital, with the consequent distribution of part of profits (in the form of interest on loans), which will however come back in the form of lent savings.

To conclude, we can present the results as follows. In an economic system with full employment, where the net income of those who organise the production process is totally saved, there exists a specific rate of profit, which is the one that has been called *natural rate*

[40] We are naturally referring to a closed system. In an open system, where the State can provide external loans from its sovereign funds, full employment could be maintained also in the case where total savings are exceeding the amount required by total investments.

of profit (since it is equal to the natural growth rate) that has the following property: if it is applied both to the price determination process and to the process for interest payments on loans, it generates an economic system *no matter what the savings decisions of the individuals may be*, whereby the amount of total savings is exactly equal to the amount of investments needed to keep pace with technical progress and population growth.

The usefulness of this simplified example, as referred to a 'socialist' system, is that it gives us a logical framework (with a really *minimal reference to institutions*), as close as possible to that foundational level of an economic system, which in this investigation has been called *natural*. There is nothing automatic in it, as I repeatedly have had the occasion to show and stress. Of course, the underlying evolving movements in technology and in the consumption patterns are always at work and may generate impulses of dynamic instability for which it will of course always be the task of the appropriate institutions to contrast.

Nevertheless, one perceives quite clearly a background of complex, but essential underlying normative characteristics towards which it would appear more than justified to address the necessary attitude, work, inventions and purposes of the complex *ensemble* of our *institutions*.

15 The Temptation of Counterfactual Hypotheses

At the end of this discourse and with reference to recent events, one must admit that the temptation becomes strong for some exercises based on counterfactual hypotheses. Especially if we consider the present deep economic crisis, what is more spontaneous than asking ourselves where would we be if, instead of following the Neoclassical and even more the Monetarist stream of thought, which has shaped the majority of the economic profession and the economic and monetary policies of the past three or four decades, we had paid greater attention to the earlier Classical and Keynesian theories and policies? One must of course be conscious that any answer given to this sort of attempts, no matter how accurately framed, cannot avoid the objection of being somewhat fanciful. Even more so in our case, where, as has been pointed out, the Classical/Keynesian approach would have been compatible with a multiplicity of institutional setups quite beyond that of a perfect competitive market economy.

All this being taken for granted, it is nonetheless surprising to note how, in a matter of a few months, the Governments of the Western industrialised nations – with the United States and the United Kingdom in the lead – have been compelled by events to intervene with unprecedented colossal bailouts to salvage shaky giant banking, financial and insurance corporations from collapsing; and then have extended the same measures to industrial corporations of world relevance, whose bankruptcy would have caused unemployment of an appalling size, which in any case would have been reputed socially unsustainable. One had to go back to Keynes's arguments, not so much to admit failure – which was done only partially – but in order to provide practical justifications for the enormous injections of public money, with financial devices and on a scale that could not be justified by any economic theory or consideration or exception on which the prevalent economic theory could rely, since according to dominant theory, the events that were happening should never have occurred.

Yet, it appears disconcerting at the very least to see that in the actual world in which we live, massive Government nationalisations should be carried out on a large scale, obviously with public indebtedness, that is of all the citizens, without any plan whatsoever, except by providing the justification that nothing different could have been done, as if what was happening was a reply to an external event, fallen upon us from the sky, not only unexpectedly but essentially inexplicably, with the sole perspective (also not explained) that it would obviously be a temporary phenomenon, to be speedily overcome, so as then to re-privatise the nationalised firms once the situation of their insolvency had been settled (i.e. had been paid off by the taxpayers).

Indeed, can we think of a clearer example of what Joseph Stiglitz himself has defined as 'American socialism',[41] that is consisting of the 'socialisation of the losses and the privatisation of the gains'?

We are left wondering why on earth public ownership (not necessarily to its full extent, that is not essentially *étatiste*, yet substantially under the control of the community, in the efficacious sense of its most variegated organisations) could not have been a little more intelligently

[41] Stiglitz (2009, p. 39).

anticipated and undertaken. Those nationalisations that were recently made could already have come about in the most natural way, that is through a sufficient accumulation of profits, so that public ownership would have come into being automatically, thereby avoiding the enormous costs which have now been undertaken and which most probably will continue to be undertaken.

A final aspect which is no longer counterfactual, but terribly relevant, cannot in any case escape attention. It seems at this point more reasonable to look with greater favour back to a Classical/Keynesian framework, perhaps with less sophisticated analytical tools than those at the bottom of mainstream economics, and yet much nearer to common sense and more suitable for incorporating that flexibility and openness of views necessary to the processes of the reconstruction of such institutions that seem more appropriate to the overall framework of an evolving and globally industrialised world.

References

Abraham-Frois, G., and E. Lendjel (2004): *Les Œuvres Economiques de l'Abbé Potron*. L'Harmattan, Paris.

Agazzi, E. (2014): *Scientific Objectivity and Its Contexts*. Springer International Publishers, Cham, Switzerland.

Allen, R. G. D. (1967): *Macro-Economic Theory*. MacMillan, London.

Allen, R. G. D., and A. L. Bowley (1935): *Family Expenditure*. King & Sons, London.

Anderson, J. (1777): *An Enquiry into the Nature of the Corn Laws, with a View to the New Corn Bill Proposed for Scotland*. Mundell, Edinburgh.

Arena, R., and P. L. Porta (2012): *Structural Dynamics and Economic Growth*. Cambridge University Press, Cambridge.

Arrow, K. (1962): "The Economic Implications of Learning by Doing," *Review of Economic Studies*, 29(3), 153173.

(1991): "Ricardo's Work as Viewed by Later Economists," *Journal of the History of Economic Thought*, 13(01), 70–77.

Arrow, K., and G. Debreu (1954): "Existence of Equilibrium for a Competitive Economy," *Econometrica*, 22, 265–290.

Arrow, K., and F. Hahn (1971): *General Competitive Analysis*. Holden-Day Inc., Edinburgh; Oliver & Boyd, San Francisco.

Baldwin, J. W. (1959): "The Medieval Theories of the Just Price: Romanists, Canonists and Theologians in the Twelfth and Thirteenth Centuries," *Transactions of the American Philosophical Society*, 49, pt IV.

Baranzini, M. (2005): "Modigliani's Life-Cycle Theory of Savings Fifty Years Later," *Banca Nazionale del Lavoro Quarterly Review*, 58(233–234), 109–172.

Baranzini, M., and C. Mari (2011): "The Cantabrigensis–Italian School of Income and Wealth Distribution," in *Gli economisti postkeynesiani di Cambridge e l'Italia, Accademia dei Lincei*, vol. 261, pp. 235–340. Scienze e Lettere, Roma.

Bauman, Z. (2009): *Capitalismo parassitario*, Il nocciolo. Laterza, a cura di B. Vecchi, trad di F. Galimberti.

Beccaria, C. (1764): *Dei delitti e delle pene*. Marco Coltellini, Livorno.

Bidard, C., G. Erreygers, and W. Parys (2009a): *The Mathematical Analysis of Linear Economic Systems: Father Maurice Potron's Pioneering Works*. Routledge, London.

(2009b): "'Our Daily Bread': Maurice Potron, from Catholicism to Mathematical Economics," *European Journal of the History of Economic Thought*, 16(1), 123–154.

Böhm-Bawerk, E. v. (1889): *Positive Theorie des Kapitales*. Marco Cortellini, Innsbruck.

Bortkiewicz, L. v. (1907): *Wertrechnung und Presirechnung im Marxschen System*. Jahrbücher für Nationalökonomie und Statistik, Berlin, English translation: *On the Correction of Marx's Fundamental Theoretical Construction in the Third Volume of Capital*.

(1952): *Value and Price in the Marxian System*. MacMillan, London, Originally published in German in 1907.

Brody, A. (1970): *Proportions, Prices and Planning – A Mathematical Restatement of the Labour Theory of Value*. North Holland Publishing, Amsterdam.

Bruni, L., and S. Zamagni (2015): *L'economia civile. Un'altra idea di mercato*. Il Mulino, Bologna.

Burmeister, E. (1968): "On a Theorem of Sraffa," *Economica*, 35(137), 83–87.

Cannan, E. (1903): *A History of the Theories of Production and Distribution in English Political Economy from 1776 to 1848*. P S King and Son, London, 2nd edition.

Cantillon, R. (1931): *Essai sur la nature du commerce en general*. Royal Economic Society, London, written in 1730 but published posthumously in 1755. Edited with supplements by Henry Higgs.

Carey, H. C. (1837): *Principles of Political Economy*. Carey, Philadelphia, Part I – 1837; Part II – 1838; Part III – 1840.

Cassel, G. (1918): *Theoretische Sozialökonomie*. C. F. Winter, Leipzig, English translation: *The Theory of Social Economy*, London 1921.

Cassidy, J. (2012): *How Markets Fail: The Logic of Economic Calamities*. Farrar, Straus & Giroux, New York, Italian translation: *Finanza e società giusta*, Bologna: il Mulino 2012.

Cavalli-Sforza, L. L., P. Menozzi, and A. Piazza (1996): *The History and Geography of Human Genes*. Princeton University Press, Princeton.

Cipolla, C. M. (1978): *The Economic History of World Population*. Harvester Press, Brighton.

Cournot, A. (1838): *Recherches sur le principes mathmatiques de la thorie des richesses*. Chez L. Hachette, Libraire de l'Université Royale de France, Paris.

Davar, E. (2014): "Walras and Contemporary Financial–Economic Crisis." *Modern Economy*, 5(5), 635–656.

De Vivo, G. (ed.) (2009): *Il Tableau Économique di François Quesnay*. Fondazione Raffaele Mattioli, Milano.

Debreu, G. (1959): "Theory of Value – An Axiomatic Analysis of Economic Equilibrium," Monograph 17, Cowles Foundation for Research in Economics, New York.

Dmitriev, V. K. (1974): *Economic Essays on Value Competition and Utility*. Cambridge University Press, Cambridge, translated by Nuti, D. M., originally published in Russian in 1904.

Dobb, M. (1940): *Political Economy and Capitalism*. Routledge and Kegan Paul, London.

Domar, E. D. (1946): "Capital Expansion, Rate of Growth, and Employment," *Econometrica*, 14(2), 137–147.

Eatwell, J. (1975): "Mr. Sraffa's Standard Commodity and the Rate of Exploitation," *Quarterly Journal of Economics*, 89(4), 543–555.

Editorial (2011): "Welcome to Anthropocene," *The Economist*, May 28.

Engel, E. (1857): "Die Productions-und Consumptionsverhältnisse des Konigreichs Sachsen," *Zeitschrift der Statistischen Bureaus des Koniglich Sächsischen Ministerium des Inneren*, Nos. 8 and 9, No. 22. Republished in *Bulletin de l'Institut International de Statistique*, IX (1895).

Ferguson, C. (1969): *The Neoclassical Theory of Production and Distribution*. Cambridge University Press, Cambridge.

Friedman, B. M. (2009): "The Failure of the Economy & the Economists," *The New York Review of Books*, May 28.

Galbraith, J. K. (2004): *The Economics of Innocent Fraud. Truth for Our Times*. Houghton Mifflin Company, Boston.

Galbraith, J. K., and J. E. Garcilazo (2009): "Unemployment, Inquality and the Policy of Europe: 1984–2000," *The Journal of Economic Inequality Volume*, 7, 189–206.

Galiani, F. (1751): *Della Moneta, Libri Cinque*. Giuseppe Raimondi, Naples, reprinted in *Della moneta e scritti inediti*, introduced by Alberto Caracciolo and edited by Alberto Merola, Feltrinelli, Milan, 1963.

Gilbert, M., and I. B. Kravis (1954): "An International Comparison of National Products and the Purchasing Power of Currencies," *OEEC*.

Gossen, H. H. (1854): *Entwickelung der Gesetze des menschlichen Verkehrs und der daraus fliessenden Regeln fr menschliches Handeln*. F. Vieweg, Braunschweig.

Graziani, A. (1989): "The Theory of the Monetary Circuit," *Thames Papers in Political Economy (Thames Politechnic)*, Spring, 1–26.

Grosse, R. N. (1953): "The Capital Structure of the American Economy," in *Studies in the Structure of the American Economy*, ed. by W. W. Leontief, pp. 185–242. Oxford University Press, New York.

Haavelmo, T. (1944): "The Probability Approach in Econometrics," *Econometrica*, 12, iii–vi+1–115, Supplement.

Haganauer, S. (1931): "Das 'justum pretium' bei Thomas von Aquino. Ein Beitrag zur Geschichte der objectiven Werttheorie," *Vierterljahrschrift für Sozial und Wirschaftsgeschichte*, 24, 161–165.

Hahn, F. H., and R. C. O. Matthews (1964): "The Theory of Economic Growth: A Survey," *The Economic Journal*, 74(296), 779–902.

Harcourt, G., and P. Kriesler (eds.) (2013): *The Oxford Handbook of Post-Keynesian Economics*. Oxford University Press, Oxford.

Harrod, R. F. (1939): "An Essay in Dynamic Theory," *The Economic Journal*, 49(193), 14–33.

(1948): *Towards a Dynamic Economics*. MacMillan, London.

Heckscher, E. F. (1955): *Mercantilism*. George Allen and Unwin, London, 2 vols. Revised 2nd edition. First published in Swedish in 1931, Vol. 2, p. 26.

Hicks, J. R. (1932): *The Theory of Wages*. MacMillan, London.

Hollander, S. (1965): "On the Interpretation of Just Price," *Kyklos, XVIII*, 615–634.

Homer, S. (1963): *A History of Interest Rates*. Rutgers University Press, Brunswick, NJ.

Houthakker, H. S. (1957): "An International Comparison of Household Expenditures Patterns, Commemorating the Centenary of Engel's Law," *Econometrica*, 25(4), 532–551.

INED (1958): *François Quesnay et la Physiocratie*. Institute National d'Etudes Démographiques, Paris.

Jensen, M. C., and W. H. Meckling (1976): "Theory of the Firm: Managerial Behavior, Agency Costs and Ownership Structure," *Journal of Financial Economics*, 3(4), 305–360.

Jevons, W. (1871): *The Theory of Political Economy*. Macmillan, London.

(1911): *The Theory of Political Economy*. Macmillan and Co., Limited, London, 4th edition.

Kaldor, N. (1961): "Capital Accumulation and Economic Growth," in *The Theory of Capital*, ed. by F. A. Lutz, and D. C. Hague, pp. 177–222. Macmillan, London.

Keynes, J. M. (1936): *The General Theory of Employment, Interest and Money*. Macmillan, London.

Koopmans, T. (1957): *Three Essays on the State if Economic Science*. McGraw-Hill, New York.

Kuczynski, M., and R. Meek (1972): *Quesnay's Tableau Economique*. Macmillan, London.

Leo III (1891): *Rerum Novarum*. Leonis XIII P.M. Acta, Romae.

Leontief, W. W. (1941): *The Structure of American Economy. 1919–1929*. Harvard University Press, Cambridge MA., 1st edition.

(1951): *The Structure of American Economy. 1919–1939*. Oxford University Press, New York, 2nd edition.

(1953a): "Domestic Production and Foreign Trade: The American Capital Position Re-examined," *Proceedings of the American Philosophical Society*, XCVII, 4, pp. 332–349.

(1953b): *Studies in the Structure of American Economy*. Oxford University Press, New York.

(1966): *Input-Output Economics*. Oxford University Press, New York.

(1970): "The Dynamic Inverse," in *Contributions to Input-Output Analysis*, ed. by A. Carter, and A. Bródy, vol. 1, pp. 17–46. North-Holland Publishing Co., Amsterdam.

(1991): "The Economy as a Circular Flow," *Structural Change and Economic Dynamics*, 2(1), 181–212.

Lowenthal, E. (1911): *The Ricardian Socialists*. Columbia University Press, New York.

Marshall, A. (1920): *Principles of Economics*. MacMillan, London, 8th edition.

Marx, K. (1867–1970): *A Contribution to the Critique of Political Economy*. International Publishers, New York.

(1869–1872): *Theories of Surplus Value (Volume IV of Capital)*. Lawrence & Wishart, London Originally published posthumously as *Theorien über den Mehrwert*, 1905–1910.

(1894): *Das Kapital*, vol. III. Otto Meissner, Hamburg, ed. FEngels, F. Otto Meissner, Hamburg.

(1959): *Capital*, vol. III. Lawrence and Wishart, London. First published in German in 1894. Lawrence and Wishart, London.

Marx, K., and F. Engels (1865): *The German Ideology*. Lawrence and Wishart, London, ed. Arthur, C. J., originally written in 1845–1846.

Meade, J. E. (1961): *A Neo-Classical Theory of Economic Growth*. MacMillan, London.

(1966): "The Outcome of the Pasinetti–Process: A Note," *The Economic Journal*, 76(301), 161–165.

Medio, A. (1972): "Profits and Surplus–Value: Appearance and Reality in Capitalist Production," in *A Critique of Economic Theory*, ed. by E. K. Hunt, and J. G. Schwartz, vol. 22, p. 1977. Penguin Books, Harmondsworth.

Meek, R. (1956): "Some Notes on the Transformation Problem," *Economic Journal*, 66(261), 94–107.

Meek, R. L. (1950): "The Decline of Ricardian Economics in England," *Economica*, 17(65), 43–62.

Menger, A. (1899): *The Right to the Whole Produce of Labour: The Origin and Development of the Theory of Labour's Claim to the Whole Product of Industry*. Macmillan, London.

Menger, C. (1871): *Grundsätze der Volkswirtschaftslehre*. Wilhelm Braumller, Vienna.

Mercier de La Rivière, P. F. J. H. (1767): *L'Ordre Naturel et Essentiel des Sociétés Politiques*. Jean Nourse, Paris.

Mill, J. (1821): *Elements of Political Economy*. Barldwin, London.

Mill, J. S. (1848): *Principles of Political Economy, with Some of Their Applications to Social Philosophy*. John W. Parker, London.

Miller, M. H. (1988): "The Modigliani-Miller Propositions after Thirty Years," *The Journal of Economic Perspectives*, 2(4), 99–120.

Mirabeau, M. d. (1762): *Tableau Economique avec ses explications*. Chez Chretien Hérold, Hamburg.

Modigliani, F., and R. Brumberg (1955): "Utility Analysis and the Consumption Function: An Interpretation of Cross-Section Data," in *Post-Keynesian Economics*, ed. by K. K. Kurihara, pp. 338–436. George Allen and Unwin, London.

Morishima, M. (1973): *Marx's Economics*. Cambridge University Press, Cambridge.

Mosak, J. L. (1944): "General–Equilibrium Theory in International Trade," Monograph 7, Cowles Foundation for Research in Economics, Bloomington, IN.

Newman, P. (1962): "Production of Commodities by Means of Commodities," *Schweizerische Zeitschrift für Volkswirtsschaft und Statistik*, 98, 58–75.

Newman, P., M. Milgate, and J. Eatwell (eds.) (1987): *The New Palgrave Dictionary of Economics*. Palgrave Macmillan, London.

(eds.) (1992): *The New Palgrave Dictionary of Money and Finance*. Palgrave Macmillan, London.

Noonan, J. T. J. (1957): *The Scholastic Analysis of Usury*. Harvard University Press, Cambridge, MA.

Pashkoff, S. (2012): *The Decline of Ricardian Economics*. Routledge, London.

Pasinetti, L. L. (1960): "A Mathematical Formulation of the Ricardian System," *The Review of Economic Studies*, 27, 78–79.

(1962): "Rate of Profit and Income Distribution in Relation to the Rate of Economic Growth," *The Review of Economic Studies*, 29(4), 267–279.

(1963): "A Multi-Sector Model of Economic Growth," Ph.D. thesis, University of Cambridge.

(1965): "A New Theoretical Approach to the Problems of Economic Growth," *Pontificia Academia Scientiarum Scripta Varia*, 28.

(1966): "New Results in an Old Framework: Comment on Samuelson and Modigliani," *The Review of Economic Studies*, 33(4), 303–306.

(1973): "The Notion of Vertical Integration in Economic Analysis," *Metroeconomica*, 25(1–2), 1–29. Reprinted in L. L. Pasinetti (ed.), Essays on the Theory of Joint Production. Macmillan, London, 1980.

(1974): *Growth and Income Distribution. Essay in Economic Theory.* Cambridge University Press, Cambridge.

(1977a): *Lectures on the Theory of Production*. MacMillan, London.

(1977b): "The Notion of Vertical Integration in Economic Analysis," in *Essays on the Theory of Joint Production*, ed. by L. L. Pasinetti, pp. 16–43. MacMillan, London.

(1977c): "'Substitution in the Real World', an Appendix to 'On Non-Substitution in Production Models'," *Cambridge Journal of Economics*, 1(4), 393–394.

(1980): "The Rate of Interest and the Distribution of Income in a Pure Labour Economy," *Journal of Post-Keynesian Economics*, 3, 170–182.

(1981): *Structural Change and Economic Growth – A Theoretical Essay on the Dynamics of the Wealth of Nations*. Cambridge University Press, Cambridge.

(1983): "The Accumulation of Capital," *Cambridge Journal of Economics*, 7, 405–411.

(1986): "Theory of Value – A Source of Alternative Paradigms in Economic Analysis," in *Foundations of Economics – Structures of Inquiry and Economic Theory*, ed. by M. Baranzini, and R. Scazzieri, pp. 409–431, 233–250. Basil Blackwell, Oxford.

(1988): "Growing Subsystems, Vertically Hyper-integrated Sectors and the Labour Theory of Value," *Cambridge Journal of Economics*, 12(1), 125–134.

(1990): "Sraffa's Circular Process and the Concept of Vertical Integration," in *Essays on Piero Sraffa*, ed. by K. R. Bharadwaj, and B. Schefold, pp. 229–239. Unwin Hyman, London.

(1993): *Structural Economic Dynamics – A Theory of the Economic Consequences of Human Learning*. Cambridge University Press, Cambridge.

(2000): "Critique of the Neoclassical Theory of Income and Distribution," *BNL Quarterly Review*, 53(215), 383–431.

(2005): "Beyond the Accumulation of Capital," in *Joan Robinson's Economics – A Centennial Celebration*, ed. by B. Gibson, pp. 247–265. Edwar Elgar Publishing, Cheltenham.

(2007): *Keynes and the Cambridge Keynesians: A 'Revolution in Economics' to be Accomplished*, Federico Caffe Lectures. Cambridge University Press, Cambridge.

(2012a): *Dottrina Sociale della Chiesa e Teoria Economica*. Vita e Pensiero, Milano.

(2012b): "A Few Counter-Factual Hypotheses on the Current Economic Crisis," *Cambridge Journal of Economics*, 36(6), 1433–1453.

(2014): "Piero Sraffa and His Books – A Foreword to the Catalogue of His Inimitable Library," in *Catalogue of the Library of Piero Sraffa*, ed. by G. De Vivo, pp. XIII–XXXI. Fondazione Luigi Einaudi and Fondazione Raffaele Mattioli, Milano.

(2015): "On the Origin of the Theory of Rent in Economics," in *Resources, Production and Structural Dynamics*, ed. by M. Baranzini, C. Rotondi, and R. Scazzieri, pp. 35–52. Cambridge University Press, Cambridge.

Petty, W. (1690): *Political Arithmetick*. Robert Clavel at the Peacock, London.

Phillip, A. (1955): "The 'Tableau Economique' as a Simple Leontief Model," *Quarterly Journal of Economics*, 69(1), 137–144.

Prais, S. J., and H. S. Houthakker (1955): *The Analysis of Family Budgets*. Cambridge University Press, Cambridge.

Putterman, L. (1988): "The Firm as Association versus the Firm as Commodity," *Economics & Philosophy*, 4(2), 243–266.

Ricardo, D. (1815): *An Essay on the Influence of a Low Price of Corn on the Profits of Stock*. John Murray, London, reprinted in Sraffa, P. (ed.) (1951): *The Works and Correspondence of David Ricardo*, vol. 4, pp. 9–42. Cambridge University Press, Cambridge.

(1821): *Principles of Political Economy and Taxation*. Murray, John, London.

(1951): *The Works and Correspondence of David Ricardo*. Cambridge University Press, Cambridge, ed. Sraffa, P., vol. 1, p. 12.

Rizvi, S. A. T. (1994): "The Microfoundations Project in General Equilibrium Theory," *Cambridge Journal of Economics*, 18(4), 357–377.

(2006): "The Sonnenschein-Mantel-Debreu Results after Thirty Years," *History of Political Economy*, 38, annual supplement, 228–245.

Robbins, L. (1935): *An Essay on the Nature and Significance of Economic Science*. MacMillan, London.

Robinson, J. V. (1956): *The Accumulation of Capital*. MacMillan, London.

Romer, P. (1990): "Endogenous Technical Change," *Journal of Political Economy*, 98(5, Part 2), S71–S102.

Roover de, R. (1958): "The Concept of the Just Price: Theory and Economic Policy," *Journal of Economic History*, XVIII, 418–434.

Ross, W. D. (ed.) (1925): *The Works of Aristotle*, vol. IX (Nicomachean Ethics). Oxford University Press, Oxford.

Samuelson, P. (2008): "Farewell to Friedman-Hayek Libertarian Capitalism," *Tribune Media Services*.

Samuelson, P. A. (1947): *Foundation of Economic Analysis*. Harvard University Press, Cambridge, MA.

(1971): "Undestanding the Marxian Notion of Exploitation: A Summary of the So-called Transformation Problem between Marxian Values and Competitive Prices," *Journal of Economic Literature*, 9(2), 399–431.

Samuelson, P. A., and F. Modigliani (1966): "The Pasinetti Paradox in Neoclassical and More General Models," *The Review of Economic Studies*, 33(4), 269–301.

Sapori, A. (1955): "Il giusto prezzo nella dottrina di San Tommaso e nella pratica del suo tempo," *Studi di storia economica*, I, 265–303.

Say, J. B. (1803): *Trait d'conomie politique*. Horace Say, Paris.

(1841): *Trait d'conomie politique*. Guillaumin, Paris.

Schelle, G. (1888): *Du Pont de Nemours et l'école Physiocratique*. Alcan, Paris.

Schumpeter, J. (1954): *History of Economic Analysis*. Oxford University Press, New York.

Schumpeter, J. A. (1951): *History of Economic Analysis*. Oxford University Press, New York.

Seton, F. (1956–1957): "The Transformation Problem," *Review of Economic Studies*, 24(3), 149–160.

Smith, A. (1776): *The Wealth of Nations*. W. Strahan and T. Cadell, London.

(1904): *An Inquiry into the Nature and Causes of the Wealth of Nations*. Methuen & Co., London, by E. Cannan based on 5th edition 1789, 1st edition 1776.

Solow, R. M. (1956): "A Contribution to the Theory of Economic Growth," *The Quarterly Journal of Economics*, 70(1), 65–94.

(1963): *Capital Theory and the Rate of Return*. North Holland, Amsterdam.

Spicciani, A. (1977): "La mercatura e la formazione del prezzo nella riflessione teologica medievale," in *Atti della Accademia Nazionale dei Lincei, Classe Scienze morali storiche e filologiche*, vol. XX of VIII, pp. 127–293. Accademia Nazionale dei Lincei, Rome.

Sraffa, P. (1960): *Production of Commodities by Means of Commodities – Prelude to a Critique of Economic Theory*. Cambridge University Press, Cambridge.

Sraffa, P., and P. Newman (1970): Exchange of letters published as an appendix to Bharadwaj, Krishna 1970.

Steedman, I. (1989): "On Pasinetti's 'G' Matrix," *Metroeconomica*, 40(1), 3–15.

Stewart, D. (1811): *Biographical Memoirs, of Adam Smith, of William Robertson, and of Thomas Reid.* G. Ramsay and Company, Edinburgh, read before the Royal Society of Edinburgh. Now collected into one volume, with some additional notes.

Stigler, G. (1954): "The Early History of Empirical Studies of Consumer Behaviour," *The Journal of Political Economy*, 62(2), 95–113.

Stigler, J. G. (1958): "Ricardo and the 93 Percent Labor Theory of Value," *American Economic Review*, XLVIII, 357–367.

Stiglitz, J. E. (2009): "Interviewed by Rana Foroohar, 'We're in a Whole New Territory'," *Newsweek*, April 6.

Stone, R. (1954): *The Measurement of Consumers' Expenditure and Behaviour in the United Kingdom.* Cambridge University Press, Cambridge, 2 vols.

Stone, R. (1997): *Some British Empiricists in the Social Sciences (1650–1900).* Cambridge University Press, Cambridge.

Sweezy, P. (ed.) (1949): *Karl Marx and the Close of His System by E.von Bö hm Bawerk.* August M. Kelley, New York.

Torrens, R. (1965): *An Essay on the Production of Wealth.* A. M. Kelly, New York, with an introductory essay by Joseph Dorfman; Originally published in 1821.

Tsuru, S. (1942): "On Reproduction Schemes," in *The Theory of Capitalist Development*, ed. by P. Sweezy, chap. Appendix A, pp. 365–374. Monthly Review Press, New York.

Volcker, P. (2010): "The Time We Have Is Growing Short," *The New York Review of Books*, June 24.

Von Neumann, J. (1945): "A Model of General Equilibrium," *The Review of Economic Studies*, 13, 1–9.

Walras, L. (1874): *Elements d'conomie politique pure.* F. Rouge, Lousanne.

Weber, M. (1967): *Storia agraria romana dal punto di vista del diritto pubblico e privato.* Il Saggiatore, Milano, Translation of Dissertation by Saverio Franchi.

Winternitz, J. (1948): "Value and Prices: A Solution of the So-called Transformation Problem," *Economic Journal*, 58, 276–280.

Wold, H., and L. Juren (1953): *Demand Analysis: A Study in Econometrics.* Wiley & Sons, New York.

Author Index

Page numbers followed by 'f' refers to footnotes.

Subject Index

Page numbers followed by 'f' refers to footnotes.

Printed in the United Kingdom by TJ Clays Ltd.